NONFICTION FILM

NONFICTION
FILM

A Critical History
REVISED AND EXPANDED

Richard M. Barsam

*Indiana
University
Press*

BLOOMINGTON AND INDIANAPOLIS

Unless otherwise noted, all illustrations are courtesy of the
Museum of Modern Art/Film Stills Archive. Other films
are courtesy of the following sources:
National Film Archive (London): *Drifters, Industrial Brit-
ain, The Saving of Bill Blewitt, The Islanders, Children at
School, Squadron 992, Fires Were Started, The Silent Vil-
lage, A Diary for Timothy, David, Every Day Except
Christmas*
Maysles Films, Inc.: *Salesman* (photo by Bob Adelman),
Grey Gardens, Christo's Valley Curtain (photo by Harry
Shunk)
Zipporah Films, Inc.: *Meat* (photo by Oliver Kool), *Near
Death* (photo by Ollie Hallowell)
Filmmakers Library: *Silent Pioneers*
National Film Board of Canada: *Waiting for Fidel*
Robert Gardner: *Rivers of Sand*

MANUFACTURED IN THE UNITED STATES OF AMERICA

Library of Congress Cataloging-in-Publication Data

Barsam, Richard Meran.
    Nonfiction film : a critical history / Richard Barsam.
    — Rev. and expanded.
        p.   cm.
    Includes bibliographical references and indexes.
    ISBN 0-253-31124-1 (cloth). — ISBN 0-253-20706-1
    (paper)
    1. Documentary films—History and criticism. I. Title.
PN1995.9.D6N57   1992
070.1'8'09—dc20   91-26985

        2   3   4   5   96   95

IN MEMORY OF MY
MOTHER AND FATHER

CONTENTS

Illustrations

Preface

The warm reception of the first edition of this book, which appeared in 1973, has encouraged me to expand its historical, geographical, and theoretical coverage in preparing this new edition. Since the scope of this critical history of the nonfiction film from 1895 to 1985 encompasses the years of its prehistory to some of its many recent achievements, I want to emphasize two basic considerations that have limited my study: the nonfiction film includes the documentary, the factual film, certain ethnographic films and films of exploration, the wartime propaganda film, cinéma vérité, direct cinema, and films on art; but it does not include experimental, abstract, or animated films.

Although I learn much from those who examine films through the apparatus of different systems of abstract thought, I believe in a simpler and more pleasurable method—a passionate engagement: in the act of looking at films; in the pleasure that derives from seeing them again and again; and, indeed, in the whole enterprise of teaching and learning about film. By continuing to explore my responses to the nonfiction films that I have seen over several decades, and by refining those responses through close consideration of the best critical interpretations of other scholars in the field, I hope to achieve an enhanced understanding of the nonfiction film: what it is, what it does, how it does it, and why it has done it so forcefully for so many of us.[1]

If, in describing the overall development of the nonfiction film, I have perhaps seemed to neglect some directors and films important to its history, it is because I am tracing the development of a genre—or, in some cases a cinematic style—and consequently include only those who most contributed to it. Unlike the first edition, however, which concentrated primarily on nonfiction films produced in the United States and Great Britain, I have, while retaining that emphasis, attempted also to include coverage of the major developments in the nonfiction films produced in Europe, Asia, and the emerging and developing countries.

A note on names, dates, and titles: Where, for political reasons, filmmakers used alternate names, those names are given in brackets (e.g., Jay Leyda [Eugene Hill]). Wherever possible, the date given for a film is the year of its release in its country of origin. As for titles of films in languages other than English, they are given in English (if the film was released in an English-language version) followed by the title in the original language. Alternate release titles are given in brackets. Television films are denoted by a bullet • preceding the date.

Acknowledgments

Seventeen years ago, the assistance and advice of many kind, generous people made possible the publication of the first edition of this book, including: Margareta Akermark, Paul Ballard, Mark Berman, Jeremy Boulton, W. Jack Coogan, Mary Corliss, Kathleen Endress, Frances Flaherty, Gillian Hartnoll, Roger Holman, Alan King, Betty Leese, Pare Lorentz, Richard Dyer MacCann, Gerald Mast, Albert Maysles, David Maysles, Jonas Mekas, D. A. Pennebaker, Barbara Shapiro, Charles Silver, Thomas Toohey, Helen Van Dongen, Willard Van Dyke, Frederick Wiseman, and Joel Zuker.

While preparing the second edition, I turned again to friends and colleagues for assistance and advice of one sort or another. I want to thank all those whose patience, good humor, and willingness to be of assistance made working on this book such a pleasure. Two deserve special mention because of their contributions: Antoinette Garber and James Manago. In addition, each of the following at some point came up with just what was needed: Ann Alter, Luis Antonio Bocchi, Jackie Cooper, Mary Corliss, Nadine Covert, Ron Magliozzi, William T. Murphy, Gudrun Parker, Richard Parker, Barbara Quart, Liz Scheines, Leo Seltzer, Aradhana Seth, Suzanne Siegel, Charles Silver, Lucy Winer, and Geert von Wonterghem.

For both editions, I worked with films and print materials at the following archives and libraries: the Film Study Center of the Museum of Modern Art, where the bulk of my work inevitably was done; the British Film Institute; the Cinémathèque Française; the libraries of the College of Staten Island and Hunter College of the City University of New York, of Columbia University, and of the University of Southern California; and the research libraries of Donnell, Lincoln Center, and the New York Public Library. I must also record my thanks to the many efficient and helpful staff members of these institutions.

For many years, Richard Dyer MacCann has been this country's wisest, most sensible, and most articulate teacher and critic of the nonfiction film; and I am deeply grateful to him for his friendship and steady encouragement. His knowledge of the nonfiction film is virtually encyclopedic; and with his familiar care and attention to details, as well as his unrivaled eye for literary excess, he read this manuscript and helped me to avoid many errors of fact and judgment.

I owe my greatest debt of gratitude to Brenda Spatt, ablest of editors and best of friends, who, though pressured to complete her own manuscript, spent countless hours both in editing this book and in bringing to it coherence and clarity. Any faults that remain are mine, not hers.

For his patient support throughout this endeavor and for his many helpful suggestions, I am especially grateful to Edgar Munhall.

PART ONE
(1820–1933)

Foundations of the Nonfiction Film

1 Reality Perceived and Recorded

FROM MEMORY TO MOVEMENT

When Auguste and Louis Lumière showed their motion pictures to the Paris public for the first time on December 28, 1895, in the Salon Indien of the Grand Café on the Boulevard des Capucines, the audience saw sights familiar from everyday life, including, in *The Arrival of a Train at La Ciotat (L'arrivée d'un train à La Ciotat),* a train coming toward them, and then *at* them—an image so large, so believable, so convincing that some people, imagining that the train was going to come right out of the screen, drew back while others reportedly ran to the back of the room in fright. The fright was justified, for, just two months before, on October 22, 1895, a railroad accident called widespread public attention to the dangers that accompany industrial progress. This occurred at the Gare Montparnasse, when a train, travelling out of control, broke through the station façade. The engine and coal tender broke off from the rest of the train and fell to the Place de Rennes below (now Place du 18 Juin 1940), thus causing the coaches to stop without damage. Only one person was killed—a lady newspaper vendor on the street.[1] Six months later, Maxim Gorky saw a program of Lumière films in Moscow, and wrote:

> Last night I was in the Kingdom of Shadows. . . . It is terrifying to see, but it is the movement of shadows, only of shadows. . . . Suddenly something clicks, everything vanishes and a train appears on the screen. It speeds straight at you—watch out! It seems as though it will plunge into the darkness in which you sit, turning you into a ripped sack full of lacerated flesh and splintered bones, and crushing into dust and into broken fragments this hall and this building, so full of women, wine, music and vice. But this, too, is but a train of shadows.[2]

Dai Vaughan points out that the most revealing aspect of these films was "that people were startled not so much by the phenomenon of the moving photograph,

Arrival of a Train At La Ciotat [*L'arrivée d'un train à La Ciotat*] (Auguste and Louis Lumière, France, 1895)

which its inventors had struggled long to achieve, as by its ability to portray spontaneities of which the theatre was not capable."[3]

The railroad, the grandest symbol of the industrial revolution, was already a familiar subject in literature, photographs, lithographs, and paintings. The steaming, rushing locomotive had become, according to Steven Z. Levine, a "paradigmatic image of modern life."[4] Robert Rosenblum writes:

> From the time of the inauguration of the first important French railway line (Paris–Orléans) in 1843, Daumier had been attracted to this new phenomenon of mid-nineteenth-century life, which for so many contemporary artists and writers, from Turner and Monet to Dickens and Tolstoi, could become everything from a Romantic symbol of energy, travel or destiny to a prosaic fact reflecting the crowds and hubbub of the expanding city.[5]

Honoré Daumier had depicted the social and psychological aspects of railroad travel, and, in his series of ten paintings made inside and outside the Gare St.-Lazare, Claude Monet had captured the immediate power and movement of trains going in and out of a great hub of railway activity. Levine observes that both the Lumières and Monet depicted the "enduring sequentiality of our experience in the world" by rearranging space, but their approaches to spatial reality are very different. Monet did not compete with the standard of representation made possible by the camera; instead, he portrayed the variations of light and atmosphere brought on by changes of the hour or season. Nonetheless, the Lumières' film of the express train and railway station is more than the cinematographic record of sequence, transportation, or communication; it is also a testament to the dynamic rhythms of industrial power that make possible both transportation and motion pictures. Thus, while the audience for the Lumières' film was familiar with the subject and the pictorial realism with which it was filmed, it was nonetheless stunned by the dynamism of the physical and human action that the Lumières had reproduced.[6] As Steven Neale emphasizes, "the cinema is an illusion of the real. But more, it is a spectacle of movement. And as such it seems at times to exceed reality itself. . . ."[7] The audience had every reason to be stunned, even apprehensive, for this moving picture not only confirmed the railroad's power to cut across the continent and into our consciousness, but also marked the end of one kind of seeing and the beginning of another.

Cinema, born in 1895, was to be the art form of the twentieth century. The Lumière brothers offered French audiences a radically different experience at a time when more experimental visual and performing arts were challenging the conventional, familiar forms. For example, French painting in 1895 was marked by a retrospective exhibition of Paul Cézanne's work, which was regarded as both a success and a scandal, as well as the artist's completion, at the age of 56, of his painting, *Boy in the Red Vest*. The year before, Claude Debussy's *Prelude to the Afternoon of a Faun* had caused a scandal in the musical world because of its alleged formlessness, a charge that in the art world had been directed at Cézanne's paintings. In 1895, Pablo Picasso was fourteen years old. In theatre, Sarah Bernhardt, continuing her distinguished career as a tragic actress, appeared in Edmond Rostand's *La Princesse Lointaine,* written for her. Audiences seeking operatic spectacle during December 1895 would have had a choice between the première (on December 14) of a new opera, *Frédégonde,* composed by Ernest Guiraud and completed by Camille Saint-Saëns, or the revival (on December 27) of Giuseppe Verdi's *Rigoletto* (composed 1851).[8] Verdi, in his 80th year, attended a performance of his *Falstaff* at the Opéra Comique, and Erik Satie, then 29, composed his *Messe des Pauvres.* Although the operetta was being expanded through many performances in the *cafés-concerts* of Paris, there was little excitement until the appearance (on December 20) of *Le Baron Tsigane,* the French translation of Johann Strauss's enormously popular *Die Zigeunerbaron* (composed 1885).[9] In literature, the mid-nineteenth century saw the transformation from romanticism to the realism of Gustave Flaubert, and was further distinguished by the fiction of de Stendhal, Georges Sand, Victor Hugo, and Honoré de Balzac. In fiction, the movement toward naturalism was led by Émile Zola, and, in poetry, the work of Charles Baudelaire, Stephane Mallarmé, Paul Verlaine, and Arthur Rimbaud was to have a profound effect on twentieth-century modes of literary expression.

By 1894, Monet had completed the group of paintings of Rouen cathedral, and had demonstrated the flickering, fleeting effects of light by breaking it down into its color components as a prism does. He had refracted the light. The Lumières had captured it. With their Cinématographe, the Lumières had solved the problem of projection and thus capitalized on the technology that had already been invented and developed almost simultaneously in Germany, Great Britain, France, and the United States. Their achievement marked one of the great turning points in the history of the visual arts, the moment in which the potentialities for representing movement were extended. Previously, paintings and photographs could only preserve a visual memory of movement. They function as the visual equivalent of the past tense; their single, static images are the remembrance of a moment in time and space. Motion pictures also record memories, but they also provide a visual equivalent of the present tense, a representation of movement itself.[10] Their kinetic images, which record temporal sequences and make space move, not only confirm the process of human vision, but also alter the spectator's psychological relationship to the visible world as projected on a screen.[11]

The success of the Lumières in making *and* projecting the first motion pictures was only one stage in a continuum of experiments and inventions related to the Western representation of reality. The Lumières did not work in isolation; their contributions to the beginnings of the nonfiction film were made on foundations established by other theorists, scientists, and artists, as well as by showmen and entrepreneurs. The experiments, inventions, and achievements of these people took place in five overlapping areas: persistence of vision, still photography, series photography, cinematography, and nineteenth-century French art. Cumulatively, these five areas demonstrate that, in late nineteenth-century France, a creative environment existed that encouraged the artist's freedom to invent a new way of viewing the world. Indeed, scientifically and aesthetically, it was virtually inevitable that the nonfiction cinema—the first manifestation of the most dynamic art form of the twentieth century—would be born in nineteenth-century France.

PERSISTENCE OF VISION: THEORIES AND TECHNOLOGIES

With the exception of such short-lived amusements as Cinerama, artists today do not attempt to fool their audiences with the illusion of a train hurtling into the station, but in the early eighteenth century, theorists and inventors explored the phenomenon of *persistence of vision*[12] not only for the sake of scientific knowledge, but also because they perceived some value in both fooling and entertaining people at the same time.[13] The invention of cinema was the nineteenth-century French culmination of several centuries of study of and experimentation with the ways in which man perceives reality. In the years preceding the birth of cinema (the "pre-history of cinema," as some historians like to call it), scientists and other thinkers propounded theories of perception and, in some cases, devised toys and machines to demonstrate those theories.[14] Early studies of persistence of vision were done in the 1820s by Thomas Young, Charles Wheatstone, Peter Mark Rôget, William George Horner, Michael Faraday, and Sir John Herschel in England, by Simon Ritter von Stampfer in Austria, and by Joseph Antoine Ferdinand Plateau in Belgium. What followed was a rapid succession of scientific, entertaining devices that literally fooled the eye. In 1825, Dr. John Ayrton Paris originated the Thaumatrope, and in 1827, he published the results of his experiment; in 1828, Faraday produced his Faraday's Wheel, an optical toy; in 1829, Joseph Antoine Ferdinand Plateau conceived the Phenakistiscope and discovered that 16fps (frames per second) produced the illusion of continuous movement (Stampfer developed a similar machine that he called the Stroboscope); in 1834, Horner invented the Zootrope, and Baron Franz von Uchatius's experiments with stroboscopic toys and the idea of projection led to his creation in 1853 of the Projecting Phenakistiscope.[15] On a different scale, there was a variety of sensational visual entertainments that were highly popular with audiences, including the Diorama, Panorama, and Phantasmagoria.[16] These inventions, less scientific than the persistence of vision devices, were essentially theatrical in conception and production, stimulating the audience with spectacular illusions, but contributing little to the development of the science and technology of realistic visual perception or representation.

By 1895, the public of Paris was already accustomed to spectacles of which the Lumières were the epitome. Spectacles of shadow plays, known as *ombres chinoises* (Chinese shadows), had been shown with great successes in Paris for several years. Some entertainments of this type, such as "Sainte Geneviève" (1894) and "Le Sphinx" (1896) took place at Le Chat Noir, a cabaret in Montmartre, which helped to prepare for the vogue of cinema by introducing such technical innovations as color, perspective, and decor to these shadow shows. The Musée Grevin, a popular wax museum, also attracted a large crowd with its realistic wax tableau and *théâtre optique,* a mechanism that was capable of prolonged projection.

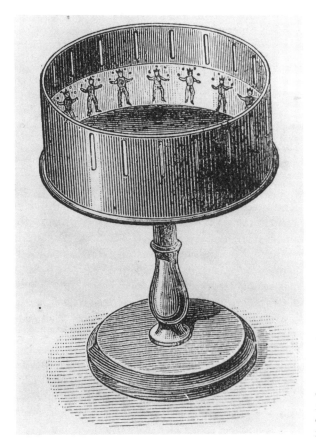

Zootrope: the circular drum of this Zootrope (or Zoetrope), a persistence-of-vision toy, was fitted with a paper strip of pictures; when the viewer looked at the spinning strip—through the slits in the drum—the alternating moments of darkness and light created the optical illusion of moving pictures.

These toys, machines, and mechanized theatrical presentations demonstrating the principle of persistence of vision, amused viewers. While they foreshadowed cinema, they were limited to depicting reality primarily through drawn figures that, while fascinating and highly entertaining, were graphically crude. As Gerald Mast says, recognizing the need for more realistic depiction of detail, "before there could be motion pictures, there had to be pictures."[17] The next step toward the development of cinema was the invention of photography.

Still Photography

While one group of scientists was working on the theoretical and mechanical principles of persistence of vision, another was almost simultaneously working on photography, the process of producing, registering, and stabilizing an optical image on a photosensitive surface. Photography is literally and technically the static representation or reproduction of light, or writing with light (*photo* means light, and *graphy* means representation). The search was for a means of capturing light and shadow that would preserve a permanent image faithful to reality as perceived by the human eye. In this search, there was little, if any, desire to regard the camera as an artist's tool (i.e., to create pictures for their own sake). Coming together were "chemistry and optics, nature and art, and memory and vision" (Neale 10) to produce an image that would, in a sense, provide documentation for the perceived world—size, mass, volume, perspective, depth. In 1901, after fifteen years of amateur picture-making, Emile Zola, the French novelist and foremost advocate of literary realism, wrote: "In my view, you cannot claim to have really seen something until you have photographed it."[18] Alan Trachtenberg writes:

> Photography denotes a process of *making meaning* through pictures. By the 1890s, this cultural process had infiltrated the entire society, establishing itself as perhaps the prime arbiter of "reality." . . . The photograph does compel its viewer to contemplate what seems an authentic token of reality, teaching viewers to read signs of life in black and white. Photography helped engender a new visibility in things and contributed to a rise in visibility itself. A high value was placed upon sight and its uses in modern culture—from surveillance to survey to spectacle to art. More intensely and urgently than in the past, to see became to know—or to hope to know.[19]

Photography—both technical and aesthetic—was envisioned by Aristotle's theoretical reference to the principle of the *camera obscura*: the Arab mathematician Ibn al-Haytham (or Alhazen) described this more fully in the ninth century; in the early fifteenth century, it was extended when the Florentine architect and sculptor Filippo Brunelleschi imagined himself as a camera to invent linear perspective; and, in the later fifteenth century, Leonardo da Vinci's first drawings for a *camera obscura* gave tangible form to the idea.[20] Other attempts to reproduce reality accurately took place in the late eighteenth century with three tracing devices: the *silhouette*; the *physionotrace*; and the *camera lucida*.

These rudimentary devices were quickly followed by progressive developments from Thomas Wedgwood in England and Joseph Nicéphore Niépce in France that produced the first images; from Louis-Jacques Mandé Daguerre, whose *Daguerrotype,* according to Daguerre, was "a physical and chemical process which gives Nature the ability to reproduce herself"; and from Sir John Herschel, who completed the process begun by Niépce and Daguerre by perfecting the "hypo" (sodium thiosulfate) that fixed the image on paper and thus arrested the effect of light on it. Herschel, the father of modern photography, first used the word *photography* in 1839 in a Royal Society lecture.[21]

What followed were primarily technological improvements on Herschel's discovery. In 1851, Frederick Scott Archer realized that glass negatives were more durable than paper, and invented the collodion, or wet glass plate, process that remained the standard photographic process until the 1870s. Between 1876 and 1881, Richard Leach Maddox and Charles Harper Bennett perfected the "dry" gelatin process, and paper photographic plates (coated with gelatin) replaced the glass plates coated with collodion. In 1887, Hannibal Goodwin sold his idea for celluloid roll film to George Eastman, who began the mass production of "American Film," paper coated with a gelatin emulsion; in 1889, Eastman improved the process by substituting clear plastic ("film") for the paper base. The invention of the gelatin dry process reduced, from fifteen minutes to one-thousandth of a second, the time necessary to make a photographic exposure and thus made it possible to record action spontaneously and simultaneously as it occurred. Beaumont Newhall writes that "the perfection of gelatin emulsion not only led to the conquest, analysis and synthesis of action, but it brought about standardization of materials and the scientific investigation of the photographic process."[22]

This experimentation with optical principles and "still photography" in the nineteenth century made it possible to fix and reproduce, first drawings, and then photographic images that could *simulate* action in the image. But this was not enough for the scientists, artists, and members of the general public who wanted to see photographs of life in motion.[23]

Series Photography

While the conquest of action was only one of the many simultaneous and rapid developments between 1875 and 1900 that modernized, simplified, and (in some cases) standardized the processes, the materials, and (occasionally) the attitudes toward still photography, it was the most important preliminary stage in the development of what was to become cinematography. In the next stage, three men— Pierre Jules César Janssen, Eadweard Muybridge, Étienne-Jules Marey—contributed to the development of a photographic process that would record a series of actions.[24] These developments, like those that resulted in photography, took place within a few years.

In 1874, French astronomer Pierre Jules César Janssen developed the *revolver photographique,* or chrono-photographic gun, a cylinder-shaped camera with a revolving photographic plate that made it possible to make exposures automatically, at short intervals, on different segments of the plate. In 1877, English photographer Eadweard Muybridge concluded experiments in California that resulted in the first series of photographs of continuous motion.[25] He used a group of electrically operated cameras (first twelve, then twenty-four) to make a series of photographs, and using a magic lantern and his Zoopraxiscope (an enlarged Phenakistiscope), he projected the first photographic images in motion in San Francisco on 4 May 1880 (Neale 34). As Erik Barnouw writes, "Muybridge had foreshadowed a crucial aspect of the documentary film: its ability to open our eyes to worlds available to us but, for one reason or another, not perceived."[26]

Although a breakthrough, Muybridge's process was cumbersome. At the same time, Étienne-Jules Marey (1830–1904), a French physiologist working in the same area, made the first series of photographs of continuous motion in 1882 using the *fusil photographique,* another form of the chrono-photographic gun, a single, portable camera that was capable of taking twelve continuous images.[27] Muybridge and Marey later collaborated in Paris, but both were more interested in using the process for their scientific studies than for making or projecting of motion pictures as such. Marey's invention solved the problems created by Muybridge's use of a battery of cameras, but the length of the series was limited to forty images—three or four seconds long; this obstacle was overcome by 1889 with George Eastman's

Motion Study (Eadweard Muybridge, USA, c. 1881)

celluloid roll film, which made it possible to take thousands of images, rather than Marey's forty. Alan Trachtenberg writes:

> Developing in the shadow of photography, moving pictures defined themselves willy-nilly by reference to their opposite. Indeed it was routine to project the opening shot of a film as a still image, which the film would then bring to life, activated as if by magic. This practice openly declared the symbiosis of still and moving photographs, acknowledging the still as the buried but essential component of film. (78)

Thus, while the technology for the invention of cinema existed, what remained was for someone to synthesize the elements first into cinematography and then into the production and projection of motion pictures.

Cinematography
Cinema, of all the arts, is the one most dependent on technology, yet its invention was the inevitable result of the artist's, as well as the scientist's, attempts to reproduce actuality.[28] The question of who was the first to develop and introduce the motion picture is another matter. John L. Fell notes that there are several compet-

ing claims: Max and Emil Skladanowsky in Germany; Louis Aimé Augustin Le Prince, Robert W. Paul, Birt Acres, and William Friese-Greene in England; Marey, Émile Reynaud, and the Lumières in France; and Muybridge, W. K. L. Dickson, Thomas A. Edison, and Grey and Leroy Latham in the United States.[29] But Steven Neale points out that

> most of the machines developed in these countries—the Cinématographe in France, the Bioscope in Germany, the Animatograph in Britain, the Vitascope in America—were in one way or another derived, inspired or affiliated to either the Kinetograph, a moving picture camera, or the Kinetoscope, a peep-show viewing machine, both of which had been invented by W. K. L. Dickson at Thomas Edison's research laboratory at West Orange in America. (41)

The invention of the first motion picture camera by William Kennedy Laurie Dickson was actually a brilliant synthesis of principles and techniques established by Muybridge, Thomas Eakins, Marey, and others.[30] We know that Thomas A. Edison's interest in the technical improvements made possible by the celluloid film was vital to the invention of the Kinetograph, the first true motion picture camera; that his fundamental interest in motion pictures was in their commercial possibilities of providing a visual accompaniment for his successful and profitable invention of the phonograph, patented in 1877; and that he, like Muybridge and Marey, was more interested in cinematography for its practical purposes than for its aesthetic possibilities. Prior to Edison, men had studied the perception of reality and invented machines for recording visual reality within the context of scientific discovery. Edison wanted to record both what he saw and heard, and, as Cook writes, "the first viable motion picture camera was invented as an accessory to a sound recording device and not for its own sake" (5). It does not detract from Edison's achievements and importance as an inventor to recognize that he was also an entrepreneur, for his attitude has profound implications in understanding the evolution of the stages by which men sought to reproduce reality.

The inherent limitations in the early technology that Dickson developed for Edison governed the films that could be made with it. They were shot from the Kinetograph, a fixed and nonmoving camera located inside the "Black Maria," which was dependent on natural sunlight; viewers saw them through the Kinetoscope, Edison's peephole viewer.[31] While the earliest results were short, unedited performances (usually comic), soon the Edison company began recording scenes from actual life itself. The first motion picture made in the Kinetograph was *Fred Ott's Sneeze* (1891); others include *The Gaiety Girls Dancing* and *Highland Dance*, and these were followed by titles that suggest the depiction of realistic, moving action: *Pile Driving* (1897), *Serpentine Dance* (1894), *Washington Navy Yard* (1897), and *Skirmish Between Russian and Japanese Advance Guards* (1904). While Edison had some interest in the documentary potential of motion pictures, his genius lay in his understanding of their entertainment potential, and his great success in infusing the narrative film with entertainment value.

For motion pictures to develop further, two problems had to be solved: the camera had to be freed from the "Black Maria," and the filmstrip had to be freed from the peephole viewer. Even though magic-lantern shows had been in existence for hundreds of years, solving the problem of motion picture projection proved to be very difficult. The challenge was to develop a machine that could project the filmstrips with a light strong enough to provide a clear image, roll the film smoothly and regularly past that light without tearing and burning it, and provide the intermittent movement of the film that would create the illusion of continuous movement. This challenge was met not by Dickson or Edison, but by the Lumière brothers (see chapter 2). Of parallel importance to this technological development was the emergence of a realist aesthetic in nineteenth-century art.

THE REALIST IMPULSE IN NINETEENTH-CENTURY ART

The birth of the nonfiction film—indeed, the birth of cinema itself—is also closely related to the diversified representations of reality in nineteenth-century art; the work of the Lumières was another manifestation of art being directed towards the objective world of things to seek a "closeness to nature."[32] Fritz Novotny explains some reasons why diversified approaches to realism were common in nineteenth-century art:

> The causes of this change which lay outside art itself have been often and amply explained: the radical changes in the structure of society; the disturbance of secular and ecclesiastical power on the Continent as a result of the French Revolution, an event which affected the history of the whole world; the subsequent beginnings of a democratic society and a new form of individualism; the consequent fundamental change in the relationship of the artist to society, both as his patron and his milieu. The significance of this new situation, involving the destruction of all links with the past and of the emergence of a new freedom for art and the individual artist, is in part obvious: it opened the way for a new view of the world. (2)

As Novotny suggests, realism and its "ever vaster fields of portrayal of the visible" (5) provide one of the contexts in which to locate and interpret the beginnings of the nonfiction film. Unlike other turning points in the history of art, the search for realism was provoked not by religion or ideology, but rather by an abandonment of ideology, by the idea that nature represented not universal beliefs, but visible phenomena. Developments in nineteenth-century French art and photography reawakened a new version of the oldest conflict in art: whether art should represent beauty or truth, the ideal or the real. There was a prevailing hypothesis that painting created the ideal and photography recorded the truth, but theory and practice varied. The commercial success of photography, and its acceptance by the public and critics, led to a competition between painting and photography; some painters (Eugène Delacroix, Edgar Degas, Gustave Courbet, Thomas Eakins) used photographs to help them to make their paintings more lifelike, and some photographers (Gustave Le Gray, Oscar Gustave Rejlander, Henry Peach

Robinson, Julia Margaret Cameron) used such techniques as unfocused lenses, retouching, and theatrical settings and costumes to compete with paintings. Steven Z. Levine suggests that the two separate arts of photography and painting "shared a common will to form" and that each wanted "to be like the other."[33] Although such a transmutation of genre did not occur, the interchange between painting and photography had at least one very important result: it helped people better to understand photography and painting as distinct modes of representation, each with its own potentialities and limitations, as well as what is meant by "originality" in art.

In painting, the new modes of representation comprised: the new romanticism of Delacroix and Théodore Géricault; the social realism of Jean-François Millet and Courbet; the social and psychological realism of Honoré Daumier; the movements of impressionism (Édouard Manet, Claude Monet, Pierre-Auguste Renoir, Édgar Degas, and Camille Pissaro) and post-impressionism (Georges Seurat, Vincent Van Gogh, Henri de Toulouse-Lautrec, and Paul Gauguin); and, finally, the directions toward twentieth-century modernism in the work of Paul Cézanne, Henri Matisse, Georges Rouault, Georges Braque, and Pablo Picasso. As these trends were developing, photographers used their skill to achieve some of the pictorial as well as the didactic aims of contemporaneous paintings, and also brought the photographic portrait as close to paintings as possible in the work of Nadar (Gaspard Félix Tournachon), Étienne Carjat, Anthony Adam-Salomon, and Napoleon Sarony. Not only in painting and photography, but also in the novel and on the stage, writers sought to portray what they saw without idealizing it, choosing their subjects from the commonplace of everyday life.

In all this great transformation of the arts, it was the realist impulse of the visual arts—recording the visible facts of people, places, and social life, for a growing middle-class audience—that helped to inspire the first motion pictures. During these years (c. 1850–90), the period immediately preceding the work of the Lumières, French painting, drawing, and caricature captured the surface look and sometimes the psychological depth of actual events and people, and also established for the audience the familiar subjects and conventions of form. Painters such as Jean-Louis-Ernest Meissonier and Édouard Manet provided a "close-up scrutiny"[34] of the grim realities of strife and death in the 1848 revolution and the 1871 Siege of Paris, while Constantin Guys chronicled activities on the battlefield as well as the society promenade.[35] Paintings served as a direct witness to life, and films were soon to follow. While the Lumières themselves did not photograph revolutions or wars, they did make some splendid records of military activities during peacetime.

Of those painters who were concerned with factual reality—among them Jean-François Millet, Jules Breton, and Rosa Bonheur—it was Gustave Courbet, a social realist of "revolutionary importance" (Novotny 143), who was preeminent in believing that "the routine events of city and country life were the only vital source of artistic truth" (Rosenblum 223). It is of course in their fidelity to recording the routine and commonplace activity that the Lumière films achieve not only archival value, but also aesthetic truth. Another kind of realism, that based on moral ideas, is seen in the work of Honoré Daumier, whose work depicts the busy, noisy world of Paris life: its streets, trains, law courts, and many other aspects of the life of its poor. Still another influence on the Lumières was that kind of realistic painting that records the commonplace in an uncommonly scientific way. In describing the work of Thomas Eakins, the American realist painter and photographer who studied in France, Rosenblum might be describing that of a filmmaker. Eakins, he writes, is a painter who "insisted on fusing the art of painting with a scrupulous study of anatomy, light, mathematics, and perspective, and who believed, with so many of his contemporaries, that the photograph was a medium which provided objective truths to support the artist's painstaking reconstructions of the visible world" (Rosenblum 357). The paintings of Gustave Caillebotte suggest yet another possible influence on the Lumières, who, like Caillebotte, recorded the dignity of manual labor. Degas, like Caillebotte, rendered activities in deep-space perspectives (Degas in the Parisian theatre, Caillebotte in the Parisian streets), and while the cinematic illusion of deep space was not possible in the first films, a well-framed depiction of street scenes was. The delight of Claude Monet in the transitory changes of light on cathedral facades (as well as on railroad stations) may have had some attraction for the Lumières, who likewise captured this evanescent phenomenon; in reviewing a Lumière program in Russia in 1896, Maxim Gorky wrote poetically of being in a "kingdom of shadows."[36]

Finally, in such paintings as Manet's *The Railroad* (1873) and *The Bar at the Folies-Bergère* (1881–82), we find the "extraordinary fusion of two worlds—that of the painting and that of the spectator" (Rosenblum 355) that was to reach an even greater complexity in the first motion pictures—richer because the moving image constantly changed the spectator's relationship to it, and more abstract because the image was black and white. The spatial and narrative structures of Manet's *Railroad* are complex. In the left foreground, our eyes are fixed on the mother's gaze; yet, in the right foreground, we look over a girl's shoulder as she watches, through the grate that separates foreground and background, the clouds of smoke in which a train leaves the station. In the Lumières' *The Arrival of a Train at La Ciotat,* there is no such artifice in the spatial and narrative structures; as a person who has come to meet the train, we are standing with the camera on the platform as the train enters the station, pulls up, and halts. In Manet's painting, the indirect event of the train is only one part of the picture; in Lumière's film, the direct event is all. We do not know if the Lumières were aware of the iconography of the railroad in nineteenth-century French art, but, despite their familiar subject, they achieved something new. They used cinematography, not in an effort to reproduce the moral vision of a Daumier or the impressionist vision of a Monet, but as servants of science, to preserve the moment, to include all the details within the frame, and to provide a true, authentic, factual record.

Before narrative, sound, or color (although these and other aspects were quickly to follow the birth of cinematography), the initial impulse of the first cinema artists was to record commonplace reality. How appropriate and natural, then, that the Lumière brothers should turn their cameras to making what they called *actualités,* or documentary views, of such ordinary subjects as a boat leaving a port, blacksmiths at work, a family at play, or military processions. The birth of the cinema in the Lumières' studio—exciting as it was in itself, in the history of human perception, and in the evolution of industrial and scientific technology—was only one of many signs that confirmed what Erich Auerbach called the "complete emancipation" of nineteenth-century French art from classical academic discipline to free experimentation and bold realism.[37]

<table>
<tr><td>**2**</td><td># The First Films</td></tr>
</table>

THE FIRST FILMS

The first motion pictures, born of the realist impulse, were "actualities," short films of actual people, conditions, or facts, constituting as Raymond Fielding writes, "unmanipulated activity of more or less general interest."[1] As there was an astounding simultaneity of invention of motion picture making and projection equipment—spurred by competition and by rapid and enthusiastic audience acceptance—so too was there a great similarity in the subject matter of these films. Events over a seven-year period (1889–1896) indicate both the speed of this technical development and the diversity of the cinematic subject matter.

In 1889, William Friese-Green made motion pictures of well-dressed London citizens walking in Hyde Park on their way to church; in 1894, Thomas Edison and W. K. L. Dickson began recording on film such noted celebrities as Sandow the Strong Man, Buffalo Bill, Annie Oakley, Bertholdi the Contortionist, the dancer Ruth St. Denis, as well as such stereotyped subjects as a Negro woman bathing her child and a farm woman feeding chickens; on March 22, 1895, the Lumière brothers showed their first films of equally commonplace subjects; on May 20, 1895, in New York City, the Latham brothers, assisted by Dickson, and using a crude projector known as the Eidoloscope, showed the first motion picture "presented to a paying audience anywhere in the world, since it preceded the [December 28] 1895 exhibitions of Lumière and [the September 1895 exhibition of Thomas] Armat and the [February 28] 1896 presentation of [Robert W.] Paul."[2] This Latham exhibition was not entirely successful, but on April 23, 1896, at Koster and Bial's Music Hall in New York City, Thomas Armat and Thomas Edison successfully employed the Vitascope to present the first motion picture show projected to a paying American audience.[3]

The subjects of these first films were limited only by the intrepidity and imagi-

Auguste and Louis Lumière (1862–1954; 1864–1948)

nation of their makers. On June 10, 1895, the Lumière brothers made the first French film of a news event at the meeting of the Sociétés Photographiques de France in Lyons—hardly breathtaking news, but nonetheless a first. On June 20, 1895, British pioneer Birt Acres made the first films of an event of international importance: the official opening of the Kiel Canal by Kaiser Wilhelm II at Brunsbüttelkoog. In May 1896, Lumière photographer Francis Doublier photographed the coronation of Czar Nicolas II in Moscow, while other Lumière photographers such as Félix Mesguich travelled the world in search of unusual subjects.[4] A year later, on June 3, 1896, another British pioneer, Robert Paul, in association with Acres, photographed the Derby at Epsom Downs. These films were soon followed by other films of important news events and suggested the format for the newsreel genre that was established in the early 1900s: royal visits, sports events, catastrophes and disasters, and public ceremonies, such as inaugurations and funerals of great leaders.

In the United States, before 1900, the major American film producers—Edison, Biograph, and Vitagraph—were also engaged in filming both conventional and extraordinary events. Fielding observes that Edison was the most prolific producer of news films during the pre-1900 period:

> At first thought, this seems remarkable, considering the bulkiness of the first Edison cameras. Appraisal of the Edison output, however, reveals that its subject

matter, almost without exception, lent itself to (1) thorough preproduction planning, (2) adequate time in advance of events for the mounting and preparation of the heavy camera, and (3) a static, never-changing camera position for the duration of the event. (16)

The subjects of the films made by these American companies included celebrated railway trains of the day, the Alaskan gold rush, New York street scenes, the inauguration of President William McKinley in 1897, and portraits of such celebrities as William Jennings Bryan, General Sir Herbert Kitchener, New York Police Chief Theodore Roosevelt, and Pope Leo XIII, photographed in the Vatican in 1898.[5] Sports films—factual and faked—were very popular; in June 1894, Edison and others made the first of a series of successful films of boxing matches.[6]

These early factual and news films by Friese-Green, Edison, Dickson, Acres, Doublier, Mesguich, Paul, Biograph, Vitagraph, and others provide a vivid and valuable record. Their achievements are all the more extraordinary considering their unwieldy equipment, the difficulty in transporting it, and the limitations imposed by the amount of footage that could be shot at any one time. It is no diminution of that achievement to note that it is also fragmentary, perhaps because of its novelty, or the exigencies of early competition for audiences, or both. By contrast, the achievement of the Lumière brothers between 1894 and 1897 stands out for the efficiency with which their organization prospered, the spontaneity of their approach to the world, and the comprehensiveness of their *oeuvre*.

LOUIS AND AUGUSTE LUMIÈRE

The significance of the work of Louis and Auguste Lumière (1862–1954; 1864–1948) is deeply rooted in both the scientific and artistic developments of the nineteenth century.[7] Their efforts connect the end of the experimental period (the experiments and inventions of Muybridge, Edison, Dickson, and others) and the beginning of the evolution of the language of cinema (the French cinema, in the achievements of Georges Méliès, who used cinema to create illusion, and Louis Feuillade, who links the realism of Lumière with the fantasy of Méliès[8]—and the American cinema in that of Edwin S. Porter, D. W. Griffith, and others). As Henri Langlois writes, "thanks to the Lumière brothers, . . . the cinema was born into the lap of daily life."[9]

Nevertheless, among cinema historians, there is some disagreement on the importance of their work. Richard Roud says that, "for all their protestations to the contrary, they were filmmakers and they were artists."[10] Erik Barnouw calls Louis Lumière a "prophet" (6); however, Alan Williams concludes that "the Lumières are more interesting and certainly more historically accessible figures when viewed as talented entrepreneurs rather than as minor gods or 'prophets.' "[11] In fact, they were all of these—nineteenth-century prophets of a twentieth-century art form, creators of the first films to record actuality, and shrewd businessmen whose superb organization made cinema a worldwide phenomenon within ten years. The foremost achievements of the Lumières lie in two broad areas: their contributions to the development of motion picture technology and the films themselves.

The Lumières' Contributions to Technology

The Lumière brothers were born into a family—called the French word for "light"—already famous in the history of photography.[12] Their father, Antoine Lumière, a photographer, founded a factory in Lyons that became the leading European manufacturer of photographic products, second internationally only to the Eastman plant in Rochester, New York.[13] Eventually, the two brothers ran the factory, which by 1895 employed some 300 workers.[14]

In 1894, Louis Lumière began experimenting with Edison's Kinetoscope and Kinetograph; making the improvements necessary for projecting filmstrips, which were lacking in Edison's machines, he invented the *cinématographe*. A portable machine, powered by hand-crank, that could be taken anywhere, the *cinématographe* was actually three machines in one—camera, developer, and projector—and it weighed about sixteen pounds, approximately one hundredth of the weight of the camera that Edison installed in the "Black Maria." Louis Lumière invented the machine, patented its technical innovations under his and his brother's name, and coined the name *cinématographe* (from the Greek for "motion re-

Cinématographe: Louis Lumière's portable machine was actually three machines in one—camera, developer, and projector—that was powered by hand-crank and could be taken anywhere.

corder") that—in its shortened name, *cinéma* —designates the art form itself. With great energy, Lumière participated in the entire process; he said:

> Not only did I make these films, but the first strips shown at the Grand-Café were developed by me in enameled iron slop-buckets containing the developer, then the washing water and the fixative. The relevant positives were similarly printed and I used as a source of light a white wall with the sun shining on it.[15]

In addition, he made other significant contributions: he set the film width at 35mm and established the silent film speed at 16fps (sound film, developed much later, runs at 24fps).[16] In 1895, in the United States, Thomas Armat independently discovered the Lumière principle of intermittment film movement, developed the "loop" (American loop or Latham loop), and sold it to Edison, who brought it all together in a projector known as the Vitascope (a projecting version of the earlier Kinetoscope). David A. Cook writes,

> The Vitascope and Cinématographe mark the culmination of the cinema's prehistory. All the basic technological principles of film recording and projection had been discovered and incorporated into existing machines—machines which, with certain obvious exceptions like the introductive of light-sensitive sound, have remained essentially unchanged from that day to this. Conversely, the history of cinema as an art form begins with these events, for if our understanding of the machines was sophisticated, knowledge of how to use them was primitive indeed. In fact, the kind of documentary recording practiced by Edison and the Lumières was to become the mainstream tendency of the cinema until the turn of the century because there was as yet no notion that the camera might be used to tell a story—i.e., to *create* a narrative reality rather than simply *record* some real or staged event which occurred before its lens. (12–13)

The Lumière Films

On March 22, 1895, the Lumières were invited to show their first film, *La sortie des ouvriers de l'usine Lumière* (*Workers Leaving the Lumière Factory*), at the meeting of a scientific group, the Société d'encouragement à l'Industrie Nationale, an event that is considered by many as the world's first successful projection of a moving picture.[17] On June 10, 1895, they showed an expanded program of eight films to the meeting of the Sociétés Photographiques de France at Neuville-Saint-Vaast near Lyons. There, they added to the excitement provoked by their invention by making films of the delegates arriving at the congress hall and projecting them two days later. Further showings for invited audiences took place in Brussels on June 12, July 11, and November 10 and at the Sorbonne in Paris on November 16. They began the commercial exploitation of their films with the first public performance for a paying audience on December 28, 1895, in the Salon Indien, a room in the basement of the Grand Café on the Boulevard de Capucines in Paris.[18] The following program is typical of what the first Lumière audiences would have seen: *Workers Leaving the Lumière Factory* (*La sortie des ouvriers de l'usine Lumière*); *Arrival of Express at Lyons* (*Arrivée d'un train en*

Workers Leaving the Lumière Factory [*La sortie des ouvriers de l'usine Lumière*]
(**Auguste and Louis Lumière, France, 1895**)

gare de Villefranche-sur-Saône); *The Baby's Meal* (*Le repas de bebé*); *The Falling Wall* (*Démolition d'un mur*); *Boys Sailing Boats in the Tuileries Gardens; The Baths at Milan; French Dragoons; Gondola Party; The Sprinkler Sprinkled* (*L'arroseur aroseé*); *Sack Race; Military Review, Hungary; German Hussars Jumping Fences; Feeding the Swans*; and *Boiler Loading*.

While there are accounts of what some members of those audiences thought as they watched these first moving pictures projected on a screen, it is almost impossible today for us to imagine the impact of this unique and curious experience, an exciting novelty that provided a view of the world that no one had ever seen this way before, what John Grierson admired as the "fine careless rapture" of their observation.[19] For us today these films are documents in cinema history and records of historical reality. But those first audiences, unaware of the cinema history that was to come, must have had a different reaction: delighted by the recognition of the familiar; intrigued, perhaps bewildered, by the unfamiliar; frightened, even, because of the size and immediacy of the image. Most of all, however, they were enthralled by the movement; indeed, once they had accepted the movement *per se*, they were ready for anything.

These first films were no more than 30 seconds long, shot by a stationary camera from a fixed point, but even with those limitations, each encompassed a new world of movement. Almost one hundred years later, viewers still find the inescapable shock of the new in these first films. To see them is to be "overwhelmed by the *potentiality* of the medium: as if it had just been invented and lay waiting still to be explored."[20]

While the traditional judgment of these films does suggest that their primary aim and pleasure was the depiction of motion for its own sake, Marshall Deutelbaum argues that these films

> draw their structure from the inherent processes selected for their subjects. . . . these processes are either linear and sequential actions in which a series of related events moves toward an inherent conclusion or circular processes in which a series of actions recurs in a regular manner, cyclically without reaching a conclusion.[21]

He concludes that, together with their sheer structural sophistication, "the expressive use of space and simultaneity of action to be seen in several of these films strongly argue that it is time to reconsider our evaluation of these films' artistic achievement" (37).

Indeed, *Barque sortant du port* (*Boat Leaving the Port*) is especially dynamic within its fixed frame, suggesting the stability within flux that was literary realism for such novelists as Marcel Proust, James Joyce, and Virginia Woolf. At the left of the frame, there is the action of men attempting to row a boat through a rough surf; at the right, there is a comparatively static scene in which several women and children watch as the boat is almost swamped by a wave.[22] *Workers Leaving the Lumière Factory,* the first Lumière film, reveals a different sense of structure, both natural and theatrical at the same time. Here, the Lumières use a theatrical device of opening and closing doors to frame the action. The camera is facing large double factory doors, which open to permit a stream of men and women workers to leave the factory; they walk towards us, and then to the left and right as they leave the frame, and, just as one man scampers back into the factory, the doors close. Within that simple structure—quite formal, as perhaps suits their first film—there is great spontaneity, a little humor, and documentary realism. The clothing, rather more formal than one might expect for factory workers, reminds us that this was not a dirty mill, but a factory producing optical instruments and equipment. This little film may also tell us something about the work ethic by reminding us that people have always moved a little faster as they quit the workplace and go on with their lives.[23]

Among the other films, the straightforward *Arrival of a Train at La Ciotat* is not likely to frighten anyone today, but *The Sprinkler Sprinkled* introduced what was to become a classic comic convention of the cinema. Several of the others offered unique moving pictures of foreign locales and customs; and *Feeding the Swans* is notable for a deeper sense of space than the others: in the middle ground, a man is leaning over a rail to feed swans in a lake in the background, when a trolley passes between the camera and the man, reminding us of the foreground.

The success of the Lumière organization is demonstrated by the speed with which they met the public's demand for moving pictures. Louis Lumière recalled that they made about fifty films in the first year, each of which was about one minute long, the maximum length of the reel.[24] By February, 1896, Lumière films were being shown at the Empire Theatre in London; by April, four theatres in Paris were showing them daily, and in May and June they were shown in New York City at three theatres: Keith's Union Square, Eden Musée, and Koster and Bial's, a music hall on Madison Square.[25] Félix Mesguich, the Lumière operator who projected the films for the Koster and Bial's showing on June 18 reports that the films were so enthusiastically received that he was brought from the projection booth to the stage, presented to the audience while the orchestra played *La Marseillaise,* and then taken to dinner. Within several days, reporters came to his lodgings at all hours to interview him and obtain more news of the *cinématographe.* Reviewing the first Lumière program in Russia, Maxim Gorky said that he was disturbed and depressed by the depiction of a gray and irrelevant world:

> Last night I was in the Kingdom of Shadows. If you only knew how strange it is to be there. It is a world without sound, without colour. Everything there—the earth, the trees, the people, the water and the air—is dipped in monotonous grey. Grey rays of the sun across the grey sky, grey eyes in grey faces, and the leaves of the trees are ashen grey. It is not life but its shadow, it is not motion but its soundless spectre.[26]

Such pessimism did not hinder the Lumière organization in introducing their films throughout the world,[27] giving "audiences—rich and poor, royalty and commoner—an unprecedented sense of seeing the world" (Barnouw 13).[28] For example, in March 1897, audiences at New York's Proctor's Pleasure Palace saw the following program, guaranteed to please everyone with its varied local and foreign subjects: *The Baby's First Lesson in Walking; The Electrical Carriage Race from Paris to Bordeaux; A Gondola Scene in Venice; The Charge of the Austrian Lancers; Fifty Ninth Street, Opposite Central Park; A Scene Near South Kensington, London; The Fish Market at Marseilles, France; German Dragoons Leaping the Hurdles; A Snow Battle at Lyon, France; Negro Minstrels Dancing in the London Streets; A Sack Race between Employees of Lumière & Sons Factory, Lyon;* and *The Bath of Minerva, at Milan, Italy.*[29]

At the end of 1897, although the Lumières had successfully exhibited and exploited more than 750 *cinématographe* films around the world, they withdrew from film production, discontinued the exhibition tours, and concentrated on manufacturing and marketing the *cinématographe* and films already in their catalog. From 358 titles in the first Lumière catalog, the 1900 catalog, *Catalogue Général des Vues Positives,* listed 1,299 titles by the Lumiéres and others, almost all of which became world famous. There were diverse subjects, such as *Barque sortant du port (Boat Leaving the Port), Scieurs de bois (Wood Cutters), Baignade de négrillons (Bathing Spot of Negro Children);* comic subjects, such as *Jury de peinture (Painting Jury);* random coverage of France in such films as *Carmaux: défournage du coke (Carmaux: Coke Oven)* and *Lyons: quai de l'archevêque (Lyons: Archbishop's Quay);* and many films of military scenes, a subject that was popular in the work of such French photographers as Gustave Le Gray and in the paintings of

Jean Baptiste Édouard Detaille and Jean Louis Ernest Meissonier.[30] The authorship of the Lumière films was clear, and the ease with which their themes were adapted by other filmmakers not only "summed up several conventions of modern mass production. . . . [but also] expressed what the public would find appealing, interesting, or moving."[31]

The Lumières and Thomas A. Edison

Between 1889 and 1897, many entrepreneurs around the world were engaged in a rapid scramble to develop motion picture equipment, produce films, and entertain audiences. The range of nonfiction film titles they produced provides not only an indication of the producers' energy and ingenuity in giving audiences films of anything that moved, but also a foretaste of the newsreel genre that was to become so popular in the United States during and after the second decade of the twentieth century. Not all participants in this were fortunate, as is most amply demonstrated by the Lumiére organization's success and the Vitascope Company's comparative

Thomas A. Edison
(1847–1931)

lack of it. The Lumières' phenomenal worldwide gain can be attributed to several factors: the novelty of their films and the delight they brought to audiences; the superiority of their industrial organization; the acumen of their marketing policy and their overall business judgment; and, according to Allen, their understanding "of the determining influence exerted upon early motion picture industrial practices by vaudeville."[32] According to Williams, the efforts of Edison's Vitascope Company "seem crude and unsystematic by comparison" (159).

In manufacturing the Kinetograph, Edison's Company could not ensure a reliable delivery schedule; moreover, even if the bulky machine was delivered on time, inconsistencies in the electrical current systems in American cities often inhibited its debut further. The Lumière's *cinématographe,* manufactured first in their Lyons factory and, by 1896, in the workshops of the engineer Jules Carpentier,[33] was hand-cranked, and thus independent of the available electrical source. In addition to the availability and reliability of the *cinématographe,* its portability and versatility further enhanced its success in contrast to the Kinetoscope. A camera/projector/printer all in one, it weighed slightly over sixteen pounds, enabling the operator to go virtually anywhere in the world to shoot live action and then to develop the footage and project it within hours.[34] The Kinetoscope, however, was a bulky, electrical driven apparatus. Operated inside Edison's famous Black Maria open-air studio in New Jersey, it was used primarily to film short versions of what audiences would have otherwise seen live on the vaudeville stage.

The Lumière and Edison films were similar in length (running from 15 to 90 seconds), with the subject determining the actual length: the stationary camera was turned on to record the action and turned off when the action was completed, and there was no editing. The films produced by both Lumière and Edison were also similar in their wide range of topics. In 1894 alone, the Edison organization made 120 Kinetoscopes on subjects different from those chosen by the Lumières: a Corbett–Courtney heavyweight fight, Buffalo Bill's Wild West Show, lady fencers, minstrels, acrobats, and many other theatrical attractions already familiar in the vaudeville theatres.[35] It seems ironic that two Frenchmen understood better than Edison (and the others who had actually photographed vaudeville acts) the potential of the motion picture for entertainment and profit within the theatrical context of American vaudeville, but the Lumières gained extensive worldwide experience while exhibiting their films, and they learned how to please the public. However, Edison's American exhibitors Raff and Gammon were the first to find a successful format for integrating motion pictures into the most available format: the vaudeville theatre.

Within about four years, the Lumières had not only established the nonfiction film but also profoundly influenced entertainment around the world.[36] Their organization was efficient not only in the manufacture of its equipment and the ease with which it could be employed, but also in its system of distribution and exhibition. When they withdrew from film production to concentration on research and manufacture—an area where Louis Lumière was, according to Barnouw, "most at home" (17)—they

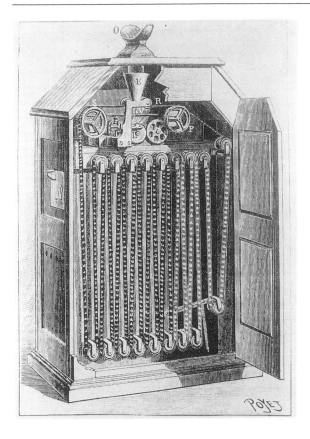

Kinetoscope: Thomas A. Edison's and W. K. L. Dickson's Kinetoscope machines showed half-minute films to single observers who looked through the viewfinder (marked *O* on the drawing).

left behind them a pattern of industrial practice that survived for the next decade: the providing of vaudeville theaters with a complete "act" consisting of projector, films, and operator. (Allen 152)

The *cinématographe* operator, like the *cinématographe* itself, was able to perform many tasks; he could be filmmaker, distributor, exhibitor, and projectionist, all at the same time. In contrast, the production and exhibition format of the new American film industry had not been firmly established, and the Vitascope Company was beset by organizational problems, further compounded by the need for several people to perform the jobs that one person could with the *cinématographe*, a fundamental misunderstanding of the market, and the desire to make a short-term profit. However, adoption of the Lumières' "marketing plan formed the basis for much of the success of the Edison and Vitagraph film companies prior to 1905" (Allen 152).

The Lumières' Overall Contributions to the Nonfiction Film
As great as the Lumières' contributions were to the technology of motion picture production and projection, their perception and recording of reality were even

more important to the history of the nonfiction film. To them, art was not an imitation of reality, but a direct, nonnarrative record of actual people doing actual things; the emphasis here is on recording reality, but, as we have seen, they also shaped this footage with a fidelity to the subject's inherent nature and structure. The Lumière factual film did not attempt what John Grierson and the 1930s' British documentary film succeeded in developing: the use of the factual record, or the deliberate reconstruction, in the service of specific educational, political, and social ends (see chapters 3 and 4). The essential triumph of the Lumière films and the secret of their beauty is what Dai Vaughan calls their "harnessing of spontaneity" (127). As such, they ensured the success and continuation of realist tradition by exploiting the audience's amazement at seeing moving pictures of familiar things; their mastery of the vernacular sublime certainly influenced the still photographs of Jean-Eugène-Auguste Atget (1857–1927), Jacques-Henri Lartigue (1896–1987), and William Rau (1855–1920). Instead of the lateral movement on one plane that viewers saw in the persistence of vision devices,

> the motion picture had at least made it possible to show an object *approaching* an audience. Lumière selected this head-on view in order to get the whole train into the picture; a side angle would have been inadequate. By doing this, he unconsciously added the one element missing from other attempts at simulating movement: dynamism.[37]

The Lumières shrewdly realized the limitations of their organization and their capital as well as the corollary need to create a demand for their new product. To further enhance the attraction of novelty and invention, they projected still color images along with the motion pictures and took pictures of a group of people one day and then showed them the next day to the same group.[38] In addition to establishing the French supremacy in production and export for almost ten years, they also set the pattern for entertainment—a program of short filmed items, predominantly of a documentary sort—that would be dominant for some years and influence the development of the newsreel.[39]

THE FACTUAL FILM AFTER THE LUMIÈRES

The years between 1894 and 1897 encompass the most important period of the Lumières' achievement. By their own choice, they had stopped making films, but their influence remained strong, and their phenomenal success prompted a score of successful imitators to compete for a share of the market. The Lumière legacy can be seen in the work of filmmakers around the world: Alexandre Promio and Ernest Florman in Sweden, Peter Elfelt in Denmark, Fructuoso Gelabert in Spain, Antonio Ramos in Spain, the Philippines, and China, Félix Mesguich in Great Britain, and Harischandra Sakharam Bhatvadekar and Abdullaly Esoofally in India.[40]

A few years later, changes began to affect the subject and the form of the nonfiction film. Known as *actualités, documentaires,* topicals, educationals, interest films, expedition films, travel films, and travelogues, these films covered a wide range of subjects.[41] As the scope of the subjects expanded, so, too, did the running times, from one to two and eventually to five and ten minutes in the first years of the twentieth century.[42] In addition to international subjects, the Lumière films concentrated on recording middle class French life which, of course, had a broad audience appeal; but their European successors recorded royal, presidential, and military subjects, which rewarded the filmmakers with the sponsorship of these high ranking officials and provided the latter with excellent publicity. Subjects included the visit of the Czar to Paris; the Alaskan gold rush; the first Wright brothers flight in France 1908; sports events such as the Henley Regatta; military exhibitions; catastrophes and disasters, such as the 1906 San Francisco earthquake and fire; and such ceremonies as Queen Victoria's Diamond Jubilee in 1897 and her funeral in 1901, Gladstone's funeral in 1898, and the funeral of the martyred British feminist, Emily Davison, in 1913.

While audiences and filmmakers alike realized that movement was the essence of cinema, they also understood, as Brownlow writes, that "it is not the movement itself that is magical, but how that movement is used" (2). The Lumières emphasized movement for its own sake, but the public grew weary of the novelty as it became increasingly aware of the medium's theatrical potentialities. In Great Britain, the public's favorite topics remained royalty and state occasions, wars, sports, and disasters. According to Rachel Low, their "attitude towards such films still showed a certain lack of sophistication, a certain indifference to whether what they saw on the screen was real or merely a reconstruction, or even a topical allusion."[43] In the United States, both movement and excitement were exploited, and typical titles, ranging from the ordinary to the bizarre, include three films shot at Coney Island: *Shooting the Chutes* (1896), one of many filmed records of an amusement park ride; *Electrocuting an Elephant* (1903), the record of the destruction of a mankilling elephant; and *Coney Island at Night* (1905); as well as such prosaic filmed records as *Market Square, Harrisburg, Pa.* (1897) and *Railway Station Scene* (1897); faked war footage, shot in New York, including *The Battle of Manila Bay* (1898) and *Raising Old Glory Over Morro Castle* (1899); footage of a natural disaster, *Searching Ruins on Broadway, Galveston, for Dead Bodies* (1900) and *Scenes of the Wreckage from the Waterfront* (1900), perhaps the first films about a natural disaster; and such unique events as the razing of a four story brick building, *A Mighty Tumble* (1901), and the beginning of air mail, *First Mail Delivery by Aeroplane* (1911).[44]

Nonfiction travel films, which were a success at the 1900 Paris Exposition, soon became popular in the United States as well. There were two film showings at the Paris Exposition, both based on the projection of realist film in an illusionist setting: the Raoul Grimsoin-Sanson's *Cinéorama*, which gave audiences the sense of looking at the landscape from a hot-air balloon, and the Lumière brothers' *Maréorama*, which simulated the view that the audience would have had from the bridge of a ship.[45] In the United States, between 1902 and 1904, William J. Keefe presented an entertainment in which the audience, seated in an open-sided railroad car, rode through a tunnel and saw scenic motion pictures made from a real train. The illusion of realism was heightened by devices that made the car vibrate as if it were on a real track. He sold the invention to George C. Hale, who introduced the "Pleasure Railway" at the 1904 St. Louis Exposition.

The "Pleasure Railway" gave audiences the illusion of actual travel: good sightlines to a life-size image on a large screen and vibrations with sound effects adding to the overall effect. The invention was not only a great success with audiences, but also played a major role in the careers of several founders of the American motion picture industry.[46] From 1905 on, the exhibition, which became known as "Hale's Tours," was installed in summer amusement parks and cities throughout the United States and Canada. The film programs of "Hale's Tours," supplied by American and European sources, were changed weekly, and offered audiences the illusion of railroad and trolley trips in many parts of the world. The theatres in which it played were sometimes designed to look like railroad depot offices, with the ushers dressed as conductors. Although the films were in black and white, the illusion was nonetheless convincing, particularly "because of the way in which the moving image of the tracks slipped away under the forward edge of the coach."[47] However, since only a limited number of titles were ever available at any one time, audiences in the major cities soon grew tired of the novelty and turned to other amusements; those in rural America, with less to divert their attention, remained fascinated with the traveling motion picture shows that introduced them to the world.[48] By 1912, Hale's Tours had ceased to be a source of international entertainment. Fielding concludes:

> Hale's crude attempts to simulate reality may seem ludicrous to us now, but the influence of his little show on the emerging motion picture should not be underestimated. It served not only to introduce and popularize the early projected motion picture, but also acted as a bridge which linked the primitive arcade peep shows and vaudeville presentations of the day with the makeshift motion picture theaters which spread across the United States between 1905 and 1910. (129)

Together with the growing need for a steady supply of short films to please the growing audiences in the nickelodeons and vaudeville theaters of the major Eastern cities, there was also a decline in the general quality, vitality, and appeal of the nonfiction film.[49] This, in turn, contributed to the rapid rise and immense popularity of the narrative format of the fiction film. As audiences tired of the formulaic travel films, they were attracted to films characterized by restaging and outright deception; these included Georges Méliès' very popular *actualité reconstituée* (reconstructed factual film) and all kinds of film fakery ranging from disasters contrived and shot in miniature to restaged foreign wars shot in New Jersey.[50] Neil Harris observes that "as audiences watched the first movies, seeing things that had never been observed before, it was not always necessary for the scenes to be literally authentic" (47). Even as the nonfiction film became less and less a part of film programs, World War I created a new audience interest in both nonfiction and narrative films about war.

THE NONFICTION FILM AND WAR: 1898–1918

Before World War I

With the sinking of the U.S. battleship *Maine* on 15 February 1898, the subsequent Cuban crisis, and the 1898 Spanish–American War, filmmakers had their first opportunities to record live combat action as well as to contribute to war propaganda. While some of this war footage was genuine, much of it, like much of the newspaper reporting of the period, was faked.[51] Shown on a typical program with comic films and nonwar films, these war films, like war coverage in the newspapers, became immensely popular with the public. Charles Musser writes that most vaudeville theaters

> showed pertinent "war films" for weeks and then months without interruption: in many cases moving pictures became a standard feature. This sudden increase in demand gave exhibitors like American Vitagraph new opportunities to move up to big-time showmanship.[52]

These early war films not only provided the public with thrill of seeing motion pictures of combat for the first time, but also roused public opinion and prowar sentiment, helping William Randolph Hearst's New York *Journal* and Joseph Pulitzer's New York *World* to exploit, distort, and exaggerate the news ("yellow journalism"). These films reflected both the nonfiction and the fiction impulses of the early cinema: "There is both the obsession with recording true events, albeit from a certain perspective, and the desire to make the cinema perform feats, through editing and double exposure, to dramatise the 'cause.' "[53] In July 1898, Albert E. Smith and J. Stuart Blackton shot actual footage of the assault on San Juan Hill in Cuba by Theodore Roosevelt and the Rough Riders. According to Fielding, their motion picture record contradicted written reports, for "Smith and Blackton's pictures of Roosevelt's attack showed not a theatrical sweep to the top but a slow, undramatic engagement extending over a long period of time" (31). Returning to the United States, they combined this actual record with staged footage, and the result was very successful with an unsuspecting public.[54] In reality, according to Smith,

> The thin line of Rough Riders halted, fired, advanced slowly, more picking their way through the heavy thicket than charging. This was the assault. Nothing glamorous or hip-hip-hooray. . . . It was not until Blackton and I returned to New York that we learned we had taken part in the celebrated "charge" up San Juan Hill. Many historians have given it a Hollywood flavor, but there was vastly more bravery in the tortuous advance against this enemy who could see and not be seen.[55]

Smith and Blackton were the first to experience a dilemma that has confronted war photographers ever since: the contrast between what photographers record in factual combat footage and how propagandists utilize it on the home front. Film exhibitors, too, "cooperated" in the war effort. Not satisfied with the realism of the actual war footage, an enthusiastic London theatre owner set off blank cartridges in the theatre to enhance his exhibition of Boer War and Chinese Boxer Rebellion films.[56]

The success of these films established a pattern for both British and American films made in the Spanish–American War and the Boer War: some filmmakers travelled to the battle to record the action, while others stayed at home and staged war scenes for their cameras. Among the former group, those concerned with verisimilitude was W. K. L. Dickson, who had been Edison's assistant for 17 years in America and who left for South Africa just after the outbreak of the Boer War to follow the troops to battle.[57] Fielding writes that his "horse-drawn Cape cart, filled with photographic equipment, eating utensils, and sleeping gear, became as much a fixture of front-line areas as Mathew Brady's mobile darkroom had been on American Civil War battlegrounds forty years earlier" (34). However, many of the faked films were carefully produced to seem authentic;[58] Thomas Edison, who "shot all his Boer War series in the Orange Mountains of New Jersey, was particularly adept in this respect."[59] British films of the Boer War of 1899–1901, according to Elizabeth Grottle Strebel, are remarkable as fact and propaganda, "undoubtedly more revealing of Victorian England than of South Africa, full of the myths and symbols of British imperialist iconography."[60]

With what appears to have been full cooperation of the warring factions, filmmakers also photographed (and faked) footage of the Chinese Boxer Uprising of 1898–1900, the Russo–Japanese War of 1904–05, the Mexican Revolution of 1910–11,[61] and the Balkan Wars of 1912–13. Jessica Borthwick, who may be the first woman filmmaker to have a place in cinema history, received some brief training in 1913 with a motion picture camera and spent a year in the Balkans making films in towns, prisons, hospitals, and on the battlefield.[62] The 1917 Russian Revolution received little attention from Russian filmmakers, although an American, Donald C. Thompson, brought back some footage that he incorporated in *Blood-Stained Russia* (1917).[63] Although Dziga Vertov began making films in 1918, it was not until 1922 that the great age of the Soviet nonfiction film began with his *Kinopravda*.

World War I: 1914–18

Kevin Brownlow writes that "the motion picture came of age during World War I,"[64] the Great War, the largest war the world had ever seen. When war broke out in 1914, film became a weapon of information and propaganda for the Allies— Great Britain, Belgium, France, the United States—as well as for the German enemy.[65] The need to mobilize opinion at home and abroad became an essential task for all countries, involved or neutral. War replaced such subjects as travel as the focus of the nonfiction film, and "for a while film people, like everybody else in Britain, could think of hardly anything but the war." (Low, 146) These silent newsreels and factual films were produced in spite of savage conditions and numerous other obstacles deliberately created by military and civilian authorities to make it virtually impossible for all but official cameramen to gain access to frontline areas and avoid the frontline censors and those at home. Helping filmmakers to overcome some of these obstacles was such specialized equipment as long-focus lenses and the De Proszynski Aeroscope camera, a lightweight, self-powered camera that was hand-held and did not require a tripod.[66] As with previous coverage of war by motion picture cameramen, faked footage was common, although, according to Fielding, "genuine footage, although of rather poor quality and coverage, did appear from time to time" (118). Moreover, the coverage tended to be specific, rather than universal, and Jack Spears points out that European films did better in Europe and the American films did better in the United States.[67]

BRITISH AND ALLIED FILMS

The British, who entered the war in late August 1914, realized early the importance of films to the war effort; in fact, although film had figured in the recruitment campaign, the British had not yet established goals or priorities for war film production. In recognition of the successful efforts of German propagandists, "the recognition of film as an important medium of official British propaganda also increased as the war progressed."[68] Soon, however, a nearly secret propaganda effort, the War Propaganda Bureau, was established in Wellington House, its headquarters, where it operated from 1914 to 1916. As might be expected, the British propaganda films were no different from those produced in other countries, which is to say that most of them were composed of either faked or reenacted scenes. According to Sanders and Taylor:

> The use of films and photographs for propaganda purposes provided an "illusion of reality" at a time when it was generally believed that the camera could not lie. The use of film montage techniques might well have been in its infancy but film, whether still or motion, could only depict what the cameraman wanted it to depict. The images presented were, in fact, carefully staged. While there were often several apparently quite realistic camera shots of wounded soldiers at the front, they were usually staged-managed in order to show fatigue being accompanied by cheerfulness. Wounds were always freshly dressed and there were rarely pictures of Allied dead, although dead Germans did feature more often. Only Allied troops in action or Allied victories were exhibited. There were realistic images of the muddy conditions at Ypres in photographic exhibitions, but their theme was symbolised by one exhibit demanding to know "Where is the pessimist?" among a line of smiling soldiers. The intention of portraying high morale was obvious, namely to convince the civilian population at home, in allied and Imperial countries that their efforts were worthwhile and producing visible effects at the front line. (155)

Because propaganda films were not always welcomed by the owners of commercial theaters, special trucks equipped with projectors took them directly to the public; as we shall see in chapter 4, following the 1917 Revolution, the Russians adopted this method with great success.

Soon after the establishment of the War Propaganda Bureau came the rapid development of government-sponsored filmmaking, and in October 1915, an important agreement was reached between the War Office and leading representatives of the British film industry. Not only did this accord solve their important differences on such matters as distribution and exhibition, but it also paved the way for a cooperative effort between government and private industry in a time of national crisis. They agreed that two categories of war film would be produced: those meant for immediate public exhibition and those designed chiefly as historical records; that British cinematographers would go to the front and send their footage back to be edited and titled most often by others, the same footage often being reused in different combinations; that the British film industry would supply the necessary equipment and expertise, while the budget and transportation would be provided by the War Office; that all negatives, prints, and copyrights were to be the property of the government; and that films were to be distributed for exhibition only in the British Empire, excluding the sensitive areas of Egypt and India.

This agreement preceded the production and release on 29 December 1915 of *Britain Prepared,* the major turning point in the development of the British film in the First World War. (Note: in the following discussion, dates are given for these films when known.) *Britain Prepared* is a compilation film that portrayed the extent of Britain's contribution to the war effort in Allied countries; ironically, the first official British film was made by an American, Charles Urban. According to Sanders and Taylor, the film

> presented in a straightforward manner the wartime activities of the British armed services, reinforced by scenes of the civilian effort in munitions factories. The film also showed basic military training, trench-digging and trench-fighting techniques (using clods of earth as weapons), as well as the various supporting services such as communications and food supply. Scenes at the Vickers munitions works recorded the contribution of women to the war effort. However, the most striking scenes of the film concerned the Royal Navy. As protector of the British Empire, the navy inspired the most impressive photography, with dramatic scenes of destroyers screening battleships, of submarines firing torpedoes, and of big guns in action. For its day, the film was an impressive production which gave the appearance of British naval supremacy even before the fleet had been tested in battle. (151–52)

According to Kevin Brownlow, *Britain Prepared* is "unusual, if not unique, in the history of propaganda films" because of its absolute honesty in showing the nation the industrial and military effort involved in preparing for war.[69] Urban screened the film in New York and Washington—to President Wilson, foreign ambassadors and members of congress—in an attempt to gain American support for the British effort and perhaps even to increase the chances that America would enter the war; however, the United States remained neutral until April 1917.

Realizing that his British patriotism may have been too strong for the American audience, Urban tried a different approach. Backed by such powerful financiers as William K. Vanderbilt and J. P. Morgan, he produced a serial that combined parts of *Britain Prepared* with *The Battle of the Somme.* The serial comprised three main parts—*Jellicoe's Grand Fleet, Kitchener's Great Army,* and *The Battle of the Somme*—and was shown with *The Munitions Makers* and *The Destruction of a Zeppelin.*[70] These films, seen by large audiences, produced large profits, part of which Morgan and Vanderbilt insisted be shared with war relief organizations. Low cites four films as conveying to the British audience "an entirely new understanding of the complexity of modern warfare, and a picture of mud, cheerfulness and death in the trenches" (157–58): *The Battle of the Somme* (1916), *St. Quentin* (1916), *The Battle of Ancre* (1917), and *Advance of the Tanks* (1917).[71] Rudimentary in cinematic terms, their impact was based on the material they presented rather than on its arrangement.

At the end of 1915, the producers of topical films were regularized as the War Office Topical Committee; in September 1917, the Committee acquired Jeapes's Topical Film and began to issue a regular one-reeler titled *War Office Topical Budget and Pictorial News*. In December 1916, David Lloyd George, the British Minister of War, became Prime Minister, and immediately reorganized the structure of government offices. To replace the war propaganda activities taking place in Wellington House, he created the Department of Information, with a Press and Cinema Branch, which, in turn, was replaced in February 1918 by the Ministry of Information, led by Lord Beaverbrook.

Despite the popularity of cinema in Great Britain before the war, it was only after 1914 that what was then still a novelty became an established phenomenon in British society. War films played an important role in this. Sanders and Taylor write:

> Screened images of the conflict served to personalize the heroism of Allied troops and the horrors of German war-making and contributed towards making the conflict one of total involvement. But if Wellington House had regarded the cinema as the "bible" of the working classes in most countries, particularly in areas of high illiteracy, the early concentration upon intellectual propaganda meant that its real potential went largely untapped, despite the occasional success. It was only with the . . . establishment of the Ministry of Information that its mass appeal was fully exploited at home and in Allied and neutral countries. (130)

Early British war films included *Men of the Moment, Termonde in Ruins,* and *Strand War Series,* and *The Great European War* (all 1914). The Allied viewpoint was provided in such films as *With the Russian Army: Artillery in Action Before Przemysl* (c. 1915), *At the Front with the Allies* (1916), *Somewhere in France* (1916), *Scenes of the First World War* (c. 1917), *On the Firing Line with the Germans, Austria at War, The Log of the U–35,* and *Retreat of the Germans at Battle of Arras* (1917), a morale-building film with scenes of German destruction. While most Allied films were made by the British, there were also French and Italian nonfiction films concerned with World War I. The French films include *Fighting with France, or, The Allies on the Firing Line* (1916), *Fighting for France* (1916), *War as it Really Is* (1917), *The Sailors of France* (1917), and *How France Cares for Her Wounded Soldiers* (1918), while Italian films include *On Italy's Firing Line* (1917), *The Italian Battlefront* (1917), *Official Italian War Pictures* (1918), and *Italy's Flaming Front* (1918).

As the public demanded more factual films about the war, this, in turn, increased their awareness of the war as well as their response to campaigns designed to boost recruitment and morale. The British films fall into the following main groups: ordinary topical issues and minor feature films, films of the Middle East, royal tours of inspection, naval films, films of particular battles, and general or interpretive treatments of larger themes.[72] Rachel Low cites *Sons of the Empire* and *Our Empire's Fight for Freedom* as being "the two films whose intellectual approach most nearly approximated to the latter-day documentary" (158), adding that the interpretation of material in these films was effected by careful structuring and the use of intertitles. An interesting experiment in film journalism was Pathé's *History of the Great War*, started in 1917, which attempted to put the events of the past three years into perspective. The Ministry of Information's notorious *The Leopard's Spots* (*Once a Hun, Always a Hun*, 1918) consolidated the German stereotypes that had been developed during the previous war years.

Other British war films include C. M. Hepworth's *Men of the Moment* (1915), *Ready, Aye Ready* (1915), *Germany's Army and Navy* (1914), *Lord Kitchener's New Army*, George Pearson's *The Great European War* (1914), *Bachlone of England* (1914), and an especially popular film, *What We Are Fighting For* (1918).[73] Films regularly showed life behind the lines and the training of soldiers, as well as troops entering towns that were currently in the news. Such films were *General Allenby's Historic Entry Into Jerusalem* (produced by Pictorial News, c. 1917); *The Men Ludendorf Fears; The British Offensive, July 1918; Ribemont Gas School; With the South African Forces*; and *Woolwich Arsenal*.[74] A number of films were made about the Middle East, most of them by Jeapes, Frank Hurley, and A. L. Varges. These include *Palestine; With the Australians in Palestine; The British Occupation of Gaza; The Advance in Palestine, 23rd–27th September 1918; With the Forces on the Palestine Front; The 44th Remount Squadron on the Egyptian Coast; The Occupation of Es Salt on May 16th, 1917; With the Forces in Mesopotamia*; and *The New Crusaders*, described by Rachel Low as "a very important film" (155).[75] There were also films featuring royal visits, such as *The King Visits His Armies in the Great Advance, The King's Visit to the Fleet*, and *The Royal Visit to the Battlefields of France*.[76] Also produced during this period were newsreels and industrial films about war materials—for example, Ernest Palmer's *Fighting German Air Raiders* (1916); biographical films, such as *The Life of Lord Roberts* (1914), *The Life of Lord Kitchener* (1914), and *The Man Who Saved the British Empire* [Lloyd George] (1918); and naval films, such as *Our Naval Air Power, The Way of a Ship on the Sea*, and *The Empire's Shield*.[77]

The British films of the First World War used all the known technical resources in attempting to overcome such limitations as the absence of sound, the impossibility of filming after dark, and the extreme difficulty of aerial cinematography. Nevertheless, they are moving in their presentation of facts and in their overall obligation to give the people at home first-hand observation of the situation on the battle fronts.

GERMAN WAR FILMS

The production and distribution of German films was placed under state control in 1915, and in 1917, the responsibility for producing training and newsreel film was given to the Picture and Film Board (*BUFA—Bild und Filmamt*). Alarmed by the growing number of effective anti-German propaganda films made by the Americans, British, and French, the German government realized that such films would also make a vital contribution to the war effort. General Erich Ludendorff, commander in chief of the German Army, wrote:

The war has demonstrated the superiority of the photograph and film as a means of information and persuasion. Unfortunately, our enemies have used their great advantage over us in this field so thoroughly that they have inflicted a great deal of damage. Nor will films lose their significance during the rest of this war as a means of political and military persuasion. For this reason it is of the utmost importance for a successful conclusion to the war that films should be made to work with the greatest possible effect wherever any German persuasion might still have any effect.[78]

Under Ludendorff's orders, UFA (*Universum Film Aktiengesellschaft*) was founded to merge, consolidate, and reorganize the disparate elements of the German film industry into a powerful production machine. Although German war film in World War I lacked the intense, sophisticated propaganda techniques that Joseph Goebbels was to develop in the 1930s, they were no less nationalistic or effective than those produced in the United States or Great Britain. Major titles include *Behind the Fighting Lines of the German Army* (1915), *The Battle of Przemsyl* (1915), *The Fall of Warsaw* (1915), *Germany on the Firing Line* (1916), *Germany and Its Armies of Today* (1917), and *On the Austro-German Battlefronts* (1917).

U.S. GOVERNMENT FILMS ABOUT WORLD WAR I

Before the United States entered the war, American commercial producers, on an ambitious scale, made a variety of war films; a brief selection includes: *The American Soldier, European Armies in Action, On the Belgian Battlefield, History of the World's Greatest War in Motion Pictures, The Great European War,* and *Uncle Sam at Work* (1915); *Somewhere in France, The American Ambulance Boys at the Front, America Unprepared, America Preparing, Uncle Sam's Defenders,* and *France's Canine Allies,* and *Uncle Sam Awake* (1916). After the United States entered the war in 1917, the titles of comparable commercially produced films reflect changing wartime priorities: *Guarding Old Glory, America is Ready, Heroic France, or the Allies in Action, How Uncle Sam Prepares, Our Fighting Forces, Rebuilding America's Merchant Marine, Saving the Food of a Nation,* and *Over Here* (1917); *War Bibles, Our Dumb Friends in War, How Stars Twinkle Away from the Studios, Kiddies of No Man's Land,* and *Rebuilding Broken Lives* (1918); and *The Salvation Army on the Job, The Girl of Tomorrow, American Women in France, Homeward Bound, New Faces for Old, Rebuilding Broken Bodies* (1919).

Meanwhile, after the sinking of the *Lusitania* in 1915, America's neutrality was seriously jeopardized. In February 1917, the United States broke relations with Germany, and, on April 6, it declared war on Germany, entering what President Woodrow Wilson called the "war to make the world safe for democracy." Eight days after war was declared, on 14 April 1917, President Wilson established the Committee on Public Information; under its director, George Creel, the Committee shaped American public policy on war films, monitored domestic production, and regulated international film trade with the United States.[79] Shortly afterward, on 21 July 1917, a photographic section of the Signal Corps was formed to make combat and military training films. Several changes in American war footage resulted from these organizational changes: military cameramen replaced civilian cameramen, the quality of the footage improved, and the emphasis shifted from recording defensive to combat actions.[80] Taken as a whole, the films produced by the U S. government during World War I reflect the "shifting national attitudes regarding the war and America's relationship to it."[81]

While the United States government had begun making films in 1911, including agricultural films from the Bureau of Reclamation and incentive films from the Civil Service, these efforts by the Committee on Public Information and the Signal Corps represented the first official efforts of the U.S. government to make war films. The responsibilities of the Signal Corps, according to Raymond Fielding,

> included receiving, censoring, and editing combat motion picture footage from front-line areas and distributing it to newsreel producers. More than six hundred cameramen and technicians—all members of the armed forces—were engaged in securing combat photographs, both still and motion pictures, for release to theaters and press associations. The task of utilizing photographic techniques for military reconnaissance, intelligence, and communication was handled independently by the Signal Corps. (124–25)

The Committee on Public Information was charged with providing information about the war for Americans and information about America for foreigners, but, according to Kevin Brownlow, the Committee "was not convinced of the superiority of motion pictures as a propaganda force",[82] and, in addition, its production was further hindered by several obstacles. Because it worked from footage sent back to Washington, and could not plan in advance, its "production of propaganda films was left entirely to chance."[83] Moreover, it lacked the close support of the American film industry, which did not want competition. As a result, there were further problems with distribution and exhibition.[84]

The nonfiction films produced by the CPI, ranging from twenty minute shorts to two hour features, were distributed both in the United States and abroad with foreign language subtitles. Their overall theme was to present the democratic way of life, to convey the basic idea that America at war was a powerful, not a violent country, and to emphasize the belief, so dear to American audiences, that the war would be won by the self-sacrifices of ordinary men and women.[85] They avoided battle scenes or anything else that would provoke reactions of revenge, and instead emphasized support activities—training, ambulance work, labor union activities, shipbuilding. About these films, Michael T. Isenberg writes:

> Death was almost continuously absent, while instruments of death were omnipresent. But the instruments were displayed as scientifically marvelous and technologically efficient. Audiences thus could enjoy American ingenuity without seeing its results. (71–72)

In 1918, the CPI's short films included *The Whispering Wires of War,* about the work of the Signal Corps, *Our Fighting Ally—the Tank,* and *Our Bridge of Ships.* Soon realizing, however, that short films were expensive and did not reach a large enough audience, the CPI produced three feature-length films for theatrical release in 1918: *Pershing's Crusaders, America's Answer, Under Four Flags,* all compilation films. (The compilation film is discussed in chapter 4.) These films, widely publicized and screened, bolstered public solidarity with the message of strength through unity. *America's Answer*—the story of America's troops in France, their activities and accomplishments—was, according to Kevin Brownlow, the most successful of the three, while *Under Four Flags,* emphasizing the Allied role, ended with a rousing tableaux of peace designed by New York theatre entrepreneur S. I. "Roxy" Rothapfel.[86] The CPI also produced a periodical newsreel, *The Allied (Official) War Review* (1918), the parts of which were very widely shown in American theatres, and which stressed good news from the Allied battle fronts and the importance of the will to win. Finally, in late 1918, just prior to the Armistice, the CPI produced six short films, including: *When Your Soldier is Hit,* about combat casualties;[87] *Our Wings of Victory,* on airplane construction; *Horses of War; Making the Nation Fit,* on the physical training of military recruits; and two films on munitions, *The Storm of Steel* and *The Bath of Bullets.* Another film, *The Yanks are Coming* (1918), raised a controversy over its depiction of aircraft production secrets. Other CPI titles include: *Flying with the Marines* (1918) and *Our Bridge of Ships* (1918). The CPI ended its activities in June, 1919.

The nonfiction war films made in and by the United States are, for the most part, uneven in quality, but they provide an important historical record of shifting

America's Answer (Committee on Public Information, USA, 1918)

national attitudes regarding the First World War and America's relationship to it. According to Isenberg, these films "did not chart a safe, nonbelligerent course between the contending European powers. Instead, they gravitated from advocating domestic preparedness to displaying Americans serving on the Allied side" (70). As a result, they presented a cross-section of America at war, actively promoting democratic ideals and stressing commitment, but never extolling the individual hero at the expense of the country's commitment. More martial in spirit than in content, these American films not only confronted the all-important issue of isolationism, but also raised morale, showed Americans the extent and price of their country's involvement, and preserved a vital historical record.

AMERICAN COMMERCIAL FILMS ABOUT WORLD WAR I

Commercial producers tried various approaches to compete with the U.S. government's virtual domination of all aspects of nonfiction film production. These included the production of such semidocumentary films as *Women Who Win* and *The Boys From Your State*, the use of color (*Our Invincible Navy* was made with the Prizma color process), or aerial photography (*Flying With the Marines*). Among the films that depicted our Allies were *Heroic France* (1916) and *Under the Stars and Stripes in France* (1917). Others followed the CPI pattern: Paramount-Bray Pictograph produced the *Uncle Sam* newsreel series; Pathé emphasized agricultural themes as well as the communications (*Whispering Wires of War,* 1918) and *War Bibles* (1918), and also praised the Russians' fight against Germany in *The German Curse in Russia* (1918), the story of a Russian woman who disguises herself as a Russian General, fights so valiantly that she is decorated, and founds the Women's Battalion of Death. Other films about the German enemy include Edwin F. Weigle's *Germany in Wartime* (1915) and *The German Side of the War* (1915), *Germany and Its Armies Today* (1917), and *Crashing Through to Berlin* (1918). Universal made the only known film on the involvement of American Indians in the war; the C. L. Chester Company made *Schooling our Fighting Mechanics, There Shall be No Cripples, Colored Americans, It's an Engineer's War, Finding and Fixing the Enemy, Waging War in Washington, All the Comforts of Home, Masters for the Merchant Marine, The College for Camp Cooks, Rail-less Railroads,* and *The Miracle of the Ships* [*Our Bridge of Ships*]; and the W. W. Hodkinson Corporation covered every stage of a soldier's life from draft to combat in *Made in America*.[88]

A different kind of propaganda followed this formula: "Take members of various minority groups, mix generously with people representing various classes, put them all in uniform, and let their racial and social differences be resolved in battle."[89] Examples of this formula in the nonfiction film genre include Edward A. MacManus's *The Lost Battalion* (1919), a semidocumentary that pays tribute to a group of plain Americans "out of the heart of Manhattan." The group includes all strata of society, but "out of this mixed, and they said, 'despicable mass,' was to be forged a thunderbolt to be hurled against the proudest army in Europe."

Nonfiction films about World War I produced after the war include *The Big Drive* (1933), *This is America* (1933), *The First World War* (1934), *Dealers in Death* (semidocumentary, 1934), *Over There* (1934), *The Dead March* (1937), and Louis de Rochemont's *The Ramparts We Watch* (1940), a "March of Time" production that provides an historical explanation of the American role in World War I, including the feelings of American isolation, and that attempts to relate that struggle to World War II.

By the end of World War I, the realist foundation of the nonfiction film had been established in the factual reportage (and sometimes faked footage) of everyday life, of war, and of travel to foreign countries. In addition, the propaganda film was originated in the films of the Spanish–American War and refined in films made during World War I.[90] Yet to be developed was the documentary film, established by the Soviets after the 1917 revolution, and the romantic film of exploration first made famous by the work of Robert Flaherty. When the aberration of the first world war had passed, audiences in the 1920s once again appeared to be more interested in films that explored primitive areas than those that recorded everyday life around them.

<table>
<tr><td>3</td><td># Exploration, Romanticism, and the Western Avant-Garde</td></tr>
</table>

FACTUAL FILMS OF TRAVEL AND EXPLORATION

Films of travel and exploration, such as those exhibited in Hale's Tours in 1904, helped to sustain the early nonfiction cinema. Kevin Brownlow hyperbolically calls factual films "cinema's most noble endeavor" (404) because they have as their primary purpose the communication of information, knowledge, and concepts about faraway and unfamiliar places. For most people in the early years of the century, unaccustomed to anything but the simplest local travel, travel films provided both fact and fantasy, a seemingly reliable window from which to view the world, as the Lumières would have it, and a liberating vision appealing to their imaginations, as Méliès would have it. In addition to their informational value, these films had what we might call a spiritual dimension as well, demonstrating the power of the camera to bring people together through a visual awareness of one another. These early travel films were so faithful in their visual depiction of other people and places that the French called them *documentaires,* not to be confused with the English term *documentary.* What Rotha calls the "naturalist (romantic) tradition"[1] of the nonfiction film began with these films, but their chief purpose soon shifted from producing factual records to promoting trade or increasing the profits of the organization that sponsored them.

By 1908, "travelogue," the word coined by Burton Holmes,[2] was being used to describe the short travel lectures with slides presented between reels at motion picture shows. These slides, the focus of Holmes's lectures, provided "a sort of Baedeker of illuminated information" (Brownlow 420). Another of the earliest informational films about travel focussed on Theodore Roosevelt, who, after his term as President, made an African safari.[3] Accompanying him was filmmaker Cherry Kearton, whose footage resulted in several films: *TR in Africa* (1909), *African Animals* (1909), *TR's Camp in Africa* (1909), and *African Natives* (1909); to profit from the publicity engendered by Roosevelt's safari, William Selig made *Hunting Big Game in Africa* (1909), a fake account of the trip shot in Chicago with animals from the zoo. Ironically, the first audiences preferred the Selig version, which had more action than the Kearton footage.[4]

In addition to Cherry Kearton, other pioneer filmmakers realized the public's interest in factual films, and provided authentic live action footage shot in exotic places.[5] These early films include the Pathé Frères' *In Seville* (1909); footage shot on a 1909 Carnegie Museum Expedition to Alaska and Siberia; Emery and Ellsworth Kolb's 1911 Grand Canyon films; Paul Rainey's *African Hunt* (1912); H. A. Snow's *Hunting Big Game in Africa* (1923); Henry MacRae's *Wild Beauty* (1927); Rear Admiral Richard Byrd's *With Byrd at the South Pole* (1930); the films made by a Dr. Haddon and Rudolf Pöch in Australia that featured sound recorded on phonograph;[6] and Alice O'Brien's *Up the Congo* (1929).[7] Other early travel filmmakers included Léon Poirier, Martin and Osa Johnson, Lowell Thomas, J. B. L. Noel, and Herbert G. Ponting. Poirier made two feature-length films about automobile journeys: *La croisière noire* (*The Black Cruise*, 1926) is about a trip across Africa, and *La croisière jaune* (*The Yellow Cruise*, n.d.) is about a similar journey through Asia. Martin and Osa Johnson, whose *Jack London in the South Seas* (1912) Robert Flaherty admired, made *Among the Cannibal Isles of the South Pacific* (1918), *Jungle Adventures* (1921), *Head Hunters of the South Seas* (1922), *Trailing African Wild Animals* (1923), and *Simba, The King of Beasts* (1928).[8] In 1914 and again in 1915, Lowell Thomas shot footage in Alaska, and his most important films introduced T. E. Lawrence to the Western world: *With Lawrence in Arabia* (1918) and *With Allenby in Palestine* (c. 1918). J. B. L. Noel photographed the 1922 and 1924 expeditions to Mount Everest and produced *Climbing Mount Everest* (1922) and *The Epic of Everest* (1924). Herbert G. Ponting's *Ninety Degrees South* (1933) was a record of Captain Robert Falcon Scott's second expedition to the South Pole between 1910 and 1912.[9] This footage on Captain Robert Falcon Scott's 1911 expedition to the Antarctic was first released in 1913 as *The Undying Story of Captain Scott*, again in 1923 as *The Great White Silence,* and finally in 1933 as *Ninety Degrees South.* Ponting edited Scott's footage into the present film, an engaging prototype for the exploration film. Although it benefits substantially from modern editing, sound, and music, the excellent cinematography retains its original power, and while it exhibits a few of the clichés of the travel film, it is also an intimate and interesting old-timer's sea yarn. The narration has the joviality, friendliness, and humor of a conversation in a men's club. The music is a whimsical complement to the scenes of penguins running about like slapstick comedians. But the film is not all description of Scott's travels with his ship, the *Terra Nova*; its final scenes record the bitter disappointment and despair that came when his grouped reached the South Pole to find that a Norwegian expedition led by Roald Amundsen had reached the destination one month ahead of them. Ponting gives the harrowing details of Scott's retreat, and using actual entries from Scott's diary, he recounts the events and finally the deaths of all members of the heroic party. And the epic drama of this British exploration film makes the events recorded in *Conquest of Everest* (1953) seem almost easy by contrast.

Ninety Degrees South (Herbert Ponting, USA, 1933)

These pioneers established the tradition which led to Flaherty's *Nanook of the North*. The most impressive of their films were those made in the American west and in the deserts, forests, jungles, and wilderness around the world.

Film and the American West
There are many factual and fiction films that, in preserving actual—and in some cases reconstructing—Western history, offer a "visual encyclopedia of Western life" (Brownlow 243). The worst of these films do distort and exploit western life: as Kevin Brownlow says, "The history of the West is as plagued by myth as the history of the cinema" (223). Nevertheless, the best of these westerns offer "unique glimpses of western history" (Brownlow 223) and recall the dispassionate clarity of the work of such masters of nineteenth century exploration photography of the American west as Alexander Gardner, William Henry Jackson, Carleton E. Watkins, Timothy H. O'Sullivan, and William Rau. Many of these films have been lost, but a typical year's inventory helps to give an idea of the extent to which the actual life of the American west was factually recorded on film.

Taking one year's output at random, the following factual films appeared in 1913: *Life Among the Navajos*; *Dredges and Farm Implements,* which showed irrigation projects and the replacement of the horse by engines; *Opportunity and a Million Acres,* about homesteading; *The Wild West Comes to Town,* which presented scenes from various wild west shows; *Camping with the Blackfeet,* showing how the once powerful Blackfoot tribe was living on a Montana reservation; *The New Red Man,* about the Carlisle Indians; *Across Swiftcurrent Pass on Horseback,* with scenes of western camp life; and a group of rodeo films, including *Duhem and Harter's 1913 California Rodeo, Pendleton Round-Up,* and *A Cowboy Magnate.*[10]

In addition to these factual films about the West, there were also Western narrative films that incorporated significant amounts of factual footage, and, in so doing, not only reconstructed Western history, but also became an extension of that history.[11] The producers and directors of many silent Western films worked with actual ranchmen, cowboys, Indians, and railroad men in their attempt to portray life and customs accurately. Some of these silent fiction films contain significant documentary footage, including James Cruze's *The Covered Wagon* (1923), with its brilliant recreation of the period of 1848; Irvin Willat's *North of 36* (1924); John Ford's *The Iron Horse* (1934), remarkable for footage that has the look of actuality; Laurence Trimble's and Harry O. Hoyt's lost film, *Sundown* (1924); and Raoul Walsh's spectacular sound film, *The Big Trail* (1930). These films established the epic grandeur of the American environment, represented an early recognition of the possibilities of nature photography, and recognized that Americans wanted to see their own country. To a larger extent, these first Westerns established what is probably the most durable story line in American film history, and, in so doing, not only recreated a substantial aspect of the American dream, but also a long series of profit-making films.

Films about Native Americans

From as early as 1910, many independent filmmakers, as well as those who worked for the United States Department of the Interior, shot a great amount of documentary footage on Native Americans.[12] Early short films include *Life and Customs of the Winnebago Indians* (1912), *See America First* (1912), and *Indian Dances and Pastimes* (1912). Longer films include Rodman Wanamaker's *History of the American Indian* (1915)—described by Brownlow as an "unusually ambitious . . . documentary record of rites and ceremonies that were already forgotten by young Indians" (335)—John E. Maple's *Indian Life* (1918), Carlyle Ellis's *Nurse Among the Tepees* (1920), a public health documentary shot on the Arapaho reservation in Wyoming, and several 1920s films shot in color, including *The Land of the Great Spirit, Life in the Blackfoot Country,* and *Heritage of the Red Man* (all n.d.). An ominous reminder of the less humane United States government policy toward Native Americans is seen in *De-Indianizing the Red Man* (1917), depicting the Sherman Institute in California, a government school devoted to transforming and assimilating Native Americans. The most gifted of these early photographers of Native Americans was Edward S. Curtis, whose films include *In the Land of the Headhunters* (1914) and *In the Land of the War Canoes* (1914).[13] By 1913, Robert Flaherty had begun to use a motion picture camera to record the lives of Eskimos; this pursuit would eventually result in his masterpiece, *Nanook of the North* (1922).[14] Both Curtis and Flaherty were criticized for their humanistic rather than scientific treatment of disappearing cultures, but it was their inherent humanism, expressed in their preferences for photographing man's essential struggle against nature, that set their films apart from those that merely record or exploit.

THE AMERICAN ROMANTIC TRADITION

The American romantic tradition contributed to one of the earliest and strongest conventions in nonfiction filmmaking, and also one of the most popular. The early nonfiction film was frequently romantic in its essential idealization of nature and overriding preoccupation with exploring man's proper relationship to the world around him. Many of the films use natural scenery and surroundings for their own sake and are concerned with conservation, demonstrating an early awareness of the need for ecological balance in a world growing more industrialized and urbanized with each passing year. The narrative generally emerges from the situation rather than from being imposed upon the material, as would be the case with Walt Disney's 1950s' nature films.

Except for the early work of D. W. Griffith (the snow scenes in *Way Down East*, 1920, for example), little had been done with the realistic use of scenery in early American films. American ingenuity has always found artificial sets more practical, especially in those Hollywood productions where all the elements—including those usually controlled by supernatural forces—could be monitored and altered when necessary. Before it became commonplace for the American Western film to glorify the sweep and stretch of the frontier plains, it was in Sweden that filmmakers began to make imaginative use of the exterior in fiction films; later, the nonfiction films of Arne Sucksdorff continued that Swedish interest in some of the loveliest nature footage ever photographed in any country (see chapter 12).

As we have seen, the American romantic approach afforded filmmakers the opportunity to investigate and glorify the American West. Indeed, throughout its history, the American nonfiction film movement has been extremely active in capturing nature not only in the West, but throughout America and around the world. Of all the early travel and exploration films, the first important American travel films were brought back from expeditions by Robert Flaherty, Merian C. Cooper, and Ernest Schoedsack.

Robert Flaherty

By far the best known and most influential director to emerge from the travel genre was Robert Flaherty. While the Lumière brothers must be credited with making the first nonfiction films, and John Grierson is regarded as the father of the documentary film, Robert Flaherty was among the first filmmakers to observe and record actual life, creating a nonfiction genre all his own. From his close observation and rich imagination, he loved to create stories, both to recount aloud for his friends and to put on film for his audiences. Robert Flaherty's passport to distinction was the combination of determined independence and romantic vision that inspired his unique films. He was in love with man and the natural world, fascinated with the crafts of primitive man and appalled by the dehumanizing technology of modern man. Flaherty's description of himself as the explorer-artist shaped

Robert Flaherty (1884–1951) [photograph taken during the production of *Louisiana Story*, 1948]

both his life and his art, yet this self-identification was sufficiently ambiguous to allow for a variety of interpretations. His films resist generic classification, and the conventional terms—realist, ethnographic, documentary—do not altogether apply.[15]

While Flaherty did not leave a formal philosophy of life or art, his vision of physical and human nature, a vision which tends to transform reality rather than affirm it, can be found in major themes that recur in his films: natural beauty, older traditions, conflicts between man and nature, families enduring together, knowledge through suffering, a longing for the past. In the Western humanist's spirit, Flaherty takes human nature as his central theme, celebrates the dignity of man, and makes man the measure of all things. In all his films, he sought to depict the same epic theme; as Calder-Marshall wrote: "People who in the midst of life were always so close to death that they lived in the moment nobly" (67).

All of Flaherty's films are variations on one ideal: happiness exists when man is free and lives simply and harmoniously with nature. Inevitably, however, there must be conflict and, in order to affirm the ascendancy of the human spirit, Flaherty concentrates on conflicts between man and nature rather than those between men. Nature thus serves both as a central motif and as a main character, symbolized by the animal and natural forces that coexist with man but are also his antagonists. It is, however, typical of Flaherty's reverence for living creatures that, in all the films, man's survival is threatened more by weather and the natural elements than by conflict with animals or other men. In *Man of Aran,* for example, the context for heroism is the raging sea that isolates the islanders and the barren rocks on which they live. The surrounding sea, a fact of life, becomes a metaphor for their unavoidable fate.

When, inevitably, he must confront nature, man survives by using the skills learned through intuition and tradition. The male protagonists of his films (specifically, Nanook, Moana, the men of Aran, the farmers in *The Land,* Mr. Latour in *Louisiana Story*) are masters of nature who survive through their skills as hunters, fighters, and fishermen. Through them, he exalts man's freedom to live as part of nature and demonstrates that those aspects that tie man to nature (his body, his needs, his sensations) are essential to him to the point that he cannot ignore them or be released from them. Flaherty's world is centered on these competent heroes and dominated by them. They are not of classically heroic stature, nor are they symbols of suffering, meant to illuminate man's condition. Rather, they serve mainly to exemplify Flaherty's view of the world, and, suffering without purpose, they are denied a full perception of their condition. In fact, they triumph over imminent death both by luck and by skill. In *Man of Aran,* the prologue states that the sea may inevitably claim the fishermen, and staging a symbolic death would certainly have been within the boundaries of Flaherty's invention; however, here they lose nothing except a small boat and some nets.[16] Flaherty's faith in mankind, as exemplified in the struggle and victory of the Aran islanders over the sea, makes him deny the tragic rhythm not only implicit in the film's narrative, but also evident in the islanders' view of life.

In Flaherty's films, man relies on the family unit that sustains and encourages him in his struggle with nature, that gives him a reason for that struggle, especially when it involves hunting for food, and that rewards him with the quiet and lasting pleasures of companionship and love. Flaherty's families, living and enduring together, are also the unit in which children learn traditions and grow into adults. As it was in his own youth, education and wisdom are found not in schools or books, but in following family tradition, a father's (not a mother's) example. In his cinematic world, childhood and adolescence include certain rites of initiation by which boys are inducted into the family, the society, and the larger culture of which these units are a part. Flaherty sought out those alien (and sometimes older) cultures which determined the social status of a young man by the nature of the ordeal to which he has submitted himself in adolescence. Through various ritualized ordeals (e.g., in the tattooing scene in *Moana,* the moments of epiphany in *Man of Aran,* the awareness of an adult world and reality in *Elephant Boy* or *Louisiana Story*), these young men do everything possible to end their reliance on the everyday patterns of their youth and break through, not only to adulthood, but also to an understanding of the rhythms of nature and man's place in it.

Flaherty's view of the world was founded not only on a humanistic faith in man, but also on a romantic neglect of human evil. Flaherty agreed with Rousseau that the most primitive and the least advanced peoples are the happiest and the least corrupt, and like Rousseau, Flaherty believed that the arts and sciences that comprise what we call civilization actually corrupt man's native goodness. But, unlike Rousseau, who never traveled to distant countries, Flaherty confirmed his belief through world travels. In fact, his travels served as a means of escape, for he succeeded in ignoring the unpleasant aspects of life—human exploitation, corruption, and misery—that he found everywhere he went to make films. He sought places—all of them corrupted by the time he reached them—where there were sufficient basic materials to permit him to fulfill this romantic vision as well as to create films that would give pleasure to his audiences.[17] Believing in mankind's essential goodness, he did not depict man's oppression of man. His films are travelogues to places that never were; they charm (but do not instruct) audiences with their narrative simplicity and cinematographic beauty.

Although Flaherty's method of developing the narrative of his films was not wholly fixed, he followed a predictable pattern, first settling down in the locality to assimilate the everyday life of the people who lived there, then making friends and earning their confidence, and finally beginning to shoot. He wished to be integrated into those societies that were the subjects of his films, so that he might arrive at a record of lives that was truthful to his vision, whether he expressed that truth through actual or restaged footage. Flaherty made his first film, *Nanook of the North,* in this unique way, in collaboration with the Eskimo subjects of the

Nanook of the North (Robert Flaherty, USA, 1922)

film, not, as has always been customary to the film industry, in collaboration with a crew. He hoped that the Inuit would accept and understand what he was doing and would work together with him as partners. The first sequence to be shot, the walrus hunt, was a test of this working method, which Flaherty and Nanook discussed:

> "Suppose we go," said I, "do you know that you and your men may have to give up making a kill, if it interferes with my film? Will you remember that it is the picture of you hunting the iviuk [walrus] that I want and not their meat?"
> "Yes, yes, the aggie [motion picture] will come first," earnestly he assured me. "Not a man will stir, not a harpoon will be thrown until you give the sign. It is my word."
> We shook hands and agreed to start the next day.[18]

This agreement secured the natives' cooperation, provided technical assistance, and, perhaps most important, helped to ensure that the film would present their point of view. There is no question that theirs was a life of struggle for food, shelter, existence—Nanook died two years later of starvation on a hunting trip; nevertheless, their willingness to help in creating a work of art that concerned elemental facts of life, not their own immediate needs, also implies that the Eskimos knew the difference between art and life. They taught Flaherty that art is more than just an expression of life's values, that it enables man to understand his relationship to life, and that it is also artifact, a utilitarian record of the moment.[19] For Flaherty, having their cooperation in delineating the difference between reality and film was a major step in bringing him closer to becoming an artist.

According to Kracauer, Flaherty took for granted that a narrative story would emerge from his approach: first, he found simple stories in the lives of people who lived close to nature, and then he created slight dramas of interest and suspense around certain heroes. In *Nanook,* he shows primitive man's realization that his destiny lay in his own hands, that it was his obligation to improve his lot on earth by working, and that the members of his family were probably his first and most important helpers. The casting of *Man of Aran* typifies Flaherty's narrative method: "We select a group of the most attractive and appealing characters we can find, to represent a family, and through them tell our story. It is always a long and difficult process, this type finding, for it is surprising how few faces stand the test of the camera" (quoted in Murphy 24). For example, the man who played Tiger-King was not an Aran islander, but an itinerant whom Flaherty thought handsome. The characters were not given individual identity, but were chosen for their typical traits and function as abstracts, known only as Man, Woman, and Boy.[20]

In order to present those romantic themes, Flaherty employed what John Grierson called "the first principles of documentary":

> (1) It must master its material on the spot, and come in intimacy to ordering it. Flaherty digs himself in for a year, or two maybe. He lives with his people till the story is told "out of himself". (2) It must follow him in his distinction between description and drama. I think we shall find that there are other forms of drama,

or more accurately, other forms of film than the one he chooses; but it is important to make the primary distinction between a method which describes only the
surface value of a subject, and the method which more explosively reveals the
reality of it. You photograph the natural life, but you also, by your juxtaposition
of detail, create an interpretation of it. (*Grierson on Documentary* 148)

For Grierson, it is the shaping of reality through this juxtaposition of detail, the
"interpretation of it," that separates the realist filmmaker from the artist who
"describes only the surface value of the subject." It is what separates the complex
re-presentation of reality found in the direct cinema approach, developed in the
late 1950s and 1960s, from Flaherty's romantic approach to reality.

In his study of existence in relation to itself and not in relation to himself,
Flaherty's work is often associated with anthropology and the anthropologist's
fascination for a way of life that has long since gone. In fact, in contrast to ortho-
dox anthropological practice, Flaherty frequently turned back the clock, attempting to restore the older way of life by altering such things as the way his subjects
lived, dressed, and hunted. The realistic day-in-the-life narrative structure of
Moana, his second film, tempts one to believe that the film provides an actual
account of Samoan life; yet the film's subtitle, *A Romance of the Golden Age,*
alludes to an earlier, prosperous period during which man lived in ideal happiness,
suggesting that Flaherty is announcing his intention of taking us to a time and place
that are not of this world. Then, as now, Flaherty's audiences probably did not
know that changes had taken place; since these were remote regions to which very
few white men had traveled, or would ever travel, they were satisfied with images
that corroborated what they believed to be true. Nevertheless, this approach,
harmless as it may seem, suggests an indifference to deeper social, psychological,
and economic realities that is exemplified by the tattooing scene in *Moana.* Before
the tattooing is shown, a title informs us that "there is a rite through which every
Polynesian must pass to win the right to call himself a man," but Ta'avale, who
played Moana, would never have been tattooed if Flaherty had not staged the
event (Calder-Marshall 113–14). Ta'avale endured the pain because he was well
paid, and because, in Frances Flaherty's words, it "was not only his own pride that
was at stake but the honour of all Samoa" (quoted in Calder-Marshall 114). Many
of the other native adult men in this scene are not themselves tattooed, suggesting
that there have been ways other than tattooing to keep the Samoan cultural tradition alive.

As Murphy observes, the Flahertys "did not understand that what appears
outwardly as a simple, primitive society, can be just as complicated and ritualistic
with similar demands and anxieties as any modern day civilization" (12). Nor did
they realize that the process of filming can have unforeseen effects on those being
filmed, as Claude Lévi-Strauss found in studying Brazilian natives; not only did the
Brazilians insist on being paid before they would pose for pictures, but, the bargain
made, they actually forced him to photograph them in order to get their wages
(156). Flaherty paid Nanook and the other Inuit people for their work, as he was to
do throughout his career with others who appeared in his films, knowing, as

Barnouw observed, that this approach would alter the people and events being filmed and recreate the past through two viewpoints: his own and the natives' (*Documentary* 36). In fact, before beginning *Nanook of the North,* Flaherty asked Nanook to agree that the process of filming his vision of reality would take precedence over the life being filmed.[21] And, indeed, the film is true to human nature, but not true to the life that the Eskimos were living when Flaherty made the film. It does not have either the wholly fictional narrative of a theatrical film or the factual reliability of an ethnographic film. As Rotha (ed. Ruby) writes: "No reference is made to social practices such as the sexual life or marriage customs of the Eskimo, so the film has little real anthropological value" (39).

Similarly, during the making of *Moana,* the Samoans were having difficulty in adjusting to the changes brought to their island by the passing of time, the British colonial government, and the Christian missionaries. Nevertheless, after several months devoted mainly to photographic experimentation, the Flahertys went forward with their plan to include within the film customs that had almost disappeared, ignoring contemporary social problems and generally altering Samoan life to fit the narrative that they imposed upon it. In addition to submitting one of their young men to the almost defunct ritual of tattooing, Flaherty required that the natives wear clothing that had long since been replaced by western dress and affect longer hairstyles than those in fashion. Felix David, the German trader who was the self-styled King of Savaii, complained that the alterations would misrepresent Samoan society, but not even this dissuaded the Flahertys. Fascinated with the simple rituals of the Inuit and the Samoan Islanders, Flaherty could overlook the complex human needs, human interrelationships, and ecological relationships that characterize any people or culture, including those that are called "primitive." For these reasons, all of Flaherty's films raise the issue of whether or not they can be considered as a truthful document.

Today, we may attempt to calculate the margin by which Flaherty missed his opportunities to preserve what would have been imperishable documents of real life, as it was lived at the moment in which Flaherty photographed it, not imagined life, as it was lived at a time before Flaherty. His romanticism, desire to tell stories, and control as an *auteur* all precluded the control and validation of the scientific method. Instead, Flaherty relied on his knowledge about the past, his intuition about the present, and his freedom to explore and improvise as he went along. Moreover, he knew that audiences did not always expect a faithful representation of reality, that they preferred the relatively superior craft of fiction films, and that nonfiction films attracted them with such devices as restaging. Flaherty realized that filmmaking is not a function of anthropology or even archeology, but an act of the imagination; it is both photographic truth and a cinematic rearrangement of the truth. When confronted with charges that he restaged scenes, Flaherty only said: "Sometimes you have to lie. One often has to distort a thing to catch its true spirit" (quoted in Calder-Marshall 97).

As a filmmaker, Flaherty's strengths are in his narrative imagination, rather than in his handling of the cinematic form that expresses it. He recognized form in nature, and took great care and attention to photographing his subject, but sometimes overlooked the formal elements within the subject that would enable him to relate it to his larger purpose. From *Nanook* on, his method was to immerse himself in the subject, to shoot everything with the hope of capturing cinematographic images that would preserve the temporal and spatial realities of what his observant eyes perceived. Although this would appear to be the ideal method of discovering a subject, of letting it unfold and reveal itself, it contributed to the lack of purpose often evident in his subsequent films. In comparing *Nanook* and *Moana*, it is evident that Flaherty's greater knowledge of the Inuit culture resulted in a more detached, objective record. *Nanook*, the more compelling film, reveals Flaherty's knowledge, while *Moana*, the more intimate one, reflects his fantasy.

His intuitive approach made it almost impossible for editors to deal with his footage along the principles traditionally associated with editing.[22] In *Moana*, for example, the Flahertys did not use editing in a traditional manner—for example, to cut from one shot to another to reveal something that the previous shot did not— nor, by the absence of editing, did they preserve realistic time and space. Examples of faulty editing include Moana's introduction with his back already tattooed, the many poorly matched shots, the confusing jump cuts to unidentified people, and the action within unedited scenes that does not justify their length. Only when he began working with Helen Van Dongen in 1940, did Flaherty begin to discover the alternative approach whereby cinematic form is achieved through a collaborative process that begins with the filmmaker's imagination of how the film will look and move, continues with the cinematographer's translation of that idea into footage, and ends with the editor's shaping of that footage to meet, as nearly as possible, the filmmaker's original conception. But even then, late in his career, he found it difficult to reconcile this process with his intuitive approach to filmmaking.

Two formal aspects of his work place Flaherty firmly within the theoretical configuration of the realist tradition: his dependence on cinematography, rather than editing, and his reliance on long-focus lenses. Flaherty's use of the long take, of re-framing to follow what is of interest, and of depth-of-field cinematography preserves the unities of place and action and creates a potentially rich ambiguity of meaning. As a cinematographer, he had an intuitive (some say "innocent") eye for capturing temporal and spatial reality. His perspectives imply a single, fixed viewpoint that remains stable even as the natural world is in flux. Realistic also are the human truth and natural beauty in his films, even though they derive from his humanism and skill as a cinematographer rather than from his fidelity to truth. Of his photography, Brownlow wrote:

> The extraordinary richness of the photography of *Moana* . . . is due in part to Flaherty's use of panchromatic film. This has been portrayed as an accident, also as an innovation. In fact, it was neither. Panchromatic had been used by Hollywood cameramen for years. It was the staple diet of the old Kinemacolor process of Charles Urban. Flaherty planned *Moana* as a panchromatic picture from the beginning, probably under the influence of Charles Stearns Clancy, whose one independent production, *The Headless Horseman*, had been shot on panchromatic and was ready for release when Flaherty left. At the request of the owner of

the Prizmacolor Company, Flaherty took a Prizmacolor camera; like all additive processes, Prizma depended upon panchromatic film. But the story that the color camera broke down and Flaherty loaded his Akeley with the panchromatic stock as an experiment is a denial of his wide knowledge of photography.[23]

A realistic "look," however, does not necessarily make a realist film. Until the last decade of his career, the primary obstacles to Flaherty's pursuit of cinematic realism were his disregard of editing and sound. Working with the Inuit Eskimos in making *Nanook,* Flaherty learned the basic organic principle that style should emerge from within the subject matter, through the selection and arrangement of details. But, in his case, practice differed from theory. He shot hundreds of thousands of feet of film, responding not only to the dictates of his "found story," but also to the requirements of his preconceptions. This method results in an extraordinary ratio of footage shot to that which is incorporated in the final cut. John Goldman, the first professional editor with whom Flaherty worked, complained that the director had sensitivity only for the shot itself and not for its place within the overall rhythm and structure of the film:[24] "His feeling was always for the camera. This wanting to do it all *in and through* the camera was one of the main causes of his great expenditure of film—so often he was trying to do what could *not* in fact be done" (quoted in Calder-Marshall 151). The advantage of not using a shooting script, a technique that many years later became central to direct cinema,[25] is that it permits the filmmaker to explore the subject freely and to realize his own vision. But this technique seldom produces impressive results without the masterful editing evidenced in the work of such "direct cinema" advocates as Frederick Wiseman or Albert and David Maysles.[26] Whatever the indisputable strengths of the early films, Flaherty's unwillingness to plan ahead, his reliance on assembling rather than editing his footage, and his reluctance to use sound more realistically have earned for these early films a controversial place in the overall development of nonfiction film realism.

Merian C. Cooper and Ernest Schoedsack

The struggle of man against nature in Flaherty's *Nanook of the North* had a great influence on Merian C. Cooper and Ernest Schoedsack, who, in the early 1920s, joined forces as explorers and filmmakers out of shared ideals—a sense of adventure and a love of travel to distant places—as well as out of the practical realization that there was a market for travel films.[27] While they are best known for producing and directing later Hollywood films, including *King Kong* (1933) and several John Wayne films, they brought back two important travel films from their early expeditions: *Grass: A Nation's Battle for Life* (1925) and *Chang* (1927).

Grass is a strangely incoherent, but fascinating film about the "forgotten people" of Asia Minor, Bakhtiair tribesmen, who make epic trips across desert and mountains to find grassy pastures for their livestock. As in *Nanook of the North,* these people struggle to survive, but unlike Flaherty, Cooper and Schoedsack do not focus on an individual. Their lengthy silent film records the nomads' travels on unmapped trails through treacherous rapids and glacier passes. Shots of the tribesmen's frozen, bleeding feet do more than the awkward title cards ("B-r-r-r. The water's cold!"), evocative of Flaherty, to depict their struggle. The Flaherty influence is also evident in the filmmakers urging the nomads to take a much more difficult route than they would ordinarily have used so that they could obtain more dramatic footage. Though *Grass* is epic in its record and pictorial impact, far more ambitious in scope than *Nanook,* it lacks the humanistic focus that makes Flaherty's film an enduring classic.[28]

Cooper and Schoedsack's second film, *Chang,* is an altogether different achievement, one that Brownlow calls "the audience picture supreme" (529). Although the subject is Siam, the filmmakers avoid accentuating its exotic aspects. Instead, their account of jungle life is so highly dramatic that the tedious, Kiplingesque captions seem totally unnecessary. Shot in the new wide-angle technique of Magnascope, and screened with a special score by Hugo Riesenfeld, *Chang* was a great critical and financial success.[29] Today, these Cooper-Schoedsack films have been overshadowed by others in the romantic tradition, but in their time they influenced two contemporary filmmakers who also combined factual and fictional footage: Douglas Burden made *The Silent Enemy* (1930), a reconstruction of Ojibway Indian life before the coming of the white man, and Varick Frissell made *The Viking* (1931), an epic of ships and seal hunting in Newfoundland.

THE SOVIET NATURALIST TRADITION

Alexander Dovzhenko

The films of Alexander Dovzhenko, like those of Robert Flaherty, develop a theme of nature, of life and death, in which human lives cannot be separated from nature around them. Like Flaherty, Dovzhenko was an idealist; unlike Flaherty, he looked ahead. Although his work falls within the Flaherty tradition that celebrates life and nature, Dovzhenko was the antithesis of that innocent filmmaker. He viewed the cycles of life on a grand and poetic scale, and his influence on the naturalistic cinema is seen in such films as Georges Rouquier's *Farrebique* (1946). Dovzhenko did not condemn modern life or idealize the past with a neo-Rousseauean view of simple man, but rather placed his emphasis on man's potential to be a more noble creature than modern society permits him to be. With what Marco Carynnyk calls his "mythopoeic imagination," he created a rhythmic, unified vision, in film after film, of three interwoven themes: patriotism, innocence, and love of nature.[30] With a playful imagination that resembles that of Marc Chagall, his fellow Russian, Dovzhenko affirms the Ukrainian peasant life he loved.

It is conventional to say that Dovzhenko is the poet among the masters of the silent Soviet film. This remains true if the term "poet" is meant to describe precisely his rich and elusive art, not vaguely avoid it. Dovzhenko is a poet in his use of symbols and rhythm, his sense of structure and unity, his appreciation of ambiguity, and his ability to see and to represent the transcendent cycle of life and death. In contrast to the other great Soviet silent directors—Sergei Eisenstein, Vsevlod Pudovkin, and Dziga Vertov—Dovzhenko did not produce a coherent body of theoretical writing that distinguished him individually or create a body of films that, however complex, was also direct and explicit. Dovzhenko's early aspirations to be an artist are reflected in his painterly concern for the composition of his images, and his lyrical films contain highly elliptical jumps in time and space. While his films are not consistent with the documentary tradition established by Eisenstein, or the direct cinema approach prefigured by the work of Vertov, they are unique in expressing the immediacy and beauty of living, the continuity of life, and the inevitability and beauty of death.

In his quest to observe and to document his Russia, Dovzhenko succeeded in serving both art and propaganda. Because Dovzhenko's poetic vision is expressed through symbolism, the ostensible subject of his films—the arsenal in *Arsenal* (1929) and the dam in *Ivan* (1932)—invariably represents a significant moment in the evolution of the Soviet economy and culture. But it is in his elaboration and expansion of these thematic symbols that Dovzhenko's art takes its shape, setting itself apart from the work of his contemporaries. As his films slowly develop their lyrical narratives, the symbols become more ambiguous, taking on new shades of meaning and providing new insights for understanding. As a true symbolist, Dovzhenko sees each thing so intensely that its poetic suggestiveness is both captured and released.

Dovzhenko's masterpiece is *Earth* (*Zemlya,* 1930), a slow, rhythmical, and dramatic film, ostensibly about the Soviet collectivization of the farms, but, in truth, a meditation on the cycle of life. In *Earth,* the everyday activities of life on the Ukrainian soil become a microcosm for life itself. The film's narrative progression suggests both sides of Dovzhenko's vision: a dying old man joyfully eating his last apple, the murder of Vasyl, a young man dancing in the moonlight, and the birth of a child to Vasyl's mother. Its larger themes are developed in the film's associative images, which are both static (the opening sea of grain, the moonlight lovers, a farmer standing between two oxen) and dynamic (the arrival of the tractor, the reaping and processing of the grain, Vasyl's dance, and the aftermath of his murder, which is told in a brilliant parallel montage that culminates in a highly lyrical, slower conclusion).

Despite the fact that *Earth* depicts life and death in the context of agricultural progress, its poignant acceptance and understanding of death were misconstrued and Dovzhenko was attacked as "defeatist" when the film was released.[31] Throughout his life and career, the government criticized his intellectual and aesthetic aloofness from the party line. In fact, his later work, including such films as *Aerograd* (*Frontier,* 1935), *Schchors* (1939), and *Bucovina-Ukrainian Land* (1940), was carried out in a climate of persecution and misunderstanding. His feeling for the heroism, suffering, and tragedy of the Ukrainian people found a very special expression during the Second World War in such films as *The Battle for Our Soviet Ukraine* (1943) and *Victory in Right-Bank Ukraine and the Expulsion of the German Aggressors from the Boundaries of the Ukrainian Soviet Earth* (1945), as well as in *Native Land* (1946), his hymn to Armenia. But after the war, although he occupied himself with several projects, Dovzhenko's energies were increasingly dissipated by late Stalinist bureaucracy. Today, he is remembered for the independence of mind

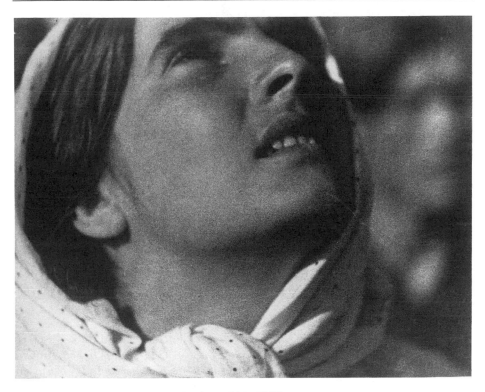

Earth [*Zemlya*] (Alexander Dovzhenko, USSR, 1930)

and action that makes the poetic beauty of *Earth* and his other early films so enchanting.

THE WESTERN AVANT-GARDE

During the 1920s, the cultural avant-garde in Europe experimented with film as they experimented with, and, in some cases, revolutionized the directions that poetry, prose fiction, music, ballet, and painting would take. In the stream of consciousness novel of James Joyce, Virginia Woolf, and Marcel Proust, the narrative expression gave way to a determination to record the importance of the immediate moment, the depth of the individual consciousness, and the cyclical and yet free-flowing nature of time. In music, the tonality and lyricism of the Romantic masters gave way to the twelve-tone technique of Arnold Schoenberg, Anton von Webern, Alban Berg, and Igor Stravinsky. The three-dimensional subjects of Cubists such as Picasso and Braque were fragmented, redefined, and presented from several points of view, all within a shallow plane or within several interlocking and often transparent planes.

Experimentation with the new medium of motion pictures was particularly evident in France, where such artists as Marcel Duchamp, Francis Picabia, Fernand Leger, Man Ray, Salvador Dali, and Jean Cocteau applied their theories of abstraction to cinema. As early as 1913, Leopold Survage, a Russian-born Cubist painter living in Paris, worked on an abstract film project, "Le Rhythme Color," but, interrupted by World War I, he abandoned it.[32] In 1915, young actor and playwright Sascha Guitry made *Our Own Crowd* (*Ceux de chez nous* 1915), a 45-minute film about Degas, Monet, Renoir, and Rodin. The first important experimental films on art were realized: by the German filmmakers Hans Richter—*Rhythm 21* (*Rhythmus 21*, 1921) and *Racing Symphony* (*Rennsymphonie*, 1928)—and Walther Ruttmann—*Light Song, Opus I* (*Lichtspiel, Opus I*); and by the Swedish filmmaker Viking Eggeling—*Diagonal Symphony* (*Symphonie diagonal*, 1921). These experiments, although serious, were short-lived, perhaps because the painters found that, as Arthur Knight writes, "film was too demanding, too expensive—and too unrewarding" (8). However, filmmakers also experimented with abstraction, repetitive patterns, recurring images, simultaneous experience, and textures of everyday life. Important European experimental and abstract films included the following French films: René Clair's *Entr'acte* (1924), Dmitri Kirsanoff's *Menilmontant* (1924), Man Ray's *Emak Bakia* (1927), Luis Buñuel's *An Andalusian Dog* (*Un chien andalou*, 1928), Fernand Léger's and Dudley Murphy's *Mechanical Ballet* (*Ballet mécanique*, 1925); Man Ray's *The Mysteries of the Chateau de Dé* (*Les mystères du château du Dé*, 1929); Eugene Deslaw's *The Electric Night* (*La nuit électrique*, 1930); Jean Gremillon's *Au tour au large*, 1927; and Jean Painlevé's *Sea Horse* (*L'hippocampe*, 1934). In Germany, they included: Wilfried Basse's *Market in the Wittenbergplatz* (*Markt am Wittenbergplatz*, 1929); *Abbruch und Aufbau, Market in Berlin* (*Markt in Berlin*), and *Germany of Yesterday and Today* (*Deutschland von Gestern und Heute*); and Alexander Hammid's *Prague Castle*.[33] The three early leaders of the Belgian avant-garde movement were filmmakers Henri Storck, Charles Dekeukeleire, and André Cauvin (see chapter 6). In the United States, early films on art include Allen Eaton's and Merwyn W. Palmer's *The Making of a Bronze Statue* (1922), Robert Flaherty's *The Pottery Maker: An Episode of the 19th Century* (1925), and the Metropolitan Museum of Art's *Behind the Scenes: The Working Side of the Museum* (1928). The avant-garde trend was seen in Ralph Steiner's $H_2 0$ (1929).

While the Americans were shaping a film tradition based on a romantic vision of life and, as we have seen, the Russians were busy adapting the dynamics of filmmaking to the necessities of politics, the experimental filmmakers of France, Germany, and Holland were working in an area unbounded by sentiment or politics. Although they occasionally produced immature films that were strident in ironic emphasis and banal in structure, their work represents an important step in the experimental approach to filmmaking, and did, indeed, create a tradition of its own. Unlike the Americans and the Russians, the filmmakers in the large European cities were not interested in pastoral or romantic hymns to nature, the strength of their people, and the grandeur of their natural resources. Instead, they examined the rushed, dehumanizing atmosphere of the urban environment. They seem to agree in their attitude toward the city: it is cramped, dirty, brutalizing, and almost unlivable; yet, at the same time, it has its charm and its beauty. Where others saw man in conflict with nature, these filmmakers saw him in conflict with urban streets. One can sing as loudly and as insightfully about the city as about the countryside; the theme and the style of the hymn may be different, but the praise remains constant all the same.

Influenced by the direct cinematography and the rhythmic montage of Dziga Vertov (see chapter 4), these continental avant garde filmmakers perfected the film genre generally called the *city symphony*. Earlier films about great cities include Julius Jaenzon's *New York 1911* (1911), Paul Strand's and Charles Sheeler's *Manhatta* (1921), Laszlo Moholy-Nagy's *Dynamics of a Metropolis* (1922), and Mikhail Kaufman's and Ilya Kopalin's *Moscow* (*Moskva*, 1926).[34] A film like the Strand-Sheeler *Manhatta* makes a strong visual statement that foreshadows such later American films as Steiner's and Van Dyke's *The City* (1939) and Francis Thompson's *N.Y., N.Y.* (1957).[35]

The later city symphonies present brief and realistic nonfiction views of city life, united within a larger rhythmic structure—a symphony—by the recurrence of images, motifs, and themes that provide continuity and progression of ideas. The least successful of these films are little more than a cross section of life, good exercises for beginning filmmakers. At their best, however, the city symphonies are poetic records of the camera's ability to capture the dynamic rhythm and kaleido-scopic pattern of city life; at the same time, they transcend their ever-changing subject matter by discovering significant human themes beneath the surface of mechanization and industrialization. It was not enough for these filmmakers merely to juxtapose the rich and the poor or the office buildings and the factory; they wanted to understand why there are rich as well as poor and why the city can be both ugly and beautiful. And such is the achievement of nonfiction films as diverse as Stig Almqvist's *The Old City* (*Gamla stan*, 1931), Steiner's and Van Dyke's *The City* (1939), and Francis Thompson's *N.Y., N.Y.* (1957), as well as of Chaplin's *Modern Times* (1936), which opens with a classic sequence that intercuts the crowds in the New York subway with herds of sheep.

Few beginning filmmakers have overlooked the opportunity to film the cities around them, expanding their sociological insights through recurring patterns and ironic contrasts. The city *is* alive, and if it reveals an aspect of the human condition less triumphant than that revealed in the cycle of nature, it is nonetheless important and very much a part of the filmmaker's concern. It was only natural, then, that Cavalcanti in France, Ruttmann in Germany, and Ivens in Holland would turn their cameras toward the city with the hope that, in documenting and interpreting it, they and their audiences might understand it better. In examining everyday life, both its prosaic and poetic moments, their films anticipate the British documentary film movement.

Alberto Cavalcanti

Alberto Cavalcanti, a Brazilian who later became an innovative force in the British documentary film movement, was influential in the French avant-garde cinema of the 1920s with such films as *Sea Fever* (*En rade*, 1927).[36] In 1934, Erwin Panofsky defined the two principal formal elements that set film apart from theatre as the "dynamization of space and, accordingly, spatialization of time."[37] Time and space are the interrelated themes of his *Rien que les heures* (*Nothing But Time*, 1926; the film is always referred to by its French title), the first and still one of the most influential films that depict a day in the life of a city. "We can fix a moment in space or immobilize a moment in time": this printed title at the end of the film confirms the paradoxical fact that the camera can simultaneously record the flow of time and stop it in space.

Rien que les heures, which is forty-five minutes in length, begins with images of morning: people awaken; a poor, old beggar woman staggers along a passage-way; and a window dresser begins to clothe a mannequin. At noon, a surrealistic clock announces the time. People stop their labors to take the midday meal: working men sit on the curb eating out of hand, while more prosperous office workers enjoy a restaurant. Some rather heavy-handed ironies (shots of men eating intercut with a cow being butchered) may have been effective the first time, but this device has been subsequently overused and become trite, and the continual reminder of the food-to-garbage cycle is overdone. The day becomes evening, and people turn their attention to leisure activities; we see an elegant card game, a street fortune teller, and the old woman (from the first part) sleep-ing in an upright sitting position (later, we will see her tottering along a passage-way again). Another heavy and unsuccessful attempt at irony results in the intercut and juxtaposed shots of two kissing couples, food, and a Rodin statue. A running news vendor is seen against the ever-increasing speed of newspaper headlines. The lights and whirling pattern of the rides at an amusement park are recorded with some very conscious use of the camera. Shots are superimposed, speeded up, and sometimes out of focus. Night falls, bringing mystery and sus-pense. A lady news vendor is robbed, and a sailor seduces a girl, but the shots of the lip-smacking lovers and of the bed are unnecessarily heavy for the weight of the irony intended.

At the conclusion of the film, we are left with the impression that life goes on, that the next day will again bring work and play, love and hate, food and garbage. Young people will enjoy themselves, artists will create, old people will wander unregarded, and lovers will kiss. Some of the images are linked through contrast, others through irony, and still others are unrelated, but the overall impression is that of a mosaic: the images relate only when they are considered in their relation to the whole picture.

In addition to establishing one approach to the city symphony, Cavalcanti's film is important to students of film technique, for it is perhaps the first nonfiction film to use the "wipe" in place of the cut or dissolve (the wipe is a form of transition from one shot to another in which a line appears to travel across the screen, removing, as it travels, one shot and introducing the next).

Other French films in the kaleidoscopic city symphony tradition are Marcel Carné's *Nogent, Sunday's Eldorado* (*Nogent, eldorado du dimanche,* 1929), a short film about Sundays at Nogent, a French working-class resort on the Marne, and Jean Vigo's (1905–34) *On the Subject of Nice* (*À propos de Nice,* 1930), another short film in the Dziga Vertov style (on which Boris Kaufman, Vertov's brother, served as cameraman), this one about the glamorous upper-class resort on the

Riviera. Like the city symphonies of Cavalcanti or Carné, Vigo's presented an ingenious vision of city life, but, unlike them, it also had a hard edge of social criticism.

Both Carné and Vigo contributed substantially to the development of realism in the French narrative film of the 1930s; Vigo is best known for the personal commitment and style that distinguished his later masterpieces, *Zero for Conduct* (*Zéro de conduite,* 1933) and *L'Atalante* (1934); Carné for his collaborations with Jacques Prévert, the most important of which are *Daybreak* (*Le jour se lève,* 1939) and *The Children of Paradise* (*Les enfants du paradis,* 1945). It is perhaps interesting to note that of the major filmmakers who established the grand tradition of French cinema—Gance, Clair, Buñuel, Vigo, Carné—only Jean Renoir, arguably the greatest of them all, began directly with narrative film without serving an apprenticeship in the experimental or nonfiction film.

Walther Ruttmann

Cavalcanti's *Rien que les heures* appeared several months before Walther Ruttmann's *Berlin: The Symphony of a Great City* (*Berlin: die Symphonie einer Grosstadt,* 1927). While both films attempt to express the life of a city on film, the rhythm of Cavalcanti's film is paced, where Ruttmann's is orchestrated; Ruttmann's vision is symphonic rather than episodic; and he relies on a unified thematic approach, not the cumulative impression of a series of images. In fact,

Berlin: The Symphony of a Great City [*Berlin: die Symphonie einer Grosstadt*] (Walther Ruttmann, Germany, 1927)

Ruttmann's *Berlin* reflects Eisenstein's influence more apparently than Cavalcanti's.[38] Ruttmann, who came out of the great tradition of the UFA studios, made *Berlin* with Carl Mayer, who wrote it, and Karl Freund, who photographed it.[39] Its spinning images and optical effects underscore its vision of a mechanized, dehumanizing city. Ruttmann's reality is a vision of madness, a composite metaphor of revolving doors and roller coasters, of scattering leaves, hurrying feet, and suicide. While it presents a day in the life of Berlin (as Cavalcanti's *Rien* shows us a day in Paris), its episodes are shaped by larger thematic concerns—movements—that give order to the many incidents depicted. In the lunchtime sequence, for example, we not only see workers eating, but also horses, elephants, businessmen in pubs, ladies in restaurants, a lion, a baby, a camel, an outdoor café, the preparations in a hotel kitchen for an elegant banquet, a monkey, and, finally, the dishwashing machines of a large restaurant and the end product of all this eating: garbage. This lunchtime sequence is complete, opening with the workers and animals eating, and closing with them all resting. All of these vignettes are rhythmically linked by the editing, as well as by the chronological continuity and overall structure of the whole film.

Without sound, musical score, or narrative comment, *Berlin: The Symphony of a Great City* creates rhythm through purely visual images.[40] Ruttmann seems concerned with presenting as many facets as possible of each city experience he records. The film opens with a fast train entering Berlin; as the train approaches the station, the film cuts to quiet city streets. Now the pace is slow, the windows are shuttered, the streets are empty, the stores closed; the few visible people include a poster hanger and a group returning from a party. The film cuts to a railroad roundhouse, and the pace slowly begins to increase. Now the day's activity begins, as men go to work, on foot, on bikes, in cars, on trains; as crowds slowly form, the pace increases, and gates and doors seem to open by themselves in response to the activity. Now it is the rush hour in the crowded railway station, and the pace of the film quickens. Men arrive at work, machines begin such diverse industrial processes as bottling milk and rolling steel; stores open, shutters open, pushcarts fill the street, children leave for school, shopping begins, trash is collected, and the postman begins his rounds. By midmorning, we see the leisure class riding in the park, the working class scrubbing-up, farmers pitching hay, and businessmen going to their offices. The pace is now rapid and the images are those of movement everywhere, from hurrying feet to ascending elevators. Offices are opened in much the same way that stores were; Ruttmann is fascinated with opening blinds, opening shutters, opening doors. The film's caustic criticism of city life exaggerates the pace of workers and of industrial processes. As with Cavalcanti's, Ruttmann's irony was once fresh, but is now trite: as agitated businessmen argue on the telephone, the film cuts to two fighting dogs, and then to two screaming monkeys. The pace and tone are set: movement becomes madness, hurrying becomes hysteria, men become machines or animals. Nevertheless, through its comprehensiveness, its contrasts, its transitions, and its thematic unity, Ruttmann's city symphony surpasses Cavalcanti's by adding intensely unified criticism to factual observation.

Joris Ivens

In Holland, Joris Ivens's experimentation with the nonfiction film form, while not as innovative as that of Cavalcanti and Ruttmann in France and Germany, was, nonetheless, impressive and influential. The early films of Joris Ivens are careful, intensive studies of the kinds of local phenomena that are of such characteristic interest to the nonfiction filmmaker. His later work in the 1930s and 1940s was more ambitious, as well as more political (see chapter 6), but his early films, shot in Holland, remain short, sharp impressions of everyday life. They include *Pile Driving* (1929), *The Bridge* (1928), *The Breakers* (1929), *Rain* (1929), *Philips-Radio* (*Industrial Symphony*) (1931), and *Song of Heroes* (1932).

The Bridge (1927–28) is a detailed visual analysis of a simple process, the workings of a railroad bridge near Rotterdam. The bridge is raised to allow river traffic to pass underneath, and lowered to connect with the railbed on the banks. This process is not complex, but it must be handled with precision and efficiency so that the maximum amount of traffic can pass over and under the bridge. Without giving it any undue dramatic emphasis, Ivens locates the event as a vital part of the region's transportation system. As the film opens, we see the bridge in the distance, followed by a few shots of the cameraman with his equipment. To provide a sense of the full function of the bridge, we see a train crossing it, and then Ivens begins a documentation of various aspects of the bridge's operation, a dynamic sequence that is heavily influenced by Eisenstein. Under the bridge, we see the large engines, turbines, and pulleys that raise and lower the roadbed, and, from above, we follow a workman at the top of the bridge as he checks its operation. The pace of the film is brisk and makes the mechanical process seem much more interesting than it probably is; shots of a horse and buggy and one of an airplane provide some whimsical contrast to the mechanization of the bridge.

Ivens must have been fascinated with this convenient and effective means of giving artistic shape to ordinary experiences, for he used it again in *Rain* (1929), a film he made with Mannus Franken. Ivens's *Rain* is to Ruttmann's *Berlin* what a sonata is to a symphony. Subtitled a "cine poem," it is a lyrical, impressionistic picture of city life before, during, and after a rainstorm. The changeability of nature is contrasted with the relative constancy of human behavior; the weather may change, but the patterns of life in Amsterdam continue. Rain fills gutters and streaks across windows, but traffic continues in the canals and on the streets. The rhythm of the film is brisk, providing a pleasant counterpoint to the high-contrast black-and-white images. The shots of the clouds forming, the wind rising, and people scurrying about opening umbrellas and closing windows are particularly evocative. A brief and charming film, *Rain* still seems as fresh as its subject; admittedly, it is a finger exercise, but the sort of exercise that only a master should undertake.

This avant-garde experimentation was only a transitional phase in the development of the nonfiction film, and soon the aesthetic approach gave way to the documentary approach.[41] It flourished in the late 1920s during the golden age of the silent visual image, but two factors at the end of the decade were to transform its energy into a different kind of filmmaking. The coming of sound gave filmmakers an entirely new language with which to work, and the worldwide depression gave them subjects about which to make films. The chief proponents of avant-garde European experimentation in the 1920s—Cavalcanti, Ruttmann, and Ivens—went on to make important political films (see chapter 6). Cavalcanti joined Grierson as a leader of the British documentary film movement; Ruttmann stayed in Germany after Hitler came to power, playing some small role in advising Leni Riefenstahl on the making of *Triumph of the Will* (*Triumph des Willens*, 1935) and making such Nazi propaganda films as *Deutsche Panzer* (*German Tanks*, 1940);[42] and Ivens went on to create an approach to nonfiction filmmaking that was to have a great influence in the United States in the late 1930s and early 1940s.

4

The Beginnings of the Documentary Film

BEGINNINGS OF THE SOVIET PROPAGANDIST TRADITION

Film was not a popular art in pre-Soviet Russia and, although the first native Russian studio was founded as early as 1908, prior to the 1917 Revolution the Soviet film industry remained small and disorganized. Ultimately, the pre-revolutionary film industry foundered after relying on European or American imports or producing its own mediocre escapist entertainment for a mostly disinterested public.[1] Nonetheless, during this period the foundations were being established for an artistic revolution that was to be both political and aesthetic. In Western Europe, this was the time of the radical reordering of the aesthetic perception of reality—the time of cubism, stream-of-consciousness, and, especially influential, futurism, which flourished after 1909.[2] A glorification of the machine age, futurism was related to cubism in its representation of several aspects of forms in motion. In turn, futurist principles strongly influenced Russian Constructivism, the Russian modern art movement founded around 1913 by Vladimir Tatlin. Like futurism, constructivism emphasized purely abstract constructions and sculptures that were also related to modern technology. David Bordwell writes that before the 1917 Russian revolution "the montage idea was distinctly in the air," and that formalist ideas "had all prefigured a technique of fragmentation and recombination of materials that was later to dominate the Soviet avant-garde." Among the few important products of the prerevolutionary industry were several films, reflecting the influence of futurism and constructivism, by artists such as Vladimir Mayakovksy, Vsevolod Meyerhold, and Yakoiv Protazanov. Although strongly influential on the development of prerevolutionary Soviet film, constructivism, with its formalist emphasis, was discouraged after the revolution as being unsuitable for mass propaganda purposes.

In contrast to the American romantic tradition in nonfiction filmmaking, which grew slowly in response to commercial factors, the Russian propagandist tradition was a product of social and political events that took place after the 1917 revolution, with both political and technological factors influencing the kind and number of films produced. What resulted was a cinema of propaganda in documentary form. In August 1919, the Soviet film industry was nationalized, and under the direction of Nadezhda Krupskaya, Lenin's wife, the Cinema Committee established a state film school to train directors, actors, and technicians, as well as to produce *agitki,* newsreels edited for the purpose of agitation and propaganda, or "agit-prop." Brought to the Russian people on specially equipped trains and boats, these *agitki* were primarily intended to provide the new masses with both a general and a political education, to serve as "one of many instruments used on the battlefronts of the class struggle for socialist construction."[3] The trains also supplied books and newspapers, as well as pictures that helped to acquaint inhabitants of the various farflung areas of the Soviet Union with each other's mode of life. These trains were a brilliant attempt at unifying the vast and shattered nation. However, the newly reconstructed film industry was soon plagued by such technical problems as lack of equipment, production facilities, and, perhaps most important, film stock. Despite Lenin's faith in film as "the most important of the arts," the newsreels remained its only major product, particularly during the Civil War (1918–21).

The beginnings of the Russian propagandist tradition in nonfiction filmmaking can be seen most clearly in the work of three directors: Alexander Dovzhenko, Sergei Eisenstein, and Dziga Vertov. The work of Vertov and Eisenstein is close in spirit to the realistic work of the Lumière brothers, while, as we have seen, that of Dovzhenko is in the romantic tradition of Robert Flaherty.[4] Of the three, Dziga Vertov is regarded as the first great theorist and practitioner of the cinema of propaganda in documentary form.

Dziga Vertov

Dziga Vertov was of his time, ahead of his time, and a victim of his time.[5] In the years between 1917 and 1929, when the Soviet government generously supported artistic experimentation and expression, Vertov was one of the most unorthodox (and self-contradictory) artists in the Soviet avant-garde movement both in his theories—which linked artistic expression and social commitment—and in his nonfiction films, which stand out among the work of his Soviet contemporaries Eisenstein, Kuleshov, Pudovkin, and Dovzhenko. His life and his work were synonymous with the decade after the Bolshevik Revolution, when, as Vlada Petric writes,

> the many avant-garde groups in search of ways to express the needs and goals of the newly liberated working class chose forms and subjects as innovative and experimental as the times. . . . This was particularly evident in cinema, which was considered the most powerful means of communication and expression. (1)

Dziga Vertov (Denis
Arkadievich Kaufman,
1896–1954)

Envious of Vertov's brilliance as a theorist and director of nonfiction film, as well
as Lenin's support of him, his colleagues were further annoyed by his insistence on
the primacy of the nonfiction mode and his rejection of the individual artistic
personality.[6] By 1929, as Stalin came to power, political terror had begun to sup-
press the originality, energy, and intense expression of the avant-garde, whose work
was increasingly replaced by commonplace socialist realism. Poetry gave way to
prose, and Vertov, never one to compromise either his originality or his audacity,
found himself out of favor, and eventually humiliated into taking intermittent jobs
as a supervisor of newsreel production.

During his lifetime, cinema theorists and historians were similarly slow to
understand and appreciate Vertov's achievements and influence, tending, as
Bordwell writes, "rather insistently, to dismiss Vertov either as a Russian Lumière,
passively recording reality, or as a monomaniacal formalist." (38). John Grierson
found Vertov an enigma, full of an enthusiasm that he could not define: "The Kino
Eye . . . is only the waiter who serves the hash. No especial virtue in the waiting
compensates for a lunatic cook."[7] Paul Rotha found Vertov to be "prophetic," but
incapable of going beneath the surface of his material.[8] Erik Barnouw acknowledged his ingenuity and originality as a "reporter."[9] Some commentators ignore his
work entirely. Although Vertov's work serves as one foundation for realist cinema,

its extensive reliance on editing is perhaps one reason why André Bazin never mentions Vertov and why Siegfried Kracauer refers to him only tangentially in a discussion of Ruttmann's *Berlin: The Symphony of a Great City* (*Berlin: die Symphonie einer Grosstadt,* 1927).[10] In fact, prints of Vertov's films were not easily obtained in either the Soviet Union or Western countries until the 1970s (in contrast to the readily available Eisenstein films), encouraging what Annette Michelson called the "forty-year history of the most distrustful and hostile reception and of systematic critical neglect."[11]

However, in the last twenty years, since *The Man with the Movie Camera* became generally available in the West, historians and critics have reexamined and reassessed Dziga Vertov's place in the development of Soviet cinema, as well as in the history of the nonfiction film. The current wealth of information confirms the magnitude of his importance and the extent of his influence, the originality and intellectual vigor of his concept of cinema, and the cinematic ingenuity and energy of his films. Vertov influenced many filmmakers of the generation to come, including John Grierson, Joris Ivens, the members of the Workers Film and Photo League, Jean Rouch and Edgar Morin (who called their technique *cinéma vérité*— the French translation of *kino-pravda,* film-truth), and those who developed American direct cinema of the late 1950's and 1960's.[12]

Dziga Vertov (born Denis Arkadyevich Kaufman) was the eldest of three brothers, each of whom earned places in cinema history.[13] Vertov was born in Bialystok, which belonged to the Russian empire until 1918, but is now part of Poland. As a youth, he studied piano, violin, and literature, reading widely in the works of American and British authors. In 1915, the Kaufman family moved from Bialystok to Moscow, where young Denis, evidently a child prodigy, not only continued his studies of music, but also began to write verse and science fiction. In 1916–17, in St. Petersburg, Vertov studied medicine and psychology at the Psychoneurological Institute, demonstrating a special interest in human visual and aural perception. But he also maintained his interest in the arts, writing poetry as well as essays and fiction, and undertaking scientific experimentation with sound and artistic experimentation with poetry. In his "Laboratory of Hearing," Vertov demonstrated an interest in sound long before his colleagues and produced verbal audio montages (a forerunner of radio documentary), reflecting the influence of Walt Whitman's incantatory free verse, the prerevolutionary cubo-futurist movement in Petrograd, Vladimir Mayakovsky's staccato-like verse, and Guillaume Apollinaire's fragment poems. Vertov, like Eisenstein and Pudovkin, seemed equally comfortable with both science and art; indeed, Bordwell (40) has identified the central tension of his work as that between the scientific precision of cinematography and the creative possibilities inherent both in cinematography and editing.

The years between 1917 and 1919 were crucial to Vertov's establishment as a filmmaker and to his growth and development as a theorist and artist who rejected mimetic (or realist) cinema in favor of technique and process. In 1917, returning to Moscow at the age of twenty-two, Vertov argued against classic art, advocating an art based on fact. As he became interested in cinema, taking the name Dziga Vertov,[14] he developed his theory of the "Film-Eye," organized the *kinoks* group, and completed his first theoretical manifesto, "About the Disarmament of Theatrical Cinema." In Spring 1918, Vertov was invited by Mikhail Kol'tsov to join the Moscow Cinema Committee and to assist—first as Kol'tsov's secretary and then as a film editor—in the production of *Film Weekly* (*Kino-nedelia*), the first Soviet newsreel, which appeared in forty-three installments between June 1918 and December 1919. *Kino-nedelia* was used as propaganda in the endeavor to build socialism by providing film portraits of the new leaders of the government, as well as of Soviet enemies. As Seth Feldman writes, "the Moscow Cinema Committee was, in effect, Vertov's film school" (4); through helping to produce this newsreel, Vertov began to develop his cinematic principles of "life caught unawares" and of montage.[15] Using footage sent in from all over the country, he experimented with editing the films that were to be carried by the "agit-trains" and "agit-steamers" and seen by the revolutionary patriots fighting on the various fronts of the Civil War, as well as by civilians in towns and villages. The work of the revolutionary filmmakers and the use of the agit-trains and steamers can be seen in two of Vertov's newsreels, *Instructional Steamer* (also known as *Red Star*, 1920) and *The Agit-Train* (also known as *VTSIK* or *On the Bloodless Military Front*, 1921).

In his first film work, Vertov was partially influenced by futurism and suprematism, by the films of Laszlo Moholy-Nagy and Jean Epstein, and by the photography of Alexander Rodchenko,[16] but constructivism was at the foundation of his most experimental film work. The constructivists considered the artist as an engineer, whose main responsibilities were to construct "useful objects" and to play an active part in the building of the new society.[17] Machines were fundamental to Vertov: for him, cinematography and sound recording were the mechanical means of reproducing reality, and the editing table the means of arranging and manipulating that reality. He was so captivated by technology that he wrote:

> Our artistic vision departs from the working citizens and continues through the poetry of the machine toward a perfect electrical man. . . . Long live the poetry of moved and moving machines, the poetry of levers, wheels, steel wings, the metallic clamor of movement and the blinding grimace of the scorching electric current. (Quoted in Petric, 6)

In addition to producing the weekly newsreels of *Film-Weekly* and writing and directing several short films, Vertov completed three feature-length compilation documentaries from the footage sent to him: *The Anniversary of the Revolution* (*Godovshchina revoliutsii*, 1919, an historical chronicle), *The Battle of Tsaritsyn* (*Srazhenie v Tsaritsyne*, 1920), and the thirteen-part *History of the Civil War* (*Istoriya grazhdenskoi voini*, 1921).[18] In this work, Vertov, like other Soviet filmmakers of the time, was plagued by severe shortages of film stock. So desperate was the need for stock that old film was sometimes scraped and recycled, sacrificing the archival value of what was removed. Despite this handicap, Vertov's work was distinguished by its dramatic reconstruction of events within the propaganda documentary form and by experimentation in length and color tinting by hand, subliminal cuts of one to two frames each, and deliberately provocative titles.

But it was in his theoretical writing during the 1920's that Vertov's main influence on Soviet silent film is to be found. Within a few years of his arrival in Moscow, Vertov's experiments had attracted a group of young cameramen, editors, technicians, and animators (including Sergei Eisenstein), whom he called the *kinoki* (or "kino-eyes").[19] With *Kinoks: A Revolution* (1923), Vertov and his collaborators began to publish a series of theoretical statements—radical in thought, eccentric in graphic appearance—attacking the conventional narrative cinema ("WE proclaim the old films, based on the romance, theatrical films and the like, to be leprous")[20] and demanding that it be replaced by an approach that integrated the processes of observation, cinematography, and editing.[21] These statements were often issued under the name of the "Council of Three," or *troika*, which consisted of Vertov; Elizaveta Svilova, his wife; and Mikhail Kaufman, his brother.[22] The target of Vertov's criticism was anything that he did not himself invent or, more likely, did not approve. The heart of his theory was his belief in the "kino-eye," a special form of cinematic observation that could penetrate the essence of actual events. For Vertov, the camera eye was better than the human eye, not only because it had the technological ability to transform reality, but also because it was not limited existentially by its human qualities and was, thus, infinitely perfectible by man.

The originality, energy, and complexity of Vertov's theories make summary difficult, but Vlada Petric has offered a brief and useful compilation of the substance of "Film-Eye":

(1) The "unarmed" human eye (the eye without the aid of the camera) is incapable of orienting itself in the "visual chaos of life"; it must be assisted by the "Film-Eye," which forms a symbiosis between the human eye and the camera objective.

(2) The cameraman does not possess any supernatural power; he is "an ordinary man" who knows how to use a mechanical tool which helps him 'veer' in the "boisterous ocean of life."

(3) The cameraman should avoid shooting "life facts" with a stationary camera; instead, he must be ready to move through as if in "a canoe lost in a stormy sea"; this contributes greater kinesthetic impact to the "film-thing" projected on the screen.

(4) The cameraman does not need a "pre-written scheme" (a script), nor has he to follow any preconceived idea about life; he does not attune himself to the "director's instructions," and the "schedule made up by a scriptwriter"; he has his own view of life and personal vision of the future film.

(5) "Speed" and "dexterity" are the most important skills of the cameraman's profession; he must "keep up with the pace of life's events," in order to maintain the genuine rhythm of the events shown on the screen as a "film-thing."

(6) The cameraman uses many specific cinematic devices to "attack" reality with his camera and to put facts together in a new structure; these devices help him to strive for a better world with more perceptive people.

(7) The cameraman should photograph persons with the intention of remain-

ing "unnoticed"; he is expected not to bother people at their work just as he would expect them not to disturb him during shooting.

(8) The cameraman must be everywhere and "observe" everything in order to obtain various choices before he decides when to shoot and what to face with his camera; only then will he be able to "keep pace with everyday life."

(9) Knowing that "in life nothing is accidental," the cameraman is expected to grasp dialectical relationships between disparate events occurring in reality; his duty is to unveil the intrinsic conflict of life's antagonistic forces and to lay bare "the cause and effect" of life's phenomena.

(10) At the same time, the cameraman is not an impartial observer of reality; he actively immerses himself in life's struggle, and once a part of it, he realizes that in life "everything has its own reason," which has to become manifest in the film.

(11) The cameraman must always take the "progressive side" of life; he is expected to support and espouse the "revolutionary attitude" toward reality, which will contribute to building "a true socialist society."

(12) All this is necessary if *kinoks* want to show on the screen "Life-As-It-Is" in its essence, including the "life" of the film itself—the process of cinematic creation from shooting and laboratory, through editing, up to the final product, i.e., the film being projected to the audience in the movie auditorium.[23]

Petric concludes that these "twelve commandments" are

uncompromising to the extreme, concerned exclusively with this medium as a means of unique cinematic expression and ideological communication, pointing to the complexity of the cinematic structure and its dialectical relationship to "life facts" and artifacts . . . a significant revolutionary document in the history of cinema. (42)

In short, Vertov invented what became known as cinéma vérité (and direct cinema), photographing "life-unawares," subsequently restructuring it through editing, and thus creating a new construction with its own aesthetic validity that is far more revealing than the life it represents.[24]

The artistic climate of the time encouraged such realistic cinematic experimentation as Vertov's *Kinopravda* ("Film-truth") film-newspaper series, which, between 1922 and 1925, appeared in twenty-three issues; its name recalls *Pravda,* the Bolshevik daily newspaper founded by Lenin in 1912.[25] In making these, Vertov used many of the experimental techniques—animation, trick photography, microphotography, multiple exposure, and hand-held cameras—that were to distinguish his later films, *Life Unrehearsed* (*Kinoglaz,* 1924), *Stride, Soviet* (*Shagai, Soviet!,* 1926), *One Sixth of the World* (*Shestaya chast mira,* 1926), and *The Eleventh Year* (*Odinnadtsati,* 1928). In 1926, he received a prize for *One Sixth of the World* at the World Exposition in Paris; however, his repeated attacks on conventional Soviet newsreels and other nonfiction films provoked controversies between Vertov and some of his colleagues, primarily Sergei Eisenstein and Nikolai Lebedev, and eventually led in 1927 to his dismissal from Sovkino (the centralized state cinema trust that had been established in 1924 to control the financing of all filmmaking in the entire Soviet Union) and to his acceptance of an invitation to work for VUFKU (All-Ukrainian Photo-Cinema Administration), the Ukrainian film studios in Kiev. It was there, in a comparatively conventional and isolated artistic climate, that Vertov created his most important films: *The Eleventh Year* (*Odinnadtsatyi*, 1928) and *Enthusiasm: Symphony of the Don Basin* (*Entuziazm: simphoniia Donbassa*, 1931), and his masterpiece, *The Man with the Movie Camera* (*Chelovek s kinoapparatom*, 1929), the most radical expression of his "kino-eye" theories.

The Man with the Movie Camera is about life (how the Russians live) and movies (how they are made) and, on first viewing, it does not seem to distinguish between the two. At first, it also seems to be a "city-symphony," the familiar cross-sectional view of how a city sleeps, wakes, works, and plays, presenting all of this action through the activities of an intrepid, peripatetic cameraman. Even if the film were regarded only as a city-symphony (and not as a work of revolutionary cinematic experimentation), it would easily surpass Ruttmann's *Berlin: The Symphony of a Great City*, to which it is often compared. Both films are concerned with images of urban reality in the present moment, not with reenactments or historical re-creations. For Ruttmann, the real city of Berlin is the literal and primary subject; for Vertov, however, the cities of Moscow, Kiev, and Odessa are secondary subject matter for the primary rendering of reality by the editor. While Ruttmann provides formal structure by borrowing movements and themes from the familiar symphonic form, Vertov creates his own personal structure by emphasizing the cameraman and his camera, his perception and ours. Ruttmann's vision broadly identifies and develops a specific personality for Berlin; Vertov's vision is inseparable from the individual perception of a single cameraman. We see the photographer (Mikhail Kaufman) taking the footage. He is in constant motion—climbing the structures of bridges, smokestacks, towers, roofs; riding in various vehicles; and lying on the ground to capture underneath views of traffic, trains, and marching men. And we see the editor (Elizaveta Svilova) winding film strips into spools, cutting and splicing the footage together.

While it reflects a great many avant-garde influences besides Constructivism, *The Man with the Movie Camera* is based on the Constructivist concept known as "art of fact." It is also the first self-defined nonfiction film, calling attention to itself, in its opening credits, as "an experiment in the cinematic communication of visible events, executed without the aid of intertitles, without the aid of a scenario (a film without a script), without the aid of theater (a film without sets, actors, etc.)." If the purpose of motion pictures is to record human life, which is to say, activity, then *The Man with the Movie Camera* must be the prototypical movie.[26] Vertov shows us how to frame reality and movement: through the human eye and the camera eye, or through windows and shutters. But, to confound us, he also shows us—through such devices as the freeze-frame, split screen, stop action, slow motion, and fast motion—how the cinematographer and editor can transform the movements of life into something that is unpredictable. He not only proves that the camera has a life of its own, but also reminds us of the editor, who is putting all of this footage together through juxtapositions of such rites as a birth, a wedding, and a death, and such movements as up, down, in, and out. Reality may be in the control of the artist, his camera, and its tricks, but it also finds definition within the editor's presentation and, ultimately, the viewer's perception. Jean-André Fieschi says that the film

> contains an astonishing play (back and forth) between document (testimony, evidence) and reconstruction; or rather, a radical and progressive *task* of fictionalizing the documentary, to a degree with a genuine *dislocation* takes place, and one finds oneself far removed from the raw material.[27]

Structurally, *The Man With the Movie Camera,* which is seventy-one minutes in length, consists of four parts.[28] It is *by* and *about* the man with the movie camera, beginning and ending with images related to the act of filmmaking and film viewing. Unlike the cameraman who is the subject of Buster Keaton's *The Cameraman* (1928), Vertov's cameraman is a Constructivist ideal—an artist among other workers who uses his tools to help build the new society; this idea "permeates the entire movie by means of visual juxtapositions that create the analogy between the filmmaker and his camera, and the worker and his tools." (Petric 80) We see the cameraman and his camera, as well as the reactions of people to them, and the film's continual self-reflexivity reminds us not only of the Constructivist practice of "baring the device" but also of its abundant cinematic inventiveness. These self-referential devices include:

> the motion picture as perceived by the viewer; the motion picture projected on the screen and simultaneously recorded by the camera (screen-within-the-screen); the "freeze-frame"; the film frames as part of the material (footage) handled by the Editor; the actual film moving through the editing table; and the film posters recorded by the movie camera and subsequently projected on the screen (like a slide). (Petric 84)

The film achieves structural unity not through conventional cinematic narrative, but through beginning, ending, and continually referring to the theme of the cameraman and his camera, as well as through sequential events that reinforce the theme of dynamic temporal progression. Vertov builds a dialectical unity of thematic opposites through the conflict of often unrelated and contradictory images, created by such devices as disruptive-associative montage, and the continual references to the filmmaker and editor at work. It is through the process of accretion that the film attains its unity, and through the process of establishing associations that the viewer makes meaning. At the same time, through cinematic illusion, Vertov continually subverts the viewers' conventional perception of space and time, thus reminding them to question that perception. Petric writes:

> Glorifying technology's capacity to aid the naked eye, examining the nature of human perception, presenting reality with a critical attitude, *The Man with the Movie Camera* does not limit itself to one particular point of view. Rather, it affords the viewer with the privilege of having looked at life from all possible

perspectives through cinematic means—a vision that is the ultimate goal of the "Film-Eye" method: not only to view life differently but above all to provide a more profound vision of reality than conventional observation can allow. (128)

As a film very much of its time, it was well-received in the domestic and international press. But it was also set apart from, and ahead of, its time by its cinematic complexity, and for that reason, it was not widely seen in Soviet theaters.[29] Ideologically, there is nothing complex, difficult, or controversial about the film. It provides a comprehensive view of Soviet life through predictable juxtapositions (of, for example, different classes of people), and its theme of temporal progression emphasizes the dynamism of the revolutionary movement. But, as "an experiment in cinematic communication," it demands a great deal from the viewer. Although it is neither as "difficult" or "inaccessible" as the prevailing critical attitude alleged for so many years, appreciating *The Man With the Movie Camera* requires the close study and repeated viewings that are more characteristic of the film scholar than the general audience. Nonetheless, the film remains readily accessible and enjoyable for any viewer, as much for its view of life, which is extensive and often humorous, as for its cinematic innovation.

With Stalin's rise to power, Vertov's position weakened in the Soviet Union, while, at the same time, his reputation grew in Europe. It can be assumed that his move to the VUFKU studios of the Ukraine was tantamount to official banishment. This departure from the mainstream of Soviet filmmaking was most unfortunate in view of the impending transformation of the cinema by the coming of sound. In fact, unlike many other serious filmmakers of the time, Vertov's early research and experimentation prepared him to make the best use of this technology, specifically for the inevitable realistic union of the "kino-eye" with the "radio-ear." Seth Feldman writes that from the beginning of the production of *The Man With the Movie Camera*, "Vertov carefully planned the musical score and may well have intended the work to be made as the first Soviet sound film" (12). Considering Vertov's previous experimentation with sound and his writings on the subject before 1929, one can imagine his frustration at not being able to create a sight-and-sound counterpoint in *The Man with the Movie Camera*.

Vertov did realize this integration in *Enthusiasm,* his first sound film, where he treated sound and visual as "separate and *equal*" elements. The tension created between the sound and visual tracks creates an audiovisual collage and makes the viewer constantly aware of their separateness as well as of their integration.[30] For Vertov, one purpose of cinematic sound is to make the viewer conscious of the human ear through the repetition of aural motifs. Another is to take advantage of the ability and mobility of these recording machines to enhance the viewer's social and political consciousness by organizing life's visual and aural chaos into a meaningful whole.

Although Vertov's next film, *Three Songs about Lenin (Tri pesni o Lenine,* 1934) was an international success, it also underscored the political and aesthetic controversy that already existed between Vertov and his contemporaries, primarily

Eisenstein. At this point, Eisenstein's career was in the ascendancy, while Vertov was headed for artistic oblivion. Vlada Petric writes:

> That Eisenstein and Vertov adopted different approaches to film is hardly surprising: Eisenstein came to cinema from theater, whereas Vertov was involved in cinematic experimentation from the very beginning of his career. Their conflicting attitudes regarding the aesthetic value and social function of cinema reflect in many ways the conceptual and ideological discord characteristic of Soviet revolutionary art throughout the 1920s. (48)

Essentially, they disagreed on the "ontological authenticity" of the nonfiction film, the extent to which the viewer accepts a cinematic account of an event as actually having taken place in the real world.[31] Eisenstein's background in theater led him to believe that the camera was not capable of both recording and revealing reality and, thus, that staging and reenactment were acceptable, while Vertov zealously believed in the primacy of the cinematic image. They disagreed on other aspects of filmmaking as well, including the use of actual people instead of professional actors, montage, and the role of sound. Politically, both opposed the state control of art, but Eisenstein eventually compromised his own artistic integrity with subservience to the party, while Vertov courageously declined to do so. However, the political oppression, artistic jealousy, and genuine aesthetic differences that fueled this dispute seem all the more poignant in that Eisenstein's and Vertov's theories and films, however different, represent significant contributions to Soviet and world cinema. It is particularly ironic that, for many viewers today, "Soviet realism" means the comparatively fresh spontaneity of his *The Man with the Movie Camera* rather than the brilliant but calculated effects of Eisenstein's *Battleship Potemkin* or *October*.

Esther Shub and the Compilation Film

Almost as old as the newsreel itself, the compilation film is that subgenre of the nonfiction film that begins on the editing table with footage that was made for another purpose. In the hands of those who would edit or manipulate such newsreel footage for their own purposes, often distorting the work of another for their own monetary gain, the compilation film can exploit the commercial purpose of cinema.[32] But in the hands of original artists with a vision of their own, the compilation film has both a history and an aesthetic validity of its own.

The first person to understand the valid historical use of the compilation film was Boleslaw Matuszewski, a Polish theorist, who, in 1897, two years after the cinema had been introduced by the Lumières, declared that it would be a new source of history.[33] During World War I, the compilation film flourished as a propaganda device on both sides of the conflict, but it was only legitimized in the 1920s through the serious efforts of Dziga Vertov and Esther Shub in the Soviet Union. Vertov's third film, *Anniversary of the Revolution* (*Godovshchina revoliutsii*, 1919), was a compilation film made from *Kino-nedelia* material, "the first indication of an interest in using compilation footage that would remain with Vertov throughout his career" (Feldman 5). It remained for Esther (Esfir) Shub, the most outstanding Russian woman filmmaker of the silent era, to create the compilation film.[34]

Esther Shub, who began her career in the Constructivist theater of Meyerhold and Mayakovsky, started to work in cinema in 1922, learning from the montage principles established by Vertov, Kuleshov, Eisenstein, and Pudovkin, and soon becoming an expert in reediting imported films. Deeply influenced by Eisenstein and Vertov, she, in turn, had an influence on both. Like them, she wanted to make films to a high artistic standard that would also educate the people to understand these new standards of art and society. Unlike Eisenstein, whose films are theatrical reenactments of history (especially *Battleship Potemkin* [*Bronenosets Potyomkin,* 1925], *October* [*Oktiabr* or *Ten Days That Shook the World,* 1928], and *Old and New* [*Staroye i novoye,* 1929]), Shub believed most strongly in preserving the onto-logical authenticity of the images with which she worked.[35] In this, her concept of the nonfiction film seems closest to Vertov's, on both the theoretical and ideologi-cal levels. Like Vertov, also, she understood the importance of sound, particularly direct sound recording, even before it became feasible.

In creating her films, Shub was faced with three major challenges: to work with the scarce footage that was available to her; to study it carefully; and to express her own ideological point of view without distorting the historical value of her material. The predominant qualities of her films are her conception of film as montage, her intuitive ability to select and put shots together, and her exact sense of rhythm and structure. In addition, Shub's patient scholarship and care of histori-cal film footage encouraged the establishment of film archives, which, in turn, provided the film materials that continue to make the compilation film possible.

Although she produced many compilation and documentary films, as well as newsreels, Shub is best known for her trilogy of compilation films: *Fall of the Romanov Dynasty* (*Padenie dinastii romanovykh,* 1927), *The Great Road* (*Veliky put',* 1927), and *The Russia of Nicholas II and Leo Tolstoy* (*Rossiya Nikolava II i Lev Tolstoi,* 1928).[36] This trilogy is a cinematic essay that utilizes existing footage to follow, according to an ideological concept, the historical course of events from 1897 to 1927. Her great achievement was to express her viewpoint without dis-torting either the authenticity or the impact of the footage she selected.[37] Shub's concept of the compilation film influenced Joris Ivens, the Workers' Film and Photo League, and Marcel Ophuls, as well as the producers of such series as "The March of Time," "This is America," "Why we Fight," "The World in Action," "The Twentieth Century," and most historical news reporting on television.

The Russian propagandist tradition in the nonfiction and compilation film was not limited to the pioneering achievements of Vertov and Shub. Other important filmmakers are Mikhail Kaufman, Ilya Kopalin, Mikhail Kalatozov, Yakov Blyokh, and Victor Turin. Their work had a direct influence not only on Russian and European filmmaking, but also on John Grierson and the British documentary film movement. Kaufman's and Kopalin's *Moskva* (*Moscow,* 1927) influenced the city-symphony genre. Blyokh's *Shanghai Document* (*Shanghaisky dokument,* 1928) is journalist reportage, important for its observation of the divided Chinese city and for its account of Chiang Kai-shek's anticommunism. Kalatosov's *Salt for Svanetia*

(*Sol Svanetii,* 1930) uses the classic problem-solution structure to show how a Soviet-built road brings both salt and prosperity to an isolated mountain community. But even more important as a direct influence on the British documentary method was Victor Turin's *Turksib* (1929), a dynamic, feature-length film that both recorded the building of the Turkestan–Siberian railway and argued for its acceptance as an economic necessity. *Turksib* was important to the British, not only because Grierson's editing of the English version helped to articulate its sociopolitical theme for a Western audience, but also because Grierson learned from it the direct style and precise statement of theme that are among the hallmarks of 1930s' British documentaries. Though *Turksib* lacks the cinematographic beauty of the British and American films of the 1930s, it is important for Turin's epic conception and dramatic, energetic organization of his themes and his use of subtitles linking the sequences. The sequence that composes swollen rivers from shots of small mountain rivulets anticipates the celebrated sequence in Pare Lorentz's *The River* (1937). Despite its importance in the history of the social documentary, *Turksib* seems ponderous today in contrast to such classics as *Night Mail* or *The River*.

While it might be argued that the British concept of the documentary film could have developed without the Russian influence, the Russians indisputably showed filmmakers around the world how political ideology and film aesthetics could be compatibly fused. Their films demonstrate that the spontaneity and flexibility of the film art can best capture the dynamic, changing political and social reality of the twentieth century. In long-range influence on the development of the nonfiction film, their imaginative, yet didactic films have proved to be more significant than the efforts of either the American romantics or the continental realists. The Russians' pioneering political films fostered the extensive experimentation with and development of the nonfiction film in England and the United States during the 1930s.

JOHN GRIERSON AND THE EARLY BRITISH DOCUMENTARY FILM

John Grierson was the father of the documentary film movement in the English-speaking world. He was the person most responsible for developing the concept of the Soviet propaganda documentary into the British documentary film, introducing Western audiences to several important Soviet nonfiction films by Eisenstein, Vertov, Turin, and Dovzhenko.[38] What became known as the British documentary film movement first began in 1927 at the film unit of the Empire Marketing Board (EMB), an organization established by the British government to promote trade and economic cooperation among members of the British commonwealth of nations, and continued at the film unit of the General Post office (GPO). By 1939, the British documentary film movement had reached the climax of its development as an influence on the British cultural and political scene. At that point, the British film units—EMB, GPO, commercial, institutional, and individual production units—had produced about three hundred films, all of them in some degree owing their existence to Grierson's leadership.

John Grierson (1898–1972)

John Grierson grew up under the influence of a Scottish socialism that was both radical and humanist.[39] Both his parents were active in politics. His father, a schoolmaster, taught him to have humanistic ideals, to adopt a liberal outlook, and to understand that individual freedom came about through education. But it was from his mother's radicalism that young Grierson learned firsthand of Scottish Socialism and of the movement for the freedom and independence of workers and women. Finally, his social attitudes reflected his observation of the Clydeside Movement in the shipyards and slums of Glasgow. As a student, first in the lower forms and then at Glasgow University, Grierson was a leader in intellectual and political activity. While his beliefs were as far left as one could go at that time without becoming a Communist, from the earliest age he shrewdly avoided any binding affiliation with a specific political party.

By the time that he was 30, Grierson had developed the humanist philosophy rooted in democracy and aesthetics that remained basic to his work for the rest of his life. He is, perhaps, best described as a progressive thinker within the system, one who was enthusiastic about social change as well as about the value and potential of human life. He believed in individual human beings and in the necessity of their collective efforts to improve society. He believed in the importance of work and in the dignity of the workers. He believed that the basic force behind art was social, not aesthetic. And he believed that the popular arts, particularly film, would replace the more traditional sources of information, such as the church and the school, as shapers of public opinion. His colleague, Edgar Anstey, said that Grierson was "sort of schizophrenic in the sense of the split between social purpose and a passionate feeling about art."[40]

Grierson's politics and aesthetics were shaped by figures as diverse as Immanuel Kant, John Stuart Mill, V. I. Lenin, Bertrand Russell, Walter Lippmann, Sergei Eisenstein, and Robert Flaherty. The works of Russell helped him to refine his passionate social conscience. While Flaherty's films reaffirmed his belief in the dignity of man, Eisenstein's films showed him that the art of the cinema could be a dynamic and powerful force in the service of man and society. Lippmann convinced him that motion pictures could help the ordinary citizen to think about social issues and to influence social reform.[41]

Grierson saw the possibilities for a new form of filmmaking in Flaherty's *Nanook* and Eisenstein's *Battleship Potemkin*. Though Grierson and Flaherty were friends, Grierson did not altogether accept Flaherty's personal approach to filmmaking; he saw Flaherty as an innocent naturalist too concerned with observation to care about making a social statement. In this Grierson underestimated Flaherty, equating Flaherty's gentleness and subtlety with indifference to social change. And as much as Grierson admired Eisenstein's *Battleship Potemkin* (he helped to prepare the English version of it) and shared his goal of making film a great social force, he referred to the film in his own inimitable way as a "glorified newsreel." Later in his life, Grierson would more readily acknowledge that revolutionary Russian attitudes toward art had more profoundly influenced him.[42] And, in fact, compared with the other possible approaches to nonfiction filmmaking—the American romantic, the Soviet propagandist, and the continental realist—the British approach, under Grierson's influence, was to be most influenced by the Soviets. Grierson also admired the possibilities of film inherent in the early film work of John Ford, James Cruze, Joris Ivens, Walther Ruttmann, and Alberto Cavalcanti. A trip to the United States broadened his social outlook, but convinced him that Hollywood filmmaking would not play a significant role in the struggle for social change.

When Grierson returned to England in 1927, he had become convinced that film was a serious medium capable of shaping public opinion, stating this conclusion:

I have no great interest in films as such. . . . Art is one matter, and the wise, as I suggest, had better seek it where there is elbow room for its creation; entertainment is another matter; education, in so far as it concerns the classroom pedagogue, another; propaganda, another; and cinema is to be conceived as a medium like writing, capable of many forms and many functions. (*Grierson on Documentary* 15–16)

In fact, at another point, Grierson chose the form and function of cinema that he would espouse:

> *Cinema is neither an art nor an entertainment;* it is a form of publication, and may publish in a hundred different ways for a hundred different audiences. . . . Of these the most important field by far is propaganda. The circles devoted to the art of cinema mean well and they will help to articulate the development of technique, *but the conscious pursuit of art carries with it, in periods of public difficulty, a certain shallowness of outlook* [emphasis added]. (*Grierson on Documentary* 185)

Grierson thus saw the filmmaker as a patriot first, and as an artist second. Nothing is more important than the common good, and, drawing a rather terse distinction between commercial and propaganda filmmaking, Grierson says, "To command, and cumulatively command, the mind of a generation is more important than by novelty or sensation to knock a Saturday night audience cold; and the 'hang-over' effect of a film is everything" (*Grierson on Documentary* 165). By "hang-over effect," Grierson must certainly have meant the lingering ideological impression that a film makes on a viewer, the effect that the filmmaker hopes will channel the viewer's mind in the direction pointed by the film. It is characteristic of Grierson that he used a blunt, familiar concept to express what the Soviet theorists took far longer to say about montage and perception.

If Grierson was a self-acknowledged sociologist, he was also a self-professed evangelist. Convinced that film was a medium of education and persuasion, Grierson devoted his missionary enthusiasm and energy to the task of convincing others that film could and should be used to further social progress. In the 1930s especially, Grierson was fortunate in having a great social laboratory in which to work. The times were economically depressed and would end in the Second World War; England was experiencing myriad social problems of education, housing, pollution, trade, and communications. As the Russians had already learned, film was a dynamic medium for educating the public, and Grierson was the right person for showing how this could be done in Great Britain. Belgian filmmaker Henri Storck commented: "Grierson always . . . saw documentary films as a weapon, as a tool for creating a society."[43] In 1939, looking back over a decade of production, Grierson observed that the British documentary film movement

> was from the beginning an adventure in public observation. It might, in principle, have been a movement in documentary writing, or documentary radio, or documentary painting. The basic force behind it was social, not aesthetic. It was a desire to make drama from the ordinary; a desire to bring the citizen's mind in from the ends of the earth to the story, his own story, of what was happening under his nose. From this came our insistence on the drama of the doorstep. We were, I confess, sociologists, a little worried about the way the world was going. . . . We were interested in *all* instruments which would crystallize sentiments in a

muddled world and create a will towards civic participation. (*Grierson on Documentary* 18)

Grierson found the drama for his films not on the battlefields, but on the doorsteps of ordinary people. He made films on subjects about which all political parties could agree: economic well-being, adequate housing, better nutrition, improved education and communications, cleaner air, and better working conditions. Though his liberal activism had much in common with the views of the British Labour Party, in fact, he had more success when the Conservative party was in power. Today, it is both apt and ironic to realize that the British documentary films of the 1930s, films advocating significant social change, were paid for by a conservative government.

Empire Marketing Board Film Unit

The Empire Marketing Board, established in 1926, was the prosaic and uninspiring name for the government department whose purpose was to promote "all the major researches across the world which affect the production or preservation or transport of the British Empire's food supplies."[44] On behalf of British products, its three principal functions were to encourage scientific research; to conduct market research; and to create publicity.[45] The EMB was headed by Sir Stephen Tallents, a specialist in what was then the new field of public relations. He built an organization which, without precedent, and within its short life (1926–33), became the largest government publicity operation during peacetime.

With its establishment of a Film Unit in 1930, the EMB also began what would result in an almost unprecedented program of state support for filmmaking (there were, of course, already nationalized film industries in the Soviet Union and in Germany). As Grierson described it, the Film Unit was

> a department among departments, and part of a very much larger scheme of educational and propaganda services. Whatever its pretensions in purely cinematic terms, it was dedicated and devoted to the usual cold-blooded ends of government.[46]

The Film Unit was only one part of this large organization of forty-five departments, but in a short time it grew in production capacity and influence to become the founding organizational source of the "documentary film" as we know it today. *Documentary* is Grierson's own term (he first used it in 1926 in reviewing Flaherty's *Moana*), and the association of this approach to filmmaking with the British is due largely to the efforts of Grierson and the EMB Film Unit.[47]

At the time the EMB was created, there was considerable interest, among official British circles, in the use of film for publicity purposes. But the suggestion that the EMB produce films came not from a bureaucrat, but rather from Rudyard Kipling, the poet and senior leader of the Conservative Party. Kipling and Walter Creighton cowrote a scenario, and with Kipling's support, Creighton was appointed as the EMB's first Film Officer. The fact that he knew nothing about film production does not appear to have been an obstacle to this appointment, but during Creighton's travels to the United States, where he went to learn the rudiments of film production, Grierson gradually assumed control and was eventually appointed Film Officer in 1930.

Grierson introduced Tallents to such Soviet films as *Battleship Potemkin, Storm over Asia, Turksib,* and *Earth,* praising them as examples of what one country could do with film as an "incomparable instrument of national expression." Grierson also wrote reports on film production and distribution that helped to shape the thinking of Tallents and others. Tallents was dedicated to the "projection" of English life and work, and he listed those national institutions and virtues in which he felt the English took most pride and in which the world would be most interested:

- The monarchy (with its growing scarcity value)
- Parliamentary institutions (with all the values of a first edition)
- The British Navy
- The English Bible, Shakespeare, and Dickens
- In international affairs—a reputation for disinterestedness
- In national affairs—a tradition of justice, law, and order
- In commerce—a reputation for fair dealing
- In manufacture—a reputation for quality
- In sport—a reputation for fair play.[48]

While these national achievements may represent the typically bland product of the public relations approach, the list was more than chauvinistic stock-taking. To achieve greater international cooperation and communication and improved status for England in the world market, it was necessary to create a more positive image. Grierson's challenge was to supervise the worldwide "projection" of that image. As part of that image, in contrast to the novels, plays, and poetry typical of England in late 1920s, the EMB presented the lives and problems of the British working class as a vital and important aspect of the contemporary scene. While, later, such poets as W. H. Auden, Stephen Spender, and C. Day Lewis would make the working class man into a hero, documentary film led the way in a culture still very much oriented to the artistic representation of the upper-class way of life. (Still later, in the 1950s, British Free Cinema performed a similar function; see Chapter 11). Throughout his career, Grierson emphasized, and encouraged others to emphasize, the presentation of a cross-sectional view of British life rather than the awakening and strengthening, as had the Russians, of the viewer's concepts of state, history, or political destiny.

In addition to being one of the first to realize the essential role that film could play in public relations, Tallents showed further foresight in suggesting that such a program of filmmaking should not rely solely on financial support from the government or from private enterprise, but, rather, should be supported jointly by them. In the later 1930s, such a balance was achieved. Thus, while both British and Soviet filmmakers were government sponsored, the British movement was not so tightly controlled by the government that its creativity and freedom of expression were regulated. The difference, of course, is in the amount of government intervention. The propaganda film, such as that made by the Soviets and later perfected by Josef Goebbels in Nazi Germany, flourishes in a totalitarian atmosphere. Vertov and Turin (under Lenin and Stalin), Riefenstahl (under Hitler), and Antonioni (under Mussolini) worked in totalitarian societies, and made important propaganda films. But the documentary film, as Grierson defined and produced it, can only flourish in a democracy, where the atmosphere of freedom of expression is more conducive to an honest investigation of social, economic, political, and cultural issues.

The EMB Film Unit was a group effort; indeed, outside of the Soviet Union, it was the only such group effort in the early history of the nonfiction film. (In the 1930s, several groups were formed in the United States for the production of documentaries with a leftist political orientation, including the Workers Film and Photo League, Nykino, and the Frontier Film Group; see chapter 6). For all his idealism, Grierson's aesthetic approach was also practical, and so he insisted that the personnel of his unit be free to experiment in a way that would in all likelihood have been denied them in the profit-making commercial studios. Even though motion picture production is, by necessity, almost always a collaborative effort, such effort is always vulnerable in matters of artistic quality; however, the EMB Film Unit was particularly successful, even though it was criticized by members of the British film industry and by those unfamiliar with, or unconvinced by, the relatively new art form. In his evaluation of their effort to bring certain aspects of modern Britain to life on the screen, Paul Rotha wrote that the EMB possessed "a sincerity and skill unapproached by any commercially operating company, at the same time bringing into existence a cooperative method of working and a spirit of loyalty which is notably absent in most other centres of film manufacture" (*Documentary Film* 97). Nevertheless, Grierson knew nothing of the practical aspects of filmmaking, so it is not surprising that his young colleagues found some of his theories to be rather solemn in contrast to the haphazard conditions under which they worked. Of the group, Harry Watt said:

> . . . we were just a bunch of enthusiastic kids, accepting the basic theme of the dignity of man from our brilliant but erratic boss, learning our job by trial and error, bubbling with ideas but making thousands of mistakes, cheerfully exploiting ourselves and each other in the absolute belief that what we did or were going to do was worthwhile.[49]

The first films produced in the EMB Film Unit in 1929 were Grierson's *Drifters* and Walter Creighton's *One Family*.[50] *One Family*

> dealt with the gathering of the ingredients for the Royal Christmas pudding from all parts of the Empire as viewed through the eyes of a small boy. The film had disaster written all over it . . . [and] was berated by the critics and ignored by the commercial cinema.[51]

In contrast, *Drifters* (1929) is a simple, beautifully photographed, well-paced silent film that established two major themes that characterized many of the British films that followed: the dignity of labor and the worth of the individual working man. Its underlying theme is the shift that transforms small, independent herring fishing efforts into a large, industrial operation. But its overall focus is on the men who brave the rough seas, do the hard work, and bring home the catch; their wonderful faces alone are enough to preserve the film's interest. Although Grierson recorded the complete process—from the time the men prepared to board their ship, through their waiting for the fish, the catch itself, and the auction, cleaning, icing, and distribution of the fish in barrels—the film is uneven, with some sequences more interesting than others. However, Grierson succeeds in relating the work of one small boat to a national fishing industry and reminds us of the economic necessity of making a quick catch and of an early return to port.

Drifters compares favorably with *Granton Trawler* and *North Sea*, later films on the same subject, and is considerably more mature than its early place in the development of the British documentary would suggest. *Drifters* was important for several reasons. First, in Grierson's understanding of montage and his emphasis on the working man, it reflected the influence of the Soviet filmmakers, particularly Eisenstein, on the foundation of the British documentary film. Second, it presents a routine activity—herring fishing—which is nevertheless brought alive, not only in terms of the physical process, but, more important, in terms of the human drama involved in this essential part of the British economy. As Flaherty had demon-

Drifters (John Grierson, Great Britain, 1929)

strated in *Nanook* and *Moana,* it demonstrates that vision can transform existing everyday material into a film of interest, quality, and drama. To Grierson, however, the film was more than a gesture in tribute to Flaherty; he said, "Its subject belonged in part to Flaherty's world, for it had something of the noble savage and certainly a great deal of nature to play with. It did, however, use steam and smoke and did, in a sense, marshal the effects of modern industry." Finally, it was the only film that Grierson himself directed, although he was responsible for the production of over a thousand films during his lifetime and closely involved with about fifty of them.

With *Drifters,* the British "at last had a factual film which made a complete break with the old illustrated lecture."[52] It was well-received by the press and the public alike, as well as by members of the House of Commons, who requested a special screening, and this success convinced Grierson and Tallents that the Film Unit should be expanded (Swann 48–49). The EMB began to grow in order to create good documentaries, "not on the basis of one director, one location and one film at a time, but on the basis of half-a-dozen directors with complementary talents and a hundred and one subjects all along the line." Grierson said:

> The documentary idea, after all, demands no more than that the affairs of our time shall be brought to the screen in any fashion which strikes the imagination and makes observation a little richer than it was. At one level, the vision may be journalistic; at another, it may rise to poetry and drama. At another level again, its aesthetic quality may lie in the mere lucidity of its exposition. (*Grierson on Documentary* 22)

Between January 1930 and July 1933, the Film Unit grew from two to over thirty people and acquired substantial technical facilities for production.

The filmmakers who formed the unit included Basil Wright, Arthur Elton, Stuart Legg, J. N. G. Davidson, Paul Rotha, Donald Taylor, John Taylor, Harry Watt, Edgar Anstey, Evelyn Spice, Ruby Grierson and Marion Grierson (Grierson's sisters), and Margaret Taylor, who later became Grierson's wife.[53] Their early films included such prosaic titles as *Canadian Apples, Sheep Dipping,* and *South African Fruit* (all c. 1929–30). Some of the notable early experiments and achievements, produced and released as silent films (the EMB was not able to convert to sound production until 1933), include Arthur Elton's *Upstream* (1931) on salmon fishing in Scotland, *Shadow on the Mountain* (1931) about pasture experiments in Wales, and *The Voice of the World* (1932) about modern communications; Basil Wright's *The Country Comes to Town* (1931) about London's market services, and *Windmill in Barbados* (1934); and Stuart Legg's *New Generation* (1932). Elton's *Aero-Engine* (1933, silent) is a well-photographed, highly detailed observation of every step in the manufacture of an airplane engine; its value lies more in its completeness of detail than in its brief, straightforward narrative. Wright's *O'er Hill and Dale* (1932) is a brisk account of sheep farming in the border hills between England and Scotland, and typical of the EMB films, it is an unpretentious, delightful picture of a valuable part of the British economy. Wright's *Cargo from Jamaica* (1933, silent) records the harvesting and shipping of bananas. This unremarkable business is enhanced by beautiful cinematography and a rhythmic sense of editing that foreshadows Wright's lyricism in *Song of Ceylon* (1934). Another silent film, Donald Taylor's *So This is Lancashire* (alternative title, *Lancashire: Home of Industry*, 1935, silent), shows the diversity of a particular region's industrial production, and although briskly edited, it is a routine and often dull account that would have been saved either by a spoken narrative or by the particular feeling for industrial craftsmanship evident in Flaherty's *Industrial Britain*. Other EMB films, some of which were released after the EMB Film Unit was disbanded, include Stuart Legg's *The New Operator* (1932); Basil Wright's *King Log* (originally titled *Lumber*, 1932) and *Liner Cruising South* (1933); Edgar Anstey's *Eskimo Village* and *Uncharted Waters* (1933); Marion Grierson's *So This is London* (1933); Donald Taylor's *Spring Comes to England* (1934), and Evelyn Spice's *Spring on the Farm* (1934).

The period 1931–32 comprised the Film Unit's most productive period, and before the government disbanded the EMB in 1933, the Film Unit had produced over one hundred films; these were distinguished as a collective effort, rather than by the particular style or vision of one director, although Flaherty's work on *Industrial Britain* (1933) was an important "outside" influence (see chapter 5). Despite critical acclaim, the EMB was not particularly successful in persuading commercial theater owners to show its films, so it established a film library in 1931, and by late 1933 was distributing 800 films to schools, libraries, and other educational institutions.[54] Rising costs were a perennial problem; in 1926, the EMB allotted less than one percent of its budget to film production, but in 1929, that allotment had risen to approximately seven percent.[55]

The development of the British documentary film movement was slowed down momentarily when a government commission recommended that the Empire Marketing Board be disbanded in 1933, not because there was any question about the quality of its achievement, but because it seemed to be an ineffective endeavor in the context of the economic depression of the early 1930s. Commercial organizations and other institutions continued to produce films, and the successful union of the documentary approach and such sponsorship can be seen, for example, in the beautiful *Song of Ceylon* (1934). However, there was tension between documentary filmmaking in the public and private sectors. Enlightened private companies recognized the public relations uses of the documentary film and envied the government's ability to produce quality films as well as its elaborate system of nontheatrical distribution, but they were generally opposed to the theatrical exhibition of these films.[56] Although the government withdrew its support from the EMB, it realized the quality of the EMB Film Unit and the necessity for continued production of publicity films. As a result, it designated the General Post Office—an umbrella organization for the government's various communications operations—to support the work of the Film Unit, under the supervision of Tallents and Grierson, as an aspect of its own public relations program.[57] The British documentary film tradition continued and prospered at the Post Office.

PART TWO

(1933–1939)

Documentary Films to Change the World

5

The British Documentary Movement: 1933–1945

GENERAL POST OFFICE FILM UNIT UNDER JOHN GRIERSON: 1933–37

While the British documentary film movement had its roots in the Soviet propaganda tradition, it developed during the Great Depression, as Andrew Higson notes, "on a complex and often contradictory ideological terrain,"[1] producing state-sponsored films that were both idealistic and practical in their treatment of social issues and problems. At the same time, there were many workers', socialist, left, or progressive films.[2] Grierson not only believed that the documentary film should provide a "creative treatment of actuality," but he also realized that the state could use film and other media to control and manipulate the audience.[3] The political implications of Grierson's approach seem Marxist: film was to be used to inform people about the material and political causes of vast social problems. But, in fact, he avoided Marxist dogma, and produced films that were intended not only to educate, but also to praise and illuminate the human condition. In this sense, the practical and aesthetic goals of the British documentary film movement were balanced much more effectively than would at first have seemed possible. Although its primary role was as a source of information and education primarily on behalf of government functions, the movement also offered filmmakers an unparalleled scope for creative experimentation.[4]

The development of the nonfiction film in the 1920s and 1930s—in Russia, Germany, and Britain, in particular—was a function of government policy and financial support. In Britain, however, filmmakers allied to this ideological use of film regarded themselves as being part of a movement, working with a common leader, from a common theoretical foundation, and towards common ends.[5] At the General Post Office, from 1933 to 1937, Grierson and his associates saw and accepted the continuing challenge to "bring the Empire alive" (*Grierson on Docu-*

mentary 166) by translating the complexities of modern communications, industry, and technology into creative, compelling films. Here, they continued their successful experiments with sound, as well as involving ranking artists from fields such as literature and music, and developing special cinematic effects with color, graphics, and animation. Given this viable creative atmosphere, supported by a solid organization and adequate funding, the British began to produce the memorable series of films that constitute their most important achievement in nonfiction film.[6]

Grierson was the first filmmaker to put British working people on the screen (other than as comic figures); he not only put them there, but observed them clearly and intimately. At the GPO, he continued the approach that he had established at the EMB: to provide a creative treatment of actuality and to make the workingman a hero; in fact, the first films produced during the transition from the EMB to GPO Film Unit introduced the workers who made Britain's new automatic telephone system: *Telephone Workers* and *The Coming of the Dial* (both 1932).[7] Other early films, made to describe and explain the myriad communications activities of the General Post Office, included *Cable Ship* (1934), *Under the City* (1934), *Six-Thirty Collection* (1934), *Weather Forecast* (1934), *Post Haste* (1934), and *BBC: Droitwich* (1934). They are all brief, succinct, and effective in their professional attempt to demonstrate the importance of simple tasks and to show that drama can be found in apparently unlikely subjects. Moreover, they exemplify some significant developments in the use of direct sound recording and narration spoken by the people whom we see on the screen. Alexander Shaw's and A. E. Jeakins's *Cable Ship* (1933) presents the work of the GPO vessel that repairs cables lying at the bottom of the English Channel. Its technique foreshadows Shaw's later *Under the City* (1934), in which the voices of a narrator and the men recount the work involved in maintaining the water, gas, telephone, and telegraph cables that run beneath London's streets. Edgar Anstey's and R. H. Watt's *Six-Thirty Collection* (1934), a commonplace explanation of the collection, sorting, and routing of mail, fails to find the human focus in this activity that distinguishes the later GPO masterpiece *Night Mail*. In *Weather Forecast* (1934), the most sophisticated of these early films, director Evelyn Spice not only provides a general presentation of forecasting methods, but also demonstrates the dramatic effect that such broadcasts have on a specific group of ships, aircraft pilots, and farmers. The film makes its major points through the use of distinctive, direct sound recording and visual images, rather than through straight narrative. Less effective, but nonetheless interesting, is R. H. Watt's *BBC: Droitwich* (1934), a clear, well-organized explanation of the function of what was then the most advanced long-wave radio transmitter in the world. Some of these were routine films on routine subjects, and others, like *Industrial Britain,* were prestige productions, intended to show the superiority of the nonfiction film over its fictional counterpart.

Robert Flaherty and John Grierson: Industrial Britain *(1933)*

As the European and American approaches to the nonfiction film developed, it seemed increasingly likely that Grierson and Robert Flaherty would one day work together; it also seemed inevitable that they would clash.[8] Although there was a great personal affinity between these two pioneers, neither altogether accepted the other's approach to filmmaking (*Grierson on Documentary* 139-44). Grierson initially planned that Flaherty would act as a master teacher, inspiring the younger filmmakers in the fledgling British documentary movement with his gift for observation and his instinctive handling of the camera.[9] He also hoped that Flaherty's name would enhance the reputation of the group. Kevin Brownlow suggests that, ultimately, the British filmmakers found Flaherty's films more important for their inspirational effect than for their integral artistic value.[10]

Flaherty accepted Grierson's proposal to make a film about the relationship between British craftsmanship and British industrial output, but, from the beginning of the project, there were temperamental and theoretical differences between the two men. *Industrial Britain* (1933), the result of this uneasy collaboration, reflects Grierson's contribution more than Flaherty's. The theme of the film—"the old changes, giving place to the new"—underscores the shift in industrial production from the steam to the steel age. The film's structure—Part I, Steam; and Part II, Steel—is meant to embody this theme, but the transition of ideas is less effectively realized than the confident narratorial voice assumes. What does link these two periods in the industrial evolution of England is Flaherty's attention to the human factor—the craftmanship and care that distinguish British products as diverse as coal, pottery, and glass. These products stand, in the narrator's words, "for the continuity of English craftsmanship and skill, for an emphasis on quality, which only the individual can give." Flaherty's images reveal a personality and dignity in the craftsmen that all the narrative about the "man at the lever" fails to communicate. In fact, in addition to its beautiful cinematography, the quality of *Industrial Britain* that most clearly identifies it as Flaherty's work remains its concern with craftsmanship. However, even though the narrator asserts that "the human factor remains, even in this machine age, the final factor," Grierson's belief in industrial progress overshadows Flaherty's feeling for individual achievement. Grierson wrote in "Robert Flaherty" of their work together:

> When [Flaherty] made *Industrial Britain* with me, his flair for the old crafts and the old craftsmen was superb, and there will never be shooting of that kind to compare with it; but he simply could not bend to the conception of those other species of craftsmanship which go with modern industry and modern organization. (n. pag.)

In some respects, *Industrial Britain* prefigures the subsequent *Night Mail;* both films attempt to relate the individual worker to the larger industrial process, to encourage their pride in their work, and to bolster their morale. However, Grierson's concept of the documentary film expanded in the five years that separate the two films. Only two minutes longer than *Night Mail, Industrial Britain* is a simple film, but its characteristically British fussiness nonetheless intrudes, with pompous narration and insistent music providing a dramatic treatment that the subject neither needs nor warrants.[11] Moreover, Grierson's attempt to praise British industry and workers omits several important factors. Grierson affirms man's

Industrial Britain (Robert Flaherty, Great Britain, 1933)

freedom to work, but seldom acknowledges his right to freedom of speech. This is a film celebrating workers; yet they never speak directly about their work. As in many other British documentaries, *Night Mail* included, we learn about them only through the narration, and we learn about their emotions only through abstract generalizations about dedication and pride. The films that depict Grierson's Utopian vision of Great Britain share a reluctance to give voice to all who might have something valid to say about the central issues of concern.

In addition, *Industrial Britain* was intended to show that beautiful products can be made among the belching smokestacks and behind the ugly walls; in order to do so and, in broader terms, to carry out his purpose of sanctifying work, Grierson must disregard the fact of air pollution, then as now a dangerous threat to the workers' health and to their community development. In fact, the clouds of smoke that we see in almost every exterior shot of *Industrial Britain* later became the subject of Grierson's *The Smoke Menace* (1937), and subsequent British documentaries also recognized urban environmental problems.

Industrial Britain illustrates what can happen when two different approaches to filmmaking are brought together, with one eventually dominating over the other. Although the subordinated style does come through almost in counterpoint to the dominant one, the end result is confusion, not fusion.

But their differences and the flawed result did not deter Grierson from continuing to appreciate Flaherty's true importance as an artist and citing Flaherty, Méliès, Griffith, Sennett, and Eisenstein as the five great innovators in the history of film. In "Robert Flaherty," he wrote:

> Flaherty, great personal story teller as he was, did not especially think of the film as a way of telling a story, developing a drama, or creating an impact, either physical or mental. For him, the camera was veritably a wonder eye, to see with more remarkably than one ordinarily saw. (n. pag.)

Subsequently, Grierson affirmed his admiration and their friendship by recommending the project that became *Man of Aran* (see chapter 6).

Basil Wright: The Song of Ceylon *(1934)*

One of the acknowledged classics of film reportage in the commercially sponsored field is Basil Wright's *Song of Ceylon* (1934).[12] Produced by Grierson for the Ceylon Tea Propaganda Board, the film was specifically intended to create a favorable image of Ceylon, now Sri Lanka, and one of its major exports. However, the film does not overtly sell tea, and, in fact, treats the subject so delicately that the viewer

Song of Ceylon (Basil Wright, Great Britain, 1934) [Basil Wright behind the camera]

may think that its real object is to depict changing customs, not to dramatize the flagging tea market. Despite the film's apparently commercial intent, the overall comment is sociological and, ultimately, philosophical. With its juxtaposition of traditional customs and modern methods, *Song of Ceylon* builds an intelligent, sensitive impression of a changing culture.

Song of Ceylon is structured in four parts, each revealing a different aspect of the Singhalese culture.[13] Slowly and carefully, the film's beautiful images are presented in counterpoint to the sound, rather than in complement, so that the resulting development is one of contrast. Part 1, "Buddha," shows and explains the natives' religion and their spiritual resources. Part 2, "Virgin Island," documents the island's natural and human resources, labor force, harvest activity, and use of dance as a means of developing poise and muscular control. Part 3, "Voices of Commerce," presents the commercial focus of the film, the harvesting and shipping of tea, and it is in this sequence that the counterpoint sound is most apparent and effective. Part 4, "Apparel of a God," returns to the subject of the spiritual life, depicting prayers, the offerings of food, and ceremonial dancing.

Song of Ceylon shows the land, people, and their customs, and most important of all, it integrates many aspects of Singhalese life into the film, so that one is left with an impressionistic, but also seemingly accurate, picture of a foreign land. In accomplishing this, it also manages to avoid the clichés and predictable juxtapositions of the travel film genre. Technically, it makes significant advances in the use of combined dissolves, superimposition of visual images, and counterpoint sound. Altogether, it is a film of refined composition, restrained impact, yet rare power.

Another film that provides insight into a complex, albeit more familiar world, is Stuart Legg's *B.B.C.: The Voice of Britain* (1935), which presents a superbly integrated picture of the complexities of radio production at the British Broadcasting Corporation. There is excellent visual unity between the sequences that show a variety of programming from children's story-telling programs to sports, drama, and the Dancing Daughters tap-dancing team. Perhaps owing to the variety of the BBC itself, this film is direct and vital, as some of the "explanation" films are not, and the fresh style of the film also has its own gentle humor. A full-length feature documentary, this is an ambitious as well as a successful attempt to capture the sounds and sights of the vast British radio enterprise.

Basil Wright and Harry Watt: Night Mail *(1936)*

The most successful and certainly the most memorable of these early GPO films was *Night Mail* (1936), produced by Grierson, written and directed by Basil Wright and Harry Watt, with music by Benjamin Britten and verse narrative by W. H. Auden.[14] Predictably, the film concerns a humble subject, the "Postal Special," the crack express train that transports the mail from London to Glasgow. The overall structure of the film follows the progress of the train; within this structure, the film presents the actual internal operation of this post office on wheels, from loading and sorting to routing and final delivery. But it is in the dramatization of this ordinary process that the film achieves its distinction, for there is mystery in the priority of this train's run on the railroad's right-of-way; excitement in the mechanized method of picking up the mail pouches at high speed; and impressions of power, strength, and even inevitability as the mail goes through. The film stresses the importance of the train to people along the route, some of whom even set their watches as it passes: "All Scotland waits for her." That all of this should come through in a film devoted to a post office train simply indicates how good a documentary film can be.

Night Mail imbues ordinary activity with drama, unlike Anstey's *Granton Trawler* (1934), which pays too much attention to the ocean and not enough to people. Anstey's achievements include straightforward cinematography and a sound track that integrates fishermen's voices with industrial sounds, but the final effect is static, not dramatic. *Night Mail* constantly focuses on the dedicated and efficient men working in the train; even the sequence that shows a new man learning how to handle the mail pouches is beautifully done, with a sense of both urgency and humor.

The film derives its impact from several sources. First, it presents ordinary people in ordinary situations in such a way that they appear to be special. Second, it keeps the speed and the sound of the train as an important part of the sound-track; underscored with a mix of Britten's music and Auden's verse, the film moves forward with a steady, compelling rhythm. Third, it emphasizes the importance and dignity of a job well done, as well as the emotional importance of mail to the lives of everyday citizens. Indeed, it makes this postal service seem the most important enterprise in the world, not only because it is an efficient human operation, but also because it facilitates communication between human beings: "None will hear the postman's knock without a quickening of the heart, for who can bear to feel himself forgotten?"[15]

In addition to the power in *Night Mail,* the power of sight and sound, there is also charm, and a characteristically British feeling for detail, efficiency, and the working man. The overall impression is of workers who are dedicated to precision and efficiency, yet the seriousness of each simple operation is occasionally lightened by a humor that is equally characteristic of the British. For example, when a man on a routine sorting assignment handles a letter with an unfamiliar Scottish address, his supervisor shows him that it is actually addressed to a place in Wales, wryly commenting, "Makes a nice change for you." The film is instructive, a pleasure to view, and a technical landmark in its use of sound and integration of image, music, and narrative. The influence of *Night Mail*'s use of direct sound can be seen in Alexander Shaw's *Cover to Cover,* Cavalcanti's *We Live in Two Worlds* and *Line to the Tschierva Hut,* and Cavalcanti's and Watt's *The Saving of Bill Blewitt* and *North Sea.*

Grierson's Influence
From 1928 to 1937, John Grierson's leadership was undoubtedly the single most important influence on the development of the British documentary film. His insistence on propaganda in the public interest, his support of cinematic experimentation, and his enlightened supervision of hundreds of major documentary films brought the movement to its high point of maturity in a relatively short time.

Night Mail represents John Grierson and the British documentary school of the mid-1930s at their best, for they successfully fuse social purpose with cinematic experimentation, responding to a dynamic and changing world. The job of the documentary filmmaker was, as Grierson originally said, to render a "creative treatment of actuality." Although this creative treatment became increasingly more professional and sophisticated, Grierson remained true to the concept that the documentary film had a didactic purpose and an obligation to enlighten, not just to entertain.

During his stewardship, many changes occurred in the British documentary film, both in form and in content. The most important technical change was the shift from silent to sound production; in the latter part of Grierson's tenure, as we have seen, there was much experimentation with sound in such films as *Song of Ceylon, Coal Face,* and *Night Mail.* Another important change came in the subject matter, as the rather narrow focus of the early films widened to include a more comprehensive vision of British society. Initially, Grierson's films, like *Drifters* and *One Family,* were concerned with dramatizing the common laborer; they were limited in scope, and, therefore, in appeal, but they served to acquaint the viewing audience with isolated and relatively unfamiliar patterns of life and industry. The second wave of films (*Industrial Britain* and *Lancashire: Home of Industry,* for example) was concerned with workers and their immediate industrial or agricultural environments; less impressionistic and poetic than the first films, these productions emphasized filmmaking technique, especially sound, and mark the turning point toward more sophisticated films. The subjects now became immediate social problems: education, housing, social services, public health, air pollution, and unemployment; and the documentary filmmakers showed their flexibility in presenting these problems and suggesting realistic solutions for an audience composed of the general public. To do so, it often became necessary to reenact certain activities using actors (nonprofessionals who are actually part of the situation being filmed) or to use studio settings. These changes were particularly evident in *The Saving of Bill Blewitt, Pett and Pott, North Sea, We Live in Two Worlds,* and *Line to the Tschierva Hut,* and, outside the GPO Film Unit, in commercial and institutional production, in *Workers and Jobs, Housing Problems,* and *Enough to Eat: The Nutrition Film.*

Moreover, films such as *Night Mail* focused on the person first and the job second; the process of dramatizing the individual worker reached its high point with films (such as *Men of the Lightship,* 1940, or *Spring Offensive,* 1940) depicting the importance of all kinds of work, including that done at the desk, in the field, or on ships at sea. Among these films, it is possible to observe three distinct stylistic variations on the documentary mode: the lyrical (*Song of Ceylon* and *O'er Hill and Dale*), the analytical (*Aero-Engine* and *Cargo from Jamaica*), and the impressionistic (*Shipyard* and *Night Mail*). During this time there was much important experimentation with narrative, sound, and music, and both in and out of the Unit, films were produced that were both more intimate in their approach to people and more technically mature. Finally, since the matters of distribution and exhibition were, perhaps, the major challenges faced by Grierson and his colleagues, he led the GPO in developing an elaborate system of nontheatrical distribution, including travelling cinema vans that brought films to audiences everywhere.[16]

In 1936 and early 1937, a number of factors combined to weaken the strength of the GPO Film Unit and, particularly, to erode the sources of Grierson's leadership. First, there was a conflict between those who wanted to continue to produce government films for nontheatrical exhibition and those who wanted to extend the influence of the documentary movement into the private sector. Second, as a result of this conflict, major talent began to leave the GPO to work for other government agencies and for private industry. They continued the Grierson tradition, and soon more films were being produced by private industry than by the government. However, those who remained at the GPO were caught in a philosophical struggle between the Grierson tradition and their interest in experimenting with it. Third, Stephen Tallents, who left the GPO for a position at the British Broadcasting Corporation, was replaced by E. T. Crutchley, who handled relations with other government agencies on which the GPO was dependent, particularly the Treasury. These and other factors resulted in a decline in Grierson's influence, and he soon was searching for an alternative home for the documentary film movement.

Grierson resigned as producer of the GPO Film Unit in June 1937. The official explanation was that he wanted to work independently, but a more plausible explanation is that the struggles became too much for him. There are several other explanations. It is apparent that the documentary film had progressed to such a point—both in its aesthetics and its influence—that it deserved more government support and a wider audience, but up to this time, the primary audience was comprised of film societies and intellectuals. Some GPO filmmakers wanted theatrical distribution for their work, a development that Grierson resisted. Other GPO filmmakers felt exploited by Grierson, and quarrelled with him over their credits on films. Although these same filmmakers have made surprisingly little comment on the reasons for Grierson's departure, what emerges is a fragmented reaction: some were happy to see him leave, believing that his departure would free them for experimentation, while others felt that he was acting prematurely. Swann (133) says that there was hostility between Grierson's supporters and opponents, and that the government's swift move to consolidate its position only further weakened Grierson's. Following Grierson's departure, the GPO conducted a complete reassessment of the purposes, policies, and procedures of the film unit. The most urgent concern was to "establish 'proper administrative control' over the unit to replace the complete autonomy it had under Grierson" (Swann 124).

As a result, filmmakers who were not considered to be part of Grierson's group were appointed to key positions, including J. B. Holmes, who was appointed to the new post of Production Supervisor. When he proved to be an ineffective administrator, Alberto Cavalcanti was appointed Senior Producer, and Holmes and Harry Watt became Senior Directors. These three supervised production at the GPO Film Unit until it was taken over by the Ministry of Information at the beginning of World War II. Grierson joined the London Film Centre (which began in August 1936 as Associated Realist Film Producers) in association with GPO veterans Edgar Anstey, Arthur Elton, Stuart Legg, and J. P. Golightly.[17] The Film

Centre, which at the beginning was mainly concerned with film production for Shell Oil, also served as clearinghouse for ideas on planning and producing them, as well as a new focal point for the whole documentary movement. In 1939, Grierson became Canadian Film Commissioner and spent the wartime years supervising the National Film Board of Canada (see chapter 8).

From time to time in cinema history, a person emerges who may truly be said to personify a period—to embody in his life as well as in his work the spirit of a certain historical moment.[18] More than any other filmmaker of his generation in England, John Grierson typified the radicalism of the period between the world wars and the special social aspirations of the pre- and post–World War II British scene. And while outside Britain there were theorists and filmmakers more radical than he—Sergei Eisenstein, Joris Ivens, Henri Storck, Paul Strand, Leo Hurwitz, even Pare Lorentz and Willard Van Dyke—Grierson possessed something that even the most gifted of his contemporaries lacked: an indispensable gift for joining radical principles to practical politics. His radicalism stemmed from the belief that people—ordinary people—were entitled to decent housing, safe working conditions, clean air, and a good education for their children. His practical politics derived from the conviction that the government (in his case, the Conservative Party in England) should demonstrate its efforts to achieve these objectives, and, by so doing, it would educate the nation and mobilize communal opinion and loyalties. In retrospect, Grierson stands out as the most liberal of radicals, not as an extremist or an iconoclast, but as one who believed that social change could be effected and that the nonfiction film would have an important part to play in bringing it about.

Grierson was not a fanatic, but he did say: "I look upon cinema as a pulpit, and use it as a propagandist."[19] In fact, it was with religious fervor that he expressed his beliefs in social welfare, internationalism, and world peace. His vision was of a world of people doing, laboring, creating together, not the Blakean vision of Jerusalem in "England's green and pleasant land," as conveyed by Humphrey Jennings in such films as *Spare Time* (1939), but the world of work and the interdependency among workers, as seen in such films as *Night Mail* or *Granton Trawler*. In his zeal, Grierson could be as tedious as a Calvinist preacher who thinks he can change the patterns by which people think and feel. And there was always a certain element of rhetoric, even of bombast, in Grierson's writing. However, there was something more valuable—his deep attachment to his morality and his vision of a future for the documentary film. And, in many ways, he was right, for, in Britain alone, the documentary film movement did influence social thinking, establish a realist tradition in film, and contribute significantly to the nation's efforts in World War II.

Because the EMB and GPO films were financed by the establishment, Grierson had to exercise caution in choosing their subjects and treatments. It would be easy to infer from this that his films were primarily advertisements for the establishment, and therefore for the status quo in a country suffering from the Great Depression. Clearly, however, as Gary Evans writes, they were not acting solely as apologists for the *status quo*. Like most left-wing bourgeois intellectuals in the thirties, they were ashamed of "poverty in the midst of plenty" and were trying to do something about raising public consciousness wherever they could. Also, they would have been the first to admit the absence of revolutionary or even radical sentiments in their films.[20]

Equally extraordinary was Grierson's subsequent rejection of the government-sponsored film, late in life, and his determination to hand down "the means of larger public expression to the people at the grass roots,"[21] embracing what Jack C. Ellis call his "anarchical conception of films of the people and for the people being made by the people."[22]

Although convinced that films should be used to analyze, inform, and educate, Grierson was the first to insist that the documentary film need not be synonymous with dullness. Feeling obligated to enlighten, not just to entertain, he tried to find drama in what would ordinarily appear to be unlikely subjects (weather forecasting, the laying of cable under the streets or under the sea, mail collection). And, as a byproduct of these efforts to depict ordinary people in ordinary situations in such a way that they appear to be special, Grierson established film as an instrument of the working class. In fact, although he liked to boast that he was the first to put the working class on the screen, that distinction must go to the Lumières' *Workers Leaving the Lumière Factory* (1895), the first nonfiction film ever made. Unlike the Lumière film, which shows actual working people, the typical Grierson documentary presents the working class as heroes; we are rarely shown the concrete facts of their lives—what they earn, how they live, or what they eat. What we do gain, however, is an awareness of the heart, warmth, good humor, and dignity inherent in Grierson's image of working class life. A film that exemplifies these Griersonian values is Harry Watt's *The Saving of Bill Blewitt* (1936), a delightfully unpretentious piece of propaganda for two national savings plans.[23] Ironically titled, the film concerns the efforts of Bill Blewitt to purchase a fishing vessel to replace the one he lost in a storm. He is "saved" by his own savings and those of a friend kept in a GPO savings account, but the film's interest in the villagers and their happiness is far more important than any sales campaign for a savings book. Despite somewhat awkward acting by the residents of a fishing village, this Cavalcanti production (with music by Benjamin Britten) is a charming reminder of the documentary film's power to translate the everyday into the memorable.

The films of the British school under Grierson are generally high in technical quality, but often insistent in narration, or music, or overall delivery of message. The best of them have a formal integrity, not only in their problem-solution structure, but also in the fusion of sight and sound images. Grierson engaged the most creative and gifted of colleagues—Alberto Cavalcanti, W. H. Auden, Darius Milhaud, Benjamin Britten—and he encouraged them to experiment in the service of this new artistic form. The cinematography is consistently excellent, for Grierson understood beauty as well as ideas and valued beautiful images and photography. Although frequently unimaginative, the sound is natural and therefore supportive of the factual nature of the films. Finally, as a formalist, Grierson also

The Saving of Bill Blewitt (Harry Watt, Great Britain, 1936)

understood that editing is crucial to the form and power of the documentary film. To a degree almost unprecedented except in the films of Pare Lorentz, Grierson understood the cinematic power to be achieved from a contrapuntal handling of visual images, spoken text, direct sound, and a musical score. It is in the editing of the sound images in relation to the visual images—in the contrapuntal collision that was his legacy to Joris Ivens, Helen Van Dongen, and Alberto Cavalcanti, among others—that one finds the greatest contribution to film form by the British documentary of the 1930s and early 1940s.

GPO FILM UNIT AFTER JOHN GRIERSON: 1937–40

The GPO under Alberto Cavalcanti placed a greater emphasis on producing straightforward government propaganda rather than the informational and enlightening documentary film of Grierson's vision, a wider and livelier focus on British society, and an increase in technical experimentation.[24] As Elizabeth Sussex writes,

> The importance of the first years of documentary, as most of the people concerned are ready enough to admit, was not the films but the creation of an environment in which experiment could begin. (43)

Although Cavalcanti, as Senior Producer, lacked Grierson's organizational skills, he was more innovative and brought a fresh approach to the work of the unit,[25] introducing many innovative techniques to documentary film production during the later 1930s and, notably, introducing to the documentary film various fictional techniques that Grierson abhorred.

Unlike Grierson, Cavalcanti did not theorize about the purpose of documentary films, saying, "I hate the word 'documentary.' I think it smells of dust and boredom. I think 'realist films' much, much the best" (quoted in Sussex 52). However, since one function of the GPO Film Unit was to serve as a training school for young filmmakers, Cavalcanti offered this practical advice, most of which distinctly criticizes the Grierson approach to making documentary films. In 1935, Grierson wrote:

> The G.P.O. Film Unit . . . is the only experimental center in Europe. Where the artist is not pursuing entertainment but purpose, not art but theme, the technique is energized inevitably by the size and scope of the occasion. How much further it reaches and will reach than the studio leapfrog of impotent and self-conscious art. (*Grierson on Documentary* 181)

Emphasizing creativity and experimentation, Cavalcanti's approach is represented by the following contrasting fourteen principles:

> Don't treat generalized subjects; you can write an article about the mail service, but you must make a film about one single letter.
> Don't depart from the principle which states that three fundamental elements exist: the social, the poetic, and the technical.
> Don't neglect your script or count on luck while shooting. When your script is ready, your film is made; then, when you start to shoot, you begin again.
> Don't trust in the commentary to tell your story; the visuals and the sound accompaniment must do it. Commentary irritates, and gratuitous commentary irritates even more.
> Don't forget that when you are shooting, each shot is part of a sequence and part of a whole; the most beautiful shot, out of place, is worse than the most trivial.
> Don't invent camera angles when they are not necessary; unwarranted angles are disturbing and destroy emotion.
> Don't abuse a rapid rate of cutting; an accelerated rhythm can be as pompous as the most pompous largo.
> Don't use music excessively; if you do, the audience will cease to hear it.
> Don't supercharge the film with synchronized sound; sound is never better than when it is suggestively employed. Complementary sound constitutes the best sound track.
> Don't recommend too many optical effects, or make them too complicated. Dissolves and fades form part of the film's punctuation; they are your commas and periods.
> Don't shoot too many close-ups; save them for the climax. In a well-balanced film, they occur naturally; when there are too many, they tend to suffocate and lose their significance.

Don't hesitate to treat human elements and human relations; human beings can be as beautiful as the other animals, as beautiful as the machines in a landscape.

Don't be vague in your story; a true subject must be told clearly and simply. Nevertheless, clearness and simplicity do not necessarily exclude dramatization.

Don't lose the opportunity to experiment; the prestige of the documentary film has been acquired solely by experimentation. Without experimentation, the documentary loses its value; without experimentation, the documentary ceases to exist.[26]

While it seems that the two producers were in agreement about the matter of experimentation, they clearly differed in their ideas of practice. Cavalcanti was more interested in the visual and literary aspects of nonfiction film than its purpose, and thus emphasized scripts and shooting. Although he was one of the first to use fully-mixed sound tracks, he de-emphasized such nonvisual elements as sound effects, optical effects, and commentary, reasoning that their excessive use can detract from the primary visual qualities of the film medium. In short, the most important difference between Grierson and Cavalcanti is probably the latter's emphasis on the interrelationship among the three fundamental elements of documentary film: the social, the poetic, and the technical. Grierson would insist that the social was more important; it is the measure of Cavalcanti's place in the development of nonfiction film that he recognized that all three elements should be important.[27]

Cavalcanti's early films reflect these cinematic principles, as well as his capacity for experimentation: *Pett and Pott* (1934), *Glorious Sixth of June* (1934), *Coal Face* (1935), and *Message from Geneva* (1936). Three, produced in collaboration with Pro-Telephon-Zürich, are concerned with communications: *Four Barriers, We Live in Two Worlds*, and *Line to the Tschierva Hut* (all 1937). *Line to the Tschierva Hut*, which deals with the bringing of telephone lines and service to a mountaineering post in the Swiss Alps, exemplifies what can be achieved when sight and sound are used with resource and ingenuity. The film demonstrates the importance of telephone service at the isolated post, depicting the rough tasks of surveying the terrain and installing poles and lines. The cinematography is excellent, especially the angle shots and the contrast between the bright snow and the darkly clad workmen. The music by Britten is very simple, but it augments and contributes to an imaginative film that is a model of subtle conception, shooting, and editing.

We Live in Two Worlds, subtitled "A Film Talk with J. B. Priestley," focusses on the extraordinarily prolific writer who worked in various genres. The film is an ambitious but generally unsuccessful statement about the beneficial political implications of communications between the so-called national and the international world. The film's subject is Switzerland, a country that is both national and international, but it is unclear whether it intends a tribute to Switzerland or to internationalism; the latter was, in itself, a common theme in many 1930s' British documentaries. Ironically, *We Live in Two Worlds* fails to communicate its points about communication. Based on the rather naïve assumption that the power of electronic communication is stronger than the power of guns—a concept that predated Marshall McLuhan by many years—this film loses in its general attempt to present an idea what *Line* gains in its fidelity to a specific incident. These two Cavalcanti films neatly demonstrate what can happen when documentary film-makers fail to focus on the immediate world around them and attempt to translate larger, abstract concepts into film. Even less effective with subject matter that was intrinsically and socially more important is *Men in Danger* (1939), a Cavalcanti production directed by Patrick Thompson. The film concerns dangerous working conditions in England's mines and factories, suggesting corrective measures and devices, yet it fails to dramatize the situation in any meaningful way, and lacks the focus, clarity, and precision of *Line to the Tschierva Hut.*

Typical of GPO production during this period is Maurice Harvey's *The Island-ers* (1939), which clearly and successfully makes its points about the power of communications to unite islands and people. After we are shown the different islands off the English coast, ranging from the remote to the near, from the agricul-tural to the industrial, we learn that the self-contained, isolated nature of island life is balanced by the contact and communication lifeline provided by mail, telegraph, shortwave radio, steamer, and ferryboat service. Moreover, in contrast to *Night Mail,* another film stressing the importance of mail as a lifeline between people, *The Islanders* lacks focus, intensity, and drama because it chooses a more general approach to the subject of communications. Of course, this film is concerned with more than the postal service, and a film about Cavalcanti's theoretical "single letter" would, in this instance, have had limited scope. However, *The Islanders* succeeds as a factual anthropological sketch and as a poetic record of the fact that air and water form bridges spanning geographical isolation when they are used to carry radio messages, letters, parcels, and merchandise; frequent contrasts between images of rock and earth, air and water, reinforce this theme. In its beautiful black-

The Islanders (Maurice Harvey, Great Britain, 1939)

and-white cinematography, *The Islanders* is similar to Flaherty's *Man of Aran,* but its musical score by Darius Milhaud is soft and complementary to the images, not strident as is the score of Flaherty's film.

Overall, the 1930s' British documentary was disappointing in its treatment of people. Aside from such films as *Night Mail,* the GPO filmmakers failed to observe humans as intimately and as wisely as Flaherty did; while they were familiar with his approach, they did not seem particularly influenced by it. But eventually they began to remedy this fault by first learning to use actual speech or written dialogue on the sound track. When their nonactors could not lend the necessary credibility, they did not hesitate to use professionals in certain roles. A distinctive landmark in the British attempt to come closer to depicting the actual person in his actual job is Harry Watt's *North Sea* (1938), the GPO's biggest commercial success. A reconstruction that uses some studio settings, this film seems "real" for the most part, although it balances on the borderline between fiction and nonfiction film, and does not fully resolve the contradiction inherent in the combination of these two approaches. The narrative, written by Watt and Cavalcanti, depicts the crew members of the fishing trawler *John Gilman;* we see the men at work and hear their actual voices. The dramatic conflict comes quickly as a storm at sea knocks out the wireless; but, before the ensuing battle with the sea reaches disastrous proportions, the men are rescued by another ship. In developing this simple conflict, the film shows the calm skipper reassuring the frightened crew, as well as the efficient land-based radio service (for, after all, this is a GPO film) that monitors ship movements and directs rescue operations. As an intimate portrait of lives of men at sea under pressure, it is superseded only by the tight, dramatic wartime documentary *Men of the Lightship* (1940).

THE INDEPENDENT DOCUMENTARY FILM: PRODUCTION OUTSIDE THE GPO FILM UNIT

As long as Grierson headed the GPO Film Unit, the British government remained the foremost sponsor of the documentary film movement. Thus, while GPO films enjoyed official status, their characteristic cinematic style also reflected the direct control the government exercised over them. At least two years before Grierson left the GPO, there were various indications that other public and private entities—quasi-governmental agencies as well as industrial corporations—were interested in sponsoring nonfiction films that would be relative to their needs. These sponsors included industrial and commercial concerns (e.g., Cadbury's Chocolate, Austin Motors, and the London, Midland, and Scottish Railway Company) and quasi-government agencies (e.g., the British Council, National Fitness Council, National Savings Movement, and the Scottish Development Council). Most of them produced conventional advertising and industrial films, works that had little relationship with the documentary film as Grierson had developed it and only a peripheral relationship to the mainstream development of the nonfiction film. But others (e.g., Shell Oil, Imperial Airways, and the British gas industry) produced documentary films that expressed a concern for human or social problems.[28] Although many of these films helped to raise production standards to a new level of achievement, they were fundamentally associated with the self-interest of the sponsor, either directly or indirectly selling goods or services and improving their image in the public's consciousness.[29]

Paul Rotha was the first leader of the independent documentary film movement, a role for which he was uniquely suited. By 1932, when the independent movement can be said to have begun, he had already established a reputation as a filmmaker, theorist, critic, and historian. More important, he was not dependent upon John Grierson. He had worked briefly with Grierson at the EMB, but was not a member of the GPO Film Unit, and laid the foundation of the independent movement with his establishment of Associated Realist Film Producers in 1935. Subsequently, three other production companies were to dominate independent production: the Strand Film Unit (begun by Rotha and then taken over by Stuart Legg), the Realist Film Unit (under the direction of Basil Wright), and the Film Centre (under the supervision of John Grierson). Film Centre was not a production company, but rather took over what Associated Realist Film Producers had set out to do, namely to serve as a broker between sponsors and filmmakers. Although Rotha was the founder of the independent movement, and an important force in its development throughout his career, he was overshadowed when John Grierson consolidated his power at Film Centre as producer and editor of *World Film News*, the influential journal of the documentary film movement.[30]

In the Strand and Realist Film Units, the early films of Paul Rotha, Arthur Elton, John Taylor, and Edgar Anstey, among others, do not resemble those produced in the Grierson-Cavalcanti GPO Film Unit tradition, nor do they seem to have had much immediate influence on that mainstream development. By contrast, these filmmakers were free to adapt their individual styles to meet the needs of varied sponsors, to treat a wider range of topics, and to introduce a variety of cinematic innovations, including the restaging of historical events, an editing style less dependent upon Soviet montage, and direct and honest depiction of working class life. In their attempt at realism, many of these filmmakers used direct interviews and came closer to the journalistic school of the American "March of Time" approach than to the carefully scripted approach of the GPO filmmakers. However,

> the most conspicuous theme, and that carried as the explicit message in the majority of these documentary films, was that benevolent corporations and similar bodies put the public's well-being before their own interests. (Swann 177)

These films, as well as those produced by the GPO, were intended for nontheatrical distribution. For several reasons, very few of them were ever shown in commercial theaters. First, the laws governing film exhibition discouraged it. The 1927 Cinematograph Films Act, adopted before the documentary film made its first impact, set exhibition quota standards that were prejudiced against nonfiction as well as short films. Although the 1938 revision of the act addressed some of these issues, the nonfiction film—documentary film, in particular—was of little importance to most exhibitors.[31] Second, the film industry, which believed that cinema audiences wanted to be entertained, also opposed theatrical distribution. Third, there was a distinct lack of interest in the nonfiction film among members of the paying theater audience, as opposed to the enthusiastic interest among those who attended nontheatrical showings.

Rotha's early work includes three conventional films: *Contact* (1933), an Imperial Airways-Shell Oil coproduction; *Shipyard* (1935); and *The Face of Britain* (1935). *The Face of Britain* presents a challenge to the future growth of English cities, but its unclear focus and emphasis on contemporary social conditions result in a superficial film. Like Rotha's later *Land of Promise* (1945), this film relies too closely on a sequential development of four separate parts ("Heritage of the Past," "The Smoke Age," "New Power," and "The New Age") and on a narration that is much less emphatic than the material requires. But, in its concern for urban planning in the rebuilding of English cities, *The Face of Britain* pioneers the way for Rotha's later and more successful *Land of Promise* and *A City Speaks*.

More immediate and more interesting, although now thoroughly dated, is Rotha's *Peace of Britain* (1936), in the imaginative "poster film" approach that Len Lye developed between 1935 and 1940. This brief film, which takes the alarming stand that there is no defense against air attack, features a cross section of Englishmen who are bewildered because the First World War—the "war to end all wars"—is apparently going to recur. Hastily assembled to support Anthony Eden's plea that Britain support the League of Nations, this overtly political film exhorts the audience to "Demand Peace by Reason" and "Write to Your M.P." One of the few British documentaries of the period that deals exclusively with politics, it has the subtlety of a banner headline, and bears no resemblance to Lye's later development of poster films into what is almost subliminal propaganda.

Rotha's *New Worlds for Old* (1938), produced for the British gas industry, is, with the Grierson-Taylor *The Londoners* (1938), notable for its use of studio sets and period costumes. These reconstructions, which are characteristic of Rotha's style, help to demonstrate the progress of the gas industry from the Victorian period to the 1930s. To enhance the dramatic development of the film's ideas, the "expert" narrator is challenged by another voice, representing the skeptical audience, a technique that Rotha used again in *World of Plenty* (1943). The comic effects, incorporated no doubt to help sell gas, at that time an unpopular commodity, often backfire and seem merely ridiculous.

Unique among early GPO films for its strong voice of social protest, Alberto Cavalcanti's *Coal Face* (1935) involved the collaboration of W. H. Auden and Benjamin Britten. Their attempts to integrate choral singing, chanting, narration, and music, while important as an experimental effort, result in a strident description of the processing and distribution of coal, rather than the successful symphonic fusion of these elements that they achieved later in *Night Mail*. The chorus of miners conveys their oppression with a tone of bitterness and futility that is surpassed in intensity and effectiveness only by Henri Storck's *Les maisons de la misère* (1937; see chapter 6).

Early in 1935, the combined forces of American journalism and filmmaking introduced a new form of screen journalism, the monthly "March of Time" series (see chapter 7). Unlike the newsreel, and unlike the documentary and factual films appearing then in England and the United States, these "March of Time" films, with their heightened drama and editorial opinion, represent a new and different nonfiction film treatment of actual current events. Among the distinctive characteristics of these films are an extensive use of actual newsreel footage coupled with reenactment footage, and a thoroughly researched and apparently factual commentary, which "voice-of-god narration" does much to make persuasive, if not convincing. This series exerted considerable influence on the course of documentary film production; and its influence in England can be seen in such films as *Housing Problems, The Smoke Menace,* and *Children at School.*

Housing Problems (1935), directed by Arthur Elton and Edgar Anstey, and produced by the Realist Film Unit for the British Gas Association, marks the first use of journalistic reporting in the British documentary. Made at the beginning of a slum clearance operation in London, the film presents what is still a remarkably contemporary picture of the human problems associated with massive urban renewal. The interviews with tenants (apparently unrehearsed) relate conditions of crowding, vermin, rats, lack of sanitation, and unsafe building construction. As a counterweight to the despair of these unrelocated slum dwellers, there are interviews with two women who emphasize the cleanliness of a new apartment building to which they have been moved. These latter interviews underscore dramatically the need for changes and demonstrate to an audience of people living in and out of slums that change is not only possible but also well worth the effort necessary to bring it about. The interviews are direct and honest, and the immediacy of the problems depicted has not been dimmed by time. *Housing Problems* is an enduring example of the power of film to encourage social reconstruction. Yet, while the unpleasantness of slum life is real and there for us to see, the gas industry relied too much on characteristic British good cheer and positive optimism to foreshadow the conclusion. Like the continental realists, the British should have let us see the dirt rather than hear about the slum dwellers' misery. Both Joris Ivens's *Borinage* (1933) and Henri Storck's *Les maisons de la misère* (1937; see chapter 6) not only bring viewers vividly in contact with degrading housing conditions, but also succeed in arousing their social consciousness through devastating pictures of the injustice of slum life. In *Housing Problems,* the viewer's response is mitigated by the sponsor's facile solutions to major problems. Later, in *When We Build Again,* another commercially sponsored British film, a similar approach was taken, but with greater success.

John Taylor's *The Smoke Menace* (1937), produced by John Grierson for the British gas industry, is a sponsored public relations film with a message. It explains that gas, a better, cleaner, and more efficient fuel than coal, helps to combat the menace of air pollution. The restraint with which the producers deliver its message is, perhaps, its own distinguishing, if dulling, feature. A straightforward film, reflecting the influence of the "March of Time," it does its job with conviction and authority, not with the unfortunate comic attack on the problem made by Rotha in *New Worlds for Old.* Like *Housing Problems,* it is a model film which balances cinematic style and content.

Basil Wright's *Children at School* (1937), which Grierson also produced for the gas industry, exemplifies changes in the British documentary during the 1930s. In fact, it remains difficult to recognize that the same director made both the beautiful *Song of Ceylon* (1934) and the forceful *Children at School*. The techniques are dissimilar although there are moments of tenderness, if not lyricism, in *Children at School*. But the subject matter of the two films is totally different, for one film depicts a land of traditional patterns, while the other demonstrates the need for rapid change to avoid decay. It is apparent that Wright would not allow a commercial message to dominate his films, and in *Children at School,* there is no apparent link between the gas industry sponsorship and the problems to be solved. Here, the deficiencies and successes of England's best and worst schools are reviewed, with emphasis on improving the entire educational system. With its theme that a "nation depends on its children," the narration suggests that education is more than a national resource; it is a national and even international priority, as references to Hitler and Mussolini demonstrate. Aside from this touch of rather heavy-handed propaganda, *Children at School* successfully represents the concern of an enlightened institutional sponsor and the influence of the "The March of Time" style on British documentary filmmaking.

Closer to the "March of Time" approach in spirit, John Taylor's *Dawn of Iran* (1938), produced by Arthur Elton for the Anglo-Iranian Oil Company, documents

Children at School (Basil Wright, Great Britain, 1937)

and celebrates the growth of Iran as an independent, industrial nation. Better as a cinematographer and editor than as a writer or director, Taylor did not succeed in giving thematic and narrative focus to this film. Despite his experience with Flaherty in Aran, with Wright in Ceylon, and with Cavalcanti in Switzerland, Taylor seems to be more concerned with the new American style of photojournalism than with the British experience in Iran that is his subject.

Not all documentary film production reflected this journalistic emphasis, for, as can be seen in two representative films, *Eastern Valley* and *Today We Live,* the British approach was too well founded and too successful to be discarded entirely. Donald Alexander's *Eastern Valley* (1937), a typical problem-solution film, is concerned with the plight of unemployed miners in a Welsh valley. Produced for the Order of Friends in London, the film suggests that the establishment of farming cooperatives would partially aid in getting the men back to work, and, at the same time, the film honestly admits that this pragmatic solution to the problem may not be the best one. Like *Housing Problems,* it uses the actual voices of those involved in the situation to create a warm, convincing account of people working together to reverse decay. *Today We Live* (1937), produced by Rotha for the National Council of Social Service, and codirected by Ruby Grierson and Ralph Bond, continues the development of the documentary form through its use of strong narrative, actual dialogue, and a fine cast of nonprofessional actors. Unfortunately, the focus of the first half of the film is not altogether clear; by the time viewers realize the film's message—that people can come together and build community centers—they may have become more interested in the ironic use of hymns on the sound track. Nonetheless, *Today We Live* is a true documentary in its searching concern for the quality of English life.

While most British nonfiction films of the 1930s are pure documentaries concerned with social reconstruction, other lines of development can be traced in the factual or informational film. Julian Huxley's *Private Life of the Gannets* (1935) is an information film with slight travel film overtones, and Edgar Anstey's *Enough to Eat: The Nutrition Film* (1936), narrated by Julian Huxley, is an information film intended to shock people into the realization that their diets are inadequate. Subtitled "The Nutrition Film," it explains the early development of vitamins and nutrition theory, but despite its reported influence on Britain's official nutrition policies, it is as dreary as British food itself once was. Also in this information category, but more effective for children, is Mary Field's *Catch of the Season* (1937), which explains, in restrained, matter-of-fact narration, the reproductive cycle of trout. Geoffrey Bell's *Transfer of Power* (1939), produced by Shell Oil, provides an interesting, fast-paced, and informative history of the evolution of the lever to the toothed wheel to gears to windmills and finally to lathes and other machines. Using diagrams, simple examples, and very lively narration, this film leaves a lasting impression of a subject that is not usually treated with such imagination; in so doing, it predates such films as Charles and Ray Eames's *A Communications Primer* (1954).[32]

British films for overseas audiences were frequently the subject of debate between filmmakers and policymakers.[33] The Travel Association, whose film unit was headed by Marion Grierson, produced films for overseas distribution; typical of these is Miss Grierson's *For All Eternity* (1935), about English cathedrals and the role that religion plays in English life, a subject that was deemed inappropriate for screening in certain countries.[34] This debate became a controversy as the British Council and the Joint Film Committee argued over what aspects of British life to emphasize in films shown at the British Pavilion of the 1939 New York World's Fair. Independent filmmakers who resented the need to make films expressing official public policy aggravated the conflict over whether to emphasize British democracy, pageantry, trade, or culture. Ultimately, the British showed many of the best GPO films, particularly those featuring the British workers, including *Night Mail, Spare Time, Men in Danger, British Made,* and *Workers and Jobs.*

OVERALL ACHIEVEMENTS OF BRITISH DOCUMENTARY FILM MOVEMENT IN THE 1930s

The achievements of the British documentary film movement in the 1930s are significant for their originality and breadth and for their consistent dedication to the improvement of public information and the awakening of social conscious-ness.[35] As a creative movement of ideological significance, it encouraged artists to develop a film form that would deal with public issues without requiring the parti-cipants' affiliation or identification with any political party or policy. Furthermore, it not only gained respect and prestige for the British film industry at a time when the feature film was failing to do so, but also established Britain's most permanent contribution to the development of world cinema: it created a tradition of realism, both for the British documentary film and fiction film; furthered the ideal of internationalism as a reasonable goal; and established and exploited the system of nontheatrical distribution. The long-term impact of the documentary film move-ment—both government-sponsored and independent—was its preparation of film-makers for the filmmaking activities of World War II. The short-term impact seems to have been less consequential; as Swann writes,

> Documentary films remained films made by elites for elites. Furthermore, these were Britain's cultural and literary elites, rather than those exercising a great deal of political influence. This tended to keep the impact of these films, in political terms, fairly small. Within conventional political circles, the documentary move-ment remained suspect. (189)

It is open to further discussion whether its most permanent achievement was the films themselves, their attempt to further the goal of unity in a time of stress, or their stimulation of free thought and argument on the vital issues of the time.[36]

Both in England and the United States, the decade between 1940 and 1950 was an important one in the development of nonfiction filmmaking. The major factor underscoring this development was, of course, the Second World War, which occupied the time and talents of many filmmakers who might otherwise have been engaged in the production of their own films. The war directly and indirectly affected the entertainment as well as the economy of the world, so that the desire for, and response to, nonfiction films fluctuated with events (see chapter 8). However, the war increased immeasurably the possibilities for the uses of non-fiction film, and provided many advances in production techniques. The postwar years were uncertain ones for sponsors, producers, directors, and the audience, yet they witnessed the development of a stronger and more independent system of production and distribution, the creation of the National Film Board of Canada, the establishment of the film program of the United Nations Educational, Scientific, and Cultural Organization (UNESCO),[37] and provided the foundations for the worldwide nonfiction film experiments in the 1950s and 1960s (see chapter 11).

6   European and Asian Nonfiction Film: 1930–1939

When World War I—the "war to end all wars"—ended in 1918, Europeans hoped that a period of peace and prosperity would dissipate the trauma of war; instead, they experienced two decades of unsettled social conditions that would result in another world war. The 1920s were marked by economic prosperity and economic collapse, but, in fact, the 1930s were even more chaotic, beginning with economic disaster, followed by the great depression, and culminating at the end of the decade in the trauma of World War II.

Against a background of ideological struggle in film during the 1930s, experimentation with film aesthetics gave way to experimentation with film politics, Fascist Germany perfected its use of propaganda, and the mass media emerged to dominate public opinion around the world. It was the golden age of the Hollywood narrative film; newsreels; print journalism, particularly American newspapers and magazines; radio broadcasting; and it also witnessed the beginnings of television. During this time, the most significant nonfiction films were made by the documentary film movement in Great Britain (see chapter 5), the government-sponsored and the leftist filmmaking movements in the United States (see chapter 7), and the Nazi Party propagandists in Germany (see below).

Meanwhile, European and Asian nonfiction filmmakers were not only working within established traditions, but also creating new forms of cinematic expression. The Russian propagandist and British documentary traditions influenced the films of Joris Ivens in The Netherlands, as well as, in a radically different way, the development of the Nazi propaganda film. The romantic tradition also progressed, notably in Robert Flaherty's *Man of Aran* (1934) and John Ferno's *Easter Island* (*Paaseiland*, 1934). The continental "city symphony" tradition influenced the Swedish film *Gamla Stan* (1931). However, the avant-garde movement, which during the 1920s had produced significant experimental films in Russia and France, seemed dead by 1930. The global center of nonfiction filmmaking remained in London, but within Europe, it shifted from the capitals of Moscow and Paris to those of Holland, Belgium, and Germany, as well as, peripherally, to such cities as Bombay and Shanghai.

This European and Asian nonfiction filmmaking was marked by intellectual curiosity in The Netherlands and Belgium, regimentation in Germany, and censorship in India and China. Some major European filmmakers—including Joris Ivens, Henri Storck, Luis Buñuel, and John Ferno—made films that were not only cinematically creative but also reflected harsh contemporary social realities; others, especially Leni Riefenstahl, created a mythical and cinematic Nazi world that lacked any foreshadowing of Nazi aggression and genocide or of the world war to come. The Asian filmmakers—then as now less well known than their European counterparts—were prevented by internal political struggles and censorship from creating a distinctive cinematic style for their nonfiction films.

Internal political struggles also repressed the development of the film art in Russia, while, in France, according to Paul Rotha,

> the events which were to lead up to war and occupation . . . stifled any clear and consistent expression of the more positive realities of the French scene and inhibited the development of documentary filmmaking.[1]

The same could be said about Italy, and, partly for that reason in both countries, filmmakers chose to focus on art or culture rather than on social issues.

BEGINNINGS OF THE FILM ON ART

A unique and influential contribution of the 1930s' European nonfiction film was the establishment of a tradition of films on art and artists. This development was at first mistakenly associated with such avant-garde and abstract "art films" as those made by Leopold Survage, Viking Eggeling, Hans Richter, Marcel Duchamp, Francis Picabia, Fernand Leger, Man Ray, Salvador Dali, and Jean Cocteau. In fact, the cinematic work of these artists was primarily experimental and, in any case, sporadic, providing stimulus, but not a model, for the development of a tradition of films on art. Films such as these did little more than encourage an interest in cinema *as* cinema—that is to say, as an art. Most early films specifically about art, created by or for museums, were "amateur productions hastily shot in the museum's basement by someone with more enthusiasm than skill."[2] The development of this genre, which flourished after World War II, was enriched in its early years primarily by Belgian and French films and only slightly by American films on art (see chapter 12).

Belgian filmmakers have consistently produced the most influential films on art. The first of these included Gaston Schoukens's *Our Painters* (*Nos peintres*, 1926); two films by Henri Storck—*Idyll at the Beach* (*Idylle à la plage*, 1929–30) and *Regards to Old Belgium* (*Regards sur la Belgique ancienne*, 1936); John Ferno's *Easter Island* (1934); Charles Dekeukeleire's *Art and Life in Belgium* and *Themes of Inspiration* (*Thèmes d'inspiration*, 1938); and André Cauvin's *The Mystical Lamb* (*L'agneau mystique*) and *Memling* (1939, see below).

In France, the film about art began impressively with Sascha Guitry's *Our Own Crowd* (*Ceux de chez nous*, 1915), a 45-minute film about the artists Edgar Degas, Claude Monet, Auguste Renoir, and Auguste Rodin[3]; and Roger Livet's *Murdered Flowers* (*Fleurs meurtrise*, 1929), about the Belgian Surrealist painter René Magritte. Pierre Chenal's *The Architecture of Today* (*L'architecture d'aujourd'hui*, 1931), explains the theory of form and function in the work of Swiss-born Le Corbusier (Charles-Édouard Jeanneret), one of the most influential architects of the twentieth century; among French films of this period, it is exceptional for its concern with urban renewal. Two films about cathedrals take a more impressionist view: Rudolph Bamberger's *The Cathedral of the Dead* (*La cathedrale des morts*, 1935) and *The Stone Wonder of Naumburg* (*Die Steinernen Wunder von Naumburg*, 1935), which Bamberger codirected with Curt Oertel. *The Cathedral of the Dead*, about the Romanesque cathedral in Mainz, Germany, is also a silent visual meditation on death. *The Stone Wonder of Naumburg*, accompanied by organ music by Bach, is not only a detailed essay on the stone sculptures of the Gothic cathedral in Naumburg, Germany, but also an influential example of how the motion picture camera can move through a great architectural space, conveying a sense of its grandeur and, at the same time, isolating the sculptures within that space for further examination. Maurice Cloche's *Mont St. Michel* (1936) surveys the architectural and social history of Mont St. Michel, the magnificent fortress-abbey off the Normandy coast. A somewhat similar film, Jean-Yves de la Cour's beautiful *Vocation* (1935) depicts the solemn grace in the daily life of Benedictine monks; ignoring the reality of everyday life, the director goes behind cloistered walls into a timeless world. Also worth mentioning are several films about individual artists: Jean Benoit-Levy's *A Great Glass Blower* (*Un grand verrier*, 1937) documents the work of the French glass designer Maurice Marinot, while his *A Great Potter* (*Un grand potier*, 1937) similarly examines the work of French ceramist Auguste Delaherche. Jean Mallon's *The Letter* (*La lettre*, 1938) provides an excellent introduction to the history and techniques of calligraphy and typography, while Jean Tedesco's *Tapestries of France* (*Tapisseries du France*, 1939) shows how tapestries are made and restored at the legendary French manufacturies of Aubusson and Gobelins.

In Italy, Luciano Emmer and Enrico Gras developed a film style that focused on the narrative content of paintings: *Earthly Paradise* (*Paradiso terrestre*, 1941) presented Hieronymus Bosch's great painting through detailed photographs; *The Drama of the Son of Man* (*Racconto di un affresco*, 1941), a similar evocation of Giotto's murals in the Arena Chapel in Padua; and *The Wars* (1941), which presented a composite of war paintings by Piero della Francesco, Simone Martini, and Paolo Uccello. Also of importance is a Swiss-German production, Curt Oertel's fictionalized documentary, *The Titan: The Story of Michelangelo* (1939). It is a highly dramatic film in its depiction of Michelangelo through his art, and, according to Arthur Knight, the Nazis showed it throughout Europe "as an example of German culture."[4] And from Japan, the early "Traditional Arts of Japan" series, which promoted Japan's industrial power as well as its cultural tradition, included *Bamboo* (1934), *The Japanese Paper Umbrella* (1935), *Japanese Paper Lanterns*

(1935), *Japanese Paper Fans* (1935), *Japanese Paper* (1935), *Jananese Noh Drama* (1938), and *Sword of the Samurai* (1939). At the same time, Japanese filmmakers were preparing a far less delightful series of propaganda films for World War II (see below).

THE NETHERLANDS

Joris Ivens

Joris Ivens, who was born in the Netherlands, is a filmmaker with an international portfolio and reputation. His films, including those made in the United States, reflect Marxist convictions and are dedicated to redressing social grievances, effecting social change, and providing the viewer with an intimate insight into the lives of working people.[5] For Ivens, film cannot be separated from politics. He believes that the filmmaker's responsibility is to participate "directly in the world's most fundamental issues" (Ivens 138). Ivens writes that a documentary filmmaker

> has to have an opinion on such vital issues as fascism or antifascism—he *has* to have feelings about these issues, if his work is have any dramatic or emotional or art value. . . . I was surprised to find that many people automatically assume that any *documentary* film would *inevitably* be objective. Perhaps the term is unsatisfactory, but for me the distinction between the words *document* and *documentary* is quite clear. (136–37)

In making this distinction, Ivens agrees with Grierson. For both, a documentary film records a fact, an event, a life, but, more important, it takes a point of view and registers an opinion. The difference between Grierson and Ivens is one of degree: Grierson seldom allowed politics to dominate his art while, at times, Ivens's politics become art (*The Spanish Earth*), and, at other times, his art is only politics (*The 400 Million*). At his best, in a film such as *Power and the Land*, he combines poetry, politics, and cinematography to make a statement of uncommon beauty and strength (see chapter 7).

Ivens's first short films record a remarkable range of subject matter and technique.[6] Some are important for their subjects: *Film Study—Zeedijk* (*Zeedijk–Film-studie*, 1927), shot in a bar and important to Ivens's development because it was made in a real setting; *Studies in Movement* (*Etudes des mouvements*, 1928) records activity on Paris streets; *The Bridge* (*De brug*, 1928) documents the operation of a railroad bridge; *The Breakers* (*Branding*, 1929) shows the variation in waves as they break upon the shore; *Rain* (*Regen*, 1929) records the pattern of rain on city streets. Other films include *Skating* (*Schaatsenrijden*, 1929) and *I Film* (*Ik-film*, 1929), two early important products of the subjective hand-held camera; *We Are Building* (*Wij bouwen*, 1929), a prefatory study to *New Earth* (1934); *Pile Driving* (*Heien*, 1928), which documents part of the process of building dikes; *New Architecture* (*Nieuwe architectuur*, 1929), made to show the best of modern Dutch architecture; and *Zuiderzee* (1930), which Pudovkin praised for its reportage and "inherent organic logic" in treating the theme of human labor (Delmar 20). With *Philips-Radio*

(*Symphonie industrielle*, 1931, also known as *Industrial Symphony*), Ivens not only experimented notably with sound, but turned to the social themes that were to characterize his later work.[7] Like Chaplin's *Modern Times* (1936) or René Clair's *Liberty Is Ours* (*A nous la liberté*, 1931), *Philips-Radio* criticizes the tyranny of modern industrialization over labor.

In 1929, Ivens made an important political and artistic decision by visiting the Soviet Union, and, on Pudovkin's invitation, becoming the first foreign director to make a film there. Sympathizing with the Russian people's cause, he made *Song of Heroes* (*Pesn o gerojach* or *Komsomol*, 1932). Here, for the first time, Ivens used not only reenactment, but also the story of an individual as a narrative device, a technique he repeated in *The Spanish Earth*. However, it was not until 1933, when he went to Belgium and joined Henri Storck, that Ivens' characteristic approach and style fully emerged.

Borinage (*Misère au Borinage*) (1933), codirected by Ivens and Henri Storck, is in both the Soviet propagandist and the British documentary traditions. A strong expression of outrage at the conditions in which Belgian miners lived and worked, it was filmed in secret under what appear to be almost combat circumstances, and later banned by both the Belgian and Dutch governments.[8] Of the Borinage, the coal region of Southwest Belgium, Ivens wrote: "That is where I went to make my next film, not as a missionary to soften or treat wounds, but as a filmmaker to reveal the wounds to the rest of the world because I thought that my best way to help in their healing" (81).

This often puzzling and ultimately unsatisfactory film contrasts life in the Borinage with that in the Dombas coalmining region of Russia.[9] Featuring people from both regions, Ivens recreated real events such as workers' parades and strikes. However, the Russian sequences are so awkward and lifeless that they appear to have been made in the studio. While the uneven effect of this direct cinematography conveys the difficult shooting conditions, it succeeds in infusing *Borinage* with a vitality that not only compensates for the technical weaknesses, but also foreshadows subsequent developments in wartime combat photography, cinéma vérité, and direct cinema. Among these memorable scenes and sequences are those depicting an underfed miner and his hungry family cramped into a tiny sleeping room; miners forced to grub for bits of coal in a slagheap while, for economic reasons, piles of coal are kept behind barbed wire; and a spontaneous, clenched-fist political march led by a man carrying a portrait of Karl Marx.

Borinage can be compared with the British *Housing Problems* (1935), Storck's *Houses of Misery* (*Les maisons de la misère*, 1937), and Flaherty's *The Land* (1941). However, Ivens believes that his cinematic style sets the film apart:

> The urgency with which this film was made kept our camera angles severe and orthodox. Or one might say, unorthodox, because super-slickness and photographic affectation were becoming the orthodoxy of the European documentary film. This return to simplicity was actually a stylistic revolution for me. . . . The style of *Borinage* was chosen deliberately and was determined by the decency and the unrelieved plight of the people around us. (87)

Arguing that *Housing Problems*, which was made two years after *Borinage*, does

Borinage [*Misère au Borinage*] (Joris Ivens and Henri Storck, Belgium, 1933)

not make maximum political use of the disagreeable living conditions it records, Ivens continues:

> Our aim [in *Borinage*] was to prevent agreeable photographic effects distracting the audience from the unpleasant truths we were showing. . . . The filmmaker must be indignant and angry about the fate of people before he can find the right camera angle on the dirt and on the truth. (88)

In contrast, Ivens praised the urgency of Flaherty's compassion in *The Land*:

> Although all of Flaherty's work had a genuine humanitarian approach, when he came to make *The Land* . . . he became so indignant and angry about the waste of people that he found, and the bad conditions that he saw in agriculture, that he made a forceful, accusing film. (89)

Ivens's next important film, *New Earth* (*Nieuwe gronden*, 1934), is an angry, ironic outcry against the progress that it set out to record: the reclamation of the Zuider Zee in the late 1920s and early 1930s. Ivens characteristically shot too much footage, and in its final form, the film seems as much a tribute to Helen Van Dongen's reclamation of the excess footage as it is to the work of the Dutch laborers. *New Earth* initially suggests the project's accomplishments by depicting the massive engineering problems that had to be solved; the first two parts of the film document the demanding labor needed to reclaim the land, construct the dams, and plant and harvest the wheat. It is not until the third part, as the re-claimed land brings depression rather than prosperity, that the film's ironic force and interest become evident.[10] The wheat, planted on the land reclaimed from the sea, is returned to the sea when the bottom drops out of the world wheat market in the early 1930s. As the wheat is dumped, we are shown hungry children and strikers, and we hear a bitter song, reminiscent of the music of Kurt Weill. Yet, the greatest irony of the film is not the waste of the harvest, reaped at such cost, but the censorship of the completed film, which could not be screened in Paris because it was judged as being "too realistic" (Ivens 99).

Joris Ivens's early films are bold cinematic statements of the artist's social consciousness, a prelude to a lifetime of committed filmmaking. See chapter 7 for a discussion of the films Ivens made in the United States during the 1930s: *The Spanish Earth* (1937), *The 400 Million* (1939), and *Power and the Land* (1940).

John Ferno

As a youth, John Ferno began his filmmaking career and his long association with Joris Ivens as the latter's assistant on *Rain* (*Regen*, 1929).[11] Like Ivens and Helen Van Dongen, he left the Netherlands early in his career to work in Europe, Asia, and the United States. The departure of these talented film artists was a loss from which the Dutch filmmaking industry did not recover until after World War II. In fact, unlike Ivens and Van Dongen, Ferno did return to his native land in 1945 to make two joint British-Dutch films, *Broken Dykes* and *The Last Shot* (1945).

Ferno's first film, *Easter Island* (*Paaseiland* or *L'île de Pâques*, 1934), is charac-terized by a sensitivity for people and an insight into hopelessness that are all the more remarkable in view of the fact that the director-photographer was only six-teen years old when he made it.[12] *Easter Island* appears to be an objective record of a Franco-Belgian expedition to Easter Island, but it provides far more than a factual account of the island's geography and its inhabitants' lives. Unlike Flaherty (in *Man of Aran*, for example), who distorted reality when it did not agree with his precon-ceptions, or Buñuel (*Las hurdes*), who expressed outrage when reality offended his sensibilities, Ferno accepts what he observes: his principal emotion is sadness for what foreigners have done to Easter Island and its traditions. In a memorable rhythm of rise and fall, the film contrasts the past with the present, using the symbolic devices of the great stone statues, representing the grandeur of the past, and a leper colony, representing the sickness brought to the island by foreigners. Through this mood of pervasive sadness, augmented by mysterious background music, Ferno creates both an anthropological record and a moving document of human life.[13]

BELGIUM

Starting in 1896, the first Belgian filmmakers—including Charles Belot, Hippolyte De Kempeneer, Louis Van Goidsenhoven, and Alberto Promio, a Frenchman—

made films about various subjects, including the new Belgian colony in the Congo, but it was not until 1922 that Paul Flon, Gaston Schoukens, Edouard de Tallenay, and André Jacquemain made what the Belgian press called "our first great national documentary": *The Prehistoric Belgian Valley (La vallée prehistorique Belge)*.[14] An exploration film about the Lesse River valley, this was typical of the numerous films about explorations in China, South America, and the Belgian Congo,[15] that Belgians produced in the early 1920s; later in the 1920s and early 1930s, they made avant-garde films that Robert Flaherty called "the most interesting in the world."[16]

From the earliest years of the century until World War II, Belgian documentary production continued to be dominated by a few filmmakers producing films that fuse strong visual qualities with penetrating social insight. With virtually no government funding, but with the great support of the film club movement, during these early years, these filmmakers, especially Gerard de Boe, made a small, but important list of social documentary films on life in Belgium and in the Belgian Congo. In addition, there were official films, made by the Ministry of Colonies about the Congo, that were primarily informational. One notable film was Armand Denis's *African Magic (Magie africaine*, 1938), a film about the Congo reminiscent of Flaherty; it preserves Denis's vision of an earlier Africa, deliberately omitting any signs of contemporary civilization.

The three most important names in the early Belgium nonfiction film were Charles Dekeukeleire, André Cauvin, and Henri Storck, all of whom made social documentaries.

Charles Dekeukeleire

Charles Dekeukeleire's career encompassed many forms of filmmaking, ranging from avant-garde to industrial films. After his first experimental and impressionist film, *Boxing Match (Boksmatch*, 1927), he began to make social documentaries, starting with *Sights of Lourdes (Visions de Lourdes*, 1931), an exposé of commercial exploitation at places of religious pilgrimage. Following *Burned Earth (Terres brulées*, 1934), which is a serious study about the human condition of the Congolese blacks, Dekeukeleire turned to the production of industrial films. Later, he returned to the avant-garde with *The Evil Eye (Het kwade oog*, 1937), followed by *Themes of Inspiration (Thèmes d'inspiration*, 1938), a short film about the way that Brueghel and other Flemish painters depicted the lives of their countrymen; it won the first prize for documentary at the 1938 Venice Film Festival.

André Cauvin

As we have seen, European filmmakers were experimenting with the many possibilities for presenting the visual arts on film, and for enriching and encouraging the experience of art through cinema. This was both a conventional attempt to teach audiences about art and also an experimental attempt to present the static visual modes in the dynamic cinematic form. Working within the tradition of such films about cathedrals as those by Rudolph Bamberger and Curt Oertel, André Cauvin expressed his great sensitivity for art through his first two films, which are masterpieces. *The Mystical Lamb (L'agneau mystique*, 1939) is about Jan Van Eyck's great altarpiece, *Adoration of the Lamb,* in Ghent Cathedral; in its simplicity and through its unobtrusive examination of the altarpiece panels, this ten-minute film ranks as an important landmark in the development of the film about art. Cauvin's *Memling* (1939) is a survey of the works of Hans Memling, the Netherlandish painter, in the Memling Museum in Bruges. The film, which features a soundtrack of music played on authentic 15th century instruments, concentrates on a detailed analysis of *The Shrine of St. Ursula.* These films, made by the Belgian government to be shown at its pavilion at the New York World's Fair in 1939, were, according to Arthur Knight, "probably the first of the new art films on an adult level, to be seen by any considerable audience in America" (10–11).

Henri Storck

Like so many European filmmakers, Henri Storck began his career participating in the activities of a ciné-club. His first short films (1929–30) are varied in approach. *Images of Ostende (Images d'Ostende)* provides a poetic account of seaside life and activity; *Idyll at the Beach (Idylle à la plage)* depicts Belgian artists James Ensor, Félix Labisse, and Léon Spillaert; *Excursion Trains (Trains de plaisir)* mocks the day-tripping vacationers who arrive at the beach. (See above for a discussion of *Borinage* [*Misère au Borinage,* 1933], codirected with Joris Ivens.) *The History of The Unknown Soldier (L'histoire du soldat inconnu,* 1931), a *montage d'actualité,* as Storck called it, is a silent film, strongly influenced by Eisenstein. An early expression of antiwar sentiment, this ironic, repetitive film is more important for its influence on subsequent compilation films using reedited newsreel footage than for its own statement; yet, without words or sound, it remains a powerful reminder, several years after the coming of sound, of the dramatic power of the silent film. Storck also produced and edited Ferno's *Easter Island* (1934), and made the art film, *Regards to Old Belgium (Regards sur la Belgique ancienne,* 1936).

Bad housing conditions and the need for slum clearance and urban planning have always been prominent themes in nonfiction film history. Henri Storck's *Houses of Misery (Les maisons de la misère,* 1937) continued the tradition begun by Joris Ivens's *Borinage* (1933) and the Anstey-Elton *Housing Problems* (1935). Filmed in a Belgium slum, and sponsored by a society dedicated to slum clearance, this film is notable for its consistently dramatic irony, its brilliant soundtrack and musical score, and its somber examination of human despair. In contrast with *Borinage,* the outrage is controlled, expressed through spoken chants and protest songs; in contrast with *Housing Problems,* the dirt and vermin seem real, not just objects for complaint in an interview. The heavy ironies in *Houses of Misery* are memorable: shots of the worn hands of a poor woman counting out coins for rent are juxtaposed with shots of the fat hands of a rich woman entering figures in her ledger; in a moment worthy of silent film comedy, the rental agent eats a banana while watching the hungry family he has just evicted, and then slips on the peel while attempting to catch a boy rescuing his bicycle from the truck carrying the confiscated belongings of the evicted family. In a classic Griersonian pattern, the statement of the problem is followed by its solution, and, as the promise of new

Houses of Misery [*Les maisons de la misère*] (Henri Storck, Belgium, 1937)

housing appears, bitter faces and songs are replaced by happiness and a choral ode at the end of the film. A model social protest film, Storck's *Houses of Misery* achieves what he and Ivens attempted in *Borinage.*

SWEDEN

The only film made during this period in Sweden that is worth noting is *Gamla Stan* (1931), directed and photographed by Stig Almqvist, Erik Asklund, Eyvind Johnson, and Arthur Lundqvist. Intended to be in the "city symphony" tradition, *Gamla Stan* presents a day in the life of Stockholm, narrated through the eyes of the lonely woman, that seems, much like Cavalcanti's *Rien que les heures* (1926), to be a chronicle of despair. Using recurrent images of water and women for thematic continuity, the film begins with an image of a doll floating face down in water, continues with the lonely, depressed, and seemingly suicidal figure of a woman wandering the streets to her hotel, and concludes with a fade-out of her being picked up by a man. The ambiguity of this ending is underscored with an ironic musical score. But music, the psychological use of the camera, and thematic repetition do not coalesce into a coherent vision of the city's life, and we are left with a detached and strangely unfulfilling impression. Unlike its European and Soviet predecessors, this short film is more a sonata than a symphony.

DENMARK

In Denmark, Poul Henningsen's *The Film of Denmark* (1935), broke even further away from the continental city symphony tradition by presenting a lyrical view of everyday life. Other films include Friedrich Dalsheim's *The Wedding of Palo* (*Palos brudefaerd*, 1934), an affectionate account of Eskimo life in Greenland in the tradition established by *Nanook of the North*, and Paul Fejos's two short ethnographic films: *The Bilo* (1936) and *Dance Contest in Esira* (*Danstavlingen i Esira*, 1936).

SPAIN

During the 1930s, American and European leftist filmmakers made films about a conflict that would foreshadow World War II: the Spanish Civil War, a struggle between those loyal to the Spanish republican government and those, led by General Francisco Franco and supported by Hitler and Mussolini, who sought to establish a fascist regime. The major films made about this conflict were either Russian—Roman Karmen and Esther Shub, *Spain* (*Ispaniya*, 1939); or American—*The Spanish Earth* and *Heart of Spain* (see chapter 7). Although the Spanish did not develop a native nonfiction film movement in the 1930s, in 1932 Luis Buñuel made the acerbic *Land without Bread* (*Las hurdes*, 1932), which, memorable for its anger, stands virtually alone among Spanish films. It should be considered in the context of other films that deal with the land, including those from the Soviet Union—Dovzhenko's *Earth* (1930) and Mikhail Kalatozov's *Salt for Svanetia* (1930); Czechoslovakia—Karel Plicka's *The Earth Sings* (1932); and the United States—Robert Flaherty's *The Land* (1942). Unlike his later *The Lost Ones* (*Los olividados*, 1950), Buñuel's early film gains in outrage what it lacks in control, and was, in fact, banned in Spain for its portrayal of the wretched conditions in Las Hurdes, a Spanish region near the Portuguese border. As a "study of human geography," as Buñuel calls it, it examines the area's lack of hygiene, nutrition, and education. Buñuel reveals the people through cruelty (the word is André Bazin's), and this approach permits him not only to see through to what Bazin calls "the bottom of reality," but also to affirm human dignity.[17] Unlike Grierson, Ivens, or Storck, however, who would have used narration to suggest solutions to these social problems, Buñuel relies only on the ironic use of themes from Brahms' Fourth Symphony and on a shot of a magnificent church rising in the middle of squalor, foreshadowing the fully developed surrealism of his later films. *Las hurdes* is a disturbing record of poverty and neglect, but the dramatic way in which Buñuel treats this tragic theme overshadows any claim it might have to being a "pure" social documentary.

GERMANY

Organization of the Nazi Propaganda Film Effort

Even before coming to power in 1933, the Nazi Party already understood that film was a powerful propaganda medium; but it did not have a well-organized or well-financed filmmaking effort, and the few rally films that were made for election purposes were shown only at closed party meetings.[18] In October 1932, Joseph Goebbels took control of all Nazi film activities; in March 1933, Hitler appointed him as Reich Minister for Popular Enlightenment and Propaganda (*Reichsministerium für Volksaufklärung und Propaganda*—RMVP), a position from which he virtually controlled literature, the theatre, music, fine arts, the press, and radio. The provisional Reich Film Chamber (*Reichsfilmkammer*) not only regulated the financing of films, but also the removal from German cultural life of Jews and others the Nazis considered undesirable. Obsessed with films, Goebbels would soon control every aspect of the German film industry.[19]

In February 1934, the Nazis adopted the Reich Cinema Law (*Reichslichtspielgesetz*), which mandated compulsory script censorship, restrictions on film criticism, and a stringent rating system for all kinds of films. Films were rated on a scale of their usefulness (the marks of distinction were known as *Prädikate*), with the highest rating awarded to those films that were both "politically and artistically valuable."

In 1938, Goebbels reorganized the German film industry, paying particular attention to the control of films that were financed either directly or indirectly by the government; he also established a National Film School (the *Deutsche Filmakademie*) for the training of new film technicians and artists. In 1942, the entire German film industry was once again completely reorganized, this time with Goebbels in supreme authority. Fritz Hippler (the director of *The Eternal/Wandering Jew* [*Der ewige Jude*] and *Campaign in Poland*) was responsible for aesthetic matters; but, in fact, as Welch concludes, Nazi filmmakers were given "few opportunities for either individual artistic expression or commercial expertise" (38). From 1943 onwards, the central line of Nazi propaganda, as conveyed through film, was that, whatever the obstacles, the Germans would win the war. This policy remained virtually unchanged until the Nazi defeat in 1945.[20]

In emphasizing the importance of film as propaganda, Goebbels was influenced by the Soviet example, particularly *Battleship Potemkin*. The Nazis, however, were never as serious as the Soviets about the aesthetic or polemic potential of the cinema. Film remained only a single element in the vast Nazi propaganda effort, the parts of which were interrelated. Nor did Goebbels ever succeed in creating a totally ideologically committed cinema that was German in character. Welch writes:

> . . . the failure of the Third Reich to produce a revolutionary "People's Culture" was due partly to the inherent contradictions of National Socialism, where romantic conservatism and revolutionary ideas formed a precarious alliance, and partly to Goebbels' own personality. . . . The results of Goebbels' *Filmpolitik* were a monopolistic system of control and organization which maintained profits, increased attendances, produced an extremely high standard of technical proficiency, yet, in the final analysis, contributed little stylistically to the history of the cinema. (312)

In fact, films commissioned by the state consisted of only one-sixth of all film production in the Third Reich. The Nazis produced fewer wartime nonfiction films than the Americans or British, although they were no less consistent in expressing their national point of view. Nevertheless, some Nazi propaganda films are memorable documents, conveying the blunt force with which the Nazis set out to disseminate their ideas.

Nazi Ideology

As the films of World War II demonstrate, propaganda is necessary to totalitarian and democratic governments alike (see chapters 8, 9, and 10). Like their democratic counterparts, Nazi propaganda films are marked by an emotional-nationalistic fervor; but they go much further, ignoring rational discourse in favor of an overt appeal to the aroused nationalism. Indeed, unlike the propaganda films produced in democratic countries, Nazi propaganda films make no attempt to appeal to the reason and understanding of their audience. Nazi ideology was built upon the essentially irrational doctrines of Aryan racial superiority, adherence to the will of the Führer, and nationalist expansion, as well as a return to "traditional German values." To promote that doctrine, the Nazis used all available means and media. In the terror within the Nazi state, Goebbels made effective use of propaganda to lead the Germans to carry out the Führer's will.

With his brilliant insight into mass psychology, Goebbels directed his most enthusiastic propaganda toward extending the supremacy of the "master race" and his most virulent propaganda against the Jews. While Goebbels wanted Nazi films to express the heart of the people and the spirit of Germany as an emerging world power, he also insisted that they express traditional German values, identified by Welch as Comradeship, Heroism and the Party, Blood and Soil (Blut und Boden), the Leadership Principle (Führerprinzip), War and the Military Image, and the Image of the Enemy. Goebbels's single-minded attempt to use propaganda became, according to Allan M. Winkler, his means of control over an entire way of life: "The truth, for Goebbels, was not important, for propaganda, he declared, had 'nothing at all to do with truth.' Rather, the real aim was success."[21] He understood that most audiences are easily swayed by propaganda because they believe the simplistic notion that "propaganda" must be lies and, conversely, that what is true cannot be propaganda.[22] In this respect, Hitler and Goebbels would sometimes disagree over the exact role of propaganda in the Third Reich, particularly film propaganda.[23] Essentially, Hitler wanted explicitly political films, based on what Welch terms the "direct lie," while Goebbels favored propaganda film that manipulated people indirectly, using an appeal to "truth" that would reinforce opinions and feelings that people already held. Thus, Goebbels preferred feature films that reflected the overall Nazi atmosphere rather than those that proclaimed its ideology.

The Nazis relied on film as an important element in the political indoctrination of young people; as Welch points out, educational film propaganda was used to create an ideological break between generations—between parents and their children—and to create a new generation of young people of heroic will (30). Even though there is very little reliable data on the composition of the German cinema audience in wartime, we can assume that women comprised the majority of the regular audience (Welch 216). Yet, even during the war, Goebbels seems to have been more interested in appealing to the youth audience.

Goebbels's success in establishing the indirect use of propaganda in film can be seen in the fact that, of the 1,097 feature films produced under his leadership between 1933 and 1945, only about one-sixth were overtly propagandistic (Welch 42–43). But the reputation and impact of the Nazi propaganda film can be better defined by the technical skill and power, rather than the numbers, of those nonfiction films—documentaries, newsreels, and educational films—that espoused the Nazi party line. Like the Americans, the Nazis used factual footage, some of it captured from their enemies, and promulgated their themes in a series of psychologically masterful, technically brilliant films.[24] Like the Russians before them, the Nazis emphasized the state as the primary force; individuals were always secondary, always subordinate to the will and good of the state. But, unlike the Russians, they were not concerned with the reality of the world, only with the distorted reality of their program for world conquest.

Prewar Nazi Propaganda Films

The first Nazi Party film, the silent *NSDAP Party Day of August 20–21, 1927* (1927), was followed by dozens of films designed to foster party unity and election victories.[25] The election films were most numerous in 1932–33, the years in which Hitler was consolidating his political strength. These include (listed by year):

1927:   *NSDAP Party Day of August 20–21, 1927 (NSDAP Parteitag August 20–21, 1927)*;

1929:   *Battle for Berlin (Kampf um Berlin)* and *Nuremberg NSDAP Party Day of August 1–4, 1929 (Nuremberg NSDAP Parteitag August 1–4, 1929)*;

1930:   *NS-Bildbericht* (No. 1–4); 1931: *Battle for Berlin (Kampf um Berlin,* an enlarged version of the 1929 title);

1932:   *Bleeding Germany (Blutendes Deutschland), German Arms, German Honor (Deutsche Wehr, Deutsche Ehr), Inflation (Federgeld), Parole Fuehrer, Zinsknechtschaft, Struggle for the Rhine (Kampf um den Rhein), The Führer (Der Fuehrer), Zuversicht und Kraft, State and Land (Stadt und Land), Hitler Over Germany (Hitler uber Deutschland), Fourteen Year Plan (14 Jahre System), Church and State (Kirche und Staat), Hitler's Struggle for Germany (Hitlers Kampf um Deutschland)* and *Bauer in Not;*

1933:   *Die Strasse frei den braunen Bataillonen, Germany Awake (Deutschland erwacht),[26] Victory of Faith (Sieg des Glaubens), Terror or Rebuilding (Terror oder Aufbau), Hitlers Aufruf an das Deutsche Volk, Germany, My Germany (Deutschland, mein Deutschland), Abrustung,* and *National Labor Day (Tag der nationalen Arbeit);*

1934:   *Unser Fuehrer—des Reiches Wiedergeburt;*

1935:   *Hande am Werk, Three Year's Struggle for Peace (Drei Jahre Kampf um Frieden), Deutsche Arbeit und Fuehrer, Day of Freedom (Tag der Freiheit), The Heir (Das Erbe);*

1936: *For Honor, Freedom, Peace (Fur Ehre, Freiheit, Frieden), Germany: Yesterday and Today (Deutschland Gestern und Heute), A Backward Look (Ein Ruckblick), Aus Eigener Kraft, Unser Brot, Arbeit und Wehr, Congenitally Ill (Erbkrank), Ewige Wache, Youth of the World (Jugend der Welt);*
1937: *Durch Kampf zum Sieg, For Ourselves (Für uns);*
1938: *Die Grosse Zeit, Word and Deed (Word und Tat),* and *Yesterday and Today (Gestern und Heute).*

Other prewar films advocating the Nazi Party line (listed with names of directors, where known) include:

1931: *Hitler's Brown Soldiers are Coming (Hitlers braune Soldaten kommen);*
1933: *We are Marching (Wir marschieren); Steel (Acciaio); Blood and Soil: Foundation of the New Germany (Blut und Boden: Grundlage zum neuen Reich)*
1934: Wilhelm Marzahn's *The First Christmas Eve Celebration During the Third Reich at the Berlin Headquarters of the German Railway (Die erste Weihnachtsfeier der Reichsbahn-Direcktion Berlin im Dritten Reich)* and Walter W. Trinks's *Up from the Depths (Aus der Tiefe empor)*
1935: Willy Zielke's *The Steel Beast (Das Stahltier),* Richard Scheinpflug's *Dr. Death—Mission and Achievement (Dr. Todt—Berufung und Werk),* Walther Ruttmann's *Metal of the Heavens (Metall des Himmels), By the Wayside (Abseits vom Wege),* Harold Mayer's *The Heir (Das Erbe), Buckeberg, Bilddokumente,* and Leni Riefenstahl's *Triumph of the Will (Triumph des Willens);*
1936: Hanns Springer's *The Eternal Forest (Der ewiger Wald), The Camera Goes Along (De Kamera fahrt mit)* and *We Conquer the Soil (Wir erobern Land);*
1937: *Mussolini in Germany (Mussolini in Deutschland), Pilots, Radio Operators, Gunners! (Flieger, Funker, Kanoniere!); Victims of the Past (Opfer der Vergangheit);*
1938: Leni Riefenstahl's *Olympia, Gesunde Frau—Gesundes Volk, Adolf Hitlers Bauten, Unsere Kinder, Unsere Zukunft,* and Richard Skowronnek, Jr.'s *Das Buch der Deutschen.*

Although many of these films provide a unique view of Nazi Germany, only a few stand out as worthy of comment in an otherwise unremarkable group of films. Johannes Haüssler's *Bleeding Germany (Blutendes Deutschland,* 1932) includes scenes of the funeral of the Nazi hero Horst Wessel, the murdered S.A. member who was supposedly also the author of the Nazi anthem that became known as the "Horst Wessel Song." Franz Wenzler's *Hans Westmar, One of the Many: A German Destiny of the Year 1929 (Hans Westmar, Einer von Vielen: Ein Deutsches Schicksal aus dem Jahre 1929,* 1933) is less important as a fictionalized biography of Wessel than for scenes—depicting the hero apotheosized against the clouds or marching columns of party members—that influenced Leni Riefenstahl's *Triumph of the Will* (1935; see below). Riefenstahl's film in turn influenced *For Ourselves (Für uns,* 1937), a sombre tribute to the party loyalists who died in the 1923 Munich Beer-

Hall Putsch. Martin Rikli's *We Conquer the Soil* (*Wir erobern Land*, 1936) is a more conventional Nazi propaganda film which praises the young men and women in the Nazi labor camps. Commending their discipline, the film shows the machinelike efficiency of corps of lean, muscular men working in agriculture, construction, and conservation; few women are seen. The cinematography here varies between soft and sharp focus, creating a mystical visual impression, but the musical score recalls the travel film genre, undercutting the mood. An exercise session that features workers stopping their ditch-digging to whistle and do calisthenics unintentionally evokes Busby Berkeley's dance routines. Nonetheless, *We Conquer the Soil* provides an excellent account of the regimentation, dedication, and energy of Nazi Party members, a theme developed to its fullest expression in Leni Riefenstahl's *Triumph of the Will.*

Machinelike efficiency was also the subject of Willy Zielke's *The Steel Beast* (*Das Stahltier*, 1935) a film that is also a rare and rarely seen example of the Nazi propaganda film gone awry. Zielke was influenced by such constructivist and *Bauhaus* artists as Lazslo Moholy-Nagy and Albert Renger-Patzsch, whose *neue sachlichkeit* (new objectivity) movement had raised objects to the status of pure works of "machine age" art. In this spirit, the German State Railways commissioned Zielke to make a film celebrating the hundredth anniversary of the railways. It was to be a major propaganda production extolling German technological superiority, but the result was something quite different: what was to have been a tribute to the German railways became *Das Stahltier*, perhaps the most compelling film tribute to machines in cinema history. With a context of the past and present history of rail travel in Germany, France, and England, emphasizing a cycle of train wrecks, Zielke creates a poetic hymn to the beauty, power, and terror of the railroad.[27] In a foreshadowing of the cinematographic flexibility achieved by Leni Riefenstahl in *Olympia*, Zielke attached the camera to the great steel locomotive—to its driving shafts, chassis, and cow-catcher—a visual process that transforms it into a living steel beast, both creator and destroyer. This poetic transformation of the train did not please Goebbels, who accused Zielke of the crime of *Shädigung des deutschen Ansehens* ("damaging the German reputation"); he not only banned the film, but had the filmmaker placed in a mental asylum, where, with the exception of a brief release, during which he was permitted to go to Greece to photograph the prologue of Riefenstahl's *Olympia*, he remained until 1942.[28]

Notable among the prewar Nazi films that reflected traditional German values are *Germany Awake* (*Deutschland erwacht*), *We Are Marching* (*Wir marschieren*), and *Terror or Rebuilding* (*Terror oder Aufbau*, all 1933). But even more important, not only for their glorification of the German peasantry and land, but also for their practical emphasis on linking agricultural recovery to national prosperity, are *Blood and Soil: Foundation of the New Germany* (*Blut und Boden: Grundlage zum neuen Reich*, 1933), which defined the genre, and *The Eternal Forest* (*Der ewigen Wald*). These and other "blood and soil" films had two purposes:

> The first was to bring the entire nation to a common awareness of its ethnic and political unity and the subsequent need for *Lebensraum* (living space); and as a

corollary, to prepare the nation psychologically to accept and rationalize future and past invasions and annexations as a justifiable liberation of oppressed German communities living abroad. (Welch 101)

Hanss Springer's *The Eternal Forest* is a very compelling Nazi film, not only for its own achievements in exalting the German people and awakening German nationalism, but also for its poetic cinematic evocation of German myth and reality. These thematic elements, as well as such impressive elements of style as cinematography and music, influenced Leni Riefenstahl's *Triumph of the Will* and *Olympia*, the latter being another film that stresses the importance of common ethnic roots. In *The Eternal Forest*, the strength of the German people is linked to their forests; while dramatic footage of staged historical events traces the history of German peasant struggles, nonfiction footage records the present need to continue the struggle against forces that threaten those forests, poetic symbols of German strength. The film may be complex, requiring a good understanding of German history; it is also a model of Nazi propaganda in its evocation of concepts fundamental to the party ideology: folk traditions, living space, a relationship to nature, and racial purity.

Triumph of the Will [*Triumph des Willens*] (Leni Riefenstahl, Germany, 1935)

Between 1933 and 1940, the Ministry of Propaganda also produced what Erwin Leiser (16) calls "Goebbels' most important political weapon": *The German Newsreel* (*Die deutsche Wochenschau*), which, like "The March of Time," was far more theatrical in its structure and presentation than conventional newsreels. The Newsreel Law of 1936 improved newsreel distribution and copyright, and 1938 legislation mandated the compulsory showing of a newsreel at every commercial film program. They were particularly popular in rural areas, where cinemas were scarce, and where mobile units ensured that practically every German "saw a film show (with a newsreel) at least once a month" (Welch 197). As newsreels—which were topical, periodical, and universal—became increasingly important to Nazi propaganda aims, their production was closely supervised and their content was subject to censorship. After the outbreak of war, the Nazis consolidated five separate newsreel production efforts into one: "The German Newsreel" (*Deutsche Wochenschau*).[29]

The newsreel had an important role to play in the Nazi propaganda effort: "to create mass intoxication and to obtain mass approval for the projected deeds of the regime in both domestic and foreign affairs" (Welch 193). For these reasons, Nazi newsreels were a more serious part of the overall propaganda effort than they were in the Allied countries. In contrast to their American or British counterparts, they were notable for "their much greater length [about 40 minutes], their use of sophisticated editing, the utilization of music for emotional effect, and a preference for visual images at the expense of the spoken commentary." (Welch 198) While their record of the speed and power of the German military could be used to terrorize their foreign audiences, at home these newsreels "served to reinforce a jubilant military self-confidence" (Welch 212). Newsreel footage was not only used in conventional newsreels but also in other propaganda films, including three large-scale nonfiction films known as the "blitzkreig documentaries": *Campaign in Poland*, *Baptism of Fire*, and *Victory in the West*.

Leni Riefenstahl

The greatest filmmaker of Nazi propaganda was Leni Riefenstahl, a dancer and actress who had achieved a reputation for her athletic performances during the late 1920s in the popular German entertainment genre known as the "mountain film." In 1931, she directed *The Blue Light* (*Das blaue Licht*), her own mountain film, transforming what had previously been a prosaic genre into a poetic statement of great beauty. Adolf Hitler admired the film and its director's talent for transferring an abstract ideal to the screen, and asked her to make a film of the fifth Nazi party rally in Nuremberg in 1933. However, a conflict with Goebbels apparently frustrated the production, and, as a result, Riefenstahl shot only several thousand feet of film. Although she was dissatisfied with the footage, Hitler ordered that it be edited, and it was released on December 1, 1933, as *Victory of Faith* (*Sieg des Glaubens*). That served as the prologue to what is widely regarded as the most powerful, influential propaganda film in nonfiction cinema history.

TRIUMPH OF THE WILL (1935)

In *Triumph of the Will* (*Triumph des Willens*, 1935), the film of the spectacle of the 1934 Nuremberg party rally, Riefenstahl created her greatest work, a film that

William K. Everson says "is not only a masterpiece entirely on its own, divorced from political or propagandist considerations, but in its emotional manipulation of the audience represents the very heart of what propaganda is all about."[30] In *Triumph of the Will*, Riefenstahl imposes her vision upon realistic footage to achieve two basic goals: the glorification of the Nazi party and the deification of Adolf Hitler.

Riefenstahl's film gives artistic expression to an heroic conception of life. Her theme is that Hitler will restore Germany to heights of ancient heroic grandeur. Much of the effectiveness of Riefenstahl's reinterpretation of German myth derives from the interplay between the heroic visual image and the heroic musical score. That is most apparent in the strong opening scene; in Albert Speer's architectural setting for the rally; in the many shots of Hitler photographed against the sun or sky; in the mists, clouds, and smoke, in the Nazi party trappings and heraldry; in the processions, festivals, and rallies; and in the awe and enthusiasm of the crowds. The world of the Nazi leaders is portrayed as Valhalla, a place apart, surrounded by clouds and mist, peopled by heroes, and ruled from above by gods. Herbert Windt's musical score evokes Richard Wagner's *Ring der Nibelungen* without extensively quoting from it, but instead suggesting the continuation of an ancient musical tradition by mixing Wagner, folk music, and Nazi Party songs.

While Riefenstahl's principal concern is the heroic portrayal of Hitler, her secondary concerns are to demonstrate party unity and solidarity and to display civilian and military strength.[31] To this end, the film depicts many groups, from aged peasants representing the oldest German traditions in dress and music, to the youngest boys representing the hope of the future. Included also are the elite secret troops, the labor service, the leaders of various party factions, and the women in the crowds. Perhaps never before (with the possible exception of Eisenstein's *Battleship Potemkin*) and never since (with the possible exception of *Woodstock*) has a film captured the spirit and consciousness of a sociopolitical movement in such a revealing way. From beginning to end, we are aware of movement, a metaphor for progress. With great care and often great subtlety, the film moves from event to event, capturing the vitality and variety of six days in two hours of superbly edited footage. Its narrative continuity does not match the chronological sequence of the actual events of the sixth party rally, nor does the film include everything.[32] To achieve the film's dramatic rhythm and progression, Riefenstahl rearranged the order of events, transforming prosaic happenings into cinematic poetry.

The slow, stately rhythm of the film is that of the imperial or religious procession. Despite Riefenstahl's complaints about their lack of variety, the events she was shooting were spectacular, and she makes this spectacle exciting. She keeps the cameras moving as much as possible, especially when the subject itself is not in motion. Through this visual movement and variety, we become involved in the speeches; we are compelled by the close-ups to look at the speaker rather than listen to his banal oratory. Even Hitler's speeches are transformed by the moving camera and the montage. There is movement everywhere in *Triumph of the Will*, and even such inanimate objects as buildings and flags are given life. We see Nuremberg through a window; as the camera moves closer for a better view, some unseen force opens the window (a few moments later, a hand opens another window); the camera pans across the rooftops, recording banners fluttering from rooftops and smoke drifting from chimneys. Through aerial photography, Riefenstahl relieves the heaviness of marching columns by picturing them as a gently wavering line moving far below. As Hitler passes crowds in his open car, we go along, for a camera is mounted on a car moving alongside his; we pass his car and then look back as it catches up to ours.

Ultimately, however, *Triumph of the Will* is more an achievement of editing than cinematography. It is divided into parts or movements, each linked to the others by narrative and by theme and motif; each section of the film has a different style, yet the overall film has unity. All of the parts come together to create a whole, a crescendo of themes at the end, as the film moves from dawn to dawn, from air to earth, and back to air at the end. Themes are stated and restated, smaller motifs are introduced and repeated, but all the individual elements of the film are subordinate to an overall structure that expressses and embodies Riefenstahl's particular vision.

When *Triumph of the Will* was first screened in Berlin in 1935, the audience acclaimed the film for its artistry. In other parts of Germany, however, audiences were not prepared to appreciate such an artistic presentation of propaganda, and so the Nazis did not disseminate the film as widely as its present reputation would suggest. Although Goebbels did not approve of Riefenstahl or her methods—the film far too explicitly glorifies the Nazi movement for Goebbels—he was impressed by her creative genius and extolled her for creating a film portrait of Hitler that was both masterful cinema and powerful propaganda. Subsequent criticism of *Triumph of the Will* has ranged from those who cannot accept its artistic achievement because they are repelled by its moral and political convictions to those who appreciate the formal beauty of the film in spite of its political vision.[33]

In *Triumph of the Will*, Riefenstahl masterfully fuses the four basic elements of cinema: light, darkness, sound, and silence. This is more than an achievement in cinematic form, for the film has other essential elements—thematic, psychological, mythological narrative, and visual interest—and it is in the interplay of these elements that Riefenstahl transcends the limitations of the documentary film and the propaganda film genres. Her art is to perceive the essence of a real situation and to transfer the form, content, and meaning of that essential moment to the screen. Through her use of myth, she extends the meaning of the immediate moment by enriching its cultural significance, transforming actual documentary footage into her own mythic vision of reality. For these reasons, no one has imitated the film directly, nor, as so often happens with propaganda and counterpropaganda films, has its footage been successfully used against it. In fact, when Luis Buñuel showed his abridged version of *Triumph of the Will* to an audience consisting of President Franklin D. Roosevelt, René Clair, and Charlie Chaplin, they all agreed that the film was too good to be used against itself.[34] Chaplin, however, recalled elements of the film in *The Great Dictator* (1940), which at times appears to be a direct parody of Riefenstahl's film. For Riefenstahl, the precision marching of the Nazi troops was an objective reality, to which her subjective photography and editing added a menacing power. For Chaplin, depicting men as if they were machines was the essence of comedy; and he tells us the same thing about Hitler and the party, but he does it in an intentionally comic mode. In the role of the dictator Hynkel, Chaplin mercilessly caricatures Hitler's manner of walking and talking, and he exposes Riefenstahl's propagandistic theme—that the *Führer* is a god—for the absurd idea that it is. Ultimately, Chaplin tells us more about Hitler than Riefenstahl can, for he probes beneath the heroic military surface to expose the insanity of humans pretending to be what they cannot be.

OLYMPIA (1938)

Throughout her career, Leni Riefenstahl was attracted by opposites—the mountains and the plains, the *Führer* and the mob, the Aryan and the Negro—a dichotomy reflected also in *Olympia* (*Olympiade*), her two-part, 205-minute record of the Eleventh Olympic Games held in Berlin in 1936. While *Triumph of the Will* depicts Hitler as a god, *Olympia* shows him as a mere mortal, a sports lover among other fans. And while *Olympia* is a great and important film, and a masterpiece of cinematic form, it is also a vehicle for Nazi Party propaganda, particularly in its celebration of the strong, healthy, athletic, and Aryan human body. Welch writes:

> With the pagan exaltation of athletic prowess, *Olympiade* succeeded in conveying something of the mystique that National Socialism claimed to introduce into all spheres of cultural life. (121)

Olympia is the ultimate sports film, presenting sports more as poetry than politics, more as a triumph of individual athletic skill than of collective will. Four years earlier, when the Olympic Games were held in Los Angeles, the film capital of the world, there were only newreel cameras to record the event. The Nazis, however, planned *Olympia* as a comprehensive film record intended to achieve the specific propaganda goals of depicting international sportsmanship on German soil; demonstrating the health and vitality of the German athletes, and, by extension, the German people themselves; and reinforcing the idea that Germany was a peaceful and friendly nation.[35] The film's impressive production arrangements in themselves provided positive publicity for Germany at a time when it needed it.

Aside from the fictional opening, picturing the flame carrier leaving the ruins of Greece, *Olympia* is a straightforward account of the event, with especially beautiful introductory passages preceding each section; it is unequaled in its appreciation of the muscular male body (a quality that also characterizes Riefenstahl's 1970s' African photographs).[36] With this film, as with *Triumph of the Will*, Riefenstahl's careful planning assured that every possible camera position and angle would be available.[37] Cameras were mounted on cars, boats, planes, cranes, tracks, balloons, and in ditches and under water. Erik Barnouw comments:

> The most startling photographic innovation involved diving; dives were followed through the air and then under water without a break. The start of the dive was photographed from the surface of the water; at the moment of impact the cameraman went under water with his special camera while changing focus and aperture. It took months to perfect the procedure. (108)

Through its almost scientific record of athletic achievement, the film established a grammar for sports cinematography that is still in use. In the sublime sequence that records the diving events, based on what Barnouw (110) calls a "simple but brilliant editing idea"—to eliminate the climactic splashes—Riefenstahl defies gravity, transcends earth, and provides a poetic experience of flight unparalleled in cinema history.

After its release (in several versions, including one that removed shots of Hitler), *Olympia* was received enthusiastically throughout most of Europe, winning the *Coppa Mussolini*, the first prize at the 1938 Venice Film Festival.[38] However, as Hitler's aggression increased, culminating in the invasion of Poland in September 1939, the film became the subject of boycotts in Europe and the United States. Today, *Triumph of the Will* and *Olympia* are both regarded as epic documentary as well as propaganda, larger and grander than their apparent subjects; they are studied as much for their expression of their creator's personal vision as for their representation of Nazi Party ideology.

JAPAN

Prior to the 1930s, Japan had a history of the usual imported Lumière and Edison films, Japanese factual films, elaborate studio productions, and newsreels. The first factual films, made in 1897 by Tsunekichi Shibata, Shiro Asano, and Kenichi Kawaura, included scenes of street activities, Kabuki drama, Japanese scenery, and the Russo–Japanese War. However, in Japan, the documentary film, according to Joseph L. Anderson and Donald Richie, "never developed into the vital form it had become in other countries."[39] Unlike early filmmaking in other Asian countries, where there was some balance between fiction and nonfiction filmmaking, the Japanese preferred a highly stylized fiction film. The development of its style was influenced by several factors, including the nonrepresentational theatrical tradition, the abstract nature of other Japanese visual arts, and the *benshi*, a commentator who explained to the audience what they were seeing on the screen.

However, in addition to the films on art discussed above, there was one radical filmmaking effort, albeit relatively minor. In 1929, Akira Iwasaki, a leader of the ciné-club movement that was influenced by European and Russian films, established the Proletarian Film League (Prokino). Like its European and American counterparts, Prokino produced newsreels and documentaries, and organized its own distribution and exhibition services. War brought the need for the propagandistic use of the nonfiction film.

The Second Sino–Japanese War (1937–45) encouraged the Japanese government to produce films that reflected national policy, including the feature-length *Japan Advancing to the North* (*Hokushin nihon*, 1934) and *Forbidden Jehol* (*Hikyo nekka*, 1936). Fumio Kamei, a Prokino veteran, and Shigeru Miki made *Shanghai* (1937), a film emphasizing sacrifice, heroism, and victory that set the tone for the Japanese propaganda films of World War II. However, Kamei's later films, including *Fighting Soldiers* (*Tatakau heitai*, 1939) and *The Poet Kobayashi* (*Kobayashi-issa*, 1940), were denounced for their ideological independence. Prior to Japan's entry into World War II, there were many other Japanese nonfiction films on China, including: *The New Continent* (*Shintairiku*, 1939); as well as films on rural Japanese subjects—*People Who Make Charcoal* (*Sumi yaku hitobito*, 1939) and *The Village without a Doctor* (*Isha no nai mura*, 1939). Anderson and Richie write that

> all these films were more influenced by the German *kulturfilm* than by the British school of documentary . . . a pseudo-scientific, pseudo-artistic approach which occasionally invalidated the subject and which one still sees in many contemporary Japanese documentaries. (146–7)

INDIA

Indian film history began, as it did in so many countries, with the introduction of the Lumières' *cinématographe* in Bombay on July 7, 1896.[40] As in Japan, there was a small output of newsreels and factual films, but no development of the documentary film until World War II. In fact, there was little recognition of the importance of the nonfiction film until 1937.

In 1885, Indian leaders of the independence movement had founded the Indian National Congress, the political party that eventually wrested Indian independence from Great Britain in 1947. During the period after World War I, there were many signs of Indian unrest, particularly between Hindu and Muslim constituencies. Gandhi's passive resistance campaigns of the 1930s encouraged reform and, by 1935, the British adopted the Government of India Act, which mandated social and cultural reforms to begin in 1937. In elections which took place in 1937, the Indian National Congress, led by Gandhi and Jawaharlal Nehru, won more than half the seats.

This relaxation of British policy also affected Indian filmmaking. Shortly after the elections, the British released a number of factual films that they had previously banned. These films, concerned with Gandhi and the independence movement, provide a vivid record of Gandhi's activities at home and at the Imperial Conferences concerning the status of India that were held in London in the early 1930s.[41] These factual records not only provided Indians with a capsule chronicle of the independence drive of the 1930s, but their banning also revealed, according to Barnouw and Krishnaswamy (123), "the extent of British determination throughout the decade to keep the passions of independence out of the film medium."

In addition to removing censorship of film coverage of the Congress Party, the British made various other efforts to win Indian public opinion. But after World War II was declared, and a divided Indian nation did not rally behind Great Britain, the British in 1942 jailed Gandhi and other Congress Party leaders. They also revived film censorship of Congress Party activities, with no photograph of Gandhi allowed on the screen. In itself, this British acknowledgement of the power of the photograph represents the astonishingly naive belief that removing the image of the Congress leaders would effectively remove them from the hearts of their followers. More positively, the Indian government established a Film Advisory Board in 1940 to encourage the production of films related to the war effort and invited British documentary filmmakers to come to India to serve as advisers (see chapter 9).

CHINA

As in India and Japan, China's cinema history began with showings made by Lumière representatives. These cameramen and others—including Burton Holmes and representatives of Edison, Urban, and Pathé Frères—followed the typical early practice, travelling to China to show their films and make additional short factual films, some of them faked, of local scenes, cultural activities, and such major political events as the Russo–Japanese War and the Boxer Uprising.[42] Enrico Lauro, an Italian, recorded local sights and customs in such films as *Shanghai's First Tramway* and *Imperial Funeral Procession in Peking* (1908), *Lovely Views in Shanghai Concessions* (1909), and *Cutting Pigtails by Force* (1911). Among the other foreign cameramen, Lauro was almost unique in providing films both for export and local exhibition.

> Here was a situation that prevailed in no other film-producing country, with the possible exception of India: of the enormous quantity of documentary material filmed in China by foreigners, from the earliest travels of film showmen to liberation, most of it was never seen by Chinese audiences. (Leyda 7–8)

Native Chinese production, which appears to have begun in 1913, and to have evolved slowly until the 1930s, concentrated almost solely on fiction filmmaking, although Leyda (19) points out that the wealthy had factual film records made of family funerals. The sporadic development of nonfiction filmmaking took place against the larger background of internal political struggles, an unreliable supply of filmmaking equipment and stock, and foreign incursions into the fledgling Chinese film business. "With some foreign investment most of Chinese film production remained in Chinese control, but the management of income, the theaters, continued in foreign control, especially in Shanghai, already recognized [by 1920] as China's film center" (Leyda 22). The films, which were predictably varied, included opera films, fiction films based on Western models (including "westerns"), and melodramatic adventure films.

Newsreels, most of them produced by foreign companies, recorded important government activities and the turbulent political history of China during the first two decades of this century: the rise and fall of Sun Yat-sen; the rise to power of Chiang Kai-shek; the beginnings in 1927 of civil war between Sun's new revolutionary nationalist party, the Kuomintang, and the communists; and the Japanese aggression in the occupation of Manchuria in 1931, the establishment of the puppet state of Manchukuo in 1932, and the invasion and occupation of China in 1937. Western viewers today are less likely to see these newsreels intact than they are to see footage from them incorporated into Western compilation films such as Frank Capra's *The Battle of China*.

On January 1, 1930, the Kuomintang, which was now firmly in power in

Nanking and Peking, established three strict principles governing censorship of film production:

> No film may be shown which is in violation of the political principles of Kuomintang or which might affect the prestige of the nation.
>
> The [Censorship] Committee must refuse license to any film, or any part of a film which may be disadvantageous to morality or to the public peace.
>
> License will be refused to all pictures which might conduce to supersititous practices, or might encourage feudalism. (Quoted in Leyda 60)

However, even before these strict principles were established, the beginnings of the civil war in 1927 had had a chilling effect on intellectuals, forcing them first into retreat and then underground. Nevertheless, Leyda writes,

> under the threat of the two most repressive political systems in modern history, the Kuomintang and the Japanese occupation, a group of Chinese revolutionaries made films that continued to reach a large public. . . . these exceptional, bitter, difficult, and often bloody circumstances resulted in the most interesting and lasting Chinese films, superior to what came before, to what was going on above ground at the same time, and, in many important respects, superior to the Chinese films made in the years well after the triumph of the Chinese revolution—whether in Peking, Shanghai, or Hong Kong—even though some of the same artists are still making films. (71)

These, however, were primarily fiction films. The best nonfiction films about China during the 1930s were made by foreigners—Yakov Blyokh's *Shanghai Document (Shanghaisky dokument*, 1928); *China Strikes Back* (1937), a Frontier Films release by Jay Leyda, Irving Lerner, and Sidney Meyers; and Joris Ivens's *The 400 Million* (1939).

<table>
<tr><td>

7

</td><td>

American Nonfiction Film: 1930–1939

</td></tr>
</table>

American nonfiction filmmakers in the 1930s were far more varied than their British, European, or Asian colleagues in the subjects they explored and the politics they represented. While most made social documentaries in the traditions of the Soviet propaganda and British documentary film, others explored the possibilities of screen journalism and independent film production. The subjects of their films include the Dust Bowl, urban planning, rural electrification, the Spanish Civil War, art, education, and automation, while their politics reflect a spectrum that includes the essentially uncommitted but fundamentally conservative attitudes of Robert Flaherty; the New Deal policies of the U.S. government as represented in the films of Pare Lorentz and the U.S. Film Service; the liberal views of Joris Ivens; and the leftist convictions of the films of the Workers' Film and Photo League and the Frontier Film Group.

However, these filmmakers differed from their European and Asian counterparts in their primary concern with domestic, rather than continental or international, issues. While some films (e.g., *Heart of Spain*, *The Spanish Earth*, *The 400 Million*, and *China Strikes Back*) focussed on events that were leading up to World War II, the majority were concerned with domestic issues; the majority of American filmmakers, like the United States itself, were not yet involved in the larger developments that would change the course of world history. Interestingly enough, where there was an affinity with European or Asian nonfiction filmmaking, it was in the relatively new category of films on art.

BEGINNINGS OF THE AMERICAN FILM ON ART

As we have seen, the beginnings of the European and Asian tradition of films on art are found in the avant-garde film, but primarily in those French and Belgian films that draw naturally on the extensive art history of their countries, films that reflect the cultural sensibilities of filmmakers who are as equally comfortable with Rubens as they are with Magritte, with Gothic architecture as they are with the architecture of Le Corbusier. These films were made by directors who not only understood painting, sculpture, and architecture, but also how to reinterpret it in cinema. Moreover, they assume a certain aesthetic sophistication on the part of the viewer, and, thus tend more to celebrate than to explain the artist and the art. By contrast, the beginnings of the American tradition of films on art are found in the more functional context of the educational film.

The first American films about art were invariably instructional; conventional in subject and in cinematic treatment, they "contributed little to adult education, nothing to adult entertainment."[1] Typical of these were such titles as *The Making of a Bronze Statue, A Visit to the Armor Galleries,* and *Firearms of our Forefathers* (all 1922); and *Furniture Making, The Etcher's Art,* and *Furniture Craftsmen* (all 1929). While a variety of government agencies, educational institutions, and independent producers (e.g., Encyclopaedia Britannica Films) also made educational films for classrooms and general training purposes, they produced only a few about art. The Works Progress Administration (WPA) of the U.S. Government produced Alexander Stazenitz's *Ercolani and Pompeii* (1936), *Sculpture Today* (1936), and Leo Seltzer's *The Technique of Fresco Painting* (1938). Other pioneering films included Robert Coffin's *Stone and Sculptor* (1931); Stewart Moss's *Eternal Athens* (1932); Kenneth Bloomer's *Ceramics* (1936); Elias Katz's *Creative Painting of Landscape* and *George Grosz at Work* (both 1937) and *Make a Mask* (1938); Lewis Jacobs's *From Tree Trunk to Head* (1939), an analysis of Chaim Gross's woodcarving technique; Evelyn Brown's *The Child Explores His World* (1938); Arthur E. Baggs's *Maria and Julian's Black Pottery* (1938), a celebration of traditional ceramic arts in New Mexico; and Francis Thompson's *The Evolution of the Skyscraper* (1939). Two films about Black artists and their art reflect the liberal but segregated social vision of the time: *A Study of Negro Artists* (1937) and *Art in the Negro Schools* (1940).

Before the 1960s, the American art museum was a comparatively elitist institution, devoted to small exhibitions that provided intellectual enrichment to a finite number of visitors, most of them knowledgeable about art, many of them collectors or scholars. Since the 1960s, that function has been augmented (in some cases almost replaced) by major educational efforts on behalf of a far wider public that is interested not only in art itself, but also in the social experience of looking at, and learning about art. Museums now offer a wide range of publications, gallery tours, lectures, audio-visual accompaniments, and films made expressly to be seen at the beginning or conclusion of exhibitions. Thus, it is all the more significant that the Metropolitan Museum of Art in New York City, which fostered these populist purposes, was, during the 1930s, the most enterprising American producer of educational films about art. Early Metropolitan Museum films on art include Robert Flaherty's *The Pottery Maker: An American Episode of the 19th Century* (1925), a film that is distinguished only by Flaherty's knowing, quiet observation of a craftsman at work; *Daily Life in Egypt* (1925), more anthropology than art; *Behind the Scenes: The Working Side of the Museum,* an account of museum support services, unusual in that patrons rarely know of these activities; *Lorado Taft, Sculptor*

(1930); *Tapestries and How They are Made* (1933), which, like many of its European predecessors, fits nicely into museum education programs; *Childe Hassam, Artist: A Short Personal Sketch* (1933); and *The American Wing* (1935).

These achievements were minor in themselves and particularly in contrast to such European films as André Cauvin's *The Mystical Lamb* and *Memling*, John Ferno's *Easter Island,* or Luciano Emmer's and Enrico Gras' *Earthly Paradise.* Nonetheless, both in the United States and in Europe, it was not until after World War II that the development of the film on art disentangled itself from the avant-garde film movement and became distinct.

ROBERT FLAHERTY: THE ROMANTIC TRADITION CONTINUES

Man of Aran (1934)

In 1932, as he sought backing in England to make a film about the Aran Islands, Robert Flaherty had found a perfect vehicle for continuing his exploration of themes in the American Romantic tradition. *Man of Aran* embodies Flaherty's concern for natural beauty and the conflict between man and nature; family life and its enduring traditions; and man's ultimate survival as he coexists with the forces of nature. At the start of this project, Flaherty seemed determined to find (or to invent) a story that would embody the conflict between man and the great sea that surrounded the Aran Islands and thus to capture the epic theme that had preoccupied him since making *Nanook*—as Calder-Marshall (67) wrote: "people who in the midst of life were always so close to death that they lived in the moment nobly."[2]

Man of Aran invites comparison with John Millington Synge's haunting play, *Riders to the Sea* (1904). In both, the lives of the islanders are defined by the raging sea that isolates them and the barren rocks on which they lived. Flaherty, like the island "family" that he depicts, was in awe of the sea's power: "The sea must never be denied its victim, otherwise it will claim the rescuer, too, for its own. It must have its victim" (quoted in Murphy 23). In Flaherty's other films, the struggle between man and nature is balanced in favor of man, who at least has a chance to win. But in *Man of Aran*, the struggle is the sea against man, not man against the sea; the sea is the stronger combatant and most frequently the winner. The dark, powerful poetry of the cinematography here affirms, better than anything else in the film, the sea's brutal power and the islanders' determined ruggedness. After the final sequence fully establishes the magnitude of the storm, a shot reminds us that the men are still far out to sea in a boat that seems useless against the huge waves. As the men slowly make their way to shore, there is no music now, only the sound of the sea and wind and the voices of Maggie and Mikeleen, who try to guide them with shouts from the shore. The juxtaposition of pounding waves and feeble shouts emphasizes the unequal struggle in the boat and the helplessness on shore. Eventually the boat is sacrificed, and the men swim in through the surf to safety; even though Maggie's husband is safe, she rails against their eternal enemy in a

Man of Aran (Robert Flaherty, USA, 1934)

mournful, unforgettable cry. Maggie's lament, interrupted by her thanks for the men's safe return, deepens the impact of this experience, reminding one of Maurya's last words in Synge's *Riders to the Sea*: "No man at all can be living for ever, and we must be satisfied." The editing of this final sequence completes the structural unity of the film: the family is once again together against the overriding image of the sea.

While scenes like this give *Man of Aran* a powerful poetic realism, they do not entirely compensate for the film's shortcomings in narrative, soundtrack, and music. Flaherty's decision to combine elements of fiction with fact by staging the shark hunt and the potato planting typifies a basic yet flawed aspect of his narrative style. As in *Moana,* by reviving disused customs and by ignoring all but the mythic elements of island life, Flaherty created an incomplete and perhaps invalid picture of that life (108).

While he always used images out of real life, Flaherty never hesitated to stage an event, as long as it was probable, if this would enhance the narrative that he imposed upon what he observed. To extend the film's dramatic conflict, Flaherty had revived a method of shark hunting that had not been used for almost one hundred years before he arrived on Aranmor and persuaded the men to learn for the first time in their lives the arduous task of working the old boats and handling the harpoons.[3] The first shark hunt, photographed from the shore where Maggie and Mikeleen keep watch, appears contrived, as, indeed, it was. Because Flaherty has invented their story and controls their action, his characters seem detached from the life their prototypes actually lived. We cannot share their fears or their victories, knowing that the shark hunt has been invented and that this particular conflict with the sea is unnecessary.

In *Man of Aran*, Flaherty continued to experiment with cinematography, and, to a lesser extent, with editing and sound. To his customary use of the moving camera, he added a finer sense of framing, camera positioning, and camera movement. And in adhering to traditional, conservative film grammar in his use of conventional establishing shots, followed by medium close-ups and close-ups, he also revealed a greater awareness of how the cinematographer prepares the footage for the editor. Flaherty's most significant cinematographic achievement on *Man of Aran* came from his continued use and experimentation with the long-focus lenses that had characterized his visual style since he had first used the telephoto lens in the making of *Nanook*. In Ireland, he used a spring-driven camera, writing in "Filming Real People" that it was "simpler in operation than any other camera I had ever seen, and not much heavier to carry around than a portable typewriter" (98). He was especially pleased with its steadiness in accommodating the variety of lenses that he used: wide-angle, two-, three-, four-, six-, nine-, and eleven-inch lenses, and an enormous seventeen-inch long-focus lens twice as long as the camera. He claimed that he owed almost everything to these lenses, and with them he captured some of the most extraordinary sea footage ever recorded on motion picture film.[4] This equipment also made possible a greater intimacy in the shots of people, reflecting Flaherty's care not only in the choice of actors but also in the selection of lenses with which to film them.

Unfortunately, the immediacy and intimacy of the photography that create a realistic context for our interest are undercut by a soundtrack of dialogue and music that was an afterthought, not an integral part of the production. In *Documentary Film*, Paul Rotha rightly observed that *Man of Aran* "avoided all the important issues raised by sound . . . " (107). In fact, for budgetary reasons, after shooting *Man of Aran* on location as a silent film, Flaherty had to work in the London studio to post record and dub in the sound effects, dialogue, and music. While this use of post-synchronous sound was an economic necessity, it challenges all the realist conventions without achieving anything that is aesthetically significant, except perhaps the substitution of music for narration, a choice that (in itself, nothing new) can be poetic and very moving. Moreover, it calls attention to itself in ways that disturb the realist context that Flaherty was trying to maintain. For example, when the boat is breaking against the rocks, we hear what sounds like mere sticks being broken in front of the microphone. Striving to create a mood of nobility, John Greenwood's musical score overwhelms the simple human activity it underscores.

By concentrating his narrative on various physical actions no longer relevant to island life, Flaherty avoided depicting accurately the physical and especially the psychological and social realities of contemporary life. As most critics of *Man of Aran* quickly pointed out, Flaherty preferred imaginary conflicts to actual ones. Paul Rotha, for example, faulted *Man of Aran* for its avoidance of social and economic reality:

> Give to Flaherty his credits; and they are many. Acknowledge our deep obligation
> to his pioneer spirit, his fierce battles to break down commercial stupidity and the
> bravery of his struggle against the despicable methods of exploitation from which
> he has suffered. But realize, at the same time, and within the sphere of documen-
> tary, that his understanding of actuality is a sentimental reaction towards the past,
> an escape into a world that has little contemporary significance, a placing of
> sentimentalism above the more urgent claims of materialism. (107)

Flaherty certainly ignored the effects of such worldwide events as the economic
depression of the 1930s, suggesting to the audience that the Aran islands were as
isolated economically as they were geographically. Oblivious to political matters,
he also avoided the very real conflict on the islands between Catholics and Protes-
tants and other civil conflicts, such as those between citizens and the police and the
exploitation of Irish tenant farmers by absentee British and Irish landlords. Nevertheless, even if Flaherty did not make use of all the potentialities of the documentary cinema, in *Man of Aran* he achieved something closer to his own aesthetics by
depicting the human struggle with richness of expression and sensitivity. Between
Man of Aran and *The Land* (1942), which will be discussed below, Flaherty made
Elephant Boy (1937), a fiction film that damaged his reputation and did little or
nothing to advance his career as a nonfiction film director.

JORIS IVENS: THE EUROPEAN POLITICAL DOCUMENTARY COMES TO AMERICA

From the beginning of his career, Joris Ivens was convinced that film could not be
separated from politics (see chapter 6). Over the years, his belief that it was the
filmmaker's duty and responsibility to participate "directly in the world's most
fundamental issues"[5] had taken him to many countries in which political ferment
or revolution was occurring: China, Russia, Indonesia, Cuba, and Vietnam. In late
1936, when he and Helen Van Dongen were working in the United States, a group
of American writers commissioned them to make a film that would explain the
Spanish Civil War to American audiences. These writers sympathized with the
Loyalist cause and thought support could be gained through a compilation film
produced from Spanish Civil War newsreel footage.[6] Ivens suggested that it would
be preferable to produce an original film, and so the group, known as Contemporary Historians Inc., produced his first film about revolution, *The Spanish Earth*
(1937).

The film celebrates the endurance of the Spanish peasants as they resist the
Fascist invaders. Although it was made under difficult circumstances with very little
money, *The Spanish Earth* accomplished their intentions: to aid the battle against
fascist aggression by raising social consciousness and funds for ambulances. In
order to reach these goals Ivens assumed that the viewer not only knew the facts
about the Fascist threat, but also agreed with the Spanish resistance. A major theme
of the film is the vital importance of agriculture and, therefore, of irrigation in the
defense by Spaniards of their country; if the Fascist aggression succeeded in cutting

The Spanish Earth (Joris Ivens, USA, 1937)

off the irrigation, the Spanish would lack the supplies necessary to feed soldiers and citizens alike. Without water, they would lose title to their land.

According to Thomas Waugh, *The Spanish Earth*, which is half-documentary and half-fiction, represents a definitive model of two basic traditions of radical filmmaking: the "international solidarity" genre and the utopian genre in which each successive revolutionary society is celebrated as an inspiration to those still struggling for liberation from oppression.[7] In fact, the film is an intelligent, moving testament to the Spanish resistance; however, it is weakened (especially for today's viewer) by its assumption that the viewer knows the facts about the Fascist threat and agrees with the moral assumptions behind the Spanish resistance. This deficiency is all the more apparent when *The Spanish Earth* is contrasted, for example, with Frank Capra's "Why We Fight" series, a group of films that had an equally hard task of explaining the background of the Second World War. Capra does not assume anything about his audience's beliefs, except perhaps that they will agree with his.

Ernest Hemingway wrote and spoke the narration, which is essential Hemingway—calm without outrage, moral without righteousness.[8] He begins, "This Spanish earth is dry and hard and the faces of the men who work on that earth are hard and dry from the sun." And when the fighting begins, he says, "This is the moment that all the rest of war prepares for, when six men go forward into death to walk across a stretch of land and by their presence on it prove—this earth is ours."[9] The intrusion of warfare into this quiet landscape seems almost unreal. The narration matches the visual images with the same direct, ironic force that Capra was later to achieve in his war films. A feeling for place and for the nuances of life infuses every image. With the exception of the combat footage, the cinematography beautifully evokes the bare, dry Spanish landscape and the hard life of the peasants. The musical score, Marc Blitzstein's arrangement of Spanish folk tunes, is a quiet and lilting reminder of prewar happiness.

After Spain, Ivens turned his attention to China, an area of conflict that would become a major battleground in the Second World War, and made *The 400 Million* (1939).[10] The film, which takes China's side in the Japanese-Chinese conflict, is too reserved, too dull, and too long to be an effective political documentary. Ivens's film shows the efforts of the Chinese resistance, but it does not evoke the same picture of Chinese peasant strength that *The Battle of Russia,* part of the "Why We Fight" series, does for the people of Leningrad. Subsequently, much of Ivens' footage was used in the compilation film, *The Battle of China* (1944), another "Why We Fight" film.

While Ivens's films about the Spanish and Chinese conflicts raised funds for these political causes in the United States, they were more important in helping to lay the foundations for the American political documentary film, particularly the work of Pare Lorentz and the United States Film Service as well as the work of the Frontier Film Group and other leftist organizations.[11] In 1939, Pare Lorentz invited Ivens to make *Power and the Land* (1940), a film for the Rural Electrification Administration of the U.S. Department of Agriculture on the subject of rural electrification and its impact on the prosperity of the American farmer. In the tradition of Lorentz's *The River, Power and the Land* (1940) evokes a strong feeling for America, but it is in direct contrast to Ivens's earlier work, and is, as William Alexander writes, "a curious film to come from a major documentary filmmaker of the thirties, so middle-class in its stolid subjects, so simple and straightforward in style."[12] That *Power and the Land* could have been made by a foreigner and yet emerge as wholly American as a painting by Edward Hopper, is both a tribute to the subject and to the vision and sensibility of the director.[13]

Power and the Land documents the tedious daily routine on the Parkinsons' nonelectrified farm in Ohio. It follows a parallel structure, so that every problem presented in the first part of the film is followed by a solution in the second part. In the first half, all the tasks are onerous, but, in the second, with the aid of electricity, they become easier to perform and, more important, bring satisfaction and profits. The film thus indirectly criticizes the private electric utilities for their reluctance to electrify outlying farms and also encourages farmers to form cooperatives financed by the government: "It wouldn't be so hard with power, but one man can't change that alone." The narration, written by poet Stephen Vincent Benét, although less forceful, resembles that in the latter part of *The River.* Soft and sentimental, rather than challenging, it incorporates soft ironies and an effective use of understatement and makes its points with easy emphasis, occasional irony, and a beautiful musical score by Douglas Moore.

Power and the Land, like *The River,* leaves a lasting impression of the American heartland and continues to affect audiences. These documentary films fuse Flaherty's poetic approach with their own particular combination of hard political realism and sentimental values, and are remarkable achievements in the power of art to transcend mere politics. Long after the issues of rural electrification, soil conservation, and dam building are answered, these films will remain forceful—as, for example, Ivens's *The 400 Million* does not—because they are ultimately concerned with lasting human values, with love of the soil, with love of hard work, and with the love that people share with each other. Ivens's affinity for the struggles of the human race is nowhere better represented than in this lovely film. It is not militant, nor does it advocate a particularly revolutionary idea; indeed, the forming of cooperatives, which itself has a long American history, is pictured as a fairly simple process. But with the visual sensibility of cinematographers Floyd Crosby and Arthur Ornitz, with Van Dongen's skillful editing rhythm, and with the integrated commentary and musical score, Ivens created a classic American documentary film.[14]

Power and the Land (Joris Ivens, USA, 1940) [left to right, Mrs. Parkinson and Joris Ivens]

During the Second World War, Ivens worked in the United States and Canada, producing films for the National Film Board of Canada and the American government. After the war (see chapter 12), the Netherlands government appointed him as Film Commissioner for Indonesia, where he made *Indonesia Calling* (1946).[15]

AMERICAN FILM ON THE LEFT: 1930-42

While the development of leftist filmmaking in the United States during the 1930s was not as cohesive as the development of similar movements in Western Europe or the Soviet Union, it was remarkable for its assimilation of foreign and native influences and for creating a political film that is uniquely American.[16] These achievements were the product of such collaborative filmmaking groups as the Workers' Film and Photo League, Nykino, and the Frontier Film Group.

The Workers' Film and Photo League of America (1930-35)

The Workers' Film and Photo League of America—founded in 1930 as "part of the cultural movement sponsored by the Communist International and its affiliated national parties in the interwar period"[17]—intended to awaken the working class, to support its political activities through meetings and boycotts, and to establish a film and photo school that would produce and exhibit politically committed photographs, newsreels, and films.[18] According to the League, by the end of 1931, it had enlisted the efforts of forty-five still photographers and nine cinematographers, including Leo Seltzer, Tom Brandon, Sam Brody, Leo Hurwitz, Irving Lerner, David Platt, Harry Alan Potamkin, Lester Balog, and Robert Del Duca, artists who shared a contempt for the Hollywood establishment and its failure to make serious films about ordinary working people.[19] In this, they were closely allied in spirit with Grierson and his followers. Despite the prominence of the film theorists in this group who admired Soviet film, they seemed to have little influence on the League's films, which, intended as an alternative to the newsreels, are quite straightforward. These films documented the struggle for jobs, unions, and civil rights, and distinctly lack any apparent references to the Russian propagandist style.

The League's early films, which were the first social documentaries produced in the United States, "tended to be formally unsophisticated, relying for their effectiveness on the *fact* of the event, on the basic power of sheer documentation" (Alexander 33). Many of these films were destroyed or lost for many years, but Leo Seltzer, the filmmaker who originally shot and edited many of the League's films, has restored six of them, including *Worker's Newsreel, Unemployment Special* and *National Hunger March 1931* (1931); *Detroit Workers News Special, Hunger: The National Hunger March to Washington 1932,* and *Bonus March* (1932); and *America Today* (1932–34). The lack of cinematic form was more than counterbalanced by an emotional intensity and political commitment that was appropriate to the historical moment in which these films were made. The films record daily breadlines, evictions, and nationwide protests against unemployment and social inequities; today, however, many of them seem dull and remote. Other problems that hindered the development of a true American style in radical filmmaking included the ideological divisions and tensions within the group and the lack of an audience large enough to justify additional production. The League's growing factionalism and the emergence of two opposing groups led to the eventual departure of the Hurwitz-Steiner-Lerner group to form Nykino at the end of 1934.[20] Although the League continued its official existence until late 1937, it was increasingly overshadowed by the Nykino group.

Nykino (1935–37)

The establishment of the Nykino group represented a realignment of some of America's most committed political filmmakers that resulted in a refocusing of their commitment to produce a viable form of political film. The Nykino group, led by Leo Hurwitz, Ralph Steiner, and Irving Lerner, also included Lionel Berman, Sidney Meyers [Robert Stebbins], Ben Maddow [David Wolff], and Paul Strand. United in their belief in social and political equality, these talented sons of immigrants, most of them Jewish, were raised, for the most part, on New York's Lower East Side or in Brooklyn, and grew up in families dedicated to various forms of socialism and labor unionism.

Among the most committed of these filmmakers was Paul Strand, already known as a great photographer as well as the maker of two films—*Manhatta* (1921) with Charles Sheeler and *Where the Pavement Ends* (1928).[21] In his desire to make films about human dignity and struggle, he was influenced by both Robert Flaherty and the Soviet documentary filmmakers. In 1934, commissioned by the Mexican government, he made *The Wave* (*Redes*, 1937; U.S. release, 1937), working in collaboration with various artists, including Carlos Chávez, Henwar Rodakiewicz, and Fred Zinnemann.[22] This impartial presentation of the conflict between fishermen off the Vera Cruz coast of Mexico and the vested interests that were interfering with their livelihood is directly in the documentary tradition, but its failure to take a firm stand weakens its force.

The careers of Pare Lorentz and Joris Ivens crossed paths with Nykino, but in different ways. Although Lorentz had little sympathy with the leftist filmmakers, he engaged several Nykino members (Leo Hurwitz, Ralph Steiner, Paul Strand, and Willard Van Dyke) in the production of two of the best documentary films ever produced in the United States: *The Plow That Broke the Plains* (1936) and *The River* (1937), both sponsored by the U.S. Government, but associated with Nykino in spirit (both films are discussed below). Joris Ivens arrived in New York City early in 1936, and had a major influence in helping the Nykino members to sharpen their theories about political films. His influence can be seen in "The World Today," Nykino's short-lived newsreel response to "The March of Time," which was among the group's early efforts. According to Alexander, "The World Today" is "not a revolutionary film; it is a film of the popular front, a film looking for an audience among those who are renewing their belief in America" (127).

By 1937, it was apparent that leftist filmmaking in the United States was moving in different and sometimes contradictory directions, the most discomforting of which were the tendencies toward either large-scale production or government-sponsored production, or both. One direction was represented by Pare

Lorentz, who helped to found the United States Film Service, working within the system to change public opinion; those moving in another direction took a more radical and more militant stand, reorganizing their forces into the Frontier Film Group.

Frontier Film Group (1936–42)

The name of the Frontier Film Group reaffirmed its American roots and paid homage to the impact of Dovzhenko's *Frontier* (1935), as *Aerograd* was known in the United States.[23] At one time or another, the group included Lionel Berman, Kyle Crichton, Leo Hurwitz, Joris Ivens, Louis Kamp, Elia Kazan, Herbert Kline, John Howard Lawson, Irving Lerner, Albert Maltz, Margaret Murray, George Sklar, Robert Stebbins [Sidney Meyers], Ralph Steiner, Philip Stevenson, Paul Strand, Willard Van Dyke, and David Wolff [Ben Maddow]. Their advisers were a distinguished group of composers and writers, including Carlos Chavez, Aaron Copland, John Dos Passos, Lillian Hellman, Archibald MacLeish, Clifford Odets, S. J. Perelman, and Muriel Rukeyser. Despite their differences, Alexander emphasizes that

> they *all* shared a critical perspective on the prevalent film forms that they associated with the values and behavior that had caused the Depression. They came together out of shared convictions, out of joblessness, out of their neglect as unestablished young artists (most of them), out of their belief in collectivism as one feature of the socioeconomic solution, and out of their young and vital conviction about their own talents and the rightness of their ideas. As a family, as a cooperative, they accorded each other high respect and support, they reached out to draw in other artists, and they attempted through their films to speak personally to their audience. (217)

The Frontier Film Group had high ambitions, but the six or so films that they succeeded in making were "a small ripple on the tide" (MacCann 83) of American nonfiction filmmaking in the 1930s. Two of their films—Herbert Kline's *Heart of Spain* and *Return to Life* (both 1937)—deal with Spain; like Ivens's *The Spanish Earth,* which was produced by Contemporary Historians, Inc., these were made to raise money for the Spanish Loyalist cause.[24] *Return to Life* is distinguished by the cinematography of Henri Cartier-Bresson. *China Strikes Back* (1937) was produced by Jay Leyda [Eugene Hill], Ben Maddow [David Wolff], Irving Lerner [Peter Ellis], Sidney Meyers [Robert Stebbins], and Harry Dunham. Similar in intent but less interesting than Ivens's *The 400 Million,* it takes a pro-China side in the Chinese-Japanese conflict. Among Frontier's other films were *People of the Cumberland* (1938)—a film by Elia Kazan, Ralph Steiner, Erskine Caldwell, Alex North, Earl Robinson, Sidney Meyers, Jay Leyda, and Helen Van Dongen—which concerns the restoring of economic security to the Tennessee mountain region; *The White Flood* (Ben Maddow, William O. Field, Sherman Pratt, Sidney Meyers, Hanns Eisler, 1940), a beautiful nonpolitical study of glaciers, and *United Action* (Lionel Berman, Ben Maddow, Sidney Meyers, 1939), a depiction of striking automobile workers in Detroit that is more characteristic of the Frontier Group.

In 1938, during the production of *People of the Cumberland,* members of the Frontier Film Group started to go their own ways, convinced that the collaborative effort was not working. In particular, Steiner and Van Dyke felt that Hurwitz and Strand had begun to dominate the organization. The split came when Steiner and Van Dyke accepted a commission from the American Institute of Planners and formed American Documentary Films, Inc., to make *The City.* Their move evoked a bitter reaction among filmmakers, and not only threatened the cohesiveness of the Frontier Films organization and its production of what was to become *Native Land,* but also had major consequences for the continued development of American leftist filmmaking. Their departure marked the turning point between films made through a group effort—committed to such leftist ideals as a Loyalist victory in Spain, a Chinese victory over Japan, the growth of trade unions, and other domestic struggles over social inequality—and films made by individual filmmakers, committed less to those ideals, regarded by some as uncomfortably close to the Communist Party ideology, than to their own careers and, not incidentally, to profit. Moreover, Van Dyke's and Steiner's move accentuated the philosophical and temperamental differences between the members of Frontier Films. Alexander points out that

> Steiner's vital, good-natured cheerfulness and Van Dyke's American romanticism grated sharply against the tougher, more caustic way in which Hurwitz and Strand regarded the ills of contemporary America. It is not surprising, therefore, that *The City* and *Native Land* are very different films. (181)

In fact, Paul Strand's and Leo Hurwitz's *Native Land* (1942), the final and most distinguished release of the Frontier Films Group, further divided the group from the beginning (when it was titled *Labor Spy*).[25]

NATIVE LAND (1942)

According to Alexander, *Native Land* was intended to reflect their sense of being outsiders—outside the mainstream of American culture as the sons of Jewish immigrants, and outside the mainstream of American film production as politically-committed filmmakers. Like Lorentz's *The Fight for Life,* it is a reenactment, using professional actors, and like the Lorentz film, it is an angry indictment of social injustice. Concerned with personal and civil rights, *Native Land* depicts violations of the Bill of Rights as recorded in actual testimony before the Senate Civil Liberties Committee hearings in 1938. The film's theme is the irony of injustice in a land of independence and freedom, the irony of tyranny and conspiracy in the land of the Bill of Rights. But this broad focus is quickly narrowed to the American labor movement in its struggle to organize in the post-Depression years. In four separate episodes (Midwest farm, big city, Southern village, and industrial town), the film depicts actual incidents of murder and brutality, atrocities committed against the "little people . . . who take the Bill of Rights for granted." It is in these episodes that the film shows its strength, yet the lack of overall cohesiveness dulls its focus and weakens its message. While the episodes are related in theme, the argument is not always clear. The "enemy within" includes spies, private armies, strike breakers, militant and armed groups such as the Ku Klux Klan, and profit-hungry indus-

Native Land (Paul Strand and Leo Hurwitz, USA, 1942)

trialists, but the film does not name these forces, and only identifies them as "the big shots," "the interests," and the "powerful corporations." At the same time, it depicts the union members as the "new pioneers" who "put the Bill of Rights into action." Although Ernest Callenbach finds that its positive patriotism "now sounds suspicious to many radicals,"[26] *Native Land* is a gripping, patriotic film; but as an indictment of the "handful of fascist-minded corporations," it remains uneven despite its realism.[27]

Made as a tribute to the common working man, *Native Land* is also distinguished by the fusion of music, narration, and photography in the development of its theme. Paul Strand's photography creates a dark, brooding, paranoid mood, full of suspicion, fear, and suspense; his restless and constantly moving camera records the ironic duality of exterior growth and interior decay. Especially in the prologue, the photography is matched by the superb editing rhythm; but in the sequences featuring the professional actors, who detract from the film's sense of actuality, another directorial hand is evident, and the visual exposition is often slow and clumsy. In Strand's sequences, however, there is superb experimentation and creative photography. David Wolff's [Ben Maddow] narrative, spoken eloquently by Paul Robeson, is stirring, not only in its recounting of past terrors, but also in its reassurance that honest men are joining together, cooperating, to combat the "enemy within."

Native Land is a strong, powerful documentary film that narrowly misses being a great one. Michael Klein argues that it deserves a special place in the history of the nonfiction film for at least three reasons:

> First of all, it is one of a handful of films (*Salt of the Earth* is another) that gives a realistic and dignified picture of average working class Americans, at the same time focusing on an experience of great social importance in their lives (trade unionism). The sense of people's faces, landscapes, and buildings that distinguishes Paul Strand's photography also characterizes his camerawork, while Howard Da Silva and the other actors portray working class roles with low key realism. Second, it presents a key aspect of the experience of the 1930's through a complex montage of incidents and genres: song, commentary, landscape (natural and industrial), symbolism, statues, documentary reportage footage, re-enactment of historical events, fictional narrative, WPA camera style, social realism, *film noir*. Third, it situates these elements in a complex structure which both unifies the film, extends its meaning, and works rhetorically in relation to the audience.[28]

As a film about the working class, it is far bolder than anything Grierson ever attempted. Trade unionism is seldom, if ever, mentioned in the British documentaries of the 1930s.

An eloquent statement for freedom and democracy, marked by deep humanistic concern, *Native Land* recalls the strengths of the past, opens the wounds of the present, and calls a challenge to the future. In this aspect, Alexander (238) compares it to Marcel Ophuls's *The Sorrow and the Pity* because it "reminds us of something potential in ourselves." After *Native Land,* Hurwitz's filmmaking career included educational films, commercial films, and films on art; among these are *The Museum and the Fury* (1956), *Verdict for Tomorrow* (1961), on the Adolf Eichmann trial; *In Search of Hart Crane* (1966), an excellent film about the elusive American poet; *Discovery in a Landscape* (1970), and *Dialogue With a Woman Departed* (1980), a complex portrait of his wife and coworker, Peggy Lawson.

After *Native Land,* the American leftist filmmaking movement continued to produce such films as Sheldon Dick's *Men and Dust* (1940) and John Ferno's and Julian Roffman's *And So They Live* (1940). Influenced by *The Plow That Broke the Plains* and *The River,* as well as by the militancy of the Frontier Film Group, the Ferno-Roffman film is about an outdated school in a backward mountain community. While it is neither so poetic as the Lorentz films, nor so direct as the Frontier films, it effectively leaves an overall impression of despair.[29] Another more effective film on the same subject is Willard Van Dyke's *The Children Must Learn* (1940). However, these films were not enough to sustain the movement, which was diminished in strength and output, not so much through any lack of commitment of those filmmakers involved, but rather through internal factors (disagreement and defection to independent or commercial filmmaking) and external ones (the impending world war).

PARE LORENTZ

Pare Lorentz was the person most responsible for the growth and development of American nonfiction filmmaking in the United States during the 1930s.[30] His achievements include directing three distinguished films (*The Plow That Broke the Plains, The River,* and *The Fight for Life*), producing two others (Ivens's *Power and the Land* and Flaherty's *The Land*), and, through his influence on President Franklin D. Roosevelt, helping to create the U.S. Film Service (USFS) in 1938. At this time, the United States was facing great problems caused, in part, by the Depression, including unemployment, a migrant population, and the need for water and soil conservation.[31] Lorentz's enthusiasm for America, for examining American problems, and for producing American films suited the period of the New Deal; he was a dedicated patriot who made films stressing the difference between American ideals and social reality.

Lorentz believed that citizens should ask the government for explanation, information, and direction to help them solve their problems, instead of just expecting the government to provide massive programs of financial support. He was also convinced that, given Hollywood's lack of interest, the government should accept the responsibility of producing films that dealt with the major contemporary problems. As we have seen, various American government agencies had made informational, training, and propaganda films since the beginning of the century, but there was no official, organized production effort until the short-lived USFS was established. As a student of film, Lorentz believed that a government-produced film could be both aesthetically pleasing and politically relevant. In theory, Lorentz and Grierson would seem to agree; however, Lorentz's films consistently achieve an

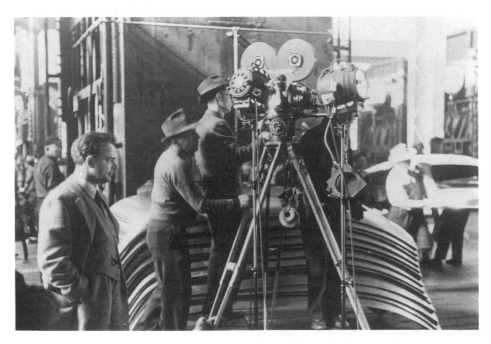

Pare Lorentz (1905–   ) [Lorentz at left of frame]

artistic distinction, blending sight, sound, and theme in a way that few Grierson productions (*Night Mail* is an exception) ever matched.

The Plow That Broke the Plains *(1936)*

Lorentz's first film, *The Plow That Broke the Plains*, depicts the social and economic effects of the Dust Bowl crisis with the sensitivity that characterizes two other works of the period: John Steinbeck's novel, *The Grapes of Wrath*, and the Walker Evans-James Agee photograph-text collaboration, *Let Us Now Praise Famous Men*.[32] Produced by the U.S. Resettlement Administration, the film sketches the history of the Great Plains—from the Westward movement and the settlement of the prairies by cattlemen and farmers, to the agricultural boom created by the First World War, to the chaos and despair caused by technological progress, the stock market crash, Depression, and drought and dust storms—combining factual footage to make a persuasive argument for the conservation of human and natural resources.[33] In its visual images, the film is as striking and as memorable as the bare, shocking photographs made by the masters of American documentary photography: Walker Evans, Dorothea Lange, Ben Shahn, Russell Lee, Margaret Bourke-White, Roy Stryker, and others. In its use of sound, it resembles *Night Mail*, begun in the same year. Like *Night Mail*, it praises men, not for their efficiency, but for their endurance in the face of inefficiency, carelessness, and greed—their own and others'. Unlike *Night Mail*, however, it has a political and social axe to grind.

The documentary argument of the film is presented in a titled prologue rather than in continuous narration, but the overall effect of its discontinuous and ironic imagery, commentary, music, and sound succeed in accomplishing what a more continuous set of cinematic elements would achieve in *The River*. Much of the film's strength lies in its often ironic juxtaposition of images and sound (such as the counterpoint image of tractors and tanks against the sound of threshing machines and bullets). Nevertheless, *The Plow That Broke the Plains* was made in the cutting room, not from a prepared shooting script, and, therefore, while the rhythm of the film's progression reflects situations as different as languorous, ripe wheat fields and whirling dust storms, it lacks the operatic buildup and excitement of *The River*. Within this flawed whole, only Virgil Thomson's music retains a lasting distinction. Thomson's score is magnificent Americana, sprightly and lively when the film depicts good times, and sonorous and ironic in its use of religious anthems and hymns when it depicts bad times after the dust storms. With insight and honesty, Lorentz reviewed his own film:

> . . . with some outstanding photography and music, *The Plow That Broke the Plains* is an unusual motion picture which might have been a really great one had the story and construction been up to the rest of the workmanship. As it is, it tells the story of the Plains and it tells it with some emotional value—an emotion that springs out of the soil itself. Our heroine is the grass, our villain the sun and the wind, our players the actual farmers living in the Plains country. It is a melodrama of nature, the tragedy of turning grass into dust, a melodrama that only Carl Sandburg or Willa Cather perhaps could tell as it should be told. (Lorentz quoted in MacCann, *The People's Films*, 66)

The Plow That Broke the Plains (Pare Lorentz, USA, 1936)

Lorentz had found his vision of America, if not the appropriate style with which to express it, and he was encouraged by the critical success that greeted the film's commercial release in major theaters across the country. Despite Congressional doubts about the film's content and intentions (was it information or propaganda, or both?) and the overtones from the presidential campaign between Franklin D. Roosevelt and Alfred M. Landon that marred its reception in some areas, *The Plow That Broke the Plains* established the direction that the American documentary film was to take until the outbreak of the Second World War. A year later, in *The River*, Lorentz was to find the style to match his vision.

The River *(1937)*

For Lorentz, American history held the key to American destiny. In *The Plow That Broke the Plains*, he had traced the history of the Great Plains; in *The River*, he traced the history of the Mississippi River and its tributaries to begin a haunting indictment of our misuse of natural resources that was, at the same time, an uplifting tribute to conservation.[34] By recounting the story of the river, Lorentz is telling the story of the precarious ecological balance of people, land, water, and crops that depend upon it. His theme is a simple one: improper planting, forestry, and harvesting deplete the land; depleted land cannot hold the top soil, and erosion results;

erosion leads to floods; and floods cripple agriculture, industry, and people. *The River* is a liberal, sentimental film, at times echoing Rooseveltian rhetoric: "'ill clad, ill housed, ill fed'—and in the greatest river valley in the world!" But Lorentz's narration does not reflect political rhetoric so much as it does the influence of Walt Whitman's transcendent free verse. The prologue begins:

> From as far West as Idaho,
> Down from the glacier peaks of the Rockies—
> From as far East as New York,
> Down from the turkey ridges of the Alleghenies
> Down from Minnesota, twenty five hundred miles,
> The Mississippi River runs to the Gulf.
> Carrying every drop of water, that flows down two-thirds of the continent,
> Carrying every brook and rill, rivulet and creek,
> Carrying all the rivers that run down two-thirds the continent
> The Mississippi runs to the Gulf of Mexico.
> Down the Yellowstone, the Milk, the White and Cheyenne;
> The Cannonball, the Musselshell, the James and the Sioux;
> Down the Judith, the Grand, the Osage, and the Platte,
> The Skunk, the Salt, the Black, and Minnesota;
> Down the Rock, the Illinois, and the Kankakee,
> The Allegheny, the Monongahela, Kanawha, and Muskingum;
> Down the Miami, the Wabash, the Licking and the Green
> The Cumberland, the Kentucky, and the Tennessee;
> Down the Ouchita, the Wichita, the Red, and Yazoo—
> Down the Missouri three thousand miles from the Rockies;
> Down the Ohio a thousand miles from the Alleghenies;
> Down the Arkansas fifteen hundred miles from the Great Divide;
> Down the Red, a thousand miles from Texas;
> Down the great Valley, twenty-five hundred miles from Minnesota,
> Carrying every rivulet and brook, creek and rill,
> Carrying all the rivers that run down two-thirds the continent—
> The Mississippi runs to the Gulf.[35]

The structure of the film's narrative is chronological, but also somewhat circular. As the narrator of the prologue suggests, *The River* begins with the growth of the Mississippi River from its tributaries all over the central part of the United States. It shows the devastating of forestry and cotton farming on the overused land, depicts the growth of the heavy industries that exploited the river valleys, records the havoc created by the flooding produced by these conditions, and finally reaches the inevitable conclusion that poor land makes poor people. The epilogue recounts the work of the Tennessee Valley Authority in helping to restore the Mississippi River and its tributary system to something approximating its earlier balance. The story, then, is simple, but its treatment is complex.

The River is a masterpiece, almost operatic in its unifying sight and sound, drama and fact. The three major sequences of the film—water, lumber, flood— open with stirring roll calls of the names of American rivers, trees, and flooded towns; these epic catalogs are repeated for emphasis and elaboration at other times. Virgil Thomson's score establishes basic motifs for each sequence, and mixes hymnlike sonorities with ragtime syncopation, not only echoing the richness of American music, but also suggesting the ambiguity and unpredictability of the great river. The superb cinematography is by Willard Van Dyke, Floyd Crosby, and Stacey Woodward, with many shots remaining vivid long after one has seen the film.[36] While most of the footage was shot directly on location without a shooting script, and assembled later in New York by Lorentz, the film also includes some footage from two Hollywood films, *Come and Get It* and *Showboat,* as well as newsreel footage. Especially in the Eisensteinian montage that depicts the history of erosion and floods from 1902 to 1937, the film's predominant visual movement—from left to right, and from top to bottom—evokes a sense of destiny. A dripping icicle begins the flow; with the passing years, this trickle becomes a stream, and the streams become rivers, later tearing across the land to become floods. As the flood expands, the shots expand in scope; to increase the tension and to prepare for the climax, Lorentz intercuts shots of turbulent water with those showing its downward flow. The narrator once again calls the roll of rivers and cities; large sections of the previous narration are repeated as the flood and the film build to a dramatic climax. Because its values are only partly literary, *The River* defies description. A synopsis cannot capture the cumulative effect of the free verse narration or the music.[37] One long remembers the drum rolls that underscore the growth of the cotton and lumber industries, the ominous sound of dripping water that is soon to become a raging torrent, and the shots of denuded forests in the dim light: "We cut the top off Pennsylvania and sent it down the river." Repeatedly, the narration questions the value of progress: "But at what a cost!"

From the film's skillful use of the images and sounds of Americana—names, maps, songs, musical themes—the viewer begins to recognize that the deterioration of the Mississippi River is an American problem, transcending state boundaries and historical periods, a problem that will ultimately deplete the entire nation economically and spiritually. Unfortunately, because Lorentz was obligated to show what the government was doing to solve the problem, the last one-third of the film (approximately ten minutes) lacks the imagination of the first two-thirds. This concluding section is devoted to a straightforward account of the progress made by the Tennessee Valley Authority and the Farm Security Administration. While it records substantial improvement and predicts great hope for the future, the sequence does not seem to be wholly integrated into the film.

Both *The Plow That Broke the Plains* and *The River* were well-received by the critics and seen by thousands of people in American motion picture theatres. According to MacCann, *The Plow* was sold by the Resettlement Administration for some 3,000 independent theatre showings (71); *The River,* released theatrically by Paramount Pictures, had an even more astonishing success for a short film in theatrical distribution (76–77). When *The River* was considered as a possible nominee for the Academy Award for a short film, Walt Disney, among other Hollywood leaders, objected on the grounds that it would create an unhealthy precedent for competition between government and private enterprise (Snyder 63–78). In London, however, *The River* was warmly received by Grierson and Flaherty, and, in competition with Leni Riefenstahl's *Olympia,* won the "Best Documentary" award at the 1938 Venice Film Festival.[38]

This international recognition had both immediate and far-reaching effects for the nonfiction film in the United States. The public had already responded favorably to the popular "March of Time" films, and now they began to show an interest in original, imaginative American nonfiction films. On another level, serious film students and critics began to pay attention to the development of the genre. And, as we have seen, in a commercial move marking a new stage in independent film production, as well as causing a major crisis within leftist filmmaking circles, Willard Van Dyke and Ralph Steiner departed from the Frontier Film Group to form American Documentary Films, Inc. In fact, at this point, the interest in documentary films dealing with contemporary problems exceeded the number of films being made. This public interest was stimulated by the success of *The Plow* and *The River* and the comprehensive program of nonfiction films shown at the 1939 New York World's Fair. As a result of this new popularity, corporations and foundations began to sponsor more films; nonfiction filmmakers formed new production groups to handle the more ambitious productions coming their way; the Rockefeller Foundation established the American Film Center to produce films for educational and public purposes; and the Association of Documentary Film Producers was established "to develop the artistic and technical standards of independent, creative documentary films."[39] Before the Second World War, Hollywood had little or no interest in producing nonfiction films, which were thought to be noncommercial, and the few independent production units could not afford to produce enough films to satisfy the potential noncommercial audience. Thus, it was left to the United States government to continue and increase its support for the production of films through the establishment of the United States Film Service.

The United States Film Service

Established in August, 1938, with Pare Lorentz as its first director, the United States Film Service (USFS) had two basic purposes: to educate government employees and to inform the public about ways of solving contemporary problems.[40] While it had the potential to become as important as the GPO Film Unit, the USFS was hampered from the beginning by Congressional discussion over the propriety and politics of the project and by a general lack of funds for film production.[41] The films produced by the unit include *The Fight for Life* (1940), *Power and the Land* (1940), and *The Land* (1942, begun by the USFS but completed under the Agricultural Adjustment Administration).

The Fight for Life *(1940)*

After devoting several years to depicting the problems of soil and water conservation, Pare Lorentz next turned his attention to an equally important national problem: public health. He was disturbed by the interrelationship of infant and maternal mortality, unemployed workers, and malnutrition. To present some solutions to these problems, he made *The Fight for Life* (1940), a feature-length film, using professional actors, real locations, and constructed sets, with a fully integrated script of dialogue and a dramatic musical score. In both theory and practice, this film combines documentary and theatrical approaches in a new form. Like Lorentz's earlier films, it deals with a powerful public issue, and like them, it is not only far ahead of its time in its hard-hitting, honest approach, but also remains a valid treatment of a continuing national problem.[42]

The Fight for Life takes an especially strong stand against what, in its view, are the "tragic accidents" that occur in the maternity wards of the nation's general hospitals. Thus, it argues forcefully that obstetricians and other doctors who handle childbirth cases should receive better training and that expectant mothers and their children should receive better prenatal and postnatal care and proper diet. Its ideal figure is the tough, dedicated doctor, concerned with his patients' health, the condition of the hospital with which he is affiliated, and the well-being of his city. In so doing, it takes the controversial stand that doctors should be prepared to serve the nation's poor, who, without money and information, often cannot benefit from proper medical care.

The Fight for Life opens with an unidentified surgical procedure taking place in a hospital operating room. We see the tense faces of nurses and doctors, and hear the sound of the patient's heartbeat on the sound track. This suspense is relieved only with the camera's revelation that a child has been born. Everything appears to be normal, but the mother's heart fails; despite a fight for her life, she dies. The young attending physician, disillusioned, decides to resume his education at a maternity clinic in the slums to learn the causes of death in childbirth. Up to this point, the film is taut, professional, and gripping. The second part of the film is a straightforward but stiff exposition of the doctor's training and internship, culminating in an actual delivery in a filthy tenement. The film graphically emphasizes the dangers inherent in childbirth at home. In the second of the two dramatic sequences of the film, we follow each step in another difficult childbirth. Here the cinematography is superbly theatrical: characters are presented almost as if in portrait, spotlighted in dark rooms and laboratories. In a home where the husband has left to look for work in another city, the grandmother tells of the hardships that have increased since she was young. Then, underscoring the succession of generations, we see her in soft distance focus in the next room as her grandchild is born in the foreground of the frame. Almost immediately the mother hemorrhages, and the doctor performs emergency surgery. But in contrast to the opening sequences of the film, this patient lives, even though the childbirth and surgery take place in squalid conditions. The crucial importance of proper planning and well-trained doctors is now self-evident.

In comparison with the other American or British nonfiction films of the 1930s, this semifictional documentary can be regarded as too theatrical and too professional. The "performances" of actual farmers (*Power and the Land*) or fishermen (*North Sea*) convey both spontaneity and believability, qualities that are lacking in the characterization of *The Fight for Life*, which uses actors speaking dialogue. On the other hand, this does not detract from the effect of the narration, which is convincing. Under all, Louis Gruenberg's musical score exploits the effect of a heartbeat with drums and strings, creating a rhythm that reminds us of mortality as well as a symphony that affirms life.[43]

Perhaps it was because he wrote and directed his own films, or because he chose distinguished collaborators; whatever the reason, Lorentz was consistently able to produce nonfiction films that have seldom been surpassed in dramatic, visual, and aural intensity. The reasons for Lorentz's success are evident in the films themselves. First, they are notable for their unity of sight, sound (music and narration), and overall sociopolitical understanding. Second, they are unmistakably "American." They resound with a naturalist's love of land, with a poet's love of language, and with a patriot's love of the traditions on which his country was built. Often, like Flaherty's films, they seem basic to the point of innocence, enthusiastic to the point of naïveté, but they are as authentic as Walt Whitman's poetry in their feeling for the country, its people, and their values. Third, while they generally conform to the documentary problem-solution structure, these films rely on varying combinations of repetition, rhythm, and parallel structure; problems presented in the first part of the films are, indeed, solved in the second part, but solved through an artistic juxtaposition of image, sound, and motif with a unity and coherence of development that distinguish them from such comparable films as the British *Housing Problems* or Ivens's *New Earth*. In short, Lorentz's films succeeded in fusing both the British and European documentary film traditions into a format intended to appeal to patriotic emotion and to move audiences to realize that one region's problems were the problems of the whole country.

By bluntly showing the erosion and loss of human and natural resources, Lorentz's films called for social change, not with Grierson's civility or Ivens's bluntness, but with the metaphor, music, and mastery of a poet. They examine the necessity for social change without sacrificing convincing realism, technical brilliance, or poetic strength. However, critics from both political parties made "bitter comments about the balance and truth of *The Plow That Broke the Plains*" (Mac-Cann 80). And Lorentz found himself with a dilemma familiar to other nonfiction filmmakers who have tangled with a government bureaucracy. Like Flaherty and Grierson, he found that a balanced, factual treatment is not easily reconciled with a sweeping, poetic approach. Like Flaherty, Lorentz approaches problems with humanitarian concern; like Grierson, he treats them with sociological realism; and like Ivens, he regards them with compassion. And to his own vision of man's condition, he adds an understanding of the integral relationship of sight and sound that is the equal of any nonfiction filmmaker.[44] Like Flaherty or Ivens, Lorentz was not only a school unto himself, but also an influence on nonfiction filmmaking that challenged the generation of filmmakers to follow.

Robert Flaherty and The Land (1942)
In 1937, Pare Lorentz invited Robert Flaherty to return to the United States to make *The Land* (1942), which Lorentz originally intended to be about the problems of rural Americans displaced by the interrelated phenomena of drought, poor farming methods, and poor management of farm production.[45] What he had

in mind was a bold treatment of the social problems that he himself had dealt with in *The Plow That Broke the Plains*. It is in some ways surprising that Lorentz would have invited Flaherty to make such a straightforward propaganda film and that Flaherty would have accepted. He was returning to the United States after many years of filmmaking around the world, and would have to reacquaint himself with a society about which he now knew very little. But he made it his first objective to explore the country and, in his customary manner, discover the story of the new film through observation. He, his wife, and his crew made three extensive trips across the American landscape to see the cotton fields in the South, mechanized farms in the West, and eroded land and abandoned farms in the dust-bowl states.

Seeing the spectacle of human suffering in America moved Flaherty as no subject had moved him before. The agricultural crisis was a specific, immediate problem of national proportions, what Flaherty called "American refugees wandering in a wasteland of their own making" (quoted in Rotha, ed. Ruby, 193). But he had to reconcile his observer's sympathy with the producer's need to provide social comment through the neat problem-solution pattern by which many traditional documentary films are made. Now, as before, Flaherty proved unable to adapt his intuitive methods to meet the social needs of the documentary film form.

The priorities of the government's task prevented Flaherty from developing some of his characteristic motifs, and the film's episodic script did not permit his customary overlay of slight fictional narrative. Before making *Nanook, Moana,* and *Man of Aran,* Flaherty had lived with members of a family until he felt that he understood them and their lives and could use them to represent the whole community. But in *The Land,* he was looking at a national rather than a local phenomenon, which could not be represented by the plight of a single ideal family.

The Land introduces the theme of the farmers' relation to the soil in highly general terms: Flaherty shows a farmhouse in time of prosperity followed by another farmhouse where "trouble has crept in," for erosion has forced people off their land and onto the roads in search of better soil and work. To emphasize that this problem has no geographical or racial boundaries, Flaherty records conditions in various places in the Midwest and South that have created problems for both white and black families. As Flaherty shows houses, farms, machinery, whole towns abandoned by the people moving westward, his narrative tone combines sentimentality and despair: "We had another name for these people once. We called them pioneers." Russell Lord's text for *The Land* had the characteristically "American" sound of films of the late 1930s and early 1940s, a Whitmanesque tone that was enhanced by Flaherty's reading the narration himself. The first-person-plural narrative effectively involves the viewer ("We came to a town . . . " or "We came upon a scene . . . "). Flaherty's flinty voice suits the expressionless faces of the people on the screen, and he expresses deep concern for them as well as a brief wistfulness for the "old ways" he likes so much.

Later, the film suggests a possible solution for the problem faced by these outcasts on the road: the mechanized government water projects that helped men to cultivate the Western deserts. But the narrator tells us that the "magic of irrigation" benefits the owners rather than the workers, for "it wasn't their water and it isn't their land." Rather, American migrant workers are shown to be exploited by this system, forced to live in filthy camps and paid low wages. The film has moments that evoke the plight of these workers, such as the shot of a boy moving uneasily in his sleep, with his mother commenting, through Flaherty's voice, "He thinks he's picking peas."[46] Suggesting that the efficient machines have become more important than the dignity of the people who serve them, Flaherty admires the machines for their size and power, yet also condemns them for displacing people.

In a juxtaposition of shots illustrating poverty amidst plenty, Flaherty emphasizes the abundance that is locked away in ships and grain elevators, demonstrating that America has enough grain to feed the world, but not its own starving children. In a bit of direct praise for the sponsor, a man comments: "I don't know what some of us would do if it weren't for the food the government gives us." Unlike Lorentz's The Plow That Broke the Plains and The River, the emphasis here is on the people, not the government. Flaherty asserts: "The strength of a man is not great. He has not in his arms and back the colossal strength of a great machine. But a man can think. He can govern. He can plan. The great fact is the land itself and the people and the spirit of the people."

By opening and closing with the framing device of a family, Flaherty attempted to provide with a simple structural device what he was unable to provide through narration. If he does not succeed, it is because, throughout the film, Flaherty's family has neither name nor identity; they are victims, barely able to accommodate their lives to the enemy of agricultural mechanization.[47]

The principal strengths of The Land are in its cinematography and editing, rather than its narrative structure. Flaherty had previously kept his camera still, but he sometimes reframed shots, or used pan and tilt shots when absolutely necessary to keep the subject in frame. Here the dominant visual style of the film is the moving camera, which not only reflects the questioning tone of the narration, but also captures the restless mood of the country. His ceaseless moving, turning, circling, and looking back says more than he does in words. Deep-focus cinematography was evident in American nonfiction film as early as The River (1937), and Flaherty's use of it reflects his nostalgic attitude.[48]

Flaherty worked intuitively, using his eye instead of an exposure meter, shooting what looked or felt right instead of following a script. Thus, his twenty-five-thousand mile exploration of the United States resulted in seventy-five-thousand feet of exposed footage. When Helen van Dongen was called in to edit this footage, she had to meet the difficult challenges of working with a sensitive artist who resisted professional assistance, of developing a visual point-of-view to unify the miles of random footage, and of providing an overall structure for the film; however, there is only so much that even a gifted editor can do with the sort of material Flaherty provided. By repeating certain shots, Van Dongen underscored the prevalence of certain problems, but repetition itself could not correct the structural imbalance of the film. No reconciliation of elements seems possible, whether in the narration, narrative structure, or musical score; in fact, Richard Arnell's insistent, dramatic music tends to overwhelm the images that it accompanies. In an attempt to make some order out of chaos, the last sequence is composed almost entirely of shots already used in the film; this effort to capitalize on their cumulative force is undercut by the narration, which, at the end, seems to have been hastily added in an attempt to add an inspirational note to a narration characterized by a tone of almost unrelieved despair.

When, in April 1942, five months after the United States declared war on Japan, *The Land* was finally released, it was withdrawn almost immediately from general distribution to prevent its use by the enemy in anti-American propaganda films.[49] Thereafter, *The Land* became as much a puzzle to its critics as its creators. Had Flaherty had been able to join his social insight to social comment, he might have produced a very powerful and influential film. Ironically, he resisted compromise with the documentary style and then seemed to abandon not only his own style, but also his traditionally humanistic viewpoint. As a result, *The Land* achieves neither the poetic realism of a typical Flaherty film, which he was not encouraged to make, nor the ideological coherence of a successful documentary film, which he was not capable of making. Both Flaherty's romantic dreams of an old Kentucky farmhouse and his realistic account of the migrant workers' camps are aspects of a larger issue which the film does not confront. Since neither Flaherty nor Lorentz seemed able to define that larger issue, it is not surprising that the film was ambivalent.

What redeems *The Land* is not any neat solution to problems that the social documentary film is supposed to provide, but its haunting images of America's poor and suffering people. It falls short of reaching Griersonian ideals, but it succeeds as a Robert Flaherty film, as a work of keen insight, rugged determination, and visual beauty.

SCREEN JOURNALISM

American Newsreel During the 1930s

Today the newsreel has vanished, but during the 1930s there were large theaters in major cities that screened only newsreels; the programs at virtually every theater included one or two cartoons, a travel film, two or more feature films, and a newsreel. It was a simple genre, relying on actual events for its raw material; the more spectacular the event, the more likely its inclusion.[50] In this colorful decade, there was plenty of action for the newsreel cameras to record. Newsreels presented this material in basic, descriptive terms, within a minimum amount of time. Usually, they were made without bias or viewpoint, although newsreels often took a humorous view of such topics as fashion. The approach to such items as transatlantic ship races or athletic events was often naïve, reflecting a characteristically American enthusiasm for achievement and progress.

Before it was replaced by radio and television news broadcasts, the newsreel provided a graphic, eyewitness account of history that neither newspapers nor magazines such as *Time* or *Life* could match. Moreover, the newsreel also served as a bridge between other forms of the nonfiction film. By the late 1920s, in the

Soviet Union, Esther Shub had discovered what many filmmakers were later to develop, particularly during the second world war: the compilation film made from newsreel footage. In the United States, the newsreel was also the source of such developments in screen journalism as "The March of Time," "This is America," and Nykino's "The World Today."

"The March of Time" (1935–51)

In 1935, producer Louis de Rochemont used the editorial and reportorial resources of Time-Life, Inc., to create the immensely popular, influential series, "The March of Time."[51] Designed to present the "news behind the news" for a mass audience, it represented a wholly original attempt at encouraging the public's awareness of contemporary events. This monthly film magazine borrowed three important features of its presentation from other sources. From journalism, it took the impartial, objective approach of the news story and the analytical approach of the editorial. From fiction films, it adapted the dramatic approach to the telling of current events. Reenactment (and preenactment) is a major issue with such screen magazines as "The March of Time" and "This is America." But while the veneer of research and the tone of authority may promise honesty and objectivity, these films had no reservations about dramatizing the facts and could often be slick and superficial. In the absence of actual footage depicting an historical event, the producers often relied on still photographs of the event or reenactments of it.

Inside Fascist Spain (from "The March of Time" series, USA, 1943)

"The March of Time" is not a newsreel. Raymond Fielding listed a number of differences that distinguished it from the common newsreel:

1. It made no pretense of reporting up-to-the-minute news. It was released only once a month. The regular newsreel was released twice weekly.
2. It dealt with a limited number of subjects in each issue (after May, 1938, with only one subject in each issue). The newsreel dealt with as many as a dozen different topics in each release.
3. Each issue ran as long as twenty minutes, allowing for a fairly leisurely and detailed exposition of subject matter. The American newsreel never ran more than ten minutes, oftentimes less.
4. It was an interpretive, discursive reel which elaborated with maps, diagrams, titles, and supplementary footage upon the issues which it treated. The newsreel, with rare exceptions, treated only the superficialities of day-to-day events.
5. It spent fifty to seventy-five thousand dollars on each issue. The average newsreel company spent eight to twelve thousand dollars on each issue.
6. Both the newsreel and *The March of Time* staged and recreated events, but *The March of Time* did so to a far greater extent, sometimes to the almost complete exclusion of authentic footage. Moreover, it frequently used impersonators of celebrities when it was found that actual footage was not available.
7. The intention of *The March of Time* was to create and exploit controversy and to provoke discussion of politically, economically, and socially touchy subjects. Newsreel producers tried to avoid controversial subject matter at all costs.
8. *The March of Time* was sometimes openly partisan; the newsreel, rarely, and never avowedly so. (*The March of Time: 1935–1951* 75–76)

Typical of "The March of Time" films is *Progressive Education* (1936), a tribute to the "late, great Horace Mann" and the new schools where fun and relevance, not facts and recitations, prepare children for the future. Or *The Movies March On* (1939), a brief history that is less notable for its historical coverage than for its support of the Motion Picture Production Code and the idea of Hollywood's responsibility to the public. Or *Story of the White House* (1936), another misleading title film, which is an account of the New Deal and Franklin D. Roosevelt, not an architectural or cultural history of the President's house. Or *Problems of Working Girls* (1936), an alarming account of the exploitation of small-town girls by New York City businessmen.

"The March of Time," which was influential on the development of the nonfiction film, and screen journalism in particular, created worldwide interest in American nonfiction filmmaking. Perhaps most influential in "The March of Time" format were the use of personal interviews and profiles of important people, the use of diagrams and charts, and the "authority" of its narrative presentation and interpretation of the news. Some scenes were reenacted, and some footage was shot directly for the films, but whatever the source, "The March of Time" capitalized on the area of research and authority that mass-produced journalism can often bring to a story.

Beyond its significance to the development of the newsreel genre, the style of "The March of Time" was frequently imitated and parodied, most memorably in Orson Welles's *Citizen Kane* (1941). The distinguishing characteristics of the Time-Life newsmagazine—histrionic style, ironic presentation, informality, and stentorian "voice of god" narration—provided the source for brilliant parody in the opening of Welles' film. Welles understood that audiences looked on newsreels in general, and "The March of Time" in particular, as reality; the search for the identity and meaning of "Rosebud" is the work of a reporter employed by a very similar series: "News on the March."[52] It is the camera that zooms in on the burning Rosebud, presumably the omniscient camera of the newsreel reporter. Welles's use of this device not only validates the importance of newsreels to the 1930s' movie audience, but also underscores the naïve belief that the exhaustive techniques of mass journalism will produce the truth. In that, Welles not only used Charles Foster Kane as a comment on William Randolph Hearst, but also on Henry Luce, the founder of Time-Life, Inc., a publisher with an influence on the American public far different but even more dominant than Hearst's.

"This is America" (1942–51)
The success of "The March of Time" prompted competition, not only from "The World Today," a Nykino venture that reached a limited audience, but also from "This is America." To provide the thousands of theaters in the RKO chain with a screen magazine, Frederic Ullman, Jr., developed "This is America" (1942–51), a lively, engaging, and sentimental series devoted primarily to the values of small-town America. Its 112 issues cover a vast range of topics, but its focus is narrow, almost always emphasizing traditional America, not, as with "The March of Time," bigness and growth, or, with "The World Today," issues of social justice.[53]

"This is America" celebrated the way of life in small town America during the Second World War: an America that seemed sure of its purpose, if doubtful of its future; an America that was proud of its traditions, if uncertain how to relate those traditions to the presence of its armed forces overseas. In their emphasis on the American way, the films find sources of strength in such familiar subjects as the editors of small town newspapers, the teachers in local high schools, and the participants in town meetings. The people featured in most of the films are the white middle or lower-middle classes, in white-collar or blue-collar jobs, who live in single-family houses located on tree-shaded streets in small towns, who have cheerful children, who attend church, and who are law-abiding. The films are all in black and white, between fifteen and twenty minutes in length, and in almost every one, the well-written narration is spoken by an off-screen narrator who speaks in the voice of an ordinary citizen, not in the "voice of God" style that characterizes "The March of Time."

"This is America" is important in the history of screen journalism, not only as a direct contrast to its better-known competition, "The March of Time," but also as a sustained series that produced many imaginative films. While the weaknesses of both series include a lack of critical focus and a reliance on clichés that reminds us of their function as mass-appeal entertainment, their strength lies in their consistently optimistic vision of America.

WILLARD VAN DYKE

As cinematographer, writer, director, and producer, Willard Van Dyke was a leader among American nonfiction film makers from 1939 when *The City* forged the link between the politics of Ivens, the poetry of Lorentz, and the nonfiction films of the 1940s.[54] After studying with Edward Weston, Van Dyke began his career as a still photographer, but soon learned the art of cinematography. In 1936, he joined Stacey Woodward and Floyd Crosby as a cameraman on *The River,* and he served as an assistant director for some sequences when Lorentz was not on location.[55] He was also associated with Frontier Films, but, as discussed above, he and Steiner broke away from the group when they received the commission to make *The City.*[56]

Van Dyke made more than fifty films, most of which have two distinguishing characteristics: an interest in cinematic experimentation and an instinctive feeling for the poetry in the lives and activities of ordinary people. Where Lorentz is at his best with the epic sweep and scope of national problems, Van Dyke excels in depicting the virtues of individual people. Where Lorentz sings of America in the Whitman tradition, Van Dyke tells stories in the tradition of Carl Sandburg. And where Lorentz achieves an operatic blend of cinematography, narration, and music, Van Dyke works with the incisive skill of a great photographer for whom the image is all.[57] Each of Van Dyke's films reveals a fresh approach, visual sensitivity, humorous insight, and reportorial objectivity. They are the films of a craftsman committed not to one ideology or vision, but to an imaginative joy in the world around him.

The City (1939)

Although *The City* (1939) is notable as Van Dyke's first important work and is often cited as Van Dyke's film, it represents the collaboration of many important talents: Ralph Steiner, the producer and, with Van Dyke, codirector and co-cinematographer; Henwar Rodakiewicz, the associate producer, whose script was based on an outline by Pare Lorentz; Lewis Mumford, the expert on cities, who wrote the narration; and Aaron Copland, who wrote the music.[58] In the words of its narration, *The City* is about "the spectacle of misapplied human power," or, more specifically, the mess of American cities. A visionary film sponsored by the American Institute of Planners, and released at the 1939 World's Fair,[59] it seeks to arouse public interest in the quality of city life by showing the evolution of city planning in four phases: the new England town, the unplanned industrial community, the congested metropolis, and the "new city" of the sponsor's dreams.

The City is a social documentary in its subject matter, problem-solution structure, and demand for change: "There must be something better. Why can't we have it?" The film derives its visionary tone from its feeling for the common man and for

The City (Willard Van Dyke and Ralph Steiner, USA, 1939)

the experiences shared by all Americans. Although the narrator regrets that American cities have grown away from the harmony between the soil and the people that characterized New England towns, his optimism seems to advocate further unchecked growth rather than careful planning: "Just watch us grow. The scales won't hold us." The film's conclusion, as idealistic as its subject, foresees a future city of white middle-class homogeneity.

In the first part of the film, the New England town, built around a central marketplace, depends on the town meeting for harmony and balance: "The town was us and we were part of it." The idyllic mood and music of this sequence give way to railroad, steam, and steel, as we shift to the dirt, smoke, and crowded living conditions of an ugly mining town: "Smoke makes prosperity, no matter if you choke on it." Now, the film becomes contemporary, pointing out problems that still plague American cities: congestion, pollution, poor education, and a sense of uselessness in many people's lives. The third episode focuses on New York City with an ironic comment on reality—"The people, perhaps"—altering the positive force of Carl Sandburg's famous phrase, "The people, yes!" In the tradition of the "city symphony," Van Dyke and Steiner capture the rhythm of New York with humor and insight. We see rush hour traffic, regimented office work, garbage and congestion, much of it in photography that has the hard-edged graphic qualities of postwar neorealism. Then, as now, it was difficult to cross the street, get a cab, or find a peaceful spot for a picnic. The film's most famous sequence depicts a high-speed lunch hour through a rapidly cut montage of efficient lunch counters, mechanized sandwich assembly, and, inevitably, indigestion. In a concluding montage of signs, New York, a "new city" once, seems to be transformed into "No York," a dead city.

As the second episode was preceded by a sequence depicting the early industrial growth brought by steam and steel, the fourth episode is introduced by sophisticated methods of construction, transportation, and, of course, city planning. The "new city" represents a move back to nature, achieved through man's command of his technology and the cooperation between the various elements of power, communications, and industry. Freeways bypass the planned town, greenbelts provide plenty of space in which to play, and children swim in a clear pond instead of a dirty city river. This visionary look into the future ignores the imminent destructive reality of the Second World War. In the "new city," there is no poverty, no race or class distinction, no misused human resources. The viewers are challenged to choose between the new city and the old. While there is little doubt that they would have chosen the new city, we now can only look back wistfully; in the fifty years since the film was released, the problems it depicts have only grown worse. Megalopolis has replaced metropolis, and the "new city" remains on the drawing boards of the city planners.

While *The City* was not altogether correct in its prophecy, it remains an excellent example of the American social documentary film, one distinguished by its cinematography, narration, editing, and sound recording. Aaron Copland's musical score, a delightful piece of Americana, strikes just the right note between a nostalgia for the past and a feeling for the present. *The City* represents a sophisticated, mature approach to a complex problem, marred only by an oversimplified solution. As the cooperative effort of several major talents, it deserves study in relation to other contemporary collaborative productions: *Night Mail, The River, The Spanish Earth,* and *Power and the Land.*

After *The City*, Van Dyke's career was prolific. In 1940, he released five films: *Valley Town*, a study of the human consequences of automating a steel town; *The Children Must Learn*, the story of an experiment in education in the Kentucky mountains; *Sarah Lawrence*, the brief biography of a Sarah Lawrence College student; *To Hear Your Banjo Play*, a study of several folk songs by Pete Seeger; and *Tall Tales*, an examination of three songs by Josh White and Burl Ives. Of these five films, *Valley Town* and *The Children Must Learn* are the most important.

The question of narration in the social documentary poses problems for filmmakers. The director can choose, among others, the omniscient narrator, the poetic commentator, the authoritative "voice of god," or the first-person narrator; he can, in addition, use prose, poetry, free verse, song, chant, or a combination of these. In *Valley Town*, Van Dyke uses narrative and song. The voice of an affable mayor delivers the first-person narration (by Spencer Pollard and David Wolff [Ben Maddow]), and although, in its feeling for America, it resembles Lorentz's style of narration, it is neither as poetic nor as effective. The emphasis in this film is on the problem, not the solution. As automation revolutionizes American industry, it creates a pool of trained men without jobs. Training for new jobs is one of the solutions suggested by the film, but it is more concerned with presenting a bitter picture of men out of work, waiting without hope for some answer to their problem. This theme is emphasized and distinguished by the film's imaginative use of song soliloquy, supplementing the narrative, to record the disillusion and despair of a typical miner and his wife. However, this soliloquy, part of a musical score by Marc Blitzstein that is an integral part of the film, is more successful as an experiment in narrative style than as communication. In *The Children Must Learn,* Van Dyke used a spoken narration that is omniscient, yet soft in its effect, as well as folk songs, sung by a chorus. Overall, the sound here solves the narrative problems of *Valley Town,* especially when the images are ironically juxtaposed with the music.

During the Second World War, Van Dyke worked with the U.S. Office of War Information (OWI) in creating a series of films designed to project the American way of life to audiences abroad (see chapter 10). After the war, he continued his career as an independent producer and director, and, in 1965, became the director of the Department of Film of the Museum of Modern Art in New York, a position he held until 1974.

The nonfiction film flourished in the United States during the 1930s, with various directors emerging as leaders. The romantic documentary advanced under Flaherty; the political documentary under Ivens; and the social documentary under Lorentz and Van Dyke. These and other filmmakers produced large numbers of films, either in collaborative efforts, such as those that characterized the leftist movement, or independent units, such as those that splintered off from the various radical movements. Experiments with cinematography, sound, narration, music, and color helped to expand the potentialities of the nonfiction film. Advances in financing and distribution made films more readily available to mass audiences, increasing their interest in films that broadened their knowledge and helped them to form opinions about contemporary events. With the outbreak of the Second World War in 1939, the American nonfiction film, which had developed almost to full maturity during the 1930s, assumed new responsibilities and created new cinematic forms.

PART THREE

(1939–1945)

Nonfiction Films for World War II

8

British Films for World War II

World War II greatly enhanced the development, use, and stature of the nonfiction film, which proved to be an important element in the wartime strategy of the global conflict. Many countries used the nonfiction film not only to make a documentary record of significant military maneuvers and related events, activities, and operations, but also to inform and report, teach and train, educate, improve morale, explain government policies, win cooperation, boost production, persuade, and, sometimes, even to entertain.

Military and civilian strategists on both sides of the conflict realized, more fully than they did in World War I, the important role that motion pictures could play in modern warfare. Mobile units could show films anywhere—in the field, in military hospitals, in jungle outposts, in industrial plants, and in civilian theatres. Films could train soldiers and industrial workers; they could create or influence opinion, strengthen attitudes, and stimulate emotions; and they could be invaluable in the scientific and tactical aspects of military reconnaissance and combat.[1] The power of the cinema as a strategic tool in wartime was demonstrated repeatedly during World War II, and a German general is reported to have declared that the opponent with the best cameras would be the victor.[2]

World War II, a military conflict between the Allies (Great Britain, Russia, and the United States) and the Axis (Germany, Italy, and Japan) also involved a conflict between the propaganda and counterpropaganda films of those powers. Their military goals and propaganda films were surprisingly similar. Each side believed it was pursuing the right goals, used all the strategic means in its power to justify its mandate, and was certain that it would be victorious. The Nazis, who were the first to produce overt propaganda films for the war, set the tone for the cinematic conflict. The British, with their documentary tradition, made a comparatively easy shift from prewar to wartime nonfiction film production. American filmmakers were influenced by the hard-hitting style of the Nazi films, and produced what was not only the largest and most consistent, but also the best body of films of the war. Each side in this global conflict made films that expressed outrage at the enemy's actions, compassion for the enemy's victims, and righteousness about its own responses. Each used formal elements— particularly music and narration—to establish and reinforce its case. From a neutral viewpoint, free from national or political allegiance, one may find little difference between Fritz Hippler's *Campaign in Poland* and John Ford's *The Battle of Midway*. Both had a report to make, and a job to do, and both did these with distinctive style.

The discussion in the following three chapters looks at the similarities, as well as the differences, in wartime nonfiction films. The British films (chapter 8) provide an eloquent record of British unity, patriotism, and humanity in a time of national peril, qualities that helped Britain to win the war. Like their predecessors of the prewar period, the British documentaries of the 1940s were professional and accomplished achievements in the film art; however, they treated social problems more directly and incisively than the earlier films. They were different also in their extensive use of written dialogue, studio sets, professional actors (in addition to the actual people of the situation being filmed), diagrams, and multivoice narration. In short, the British documentary filmmakers continued to be professional in their treatment of subject, accomplished in their cinematography and editing, unrestrained by earlier notions of realism, and experimental in their use of sound. Above all, their films preserved the familiar British characteristics of understatement, thoroughness, clarity, and humor.

Unlike the British or the Americans, who had used the nonfiction film primarily for social purposes during the 1930s, the Nazi Party had perfected the use of propaganda film primarily for its own political purposes (chapter 9). Their films aimed at repressing the viewers' ability to think critically or to form their own conclusions. They created a vision of a new world that exalted Aryan supremacy and promoted anti-Semitism, the "final solution," an antilabor position, and world conquest. Their policies are bellicose, their tone strident.

Many American wartime films (chapter 10) were equally rough in tone, for American strategists and filmmakers had studied the Nazi examples and recognized their quality. The United States entered the war almost two years after the other major powers, and thus had the advantage of adopting both Axis and Allied methods in their production or using their footage in compilation films such as those in the "Why We Fight" series. In that time, the American government also saw how effectively both the allies and the enemy were using nonfiction film and provided a substantial budget for its production in this country.[3] The net result of this effort was hundreds of films, many of which remain important to nonfiction film history, as well as to social and military history.[4]

Before the war, the documentary genre, in particular, was principally concerned with stimulating constructive and critical thinking and with shaping or spreading opinions and ideas for the good of mankind. The majority of nonfiction films made during the war were also concerned with teaching and information, but they were based on the fundamental values of the countries which made them. They may not have called upon the audience to think critically or to draw logical conclusions, but they were quick to be righteous about their own motives or to pass judgment on the motives of their enemies.

ORGANIZING FOR WAR-FILM PRODUCTION

During the 1930s, nonfiction filmmakers developed diverse cinematic styles appropriate to their various goals and different audiences. In the sense that they were creating new forms, their work was experimental; in fact, the films that they made were regularly misunderstood as educational, mistrusted as propaganda, and misused as advertising. Overall, documentary and factual films were a force for social reconstruction during the years of the great Depression; but, toward the end of the decade, World War II war turned the world's attention from national to international problems, and such issues as improving education, housing, and environmental conditions became secondary to the larger issues of war and peace.

By September 1939, when Great Britain declared war on Germany, British documentary filmmakers inside and outside the GPO Film Unit were ready to turn their attention to the production of factual, informational, and propaganda films for the Second World War. Just as they had systematically and collaboratively developed their film aesthetics to fulfill social goals, they would now confront such challenges as planning for civilian and military communications in wartime. Just as government sponsorship of films was being phased out in favor of commercial and institutional sponsorship, the government would once again provide support for a full program of propaganda and counterpropaganda. And just as cinematic experimentation appeared to have reached its peak, the war would bring a need for innovative filmmaking. The British could accommodate to these broad changes because they had a strong background in many formats of nonfiction film production, as well as an audience familiar with, and supportive of, their work.

1940 was the turning point, both for British politics and the British film industry.[5] In May 1940, Winston Churchill replaced Neville Chamberlain as prime minister. Under the wartime reorganization of the cabinet, the Board of Trade became responsible for the economic health of the film industry, while the Ministry of Information (MOI) was responsible for involving the film industry in the war effort and for supervising all film production. However, in their early planning for the role that nonfiction film might play in the war effort, British government officials neither involved the leaders of the documentary film movement nor anticipated that official film production would take place on the massive scale that it eventually did. In time, the bureaucrats relinquished their early misgivings about the filmmakers' positions on public policy issues, and with Grierson—the principal source of their antagonism—busy establishing the National Film Board in Canada, the documentary group "became a major influence in film production policy" (Swann 250). The movement was without a leader, and although the government did not want the documentarists to take part in formulating the strategy for wartime production, they did want the various production units to remain in operation. Yet, during the first year of the war, several major figures—among them, Basil Wright, Arthur Elton, Edgar Anstey, and Paul Rotha—were not involved in MOI production. In contrast to what was occurring in England, Grierson became a leading influence upon Canada's official propaganda policy.

The work of the MOI, like that of most bureaucracies, was perennially hindered by issues of policy and personnel, and, because of this, war film production began slowly. Throughout the war, there was no uniform British policy on the role or importance of film in the information effort (radio and the press were considered more important); as a result, questions relating to morale and propaganda (particularly as defined by the Nazis) were often the subjects of debate and disagreement. Most people acknowledged that film had a considerable value in entertaining, informing, and raising morale, both at home and among the troops; but inside and outside the government, many expressed serious reservations about using the British film industry for propaganda, doubting the importance of propagandist films to British strategy. Valuable production time was lost as the MOI engaged in this internal policy struggle between the idealists and the realists. However, as did their counterparts in the United States, the realist filmmakers prevailed, arguing, as did Ralph Elton, that "the public, if they were going to fight at all, had better know what they were fighting about" (quoted in Sussex 119–20). However, Paul Rotha accurately observed that ultimately "there was no real common policy except that their [the MOI's] films, good though some of them were technically, were alleged to be what was called in the 'national interest.' "[6]

As the war progressed, these issues became less important, with the general practice of "projecting" Britain taking the place of a more carefully articulated policy.[7] As Grierson had already learned, the British government preferred to use the nonfiction film to preserve and project the national image rather than to change public opinion. Gary Evans writes:

> Britain's Ministry of Information became an indifferent step-parent to the first documentary school and bore a large part of the responsibility for undermining the morale and sense of élan which Grierson had nurtured so carefully for so long. The British documentary movement floundered about during the conflict. Its wartime documentaries suffered a lack of thematic coherence because the Churchill government chose not to enunciate war aims. . . . Churchill treated information as a whole with relative indifference. (49)

Thus, without a sole leader of Grierson's stature to keep the documentary idea alive, and with an official reluctance to make tough films, the British produced competent films, but, for example, never achieved the hard, swift, stirring precision of Frank Capra's "Why We Fight" series. Their highest achievement lay in another kind of propaganda: the comparatively soft, slow, and lyric films of Humphrey Jennings. In short, while the wartime films reached a vast audience, the quality of these films reinforces Sussex's conclusion that the MOI never believed that government-produced wartime nonfiction film could be as effective as the products of the commercial studios (Sussex 160).

At the outset, the MOI Films Division also had problems with leadership. In the eight months between September 1939 and April 1940, two people held the position of Film Liaison Officer.[8] Meanwhile, the GPO Film Unit was renamed the Crown Film Unit and incorporated into the Films Division, where it continued to be the official film production unit. In April 1940, the situation improved when Jack Beddington was appointed the Film Liaison Officer and overall head of MOI film production. He assigned film projects either to Crown or, through Arthur Elton, his contact with the independent film industry, to such production units as Realist, Strand, Shell, Paul Rotha, Spectator, Verity, Merton Park, Green Park, and Film Centre.[9] Beddington supported many of the principles of the British documentary movement, and in his professional public relations work for Shell Oil, he had established the influential and successful Shell Film Unit. With his stable leadership, film production increased rapidly, but there continued to be other personnel problems within the organization. When GPO became Crown, Cavalcanti remained as the head of production; but, as a foreigner, he was thought to be inappropriate as the head of the government's official propaganda film unit during war. Thus, Calvancati was replaced by Ian Dalrymple, who himself resigned in 1943 because of continuing problems related to the policies of production and distribution.[10] After Dalrymple, J. B. Holmes again assumed control of the unit, but was no more successful than he had been in 1937, when he was forced to relinquish control to Cavalcanti. In January 1945, after two years in which the Crown Film Unit had "floundered" (Swann 265), Basil Wright took control.

As a result of the November 1940 Boxall Report, the Crown Film Unit was reorganized and streamlined along the lines of the commercial film industry. Before the war, there were marked differences between documentary filmmaking operations at the GPO and independent units; now, the Crown's "bigger budgets, better facilities, and special status . . . helped to accentuate the differences" (Swann 267). Not only was production relocated in the splendid commercial facilities at Pinewood Studios, but the narrative form, the staple of the commercial film industry, became an important factor in documentary production. These narrative films were more widely distributed than any of the other MOI documentary films, and also gained greater critical attention. However, as Swann points out, this success with

> feature length films portraying the heroic British people at war steered it away from films dealing with social problems and particularly, the problems resulting from the war. (265)

The MOI Films Division was ultimately successful both in identifying subjects for films and in securing the necessary facilities and staff to make them.[11] In the standard categories—training, combat, anti-enemy propaganda, incentive, and information films—these films covered a wide range of subjects and fulfilled many purposes, including bolstering British courage in the face of Nazi aggression; preparing white-collar workers to undertake industrial jobs; introducing citizens to the social and medical services available to them; instructing people in childbirth and childcare; orienting them to new modes of living or routes of transportation; and documenting the living conditions of British cities, towns, and villages. Other films projected British strength abroad, particularly to the United States and other allies. The Colonial Film Unit made special movies for instructional work in Africa and India; and still other films were produced by the film units in other countries of the Empire, including Australia, Canada, India, New Zealand, South Africa, and the West Indies. All this film activity was, in short, intended to improve the flow of essential and useful information and, thus, to strengthen national defense. Meeting the challenges of wartime production proved to be the peak of achievement for British nonfiction film makers, who, in consequence, gained more influence over public information and attitudes than they ever had before or were ever to have again. One reason for this influence was a mandate to engage in the steady production of films; another was the establishment and publication until 1947 of *Documentary News Letter,* which served as a chronicle of production information and a forum for policy. Finally, an exchange of artists between the documentary production companies and the feature film studios resulted from the increased demand for documentary films, the shortage of facilities for making features, the shortage of technicians (many of whom had enlisted or who were working in combat film production units), and the involvement of the feature companies in making the famous "five minute" and "fifteen minute" factual short films for the Ministry of Information (Dickinson and Street 114). According to Swann, these short formats "provided virtually the only opportunity which the rest of the documentary movement had to reach audiences in the commercial cinemas" (269).

Because there is still no accurate account of the numbers of films produced, the audiences who saw them, or the revenues from them, it is practically impossible to measure their precise impact on the war effort. In contrast to the patriotic quality of many of the films, which stress selfless sacrifice, the British exhibitors resented having to show government propaganda films. Audiences, who went to the cinema primarily for escapist entertainment were largely hostile to propaganda films, and exhibitors provided the MOI with free screenings partially because they feared that otherwise they would be regarded as unpatriotic (Swann 270). As a consequence, nontheatrical distribution prospered, creating forums for both cinematic experimentation and public debate.

Although British wartime films undoubtedly constitute an extraordinary achievement in the overall history of the nonfiction film, most have, unfortunately, become archive films, rarely screened for general audiences, having served and outlived the purposes for which they were made. Shortages of film stock restricted many of these films to lengths of five to fifteen minutes, but this encouraged a cinematic shorthand of admirable clarity and directness. A few short films were called "poster films," because of their direct, single-idea messages, and some of the longer films are equally blunt. Nonetheless, a great many of them are successful *as* film, reflecting the ten years of cinematic experimentation that preceded the war and conveying sincerity and emotion that remain effective and moving.

CONCERNS OF BRITISH WARTIME FILMS

In this chapter, films are discussed according to the following subject and production categories: domestic defense; firefighting; wartime living conditions; training films for civilians and armed forces; farming, gardening, food, and nutrition; health; wartime industry; Britain and the sea; labor, women, and youth; strategy and combat; anti-enemy propaganda; and envisioning the postwar world. Some war films appeared in different versions—under different titles, in different lengths, and at different dates—depending on whether they were being adapted for theatrical, nontheatrical, domestic, or overseas distribution; thus, in this chapter, the dates given are those for the first known release of a film, whatever its format.

Domestic Defense

Ironically, the first British wartime film appeared three years before Britain declared war. Len Lye's *Peace of Britain* (1936) was a hastily assembled "poster film" reinforcing Anthony Eden's call for British support of the League of Nations. It presents a cross section of Englishmen who are bewildered that World War I—the "war to end all wars"—is likely to be repeated. As part of its effort to avert war, it argues that there is no defense against air attack. One of the few British documentaries that is overtly political, its bold messages were meant to alarm people into action: "Demand Peace by Reason" and "Write to Your M.P." These crude tactics were supplanted by Lye's later development of the poster film into a form of propaganda that was, by contrast, almost subliminal in its appeal.

From the time that war was declared in 1939, the British made many nonfiction films concerned with domestic defense, including such subjects as the dangers of gossip (*Hitler Listens*, *All Hands*, and *Dangerous Comment*, 1939; *Now You're Talking*, 1940; *War and Order*, *You're Telling Me*, and *Telefootlers*, 1941; and *Next of Kin*, 1942); wartime precautions and preparations (*Britain Shoulders Arms*, *War Comes to London*, *Do It Now*, *The First Days*, 1939; *A Job to be Done*, *Empire Round the Atlantic*, *On Guard in the Air*, *Ring of Steel*, *Coastal Defense*, 1940); air raid patrols (*Control Room*, 1942); the problem of keeping supply lines open (*Battle of Supplies*, 1942); and home guard training (*Home Guard*, 1941).[12]

A more direct approach to domestic defense was evident in two films: Harry Watt's *Dover Front Line* (1940) and, more important, *London Can Take It!* (codirected by Harry Watt and Humphrey Jennings, 1940).[13] *London Can Take It!* recounts, through a narration by American journalist Quentin Reynolds, the strength of Londoners during a night of the German blitz. A common theme in many of these films is that traditional British institutions, such as religion and democracy, directly contributed to the strength of the British people. Films on these subjects include *Home Front*, 1940; *All Those in Favour* and *Words and Actions*, 1942; and *Religion and the People*, 1940, and *Chacun son Dieu*, 1942.

Whether they were working together (as on *London Can Take It!*) or alone, the films of Harry Watt and Humphrey Jennings were of prime importance to the British war effort.[14] Of their early films concerned with domestic defense, three stand out: Harry Watt's *Squadron 992* (1939) and *Target for Tonight* (1941) and Humphrey Jennings' *Spare Time* (1939). *Squadron 992* (1939), produced by Alberto Cavalcanti and directed by Harry Watt, was intended to inform the public about the work of a Royal Air Force balloon squadron. Watt writes about making the film:

It was a ghastly job. Balloons were boring things to start with, lunging around at the end of their cables like elephants that have had bad news, liable to break away in the middle of the night and have to be chased across the countryside, and the sites themselves were often in the dreariest and most inaccessible places. They were never meant to stop bombing but to prevent the Germans diving on the target, their terrifying new technique, and force them to bomb from a height, a very inaccurate method in those days. (130)

The film quickly explains the balloon squadrons so that it can urge the public's cooperation with this work and instill pride in the British armed forces. For example, it depicts the courtesy with which the Royal Air Force commandeers farm buildings and fields, and the equally good-natured response of those who cooperate with them. *Squadron 992* is noteworthy for its patriotic sequences and its use of familiar songs associated with military camaraderie. An early and influential example of the use of documentary film for war purposes, *Squadron 992* is a landmark in the development of documentaries made at the beginning of the war effort.[15]

Harry Watt's *Target for Tonight* (1941) was very popular with civilian audiences, because, as Watt says, it was a "hitting back film, instead of these interminable 'taking it' efforts" (146). It remains one of the most widely mentioned British

Squadron 992 (Harry Watt, Great Britain, 1939)

war films, for, like *Fires Were Started* (a "taking it" film), it presents war operations through the eyes of the men involved rather than through the filter of politics or propaganda. *Target for Tonight,* which uses considerable reenactment, details a typical Royal Air Force bombing raid on Germany; we see and hear the crew of one bomber discussing the plan, carrying out the mission successfully, and returning their damaged craft through a heavy fog to a safe landing. The film describes the careful planning and apparent ease with which the offensive operation is handled. Beneath this routine activity, we see the British: confident, yet afraid; humorous, yet wary; convivial, yet alone with their thoughts. Watt does not dramatize ordinary activities, as he and Wright did in *Night Mail,* but rather provides an intimate, natural picture of men at war. Unlike Capra, who, in his "Why We Fight" films, sees war as a vast struggle between the forces of right and wrong, Watt sees war in human terms, as the combined operations of many small units of men. Generally, this approach is typical of other British war films, which are concerned with people, not battles, which focus on defensive planning, not propaganda, and which imbue the war effort with a sense of mission, not destiny.

In 1934, Humphrey Jennings began work in the GPO Film Unit not only as an editor, set designer, and actor on other people's films, but also as a director: *Locomotives* (1935); *English Harvest, Design for Spring, Penny Journey* (1938);

Target for Tonight (Harry Watt, Great Britain, 1941)

Spare Time, Speaking from America, S.S. Ionian (Her Last Trip), The First Days (codirected with Pat Jackson) (1939); *Spring Offensive (An Unrecorded Victory), Welfare of the Workers* (codirected with Pat Jackson), *London Can Take It! (Britain Can Take It)* (codirected with Harry Watt) (1940); *Heart of Britain (This is England)* and *Words for Battle* (1941); *Listen to Britain* (codirected with Stewart McAllister) (1942); *Fires Were Started* and *The Silent Village* (1943); *The Eighty Days* and *The True Story of Lili Marlene* (1944); *A Diary for Timothy* (1945); *A Defeated People* (1946); and *The Cumberland Story* (1947).[16] Beginning with *Spare Time* (1939) and continuing through *The Cumberland Story* (1947), he was the filmmaker whose work best captured Great Britain at war, using what Barnouw described as his specialty: "the vignette of human behavior under extraordinary stress" (*Documentary* 145). Jennings's overall approach to filmmaking reflected and extended the careful, quiet observation of everyday behavior that distinguished his prewar sociological project titled "Mass Observation." This approach was first used in *Spare Time,* which surveys ordinary people doing ordinary things and thus provides multiple points of view.[17] Jennings precisely records simple details of the leisure time behavior of people from all walks of life. The spontaneity and sincerity of their actions give the film the appearance of an objective record, but, as is typical of this kind of sociological observation, Jennings is reluctant to pass judgment, and his ambivalence frequently leaves the viewer both bemused and irritated. Nonetheless, the film is interesting because of its sensitivity to the details of daily life, the director's awareness of how sight, sound, and music can be harmonized in a work of art, and also because he regards all activities—sports, fairground amusements, dancing, or the relatively solitary pursuits of gardening, cycling, or training pigeons or dogs—as contributing individual fulfillment as well as social cohesiveness. While not entirely successful, *Spare Time* hints at the strengths of Jennings's later films.

Firefighting

Because of the widespread devastation caused by the German blitz bombing of London and other English cities, fighting the resultant fires was a major British concern, and films were produced to help train people in the skills necessary for firefighting, as well as to raise the morale of people involved in this dangerous work, many of whom were volunteers. These include *Fire* (1940) and *Fire Guard* (1942), both about the training and functions of the organized fire services; *A New Fire Bomb* (1942) and *Butterfly Bomb* (1943), which provide instructions on dealing safely with explosive fire bombs; *Go to Blazes* (1942), concerned with fires caused by blitz bombing; and *Factory Fire Guard* and *Fire Guard Plan* (1943), which encourage systematic training to combat fires in congested areas.

Among these, however, one film stands out: Humphrey Jennings's masterpiece, *Fires Were Started* (1943). In this film, Jennings fused his strengths as poet and realist to depict British endurance in action. Like so many British nonfiction films, the subject is deceptively simple: the National Fire Service going through a typically dangerous day during the London blitz. Jennings did not impose dramatic situations or caricatures upon this routine activity (as Dickinson did in *Next of Kin*), nor did he attempt to make heroes out of dedicated men doing their work.

Fires Were Started (Humphrey Jennings, Great Britain, 1943)

Rather, after establishing the individuality of the men who form the unit, he merely depicted their activities, from maintaining equipment to fighting a warehouse blaze. Jennings understood these working men, their informality, conviviality, and anxiety. There is an excellent sequence showing them waiting for the alarms to sound, singing, dancing, playing pool, teasing each other, seemingly unaware that a dangerous and perhaps even deadly fire awaits them, as it does almost every night.

Unfortunately, the fire itself, shot under actual conditions, does not prove exciting enough to fulfill the expectations created by the first half of the film. To the viewer, the scene of fire fighting may seem long, tedious, and curiously devoid of anticipated drama; to the men, it is just another fire, another effort in the defense of London. Only at the conclusion, as a fireman's funeral is crosscut with shots of the ammunition ship that the dead man helped to save, do we understand the importance of this work. And while the nighttime cinematography is excellent, the music fails to complement the action, as it does so perfectly in the first half of the film. Still, were it not for the absence of tension between the two parts of the film—the preparation and the fire—and the lack of dramatic intensity in the fire sequences themselves, *Fires Were Started* would be an almost perfect documentary film. As a particularly imaginative treatment of a thoroughly prosaic subject, it transcends its praise of the dedicated men and women of the Fire Service. Like *Night Mail, Fires Were Started* is an impressive work of art.[18]

Closely allied to these firefighting films are several concerned with survival techniques and rescue services. These, too, are information and training films, helping people to better understand how to help one another after a catastrophe (*S.O.S.* and *Neighbours Under Fire,* 1940), how to locate people trapped in bombed buildings (*Rescue Reconnaissance,* 1943), how to get people out from under debris by means of a tunnel (*Debris Tunnelling,* 1943), and how to clean up after bombing (*Debris Clearance,* 1943). Others concern rescue operations in the water by the Channel Rescue Service (*The Pilot is Safe,* 1941), and in coal mining accidents, including *Dai Jones* (1941) and *Accident Service* (1943).

Wartime Living Conditions

The cinema made its greatest contribution to maintaining civilian morale through those films that showed people how to cope individually and collectively under wartime living conditions. Early on, these were city symphonies—in spirit, if not always in form—that presented a general view of London life: *The New Britain* (1940), *London, Autumn, 1941* and *Ordinary People* (1941), *London 1942, The Big City,* and *London Scrapbook* (1942), and *Doing Without* (1943). The majority of films, however, focused on more specific subjects that were chosen not only to evoke and reinforce the British way of life at home, but also to project its characteristics and stereotypes around the world. Subjects include horses (*Thoroughbred,* 1940), handicrafts (*Handicraft Happiness,* 1940), pubs (*Sport at the Local,* 1940), traditional village life (*Medieval Village,* 1940), living conditions for war plant workers (*Lady be Kind,* 1941), evacuation and relocation (*Living With Strangers,* 1941), the relief work of the Salvation Army (*The Serving Army* and *A Good Landfall,* 1941), civic issues (*Citizens' Advice Bureau,* 1941, *Rush Hour,* 1942), building (*New Towns for Old, Builders,* 1942) transportation (*Transatlantic Airport,* 1943), fuel economy (*The Burning Question,* 1944), sports (*Some Like it Rough,* 1943, and *Cine-Sports,* 1943, a series produced for armed forces at the front), teamwork (*The Team,* 1941), and welcoming allied soldiers (*A Visit from Canada,* 1941, and *Welcome to Britain,* 1943).

Because the war affected all forms of communication, several nonfiction films depicted typical problems ranging from newspaper delivery during the blitz (*Newspaper Train,* 1942) to radio broadcasting (*Freedom Radio* and *B.B.C. Brains Trust,* 1942). The continuing need for entertainment and culture during the war was depicted in *The Battle of the Books* and *Words for Battle* (1941) and in *Breathing Space* (1942). Perhaps because the government was more concerned with evacuating children than with educating them, there were only a few films about the nation's schools, including *Ashley Green Goes to School* (*Village School*) (1940), *Our School* (1941), and *Children's Charter* (1944), which explains the new Education Act. How war changed the celebration of Christmas, both at home and at the front, was depicted in *Adeste Fideles* and *Christmas Under Fire* (1941).

Perhaps the best of all these films devoted to the effect of war on ordinary living conditions is *Listen to Britain* (1942), a film codirected by Humphrey Jennings and Stewart McAllister; both before and after this film, McAllister was best known as the editor of Jennings' films.[19] With characteristic affection for ordinary people and activities, Jennings and McAllister presented a convincing cross-sectional picture of a nation resolute in its stand against Nazi aggression. *Listen to Britain* continues the tradition, begun with *Night Mail,* of exploring the uses of sound in the documentary film, including directly recorded sounds, poetic commentary, and music. Similar in approach to American cross-sectional war films (*The Ramparts We Watch,* 1940, and *War Comes to America,* 1945), *Listen to Britain* demonstrates that sound can provide not only accompaniment but also counterpoint to images and attempts to create a "symphony" of the sounds of Britain at war. With careful understatement and reserve, the film carefully portrays a strong nation, ready for war, but continuing in its traditional activities. Children dance in a circle at school, miners go down into the pit, and the Queen appears amid the office workers at the lunchtime concert. All are aware that, sooner or later, they may become the "target for tonight." To complement the sense of anticipation and waiting that is visible on every face, Jennings and McAllister mix fervent patriotic narration, familiar dance-hall and folk songs, the ominous sounds of mechanized military vehicles, and the reassuring sounds of a lunchtime recital by Myra Hess in the National Gallery of Art. Irony is apparent in shots of dirigibles keeping watch, in a mix of traffic and factory sounds over a Mozart piano concerto, in the shots of empty galleries and empty frames in the National Gallery, now evacuated of its treasures. Through the film's artistry and candor, we become familiar with the qualities of human endurance that would preserve England through the war.[20]

Our Country (1944), the result of a collaboration between John Eldridge and Dylan Thomas, attempts to present wartime Britain to overseas audiences. Similar to the American *War Comes to America* (1945), *Our Country* aims at presenting a spectrum of cultural and social patterns, from the activity of London to the comparative quiet of a Welsh town, seen through the eyes of a wandering British seaman. However, it is overly sentimental (an understandable fault of nationalistic films, especially in wartime) and often superficial, and with the exception of a sequence in which a munitions plant worker expresses her relief at surviving a nighttime bombing raid, there is little sense of the personal emotions and values of the British people that come through so solidly in such films as *They Also Serve* and *Listen to Britain.* What remains memorable is Thomas's commentary, a lyrical tribute to the strength and determination of the British people.

As their contribution to the war effort, people were encouraged to save both money and those vital materials that could be salvaged for future use. The national savings plans that were the subject of several GPO films in the 1930s (including *The Saving of Bill Blewitt*) remained relevant in wartime, as seen in such films as *Albert's Savings, Save Your Way to Victory,* and *Young Folks Show the Way* (1940). Encouraging people to save waste materials was the object of such films as *Salvage with a Smile* and *Raw Material is War Material* (1940), *Any Old Iron* (*Feed the Furnaces*) (1941), and *Arms from Scrap* (1942).

Although the majority of these films were made about people living in the British Isles, there were others, on similar subjects, made by filmmakers in England and in other countries of the British Empire about life in Africa, Australia, Canada (see discussion below), India, and New Zealand. Scotland, notably, consistently contributed excellent nonfiction films that depicted the work of the Scottish people in the war effort, including *The Freedom of Aberfeldy* (1942), which shows Scottish hospitality to the armed forces, and *Crofters* (1943), about life in a remote Scottish village.

Training Films for Civilians and the Armed Forces

As war altered the British pattern of living in large and small ways, civilians and members of the armed forces were taught to meet new challenges through the use of the nonfiction training films. Films for civilians covered such subjects as farming, gardening, food, nutrition, and health (discussed in sections below), while others provided routine training in domestic areas such as traffic safety (*Dangers in the Dark*, 1941), metalworking (*How to File*, 1941) or industrial safety (*No Accidents*, 1942), as well as in wartime matters (e.g., *Street Fighting* (1942) taught the principles of hand-to-hand combat as practiced by the British Army).

Films helped to recruit and train members of the armed forces, who were trained by film for such specific tasks as stalking a sniper (Len Lye's *Kill or Be Killed*, 1942) or clearing a minefield (*Minefield*, 1943). *A Nation Springs to Arms* (1940) recounts the beginning of war training efforts, *The Right Man* (1942) explains Army testing methods, and *Personal Selection: Recruits* and *Personal Selection: Officers* explain the psychology of recruitment. Other films are concerned with individual units, including the air force (*Raising Air Fighters*, 1939; *Fighter Pilot* and *Into the Blue*, 1940; and *R.A.F. in Action*, 1942); army (*Raising Soldiers*, 1940); navy (*Raising Sailors*, 1940; *Sam Pepys Joins the Navy*, *Sea Cadets* (*Nursery of the Navy*), and *Naval Operations*, 1941); and paratroops (*Paratroops*, 1942).

Farming, Gardening, Food, and Nutrition

While dozens of films throughout the war were concerned with broad martial themes of maintaining morale and training for the defense of democracy, other films dealt with more domestic needs, such as farming, gardening, food, and nutrition. The first major film about farming was Humphrey Jennings's *Spring Offensive* (*An Unrecorded Victory*) (1940), a skillful documentary that not only depicts British farmers supplying food for people at home and troops abroad, but also honors them for sheltering city children during the bombing. Primarily an information film, with the untroubled appearance of a lyrical documentary, it makes the wartime agricultural effort seem an effortless task, one that scarcely seems to alter the lives of farmers and their families. In addition to capturing the genial, steadfast spirit of the British people, *Spring Offensive* also served a more explicit propaganda function, pointing to the neglect of British farmland since the First World War and demonstrating that a nation must keep its farms in full production if it is to remain strong. Comparable films on encouraging greater productivity from available land include *Fighting Fields* and *New Acres* (1941) and *A Farm is Reclaimed* and *Motive Power* (1943). Some farming films were intended to provide training in specific tasks: *Protection of Fruit* and *Silage* (1940); *A Way to Plough*, *How to Dig*, *Dig for Victory* (1941); *How to Thatch*, *Clamping Potatoes*, and *Making a Compost Heap* (1942); and *Stooking and Stacking*, *Reseeding for Better Grass*, *Making Good Hay*,

Making Grass Silages, Clean Milk, Welding Helps the Farmer, and *Simple Fruit Pruning* (1943). Others taught farmers how to use equipment (*Farm Tractors,* 1940, *The Turn of the Furrow,* 1941), showed urban workers how to help farmers during harvest (*Start a Land Club,* 1942), and depicted the cycle of seasons on a farm (*Spring on the Farm* and *Winter on the Farm,* 1942, and *Summer on the Farm* and *Autumn on the Farm* [*The Crown of the Year*], 1943).

While gardening is a traditional English pastime, in wartime what was once leisure activity became survival activity, as the flower gardens were transformed into vegetable "victory" gardens that significantly increased the nation's food supply. In itself, the transformation might have served as the subject of rather more powerful films than *Backyard Front* (1940) and *Filling the Gap* (1942).[21] There were also many films on the inevitable relationship between farming, gardening, food, and nutrition. As was appropriate to the stodgy British food of the time, these films focus on basic subjects: essential foodstuffs for children (*For Children Only,* 1942), casserole cooking (*What's for Dinner?,* 1940), office and factory canteens (*Queen's Messengers, Eating at Work, Canteen on Wheels,* 1941; *Canteen Command,* 1943); common foods (*Choose Cheese,* 1940, *Two Cooks and a Cabbage,* 1941, and *All About Carrots,* 1941), and, inevitably, food rationing (*Fruits From the Garden,* 1940; *The New Bread* and *When the Pie Was Opened,* 1941; *Keeping Rabbits for Extra Meat,* 1942; and *More Eggs from Your Hens* and *Twelve Days,* 1942).[22]

Health

Emphasizing the close relation between food and health, particularly during a time of national emergency, British nonfiction filmmakers produced a series of films that showed people how to maintain good health, including *Vital Service* (1939), *Health in War* and *The Gift of Health* (1940), *Fitness for Service* (1941), *A.B.C.D. of Health* (1942), and *First Aid on the Spot* (1943).[23] Some provide health education on specific diseases or health problems such as malaria (*Malaria,* 1941), venereal disease (*Subject for Discussions,* 1942), tuberculosis (*Defeat Tuberculosis,* 1943), scabies (*Scabies,* 1943), and blindness (*Out of the Night,* 1941, and *Victory Over Darkness,* 1942).[24] Finally, other films cover a range of topics: sneezing into one's handkerchief to prevent the spread of the common cold (*A-Tish-Oo!,* 1941, and *The Nose Has It,* 1942); neuropsychiatry (*Neuropsychiatry,* 1943); diseases carried by rabbits (*Rabbit Pest,* 1941); and a group of films about rats (*We've Got to Get Rid of the Rats,* 1940, *Kill That Rat,* 1941, *Rat Destruction,* 1942, and *Killing Rats,* 1943).

Wartime Industry

Prewar GPO films had stressed the expertise of British craftsmanship and the excellence of British manufactured goods, and several wartime films continued this theme, including *The Obedient Flame* (1940), an early film about the wartime economy. A variety of films demonstrated the wartime productivity of the railways (*Carrying On,* 1939), road transport (*66 Northbound,* 1940), steel (*Furnaces of Industry,* 1940, *Teeth of Steel,* 1942), oil (*Distillation,* 1940, and *Wartime Shipment of Packed Petroleum,* 1943), and chemicals (*This is Colour,* 1942), as well as construction (*Building for Victory*, 1942) and the methods of increasing industrial output (*Planned Electrification*, 1940). The wool industry and its vital contribution to the British economy was the subject of several films, including *The Story of Wool* (1940) and *Border Weave* and *Western Isles* (1942), the latter two of which depict the making of Scottish tweed.

Filmmakers naturally stressed the essential industries that supplied the fighting forces with armaments, materials, and supplies. *Wartime Factory* (1940) provided an overview of industrial production; *Raw Materials* (1940) emphasized the importance of natural resources; and *The Big Pack* (1943) explained the logistics of supplying a major overseas military campaign. As we have seen from the films of the 1930s, such as *Drifters* (1929), *Industrial Britain* (1933), and *Night Mail* (1936), British filmmakers excelled at depicting how things were done or made. During the war, a comparable film was Arthur Elton's *Airscrew* (1940), which, like his earlier *Aero-Engine* (1933) or *The Transfer of Power* [*Lever-Age*] (1939), is an ingenious explanation of an otherwise unremarkable technical process, the manufacturing of a metal, variable pitch airplane propeller, which also served as an incentive film to raise pride among British industrial workers. Films describing the munitions industry included *Factory Front* (1939), *The Voice of the Guns* (1940), and *Danger Area* (1943), which, like *Speed-up on Stirlings* (1942) and *Britain Beats the Clock* (1943), explained the need for fast production under difficult conditions. *We Sail at Midnight* (1942) depicted the lend-lease arrangements that supported a British tank factory, while other films (*Shipbuilders*, 1940, and *Clyde Built*, 1943) dealt with the shipbuilding industry.

Britain and the Sea

Living on a tight, little island, dependent upon the sea for trade, transportation, and defense, the British made films that emphasized not only the economic importance of their ports, fishing industry, and worldwide shipping trade, but also their country's strategic vulnerability to enemy bombers from the European continent and submarines in the surrounding waters. In addition to *Ports, Cargoes*, and *The Merchant Navy* (1940), *A1 at Lloyds* (1941) describes insuring British war ships and *A Few Ounces a Day* (1941) focuses on Atlantic convoys. In the tradition of *Drifters, Granton Trawler*, and *North Sea*, David MacDonald's *Men of the Lightship* (1940) became the first and the best of these British wartime films about the sea. Designed to arouse humanitarian feelings, this film depicts the Nazi bombing of a lightship patrol boat. In excellent scenes of reenactment, it portrays the daily life of the ship's crew, their efforts to survive after the bombing, and, finally, their deaths by exposure as their lifeboat is lost in the fog.[25] *Men of the Lightship* is not only a tribute to the civilian heroes of the lightship service, but also a dramatic, controlled, propaganda film that condemns the ruthless Nazi pattern of attack, yet does not arouse the outrage of the audience. With the later *Target for Tonight*, it helped prepare the British and their allies for the blitz attacks that were soon to devastate London and other English cities.

Three films emphasize the strategic importance of the sea: Pat Jackson's *Ferry Pilot* (1941) and *Western Approaches* (1944), and J. B. Holmes's *Coastal Command*

(1942). *Ferry Pilot* covers transportation between the British Isles, while *Coastal Command* (1942) presents a dramatic, intimate picture of the work of the Royal Air Force and the Royal Navy in protecting British shores during World War II. Pat Jackson's *Western Approaches,* somewhat similar to Harry Watt's *North Sea* (1938), is a dramatized documentary about wartime convoys in the "western approaches," contrasting the American and British methods of transporting men and materials around traps set by the Nazis. It is rare among its contemporaries not only for its feature length (85 minutes), but also for Jack Cardiff's color cinematography.[26]

While some wartime films—such as *Give Us More Ships* (1941)—stressed the need to increase the production of ships, others reminded the British of the economic importance of the fishing industry and the men who make their livelihood from it: *Sailors Without Uniform* and *Herrings* (1940), *Merchant Seamen* (1941), and *Atlantic Trawler* and *Men from the Sea* (1943). Wartime life on military ships was the subject of *H. M. Minelayer* (1941), *Troopship, We Dive at Dawn, H.M.S. King George V* (1942), and *Close Quarters* (1943).

Labor, Women, and Youth

Before the war, the British documentary movement excelled in producing incentive films that raised workers' self-esteem and morale, and, at the same time, depicted a social structure that was deeply stratified. During the war, British society retained its characteristic consciousness of class divisions, while becoming more aware of gender and age divisions. Almost overnight, the labor force changed. As men joined the armed services, women and youth routinely took their places in factories, offices, and shops, and in operating essential services, such as public transportation. Thus, essential to maintaining the unified cooperative effort necessary to winning the war were films that extolled the importance of labor, as well as the vital roles played by women and youth. Some films stressed the importance of every kind of job (*Voice of the People* and *Welfare of the Workers,* 1940, and *Essential Jobs,* 1942), the construction industry (*The Builders,* 1940), dockworkers in wartime (*Dockers,* 1942), and coal mining (*Coal Front* and *It Comes from Coal,* 1940, and *Coalminer,* 1943). Others depicted dangerous wartime work (*Shunter Black's Night Off,* 1941); still others encouraged workers to enter the wartime workforce (*Jane Brown Changes Her Job,* 1942) or celebrated workers who devoted their weekends and free time to their jobs on a bomber assembly line (*Workers' Weekend,* 1943), or saluted those who worked at night (*Night Shift,* 1942) or who participated in the cooperative labor movement (*Men of Rochdale,* 1943). A popular series, *Worker and Warfront* (1942–44), presented a composite of British life that both entertained factory workers and kept them informed about the progress of the war.

Women were of paramount importance to the war effort and to the wartime economy, not only in their more traditional roles as mothers, housewives, and nurses, but also as replacements for male factory workers who had enlisted in the armed forces. Films that depict women in factories include *Her Father's Daughter* (1940) and *They Keep the Wheels Turning* (1942). Other films depict women in munitions factories (*Work Party,* 1942); volunteer service (*A.T.S.,* 1941, and *W.V.S.,*

1942); and the armed forces (*Britannia is a Woman* [*Women in Wartime*], 1940; *W.R.N.S.* and *Airwoman,* 1941; and *Balloon Site 568,* 1942).[27]

In the film industry, too, women took over men's jobs and played a significant role as directors, producers, actors, writers, narrators, editors, designers, and other artists and technicians; they served also as film critics and journalists. Margaret Thompson made over a dozen films on agricultural subjects;[28] Mary Field, who established a reputation in the 1930's for making outstanding nature films, continued to produce similar films; and Evelyn Spice, a member of the original Grierson GPO group, made several memorable films—including *Weather Forecast* and *Job in a Million*—that are distinguished by her humanism. Other women directors included Jane Massey (*Your Children's Teeth,* 1944), Louise Birt (*W.V.S.* and *Fighting Allies,* 1942), Muriel Baker (*Action,* 1942), Rosanne Hunter (*Stooking and Stacking,* 1943), and Yvonne Fletcher (*The Children See It Thru',* 1941).[29]

John Grierson's two sisters, Marion and Ruby, were also active in the British documentary movement. Before the war, Marion Grierson had directed such noteworthy travel films as *So This is London* (1933) and *For All Eternity* (1934). Ruby Grierson's *They Also Serve* (1940) depicts the active role that British housewives played during the war; this brief, thoroughly charming, and unpretentious film touches upon human moments that embody the entire war effort at home.[30] Sim-

They Also Serve (Ruby Grierson, Great Britain, 1940)

ilar films include *Women at War* (1941), *The Country Women* (1942), and *Millions Like Us* and *Women of Britain* (1943).

Young people were a focus of great public concern during the war. Mindful of the destruction of almost an entire generation during the First World War and anticipating the devastation that would be caused by German bombing raids, the British evacuated many young children from the cities either to the comparative safety of the countryside or to the homes of relatives and friends in the United States and Canada. These efforts to save the children are the subject of *These Children are Safe* (1940), and *The Children See it Thru'* and *Five and Under* (1941). Young people expressed their views on war in *They Speak for Themselves* (1942), and the important task of encouraging youth to cooperate in the war effort was the subject of such films as *Venture, Adventure* (1941), *Youth Takes a Hand* (1942), and *Citizens of Tomorrow* (1944). Older youth became a part of the labor force, both in an organized and in an informal fashion, taking jobs they could do or helping out wherever they could; they were encouraged to organize young farmers' clubs (*Young Farmers*, 1942) or to join the construction industry (*New Builders*, 1943).

Anti-Enemy Propaganda

In retrospect, British wartime filmmakers were mainly concerned with emphasizing the positive aspects of life at home, rather than producing anti-enemy propaganda. Like American filmmakers, they seemed confident enough in their own strengths as a free people to show "how" and "why" rather than "who" they were fighting. A few anti-enemy films are memorable for their humor, including Alberto Caval-canti's *Yellow Caesar* (1940), a compilation of footage on Benito Mussolini that makes the Italian Fascist leader appear ridiculous, and *Germany Calling* [*Lambeth Walk*] (1941), in which footage of goose-stepping Nazi soldiers is re-edited to a soundtrack that features the popular "Lambeth Walk."[31] While Cavalcanti's *Three Songs of Resistance* (*Trois chansons de resistance*, 1943) is an attempt to bolster the morale of resistance groups on the continent, who actually received prints of it dropped by parachute, other films took the form of warnings: *Italy Beware* [*Drums of the Desert*] (1940) warns against Italian aggression in Ethiopia, and *Musical Poster #1* warns against enemy spies. *Invincible?* (1942) contains captured German newsreel footage transformed by the British into anti-German propaganda.

In anti-enemy propaganda, as in other genres of wartime films, Humphrey Jennings excelled with two memorable anti-Nazi statements—*The Silent Village* (1943) and *The True Story of Lili Marlene* (1944); after the war, he followed these with *Defeated People* (1946), which is equally memorable for recognizing the hu-manity of Germans.[32] *The Silent Village*, a reenactment similar in some ways to the "it can't happen here" format of Peter Watkins's *The War Game* (1966), is essen-tially a fiction film with a propaganda intent. Honoring the victims of Nazi attack on the Czechoslovakian mining town of Lidice, it was actually filmed in the Welsh mining town of Cwmgiedd. This is a lyrical view of quiet village life interrupted by Nazi occupation. The villagers' resistance is shown in strikes, acts of sabotage, and rebel attacks on occupying soldiers. Although much of the dialogue is in Welsh, the

The Silent Village (Humphrey Jennings, Great Britain, 1943)

townspeople's emotions penetrate the language barrier. However, through its parallels, this film does more than reinforce the horror of war at home in contrast to horrors abroad, for it depicts in cruel terms what the British would experience if the Nazis were to occupy their land. It is thus both a mythical analog and real warning, intended to strengthen morale and sharpen awareness of the urgent need for total defense against the enemy. A similar, but less effective, American film is *Fellow Americans* (1942), which attempts a parallel between the attack on Pearl Harbor and an attack on actual American homes.

Combat Films

Most of the films in the preceding discussion depicted the imminence or potential threat of war to Britain; in contrast, combat films actually recorded the horrors of war on various fighting fronts. Such films as *Wavell's 30,000* (1942), *Tunisian Victory* (1943), and *Desert Victory* (1943) are full-length campaign films, similar to shorter American films such as *Report from the Aleutians, The Battle of San Pietro,* and *The Liberation of Rome.* The best of these British combat films is *Desert Victory,* an account of the battle at El Alamein, in which allied troops, led by British General Montgomery, defeated Nazi troops, under General Erwin Rommel. This graphic document brought the reality of war home to the civilian audience,

Desert Victory (David MacDonald, Great Britain, 1943)

describing the geographical and military background of this major turning point in the allied efforts against the Nazis, and, in particular, depicting the physical hardships and obstacles that proved a more formidable threat to victory than Rommel's German-Italian army. *Desert Victory* is incisive, lucid, and complete in its handling of actual close-range combat footage, some of it captured from the Germans in their retreat. The shots of nighttime artillery attack are spectacular. *Desert Victory* contrasts the immediate strategy of battle with the lives of individual fighting men, from the general in command to the infantryman in a trench; this technique was also used in such later American films as *With the Marines at Tarawa* and *To the Shores of Iwo Jima*. The narration here is much less strident than that of American combat films, and, for the most part, the sound was directly recorded on the scene.

Combat cameramen worked in the line of fire, producing films of great immediacy and impact; *Front Line Camera* (1942) and Len Lye's *Cameramen at War* (1943) demonstrate their bravery and cinematographic skill in the face of danger. The latter is a compilation film that provides a brief history of the work of specialized combat cameramen, including a memorable shot of D. W. Griffith in the trenches of the First World War. Lye's film demonstrates the extent to which filmmakers concentrated their energies on the war effort, and its somewhat plodding seriousness is all the more noticeable in contrast to his more characteristic experiments with color and animation.

Envisioning the Postwar World

Determined to be optimistic about war's outcome, cinematic visions of the postwar world were hopeful yet realistic in their responses to such challenges as alleviating hunger, providing for veterans,[33] and planning for the future. Many of these films, made during the war and immediately after, were produced by commercial sponsors under the overall auspices of the Ministry of Information. Before the war, as we have seen, the basic themes of the British documentary film movement were reform, action, and results. Under government sponsorship, British filmmakers undertook the challenges to explain major issues of great social importance and suggesting solutions, supplying useful information, and encouraging people to think critically about these issues. But the growing documentary film movement began to require sponsorship of sufficient magnitude to foster both the creative development of individual filmmakers and the dissemination of the sponsors' ideas.[34] The risk was that unenlightened commercial organizations would incorporate films into an advertising or marketing scheme, and not, in the larger and more idealistic sense, as Grierson had envisioned.

Nevertheless, many commercial and industrial organizations that were persuaded to use documentary films during the 1930s and 1940s produced imaginative and effective films; films such as *The Harvest Shall Come* and *When We Build Again* remind us that commercial organizations, despite a relatively weak system of distribution, can both support and benefit from films of social significance. Max Anderson's *The Harvest Shall Come* (1942), a film about the refertilization of depleted soil, focused on the problems of individual farmers, the necessity for an expanded agricultural effort, and the agricultural challenges of the postwar future. It is in the tradition of Ivens's *Power and the Land* and Jennings's *Spring Offensive,* and while it is neither as dramatic nor as challenging as *The Plow that Broke the Plains* or *The Land,* it is an effective variation on the same theme. Its cautious, but hopeful ending—"this time it's got to be different"—characterizes the understatement of the film. Produced by Basil Wright for the Imperial Chemical Industries, this film is far-sighted in its realization that the world's depleted soil must be made fertile for a hungry world. Essentially a history of post-Victorian farmers, it reviews the problems incurred by the shift from an agricultural to an industrial economy and uses actors in its semifictional approach to the "neglected and forgotten" farm workers. It was not only a far-sighted educational treatment of a major social problem, but also good advertising for its sponsor. By contrast, another John Eldridge–Dylan Thomas collaboration is limited by its narrow scope. *New Towns for Old* (1942) is an information film on city planning, but in eight minutes it can provide only a simple and unfortunately superficial question-answer narration regarding a subject that was so expertly handled in the earlier American film *The City* (1939) and in the later British film *When We Build Again* (1945).

Ralph Bond's *When We Build Again* (1945), sponsored by Cadbury Brothers, a manufacturer of chocolates, is an excellent documentary on urban planning in the tradition of *Housing Problems* and *The City.* Like *Housing Problems,* it incorporates interviews with people in their own houses, but unlike the earlier film, it strongly advocates the integrated planning of new cities. Like *The City* (codirected by Willard Van Dyke and Ralph Steiner), it emphasizes the advantages of light, quiet, and open spaces. The film begins with a commentary written and spoken in part by Dylan Thomas, the theme of which is summarized in this line: "when we build again, we must build for people." A good example of the problem-solution film, *When We Build Again* integrates visual image, commentary, and music in a persuasive and pleasant social documentary.

Paul Rotha's *World of Plenty* (1943) is compiled from footage that not only documents the problem of wartime food shortages, but also explains some of the efforts that would be necessary to prevent the famine and pestilence that followed the First World War. It attempts to educate viewers about postwar food production, equitable food distribution, food imports and exports, subsidies to farmers, the Lend-Lease Plan, and the overall duty of the British government to ensure the nation's nutrition and health. Finally, the film recommends science as the remedy for devastated farmlands and advocates the adoption of a world food plan based on man's right to be free from hunger. In addition to depicting the worldwide paradox of plenty existing alongside poverty, *World of Plenty* was also intended to show British citizens that rationing was also a problem in the United States and that everyone would have a voice in postwar planning for prosperity. To fix the viewer's attention on these complex issues, as well as to promote postwar plans, Rotha uses

World of Plenty (Paul Rotha, Great Britain, 1943)

many characteristic devices, most at the expense of Americans, and some that had been used in his earlier *New Worlds for Old*. These include a ponderous "voice-of-god" narration challenged by a colloquial American voice; graphics and diagrams, also questioned by an American; and British housewives being interviewed about the ration system by an American visitor to London. *World of Plenty* is a slick, somewhat superficial, but extremely ambitious film, whose attempt to cover such a vast subject makes it lose focus and direction. Still, if it is not wholly effective in its presentation, *World of Plenty* is an excellent example of how much shape and style could be given to footage shot at different times and places.

Rotha's *Land of Promise* (1945) and *The World is Rich* (1947; see chapter 11) are also concerned with the related wartime problems of agriculture, food, and starvation, while *A City Speaks* (1946) deals with postwar rebuilding. *Land of Promise* is a hard-hitting, comprehensive feature-length documentary that criticizes the British government's handling of housing problems between the First and Second World Wars. Utopian as *Land of Promise* is, however, the film is ultimately less successful than *The City* in its plea for uniform planning. Like most of the films written and directed by Paul Rotha, its cinematic technique tends to overwhelm its content; that is to say that the film's technique does not fully serve the film's idea. Rotha favors the well-organized film; here, there are three parts: homes as they were, as they are, and as they might be. Predictable and neat as such organization may at first appear, it is hardly imaginative, even though this particular film is beautifully paced and edited. Eager to further the development of the modern documentary film, Rotha combines several incompatible techniques. *Land of Promise* uses a question-answer narration, a skeptical man-on-the-street narrator (actor John Mills), in addition to other narrative voices, and diagrams for clarification. Detailed in explanation, graphic and convincing in argument, and almost militant in intent, the sheer variety of these technical devices tends to blur the film's focus on the need for urban planning. *Land of Promise* is a fascinating example of all that can be done with the documentary approach; unfortunately, not all of it should have been done in one film.

Humphrey Jennings's *A Diary for Timothy* (1946) takes the form of a story told to a newborn baby, recounting the sacrifices and struggles of the British people and emphasizing the baby's good fortune in being born after the worst of the war. E. M. Forster's commentary is beautifully read by John Gielgud, and while its sad, sentimental tone is appropriate to the valedictory mood, it offsets Jennings's attempt to be optimistic, particularly as the film ends with a challenge to Timothy and others of his generation: "Are you going to let this [war] happen again?" Although *A Diary for Timothy* is blurred in its thematic focus and development, its emotional uncertainty reflects one aspect of the national mood at the time.

GRIERSON AND THE NATIONAL
FILM BOARD OF CANADA

Canada was one of the first countries in the world to understand and appreciate the role that film could play in national affairs. As early as 1900, the Canadian

A Diary for Timothy (Humphrey Jennings, Great Britain, 1946)

Pacific Railway had produced the "Living Canada" series of "scenic films" designed to encourage British immigration to the vast Canadian frontier.[35] During the First World War, Canada produced propaganda films under the direction of Max Aitken (later Lord Beaverbrook), who extended his influence to the British Empire when he was appointed as the British Minister of Information in February 1918 (see chapter 2). During the 1920s and 1930s, the films produced by the Canadian Government Motion Picture Bureau were primarily concerned with promoting tourism from the United States. By all accounts, they were mediocre achievements that received scant attention at home and a poor reception abroad (Evans 51). In 1930, the Imperial Conference, which was held in London, recommended that there be contact between the film activities being undertaken throughout the Empire, and in 1931, Grierson made his first trip to Canada to establish such contacts. When Grierson resigned from the GPO, the Canadian government invited him in May 1938 to study and report on its worsening film situation.

Grierson's report, which was the genesis of a new government film policy, eventually transformed the Canadian film program. Among other things, Grierson recommended a central agency to coordinate government film production and distribution. By 1939, this central agency was established as the National Film Board of Canada (NFB) with Grierson appointed as its commissioner. Although he wanted to keep the Board small and to avoid bureaucratic squabbles he had known in Britain, and which had already begun to plague the Ministry of Information in London, he was soon heading a large organization of nearly eight hundred people producing films for national and international purposes. According to its 1942 annual report, the NFB films were

> designed deliberately to promote a sense of national unity and a national under-
> standing between the many groups which go to make the Canadian nation. They
> are designed to interpret the interests of each section of Canada to the others, and
> to integrate sectional interests with the interests of the nation as a whole. Many
> of them serve also in an important way to interpret Canada to the world at large.
> (Quoted in Evans 117)

Fundamentally, Grierson's concept of the documentary film remained the same in Canada as it had been developed in England: film as a means of educating people and as a source of communication between a government and its citizens. With the outbreak of war, he was less concerned with the broad social issues than with propaganda that would further national goals and institutions. Grierson was in Canada "to inspire, not question, and to promote hope over cynicism or despair" (Evans 11).

The National Film Board began production and distribution on a large scale, and created as many as three hundred films by the end of the Second World War, at which time allegations about his political loyalties forced Grierson to resign.[36] NFB production was varied and popular. The outstanding "Mental Mechanism" series not only widened the nonfiction film audience, but also influenced American production of films concerned with psychological and psychiatric matters. To enable the NFB to carry out its mission of public information and education, Grierson created two major series of films: "Canada Carries On" and "World in Action," both influenced by "The March of Time."[37]

"Canada Carries On," a series produced by EMB and GPO veteran Stuart Legg, was devoted to Canadian wartime strategies, activities, and achievements in such areas as transportation, communication, industrial and agricultural production, as well as in military efforts.[38] Its primary intention was to educate Canadians about Canadian efforts in an international context, and its principal accomplishment was presenting a national image of Canada and inspiring a receptive audience of millions in theatres, community halls, schools, and churches across the country. Many of the early films in the "Canada Carries On" series were of limited concern to such audiences as farmers or factory and munition workers, and in April 1942, Grierson and Legg launched a new series, "The World in Action" (April 1942 through July 1945) for international audiences. Ostensibly, they were concerned with great world events, but according to Evans, "what they were attempting was to influence and direct the political attitudes of international audiences toward an internationally oriented postwar ethic" (167). Despite this controversial mission of internationalism (the allegations stemming from this helped to ruin Grierson's Canadian career), the new films were successful critically and financially, particularly in the United States. Nonetheless, while Canadians in general acknowledged that one of the lessons of the Second World War was the interdependency of nations, the Canadian politicians in power saw these propaganda films as a threat to nationalism and the actual world as it existed at home. Notable titles include *Churchill's Island* and *Warclouds in the Pacific* (1941); *High Over the Borders* (1942); *Action Stations* and *Battle is Their Birthright* (1943); and *When Asia Speaks* (1944).

The success of the National Film Board of Canada during the 1940s can be measured by the extent of government support, the enthusiastic audience reception at home, and the positive image that its films created for Canada throughout the world. If it was too highly organized and too much restrained by the necessity of spreading government information, it was, nonetheless, the force that helped Canada to become a major contributor to the world nonfiction film market in later years, particularly in the 1950s and 1960s, when Canadian nonfiction films proved to be a principal influence on the Americans and the British working to develop such new forms of cinematic expression as Cinéma Vérité, Direct Cinema, and Free Cinema.[39]

9	European and Asian Films for World War II

The Second World War, a military conflict between the Allies (Great Britain, Russia, and the United States) and the Axis (Germany, Italy, and Japan), was also a conflict between the propaganda and counterpropaganda films of those powers. The chapters preceding and following this one are concerned with the wartime nonfiction films of the Allies, while this chapter presents the wartime nonfiction films of of the Axis powers—Germany, Japan, and Italy—and the anti-Axis films of Russia, China, and the French Resistance.

AXIS FILMS

The Nazi Propaganda Film
The Nazis had already perfected their propaganda tactics in many films (see chapter 6) before they began World War II with their invasion of Poland on September 1, 1939.[1] Like the Soviets before them, the Nazis believed in the political power of cinema, but unlike them, they differentiated between narrative and nonfiction approaches and in their uses of cinema. Goebbels, who loved the cinema and had a perceptive insight into mass psychology, encouraged German filmmakers to produce narrative films that offered entertainment and escape, as well as newsreels and nonfiction films that carried party propaganda. These overtly propagandistic nonfiction films were aimed at repressing the viewers' ability to think critically or to form their own conclusions. Among other goals, the Nazis used such propaganda films in their attempts to stir the patriotic emotions of the faithful and to weaken the resistance of the enemy.

In their use of commentary, the Nazis told what the visual images did not, impressing rather than instructing the audience. They exploited the graphic similarities of maps and the human nervous system to suggest that conquest was a natural phenomenon. The Nazis used large quantities of newsreel material, especially shots taken at the various military fronts, for the "German Weekly Review" (*Deutsche Wochenschau*) and features,[2] and used captured enemy film to work against the country from which it was seized. They also contrasted close-ups of Negroes with those of Germans to support their theory of the "master race." Music was used to intensify and manipulate, much as it was in British and American war films; but in the Nazi films, the music was also used suggestively to transform an English tank into a child's toy, erase the fatigue from a German soldier's face, or create the impression that a few German soldiers were an advancing German army.

The formality, grandeur, and unrealness of these Nazi propaganda films suggest a Utopian fantasy similar to that of Fritz Lang's *Metropolis* (1926), not surprisingly, since *Metropolis* was reportedly Hitler's favorite film. Its vivid contrasts between automaton ruler and his robot-like subjects created a paradigm for the contrast between the *Führer* and the people that is exemplified in such a film as *Triumph of the Will* (see chapter 6). In that film, Hitler and his activities are depicted with a solemn devotion, while ordinary people and events are often depicted with a false sentimentality about home, family, and religion, not portrayed as individuals, but rather as tiny parts of a vast superhuman machine.

The Nazis created a broad, general vision of a new world, depicting the anticipated glories of the "Thousand Year Reich" and exalting Aryan supremacy, but they also promote anti-Semitism, the "final solution," antilabor, and world conquest. However, with the exception of one nonfiction film—Fritz Hippler's *The Eternal/Wandering Jew* (*Der ewige Jude,* 1940)—the strongest anti-Semitic sentiments appeared primarily in narrative films made for theatrical distribution, such as Erich Waschneck's *The Rothschilds* (*Die Rothschilds,* 1940) and Veit Harlan's *The Jew Süss* (*Jud Süss,* 1940). Although the Nazis believed in the power of cinema to entertain and to enlighten, their art was shackled to a degenerate ideology of racial supremacy and military tyranny, and they were beaten by forces who used cinema in the service of freedom. Nazi propaganda films demonstrate the complete moral bankruptcy of the Nazi vision.[3]

Wartime Nazi Propaganda Films

The period between the outbreak of war in 1939 and the first Nazi defeats in Russia in 1942 "marked the highest concentration of overt Nazi political propaganda in feature and documentary films during the Third Reich" (Welch 187–88). The outbreak of war brought a turning point in Nazi propaganda tactics and in film production, which shifted from the overtly political film to the overtly escapist narrative film. But the themes of these films remained essentially the same: self-sacrifice, comradeship, and heroic death in battle. The political film was exempt from budgetary restrictions and may have been less expensive to produce, but it required more government supervision, and thus was more difficult to complete. The entertainment film, produced under controlled studio conditions, pleased not only audiences but accountants as well. Overall, however, the number of feature films declined almost as rapidly as the cost of production increased. Other factors besides this change in focus affected production: many film studios were badly damaged by Allied bombing and film stock was in short supply.

During the first year of war, the Nazis produced several films, including *Bauten im Neuen Deutschland, Einsatz der Jugend, Das Wort aus Stein* (all 1939), and Walther Ruttmann's *German Tanks* (*Deutsche Panzer*, 1940), but three titles stand out for their cinematic power and notorious lies—two are about Germany's invasion of Poland, the event that began the war: *Baptism of Fire* (*Feuertaufe*, 1940) and *Campaign in Poland* (*Feldzug in Polen*, 1940); the third—*Victory in the West* (1941)—concerns the Nazi invasion of Belgium, Denmark, France, Holland, and Norway.[4]

FILMS ABOUT GERMANY

Hans Bertram's *Baptism of Fire*, a model of Nazi propaganda, was successful because it romanticized warfare and thus appealed to the German ideal of heroism. In content, it deceitfully recounts the Nazi invasion of Poland and self-righteously justifies the use of brute force; in form, it is lyrical in its celebration of Nazi air power and ecstatic in its delight in victory, evoking a Wagnerian world of heroes, fire, and clouds. It avoids the grim reality of warfare, suggesting instead that the German military tradition is a central part of German destiny. Made for Hermann Goering, the head of the German Air Ministry, and featuring commentary by him, it has three practical objectives: to praise the German air force, which was responsible for the victory over Poland; to humiliate Britain, which, through Prime Minister Neville Chamberlain, had pledged its support to the Polish defense; and to frighten Britain and other Allies in its foreshadowing of how Nazi air power would be used in the bombardment of British and European cities. The film blames the destruction of Warsaw on the British, who had encouraged the Polish people to defend the city; the narrator says:

> What have you to say now, Mr. Chamberlain? Here you find conclusive evidence of the catastrophe you brought about in the Polish capital. Do you fear the curse of a betrayed people? . . . All this is your work, yours is the guilt, and you will have to answer for it at the last judgment. And remember one thing: this is what happens when the German Luftwaffe strikes. It will also know how to strike at the guiltiest of the guilty.

According to Nazi filmmaker Karl Ritter,

> the ultimate purpose of all National Socialist films is to show the test of an individual within the community—for the individual's fate only has meaning when it can be placed at the service of the community, whereupon it becomes part of a people and nation. (Quoted in Welch 215)

Films like *Baptism of Fire* and *Campaign in Poland* exemplified this purpose, extolling the image of the German warrior as a brave and fearless man willing to sacrifice his life for his Führer and his country.

Fritz Hippler's *Campaign in Poland*, as deceitful as *Baptism of Fire*, presents the official Nazi explanation of the German invasion and defeat of Poland that began the war. However, it is an insidious account that assumes the moral imperative of the Nazi mandate and puts all the blame for World War II on the Poles. Its dishonesty is symbolized by the title, in which the neutral words "campaign in Poland" are substituted for what the free world called the "rape of Poland." Throughout, the narration of the English language version is delivered in this matter-of-fact tone. The siege of Warsaw (with no reference whatsoever to the brutal massacre in the Jewish ghetto) is explained in civil terms. This discretion extends to the images, which include destroyed buildings, but no bodies. The film ends with Hitler's arrival in Warsaw, a victory march—"Germany ought to feel safe under the protection of such an army"—and the ringing of the victory bell, an image that also concludes the "Why We Fight" films. Throughout the film, but especially in this final sequence, Herbert Windt's music recalls the score he composed for Riefenstahl's *Triumph of the Will* (Windt also wrote the score for *Olympia*). Hippler's *Victory in the West* takes a similar approach in its gloating account of the invasion and defeat of Belgium, Denmark, France, Holland, and Norway.

FILMS ABOUT THE ENEMY

While the Nazi propaganda film attempted to influence opinion or change attitudes, it was most effective in reinforcing opinions that the audience already held, particularly their hatred of enemies. Some groups, like the Russians and the Jews, were traditional enemies; others, like the British and the Americans, became enemies as World War II progressed. The Nazis used blunt contrasts and familiar stereotypes to attack Soviet Communists in many feature films, and they attacked their other enemies in nonfiction films. As tensions between Germany and Britain increased, Britain became the object of hatred in Nazi cinema. *Gentlemen* (1940?) accuses such stereotypical British gentlemen as Churchill, Chamberlain, and Eden as warmongerers. *The English Sickness* (*Die englische Krankheit,* 1941) accuses the British of spreading disease in World War I. Among the few anti-American propaganda films, *Around the Statue of Liberty* (*Rund um die Freiheitsstatue,* 1942) stands out.

The Nazis were obsessed with producing a racially pure Aryan people, with maintaining their health, and with providing sufficient living space (*Lebensraum*) to ensure their individual development and collective security. They pursued these goals through laws governing sterilization or euthanasia of persons suffering from incurable hereditary disabilities, through anti-Semitism, and through the methodical extermination of the Jews. These subjects were central to the Nazi *Weltanschauung*, and Nazi propaganda films dealt with them as routine solutions to social problems that threatened the purity of German life. Films argued that euthanasia— the selective "mercy-killing" of physically and mentally sick persons—would help to maintain German ethnic unity, racial purity, and political unity. Other films argued for the mass extermination of the Jews by exploiting "the historical predisposition of the audience towards an anti-Semitic explanation for Germany's cultural, economic, and political grievances" (Welch 282). *Abseitz vom Wege* (*By the Wayside*) and *Erbkrank* (*Congenitally Ill,* both 1936) were short films that drew a parallel between physical fitness and the fitness to survive. They were "intended primarily for internal 'ideological' education and were not released to the general public," but *Opfer der Vergangenheit* (*Victims of the Past,* 1937), which explained the Nazi policy of euthanasia of the mentally handicapped, was released in com-

Victory in the West [*Sieg im Westen*] (Fritz Hippler, Germany, 1941)

mercial theatres throughout Germany (Welch 122). The fullest exposition of these ideas about euthanasia is made in the feature film *Ich klage an* (*I Accuse*, 1941).

These films are based on the potent myth of German invincibility and on the equally potent myth of the evil enemy. Nowhere was this more apparent—and nowhere was it more "natural" to the way of thinking of many Germans—than in the films of anti-Semitism. Anti-Semitic films scarcely existed before the war, but as Hitler began the full implementation of his "final solution" to the Jewish "problem," Nazi propaganda films exploited the German fear of the "international Jewish conspiracy" and encouraged German audiences to understand and accept genocide. The most scurrilous of them is a nonfiction film: Fritz Hippler's *The Eternal/Wandering Jew* (*Der ewige Jude*, 1940). The film's essential contrast is between myths and stereotypes of Jews and the Nazi ideal of a "master race," between the alleged inferiority of the Jews and the superiority of the Germans. Through footage which Hippler took during the German invasion of the Jewish ghetto in Warsaw (and the subsequent massacre therein), he bluntly demonstrates what the Nazis would do to introduce their form of "civilization." And through the equally offensive use of footage from fiction films (including George Arliss's portrayal of a Rothschild in *The House of Rothschild*, 1934, and Peter Lorre's—described as "the Jew Lorre"—portrayal of the child murderer in *M*, 1932), Hippler ironically attempts to "validate" his documentary footage. In a structural pattern that emphasizes the need for exterminating the Jews, the film begins in the darkness and squalor of the Jewish ghetto and ends in a light-filled sequence depicting triumphant Nazi youth against the sky. Jews are equated with rats—a menace of restless parasites that spread disease and bring ruin. Jews are indicted for their dominance of international banking. They are criticized for their decadent art forms, for their religious beliefs and ceremonies, and, finally, for their rites of kosher butchering, which Hitler outlawed as cruel and heartless: "And just as it dealt with this cruel slaughter, so will the Germany of National Socialism deal with the whole race of Jewry." The film argues that Jews are criminals; that they have no soul; that they are different in every way; that killing them is not a crime, but a necessity—just as killing rats is a necessity to preserve health and cleanliness.

This film, insidious in content and form, is as strongly anti-Semitic as any film the Nazis ever made. Its theme is clear: only through extermination of the Jews will the Nazi ideal of racial purity prevail. In the form of a "documentary," its style is equally manipulative, not only reinforcing old beliefs and stereotypes, but also showing the inevitable outcome of Nazi ideology. Despite its use of graphic animation and actuality footage that are equally disgusting, this does not appear to have been a popular film with the German cinema audience, who by then may have had enough of anti-Semitic films, or, as Goebbels predicted, may have wanted their ideology in the form of entertainment rather than in a didactic lesson. Nonetheless, the film had a purpose other than preparing Germans for the "final solution," and that was to "divert public attention from genuine social and political problems" (Welch 303).

As the war progressed, the Nazis continued to produce such films as *Soldaten von Morgen* (1941); *Die Grosse Deutsche Kunstausstellung Munchen 1943, Herr Roosevelt Plaudert, Das Sowjetparadies* (1943); *Der Fuhrer Schenkt den Juden eine Stadt* and *Rundfunk im Kriege* (1944), and they concentrated much of their filmmaking energies on producing the notorious propaganda newsreel, *German Weekly Review (Deutsche Wochenschau)*.[5] With the turning point in late 1942 and early 1943, and the subsequent Allied victories in Europe in 1944, the Nazis were preoccupied with a desperate attempt to avoid the total collapse that occurred nonetheless in April, 1945. As a result, Nazi filmmaking—narrative and nonfiction— declined after 1943.[6]

Although Welch says that "no reliable information exists with which to measure the success or failure of Nazi film propaganda" (308), it is important to remember that film was only one part of the vast Nazi propaganda effort, the parts of which were interrelated. In fact, films commissioned by the state consisted of only one-sixth of all film production in the Third Reich. The Nazis produced fewer wartime nonfiction films than the Americans or British, although they were no less consistent in expressing their world view.

Japan

The outbreak of World War II brought significant changes in the Japanese film industry. The Proletarian Film League (Prokino), which helped to develop the Japanese nonfiction film in the 1930s, was outlawed, and the Japanese government decreed that films could be directed only by those who held a government license. Moreover, Fumio Kamei, one of Japan's most promising directors (see chapter 6), angered military officials with his *Fighting Soldiers* (*Tatakau heitai,* 1939) and was not only denied a license, but was also imprisoned for two years during the war. The Japanese film industry, which was mobilized for war "to an extent undreamed of in the Allied countries" (Anderson and Richie 147), produced feature-length films recording Japan's military victories. And their prewar nonfiction films on China had created a demand for documentary and newsreel films, which were also shown by official decree in most Japanese theatres. These include *Malayan War Record* (*Marei senki,* 1942), a compilation of combat footage; *Divine Soldiers of the Sky* (*Sora no shimpei,* 1942), a story of parachute troops in action; and *Sunk Instantly* (*Gochin,* 1943), films "which made the war more real to those on the home front than any dramatic film could" (Anderson and Richie 147).

Most of these government propaganda films were designed—as were the feature-length fiction films—to inspire Japan's population with the need for personal sacrifice (including suicide) in its determination to win the war. From 1944 on, with the scarcity of film stock and the increase of bombings, Japanese films became even more fanatical about instilling in ordinary people the selfless *kami-kaze* spirit traditionally reserved for the warrior (*samurai*) class. In distinct contrast to both Allied and Axis propaganda films, these Japanese films were characterized by an almost complete lack of the enemy presence.[7] There were, however, several notable exceptions in films intended to promote Japanese interests in Indonesia and Australia, countries that would become Japan's enemies, but which were essential to Japan's strategic position.[8]

Italy

In Italy, the Fascist dictator Benito Mussolini not only understood the political potential of cinema, but also demonstrated an interest in the Italian film industry. In 1924, he created Instituto LUCE (L'Unione Cinematografica Educativa) to produce Italian nonfiction films (including newsreels and documentaries) and to censor similar foreign films.[9] In 1934, following the German model, he transferred his regime's responsibilities for the propagation of Fascist ideas and for censorship to the Ministry of Press and Propaganda. In the same year, Mussolini also took another step to stimulate filmmaking by establishing a national film school, the Centro Sperimentale della Cinematografia, where many leaders of *neorealism* and the postwar renaissance of Italian film were trained (see Chapter 12).

In 1940, Mussolini's forces entered World War II in a major combat on the deserts of North Africa. By 1941, the Italian army had failed in this campaign, as well as in those in Greece, and by July–August 1943, the Allies had invaded Italy. Mussolini was then virtually powerless, and Italy was in chaos. Italian cinema during 1940–44 was almost entirely profascist, but with the arrival of neorealism in the postwar years, which was a product of both political and social circumstances, it underwent a radical change that not only broke completely from its past, but also had an enormous influence on modes of representing reality in the nonfiction film.

Perhaps because of their relatively brief and troubled hold on power, the Italian fascists produced few nonfiction propaganda films. Several deserve mention. Although German director Walther Ruttmann's *Acciaio* (*Steel,* 1933) is a fiction film, from a script by Luigi Pirandello, it incorporates nonfiction footage to celebrate work and technology.[10] *A Look at Japan* (*Uno sguardo al Giappone,* 1941) celebrates the monuments, industrial factories, folkore, and life of a Far Eastern ally. Giovacchino Forzano's *Camicia Nera* (*Black Shirt,* 1933), a propaganda film telling the story of a simple family under Fascism, prefigures neorealism by using actual people playing themselves. *Path of the Heroes* (1936), according to Rotha, "purported to tell the Italian view of the Ethiopian massacre" (*Documentary,* 203). Another film, *Hitler in Florence* (1938), shows Mussolini nervously awaiting Hitler's arrival at the Florence train station. While the official Italian filmmakers did not intend this, Mussolini's behavior in this film makes him appear to be ridiculous,[11] an effect that Alberto Cavalcanti deliberately intended in *Yellow Caesar* (1940). In this compilation film, Cavalcanti cleverly edits sight and sound images to produce a heavily satiric portrait. When Italy was liberated and the war was over, *neo-realismo* not only revealed the great potential of the Italian cinema but also set the cinematic style for years to follow (see chapter 12).

ANTI-AXIS FILMS

The power of the cinema as a strategic tool in wartime was demonstrated over and over again, on both sides of the conflict. A German general noted that it might even prove to be the decisive factor; according to Richard Griffith,

> [he] declared that the opponent with the best cameras would be the victor. His statement was open to two quite different interpretations: either he implied that motion pictures can be a powerful weapon as an opinion-building attitude-directing and emotion-stimulating medium; or he was speaking purely as a militaryman and had already foreseen that motion pictures were capable, in quite another manner and on a more technical level, of providing a new guide and a new arm to any High Command foresighted enough to utilise them.[12]

The films made by the Allies and by other anti-Axis forces in Russia, China, and the French Resistance demonstrate the power of cinema to support the defense effort, raise and sustain morale, and provide news from the fighting fronts.[13] Not incidentally, they were also the films of the victors.

Russia

In 1939, after a series of victories, Nazi Germany held strongholds in both Western and Eastern Europe. The Soviet Union, unable to reach an alliance with Great Britain and France, signed a nonaggression pact with the Germans in August 23, 1939, removing the German fear of a possible two-front war. On September 1, World War II began as Germany launched its attack on Poland. During the next two years, in a series of campaigns, Germany consolidated its European strength, and on June 22, 1941, in a move that was to prove one of the principal causes of the German collapse in 1943, the Nazis ignored its nonaggression pact and launched a three-pronged attack on the Soviet Union. That same week, the Soviet film industry mobilized, led initially by such major filmmakers as, among others, V. I. Pudovkin, Mark Donskoy, Grigori Alexandrov, and Sergei Eisenstein.[14] They planned combat films, newsreel "albums," and instructional films at the Documentary Film Studio, which during the war was under the leadership of Sergei Gerasimov. Most of these films were strongly antifascist. As the war activity increased, vital production facilities were moved from major cities to less vulnerable places.[15] Leyda writes:

> The magnitude of this operation may be imagined, if at all, if one could realize the mechanics of shifting the entire organization of Twentieth Century-Fox from Beverly Hills to Minneapolis, and that of Paramount to New Orleans, while the whole U.S. Army moves in the opposite direction towards the West Coast. (369)

They also dispatched combat and newsreel cameramen to the various fronts; Leyda says that "no assignment seemed impossible to the newsreel cameramen" (374), who were widely honored for their bravery. As a result of their efforts, excellent footage of individual battles was featured in many films. The Nazi determination to conquer the Soviet Union was severely hampered when the Germans were halted outside of Moscow in December, 1941, an event that is documented and celebrated in "the most widely shown film of the war" (Leyda 370): Leonid Varmalov's and Ilya Kopalin's *Defeat of the German Armies Near Moscow* (1942; English title: *Moscow Strikes Back*). As the production companies evacuated Moscow, they left most of the film archives behind, a fact that helped the Documentary Film Studio, the one large film organization to remain in Moscow, to compile this film.[16]

Three unique films—*A Day in the New World* (1940), *A Day of War* (1942), and *A Day in a Victorious Country* (1948)—use techniques similar to the "day in the life" technique of Dziga Vertov's *The Man with the Movie Camera*, the European "city symphonies," and the sociological comprehensiveness of Humphrey Jennings's "mass observation" project. The idea for the film was conceived by the novelist and dramatist, Maxim Gorky, who proposed that on a predetermined day, all documentary cameramen, all over the Soviet Union, should shoot everything they saw around them. He believed that the footage would provide a comprehensive insight into Soviet life. Of these, Mikhail Slutsky's *A Day of War* provided an excellent cross-sectional view of the progress of the war on June 13, 1942. Paul Rotha, who preferred the studio documentary to the compilation of newsreel film, commented:

> Despite the intrinsic interest of certain of the sequences and the general impression of vastness, the link of authenticity alone was too weak. There was no really convincing reason why the whole thing should have been shot in a single day. (*Documentary Film* 289)

A major turning point in the war, and a landmark in military history, was the

Moscow Strikes Back [*Defeat of the German Armies Near Moscow*] (Leonid
Varmalov and Ilya Kopalin, USSR, 1942)

Nazi siege and destruction of Stalingrad (Volgograd) in 1942. Although the combined German and Soviet losses were staggering, and the Soviets lost a great city,
they ultimately won the battle and remained on the offensive for the rest of the
war. The Siege of Leningrad became the subject of several films—among them, the
newsreel compilation, *The Siege of Leningrad*; Roman Karmen's *Leningrad in Combat* (1942); Lydia Stepanova's and Sergei Gurov's *Komsomols* (1943); and two reenactments, Friedrich Ermler's *Turning Point* (1946) and Nikolai Verta's *The Battle of
Stalingrad* (1949)—but the most important of them was Leonid Varmalov's *Stalingrad* (1943).

During the war, Pudovkin appears to have been a tireless source of encouragement for Soviet filmmakers. In *Moscow Strikes Back,* he found the paradigm for
the kind of film needed in wartime:

> This is the feature-length documentary film which uses the facts of living actuality
> as filmed by the motion picture camera, but which unites them in montage with
> the aim of communicating to the spectator certain, sometimes quite general and
> abstract, ideas.
>
> Such a documentary film is not merely informational. It differs from the
> newsreel in the same way that an editorial or article in a newspaper differs from
> the news item in the next column. (Quoted in Leyda 371)

During the first part of the war, Dovzhenko was so dissatisfied with the widespread use by his colleagues of artificial settings and actors that he worked in media other than cinema. But he found in Pudovkin's theory of the feature-length documentary the inspiration for "supervising" two passionate and patriotic films: *The Fight for Our Soviet Ukraine* (1943) and *Victory in the Ukraine and the Expulsion of the Germans from the Boundaries of the Ukrainian Soviet Earth* (1945).[17] The fighting in the Ukraine caused Dovzhenko great personal suffering, and he wrote about the first film with characteristic pessimism:

> I don't know what the government will say about it. Maybe the film will be banned or I will be forced to mar it by cutting the difficult and unheroic scenes. But I am convinced of one thing: the film is absolutely correct. In what does its truth inhere? In the grandiose woe of retreat and the incomplete joy of advance. (*Alexander Dovzhenko: The Poet as Filmmaker* 91)

Other film production changed also as the war turned against the Axis powers. At the Documentary Film Studio, "possibly inspired by Dovzhenko's work with the newsreel feature" (Leyda 386), Gerasimov produced five important films that incorporated Russian and captured footage: Yuli Raizman's *Towards an Armistice with Finland* (1944) and *Berlin* (1944), Alexander Zarkhi's and Josef Heifitz's *The Defeat of Japan* (1945), Sergei Yutkevich's *Liberated France* (1945), and Maria Slavinskaya's *A Cameraman at the Front* (1946), a memorial to cinematographer Vladimir Sushinsky, whose death is recorded in the film.[18] Other films of the period include Vasili Belayev's *The People's Avengers* (1943), Alexander Zguridi's *In the Sands of Central Asia* (1943), and Boris Dolin's *Law of the Great Love* (1945).[19]

The war's end reinforced the strategic importance of the Soviet cinema, for, as Leyda writes, "Soviet cinema honours almost equalled the military honours conferred on the victors. . . . " (387). Soviet cameramen, editors, and sound technicians, along with their Allied counterparts, proved again how prophetic the German general was in his remarks, cited earlier, that the opponent with the best cameras, among other strengths, would be the victor.

China

Chinese film production, immediately preceding and during World War II, was largely determined by the complex and unstable internal situation (see chapter 6).[20] Discussing film production in Changchun, Peking, Shanghai, and Yenan, Leyda indicates that the Chinese appear to have made numerous nonfiction and newsreel films, some openly propagandist, but that the lack of accurate records makes it difficult to establish their chronology or classification. However, he specifically cites *Yenan and the Eighth Route Army* (1939), made by Yuan Mu-jih and the Yenan Film Group with the help of equipment donated by Joris Ivens, and according to Leyda, "the most ambitious of the twenty-one films made between 1939 and 1945" (151).[21]

FRENCH CINEMA OF THE OCCUPATION
AND RESISTANCE

In May–June 1940, Germany invaded, defeated, and occupied France. Marshal Henri Philippe Pétain, the 84 year old hero of World War I, became the head of the Vichy Government of "unoccupied" France, while General Charles De Gaulle, in London, proclaimed the continued resistance of the "free French." In collaborating with the Nazis, the Vichy government itself became fascistic. Although Pétain remained the titular head of the government until 1944, Pierre Laval took the power from him in 1942. In 1943, the Allied invasion of North Africa resulted in the establishment of De Gaulle's Free French government at Algiers and in the complete German occupation of metropolitan France. Following the victorious Anglo-American landing at Normandy on June 6, 1944, and the subsequent liberation of Paris, De Gaulle's government moved to Paris. By the end of 1944, the Allies, with heroic aid from the French Resistance, had driven the Nazis out of France. Between 1944 and 1946, De Gaulle was provisional president, and the Fourth Republic was proclaimed in 1946.

This was a deeply troubling time for the French, as revealed in Marcel Ophuls's *The Sorrow and the Pity* (see chapter 15). It was also a major turning point for French commercial cinema.[22] Most of the great directors—René Clair, Julien Duvivier, Jacques Feyder, Max Ophuls, and Jean Renoir—were either in hiding or in self-proclaimed exile in the United States or Great Britain, or, because they were Jewish, detained in prison camps, or otherwise out of work. But there were also positive developments. Many directors remained in France—among them, René Clément, Jean Cocteau, Henri-Georges Clouzot, Robert Bresson, Marcel Pagnol, Sascha Guitry, Marcel Carné, and Maurice Tourneur; there was a large French audience for films, including imported American and German narrative films; the government established a film school—the Institut des Hautes Études Cinématographiques—in 1943; and a new generation of directors emerged. Equally important, both the Vichy and Berlin governments were interested in the economic vitality of the French cinema, and so it survived by sacrificing "the freedom, the near anarchy, that had prevailed in the 1930s" (Ehrlich 190).

During the War, the French commercial cinema prospered with films of escape and entertainment, many of which were in the tradition of French cinema of the 1930s. André Bazin asserts that "it is a mistake to oppose realism to escapism," and that "a captive nation that refused to exalt its slavery and yet could not proclaim its desire for freedom naturally had to develop an escapist cinema" (98). Roger Régent emphasizes that, of the more than two hundred narrative films made during the Occupation, none contained German propaganda; Jacques Siclier says that French audiences regarded the cinema as distinct from politics:

> I never heard anyone say the words "cinema of Vichy." . . . Vichy was the city in which the government of France was located. The cinema was something else: a spectacle of which we demanded distraction, the passing of daily difficulties and trials, pleasure, and a form of freedom.[23]

The emphasis on filmmaking in France during the Occupation was, as it was during the 1930s (see chapter 6), on the narrative film. The French nonfiction film continued to treat ordinary subjects in an ordinary way. However, between 1939 and 1945, more than four hundred nonfiction films were made, including films that observe everyday life (e.g., Georges Rouquier's *Le charron*), films of scientific observation (e.g., Jacques Cousteau's *Epaves*), and films about art, architecture, sports, country life, craftsmanship, and the historical past.[24] Nonetheless, most of these short films, which were shown in commercial theatres along with feature films, remain unfamiliar and are not cited as having advanced the art of the nonfiction film in France.

Vichy Government Propaganda Films

The Vichy Government produced propaganda films favorable to Pétain, the "national revolution," and Germany, as well as films unfavorable to prewar government, the Resistance, Jews, Allies, and Communists.[25] These propaganda films include *Maréchal Pétain in Pictures and Words* (*Images et paroles du Maréchal Pétain*), which depicts the French leader in his country home and in his Vichy office; other films depict his travels around France. *One Year of National Revolution* (*Un an de révolution nationale*) praises the stability that the Vichy government has returned to French life. *The French Have a Short Memory* (*Français vous avez la mémoire courte*) recounts the history of the Russian Revolution and laments the expansion of world Communism. *The Tragedy at Mers-el-Kebir* (*La tragédie de Mers-el-Kebir*) depicts the British destruction of the French fleet in the Algerian port. *The Corrupters* (*Les corrupteurs*) and *The Jewish Peril* (*Le péril juif*) use German footage to propound anti-Semitic ideology. *Free America* (*Libre amérique*) uses American nonfiction footage against itself to present a distorted picture of a country where Jews allegedly provoke misery, strikes are severely reprimanded, and the human condition is degenerate. Other propaganda films extolled the pleasures of work and travel in Germany, explained the treatment of French prisoners in German camps, praised the anticommunist activities of the French Foreign Legion, and labelled the Resistance as a terrorist movement.[26] While French audiences saw these films, as well as German propaganda films about Nazi military victories—and, after the war, films about Allied victories and the German defeat—they clearly preferred to see entertaining narrative films.[27]

Films of the French Resistance

The work of the Resistance, which necessarily had to be clandestine, did not lend itself to filmmaking. It should be noted, however, that countries that were sympathetic to the Resistance made films about underground activities. These include Alberto Cavalcanti's *Three Songs of Resistance* (*Trois chansons de resistance*, 1943) from England and Theodor Christensen's *Your Freedom is at Stake* (*Det gaelder din frihed*, 1946), a two-and-a-half hour compilation film from Denmark. The Danish film is all the more remarkable for containing footage actually made during the German Occupation of that country.[28] While its subject is the growth of the Danish Resistance Movement, the film also shows the changes in daily life during the

Occupation. It depicts the mass terror by which the Nazis attempted to break the resistance movement, which included direct sabotage and the diversion of the Jews from routes leading to concentration camps to those that led to safety in Sweden. *Your Freedom is at Stake* is a great record of bravery, shot by brave men. Also of interest are Carl Th. Dreyer's wartime and postwar documentaries, made for the Danish government.[29]

The French films of the Resistance, which also had to be made after the liberation, include such narrative films as Christian-Jaque's *Boule de suif* (1945), René Chanas's *Le jugement dernier,* Henri Calef's *Jéricho,* Yves Allégret's *Les démons de l'aube,* and Louis Daquin's *Patrie* (all 1946). The official nonfiction film, *Resistance Journal* (*Le journal de la résistance,* 1945), an exceptionally moving film, was compiled almost completely of newsreel footage shot during the war by Jean Painlevé, Jean Grémillon, Louis Daquin, and Pierre Blanchar, among others.[30] Jean Cocteau's *Black Friendship* (*L'amitié noire,* 1944) is unique, not only as a sensitive ethnographic film about Negroes, but also as having been made during a time when the Nazis promoted the theory that black peoples were inferior. But the most successful and most familiar of these films is René Clément's *Battle of the Rail* (*La bataille du rail,* 1946).

Battle of the Rail is, like two other postwar masterpieces—Roberto Rossellini's

The Battle of the Rail [*La bataille du rail*] (René Clément, France, 1946)

Open City (Roma, città aperta, 1945) and Vittorio de Sica's *Shoeshine (Sciuscià,* 1946)—a narrative film that was strongly influenced by the nonfiction approach. This was Clément's first feature-length film, although he had previously made *Ceux du rail* (1943), a documentary about French railway workers. Originally conceived as a nonfiction film, *Battle of the Rail* uses a script and actors to depict the sabotage activities of French railway workers who were part of the Resistance during the period of the Allied invasion of the Normandy Coast; the narration of the English language is spoken by Charles Boyer. With what Bazin praises as "artistic honesty" (125), Clément not only captures the great integrated power of the railroad (as did Willy Zielke in *Stahltier*), but also, and more important, shows the necessity for the equally integrated sabotage activities. Here, as in Buster Keaton's *The General* (1927), the most exciting sequence features a train that has been abandoned by its crew to function as a demonic engine of destruction; as with the Keaton film, this culminates in a terrifying derailment. However, as propaganda, the film can also be slightly smug and self-congratulatory, particularly in making the French seem to be as clever as the Germans are overbearing and stupid. Similar in their liveliness and intensity are Clément's *The Damned (Les maudits,* 1947), a suspenseful thriller about an escaping German submarine that also combines narrative and nonfiction footage, and Jean Grémillon's *The Sixth of June at Dawn (Le 6 juin à l'aube,* 1946), which depicts Normandy from the perspective of the Allied invasion on June 6, 1944.

During the Occupation, Georges Rouquier developed a reputation for sensitive observation in the Flaherty mode with such films as *Le charron* (1943), a short film about a wheelwright, and *Le tonnelier* (1945), about a barrelmaker. While both of these films emphasize a return to craftsmanship, which the Vichy government valued, Rouquier says that both films record traditional crafts that became all the more important in view of shortages of crucial materials.[31] Thus, to some, these films are propaganda; to others, realism. His *Farrebique* (1946), a poetic film that features members of the Rouquier family, takes a look at everyday life on a French farm as well as a look toward the future, and might be called a "country symphony." The history of the family and its farm are balanced by daily concerns and set within the cycle of the seasons, a progression that is advanced by time-lapse photography. Its narrative cross-cuts between various farm activities and the central subject of bread baking, a device that not only provides continuity but stresses the almost spiritual role that bread plays in the family's life. When the grandfather dies, the cutting of bread, which was the old man's task, passes to his eldest son. This lyricism is broken by a concern for the future. As one era ends, and another begins (in the family as well as in France), the Rouquiers debate whether or not to use the grandfather's money to bring electricity to their farm or to repair the old farmhouse. In 1950, he continued this tradition with *The Salt of the Earth (Le sel de la terre),* about life in the Camargue, and returned to the family and its life with *Biquefarre* (1984), which includes shots from the first film and depicts the family at another turning point in its history.

Despite the war, the French continued to make films on art and artists. Notable titles include René Lucot's *Rodin* (1942); Jean Lods's *Aristide Maillol* (1943);

Gilbert Prouteau's *God Chose Paris* (*Dieu a choisi Paris*) and François Campaux's *Henri Matisse* (1945). Finally, in Belgium, where nonfiction film production had virtually stopped during the war, there were films by André Cauvin and Henri Storck. Cauvin's *Congo* (1943) documents the "tropical help" that the Congolese provided to the allied war industry, and Storck's *Peasant Symphony* (*Symphonie paysanne* or *Boerensymfonie*, 1944), one of his masterpieces, recalls *Farrebique* in its celebration of natural cycles, the earth, and farmers.

10 American Films for World War II

If, among the nonfiction films made during World War II, the British films were characterized by their humanistic vision of man's ability to endure and prevail, and the Nazi films by their threatening bellicosity, the American films were distinguished both for their bold, patriotic, and shrewd explanation of why we were fighting, and for their sophisticated cinematic artistry. The wartime nonfiction film propaganda of Allied and Axis nations alike present an inflated picture of traditions, values, and strengths. The American films depict a powerful and righteous nation, self-confident in its destiny to save the world from tyranny. According to Allan M. Winkler, such propaganda "reflected the way that most ordinary Americans viewed themselves as they worked to defeat the Axis powers. In the end American propaganda reflected American policy, and indeed America itself."[1]

Many of the nonfiction films made during World War II were characterized by the same traits that distinguished the feature films of the previous decade: sentimental and corny, witty and intelligent, simplistic and superficial, hard-hitting and zealous. And, in fact, unlike the American nonfiction films of the 1930s, which were made primarily by independent or group filmmakers on the East coast, many of the wartime films were made, under the supervision of Washington, by Hollywood professionals in the world's motion picture capital. This enterprise involved an impressive collaboration between industry and government. As Americans were drafted into military service, so, too, were directors, cinematographers, editors, and writers of Hollywood and independent films drafted into the film units of the armed forces, with the resources of major studios, distributors, film archives, and motion picture equipment manufacturers put at their disposal.[2] The Hollywood part of this effort was coordinated by the War Activities Committee of the Motion Picture Industry, which was organized into seven divisions that reflected the complex American film industry: theaters, distributors, Hollywood production, newsreels, trade press, foreign markets, and public relations. Involved in Washington were the major government agencies—State, Treasury, War, Justice, Interior, Agriculture, Transportation, Civilian Defense, Inter-American Affairs, War Information, War Production Board, and War Relocation Authority. Together, the film industry and the government produced an astonishing number of films of many kinds, for many purposes.[3] Some provide documentary records of combat; others illustrate the civilian contributions to the war effort; and still others honor human bravery and strength.[4]

In the United States, the only Allied country untouched by war activity within its continental borders, civilians had to rely for their war news on personal correspondence from military personnel in the war zones, newspapers, radio, motion pictures, or media prepared by the Office of War Information. National television broadcasting, the chief source of public information in the Vietnam War, did not exist in the 1940s, and neither did the concept of the "living room war." Indeed, through their weekly attendance at the movies, audiences saw up-to-date newsreels and government combat films, as well as narrative films, which provided information, entertainment, and escape from their anxieties about the war. The partnership between Hollywood and Washington ensured a steady flow of timely information to motion picture screens in the nation's theaters, military camps, military and civilian hospitals, and to industrial plants. These films helped Americans to understand the vital importance of many new things, including the necessity for combat in places they had never heard of before, twenty-four-hour industrial production, and food rationing. This information not only informed and educated the public, but also encouraged their generous support of the war effort. During the war, attendance was high at local movie theatres, which proved to be an ideal location for selling war bonds or for collecting money for such purposes as war relief.[5]

In the United States, mustering support for the war effort was not always easy, for many Americans had not only a stalwart isolationist tendency, but also a deep-seated distrust of government propaganda. Industry and government leaders, who were impressed by the Nazi and British film programs, were certain that film could be successful in informing the predominantly isolationist Americans of how, where, when, and why they were fighting and thus awaken their patriotic sympathies. According to Elmer Davis, the wartime head of the Office of War Information (OWI), there were at least three other obstacles to wartime film production: the danger that the propaganda would reflect partisan views, especially the president's; the lack of military cooperation in gathering and reporting facts, especially when it might aid or give comfort to enemy; and the belief among some members of the press that they should be free to gather the news without having to rely on a government spokesperson.[6]

During the Second World War, nonfiction film helped to unify the public in its patriotism and to encourage its support of military involvement. Although Allied films do not idealize war, they attempt to justify World War II by explaining it in clear, non-ambiguous terms. Still, bound together by a common goal—freedom from Fascist aggression and tyranny—Allied filmmakers often set aside logic and convention, as well as civic and personal values, to support the overriding idea of victory over the enemy.[7]

AMERICAN PROPAGANDA AND COUNTER-PROPAGANDA FOR WORLD WAR II

Louis de Rochemont's *The Ramparts We Watch* (1940) is the earliest example of an American wartime documentary, although it was released before the United States declared war and cannot be easily categorized among the films produced during the war. A "March of Time" production, it is a daring and successful attempt to counter the feelings of American isolation before the Second World War. *The Ramparts We Watch* is both a fictional reenactment and a compilation of newsreel footage. It is set apart from the other "March of Time" films by its feature length, dramatic narrative, use of patriotic and popular war songs, and Lothar Wolff's skillful editing of newsreel, Nazi propaganda, and reenactment footage. While its sense of small-town America is somewhat trite, it presents a convincing and accurate analysis of American attitudes before the Second World War, explaining the American role in the First World War and, through its sentimental appeal to a sense of justice and democracy, directly attempts to relate that struggle to the impending conflict. In its attempt to inform Americans about the war, *The Ramparts We Watch* is superseded only by Frank Capra's *War Comes to America,* a similar film in the "Why We Fight" series. Aside from Samuel Spewack's *World at War* (1942), a compilation film that provides historical background to America's entry into combat, other early films had more mundane objectives, as reflected by some of their titles: *Meat Rationing, Send Your Tin Cans to War,* and *Rent Control.*

The following discussion is divided into these categories: films produced by the U.S. Office of War Information; military training and civilian information films, including the "Why We Fight" series; incentive films; combat films; and films on the effects of war. Many films overlap these categories. Some war films appeared in different versions—under different titles and in different lengths—depending on their use in theatrical, nontheatrical, domestic, or overseas distribution. In this chapter, the dates, where given, are those for the first known release of a film.

United States Office of War Information

Between the outbreak of the war in Europe on September 1, 1939, and the Japanese attack on Pearl Harbor on December 7, 1941, the United States government made no organized attempt to produce propaganda and counterpropaganda films. But with Pearl Harbor and the American declaration of war on Japan, which followed the next day, Washington recognized the need for an organized information effort to gain the attention and support of the American public and its allies. Soon after Pearl Harbor, President Roosevelt endorsed the motion picture as "one of our most effective media in informing and entertaining our citizens," declaring that it could make "a very useful contribution" to the war effort (Roosevelt quoted in Winkler 57). Before the declaration of war, however, the American government's attitude toward the arts—motion pictures, in particular—went no further than the issue of "art or propaganda." In England, as Richard Griffith writes, Grierson built "his successful British documentary movement on a principle of compromise between the interests of adult education on the one hand and the interests of big business and big government on the other."[8] But except for the pioneering but limited efforts of Mary Losey to organize the Association of Documentary Film Producers between 1939 and 1942, no one in the United States—and certainly not the government—had yet been able to unite filmmakers as diverse, for example, as Lorentz, Van Dyke, Strand, and Hurwitz into one production group.

The outbreak of war provided the impetus for change. In 1942, the U.S. government created the Office of War Information (OWI) and consolidated government information services under the direction of Elmer Davis, a prominent radio newscaster.[9] The OWI served as liaison between the Government and the motion picture industry to help coordinate the production, distribution, and exhibition of films. Through its Domestic Branch, the OWI coordinated the release of war news for distribution at home; through its Overseas Branch, under the direction of noted playwright and screenwriter Robert E. Sherwood (*The Petrified Forest, Abe Lincoln in Illinois, The Best Years of Our Lives*), it launched a huge information and propaganda campaign abroad. The films produced by the OWI's Domestic Branch, including the "Magazine of the Screen" (a monthly release of very short subjects), were released in nontheatrical distribution through community organizations, libraries, and educational institutions. Its overseas distribution included the "United Newsreel," designed for counter-propaganda in enemy countries and produced cooperatively by five major American newsreel firms—Paramount, Pathé, Fox Movietone, Universal, and News of the Day;[10] other productions intended for foreign use included monthly screen magazines, other newsreels, and approximately forty original nonfiction films produced in seventeen languages.[11] As the war continued, Congressional opposition to the domestic operations of the OWI curtailed funding, and by 1944 the OWI operated mostly abroad, where it helped to maintain Allied confidence and to undermine enemy morale. The Office of Strategic Services (OSS) was created in 1942 to obtain information about the enemy, to sabotage their war potential, and to weaken morale. Both the OWI and OSS were abolished in 1945. The OWI's foreign functions were transferred to the State Department, while many of the functions and activities of the OSS were absorbed by the Central Intelligence Agency (CIA) when it was established in 1947.

The OWI was challenged to make films that would carry the American message at home and abroad and, at the same time, avoid provoking partisan Congressional criticism, censorship, or other attempts at interference. To strengthen not only the OWI cause, but the American feeling of dominance, its theme, as Davis repeatedly stated, was "that we are coming, that we are going to win, and that in the long run everybody will be better off because we won" (Davis quoted in Winkler 155). As Philip Dunne has said, the wartime filmmaker had to assume that "the audience must be *for* one thing, *against* something else."[12] The OWI's task was difficult, for many Americans had vivid memories of World War I and were reluctant to get involved in another major conflict. Thus, especially at the beginning of the war, despite the news from the European fronts, the frequent air raid drills at home, and the devastating loss at Pearl Harbor, the American public at large, as well as the new military personnel, remained ignorant, confused, or in conflict about the new war (Barnouw 155).

Providing the facts and gathering support for the war effort was a mission by no means unique to OWI and World War II. MacCann points out that

> The pattern of the OWI's campaigns was not very different from the activities of George Creel . . . in World War I—and not much more ambitious. The big difference was in tone, temper, and taste, not in fundamental objectives. (120)

While many of the films made by the OWI Domestic Branch were straightforward informational films (*World at War, Colleges at War, Doctors at War*), a more aggressive stance appeared in the OWI Overseas Branch films intended for counter-propaganda use in enemy countries. Films like *Hymn of the Nations, The Town,* or *The Cummington Story* were more ambitious and earnest in, for example, their advocacy of domestic preparedness or warning against Fascist evil. Following Pearl Harbor, the OSS made various films about Japan; these include *Japanese Behavior,* an attempt to introduce Americans to Japanese ways of thinking and living, and two films about Japan's strategic position and advantages: *Geography of Japan* and *Natural Resources of Japan.* Far more insidious was *Japanese Relocation* (1943). People of Japanese descent were considered security risks, particularly since the majority of them were living on the West Coast, a likely target for invasion; therefore, the U.S. Government forced more than 110,000 people, two-thirds of them U.S. citizens, from their homes, farms, and businesses to spend the duration of the war in "relocation" camps in the American interior. This short film is an attempt to provide an explanation for what the government regarded as a necessary precaution. Similar in intent were the films of the War Relocation Authority: *Challenge to Democracy,* another favorable description of the detention camps; *The Way Ahead,* which shows relocated Japanese in new jobs; *Go For Broke,* which describes the training of Japanese-American recruits, and *For Valor,* which celebrates Japanese-American war heroes. Seen today, these films are simplistic, particularly since the establishment of these detention camps is now believed to have abrogated the civil liberties of those Japanese who were U.S. Citizens.

The OWI overseas branch, which received over three times the funds as the domestic branch, made films designed to inform military and civilian audiences abroad about the American way of life. MacCann confirms that, although the films of both divisions emphasized news, facts, and "the strategy of truth," the

> dominant and continuing purpose of film production by the Overseas Branch was the indirect support of the armed forces and the foreign policy of the United States by telling the story of America to its friends and acquaintances. (138–39)

The films for the overseas audience conspicuously avoid depicting social problems, but rather present an oversimplified, patriotic vision of traditional small-town America. Nonetheless, they are films of simple beauty and deep feeling, emphasizing the values for which Americans were fighting. Some of these films are humorous (*The Autobiography of a Jeep,* 1943); educational (*The Grain That Built a*

Hemisphere, 1943); or instructional (*Water: Friend or Enemy,* 1943). But, overall, these OWI films are concerned with life in America as it had been, as it was, and as the filmmakers hoped it would be after the war.

Like many Hollywood films of the 1930s, these nonfiction films present a romanticized view of America, in an effort to convince foreign audiences that the United States was a country of small towns, quiet church-going citizens, and lazy leisure-time activities. Such an image is suggested in Josef von Sternberg's *The Town* (1944), a short account of the cultural and architectural traditions that Americans inherited from Europe. Helen Grayson's and Larry Madison's *The Cummington Story* (1945) is more effective in depicting America's ability to absorb foreign influences. This lovely film captures all that is best in a small New England town, and, by implication, in the country as a whole. The story concerns four foreign families who leave Europe's turmoil for a new life. When they arrive in Cummington, townspeople are cool, even aloof; eventually, the minister, who narrates the film, helps both Americans and foreigners to understand and overcome their self-consciousness and, in time, to build mutual confidence and respect. Despite *The Cummington Story*'s sentimentality, which is intensified by Aaron Copland's music, it remains a successful variation on the familiar melting pot theme. Seeing such a film, together with the films about the Japanese relocation camps, can give audiences today a deeper understanding of American social conditions during the war and the challenges met by the OWI filmmakers who produced these films.

Willard Van Dyke's *Northwest U.S.A.* (1945)—more folksy than *The Cummington Story,* but also more factual—depicts the Northwest as a trade crossroads for over-the-pole flights and documents the building of the Grand Coulee Dam, emphasizing its role in supplying power to wartime industries. Van Dyke's *Oswego* (1943) is a study of a small American town located on Lake Ontario; during the Westward movement, its strategic position made Oswego vital to defense against the Indians and it remained vital during wartime for its harbor and munitions plants. Van Dyke also presents the town as a bulwark of such values as freedom, tolerance, and peace, as exemplified by Main Street and the town's newspaper, courthouse, schools, and houses of worship. The freedoms represented by these institutions are linked to the real purpose of the film: its record of United Nations Week, in which members of the UN forces are invited to see America firsthand. The film, which explains that the purpose of this visit is world peace, was released one year before Oswego was designated as the site of a major shelter for war refugees.[13] Van Dyke's other films for the OWI include *Steeltown* (1944), a picture of life and work of American steelworkers; *Pacific Northwest* (1944), a film about the importance of Oregon and Washington to world trade and transportation; and *San Francisco: 1945* (1945), which records the founding conference of the United Nations and emphasizes that the world looked to the United Nations to prevent future wars.

Highlighting another region of the United States, Alexander Hammid's *Valley of the Tennessee* (1944) examines the Tennessee Valley Authority (TVA) project, emphasizing the development of human resources through the development of natural resources. However, it minimizes the complex social and political issues

The Cummington Story (Helen Grayson and Larry Madison, USA, 1945)

that surrounded the project without placing appropriate emphasis on the communal aspects of the project. Hammid's *A Better Tomorrow* (1945) is even more superficial in its view of the New York City school system. Filmed in a high school, it concentrates on the new aspects of progressive education, with minimal attention given to the schools' inability to improve poor teaching and cope with racial problems. *A Better Tomorrow* was effective war propaganda, but, as information, it is as unfair to its subject as it is to the country, for by avoiding the present, it distorts the future.

In a completely different manner, Jules Bucher's *The Window Cleaner* (1945) provides a brief account of a day in the life of a Manhattan window cleaner. The film's attitude is realistic and independent, implying that the window cleaner is as much a part of the American scene as the skyscraper in which he works. This simple subject is enhanced by a whimsical jazz score and a plucky commentary spoken by the window cleaner himself.

While some OWI films concentrated on regional values, towns, or projects, others were concerned with general American institutions and the people who were a part of them. Henwar Rodakiewicz's *Capital Story* (1945) recounts the work of the U. S. Department of Health; John Houseman's *Tuesday in November* (1945) explains the American electoral process; and Hammid's *Library of Congress*

(1945) presents a lively picture of the institution's work in preservation, education, and service to scholars and the general community. Hammid's *Toscanini: The Hymn of Nations* (1945), reportedly the most famous and most popular of the OWI overseas films, presents a sensitive portrait of maestro Arturo Toscanini conducting a radio broadcast of Verdi's "Hymn of the Nations," programmed in celebration of Mussolini's fall and the liberation of Italy.

These OWI films produced for overseas audiences clearly share an unpretentious, sentimental, and romantic view of America; they tend to overlook the faults and concentrate on the virtues of American life, especially when those virtues foster hope for the postwar future. These films were produced, written, and directed by people who had already established a reputation for quality in American nonfiction film; and so they are almost always uniformly excellent in their cinematography, editing, and musical scoring. Indeed, within the limited context of war propaganda for overseas distribution, they must be excused for what they omit, only because what they provide is so good. These films reinforced our self-image and showed the peoples of other countries what we wanted them to see. Acknowledging their simplistic tendency to overlook America's diversity, MacCann writes that these "were earnest, honest efforts to pin down some part of the American scene in terms that could be understood by audiences of varying literacy and background" (MacCann 143).

In addition to making films under OWI sponsorship, many of these same filmmakers continued to create nonfiction films for commercial and institutional organizations. In 1944, Willard Van Dyke and Ben Maddow made *The Bridge* for the Foreign Policy Association. This low-key film assesses the effects of World War II on the trade and transportation problems of South America, and is as much an affirmation of the power and efficiency of air transport (which is "the bridge") as it is an analysis of the social and political problems that hinder international transport and trade.[14] However, the film's narration is too general to give real meaning to the significance of air transport. A similar narrative vagueness also detracts from the effectiveness of Van Dyke's *Journey Into Medicine* (1947), produced by Irving Jacoby for the State Department; the same fault is evident in Van Dyke's and Jacoby's *The Photographer* (1948) (see chapter 13). Jacoby's *The Pale Horseman* (1945) is an excellent compilation film about the work of the United Nations Relief and Rehabilitation Administration (UNRRA) and the members of the Allied armies to relocate people, stop epidemics, and provide shelter. In a departure from his earlier work, Jacoby wrote a sincere and gentle narration to offset the grim reality of the scenes of famine and epidemic disease. Like David Miller's *Seeds of Destiny* (1946), the value of *The Pale Horseman* does not lie in its presentation of fact, but rather in such extraordinary images of human suffering as a child sitting on a pile of rubble, shaking so much from hunger and exhaustion that he is unable to accept the food being offered by a soldier.

Frank Capra: Military Training and Civilian Information Films

Frank Capra made the most distinctive contribution of all the Hollywood directors involved in the production of nonfiction films for the education and training of the armed forces. The outstanding example of his achievement is the "Why We Fight" series, representing American war documentary at its best. But Capra was also responsible for producing, directing, or supervising other important military training and civilian information films. The unmistakable style of Capra's wartime films—fresh, imaginative, and, above all, enthusiastic—sets them apart from routine training films, many of which are precise but also pedantic. Such films guided personnel through every stage of military life from induction, orientation, and training, to off-duty activities, demobilization, and preparation for postwar life. These lessons included how to regard the enemy, how to dress, how to keep clean, how to care for equipment, how to survive on the desert, and how to avoid disease. These military training films range from John Ford's vivid *Sex Hygiene* (1941) to Walt Disney's animated color films that transform the complexities of meteorology and navigation into fun.

Capra and his collaborators—who included Anatole Litvak, Anthony Veiller, Theodor ("Dr. Seuss") Geisel, Dimitri Tiomkin, Joris Ivens, and Carl Foreman, among many others—made several information films about the enemy in the "Know Your Allies—Know Your Enemies" series. These include *Know Your Ally, Britain* (1943); *Know Your Enemy—Japan; Here is Germany* (1945), begun by Ernest Lubitsch as *Know Your Enemy—Germany* in 1942; *Your Job in Germany* (1945); and *Our Job in Japan* (1946). A good example is *Know Your Ally, Britain.* Just as the British depicted themselves in *Listen to Britain* (1942), a film very popular in the United States, so the Americans attempted to understand and project British character and culture in *Know Your Ally, Britain.* A tough, simple film, it stresses our roots in England's history, our similarities, rather than differences, and our need for unity in the war effort. Through the use of homely figures of speech, as well as athletic metaphors and analogies, the film succeeds in creating a lively image of the British people. Still, while it strongly refutes Hitler's anti-British propaganda, *Know Your Ally, Britain* perpetuates certain silly stereotypes about English life; it does, however, remain scrupulously fair in trying to understand the truth behind these stereotypes. In human terms, it is an interesting and effective film.

"The Army–Navy Screen Magazine," another example of the work of the Capra unit, was one of the most instructive and successful of the training films made by the United States Army exclusively for the armed forces. The twenty-minute films in this biweekly series were designed to accommodate audience requests. Folksy, humorous, optimistic, they were intended to provide information in a flexible, informal format and to build morale. If a man requested a picture of his home town, he usually got it. Another soldier sent in lyrics of his own composition, asking without much hope that they be set to music and that the Army get "some dame to sing it." If they did, "I'd faint!" Shortly thereafter, the song was recorded and filmed; the commentator remarked, "Here you are, soldier, go ahead and faint." A typical issue of this screen gazette would range from the silly (a "Private Snafu" cartoon) to the serious (a report by J. Edgar Hoover on Nazi espionage in the United States). Nonetheless, because they served as the G.I.'s own films, they carried less government propaganda and more entertainment than other wartime films.

In addition to the educational "Know Your Allies—Know Your Enemies" series, and humorous "Army–Navy Screen Magazine," Capra also produced inspirational films. *The Negro Soldier* (1944), directed by Capra and Stuart Heisler, is film whose honest intentions are unfortunately weakened by its use of stereotypes. Meant to instill pride in the role that black people have played in the nation's defense since the Revolutionary War, the film also shows prominent blacks in sports, the arts, and professional life. It discusses the prejudice against Negroes in Nazi and Japanese propaganda, but totally avoids the issue of segregation in the United States armed forces. The only scenes of military life that integrate blacks and whites depict a church service and an officer's training course. While there is no direct reference to segregation, we see it, indirectly, and unintentionally, in the depiction of a typical Negro soldier's experiences (through a letter read by his mother). We see him going through enlistment, training, and combat in a segregated company. In creating these undeniably accurate scenes, the filmmakers lost an opportunity to acquaint fighting men with their black counterparts, just as they had acquainted them with their European allies. Moreover, the film not only depicts segregation without the slightest degree of criticism, but also uses degrading stereotypes such shuffling jazz rhythms and a musical comedy ending that is as offensive to black fighting men as it is destructive to the whole intent of the film. In a final montage, utilizing four images on the split screen, we see black soldiers marching to a jazzy version of the Negro spiritual "Joshua Fought the Battle of Jericho," a frivolous conclusion for a film that begins by pointing out that the first man to die in the Boston Massacre of 1770 was a Negro patriot.

As the war in Europe drew to a close, victorious but homesick troops looked forward to returning to the United States. To boost their morale, but also to prepare them for the possibility of their transfer to the Pacific front, Capra made *Two Down, One to Go* (1945).

THE "WHY WE FIGHT" SERIES

The films in Frank Capra's "Why We Fight" series constitute the single most powerful nonfiction film achievement in the war effort.[15] Addressed to those in civilian and military audiences alike who doubted the need for another world war, these films, in Capra's view, "not only stated, but, in many instances, actually created and nailed down American and world pre-war policy."[16] There are seven titles in the series: *Prelude to War* (1943), *The Nazis Strike* (1943), *Divide and Conquer* (1943), *The Battle of Britain* (1943), *The Battle of China* (1944), *The Battle of Russia* (1944), and *War Comes to America* (1945). They were made in historical order, depicting Nazi aggression and brutality, the major battles of the war, and, finally, the impact of prewar and war efforts on American public opinion. These are remarkable both as propaganda, made by film experts who had studied and restudied the best of the Nazi and British films, and as compilation films, lucid and fresh in their handling of many cinematic sources, historically balanced, and persuasively and dramatically presented.[17]

Prelude to War is not only the first, but also the most patriotic and bellicose of the series. Its purpose is to tell its audience "why we fight," and it proceeds toward this goal by contrasting the "free world" with the "slave world" of German and

Prelude to War (from the "Why We Fight" series, Frank Capra, USA, 1943)

Japanese militarism and their organizations of "Fascist stooges led by dictators." The film documents terrorist executions, the destruction of churches and synagogues, brainwashing of German and Japanese citizens, and the indoctrination of children. In a brilliant montage of goose-stepping Nazi soldiers, the film makes its strongest point about military repression. As contrast, Capra stresses the free world's freedom of the press, worship, and elections. But he is tough in answering allegations of American isolationism and lack of support for the League of Nations. His blunt logic—"It's their world or ours"—is matched by his incisive toughness—"The chips are down." In its vigorous handling of an explosive question, this film sets the tone for the films that follow.

Perhaps the most fervently anti-Nazi film in the series, *The Nazis Strike* describes the "maniacal will," the "madness," and the "insane passion for conquest" of the Nazi leaders. It stresses their terrorist tactics and use of propaganda and explains their pincer strategy (an aspect more fully detailed in *Divide and Conquer*). However, its use of music ("Warsaw Concerto" and "Onward, Christian Soldiers") creates a mood of moral righteousness that, despite its good intentions, seems, at least today, to diminish its effectiveness. Indeed, all of the "Why We Fight" films lack some degree of subtlety and reserve.

Divide and Conquer records the high point of the Nazi offensive, when Germany invaded Belgium, Holland, Denmark, Norway, and France in preparation for its bombing and planned invasion of Britain. The title refers to Hitler's use of propaganda to confuse and conquer the smaller free countries through sabotage, the fifth column, strikes, riots, and hate literature. Counterpointing the remarkably factual narrative tone is a comparison between Hitler's lies and "efficiency" and the tactics of the gangster Dillinger. There is also heavy irony—a Capra specialty in these films—in the juxtaposed comments on the neutrality of the Low Countries and on the Nazi betrayal of the Dutch surrender in the bombing of the shipyards and civilian population of Rotterdam. France is portrayed as disillusioned and cynical, mindful of her heavy First World War casualties, dismayed at the failure of the League of Nations, and weary of her own ideals. Such criticism characterizes this series' attitude toward countries reluctant to fight, isolationism, and inaction by allies of the League of Nations. A well-organized film, clear, explanatory, persuasive in its use of charts, maps, and diagrams, *Divide and Conquer* is an especially hard-hitting attack on Nazi policies, which it describes as "a new low in inhumanity."

Three films in the "Why We Fight" series are devoted to specific military campaigns. *The Battle of Britain,* which lauds the Royal Air Force, provides a dramatic account of the strength of the British people after the defeat at Dunkirk and during the blitz of London and Coventry: "Hitler could kill them, but damned if he would lick them." Here, the music—the familiar British "Land of Hope and Glory" and "British Grenadier"—provides ironic musical comment on the fiery swastikas burning across the film's graphic map of Europe.

The Battle of China, the weakest of the three, supports China, but its tone of moral outrage is less effective in conveying the horrors of war than the terrifying images of the wounded and killed. Like *The Battle of Russia,* the film is a record in praise of the popular resistance against aggression, and, like the other films in the series, it uses colorful figures of speech to make its points. For example, the Burma Road brings the "blood plasma of supplies" and the Yangtze River is "China's sorrow." Ending with the assertion that "China's war is our war," this film, like the others, depicts enemy aggression and the necessity for resistance and defense. And, like the others, it makes the indirect point that we must fight over there so that we will not have to fight at home.

Much the strongest of the three battle films, *The Battle of Russia* is a tough, fast, informative film that presents a thorough coverage of the depth and breadth of the massive Nazi attack on Russia. Compiled like the other films from actual and staged footage, it is almost one-half hour longer. While the lengthy cross-sectional view of Russia's natural and human resources is less exciting than similar sequences in *War Comes to America,* the last film in the series, it is hard-hitting, heavily ironic, and full of praise for the strength and determination of the Russian people in their fight against the Nazis: "Generals may win campaigns, but people win wars." In these films, Capra and his staff made effective use of music native to the countries whose plight they were portraying; here, they include many types of Russian music, including choral songs, folk ballads, and themes from classical works. More analytical than the other films, *The Battle of Russia* discusses specific reasons for the final Nazi failure in Russia. More dramatic than the other films, it reaches its climax in the Siege of Leningrad and a final, unforgettable shot of a captured German soldier trudging across the ice in a pair of makeshift paper shoes, an ironic comment on the "invincible" Nazi juggernaut. And like the other films in the series, it concludes with the ringing of the Liberty Bell and a superimposed "V" for victory.

The final film, *War Comes to America,* resembles the "March of Time" production *The Ramparts We Watch* (1940) in its cross-sectional view of an isolationist America reluctant to enter another world war. Capra's film is very persuasive propaganda, showing American values and the great shift in public opinion that led to our entrance into the war, while the de Rochemont film is a dramatic reenactment that compares American reactions before the First World War with the period prior to entrance into the Second World War.

War Comes to America begins with the standard disclaimer: this is a War Department film, compiled from authentic newsreels, official allied films, and captured enemy films; when necessary, for purposes of clarity, reenactments have been made. In its attempt to explain America's gradual shift in public opinion from isolationism, it carefully establishes several important background points. First, it traces the American fight for freedom from landing of the pilgrims, through the frontier and immigration movements that built the country, to the First World War. Second, it emphasizes the positive attributes of the American people, showing them to be hardworking, inventive, enterprising, eager for education, and sports- and pleasure-loving. But, more important, it depicts Americans as free people who believe in the future, in peace, and in the liberty and dignity of man: people who hate war, but who will fight to preserve freedom. Third, to the question—"Is the war necessary?"—it answers that world events make it so. To appeal to the average soldier in the audience, it parallels typical events from his childhood and adolescent years with actual world events, from the Depression through the Neutrality Act, through the Japanese-Chinese conflict to the Munich Pact. It utilizes figures from the Gallup Poll (referred to as an expression of "we the people") to substantiate the rising sympathy for war among Americans. The German-American *Bund* was affiliated with the Nazis, and footage from its rally in Madison Square Garden, where Nazi symbols were numerous, demonstrated the immediacy of an enemy that some might have thought was confined to foreign shores. As the war effort builds, we see a cross section of enlisted men ("This is the Army, Mr. Jones" on the sound track), Hitler's invasion of Paris ("The Last Time I Saw Paris"), and the bombing of Pearl Harbor. The film's method skillfully combines public opinion polls, official testimony, and historical fact and reference in providing a comprehensive picture of the diversity of American life. Perhaps the most carefully documented answer to the overriding question "why we fight," *War Comes to America* is a fast-moving, patriotic, and ultimately convincing film.

The "Why We Fight" series is persuasive, dramatic, and forceful in its presentation of facts, and especially sophisticated in its use of sound, music, narration, and speech. The films are masterful in their compilation of many kinds of film footage, a brilliant triumph of form over content. The narration is tough and ironic, wholly American in its rhythms, figures of speech, and attitudes toward the enemy. Refusing to admit that the United States might be defeated, they juxtapose the bestial Hitler and the heroic ordinary citizens who were his victims, and urge Americans to muster the strength and determination to prevail against the enemy. These strong films are determined to help American fighting forces to fight, persist, and win, to believe in the moral necessity of their mission, and, throughout, to retain faith in the principle on which these complex films were made: the right to enjoy freedom, justice, and happiness is undeniable, worth the fight, and within grasp. The "Why We Fight" series remains the best group of films to have been made during the Second World War, and, in addition, the best record on film of the reasons behind that war, the most dramatic account of its battles, and the most eloquent tribute to the civilian and military men and women who fought and died fighting.

Incentive Films

Incentive films, which frequently fall into the category of other wartime informational films, were produced by a variety of government agencies to foster the idea that everyone could have a role in the war effort. The films of the War Production Board, directed mainly at industrial workers, were intended to train industrial workers, to boost their morale and production output, and to demonstrate the importance of their work and products to the general war effort. Examples include *The Story of Big Ben* (1944), a tribute to shipyard workers, and *How Good is a Gun?* (1944), designed to praise and motivate munitions workers. These are the people pictured in *War Town* (1943), an OWI film that provides a brisk, straightforward presentation of the problems in an Alabama town overcrowded with defense workers and their families. Another kind of incentive film was designed to encourage civilian cooperation in government initiatives. These films include the whimsical *Out of the Frying Pan into the Firing Line* (1944), a Walt Disney–Minnie Mouse collaboration on the saving of fat scraps; *Road to Victory* (1944), in which Bing Crosby and Frank Sinatra promote the purchase of war bonds; and *America's Hidden Weapon* (1944), similar to Britain's *They Also Serve*, which documents the work of farmers and "victory" gardeners in supplying increased wartime agricultural needs. Similar films explained the need for the mobilization of women in industry and the military, the protection of the health and physical vigor of all citizens, including the care of children, and the need for blackouts, food rationing, and saving scrap metal.

Combat Films

While many filmmakers were producing training, propaganda, and incentive films for use at home and abroad, scores of combat cameramen, most of them from the Signal Corps, were on various battlegrounds gathering direct photographic records of the war. The coverage includes operations on the ground, in the air, and at sea. Often working and sometimes dying under live fire, these cameramen brought the war home to civilians. Among the first combat films were *Our Russian Front*

(1942), by Lewis Milestone and Joris Ivens, and *United We Stand* (1942), a newsreel compilation.[18] In an effort to relate the soldiers of World War II to those who have protected America since the eighteenth century wars of revolution, Garson Kanin directed two films designed to instill in their audiences a sense of history and a realization of the present conflict: *Ring of Steel* (1942) and *Fellow Americans* (1942). *Fellow Americans*, the more effective of the two, is an impassioned cry for vigilance that recounts the bombing of Pearl Harbor as if it occurred over four typical American cities. By telling us that the bombs fell, but "no one heard, no one saw," the narrator is convincing the audience that direct attacks on troops abroad are also indirect attacks on civilians at home. Both films were narrated by prominent actors—the first by Spencer Tracy and the second by James Stewart—whose familiar voices brought their arguments close to the audience. As it is with many war films, Oscar Levant's music is very effective here, utilizing a crescendo of American patriotic themes to overwhelm the sounds of warfare.

As the war progressed, the planning, organization, narrative, and cinematography of combat films improved, not only through experience, but also through the gradual influence of specific theatrical elements brought to the films by the Hollywood directors who made them. William Wyler's *Memphis Belle* (1944) and Walt Disney's *Victory Through Air Power* (1943) are among the films exemplifying this influence, while more routine combat films include *War Department Report* and Darryl F. Zanuck's *At the Front in North Africa* (1943); *AAF Report, Attack: The Battle for New Britain, The Liberation of Rome, With the Marines at Tarawa, The Battle of the Marianas, Guam: I Saw it Happen, Beachhead to Berlin* (1944); and *Brought to Action* (1945). The combat films of two Hollywood masters—John Ford and John Huston—deserve further discussion.

John Ford

John Ford made a major contribution to the wartime nonfiction film. As chief of the Field Photographic Branch of the Office of Strategic Services (OSS, later the CIA), he, like Capra, had his own production unit and, according to Tag Gallagher, "made a great many films, some of which were only projected once, and in the greatest secret, before a few government leaders."[19] Their strategic importance is suggested by some of the titles: *How to Operate Behind Enemy Lines; How to Interrogate Enemy Prisoners; Living Off the Land; Nazi Industrial Manpower; Dunkirk in Reverse*; and *Inside Tibet* (Gallagher 529). Other Ford titles include *Sex Hygiene* (1941), *Scorched Earth* and *Torpedo Squadron* (1942), *Victory in Burma* and *We Sail at Midnight* (1943). Ford's most memorable wartime nonfiction film is *The Battle of Midway* (1942).

Like Huston's *The Battle of San Pietro*—indeed like all combat films—*The Battle of Midway* is remarkable because it is authentic. Unlike Huston, who makes an ironic anti-war statement, Ford makes a tribute to fighting men that is both supportive and sentimental. But *The Battle of Midway* is more than an authentic and enthusiastic record of the naval battle that was one of this war's great turning points. It is what Gallagher calls a "directly manipulative" (203) propaganda film, designed to provide Americans with a view of actual combat that is direct in its realism, stirring in its patriotism, and unflinching in its opposition to war.

No wartime filmmaker knew better than Ford how to manipulate cinematography, narration, and music to make a point. *The Battle of Midway* was intended primarily for the parents (especially the mothers) of the fighting men who were involved, and its images provide the audience with the rare, direct immediacy of being there. Midway, seen on a map as a speck of land in the Pacific, is described as "our outpost, your frontyard." Accompanied by several cameramen (including Gregg Toland), Ford, who was often in the line of direct fire, shot most of it himself in color. The power of the shellfire makes the film jump in the camera, and the narrator says, "Yes, this really happened." The folksy narration, read by some of Ford's favorite actors—Jane Darwell, Henry Fonda, Donald Crisp, and Irving Pichel—creates a theatrical tension between the people in the theatre and those on the screen: "Men and women of America, here come your neighbors' sons. You ought to meet them." The music—including "Red River Valley," "Anchors Aweigh," "Onward Christian Soldiers," and "My Country 'Tis of Thee"—evokes strong memories and patriotic emotions and is an integral part of the film's emotional impact.

The Battle of Midway is a deeply humanistic statement about those who fight, who are injured, who survive, and who die. But it is also ultimately and unashamedly about American values, American fighting strengths, and an American victory. For a film that shows and says so much, *The Battle of Midway* is remarkably short (only 17 minutes), but during that brief span, it leaves its audience defenseless. Not surprisingly, it caused a sensation in American theatres and won the Academy Award for the Best Documentary of 1942.[20] Today, it still retains much of its emotional and patriotic power.

John Huston

John Huston made several films for World War II, two of which—*The Battle of San Pietro*, a combat film, and *Let There Be Light*, a film about the effects of war—are classics of the nonfiction film. Huston describes his *Tunisian Victory* (1944), a film co-produced by the United States and Great Britain, as having been compiled from staged scenes shot in the California desert.[21] His *Report from the Aleutians* (1943) is an intelligent account of the ground activities and flying missions of an isolated bomber squadron. Unlike *The Battle of Midway*, which is remarkably short, it is overly long incorporating an excessive amount of material.[22] The film's tough conception, direction, color cinematography, and ironic narration set it apart from some of its contemporaries and reserve for it a special place in the effort to bring home a graphic account of the war to civilians.

Huston's masterpiece is *The Battle of San Pietro* (1945), one of the most distinguished films produced during the Second World War.[23] Like Ford's *The Battle of Midway*, it is both an informative, authentic account of combat and a moving human document. It uses diagrams to explain the military strategy behind the long battle in the Italian mountains, and shots of peoples' faces to reveal the brutal impact of that battle. Made in the heat of fire, the cinematography includes

The Battle of San Pietro (John Huston, USA, 1945)

(with the films that were to come from the Pacific front) some of the best footage from the war. There is direct footage of soldiers being shot and killed, of bodies being placed in unlabeled white sacks, and of townspeople returning to a devastated mountain village. And through these harrowing sequences, we are never allowed to forget the bravery of the infantry, the tenacity of the townspeople, and—remarkable for a propaganda film—lack of narratorial certainty about the ultimate victory over the fascists. All of Huston's war films reflect a deep pacifism, which explains the continual editing required by the War Department. Because *The Battle of San Pietro* was alleged by some Washington military officials to be "anti-war," its release was delayed by almost a year. *Let There Be Light* (1946), one of the most moving antiwar statements ever put on film, was not released until 1986. But neither of these films is directly or intentionally a "pacifist" film; rather, they reflect, with grim immediacy, the need to stop the Nazis and the awful toll taken by the politics of war. Hardly concerned with the policy or rhetoric of war, each tells its version of the real story of war through the faces of little children returning to the bombed-out ruins of San Pietro or through the dazed, uncomprehending reactions of shell-shocked veterans.

The combat films made in Pacific and European battles during the latter part of the war reflect a considerable improvement in cinematic style. Among these combat films from the Pacific are *Brought to Action* (1944), *The Battle for the Marianas* (1944), *Guam: I Saw It Happen* (1944), *The Fleet that Came to Stay* (1945), and *Appointment in Tokyo* (1945). Two films that provided a well-prepared buildup to victory, with intercut shots of the combat and the dead, are *With the Marines at Tarawa* (1944) and *Fury in the Pacific* (1945). The former, in color, is a tribute to the Marines, while the latter provides a more dramatic picture of combat and casualty. William Wyler's *Memphis Belle* (1944) depicts an American bombing raid over Germany, and, in its focus on the men involved, resembles *Target for Tonight*.[24] Wyler and John Sturges codirected *Thunderbolt* (1945), which records the air war in Italy. No war film better captures the intensity of fighting in the Pacific than *To the Shores of Iwo Jima* (1945), a color compilation of footage by Navy, Marine, and Coast Guard combat cameramen. Their organized, efficient, and professional work provides a vivid record of the complex invasion and capture of this strategic Japanese stronghold.

Behind the scenes of combat, other military camera crews recorded the day-to-day activities that made combat possible. Less a combat film than a theatrical record of these workings and their importance is *The Fighting Lady* (1945), a film by Edward Steichen and Rear Admiral Arthur W. Radford. The narration takes a tough attitude ("Remember Pearl Harbor") as it relates the attack on Truk Island, the massive Japanese naval base, but it is also folksy and sentimental in its emphasis on the average sailor and his duties. Steichen's cinematography includes some thrill-

Memphis Belle (William Wyler, USA, 1944)

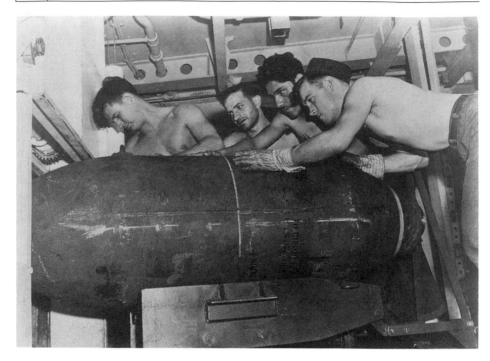

The Fighting Lady (Edward Steichen and Rear Admiral Arthur W. Radford, USA, 1945)

ing color combat footage, but as a record of the work of aircraft carriers at sea, it is essentially a propaganda film made for civilians at home.[25]

Films on the Effects of War

Most wartime films were made for specific military and civilian purposes, for training and for propaganda, and most of them depict, in one way or another, the effects of war on its participants. Another category of films was specifically concerned with the psychological, physical, and emotional results of war. They depict the casualties of the spirit and document destruction and despair, poverty and disease, hopelessness and fear. These documents of war reflect the humanity that helps men endure in the face of battle.

Frank Capra's "Why We Fight" films may explain the political and military reasons for war, but they do not present the psychological and physical effects of war on soldiers. His graphs, charts, maps, and narration may build a persuasive case for waging war, but that kind of information alone does not itself provide sufficient justification, for the destructiveness of war defies and transcends objective explanation; it can be understood only in subjective human terms. The greatest films to come out of World War II—*The True Glory, Let There Be Light,* and *Le Retour*—record man's inhumanity to man, but they seek, also, to preserve that humanity.

The True Glory (1945) portrays war on a grand scale, stressing both the individual soldier and military teamwork in a cross-section view of the Allied war effort from the Normandy invasion to the occupation of Germany. A British-American production, this compilation film relies on footage coedited masterfully by Carol Reed and Garson Kanin, and underscored by the voices of men telling their own stories. In its use of sound, *The True Glory* provides a detailed account of war, expressed in human terms. There is narration—serious, ironic, and humorous—from all kinds of soldiers (young, old, black, white, American, British, enlisted men, and officers) with General Eisenhower adding occasional authoritative comments. The composite of pictures and episodes moves forward progressively, both in military and cinematic terms, but the ending seems abrupt and inconclusive. Since the war was not over when the Allied Forces entered Germany, the meaning of the "true glory" remains incomplete, despite a quotation from the English Book of Common Prayer that attempts an explanation: "It is not the beginning but the continuing of the same, till it be thoroughly finished, which yieldest the true glory."[26] Eisenhower's narration suggests that the true glory is the teamwork of a complex force of men, and the men's voices attest to this miracle of cooperation and tenacity. The overall film seems to confirm that "the true glory" is not victory itself, but the common pursuit of victory by men dedicated to peace

The True Glory (Carol Reed and Garson Kanin, 1945)

and freedom. What the film lacks in climactic focus, it more than compensates for in editing, rhythm, musical score, and overall impact.

John Huston's *Let There Be Light* (1946) at first appears to be a training film designed to convince the general public, especially employers, that soldiers suffering from neuropsychiatric damage can be rehabilitated and resume civilian life.[27] But this film does more than explain psychiatric therapy. It is a record of war, not in combat terms—in the numbers of rounds fired or enemy tanks captured—but in human terms, in the numbers of soldiers reduced to uncontrollable weeping, or resigned to loss of memory, speech, muscle control, or spirit.

The film opens in shadow; we see the stretchers being carried off ships and planes into hospitals. Huston reads the narration: "Here is human salvage—the final result of all that metal and mortar can do to violate human flesh." Using a concealed camera, Huston records actual interviews in which soldiers tell of their hopelessness, grief over lost buddies, insomnia, nightmares, and fears of death. Balanced against the emotional impact of this footage is a detached explanation of mental illness and of the complex therapy by which it is controlled and cured. Indeed, because of its technical vocabulary and disturbing realism, this film may not be for the average viewer. Its primary purpose is to show the techniques of psychiatrists as they attempt to locate the sources of illness; actual footage records narcosynthesis, hypnosis, and group therapy. But it is not in these informational sequences that the film carries its power, but rather in the unforgettably poignant moments before, during, and after therapy. A soldier, believed to be mute, cries out: "God, listen, I can talk; I can talk. Oh, God, listen." A soldier overcome with homesickness and nostalgia sobs when remembering a letter that contained a picture of his girlfriend at home. Another scene depicts a group of soldiers learning to play "When I Grow Too Old to Dream" on the guitar. In the hands of another director, this scene might have been overly sentimental, but under Huston's direction, it rings true.

The theme of *Let There Be Light* is universal: human relationships and human love can provide happiness, safety, and security. To be healed, these returning soldiers have to be supported not only by professional therapy, but also by understanding families, patient employers, and an enlightened public. William Wyler says it another way in *The Best Years of Our Lives* (1946) when the amputee Harold Russell steps out of the cab on his first day home. In that moment are crystallized all his fears about a world that he hopes will understand what it has done to him. Such a subjective experience cannot easily be conveyed. Although *Let There Be Light* ends a little too lightly with a ceremony of discharge from the hospital, it does not leave the impression that war-induced neuroses are quickly treated.

Prior to its release in 1986, the U.S. government suppressed the film from the public, restricting its use to professional study. Considering the positive benefit it might have had, the government sadly underestimated the public's capacity to accept the truth of war.[28] As a war film, *Let There Be Light* is without compare: it records the factual realities; it reacts to them with moral vigor; and it tells the truth.

Films like *Let There Be Light* remind us that the truth of war lies in its human cost—those who died or were mutilated in combat, those who perished in concentration camps, those who were left homeless and starving. The record of war is a record of victory and defeat, of man's humanity and inhumanity, of joy beyond belief, and of despair beyond imagination. The devastation of war was also recorded and preserved by such nonfiction films as *Nazi Concentration Camps* (1945), the Allied official record of the death camps, and *Death Mills* (1946), produced by the U.S. War Department, which, with a strong narration, also presents an appalling documentary record, and Theron Warth's and Richard O. Fleischer's *Design for Death* (1948), compiled from confiscated Japanese footage. David Miller's *Seeds of Destiny* (1946) is a haunting record of the millions of children who were left at the end of war with minimal food, clothing, and medical attention. *Nuremberg* (1948), a film compiled by Pare Lorentz and Stuart Schulberg, records the Nuremberg trials, including the devastating footage of atrocities used by the prosecution. The Nuremberg Trials are also the subject of Marcel Ophuls's *Memory of Justice* (see Chapter 15).

In the face of great catastrophe and human tragedy, many artists find that simplicity can best record the magnitude of overwhelming events. Henri Cartier-Bresson is such an artist. His years as a photographer proved to him the value of capturing the meaning of the moment in the passing of time, what it means to be alive. Some moments of the human experience need no comment or elaboration; with minimal commentary (the narration is in French), his *Le Retour* (1946) stands as the most moving document of human agony and joy to come out of World War II. *Le Retour* is about the liberation of French prisoners from Nazi concentration camps: their removal, half dead, on trucks; their hospitalization and recovery; and, finally, their return to France and reunion with families and friends. It is a subtle film in its factual presentation of horror and happiness; neither of these extremes requires dramatic emphasis, and, given his artistic background, it is not surprising that Cartier-Bresson moved his camera very little as he recorded the triumph of life over death. This story is manifest in the record of haunted eyes in sunken faces and the tense, gripped hands of waiting relatives. The rhythm with which *Le Retour* shapes the overwhelming emotion of great tragedy leads us to the triumphant catharsis of joy.

In the Pacific, as the war came to an end with the dropping of atomic bombs on Hiroshima and Nagasaki, Japanese and American cameramen recorded the physical damage caused by the bombs and their radioactivity on the physical environment and the human body. This footage forms the basis of Erik Barnouw's and Paul Ronder's *Hiroshima-Nagasaki: August, 1945* (1970).[29] This stark, simple compilation film is mainly a visual record of the physical and human destruction caused by the bombs, of cities reduced to ashes, of women with patterns of their kimonos burned into their skin, of children mutilated. There is narration by three voices: the poetic comments of a Japanese woman victim; the factual, but ironic comments of the American writer-editor, Paul Ronder; and the voice of Robert Oppenheimer, one of the inventors of the bomb, repeating words from the Bhagavad-Gita, the Hindu book of devotion, to describe the weapon: "Now I am become death, the destroyer of worlds." The film neither accuses those who developed the bombs and authorized their use, nor pleads for their victims, but ends simply with a statement condemning the testing of nuclear weapons. The title, *Hiroshima-Nagasaki: August, 1945,* suggests a factual film, but the facts are too awesome to be treated objectively; instead, this is a film made in a genre all its own, but one, like all the others discussed in these chapters on World War II films, that helps us to understand the meaning of war.

PART FOUR
(1945–1960)

Nonfiction Film after World War II

11

British Nonfiction Film after World War II

GREAT BRITAIN AFTER THE WAR

Under the leadership of Winston Churchill, Great Britain rose to a supreme and victorious effort during the Second World War. Nonetheless, while Great Britain shared with its allies a triumph over the Axis countries, it suffered greatly: the nation lost 420,000 men and women; many of its large urban areas and industries, devastated by bombing, had to be rebuilt and modernized. The end of the war also began a period of postwar decline in which it lost much of its former global, social, and economic power. As the United States assumed preeminent leadership in world affairs, including international trade, shipping, and banking, the British empire began to shrink after independence was granted to many countries, most notably India, which was partitioned into India and Pakistan, and Palestine, which became Israel.

In 1945, Clement Attlee and the Labour Party were unexpectedly elected to replace Churchill's Conservative government. In response to the worsening social and economic situation, the Labour government vigorously nationalized many major industries and enacted considerable social reforms. In 1951, Churchill and the Conservative Party resumed power, and while they reversed the nationalization of some industries, they retained Labour's social reforms. During the 1950s, as Britain allied itself closely in world affairs with the United States and the North Atlantic Treaty Organization (NATO), it also became embroiled in numerous foreign difficulties in the Middle East, Near East, Africa, and Asia. The mid-1950s continued to be a period of economic and social transformation, particularly for the working class, young people, women, and immigrants.

The British Film Industry
Immediately after the war, between 1945 and 1950, the British government and the film industry worked together to ensure the future of British film. This effort

included considerable discussion of the potentiality of the British film in general, and the nonfiction film in particular.[1] Issues in the general debate included financing, production, distribution, exhibition, trades and tariffs, and American competition. During the 1930s, the British documentary film, with its concern for the examination of domestic social issues, and with substantial government support for production, distribution, and exhibition, had gained stature and influence, both in Great Britain and the United States.[2] By 1940, the British documentary film, sponsored both by the government and by nongovernment organizations, had been firmly established as a prominent creative movement of ideological significance. In the postwar debate on the future of nonfiction film, leading filmmakers expressed substantial dissatisfaction with its declining quality and with the role that government policy was alleged to have played in this decline. Some participants in this debate argued for a thorough reexamination of the entire medium of cinema. Others argued for the production of nonfiction films that would be educational and enlightening, films that could return to "the schoolmasterly approach which characterized some of the work of the documentary movement" of the 1930s (Dickinson and Street 155).

In 1947, a government report, *The Factual Film in Great Britain,* proposed transforming not only the objectives of the British Film Institute, but also the future of the cinema and television industries as a whole. In the government, the Ministry of Information (MOI) was replaced by the Central Office of Information (COI), which subsumed the MOI Films Division and the Crown Film Unit. The 1948 Films Act dealt with the need to support British domestic film production as well as to find a place in British theaters for films of other countries, particularly the United States. Although the government stopped short of nationalizing the film industry, it did exercise extensive control. Measures taken by the government included the establishment of the National Film Production Council, a committee designed to promote cooperation within the film industry; the establishment of National Film Finance Corporation, an agency to provide public funds for film production; and the formation of three new production groups, including Group Three, headed by John Grierson and dedicated to providing a showcase for new talent. Subsequently, the 1951 Festival of Britain provided commissions for several outstanding films.

During the early 1950s, the British film industry was also beginning to adjust to the devastating impact of television on the cinema. Dickinson and Street write:

> The BBC reintroduced its television service in 1947, and two years later cinema admissions began to fall. In the mid-1950s, when commercial television was on the air, this downward slide continued, and it was soon aggravated by a spate of cinema closures. By 1960 the cinema had lost two-thirds of its 1950 audience; in the next decade it lost half of what remained. (227)

However, television ultimately helped to revitalize the nonfiction film by encouraging two elements that had contributed to the early British documentary movement: a group, working in a creative atmosphere and dedicated to a common journalistic purpose, and sustained sponsorship.

In the nonfiction film, the postwar period saw an increase in commercial sponsorship, the increased production of films on art, the use of longer formats and color film stock, and the production of films specifically for showing in public theatres. Other developments included films that incorporated written dialogue, studio sets, professional actors (in addition to the actual people of the situation being filmed), diagrams, and multi-voice narration. However, many successful features of the traditional British documentary approach were retained, including the intelligent handling of subject matter; excellent cinematography, sound recording, and editing, much of it experimental; and the characteristic British traits of understatement, thoroughness, clarity, and humor.

This period of development also reflected another long-term change: the blending of narrative and nonfiction approaches in the same film. Filmmakers began to argue for a nonfiction film (the "story documentary") that, in addition to its independence and traditional concern with social responsibility, would also integrate aspects of the narrative film and thus appeal to a wider audience. Earlier British examples of this effort include such films as Harry Watt's *North Sea* (1938) and *Target for Tonight* (1941); films that fuse the "poetic" with the narrative, such as Humphrey Jennings's *Spare Time* (1939), *Listen to Britain* (1942), and *Fires Were Started* (1943); and, reversing the emphasis, studio-made narrative films with documentary overtones, such as Launder and Gilliat's *Millions Like Us* (1943).[3] Outstanding among the postwar British examples of this hybrid form are Humphrey Jennings's *The Cumberland Story* (1947) and Paul Dickson's *David* (1951).

Rather than leading to some new form of nonfiction film, this blending of the nonfiction and narrative approaches led, between 1945 and the mid-1960s, to the dominance of the narrative over the nonfiction film.[4] While the dual effects of the shift to commercial sponsorship and the infusion of narrative into the nonfiction film are too complex to delineate in this context, the British documentary of the postwar years reaffirmed its abiding commitments to cinematic realism, to extending conventional social discourse primarily on working-class issues, and to furthering humanistic values. The following discussion considers the two dominant strains of postwar British nonfiction film: the continuing documentary tradition and the Free Cinema movement.

The Continuing Documentary Tradition

During World War II, commercial sponsorship was responsible for such British nonfiction films as *The Harvest Shall Come* (1942), *New Towns for Old* (1942), *World of Plenty* (1943), and *When We Build Again* and *Land of Promise* (1945) (see chapter 8). After the war, commercial sponsors continued to produce films about a broader range of subjects; some of these were directly related to postwar recovery, while others treated subjects more reminiscent of prewar films.

Paul Rotha's *The World is Rich* (1947) is an ironically titled film about hunger in those countries that directly participated in the war. Essentially a compilation film, it shares some of the same footage that comprises Irving Jacoby's *The Pale Horseman* (1946; see chapter 10), but lacks the impact achieved by the editing of that film. It is also similar to Rotha's *Land of Promise* (1945) in its use of multivoice

The World Is Rich (Paul Rotha, Great Britain, 1947)

narration and diagrams. Rotha next turned to British concerns in *A City Speaks* (1947), a full-length film about the processes of local government in Manchester. An aggressive but pleasant public relations film sponsored by the Manchester Corporation, it recounts the history of this important manufacturing center, carefully explaining local elections and government. While taking an optimistic and idealistic view of bureaucratic democracy, it does not shirk from showing realistically the "rotten leftovers of yesterday" in the city's slums. However, as a sponsored film, *A City Speaks* lacks a sense of genuine social responsibility, and demonstrates that professional skill, technical virtuosity, and comprehensiveness do not necessarily make an effective documentary film when genuine commitment to social problems is absent.

After the war, some British filmmakers turned to foreign subjects, among them Ralph Keene and John Eldridge. In addition to making *Cyprus is an Island* (1945), Keene travelled to Ceylon to make *String of Beads* (1947) for the International Tea Bureau. Like Basil Wright, who made the classic *Song of Ceylon* (1934), Keene used black-and-white cinematography, but he lacked Wright's feeling for the culture and imaginative control of cinematic form. John Eldridge's *Three Dawns to Sydney* (1948), made for the British Overseas Airway Corporation, is a fragmented tribute to air power that was also intended to promote air travel, while his *Waverly Steps* (1949), made for the Scottish Office, was intended to promote interest in and travel to Edinburgh. *Waverly Steps* owes something to the films in the "city symphony" tradition in its attempt to capture the diverse cultural interests, sights, and sounds of the Scottish capital. However, it is more about actual people in the city (as in Arne Sucksdorff's *People in the City*) than the patterns of a city (Ruttmann's *Berlin*). More straightforward than the typical "city symphony" film, it warmly depicts the cordial reception given to a non-English-speaking Danish visitor. While *Waverly Steps* lacks the mysterious emotional mood of such films as *Rien que les heures, Berlin: Symphony of a Great City,* and *Gamla Stan,* it is remarkable for its avoidance of clichés (only once do we hear bagpipes), its imaginative and rhythmic editing, and its use of the moving camera.

Humphrey Jennings's *The Cumberland Story* (1947) would have been an ideal project for sponsorship by the coal industry, but it was, instead, produced by the Crown Film Unit of the Central Office of Information. Ironically, it exhibits the faults that might be expected in a commercially sponsored film: it lacks the social consciousness characteristic of a social documentary produced by the government. *The Cumberland Story* is concerned with the redevelopment of an outdated coal-mining operation in a depressed area. Narrated by the new manager of the mines, a well-intentioned and progressive individual who must contend with fear and resistance among the villagers, the film takes a dogged, but predictable, approach to the resolution of the region's problems. Jennings' view of the situation is straightforward and comprehensive, incorporating some excellent dramatic reenactment, but it lacks the humanism of his earlier *Fires Were Started.* Although the British Film Institute chose it as the outstanding documentary of the year, it is little more than an interesting variation on a dominant theme in British documentary: the importance of the individual worker to industrial production.

The Cumberland Story is an example of what can happen when a government-sponsored film fails to do justice to subject matter that is essentially commercial. Terry Bishop's *Daybreak in Udi* (1949), made by the Crown Film Unit for the Colonial Office, is a film about Nigerian social development, and illustrates what can go wrong when government policy takes precedence over people. The issue is the construction of a maternity hospital in the jungle, as seen through the eyes of the British district officer. Unfortunately, and, perhaps, unintentionally, the film reflects an imperialist attitude that is particularly offensive: on one hand, the officer encourages the preservation of native tradition and, on the other, uses a sort of persuasive logic that ignores local traditions and feelings. In contrast to the natives, who appear to be both intelligent and reasonable, the officer seems uncivil and paternalistic. *Daybreak in Udi* ignores all of Grierson's teachings about balancing presentation and propaganda, and ultimately betrays its sponsor.

The news-magazine film, established in the United States with "The March of Time" and "This is America" series and in Canada with the "World of Action" series, was less popular in Great Britain. The British "Wealth of the World" series was concerned with various natural and industrial resources, but its superficiality precluded accuracy and depth. For example, *Transport* (1950), which praises the overall efficiency of the transportation system that the Labour government had nationalized, recounts the history of railways, coaches, buses, and trucking, avoiding any reference to labor union problems. As such, it functions as a public relations piece for transportation interests while eschewing the responsible social comment that is basic to the British documentary film.

During the 1950s, several major public events gave stimulus to British nonfiction film production. The Festival of Britain, celebrating the one hundredth anniversary of the Crystal Palace Exhibition, provided filmmakers with commissions, theaters, and large audiences. International exhibitions like the Festival of Britain and the 1967 Montreal Expo focused attention on the creative potential of the medium and on its superior ability to provide information in an imaginative way. Among the outstanding Festival films were *The Waters of Time, Forward a Century,* and *David.* Basil Wright's and Bill Launder's *The Waters of Time* (1951) is about the locks and docks of the Thames River. It is in the GPO tradition of explaining a process with the direct comments of working people, but its slow, tedious portrayal is further hindered by a pretentious poetic narration that attempts to capture the spirit of the Thames in the Elizabethan period. *The Waters of Time* tries to make poetry out of a prosaic subject, but unlike Lorentz's *The River,* it does not succeed.

Napier Bell's *Forward a Century* (1951) records the hundred years' growth since the Great Exhibition of 1851, which celebrated 19th century industrial progress, and suggests that 20th century Great Britain must meet the challenge of human progress. These contrasts between nineteenth- and twentieth-century exhibitions provide a good structural framework, but lack insight into modern British economy and culture. Using still photographs and engravings, the film reviews Britain's past industrial strength; its narrator and a voice representing Queen Victoria claim that the British prefer humanity to imperialism and material progress. The pictures are brought alive by an imaginative mix of sound effects, narration, and music; however, while the old photographs are interesting, the film lacks conviction and direction. Like *The Waters of Time, Forward a Century* is a commemorative film, too consciously cheerful to be honest about its subject.

In its humanistic study of the rehabilitation of war casualties, Paul Dickson's *The Undefeated* (1950) not only recalls John Huston's *Let There Be Light,* but also foreshadows Dickson's next film, *David* (1951). More than any other film of the period, *David,* produced for the Welsh Committee of the Festival of Britain, demonstrates the continuing vitality of British nonfiction filmmaking. Its national pride and reverence for tradition set it far apart and high above its contemporaries. *David* tells the story of a Welsh school, its students, and its elderly caretaker's bid for the first prize in the Eisteddfod, the Welsh national competition of poetry and singing. Dickson appears to have been influenced by Flaherty in telling this true story, for it takes a more narrative and more fictional approach than the conventional nonfiction film. While the film is notable for its warm presentation of the actual inhabitants and customs of the Welsh village of Ammanford, it is also memorable for its emotional strength and evocation of friendship and love. Like the old man himself, it is not a film to be forgotten; like Lindsay Anderson's *Every Day Except Christmas* (1957), it proves that nonfiction films celebrating human warmth and beauty outlast tributes to transportation systems and oil resources.

Before the 1950s, in contrast to filmmakers in Germany, Belgium, France, and

David (Paul Dickson, Great Britain, 1951)

Italy, the British had not produced any significant films on art. Slowly, through commercial sponsorship, and then under the aegis of BBC Television, this situation changed, with Dudley Shaw Ashton emerging as the major filmmaker. Among the earlier titles were *Looking at Sculpture* (1950), by Reginald Hughes and Dudley Shaw Ashton, John Read's *Henry Moore* (1951), and Guy Brenton's *The Vision of William Blake* (1958). Important British films on art during the 1960s include Read's *Barbara Henworth* (1961) and *An Act of Faith* (1967), Ashton's *Francis Bacon: Paintings, 1944–1962* (1963),[5] *Poussin: The Seven Sacraments* (1968), *The Art of Claude Lorrain* (1970), and *Mantegna: The Triumph of Caesar* (1973), and Ken Russell's *Always on Sunday: Henri Rousseau* (1965).

The year 1953 was marked by two events of major historical importance for Great Britain: the Coronation of Queen Elizabeth II (June 2, 1953) and the conquest of Mount Everest by Edmund Hillary and his Sherpa guide, Tenzing. Both events took place within four days. Although several newsreel-type narratives of the Coronation were filmed, Castleton Knight's color production, *A Queen is Crowned* (1953), is the official film. Its ninety minutes, shot from superb vantage points and edited from six hours of procession, pageantry, and ceremony, preserve a complete record. The narration, written by playwright Christopher Fry in a style that incorporates both the factual and the poetic, is spoken by Laurence Olivier in a tone that alternates between excitement and awe. Ultimately, however, *A Queen is Crowned* is no more than an historical record; it does little to help the viewer to understand the meaning of monarchy. Sixteen years later, two British films about the function of a constitutional monarchy within a democratic political system proved to be as analytical and insightful as they were entertaining: *A Prince for Wales* and *Royal Family* (both 1969).

Other crowning achievements of the period included the 1950 conquest of Annapurna as well as the 1953 conquest of Mount Everest, two of the world's highest mountains. *The Conquest of Everest* (1953), a film by Thomas Stobart and George Lowe, effectively presents a straightforward account of the efficient preparations for the expedition. However, their depiction of the expedition itself relies on the ominous background sounds of falling snow and ice, heavy breathing, and an occasional avalanche to add some drama to what is, otherwise, a highly scientific and carefully planned event. A series of anticlimactic sequences make the crest seem impossible to reach, and the narrator seems confused as to who was actually leading the expedition. (This confusion perhaps foreshadows the later debate on Tenzing's role, which appeared to have been more significant than Hillary admitted.) But there is only excitement when we finally see Hillary and Tenzing conquer the highest mountain peak in the world. Although the summit was actually reached on May 29, the news was announced in England as "the crowning glory" of the coronation on June 2. *Annapurna* (1953) attempted to give human drama to a scientific expedition that lacked the element of human struggle and suffering that made an earlier record—Ponting's *Ninety Degrees South* (1933)—such a memorable film. *Annapurna* is an uneven film, combining reenactment with actual footage shot on the ascent; like *The Conquest of Everest*, it is beautiful and striking, but essentially unmoving.

Other films also presented subjects of international significance. Basil Wright's *World Without End* (1953), a film made for the United Nations Educational, Scientific, and Cultural Organization (UNESCO), demonstrates one of the major challenges of making films for that world organization: how to present a country's social problems without offending its political sensibilities. Wright's challenge here was to contrast the problems and the progress of peoples in Mexico and Thailand who were abandoning their traditional way of life for more modern approaches to agriculture, health, sanitation, and education. He successfully balances the need to report appalling conditions with the desire to educate. He takes the "land of contrasts" approach without the obsequious narrative of the traditional travel film, and by combining native music, beautiful soft cinematography, and an intelligent, informative narration, he successfully presents both problems and solutions. Another challenge faced by filmmakers working for the United Nations is the question of language. UN policy stipulates that films for an international audience be narrated in English or French, and that those for a specific country should be in the language of that country; when UN films are for both audiences, separate narrations must be prepared. This did not appear to be a problem for the makers of *World Without End* (Paul Rotha directed the Mexican sequences, while Basil Wright directed those in Thailand), and it succeeds as a clear, imaginative film. Another notable British film of the period is Robin Carruthers's *They Planted a*

Stone (1953), a succinct account of the harnessing of the Nile River for hydroelectric power and industrial growth.

The Griersonian tradition in documentary filmmaking was rapidly being adapted to meet new needs in England. An example of one adaptation of this older tradition is Thorold Dickinson's *Power Among Men* (1958), made in color and black and white. A film about the work of the United Nations Relief and Rehabilitation Administration (UNRRA), it is, like Dickinson's *Next of Kin* (1942), a blend of the narrative and nonfictional approaches; unlike the former film, it uses narration by actor Laurence Harvey rather than performances by professional actors. Based on a general theme—"men build, men destroy"—it is, like a Rotha documentary, neatly divided into four parts that correspond to efforts in four geographical areas. The inherent limitations of UN sponsorship weaken what might have been an interesting film; as it is, *Power Among Men* is but a weak reminder of the strong documentary tradition out of which it came.

Any account of postwar British nonfiction filmmaking would not be complete without mention of Peter Watkins, who worked outside the Free Cinema movement and is notable primarily for *Culloden* (1964) and *The War Game* (1965), two films that combine narrative and nonfiction techniques in developing an antiwar theme. Both films use historical reenactments to convey the brutalities of war, and, consequently, they helped to reinforce the anti-Vietnam protests of the late 1960s. *Culloden* depicts the 1745 massacre in which English forces defeated the Highlanders under Prince Charles Edward Stuart ("Bonnie Prince Charlie") to end the Jacobite uprising and secure the union between England and Scotland. *The War Game*, which, to a certain extent, resembles Humphrey Jennings's *The Silent Village* (1943), depicts England after a nuclear attack. Although its showings were restricted because of its intense subject matter, during the late 1960's the film was widely screened in the United States, and was a particular favorite of college students.

The Griersonian tradition had been broken by World War II, and it was clear by the mid-1950s that the British nonfiction film—the documentary film in particular—needed to rediscover its traditional humanism and lyricism. In 1956, the Free Cinema Group provided this impetus.

BRITISH FREE CINEMA: 1956-59

In the mid-1950s, a group of young British filmmakers, led by Lindsay Anderson, Karel Reisz, and Tony Richardson, took the problems and language of ordinary people as the rallying point for a new filmmaking movement that they called Free Cinema. They hoped to create a lyrical nonfiction film form that would restore an appreciation for the commonplace similar to that which had characterized the great British films of Humphrey Jennings,[6] to spark an interest in the styles of foreign nonfiction films,[7] and thus to revive the genre. The Free Cinema Group, like Vertov and the Italian neorealists, rejected prevailing cinematic convention; in so doing, they also rejected a cinema and a society "still obstinately classbound,"[8] turned their cameras on ordinary people and everyday life, and proclaimed their freedom to make films without worrying about the demands of producers and distributors, or other commercial considerations.[9] Because the films of the Free Cinema movement were entirely the free expression of the people who made them, they serve as one more link between the growing postwar movement in Europe toward a new cinematic realism and the first experiments in 1953 in the United States with direct cinema.[10] Like the French New Wave, the Free Cinema movement believed that filmmakers should use the cinema not only for personal expression, but also for social comment.

With his fellow Englishmen, Karel Reisz and Tony Richardson, as well as with such European directors as Michelangelo Antonioni and Alain Resnais, Lindsay Anderson began his career in nonfiction films. Anderson defined his own approach: "The first duty of the artist is not to interpret, nor to propagandize but to create."[11] Moreover, he believed that the traditional realism and authenticity of the British documentary were obstacles to that creativity. Anderson further argued that the documentary film approach inhibited a filmmaker from imposing his own ideas on his raw material and that the sociological base of the Grierson approach was no longer applicable in a complex world.[12] And he understood that the Griersonian problem-solution model is successful only when it is directed at an audience predisposed to the thinking behind the solutions.[13] Despite his harsh response to tradition, Anderson nevertheless acknowledged his debt to Humphrey Jennings, whose influence is apparent in such Anderson films as *Every Day Except Christmas*.[14] It is a feeling for people, not social issues, that Anderson admired in the work of Jennings, Flaherty (whose *Louisiana Story* he praised), and John Ford. In Ford's films, he found a feeling for individual values and for rooted tradition that proved to be a major influence on his depiction of his own country's culture.

The achievements of Anderson and his colleagues in the nonfiction film were limited; as Marcorelles observes, their films

> came out of a particular moment in history, as a reaction against the conformity of the British cinema at the time, but they did not really break through into any kind of revelation, did not actually question the nature of reality. They merely scratched at the surface of Victorian puritanism at the appropriate moment; their use of direct cinema was just an accident, it was not, in their case, a tool deliberately used to scrape off all the varnish of social convention. (43–44)

Since these directors went very quickly into making feature films, their most important contribution to British cinema was not the Free Cinema movement itself, but rather their influence on the British narrative films that were the best known product of this "new realism": Jack Clayton's *Room at the Top* and Tony Richardson's *Look Back in Anger* (1959), Karel Reisz's *Saturday Night and Sunday Morning* (1960), Richardson's *The Loneliness of the Long Distance Runner* (1962), and Lindsay Anderson's *This Sporting Life* (1963).

Lindsay Anderson's early films are conventional, sponsored industrial documentaries: *Meet the Pioneers* (1948), *Idlers That Work* (1949), *Three Installations* (1952), and *Wakefield Express* (1952). *Thursday's Children* (1953), written and directed by Guy Brenton and Anderson, forms a link between the familiar British documentary film and the direct cinema of the 1960s.[15] Traditional in subject, it concerns the Royal School for the Deaf in Margate; contemporary in approach, it achieves an extraordinary degree of intimacy—in both camera and sound work—in its observation and explanation of the teaching of the deaf. Without sentiment, *Thursday's Children* details the painstaking process by which a deaf child is taught to read lips and printed matter and to speak. The film is optimistic at times, but never at the expense of the subject matter. It can be compared with Sidney Meyers's *The Quiet One* or Allan King's *Warrendale* in its concern with a special school but, unlike those films, it does not portray the inevitable emotional problems, nor does it investigate the youngsters' family backgrounds. This is an isolated school where children live together with others sharing the same handicap; homes are mentioned only in terms of friendly letters and parcels of goodies. However, the school situation resembles that depicted in the other films in that it relies on a communal spirit to reinforce the awareness and the concentration needed to cope with the impairment of hearing. The lyrical commentary, read by Richard Burton, only emphasizes the silent world of those who cannot hear it. Still, for Anderson, people are not alone, no matter how different they may be. From the quiet world of *Thursday's Children,* to the bizarre world of *O Dreamland,* to the flower-fresh, nighttime world of *Every Day Except Christmas,* Anderson reveals the unique man as he celebrates all mankind.

While *Thursday's Children* is an important achievement in nonfiction film reporting, *O Dreamland* is more typical of the Free Cinema Group. *O Dreamland* (1953) is a satiric, heavy-handed comment on a popular and tawdry British amusement park. As a film, it is an elementary exercise, but it influenced contemporary filmmakers not only because it was almost directly opposite in approach to a similar film—Humphrey Jennings's *Spare Time* (see chapter 8)—but also because it dared to criticize the tasteless ways in which the British working classes use their leisure time. While the Jennings film appears to some viewers as an ambiguous comment on leisure, Anderson's steers a careful course between outright criticism of the pleasure seekers and the park's proprietors. The theme of class is a major one in Anderson's fiction films of the period, including *This Sporting Life* (1963) and *If . . .* (1968). In his later nonfiction film, *Every Day Except Christmas,* Anderson is concerned with the very same working people who might spend a Saturday or Sunday at Dreamland, but there he ennobles, rather than criticizes, the working class, making them seem the most important element in England's social fabric. *O Dreamland* was a diversion for Anderson rather than an indication of the direction in which his films were to move.[16]

Following Anderson's lead, Karel Reisz and Tony Richardson took their cameras into a London jazz club to observe the working classes at a different kind of leisure. *Momma Don't Allow* (1955) shows genuine affection for mid-1950s British popular culture, but seems more interesting as a record of clothes, hairstyles, and music than as a film. Like many experimental films, in contrast with the documentary tradition, it seems content with asking questions rather than providing answers. Similar in approach to *Momma Don't Allow,* but pointing the way toward the direct cinema of the 1960s, is *Nice Time* (1957), a film by Claude Goretta and Alain Tanner that observes the various pleasures offered in London's Piccadilly Circus, and Karel Reisz's *We Are the Lambeth Boys* (1959), which is a serious attempt to understand working class youth. As in *O Dreamland,* Goretta and Tanner use music to comment ironically on the people who are there for amusement. The film is overdone and overlong, but it freshens one's visual sense of a familiar location.

Anderson supervised the editing of Lorenza Mazzetti's *Together* (1955), a well-intentioned but unsuccessful film about the lonely, isolated lives of two deaf-mutes. Although Mazzetti clearly understands how insensitive hearing people can be to those who are hearing-impaired, she indulges in an overly dramatic conclusion—the accidental death of one of the boys—that distorts the focus of the film. If she had been more influenced by *Thursday's Children* than by such fiction as John Steinbeck's *Of Mice and Men* or Carson McCullers's *The Heart is a Lonely Hunter,* she might have created a film that would have helped us better to understand deafness; instead, she concludes rather despairingly that "life goes on," an observation that reflects the angry British culture, as well as the prevailing existential philosophy, of the 1950s. Daniel Paris's music helps redeem the film by successfully distinguishing the different worlds of those who can and cannot hear.

In his program notes for *Every Day Except Christmas* (1957), Lindsay Anderson, with an idealism characteristic of the period, stated: "I want to make people—ordinary people, not just Top People—feel their dignity and their importance, so that they can act from these principles. Only on such principles can confident and healthy action be based."[17] This lyrical film is in the British tradition of clear explanation, excellent cinematography, and imaginative sound; in addition, it restores an appreciation for the commonplace that had been missing since Humphrey Jennings's wartime films. Here, Anderson joyfully celebrates the simple virtues of ordinary working people in London's Covent Garden, which was then the city's central market for fruit, flowers, and vegetables. His film offers a thorough, interesting, light observation of the typical activity that goes on behind the scenes of this vast market. Its charm, narration, and delightful musical score create a gentle tribute to ordinary people who work with pride and satisfaction at uncomplicated tasks.

Anderson is concerned not only with the work activities of these people, but also with their friendly relations with one another, their careful handling of perishable produce and flowers, and their pleasure in serving their customers. In the Griersonian tradition that sought nobility in the craftsman, Anderson finds dignity in the work of Alice, the last of the market's renowned women porters. Watching her, we feel past and present eras come to life on the screen, from the days when "Victoria was Queen, and every gentleman wore a buttonhole," to the present, when elderly flower sellers look for bargains later in the morning. Anderson pictures more than a genuine vignette of London's commerce; he shows us the people behind the tradition. His camera and sound equipment capture and celebrate life. In the direct cinema mode, the sound, which is asynchronous, provides contrapuntal comment on the activity we see. But long after we forget what was then a new

Every Day Except Christmas (Lindsay Anderson, Great Britain, 1957)

film technique, we remember the faces—"Alice and George and Bill and Sid and Alan and George and Derek and Bill and all the others . . . " to whom the film is dedicated. Like Flaherty's *Nanook of the North* and Jennings's *Fires Were Started,* Anderson's *Every Day Except Christmas* finds beauty in the ordinary and creates art out of the unexpected.

The contributions and influence of Free Cinema were most apparent at the February 1956 screening of the first Free Cinema program at the National Film Theatre; it included the films discussed above, films from France by Franju, Truffaut, Chabrol, and Lionel Rogosin's *On the Bowery* from the United States. On the stage, it was the year of John Osborne's *Look Back in Anger,* and in the streets, "mods," "rockers," and "teddy boys" captured the imagination of filmmakers, playwrights, and emerging rock music groups. What the Free Cinema filmmakers achieved was not so much the films themselves, but rather a spirit of free, uninhibited inquiry. The films are important, especially for their inventive handling of sound, but even more for their place in the development of direct cinema. They foreshadowed a new kind of filmmaking that questioned conventional film symbolism, pioneered new methods of sound recording, and encouraged the development of lightweight equipment that allowed the cinematographer to move freely.

In the postwar years, an emphasis on social realism revitalized the British cinema, in general, and, through the Free Cinema movement, the nonfiction film, in particular. In the changing postwar socio-economic climate, British social realism was outspoken on the subjects of class and power and focussed new attention on such subjects as sexuality, gender, and race. Like the French New Wave, however, the British "new cinema" lost its cohesiveness around 1963 as its major directors, who had their start in the nonfiction film, broke away for independent careers in fiction films. Among their notable achievements were Tony Richardson's *Tom Jones* (1963), Karel Reisz's *Morgan* (1966), and Lindsay Anderson's *If . . .* (1968). Their concern with social realism had helped to revitalize the British nonfiction and fiction film, but the British film industry as a whole was having increasing difficulty withstanding the impact of television and the increasing American investment in the British film industry. Thus, this unique British style of cinematic realism had little opportunity for further development as national film industries became more and more dependent on an increasingly international environment of film financing, production, and distribution.

12

European, Asian, and Canadian Nonfiction Film after World War II

In the fifteen years after the Second World War (1945–1960), a new nonfiction film emerged in Europe, Asia, and Canada. Although production varied widely in subject, style, and quality, filmmakers seemed to share a common impulse to explore uses for the nonfiction film that went beyond the Griersonian documentary film or the wartime propaganda film. Filmmakers in the allied countries of Europe were able to resume production more quickly than their counterparts in the defeated nations. The largest number of films, and the most influential, were produced in Italy, Belgium, and France. In Asia, after the war, as before it, nonfiction film production derived primarily from filmmakers in India and China. In Canada, the National Film Board continued its impressive development. The result of this diverse activity offers rich evidence not only of the adaptability of the nonfiction film, but also of its continuing power to advance the goals of social reconstruction, cultural enrichment, and world peace.

EUROPE

Italy
NEOREALISM

Italian Neorealism was to have a major influence on the subsequent development of realistic cinema worldwide.[1] The work in the early 1940s of Alessandro Blasetti and Vittorio De Sica, with scripts by Cesare Zavattini, prefigured the emergence of neorealism. As early as 1942, Zavattini expressed his beliefs in a new realism; a year later, critic and theorist Umberto Barbaro, using the term *neo-realismo,* also called for a fresh approach to the Italian film. In their hope for the future of Italian cinema, they seemed to yearn for a return to the traditions of Soviet expressive realism and even French poetic realism, rather than looking forward to the development of cinéma vérité or direct cinema.

The immediate impact of Italian neorealism was to free Italian post-war film-making from studio conventions, to create a realistic look that went below surface appearances, and to foster both a humanistic viewpoint and a social commitment.[2] In some ways like Vertov before him, Zavattini rejected many of the prevailing cinematic conventions:

> Neo-realism breaks all the rules, rejects all those canons which, in fact, only exist to codify limitations. Reality breaks all the rules, as can be discovered if you walk out with a camera to meet it.[3]

And in some ways like Flaherty, Zavattini wanted cinema to reflect the authorship of an individual filmmaker, to avoid scripting, and to take "a direct approach to everyday reality . . . " (64). While Zavattini's major importance to cinema history was within in the neorealist movement, he also ultimately influenced the development of direct cinema through his beliefs in reality and in the potentialities of an uncontrolled realistic film.

By blurring the traditional boundaries that had separated the narrative from the nonfiction film, the major neorealist films created a new approach to filming reality. Yet, despite their concern with postwar life (a reaction to Fascism) and their "documentary look" (a function of the creative hardships under which they were produced), these films also used scripts and actors and thus do not fit this study's concern with the mainstream development of the nonfiction film. On the other hand, many of them have had an extensive influence on both Italian and world cinema. Their titles are familiar to all students of cinema history. Rossellini's *Open City* (*Roma, città aperta*, 1945), perhaps the most important example, had the singular purpose of recapturing as faithfully as possible life under German occupation and the role of the Italian resistance.[4] In subject, it resembled René Clair's *Battle of the Rail* (*La bataille du rail*, 1946). In style, it set the tone for the subsequent revitalization of the Italian film industry in succeeding years. The other masterpieces of Italian neorealism are also well-known: Rossellini's *Paisan* (*Paisà*, 1946) and *Germany, Year Nought* (*Germania, anno zero*, 1947); Luchino Visconti's *Obsession* (*Ossessione*, 1943) and *The Earth Trembles* (*La terra trema*, 1948); and Vittorio de Sica's *The Bicycle Thieves* (*Ladri di biciclette*, 1948). *Open City* had shown Italians fighting to liberate themselves both from the Fascists and from their own self-imposed history of civil oppression. This theme, developed in a style far less original than Rossellini's, is evident in two other antifascist nonfiction films: *Days of Glory* (*Giorni di gloria*, 1954), directed by Giuseppe De Santis and Mario Serandrei with the collaboration of Luchino Visconti and Marcello Pagliero, and *Our War* (*La nostra guerra*, 1947), a short by Alberto Lattuada about the liberation of northern Italy.

Wartime political and social factors did not, as in some other European countries, foster the Griersonian documentary film. As Pierre Leprohon writes:

> . . . the documentary was not to be the Italian filmmakers' preferred form; they chose to reconstitute actuality, in fictional narratives directly inspired, as in Rossellini's work, by revolt, hope, or fear.[5]

Michelangelo Antonioni was, however, an exception to this model. Early in this period, when Visconti was making *Ossessione,* Antonioni began making straightforward documentaries about ordinary human lives. Throughout his career, according to Ian Cameron and Robin Wood, Antonioni was "interested in people first as individuals, rather than as symbolic figures, or representatives of a social condition."[6] His *People of the Po* (*Gente del Po,* 1943; 1947), which was partly lost and then partly restored, is a simple account of life along the Po River; *Dustmen* (*N.U.—nettezza urbana,* 1948) is an equally plain account of a day in the life of Roman street cleaners; *Superstizione—non ci credo!* (1948) is a brief film that catalogues the strange and illegal superstitions of a small Italian village; *L'amorosa menzogna* (1948–49) is about the private lives of the actors who are photographed for the unique Italian comic strips known as *fumetti; Sette Canne, un vestito* (1950) concerns the manufacture of synthetic fibers; and *The House of Monsters* (*La villa dei mostri,* 1950) records the grotesque statues at Bomarzo. While these short, rudimentary films are a world apart from the existential complexities of Antonioni's later work, they reveal unmistakable stylistic traits that were subsequently more fully realized in fiction films.

The other nonfiction filmmakers who produced traditional films included Giovanni Paolucci, *The Cassino Valley* (*Valle di Cassino,* 1946); Domenico Paolella, *Italy is Awakening* (*L'Italia s'è desta,* 1947); Luciano Santoro, *Building in the Post-War Period* (*Dopoguerra edilizio,* 1949); Carlo Infascelli, *Cavalcade of a Half Century* (*Cavalcata di mezzo secolo,* 1951); Romolo Marcellini, *Italy and the World* (*L'Italia e il mondo,* 1953); Giorgio Ferroni, *Yesterday and Today* (*Ieri e oggi,* n.d.); Carlo Lizzani, *Nel mezzogiorno qualcosa e cambiato* (1950), *Achtung! Banditi!* (1951), *Ai margini della metropoli* (1952), an episode in *L'amore in città* (1953), *Cronache di poveri amanti* (1954), *Lo svitato* (1956), *La muraglia cinese* (1958), and *Esterina* (1959).

FILMS ON ART

Unlike the governments of Great Britain, France, or Belgium, the Italian government did not support Italian nonfiction filmmakers to any appreciable extent. While the Italian government preferred financing opera, it did fund the production of those nonfiction films that it believed would appeal to audiences in the commercial theatres, films that celebrated such popular subjects as Italian art and architecture rather than deal with the social issues.[7] Here, according to Jarratt, "the names of Luciano Emmer and Enrico Gras stand out as pre-eminently as that of Rossellini among the realists."[8]

Emmer and Gras—they worked together, although several films are signed by Emmer alone—developed a new approach to filming art. Using a variety of cinematic properties, they gave life to static images, recounting the narrative of a painting that, itself, tells a story. In Emmer's *Story of a Fresco* (*Racconto da un fresco,* 1941), a film about Giotto, they follow the painter's career from the St. Francis cycle attributed to him at Assisi, through his great frescoes in the Arena Chapel at Padua, to the frescoes in Bardi and Peruzzi chapels in Santa Croce in Florence.[9] Following this ramble through pre-Renaissance art, the film concludes with a concise summary of the importance and influence of the stylistic elements in

Giotto's work. Emmer's cinematographic technique—photographing static images with a moving camera, using the zoom lens for detail and the fisheye lens to open up tight spaces—reinforces the movement and rhythm of Giotto's narratives; however, his sound track—a mixture of wind, voices, sighs, drumbeats, and eerie music—is less successful in its attempt to convey Giotto's sense of the mystery of time and eternity. Yet, despite its faults, *Story of a Fresco* is a pioneering educational film of high quality.

Emmer and/or Gras used a similar technique in other films: *Il cantico delle creature* (1942), also on Giotto; a film on Hieronymus Bosch, *Earthly Paradise* (*Paradiso terrestre*, 1941); and one on the life of St. Paul, *On the Road to Damascus* (*Sulla via di Damasco*, n.d.). In 1948, they followed *White Pastures* (*Bianchi pascoli*), a sensitive study of the Allied cemeteries in Italy, with two films about Venice: *The Romantics of Venice* (*I romantici a Venezia*) and *Islands of the Lagoon* (*Isole della laguna*). Among their other films are studies of Carpaccio: *The Life of St. Ursula* (*La leggenda di Sant'Orsola*, 1948); *Piero della Francesca* (1949); Botticelli, *Primavera* (*Allegoria della primavera*, 1949); and four films on Picasso: *Life and Death in Painting* (*Vita e morte della pittura*), *Il sonno della ragione*, *I fauni*, *Colombe* (all 1954).

Other Italian films on art include G. Betti's *Paolo Uccello* (1949); Henri Alekan's *The Cubist Experience* (*Experienza del cubismo*, 1949); Rafael Andreassi's *Georgio de Chirico* (1952); Primo Zeglio's *Borromini* (1959); Giovanni Caradente's *Alberto Burri, The Artist in his Studio* (*Alberto Burri, l'artiste dans son atelier*, 1960); and Marcello Grottesi's *Borromini* (1974).

Belgium

In reestablishing the nonfiction film genre after the war, Belgian filmmakers were encouraged by several factors: government and private support; television broadcasting, which brought nonfiction films to a larger audience; and a National Festival of Belgian Films in 1954, which, although short-lived, helped to stimulate the industry. This growth of the Belgian arts, in general, and the cinema, in particular, in no way reflected a strengthening of national unity, for the major ethnic groups that made up Belgian society—the Flemish and the Walloons—remained separated by cultural and linguistic differences. The Flemish filmmakers enjoyed a higher proportion of state funding for the arts than did any other group.[10]

Between 1945 and 1959, film production in the public sector, especially by and for television, followed the model established by the British Broadcasting Corporation (BBC) in which information and education took priority over entertainment. The private sector, which traditionally had neglected the sociopolitical documentary, continued to produce a variety of nonfiction films on art, travel, industry, exploration, folklore, and science. Among the independents, Charles Dekeukeleire, André Cauvin, and Henri Storck—the three most important names in the early Belgium nonfiction film—continued to make social documentaries and films on art. They were joined by Gerard de Boe, as well as by several major new talents, including Luc de Heusch and Paul Haesaerts. These films can be divided roughly into three major categories: films on domestic subjects, colonial subjects, and art.

FILMS ON DOMESTIC SUBJECTS

During the war, Henri Storck set for himself the challenging goal of making a film that would pay tribute to the Belgian people—specifically the wartime efforts of Belgian farmers—without mentioning the most dominant fact of wartime life, the Nazi occupation. He accomplished this admirably with *Peasant Symphony* (*Boerensymfonie*, 1944). After the war, Charles Dekeukeleire also paid tribute to the Belgian people. Instead of reporting on postwar reconstruction, he used an ingenious montage of medallions, paintings, coins, and stamps in *The Founder* (*Le fondateur*, 1947) to recall those strengths that Leopold I (1790–1865), the first King of Belgium, had left to succeeding generations of his countrymen. In a similar film, *Charles the Fifth* (*Karel de Vijfde*, 1956), Dekeukeleire told the story of the Holy Roman Emperor. While Dekeukeleire's *Living Space* (*L'espace d'une vie*, 1949) is seemingly concerned with postwar reconstruction, it also contrasts postwar Belgian freedom with the Nazi occupation, for its title is a sarcastic allusion to Hitler's claim that Nazi aggression was justified by the need to provide Germans with *lebensraum* (living room). He also made *Houses* (1948), a film about urban social planning. After the war, Storck also made *Crossroads of Life* (*Op de viersprong van het leven*, 1949) about juvenile delinquency.

FILMS ON COLONIAL SUBJECTS

From the early days of Belgian filmmaking, the Belgian Congo had remained of interest to filmmakers. After the war, several outstanding films contributed to international understanding of the region by avoiding the usual faults of colonial filmmaking: paternalism and the presentation of exotic imagery for its own sake. André Cauvin, whose prewar work included two films on art (*The Mystical Lamb* and *Memling*), made *Congo* (1944) and *The Equator with 100 Faces* (*L'equateur aux cents visages*, 1949); the latter is a feature-length film that provides a mosaic of casual observations, some of which (the chase of a gorilla, for example) are very exciting. Six years later, he returned to make *Noble Lord* (*Bwana-kitoko*, 1955), a record of King Leopold III's visit to the Congo. Henri Storck's *Barons of the Forest* (*Vrijheren van het woud*, 1958), an international coproduction, presents an ethnological view of the people of the East Congo. It offers a comprehensive set of observations that show us much, but tell us little, in analytical terms, about the region. Gerard de Boe's *Tokèndé—We Go* (*Tokèndé—wij gaan*, 1958) is remarkable not only because it was filmed in CinemaScope, but also because, as a sponsored film designed to promote Belgian interests, it nevertheless succeeds also in being prophetic about colonial independence. Although commissioned by the Catholic Church to recount the history of sixty years of missionary work, it expresses the filmmaker's personal support for independence, a view that, at that time, was unpopular with most Belgians. Using an approach pioneered by Robert Flaherty, and used more recently by Jean Rouch and Robert Gardner, among others, Luc de Heusch worked intimately with a tribe in the Belgian Congo to make *Rites of the Hamba* (*Fêtes chez les Hamba*, 1954), which presents an internal view of native customs, including initiation rites. A film by Gerard de Boe and Emile Degelin took another approach. Filmed in the Colonial Museum in Brussels, rather than in the Congo, *She Will Be Named His Woman* (*Deze zal zijn vrouw genoemd worden,* 1954), presents the various roles of Congolese woman through art and artifact. Demonstrating great sensitivity for Bantu sculpture, it succeeds both as an ethnographic film and as a film on art. Gerard de Boe added to the list of important colonial films with *The Wagenia Fishermen* (*Les pecheurs wagenia,* 1951).

When the Belgian Congo achieved its independence in 1960, colonial filmmaking stopped. However, in 1986, Jan Neckers, a director for Belgian television, made *As Big As a World Where Your Flag is Planted* (*Als een wereld zo groot, waar uw vlag staat geplant*), an impressive compilation film—using photographs, scenes from narrative and documentary films, and a few interviews—that recounts the history of the Belgian colonization of the Congo.

FILMS ON ART

After the Second World War, many filmmakers celebrated the artistic legacy that remained one of the glories of a European civilization almost destroyed by war. Belgian filmmakers pioneered in this genre during the late 1920s and 1930s and continued after the war to produce an excellent body of films on their rich history of art.

Henri Storck's art films are notable for a cinematic style that complements the style of the artist whose work is being filmed. In *The World of Paul Delvaux* (*De wereld van Paul Delvaux,* 1947), the dreamlike images of the Belgian Surrealist painter are underscored by verbal images by Surrealist poet Paul Eluard; many years later, Storck made a second film on Delvaux, *Paul Delvaux, or The Women Defended* (*Paul Delvaux, ou Les Femmes Defendues,* 1970). Storck's *Rubens* (1948), made in collaboration with art critic Paul Haesaerts (see below), is, with the work of Emmer and Gras (see above), among the first great postwar films on art; it is not only intelligent and informative, but worthy of its subject. Storck uses a variety of cinematic properties for pedagogical purposes—split-screen, crosscutting, close-ups, superimposition, fast-motion cinematography, microcinematography, distortion, and animation—to reveal and analyze the composition, themes, and evolution of Rubens' paintings. In contrast to the extraordinary *Rubens,* Storck's other films on art are less effective: *The Open Window* (*La fenetre ouverte,* 1952), about landscape painting, and two studies of the work of Felix Labisse: *Felix Labisse or the Happiness of Being Loved* (*Félix Labisse ou le bonheur d'etre aimé,* 1962), *The Misfortunes of War* (*Les malheurs de la guerre,* 1962).

René Magritte, the Belgian Surrealist, was the subject of several Belgian films, including Luc de Heusch's *Magritte, or the Object Lesson* (*Magritte, ou la leçon des choses,* 1960) and Roger Cocriamont's *René Magritte* (1946).[11] The de Heusch film, made in collaboration with Jacques Delcorde and Jean Raine, includes Magritte's personal observations and interpretations of his work. De Heusch also made *Alechinksy from Nature* (*Alechinsky d'après nature,* 1971), about the painter Pierre Alechinsky, famous for his violent expressionist style.

Paul Haesaerts's prolific output of films on art and artists reveals great curiosity about a comprehensive range of art historical subjects, ancient and contemporary. Typical of his early work is *Visit to Picasso* (*Visite à Picasso,* 1950), which, in contrast to a sombre, worshipful film like Henri-Georges Clouzot's *The Picasso Mystery* (*La mystère Picasso;* see below) is remarkable for its fresh, light approach. Haesaerts's brief survey of Picasso's work is set in the context of a visit to the artist's studio at Vallauris. Like the Clouzot film, we see the artist working; but unlike the Clouzot film, where Picasso paints on an opaque surface, here Picasso paints on a piece of plexiglas, through which we see him, seemingly bemused by his work. Haesaerts's portrait is much more intimate and revealing than Clouzot's, which it influenced; moreover, it captures the joy of creativity, a spirit reflected not only in Picasso's playful draftsmanship, but also in his nonchalant puffing on a cigarette as he signs his name to end the film. Haesaerts's other films include *From Renoir to Picasso* (*De Renoir à Picasso,* 1950); *Four Belgian Painters at Work* (*Quatre peintres belges au travail,* 1952); *Masks and Faces of James Ensor* (*Masques et visages de James Ensor,* 1952); *The Golden Age: The Art of the Flemish Primitives* (*Een gulden eeux, de kunts der valaamse primitieven,* 1953); *Humanism, The Victory of the Spirit* (*L'humanisme, victoire de l'esprit,* 1954); *Laethem Saint-Martin, The Village of Artists* (*Laethem Saint-Martin, le village des artistes,* 1955); *Under the Black Mask* (*Sous le masque noir,* 1958), on African art; *Cri et connaissance de l'expressionisme dans le monde à l'expressionisme en France* (1964), a film on Edvard Munch, Marc Chagall, Oskar Kokoschka, Francis Bacon, Constant Permeke, Gustave de Smet, and Oscar Jespers; *Ric Wouter's Joyous Folly* (*La folle joie de Ric Wouters,* 1966), about the leading Belgian exponent of Fauvism; *The Key to the Surrealists' Songs* (*La clef des chants surréalistes,* 1966), about Giorgio De Chirico, René Magritte, Paul Delvaux, Brauner, André Breton, Pablo Picasso, Max Ernst; *Brueghel* (1969); and *Henri Evenpoel, Painter of Tenderness* (*Henri Evenpoel, peintre de la tendresse,* 1970), about the tragic early death of an artist known for his sensitive portraits of children.

Other important Belgian films on art include those by Jean Cleinge: *Ink* (*Encre*) (1964), about Pierre Alechinsky, Karel Appel, and Ting; *Van Eyck, Father of Flemish Painting* (*Van Eyck, père de la peinture flamande,* 1972) and *Memling* (1972); and those by André Delvaux: *With Dieric Bouts* (*Met dieric bouts,* 1975); Charles Leirens: *Visit to Chagall* (*Visite à Chagall,* 1950); and René Micha: *Paul Klee, or The Genesis* (*Paul Klee, ou la genèse,* 1958).

France

Postwar nonfiction filmmaking in France actually began with the release of several French resistance films that have become classics: René Clément's *Battle of the Rail* (*La bataille du rail,* 1946), Jean Grémillon's *The Sixth of June at Dawn* (*Le 6 juin à l'aube,* 1946), and Georges Rouquier's *Farrebique* (1946; see chapter 9). While French filmmakers were somewhat slower than their counterparts in Italy or Belgium to resume production, they were eventually more prolific in output. Their efforts continued and flourished in the nonfiction movement of the 1950s, which itself provided one of the sources for the French New Wave (or *nouvelle vague*) of the 1960s (see chapter 14). This postwar revival of the French nonfiction tradition was not only strengthened by the leadership of innovators such as Georges Rou quier, Jean Grémillon, and Roger Leenhardt, but also provided the training ground for newer artists such as Alain Resnais and Georges Franju.[12]

ALAIN RESNAIS

Alain Resnais began his filmmaking career in the French nonfiction film movement and, in the first eleven years, made many short films on art, including *Portrait of Henri Goetz* (1947), *Visit to Hans Hartung* (1947), *Lucien Coutaud* (1947), *Christine Boumeester* (1947), *Cesar Domela* (1947), *Malfray* (1948), *Van Gogh* (1948), *Paul Gauguin* (1950), *Guernica* (1950) (with Robert Hessens), and *Les Statues Meurent Aussi* (with Chris Marker, 1951). Typical of these films is *Van Gogh*, which recounts the artist's life through his paintings and drawings, and is especially effective in telling of Van Gogh's years in the Asylum at Arles. There is no live action; in photographing the static images, Resnais uses cinematic elements common to other films on art, including the moving camera, close-ups, and the zoom lens. This black and white film depicts the life of a painter associated with vibrant color; the heavy paint on Van Gogh's canvases helps to convey the movement and intensity, if not the color, of his later work. This period of Resnais's career concluded with two remarkable films: *Night and Fog* (*Nuit et brouillard*) (1955), a film about the Nazi death camps, and *The Memory of the World* (*Toute la mémoire du monde*) (1956), a cinematic essay on the effect of time on books in the library. Resnais links music to his cinematography of the baroque interiors of the Bibliothèque Nationale, making *The Memory of the World* the more significant film cinematically, but *Night and Fog* is ultimately the more important not only in the context of nonfiction film history, but also in its relation to the ethical foundations of the genre.

Resnais made *Night and Fog* in collaboration with two artists who had first-hand experience with the Hitler era: Jean Cayrol, a novelist, poet, and former concentration camp prisoner, and Hanns Eisler, a composer, former associate of Bertolt Brecht, and refugee from Hitler's Germany.[13] The film juxtaposes meditative color footage of ruined concentration camps with shocking archival black-and-white footage of the activities and atrocities that took place there. Past and present film combined together makes the truth more painful for an audience to see than would the archival footage alone, as it appears in newsreels and compilation films about the Nazi holocaust. In this juxtaposition of memory and actuality, this merging of past and present time, Resnais prefigures the principal thematic concerns of his later narrative films. In *Night and Fog*, the contemporary footage, shot with a slowly moving camera, seems dispassionate in providing a record of weed-filled yards, crumbling buildings, and cold ovens. The time is autumn, and the colors are gentle and somber. By contrast, the archival footage is sharp and unambiguous in showing us what actually occurred in these places: the Nazis' degradation and final destruction of millions of Jews and others they judged as undesirable and expendable. People are herded like cattle into anonymous trains, which, shrouded in night and fog, deliver them to unknown camps. There, they are shaved, tattooed, numbered, and forced in extreme heat and cold to work at hard labor. The food is filthy, the sanitary facilities are inadequate, the sleeping conditions are crowded, and the hospitals are sham excuses for the torture of unspeakable "medical" experiments. The film makes the viewer feel the terror of the "shower rooms" that in actuality are gas chambers, of the pyres where some of the human remains are burned, of the open pits where bulldozers bury piles of bodies so high that the images are unreal. Unreal, also, are the images of human hair made into rugs, bones into manure, and flesh, muscle, and fat into soap.

In spite of this devastating evidence, Resnais remains reflective, not moralistic. At the conclusion, against a color sequence showing the ruins of one of these camps, the narrator says:

> And there are those of us who sincerely look upon the ruins today, as if the old concentration camp monster were dead and buried beneath them. Those who pretend to take hope again as the image fades, as though there were a cure for the plague of these camps. Those of us who pretend to believe that all this happened only once, at a certain time and in a certain place, and those who refuse to see, who do not heed the cry to the end of time.[14]

For the audience, the issue, then, is not what we have seen, but how we choose to perceive and remember it; this is also the subject of Marcel Ophuls's *Le chagrin et la pitié (The Sorrow and the Pity)* (see chapter 15). Such intellectual speculation—especially the apparent refusal to reach conclusions or to be outraged—disturbs some viewers. But while Resnais does not pretend to answer the larger questions about life, good, and evil, he is not neutral except in his narrative tone. Building upon the evil that we have seen, *Night and Fog* leaves us with unforgettable memories that provide answers and warnings of their own. Appropriately, then, Resnais uses images, not narration, to embody and sustain his humanistic theme.

GEORGES FRANJU

Georges Franju is perhaps best known for his first film, *Blood of the Beasts (Le sang des bêtes,* 1949). Like Frederick Wiseman's *Meat* (1976, see chapter 15), Franju's subject is a slaughterhouse, and, like Wiseman, Franju looks objectively at a process that most viewers—meat-eaters and vegetarians alike—would probably prefer not to see. Both artists present the slaughterhouse without identifying problems or suggesting solutions, and both accept the process by which animals are butchered and its justification—the human need for meat. There is nothing in Franju's film, made shortly after the Second World War, to suggest parallels between the slaughterhouse and the Nazi death camps. He does not pity the animals, nor condemn their butchers, but, like Wiseman, shows us an ordinary industrial process to which most of us have never been introduced. Unlike Wiseman, however, Franju is not concerned with the slaughterhouse as an economic entity, nor is the process that he depicts so highly mechanized and computerized.

Blood of the Beasts begins with lyrical, sunny images of the world outside the slaughterhouse—the sort of mundane reality that fascinated the Lumière brothers—and then takes us inside the shadowy buildings where horses, cows, and sheep are butchered for market. Despite Franju's objectivity—perhaps because of it—these are harrowing places. The men and women who work here stand in small rivers and pools of blood as they stun, flay, dismember, and butcher the animals. While the slaughterhouse may seem to be a frightening place, Franju photographs it objectively. Some of the most memorable images are those of ordinary people with cigarettes dangling from their lips, sharpening their knives, and going about their business as if they were not working in a place awash with blood and reeking of animal's intestines. As Noel Burch suggests, Franju transcends his subject to "get at the heart" of the subject.[15] That subject is actuality, neither beautiful nor terrifying, but both.

As Franju states in the epigraph to his *La première nuit,* "It only requires a little imagination for the most ordinary action to become imbued with disquieting meaning, for the décor of everyday life to engender a fantastic world." Although Franju is heavy-handed in *Blood of the Beasts*—especially in the chiaroscuro of his cinematography, his repeated shots of blood, and his use of music—he, like Wiseman, understands the multiple ambiguities of reality. For example, at one point, he makes one of Franju's butchers appear to be singing a melody from Debussy's "La Mer," a reference that could easily allude to the sea of blood on the floor as appeal to the audience to prefer a diet of fish. In this aspect, his work forms an important link between the nonfiction film of postwar France and the British Free Cinema of the 1950s and cinéma vérité and direct cinema of the 1960s (see chapter 14).

While he made twelve other short films between 1950 and 1958, only *Hôtel des invalides* (1952) had the impact of *Blood of the Beasts*. It, too, begins ostensibly as a straightforward account of the French War Museum and veterans' hospital, but Franju soon transforms the film into a scathing attack on war. Franju's other nonfiction films include *Passing by Lorraine* (*En passant par la Lorraine*) (1950), in which the steel mills consume the workers almost as viciously as the slaughterhouse consumes the animals; *Le grand Méliès* (1952) and *Monsieur et Madame Curie* (1953), tributes to the pioneers of French cinema and science, respectively; *Notre Dame, cathédrale de Paris* (1957), a melancholy view of the broken and decaying parts of the cathedral; and *La première nuit* (1958), a descent into the reality and then the nightmare of the Paris subway.

Throughout the 1950s, there was a revival of interest in nonfiction films about the natural world; such films were produced by anthropologists and other scientists, including Jean Rouch, Jacques-Yves Cousteau and Louis Malle, Gregory Bateson and Margaret Mead, John Marshall, and Robert Gardner. Notable among these is Jacques-Yves Cousteau and Louis Malle's *The Silent World* (*Le monde du silence*) (1956). The first of Cousteau's many films, *The Silent World* is an intriguing and educational account of oceanographic exploration on and beneath the surface of the sea. The superb color cinematography provides an intimate look not only at Cousteau's team of divers, but also at a stunning variety of underwater life. Although many imitated Cousteau's and Malle's original approach to filming underwater, Cousteau continued to have great success in succeeding years with his films for television. These, too, were concerned with observing and preserving the natural world, especially its seas. In this same genre of exploration are Thomas Stobart's and George Lowe's *The Conquest of Everest* (Great Britain, 1953; see chapter 11), which documents and celebrates the successful feat of Sir Edmund Hillary and Tenzing Norkay of Nepal to reach the summit, and Thor Heyerdahl's *Kon-Tiki* (Norway, 1951), which records his travel from Peru to the Tuamotu Islands of

Polynesia in primitive rafts. Enormously popular with the public, both films won major prizes.

FILMS ON ART

Even during the war, the French made films on art, including Jean Lods's *Aristide Maillol* (1943) and *Aubusson* (1946), and Gilbert Prouteau's *Dieu a choisi Paris* (1945). Beginning with the postwar period, and extending into the present time, the French film on art became a minor industry. Early titles include Jean-Paul Ceria's *Paul Cezanne's Provence* (*La provence de Paul Cezanne,* 1946); Philippe Este's *Rediscovered Art* (*L'art retrouvé,* 1946); Victoria Spiri Mercanton's, Marguerite de la Mure's, and Albert Saboul's *1848 or the 1848 Revolution* (*1848 ou la révolution de 1848,* 1948); Pierre Braunberger's and Nicole Védrès' *Paris 1900* (1948); and Henri Alekan's *Rodin's Hell* (*L'enfer de Rodin,* 1949). Perhaps the most impressive among these is François Campaux's *Henri Matisse* (1946), which like Haesaerts's film on Picasso (see above), is remarkable for its intimate, unpretentious profile of one of this century's greatest painters. After a straightforward survey of Matisse's early years, we see the artist at 85 in his Paris apartment making several sketches of his grandson. Although the narrator gravely explains the creative process as "hesitation, decision, search, and execution," Matisse says frankly that it is "hard work." The film includes a fascinating account of the evolution of "The Peasant Blouse," as well as a slow-motion analysis of Matisse painting from a model.

William Novik's *Images medievales* (1949) was the first film on art to present medieval life through illuminated manuscripts, and remains an extraordinary contribution to teaching art and history through film. It assumes—a little too neatly perhaps—that these stylized images actually depicted daily life, but its use of music of the period helps validate its claims to being an authentic document.

One of the most popular of all French films on art, Henri-Georges Clouzot's *The Picasso Mystery* (*La mystère Picasso*) (1956), explores the idea that the spatial freedom enjoyed by the visual artist is compromised by the temporal restraints imposed upon the filmmaker by his available footage. To dramatize this, Clouzot plays a tyrannical director who seems to bully the bare-chested artist into finishing his work before the available film stock runs out. This witty conceit (if that was the filmmaker's intent) fails because we know that, with an artist of Picasso's stature in the studio, Clouzot could have had as much film stock as he needed. We see Picasso creating over fifteen images on an opaque glass screen, with the camera recording from both sides. (By prior agreement, the images were destroyed when the film was completed.) Ostensibly, this approach offers an extraordinary opportunity to watch the artist in action, but the premise on which the film is based seriously weakens its value as a serious record. Furthermore, the pretentious score does not succeed in matching musical equivalents to the lines and color that Picasso adds to his work. Clouzot, usually a master at revealing the darkest human psychology, only succeeds in revealing to us some of Picasso's astonishing vitality and creativity and considerably more of his own eccentricity. The "mystery" referred to in the title—the ultimate cliché, the mystery of creation—remains mysterious.

During the 1950s, the French made films on an remarkable range of art and artists, including: Jean Grémillon's *Life's Charms* (*Les charmes de l'existence*, 1950) (with Pierre Kast), about Bouguereau; Frédéric Duran's and Abbé Morel's *Miserere* (1951), about Rouault; *The House of Images* (*La maison aux images*, 1955), about Miró, Masson, Dunoyer de Segonzac, Trémois, Dali, Derain, Laboureur; and *André Masson and the Four Elements* (*André Masson et les quatre éléments*, 1958). Pontus Hulten's and Robert Breer's *Movement* (*Le mouvement*, 1950) is about such "action artists" as Tinguely, Breer, Mortensen, Jacobsen, Vasarely, and Agam. The focus of Nicole Védrès's *Life Begins Tomorrow* (*La vie commence demain*, 1950) is Jean-Paul Sartre and Jacques Prévert, while Henri Bonniere's *The Unleashed Ones* (*Les dechainés*, 1950) is about "les lettristes." Other films about specific artists include Rene Lucot's *Antoine Bourdelle* (1950); Andre Bureau's *Georges Braque* (1950); Roger Livet's *Histoire d'Agnes* (1950), about Henri Goetz; and Philippe Este's *Living Art* (*L'art vivant*, 1950), about Chagall, Léger, Lhote, Lorjou, Minot, and Villon. The subject of Pierre Kast's *The Disasters of War* (*Les désastres de la guerre*, 1951) is Goya, while that of Jean Aurel's *Les fêtes galantes* (1951) is Watteau.

In the midst of his most creative period, Jean Cocteau made *Santo Sospir* (1952), which, without the master's hand, would be regarded as little more than a home movie about a vacation house. Other films on art by lesser-known artists include Edgar Pillet's *Henri Laurens* (1952); Arcady's *The Cruel Fable* (*La légende cruelle*) (1952), about Léonor Fini; Georges Bauquier's *The Builders* (*Les constructeurs*) (1956), about Fernand Léger; Jean Aurel's, Charles Estienne's, and Jean-Claude See's *Kandinsky* (1950), *The Manet Affair* (*L'affaire Manet*) (1951), *Jules Verne* (1952), *Heart of Love* (*Coeur d'amour*) (1952); Enrico Fulchignoni's *Leonardo da Vinci, or The Tragic Search for Perfection* (*Leonardo da Vinci, ou la recherche tragique de la perfection*) (1952); Jean-Claude Bernard's *Chez ceux de Montparnasse* (1957); Étienne Périer's *Bernard Buffet* (1957); Yves Alain's *Montparnasse and its Painters* (*Montparnasse et ses peintres*, 1957); Pierre Alibert, *Cubism* (*Le cubisme*, 1957); Pierre Alechinsky's *Japanese Calligraphy* (*Calligraphie japonaise*, 1957); and Jean Lods's *Zadkine* (1960).[16]

Finally, there is Roger Leenhardt, who, with Resnais and Franju, can be regarded as a bridge between the nonfiction film, the film on art, and *la nouvelle vague*.[17] Leenhardt was not only a film theorist and critic, but also a prolific filmmaker, whose nonfiction films include *Daumier* (with Henri Sarrade) (1958), *The Master of Montpellier* (*Le maitre de Montpellier*, 1960), *The Man with the Pipe* (*L'homme à la pipe*, 1962), *Women and Flowers* (*Des femmes et des fleurs*, 1963), *Corot* (with Guy Bernard) (1965), and *Monsieur Ingres* (1967).

Other European Films

Several trends emerged in the postwar production of the nonfiction film in European countries other than Italy, Belgium, and France. Topics included art, poetic celebrations of nature, personal observations of everyday life, and historical chronicles—particularly accounts of the German atrocities of the Second World War.[18]

These historical chronicles, continuing the traditional role of the nonfiction film as documentary witness, were based on the extensive archives of wartime film made and preserved by the Nazis. In a postwar Germany divided into Western and

Eastern zones, the Allies strictly controlled film production in West Germany, while the former UFA film production facilities and equipment, renamed DEFA, were under Soviet control in East Germany. In the years immediately following the war, West Germany was consumed by the Nuremberg trials, where Nazi wartime footage was screened as evidence against the Nazis and their collaborators.[19] Many West Germans were shocked by this dreadful record of their recent history and filmmakers made little further use of it; the East Germans, equally obsessed with what the evidence depicted, used it to make a group of outstanding compilation films. Barnouw (178) writes that "the films reflected the bitter antagonism between the East and West German regimes, and made their contribution to the bitterness. They also put continued pressure on West Germany for action against war criminals."

Andrew and Annelie Thorndike are the leading filmmakers of the East German historical chronicle. Their work in compiling archival footage is in the tradition established by Esther Shub (see chapter 4) and continued by Vertov, Cavalcanti, Capra, and Dovzhenko; their success ensured the continuation of this tradition in the work of Marcel Ophuls (see chapter 15). The Thorndikes not only made a thoughtful use of compilation techniques to recount German history; their major achievement was the use of the archival footage as a warning, even an indictment, against the repetition of the abuses depicted in that history—what Leyda calls "trial by document."[20]

The Thorndikes' first film, *You and Many a Comrade* (*Du und mancher Kamerad*, 1955), focussed sharply on the alliances between German military and industrial leaders that had involved Germany in two world wars. They were particularly incensed by Nazi criminals who remained alive and free, and they exposed Hans Speideland and Heinz Reinefarth, respectively, in *Operation Teutonic Sword* (*Unternehmen Teutonenschwert*, 1958) and *Holiday on Sylt* (*Urlaub auf Sylt*, 1959). Another Thorndike film, *The Russian Miracle* (*Das Russische Wunder*, 1963), presents a chronicle of modern Russian history.

In the spirit of indictment established by the Thorndike films, Joachim Hellwig made *A Diary for Anne Frank* (*Ein Tagebuch für Anne Frank*, 1958), a film unique among the other works on this subject for its probing into the lives of those responsible for the young martyr's death. Working in Switzerland, German refugee Erwin Leiser made two powerful films about the Hitler era: *Mein Kampf* (1960) and *Eichmann and the Third Reich* (*Eichmann und das Dritte Reich*, 1961). Leiser's objective and analytic insight cuts deep into the collective German soul.[21]

Not all postwar German films were chronicles of the war. Joris Ivens, who was also interested in the uses of archival footage, produced several films for DEFA, the East German studios: *Song of the Rivers* (*Lied der Ströme*, 1954), made with Vladimir Pozner, about people who work on and around the world's six great rivers;[22] *My Child* (*Mein Kind*, 1956), about the role of motherhood around the world; and *The Wind Rose* (*Die Windrose*, 1956), made with Alberto Cavalcanti, about the role of women in five different countries. Like Paul Rotha's *Land of Promise* (1945) and *The World is Rich* (1947) (see chapter 11), Ivens was concerned in *The Wind Rose* with worldwide reconstruction, growth, and peace in the postwar era.

Other Eastern bloc nations also used archival footage to document wartime history. In Yugoslavia, Gustave Kasvrin's and Kosta Hlvavaty's *Jasenovac* (1945) documented concentration camp atrocities. In Poland, a similar film was Aleksander Ford's and Jerzy Bossak's *Majdanek* (1944). Bossak and Waclaw Kazimierczak compiled Nazi footage showing their destruction of the Warsaw Ghetto in *Requiem for 500,000 (Requiem de la 500,000,* 1963). Other Polish films concerned with wartime crimes and atrocities were Janusz Majewski's *Fleischer's Album (Album Fleischera,* 1962) and Jerzy Ziarnik's *The Everyday Life of Gestapo Officer Schmidt (Powszedni dzien Gastapowca Schmidta,* 1963). Still other Polish compilation films recounting wartime history are *The Last Parteitag at Nuremberg* (1946) by Antoni Bohdziewicz and Waclaw Kazmierczak and *September 1939 (Wrzesien,* 1961) by Bossak and Kazmierczak. Working for Films Polski, American filmmaker Leo Hurwitz (*Native Land,* 1942) produced *The Museum and the Fury* (1956), an impassioned film about Auschwitz.[23]

Postwar Soviet films include Roman Karmen's film about the Nuremberg trials, *Judgment of the Nations (Sud naradov* in Russia, *Gericht der Völker* in Germany, 1946); Ilya Kopalin's *The Unforgettable Years (Nesabyvajemyje gody,* 1957), celebrating the fortieth anniversary of the Soviet revolution;[24] and Mikhail Romm's *Ordinary Fascism (Obyknovennyi Faschism,* 1965).

Poetic celebrations of nature and everyday life, as well as films on art, were among the other European trends in the nonfiction film to emerge in the postwar period. The Swedish filmmaker Arne Sucksdorff was preeminent among the European filmmakers who lived close to nature, especially animals. Unlike the nature films produced by the Walt Disney Studios—which, however colorful they may be, always seem condescending to the life they are ironically attempting to celebrate—Sucksdorff's films depict natural life not only with first-hand knowledge and observation, but also with respect and love. Several of Sucksdorff's wartime nature films can be interpreted as parables about Nazism, including *A Summer's Tale (En sommarsaga,* 1941), *Gull! (Trut!,* 1944), and *Shadows on the Snow (Skuggor över snön,* 1945). Sucksdorff's other wartime films include *Wind From the West (Vinden från väster,* 1942), *Reindeer Time (Sarvtid,* 1943), and *Dawn (Gryning,* 1944).

After the war, Sucksdorff turned briefly to the city. His *People of the City (Människor i stad,* 1947) is more about actual people living in the city (as in John Eldridge's *Waverly Steps,* 1949; see chapter 11) than it is about the patterns of city life (Ruttmann's *Berlin: The Symphony of a Great City,* 1927). His other films include *A Divided World (En kluven värld,* 1948), and two short films made in India: *Indian Village (Indisk by,* 1951) and *The Wind and the River (Vinden och floden,* 1951).

Sucksdorff's *The Great Adventure* (1953), a beautiful, lyrical film and his best-known work, recounts a boy's coming of age as he learns about nature. It includes a parable about animals—the fox and the lynx—that reinforces a child's wishful belief that pets don't betray people. Sucksdorff may have been influenced by Flaherty's *Louisiana Story* (1948; see chapter 13) in his depiction of man's selfishness and his celebration of nature's harmony, for the ostensible theme here is that man should learn wisdom and common sense from nature. But the film's dominant

The Great Adventure (Arne Sucksdorff, Sweden 1953)

theme is predators, and is startling in its portrayal of animal cruelties. *The Great Adventure* has been praised for its acute, patient observation of animal behavior and its beautiful cinematography.[25]

Other European films of the postwar period include those that record the personal and sometimes poetic sensibility of the individual film artist. In Denmark, the legendary director Carl Theodor Dreyer made eight short films for the Danish government between 1942 and 1954, including *Thorvaldsen* (1948), a study of the sculptor Bertel Thorvaldsen, that, in its cool, precise observation of his work, matches cinematic style with sculptural subject. In Holland, a young filmmaker, Bert Haanstra, took an entirely different approach, making films of great style about simple subjects. *Mirror of Holland* (*Spiegel van Holland*, 1950), a chronicle of Dutch life, much of which was photographed in watery reflection, recalls the observations in early work of Joris Ivens (see chapter 6). *Panta Rhei* (1951) is an experimental film concerned with the movements of clouds, birds, and leaves, all juxtaposed against one another; it, too, recalls Ivens. Haanstra's other films of the period include *Rembrandt: Painter of Man* (1957); *The Human Dutch* (*Everyman* or *Alleman,* 1963); and his masterpiece is *Glass* (1958).

Glass is a short, delightful visual essay on glassblowing that juxtaposes the traditional handcrafted methods with a modern mechanized process. The former process produces original works of art—vases, goblets, and platters—while the latter produces identical and utilitarian bottles and ashtrays. In the tradition of such films as the Flaherty-Grierson *Industrial Britain,* Haanstra uses frequent images of hands at work to pay tribute to serious craftsmanship. By contrast, he depicts mechanization going awry; for example, humans must intervene when a robotic arm programmed to pick up bottles cannot cope with a damaged one. Haanstra counterpoints the color images further with a whimsical jazz score, and the titles and credits, which transform themselves into several different languages, underscore his universal perspective.

Following in this lyrical mode were several short films from Poland: Andrzej Munk's *A Walk in the Old City (Spacerek staromiejski)* (1958), Kazimierz Karabasz's *Musicians (Muzykanci)* (1960), and Jan Lomnicki's *A Ship is Born (Narodziny statku)* (1961).

ASIA

India

When the war was over in 1945, Clement Atlee, the British Labour prime minister, proposed that Great Britain grant India its independence by 1948, a status that, in actuality, was achieved in August, 1947. Under British rule, the Indian film industry had been burdened by entertainment taxes, restrictions on what could be exhibited, and censorship; Indian filmmakers believed that independence would alleviate these obstacles.[26] In fact, the government of the new Indian republic increased taxes and required that a minimum number of "approved" films be included in every theatrical screening. These films were to be produced in a new government Films Division, which replaced—but was modeled on—the British Information Films of India. Although the film industry resisted, demonstrating its protests by closing all theatres for a day, the government moved forward in the production of nonfiction films, including documentaries and newsreels. Thus began a feud between the government and the film industry, located in the three major film centers—Bombay, Calcutta, Madras—that lasted almost ten years.

The Indian government believed that the production of nonfiction films would create a market for the genre and thus stimulate the private film industry. To a small extent, it did; industries such as Burmah-Shell, for example (whose film division was under the direction of British filmmaker James Beveridge) produced such films as Paul Zils's *Textiles* (1956), Fali Billimoria's *A Village in Travancore* (1957), and Hari Das Gupta's *Panchtupi: A Village in West Bengal* (n.d.), all of which won awards at the Edinburgh Film Festival.[27] However, these encouraging signs of revived commercial production of the nonfiction film were short-lived. In 1958, the Burmah-Shell unit was disbanded, and the magazine *Indian Documentary,* the rallying point of the commercial film industry, ceased publication. The only other commercially sponsored film of note was Satyajit Ray's *Rabindranath Tagore* (1961), a haunting tribute to one of India's great poets. It seemed apparent that the future of the Indian nonfiction film lay in the government's Films Division.

The Films Division, under the direction of Ezra Mir, its head of production, met a staggering challenge with overwhelming success. At its peak, it was producing 104 nonfiction films and 52 newsreels per year for theatrical showing. The Films Division's activities were modelled on the well-known pattern established by the British documentary film movement in the 1930s. It stationed a newsreel cinematographer in each state, with additional camera staff in larger cities, and produced cartoons and other films for special purposes, such as screenings in mobile vans, schools, and overseas locations. Because the Division had to release each film produced in five languages, filmmakers tended to emphasize narration over other cinematic elements, but, according to Barnouw and Krishnaswamy, "its films were modest and factual in manner and well photographed" (203). These films helped to inform and to educate many Indian audiences about aspects of their culture, and some of them won major awards, adding to the acclaim that Indian films had already begun to garner at international film festivals. Important films produced by the Films Division include *Jaipur* (1951), *Symphony of Life* (1956), *Khajuraho* (1956), *Gotama the Buddha* (1957), Fali Billimoria's *The House That Ananda Built*, P. D. Pendharkar's *Weave Me Some Flowers*, Vithalbhai K. Jhavari's important compilation film, *Mahatma: Life of Gandhi, 1869–1948* (1968), G. Aravindan's *Circus Tent* (1978), and *Where Centuries Coexist* (1975). After the 1975–77 "emergency" imposed by Prime Minister Indira Gandhi, the government relaxed some of its control over the Indian film industry, which continues to be the largest in the world.

Japan

Despite a few attempts at producing nonfiction films, the Japanese never really developed the genre.[28] Prior to World War II, their cinema history was limited to narrative films whose aesthetic influences were outside the western cinematic and aesthetic tradition. In the postwar period, during the American occupation (1945–52), Japanese filmmakers worked under severe ideological restrictions—they could not celebrate important cultural traditions such as feudalism, imperialism, or militarism—and Japanese audiences were increasingly able to see European and American films. The golden age of Japanese cinema occurred after the occupation, with the films of Akira Kurosawa, Kenji Mizoguchi, and Yasujiro Ozu. Unlike some of their European counterparts (Alain Resnais and Michelangelo Antonioni, for example), who began their filmmaking careers in the nonfiction mode, they began directly in the heavily stylized world of the Japanese motion picture studio.

China

Several factors make it difficult to form a clear impression of the development of the Chinese nonfiction film: the succession and complexity of the political changes within the country itself; the comparative unavailability of Chinese nonfiction films for study by the Western scholar (compounded by language barriers, even when they are available), and the absence, thus far, of a body of significant scholarship on the subject.[29] The course of Chinese history, after the Second World War, was directed by the actions and achievements of the nationalist and revolutionary movements, specifically by the rise and fall, first, of Chiang Kai-Shek, and, then, of

Mao Tse-Tung. These political movements also affected the film industry. With each wave of political change came changes in the policies that governed propaganda and art.

Between 1945 and 1949, the Nationalist government under Chiang Kai-Shek faced many major challenges, most importantly the struggle against communism. In the first years of the postwar period, filmmakers were divided by their prewar and wartime loyalties, film production was sporadic, and the relatively few films that were produced invariably reflected the anticommunist line. After Mao came to power in 1949, figures indicate that nonfiction films accounted for more than half of the nation's film production. Moreover, a new link between the Chinese and Soviet film industries helped to revitalize not only production methods, but also the cinematic style of Chinese films. Soviet filmmakers visited China, Chinese filmmakers visited the Soviet Union, and the overall result in China was the elevation of the study and production of cinema to a new degree of seriousness. Chinese filmmakers reorganized and improved their film schools, and the Soviet influence resulted in a marked increase in Chinese nonfiction films about such subjects as civil engineering and construction, land reclamation, farm collectivization, and military achievements.

Mao's proclamation of the "great leap" in 1957–58 further inspired the Chinese filmmakers. However, the achievement of a truly revolutionary Chinese cinema was slowed by several factors, including the potential audience's preference for literature and theatre; the restrictions imposed by policy and censorship; and the internal shifts in cultural ideology and priorities, particularly those brought by the purges and changes of Mao's continuing revolution in the late 1960s. Much of this history of the People's Republic of China is recounted in a film by Fu Ya Huang and Bao-Shan, *A Spark Can Start a Prairie Fire (Hsing hsing chih huo keyi liao yuan*, 1961). A more typical film, concerned with a large-scale water construction project, was *The Red Flag Canal (Hong Chi Chu*, 1969).

Throughout this period, more and more Western filmmakers visited China, some to lecture, some to make films, others to observe the Vietnam conflicts through a Chinese perspective. Joris Ivens made *Early Spring* (1958), which, according to Leyda, was "the only Chinese actuality film that seemed to grow as you watched it" (251).[30] Felix Greene's *China!* (1963) provided many Western audiences with their first sustained view of the country, but it angered American authorities, who were pursuing the anticommunist line and who objected to a favorable view of China. Another controversial film was Michelangelo Antonioni's *China (Chung Kuo)*(1972), a two-hour film made for Italian television; like Louis Malle's much longer and more ambitious *Phantom India*, which was misunderstood by many Indians, it provoked a reaction from some Chinese who believed that Antonioni had underestimated their revolution.

CANADA

The National Film Board of Canada

During the war, the National Film Board of Canada (NFB), under John Grierson's leadership, had devoted its activities primarily to propaganda (see chapter 8). There

China (*Chung Kuo*) [Michelangelo Antonioni, Italy, 1972]

were problems with his stewardship and approach, and, after the war, propaganda seemed, according to Evans, "to have become again a suspect activity, desite Grierson's long campaign to equate it with education."[31] After Grierson's departure in 1945, without changing measurably its emphasis on films that focused directly on human beings, the National Film Board, under the new direction of Ross McLean, embarked on some major new ventures, producing films on art and psychology, the historical chronicle, films of personal observation, and animated shorts. In the early 1960s, the work of Canadian filmmakers had an influence on the development of cinéma vérité and direct cinema (see chapter 14).

The NFB pioneered in producing outstanding films about psychology, including those in the "Mental Mechanisms" Series: *The Feeling of Rejection* (1947), *The Feeling of Hostility* (1948), *Overdependency* (1949), *The Feeling of Depression* (1950), and *Shyness* (1953). (In the next decade, Allan King's *Warrendale* (1966) would bring direct cinema techniques to bear on a study of emotionally disturbed children; see chapter 14.) Other Canadian films were concerned with art, including Albert Tessier's *Four Canadian Artists* (*Quatre artistes canadiens*, 1948), and with subjects indigenous to the region, including Douglas Wilkinson's *How to Build an Igloo* (1950) and *Land of the Long Day* (1952), which, as Flaherty did in *Nanook of the North*, takes as its subject matter the life of an Eskimo family.

Among the distinguished Canadian film achievements of this period are Roman Kroitor's *Paul Tomkowicz: Street Railway Switchman* (1954), which, made in the emerging cinéma vérité style, offers a touching account of the life of an extraordinary working man; *City of Gold* (1957), a chronicle by Tom Daly, Colin Low, and Wolf Koenig; and Roman Kroitor's and Wolf Koenig's *Glenn Gould: Off the Record* and *Glenn Gould: On the Record* (1959), which provides an intimate look at the Canadian pianist, who, twenty-seven at the time it was made, was already one of the greatest artists of our century.

City of Gold, which pioneers in the use of still photographs to illuminate an historical moment, provides an original and enchanting account of the history of the late nineteenth-century gold rush to the Yukon.[32] The film begins by conventionally recounting the old days of Dawson City and memories from the narrator's youth, set against motion picture footage of the city as it was when the film was made. The filmmakers had access to a major collection of glass-plate negatives, taken in 1898, at the height of the gold rush, that illustrate the gold's spectacular lure. Through these photographs, in a departure from the conventional cinematic approach to history, we see the rapid transformation of Dawson City from a tiny mining village to a city that is, at once, rough and sophisticated. Underlying the factual history related by these wonderful photographs is a narration of genuine feeling, full of wonder, nostalgia, and sentiment, but also analytical, objective, and refreshingly free of any pretentious interpretation of the sociological phenomena

City of Gold (Tom Daly, Colin Low, and Wolf Koenig, Canada, 1957)

that it reveals. Pierre Berton speaks the narration with such perfection that he demonstrates (as does Richard Burton in *Thursday's Children*) the extra enchantment that is produced by matching the right voice to visual images.[33] While this narrative lacks the dynamic rhythm of *The River*, or the poetic intensity of *Night Mail*, or the charm of *Every Day Except Christmas*, *City of Gold* ranks with these films as a landmark in the narrative development of the nonfiction film.

13

American Nonfiction Film after World War II

With the war's end, the excitement of victory temporarily replaced the terrors of war abroad. For Americans, the victory brought a postwar standard of living that far exceeded anything that they had ever known. However, many Americans began to see that the tidy image of the United States, created by the government's propaganda effort during the war, was an illusion of domestic tranquility. They had been told to believe that the United States was a truly democratic society, one in which everyone lived together in harmony, but when the troops returned, many veterans had difficulties in reentering civilian life. It was not long before the postwar euphoria was replaced by a mood of disenchantment and pessimism. Both at home and abroad, the United States was confronted with major forces that undermined the peace and prosperity.

At home, these forces included social inequities, racial prejudice, economic readjustment, and the ascendency of a new political conservatism—exemplified in the policies of the Eisenhower administration and in the climate of repression established by Senator Joseph McCarthy's investigations into the activities of alleged Communists. Abroad, they included United States entry into Korean War—a struggle (1950–53) between Communist and non–Communist forces that resulted in 54,246 U.S. dead,[1] and the emergence of the Cold War (dating from the end of the Second World War to the early 1960s)—a term used to describe the shifting struggle for power and prestige between the Western powers and the Communist bloc nations.

In the postwar period, the entire film industry—Hollywood and independent, narrative and nonfiction—faced a different world. Hollywood confronted major changes: movie box-office income fell, production costs rose, studio-owned theatre chains were dissolved by court order, the loyalty of creative artists was challenged by the House Un-American Activities Committee, and the arrival of television prompted such Hollywood reactions as increased color and widescreen production. In Italy and France, the new realism had begun to transform the national film industries. In Hollywood, socially conscious directors merged non-fiction "realism" and narrative to produce such a new genre, known as the "semi-documentary."[2] Louis de Rochemont, a pioneer in making films that crossed traditional boundaries, produced four films by director Henry Hathaway that remain models of the new genre: *The House on 92nd Street* (1945), *13 Rue Madeleine* (1946), *Kiss of Death* (1947), and *Call Northside 777* (1948). Other notable titles include Elia Kazan's *Boomerang!* (1947) and Jules Dassin's *Naked City* (1948). While the semidocumentary genre was relatively short-lived, its influence was readily apparent both in the subject matter and cinematic style of such narrative classics as John Huston's *The Asphalt Jungle* (1950), Elia Kazan's *On the Waterfront* (1954), and Alfred Hitchcock's *The Wrong Man* (1957), and, in combination with the influence of Italian neorealism, in the hard-edged style of *film noir*.

Before the war, the American nonfiction film was characterized by two basic forces: independent films produced for the competitive marketplace and government-sponsored films produced for public information and education. This dual development was halted during the war as the government's production of films for official and propaganda purposes took precedence over other kinds of filmmaking. In the postwar conservative atmosphere, most filmmakers avoided both cinematic innovation and political dissent, and, overall, their films contributed little to an understanding of the social and political issues of the time. Instead, many filmmakers moved away from the nonfiction tradition, which had traditionally presented people as members of a group rather than as individuals, and began producing more personal, more direct films concerned with the individual problems that mirror national ones.

Three patterns emerged: a revival of government-sponsored filmmaking provided commissions for filmmakers and international exposure for their work; the emergence of television provided a new format and attracted new audiences; and, as before the war, independent production flourished.

POSTWAR GOVERNMENT FILM PRODUCTION

The first postwar government information activities were built on precedents set by the Office of War Information (OWI). When the government suspended the OWI operation at the war's end, its activities were taken over in August, 1945, by the State Department's new Division of International Information. Although the first postwar foreign information activities were the result of "the ritual of cold war competition,"[3] designed "to counteract in some measure the anti-United States propaganda flowing out of Moscow,"[4] President Harry S. Truman set a higher tone for future information activities:

> This government will . . . endeavor to see to it that other peoples receive a full and fair picture of American life and of the aims and policies of the United States government. (Quoted in MacCann 175)

It was apparent that the government needed to establish a systematic governmental program of information and cultural activities overseas. This need was met by two basic pieces of legislation: the Fulbright Act of 1946, which mandated a peacetime international exchange program, and the Smith-Mundt Act of 1948, which serves as the charter for a peacetime overseas information program. Although Truman wanted a permanent information organization, such an operation did not become a reality until 1953 when the United States Information Agency (USIA) was established. Between 1945 and 1953, there were various governmental agencies charged with domestic and international information activities.[5] One of these agencies, the Economic Cooperation Administration (ECA), achieved Truman's goal through films that documented the Marshall Plan's contributions to the economic recovery of Europe. Typical ECA titles are *Village Without Water* (the building of a new aqueduct), *Adventure in Sardinia* (the eradication of malaria), *Project for Tomorrow* (the organization of a 4-H club in Austria), and *Rice and Bulls* (the story of a French farmer who responds to changing needs by planting rice rather than raising bulls). The Marshall Plan films, which follow the traditional problem-solution pattern of the nonfiction film, did not contribute much to the stylistic development of the genre, but they had a more important goal to accomplish. As MacCann writes, they

> were not about American life. They did reflect the American spirit of change and progress—the ingrained attitude that "there must be some better way." They accompanied a historic moment and a magnanimous concept of free giving in the wake of disaster. It was a time when hearts were full, actions were generous and gratitude was freely spoken. The documentary film did its part by multiplying, intensifying and recording for posterity one of the greatest achievements of American foreign policy. (182)

Another postwar government filmmaking activity, under State Department jurisdiction, was the International Motion Picture Service (IMPS), which, in early years, assigned film projects to such prominent independent nonfiction directors and producers as Willard Van Dyke, Irving Jacoby, Henwar Rodakiewicz, Julien Bryan, and Louis de Rochemont. Their films, which were shown through a vast worldwide network, included Rodakiewicz's *International Ice Patrol* (1947), a workmanlike film, that in the G.P.O. tradition, salutes a Coast Guard vessel that keeps track of icebergs, and Van Dyke's *The Photographer* (1948; see below).

Aside from these titles, however, the IMPS films are not memorable. This is hardly surprising, considering the overall political climate. On the domestic front, while the government seemed to agree that its information policy should maintain a strong anticommunist stance, it was also apparently uncommitted to financing films that would carry this message. On the international front, the cold war intensified, and in 1950 the United States entered a devastating war in Korea. With the establishment of the United States Information Agency, the government's information activities entered a new era, sophisticated in both policy and product.

The United States Information Agency
The United States Information Agency (USIA), created by President Dwight D. Eisenhower in August, 1953, consolidated all international information programs.[6]

From its beginnings, it was intended to be different from the government information efforts of the Second World War, and its mandate deserves quotation in full.
The purposes of the USIA are to:

> (1) strengthen foreign understanding and support for United States policies and
> actions; (2) counter attempts to distort the objectives and policies of the United
> States; (3) advise the President . . . and other key officials on the implications of
> foreign opinion for present and contemplated United States policies; (4) promote
> and administer educational and cultural exchange programs in the national inter-
> est and in order to bring about greater understanding between the people of the
> United States and the peoples of the world; (5) cooperate with the American
> private sector to enhance the quality and reach of America's overseas information
> and cultural efforts; (6) assist in the development of a comprehensive policy on
> the free flow of information and international communication; and (7) conduct
> negotiations on information and educational and cultural exchanges with other
> governments.[7]

Despite this clear mandate, the USIA did not in its early years have a dynamic
director or develop a strong sense of direction until March, 1961, when President
John F. Kennedy appointed Edward R. Murrow, a veteran of radio and television
broadcasting, to head the USIA. Kennedy's appointment was astute—Murrow had
an international reputation for journalistic integrity—and it had a precedent in
President Franklin D. Roosevelt's appointment of professionals like Frank Capra to
supervise wartime film production and Elmer Davis to head the OWI.

The USIA's Motion Picture and Television Service (IMV), headed by George
Stevens, Jr., was responsible for producing films and television programs, both
original and in compilation format; for distributing these products worldwide and
for assessing their impact on foreign audiences; for selecting, in cooperation with
representatives of the film industry, films to represent the U.S. government at
international film festivals; and for fostering the international exchange of educational and cultural audio-visual materials.

The majority of USIA films are

> documentaries, supporting long-range objectives, topical shorts, newsreels,
> and filmed official visits by heads of state and other foreign officials. USIA-
> produced films are supplemented by those acquired from private sponsors and
> other agencies, from which overseas exhibition and adaptation rights are pur-
> chased. (Henderson 79)

Because these films were intended only for showing in foreign countries, American
audiences were not familiar with them. However, two USIA films have been released for U.S. theatrical showings. The first was a color film of Mrs. John F.
Kennedy's visit to India and Pakistan: Leo Seltzer's *Jacqueline Kennedy's Asian
Journey*.[8] The reasons behind this special release of a government propaganda film
are easy to understand: Murrow was persuasive, the trip was successful, and Mrs.
Kennedy was the subject of considerable interest. *Jacqueline Kennedy's Asian Journey* is a conventional travelogue that contrasts old cultural traditions with modern

progress. Mrs. Kennedy looks radiant and happy as she tours India and Pakistan, and although there is nothing controversial in the film, the domestic screenings were the target of partisan criticism. Nonetheless, the film was very popular with audiences at home and abroad. The second USIA film to be screened for American audiences was Bruce Hershenson's *JFK: Years of Lightning, Day of Drums* (1967), a biography of the assassinated President.

Stevens's major achievement was using (and sometimes discovering) such talents as Leo Seltzer (*Jacqueline Kennedy's Asian Journey*); Charles Guggenheim (*United in Progress, Nine From Little Rock, Night of the Dragon*); Bruce Hershenson (*Friendship Seven, Five Cities of June, JFK: Years of Lightning, Day of Drums*, and *The President*); James Blue (*The School at Rincon Santo* and *The March*). Stevens also established programs in film schools that supported such fledgling filmmakers as Kent Mackenzie (*The Exiles* and *A Skill for Molina*), Ed Emshwiller (*Faces of America*), Gary Schlosser (*Cowboy*), Carroll Ballard (*Beyond This Winter's Wheat*), Robert K. Sharpe (*Labor of Love*), and Gary Goldsmith (*Born a Man*). With the best of these films, he joins the ranks of such great nonfiction film producers as Pare Lorentz and John Grierson.

TELEVISION DOCUMENTARY

While television, with its abundant opportunities to inform, educate, and entertain, has become a dominant force in American life, its nonfiction programming varies widely in quality. Nonfiction films produced for television are not within the scope of this study, except to outline their considerable influence on the development of the nonfiction film. After the war, the nonfiction film was in a period of decline worldwide. As A. William Bluem writes:

> The intent to persuade and influence, to involve great audiences, to make exciting the great issues and causes of our time, lost its force with the end of violence; and by the time the crises of the world loomed large once more, television had arrived and was ready to assume this documentary responsibility.[9]

In 1955, Paul Rotha and others had doubts about the role that nonfiction film might play in television,[10] but television producer Burton Benjamin has since argued that the television industry, in its first years, did "more for the documentary than the motion picture industry did in six decades."[11] Now, there is no question that, throughout its history, television has continually provided new possibilities for the nonfiction film.

Bluem sees the television documentary (and he consistently uses the term *documentary*) as the product of two influences: the radio documentary programs of the 1930s and the overall nonfiction film tradition. Television mediated between these two influences, offering not only an instantaneous record of our times, but also a reporter-narrator to interpret them. The first television documentaries were essentially newsreels that provided on-the-spot journalistic coverage. Eventually, stylistic landmarks began to appear in two memorable series: "See It Now," begun in 1951 by Edward R. Murrow and Fred W. Friendly, and "Victory at Sea," begun in 1952 by producer Henry Salomon. Both series had their roots in nonfiction film history—"See It Now" in "The March of Time" (both radio and film versions) and "Victory at Sea" in such wartime films as *Desert Victory, The Fighting Lady, The Battle of Midway, Battle of San Pietro,* and the "Why We Fight" series. Murrow and Friendly were the most influential forces in the development of the television documentary during the 1950s, but it is perhaps not surprising that their backgrounds in radio broadcasting, journalism, and public affairs made them somewhat more sensitive to words than to images. When television producers and filmmakers during the 1960's began to incorporate techniques learned from cinéma vérité, the image became a more integral part of television reporting.

There are, according to Bluem, three approaches to the making of television documentary: the compilation approach, the biographical approach (often utilizing compilation techniques in addition to dramatic structure), and the dramatic approach. The compilation approach, one of the most familiar, characterizes two of the most memorable of the early television series: "The Twentieth Century" (CBS, 1957–64) and "Victory at Sea" (NBC, 1952–53). The biographical approach, which was generally very popular, is particularly evident in the historical biographies produced by such series as Henry Salomon's "Project XX" (NBC), "The Twentieth Century," Donald B. Hyatt's "The World of _____ " and "The Story of _____ " (NBC), and David Wolper's "Biography" (NBC). The dramatic approach to early television documentary is evident in countless films, from those that recorded inherently dramatic events to those that imposed a dramatic framework upon events. Among the noteworthy achievements in this field are "Circle Theatre" (1950–55), Robert Drew's "Living Camera" series, which included *The Chair* (1962; see chapter 15), and William Jersey's *Manhattan Battleground* (1963) in the NBC "Creative Projects" series. On CBS, "Omnibus," a transformation of the screen magazine format, used all three of these approaches in an urbane series of programs that distinguished itself in the television wasteland.[12]

The nonfiction film made for television enjoys one distinctive advantage over its counterpart made for theatrical showing: immediate screening that reaches millions of viewers in their homes at practically no direct cost to them. Moreover, the television networks have often advertised them as "specials," thus stimulating audience interest and increasing their apparent stature. Today, the carefully produced "special" still exists, but, with remarkable advances in video production methods, television stations can now produce two- and three-hour "specials" on the same day the events are occurring. Television seems to realize much of its potential when covering national or international tragedies.

POSTWAR INDEPENDENT FILM PRODUCTION

Postwar independent films extended the range of the American nonfiction film in several ways. They served the special interests of business and nonprofit sponsors; extended the range of television broadcasting; fostered the development of the cinematic art for its own sake; and, in the Griersonian tradition, addressed human concerns. These films explored new social issues, exhibited new cinematic approaches, attracted new money, fostered new talent, and won new audiences. Robert Flaherty's *Louisiana Story,* which reflected the director's exploration with new production methods, was a major link between pre-war and post-war production.

Robert Flaherty and Louisiana Story (1948)

Louisiana Story (1948), Robert Flaherty's most ambitious and most beautiful film, is made out of myth, memory, and actuality.[13] It culminates his career by recapitulating the central motifs and philosophy of the films that preceded it. In *Nanook, Moana,* and *Man of Aran,* Flaherty portrayed life free from industrialization, and in *Industrial Britain* and *The Land,* he considered the effects of technology on manual labor. In *Louisiana Story,* with Standard Oil as the sponsor, he represented industrialization as neither threatening nor beneficent, but instead created a rich ambiguity of meaning in depicting the coming of the oil industry to the Louisiana bayou. Flaherty, acknowledging the film's dreamlike mood, called its narrative a "fantasy," but in presenting a world out of time—a world that does not refer in any way to America after World War II—he is also offering a world out of mind, the autobiography of a romantic who, at the age of sixty-two, retained the wonder of a boy exploring the world around him.

Flaherty sees this world through the eyes of Alexander Napoleon Ulysses Latour (the fancifully allusive name that he gave to the character played by Joseph Boudreaux), and evident throughout is a rapport between the director and this winsome youth that recalls not only Flaherty's collaboration with Nanook and Moana, but also his affectionate relationships with Mikeleen (*Man of Aran*) and Sabu (*Elephant Boy*).[14] The principal characters of both *Nanook* and *Louisiana Story* are explorers: Nanook (the father) and Alexander (the son). Here, Flaherty records and celebrates the boy, who, through his innocence, curiosity, superstition, and powers of magic, seems, in Wordsworth's sense, the father of the men who come to the bayou in search of oil. He is there before they arrive, amused by their behavior while they are working there, and remains after they leave. The bayou provides his experience and circumscribes his life, and even though he might have been spoiled by contact with the world outside, the impression left at the film's conclusion is that his innocence has, if anything, been confirmed.

Thus, in *Louisiana Story,* Robert Flaherty met a challenge that had bested him in making *The Land*: the reconciliation of opposing forces. On the mythic level, he succeeded in reconciling the opposite worlds of the boy and the men, the alligator and the oil derrick; on the personal level, the integrity of the independent filmmaker was reconciled with the needs of the industrial sponsor, his views with those of his collaborators. It had taken Flaherty a lifetime of exploring his own artistry to reach this point, and he brought to its production everything that he had learned.

In one important aspect, this film was different from any previous film Flaherty had made. He chose an impressive group of artists with whom to work as his collaborators, including Richard Leacock, the cinematographer; Helen van Dongen, the editor, who also served as associate producer; and Virgil Thomson, whose beautiful musical score is one of the most successful elements of the film.[15]

Louisiana Story (Robert Flaherty, USA, 1948)

Flaherty's wife Frances worked with him on the story. They were not asked to join him midway, to help solve a problem (as Helen Van Dongen was asked to join him on *The Land*), but, rather, were with Flaherty from the beginning through the completion of the film. Although all of them helped Flaherty bring *Louisiana Story* to completion, it is without a doubt that Helen van Dongen played the most important role by giving the film its clarity, coherence, structure, and rhythm. Flaherty realized that, even though they disagreed on many points, he could not complete the film without her.

Flaherty had a simple view of the world, but he was not innocent. As his other films demonstrate, Flaherty did not wholeheartedly espouse Standard Oil's message: he knew that men could spoil, even destroy, the natural environment, that innocence was virtually meaningless against the material strength of the industrial world, and that human beings paid dearly for the benefits provided by technology. Flaherty also knew that his film would be worthless if the sponsor's message took precedence over those values that characterized his other films. Yet he could not wholly ignore his sponsor's reason for making this film. Thus, he made the best choice possible under the circumstances and narrated the film through the viewpoint of a boy who is so close to nature that his only friend is a gentle raccoon and who will fight the alligator he believes destroyed that friend. This proved to be a brilliant decision for the film, for it not only provided a persona to serve as Flaherty's advocate, but also preserved the wondrous spirit of boyhood that is among its most enduring qualities.

Louisiana Story served both the practical needs of Standard Oil and the poetic spirit of Robert Flaherty. Out of materials that might otherwise have become a prosaic industrial film, Flaherty made a dramatic film showing the difficulty and the danger involved in the discovery of oil. To all members of his audience—stockholders, environmentalists, schoolchildren, and the general public—the film explained not only the process by which oil was discovered in the bayou, but also confirmed something of the mystery of nature. It told the story of men—the hardworking, experienced younger men on the drilling rig; the older, skeptical Mr. Latour—and, through the eyes of a boy, it created a special world, haunted by werewolves and mermaids. The film is a study in contrasts between technology and superstition, men and boys, the bayou and the world beyond, and success and failure. The noise and power of technology, developed so beautifully in the sequence known as the "Ballet of the Roughnecks," are contrasted with the beautiful, quiet, and lyrical scenes depicting Alexander in the bayou, exploring, watching, listening, or fishing.

Flaherty had been free to indulge himself and his view of the world. Not only did he have a contract that ensured him complete artistic freedom, and collaborators who would help him realize his vision, but he had conceived the unusual idea of revealing his story through the eyes and thoughts of a boy. Alexander Napoleon Ulysses Latour was not a one-dimensional character like Mikeleen (*Man of Aran*), but a real boy, living in a world of reality, myth, and memory, and it is no wonder that Flaherty took such care in directing the boy who played him. Flaherty's wonder and curiosity about life become Alexander's and thus become ours. The film is a fable, both simple and complex, raising more questions than it answers and using both subconscious symbols and newspaper headlines to reveal actuality. Today, when oil is both a natural and a political resource, treasured by virtue of its scarcity and value, the film gains new worth, tantalizing us with the precious, mysterious balance that exists between man and nature in an imaginary world without politics.

In *Louisiana Story*, there is realism in Flaherty's treatment of the oil industry, but also poetry in his love of nature and elegy in his celebration of innocence. *Louisiana Story* is a lyrical film whose images linger in the memory. From its beginning in the dreamlike images and the narrative tone set by Flaherty's voice, through the formal structure of the oil drilling sequence, to the conclusion, *Louisiana Story* is a film based on myth, memory, and actuality. The six sequences unfold leisurely; the first engages the viewer with images of mysterious shapes and shadows, and the others tell the chronological narrative. Circular in construction, the film moves from peace and quiet to activity and noise and finally back to peace and quiet. The crew enters the isolated bayou, drills for a well and establishes a pumping unit, and then departs. The boy is there at the beginning and ending of the film; although the central section concentrates on the industrial operation, his view of the world is not changed, but rather confirmed, by the activity. The fundamental aim of this narrative is to express the feeling and atmosphere of the place, not just the actuality of the situation.

As had happened before in his career, Flaherty eventually realized that he had a problem in attempting to discover a narrative within nature and letting that narrative reveal itself. Although he had the overall concept, and had no difficulty in translating the moods he wanted into expressive visual images, the larger design would have eluded him without the contributions of his collaborators in scenario, photography, editing, and music. Thus, the film's beauty is partly a result of Flaherty's insistence on many of his traditional ways of working, and partly a product of his collaborative experiments with cinematography, particularly with the synchronous sound camera. He was agreeable to the overall use of sound, music, and, for the first time, directed scenes with dialogue.

In Robert Flaherty's *oeuvre, Louisiana Story* stands alone as a small masterpiece—lyric, poetic, humanistic, as a realistic account of a major industrial process, and as a romantic elegy to a world that Flaherty envisioned and illuminated more completely here than in any of his other films. He had never before made a more ambitious film than *Louisiana Story,* and, despite its success and his subsequent involvement in several filmmaking projects, it was his last film.[16]

Independent Films of the 1950s
Throughout its history, from Flaherty to Lorentz, from Van Dyke to Leacock, the American nonfiction film has been distinguished by an insightful social consciousness. Thus, during the 1950s, many films were concerned with such issues of social, scientific, and economic importance as the environment, physical and mental health, hospitals, and alcoholism. Whether photographed directly or reenacted, the best of them, as Lewis Jacobs writes, "campaigned for improving man's knowledge of himself."[17] There were, of course, other aspects to the postwar development of the American independent nonfiction film. Television demonstrated its ability to produce instantaneous news reports, and "art houses"—theatres that featured foreign and domestic films *as* art—introduced audiences not only to international film production, but also to the American revival of the European experimental (or underground) film tradition.[18]

Traditional concerns typical of the 1950s' American independent film included domestic issues and social conditions (children, health, labor, urban life); observing the varied phenomena of American life; preserving a record of foreign cultures; illuminating art and artists; presenting biographies of famous persons; and documenting war.

CHILDREN
The welfare of the world's children was a major concern in the 1950s, and the first American nonfiction film on this subject, made shortly after World War II, was Leo Seltzer's *First Steps* (1947), which won the Academy Award (Oscar) for the Best Documentary Short in 1948. Seltzer, who started with the Film and Photo League (see chapter 7), made over sixty films for various public and private agencies, including the USIA, the United Nations, foundations and philanthropic organizations, and television networks. His work encompasses almost the entire span of the

history of the American nonfiction film and has made a distinguished contribution to its development. *First Steps,* a short film made for the United Nations, documents the rehabilitation of children who are afflicted with cerebral palsy. It is straightforward and hopeful, following one boy's progress with physical therapy and group activities at a special camp. Seltzer also directed *Fate of a Child* (1950) in which the death of a child illustrates the extensive problems of an underdeveloped Latin American country.[19] A routine problem-solution film, it hardly examines the issues in detail; but, instead, shows the various ways in which the United Nations can provide technical assistance.

Shortly after the war, a group of talented artists, working together in various combinations, produced several outstanding films about children. These include *The Quiet One* (1948), produced by Sidney Meyers, Janice Loeb, Helen Levitt; *Steps of Age* (1950), produced by Sidney Meyers and Ben Maddow; and *In the Street* (1952), produced by Helen Levitt, Janice Loeb, and James Agee.[20] Of these, *The Quiet One,* along with Flaherty's *Louisiana Story,* brought the greatest hope of revitalization for the commercially distributed, feature-length nonfiction film.

The Quiet One concerns a boy's private world. Like Flaherty, the filmmaking team of Meyers, Loeb, and Levitt present the odyssey of a boy who is searching for himself in a world that he does not yet fully understand. And, like Flaherty, they allow the film to move at the boy's pace and rhythm. But unlike Flaherty's Cajun

The Quiet One (Sidney Meyers, Janice Loeb, Helen Levitt, USA, 1948)

boy, free to roam the Louisiana bayous in his own canoe, the subject of *The Quiet One* is a young black boy, the child of an unhappy and broken home, who is trying to find himself in a remarkable school established for boys like himself. In a straightforward documentary approach, the filmmakers of *The Quiet One* observe the boy in a world that he perceives to be almost unbearably boring, isolated, and frustrating.

The first half of *The Quiet One* depicts the experiences that bring Donald to the Wiltwyck School, while the second half, narrated by the school's doctor, details his experiences there. Through Donald's courage and determination to overcome his inability to communicate, the film demonstrates that this environment provides boys like Donald with the security to take the first steps in healing themselves. The dramatic sequence in which he runs away from Wiltwyck exemplifies the serious and complex way in which the film presents Donald's problems. At one point, Donald is hiding on a railroad track, trapped against a wall by a passing train, and moments from his young life flash before him as one frightening memory. As a result of this cathartic experience, he decides to return to school and continue his recovery. *The Quiet One* makes no compromises in its presentation of Donald; he is a child, but not a child actor, and his unaffected appearance in the film is memorable. Like Flaherty, the team of Meyers-Loeb-Levitt had the patience and ability to capture a child's spontaneity on film. The commentary, written by James Agee, is gentle and factual, serving to unify the film's content and visual style. Unlike most commentaries, it is informative without being didactic, illuminating without being strident, poetic without self-conscious lyricism, and, above all, infused with understanding and compassion.

After the war, it was rare for directors of Hollywood narrative films to make nonfiction films. For that reason alone, *Benjy* (1951), directed by Hollywood veteran Fred Zinnemann, is worthy of attention. *Benjy* tells the story of a crippled boy; of his parents, who cannot reconcile themselves to his condition; and of the work done by the Los Angeles Orthopedic Hospital in rehabilitating him and changing his parents' attitude. Using a script and professional actors, Zinnemann moves briskly toward a predictable conclusion, overpowering the subject and its emotion with his cinematic approach. In style, *Benjy* seems a forerunner of the television hospital series. The extent to which handicapped children are capable of conveying an immediate sense of their own problems is better presented in Lindsay Anderson's and Guy Brenton's *Thursday's Children* (see chapter 12).

HEALTH

A major contributor to the nonfiction film (see also chapter 14), George Stoney has produced or directed almost fifty films since 1950, many of them on the subjects of physical and mental health care.[21] Stoney's work is marked by a concern for the disadvantaged, especially blacks and native Americans. Like Pare Lorentz, Stoney often formulated his early nonfiction films with a fictional framework, controlling their dramatic conflict so that it did not overshadow the resolution of the problem at hand.

Following *Palmour Street* (1950), which is about health education in the black community, Stoney made his most famous film, *All My Babies* (1952), which represents a breakthrough not only in its careful approach to the training of Negro midwives in Georgia, but also in its direct cinematography of an actual childbirth. Like Lorentz's *Fight for Life, All My Babies* begins with a sequence in which a classroom of midwives is admonished for not preventing one baby's death. But unlike the opening of *Fight for Life,* which shows how a training program for midwives is established, *All My Babies* is concerned with improving a midwifery system that is already in operation, with most of the footage shot in the cabins and houses of the people depicted. Lorentz relied on a tight conflict to bring drama to his treatment of the theme; his approach is professional, but often as cold as steel. Stoney works more simply, contrasting fear and ignorance with safe, successful childbirth methods. Like Lorentz, Stoney contrasts a dirty home whose residents are unprepared and apprehensive, with a home in which the residents have made the appropriate physical and psychological preparations for both prenatal and post-natal care, as well as for the birth itself. The scene of childbirth is directly photographed in close-up, the details of which provide an unexpected dimension to the film's instructional value. Stoney's film was made with great care and especially noteworthy editing by Sylvia Bettz. The soundtrack, which mixes Negro spirituals with gentle narration by the midwife, Miss Mary, effectively complements the straightforward cinematography. *All My Babies* presents a sentimental, easy solution to the very real problem of infant mortality in depressed, disadvantaged areas; although it might easily be criticized for that approach, the film continues to show audiences the power of community, the work of loving hands, and the beauty of childbirth.

In the postwar period, the general public and filmmakers alike paid increasing attention to mental health. While the Canadians pioneered in producing outstanding films about psychology, including those in the "Mental Mechanisms" series (see chapter 12), several American films deserve brief mention even though they use fictional techniques within a nonfiction framework. These include *Steps of Age* (1950), directed by Sidney Meyers and Ben Maddow, a sensitive film about the problems and pressures of growing old; *Angry Boy* (1951), directed by Alexander Hammid and Irving Jacoby, which shows how a guidance clinic helps to reform a young boy caught stealing; and Irving Jacoby's *The Lonely Night* (1954), a frank account of how a young woman and her therapists cope with her problems. All of these films on health, Stoney's included, were intended to convince audiences of the need for good physical and mental health, and to appreciate the work of the agencies that help people maintain their health.

LABOR

During the 1930s, many American nonfiction filmmakers found inspiration in left-ist and radical social movements and in the work of such groups as the Workers' Film and Photo League, Nykino, and Frontier Films (see chapter 7). It is thus surprising that these filmmakers have produced relatively few memorable American nonfiction films on labor issues. Certainly, some films have been concerned with the importance of labor in our society—including the films of the Film and Photo League and Paul Strand's and Leo Hurwitz's *Native Land* (1942)—but many others have only touched lightly on subjects such as labor unrest, strikes, and union organization.[22] This tendency to avoid labor issues continued into the 1950's, a decade of conservatism and economic well-being. However, two exceptions deserve mention: *Salt of the Earth* and *Harvest of Shame*.

Herbert J. Biberman's *Salt of the Earth* (1954) has three themes: the struggle of Mexican-Americans for equality with Anglo-Americans; the struggle for better working conditions; and the struggle between married partners for equality. With its radical inspiration, the film explores the interrelations between workers' and feminists' concerns. However, as a prolabor statement, it unfortunately uses melodramatic stereotypes to create a simple world in which good workers are victims of bad mine owners and police officers. Nonetheless, the film is notable for its scripted reenactment, use of nonprofessional actors, and cinematography.[23]

David Lowe's *Harvest of Shame* (1960), an outstanding CBS social documentary on migrant labor, has had a major influence on the nonfiction genre because of its strong editorial stand on a subject that many people would prefer to ignore. Some of the footage that records the squalid life of migrant workers is familiar: unsanitary, rat-infested housing; unwholesome food; the lack of day care for children; and wretched travelling conditions. But, in the world of television broadcasting, this was largely unexplored territory.

Harvest of Shame, narrated by Edward R. Murrow shortly before he left CBS to head the USIA, was first broadcast during Thanksgiving week when Americans were celebrating the harvest; in that context, the film shocked viewers as *The Grapes of Wrath* had twenty years before. In his earnest voice, Murrow told the audience about pending legislation that, if passed, would alleviate many of the migrant workers' problems. The implied suggestion here was that viewers might feel strongly enough to write to their representatives in Washington. Such a call for action on the viewers' part was something new in the history of the nonfiction film, for even the most hard-hitting social documentaries stopped short of using such a direct tactic. But immediacy was one of the advantages of television, and "CBS Reports," like "See It Now,"

> functioned at its journalistic best in detailing those continuing stories which set contemporary issues squarely before the public—issues in which the element of controversy was inherent. . . . The treatments took two basic forms: either the balanced and impartial analysis, or, more rarely, the undeniably editorial statement. (Bluem 103)

Harvest of Shame was one of these rare films. Although it included a few dissenting views, it did not attempt to be neutral by balancing its arguments. Its editorial bias provoked strong criticism; in response, CBS stated that it had "presented facts and issues so as to stimulate people into doing their own thinking" (quoted in Bluem 105). Although *Harvest of Shame* is in the American tradition of the engaged social documentary, the tradition of *The Plow that Broke the Plains, The River*, and *Native Land*—it broke new ground in that genre. As television grew more commercial, however, such committed editorial statements were the rare exception, not the rule.

URBAN LIFE

From the advent of the European "city symphony" tradition through such American classics as *The City* (1939), urban life has fascinated nonfiction filmmakers. Before the war, most of the films in this tradition were about the rhythm and excitement of city living. After the war, the most vibrant tribute to the city was Francis Thompson's *N.Y., N.Y.* (1957). Working in the surrealist rather than the documentary tradition, Thompson presents a scintillating "day in the life" of New York City that is linked to two landmarks in the "city symphony" tradition: Cavalcanti's *Rien que les heures* (1926) and Vertov's *The Man With the Movie Camera* (1929). However, unlike these city symphonies, which pay realistic tributes to urban excitement, Thompson's view of New York is neither realistic nor complacent. Shot in color, with jazz underscoring the city's rhythm, *N.Y., N.Y.* splits images into so many fragments that the city appears as if it were being observed through a kaleidoscope. Other typical lighthearted salutations to city life include Frank Stauffacher's *Sausalito* (1948) and *Notes on the Port of St. Francis* (1952), Carson Davidson's *Third Avenue El* (1955), Willard Van Dyke's and Shirley Clarke's *Skyscraper* (1960), and Shirley Clarke's *Bridges-Go-Round* (1959).

In his rich and varied career as a filmmaker, Francis Thompson travelled extensively to make a variety of films, most of them sponsored by large corporations or philanthropic foundations.[24] Like many independent filmmakers of the postwar period, he believed in cinema as an art form as well as a forum for the discussion of social issues. And, with his collaborators, he was also an important pioneer in the

N.Y., N.Y. (Francis Thompson, USA, 1959)

use of large-scale, multi-image film technique. Thompson and Alexander Hammid began experiments with huge multiscreen projection in *To Be Alive!* (1964), one of the great attractions at the 1964 New York World's Fair; later, Thompson made *City of Wilderness* (1974), about the growth and development of Washington, D.C., from its early beginnings to the present day. Thompson's later films in the Omnimax/Imax technique are truly spectacular in their screen proportions and use of multi-images. These include *We Are Young!* (1965) for Expo '67; *US* (1968), with a narration written by W. H. Auden, for HemisFair '68; *American Years* (1976), for the bicentennial celebration in Philadelphia; *To Fly!* (1976), which remains the greatest attraction at the Smithsonian's National Air and Space Museum in Washington, D.C.; *Living Planet* (1979) and *On the Wing* (1986), both for the Smithsonian's National Air and Space Museum; and *Energy! Energy!* (1982), for the 1982 World's Fair in Knoxville, Tennessee. Because most of these films were designed for special projection and auditoriums, usually at world's fairs and exhibitions, they are not generally available for viewing; however, *To Be Alive!* is screened daily for visitors to the Racine, Wisconsin, headquarters of its sponsor, the Johnson's Wax Company.

Despite a technology that limits their audiences to special theatres, these works remain major contributions to nonfiction film history. With their overwhelming size and compelling use of many screens projecting simultaneous images, they encourage audiences to see cinema in a unique way. And through their intelligent commentary, they encourage audiences to think about social issues without stereotypes. Thompson's and Hammid's *US*, for example, was anything but a world's fair entertainment. Although sponsored by the United States Department of Commerce, it does not offer a predictable government message. Rather, it bluntly criticizes the United States for not having realized its potential. On a cinematic scale that is commensurate with the issues it covers, the film focuses on poverty and racism, the betrayal of Native Americans, pollution, the devastation of our natural resources, the difficulty of finding solitude and privacy, and the ugliness of the man-made environment. Auden's commentary calls our attention to these problems, inviting our further contemplation of them. He concludes:

The eyes of the world are upon us
And wonder what we're worth,
For much they see dishonors
The richest country on earth.

Shamefully we betray
Our noble dead if we,
After two hundred years,
Cannot or will not see,
More clearly what is meant
By certain truths that they
Believed self-evident.

On each of us depends

> What sort of judgment waits
> For you, for me, our friends,
> And these United States.

If this reminds one of Pare Lorentz's narration for *The River,* that is, perhaps, intentional, for that film, too, lists our national failures; however, like *US,* it also assumes that American audiences can accept the truth about deplorable social conditions and take positive steps to correct them.

Other 1950s' nonfiction films dealt with the struggle for equal rights, which entered a new phase with the 1954 Supreme Court decision mandating integration in the schools. From that point forward, new battle lines were drawn, especially in the cities, over such issues as integrated schools, voter registration, and equal housing and job opportunities. Television, predictably quick to cover the struggle, did so courageously and, later, during the 1960s, documented the civil rights era with journalistic distinction (see chapter 14).

Leo Hurwitz's *Strange Victory* (1948), an unusual compilation film, was among the first postwar film statements on racism.[25] Consistent with Hurwitz's earlier work (e.g., *Native Land*), it is a bitter film that moves outside the mainstream development of the American nonfiction film. Warren Miller writes that it alienated many viewers with its

> refusal to compromise with fact: the fact of the exploitation and oppression of the Negro people in America, the fact of anti-Semitism, of native fascism; and the disquieting idea that the recent war had indeed produced a strange victory, the values of the loser being adopted by the victor.[26]

Hurwitz uses sharp, swift juxtapositions of images and ideas, some of which are less than subtle (e.g., a "colored only" sign is juxtaposed with the tattooed number on the arm of an inmate of a Nazi concentration camp). He creates the image of an America that is complacent in its victory, prosperity, and racism; the narrator warns: "Nigger, kike, wop, take my advice and accept the facts—the world is already arranged for you." In William Wyler's *The Best Years of Our Lives* (1946), the fighter pilot (played by Dana Andrews) cannot get work when he returns home; his heroism means little in a postwar economy whose values are material, not human. Hurwitz replicates that theme—here it is a black fighter pilot who cannot get work—but he goes farther than Wyler, documenting the racism that is more concerned with a man's color than his valor. *Strange Victory* is a brilliant, hard-hitting film that not only continues the radical traditions of certain films made by The Film and Photo League and Frontier Films, but also offers a potent challenge to democracy in a time of national complacency and conservatism.

Charles Guggenheim's *A City Decides* (1957) analyzes how the 1954 Supreme Court decision on school integration affected the urban community of St. Louis. Guggenheim's scripted dialogue and use of actors lacked the immediacy of television news reportage, a style with which viewers were becoming increasingly comfortable; still, *A City Decides* is an important cinematic landmark in the study of integration and education.[27]

Before 1956, when Allan King made *Skid Row* and Lionel Rogosin released *On the Bowery,* no nonfiction filmmaker had ever taken a thorough look at alcoholism and the sustained suffering of the alcoholics' world. Later, in the 1960s, nonfiction films became concerned with problems of alcoholism and drug addiction (for example, Pennebaker's *David,* a film about synanon), but Rogosin deserves the credit for first examining this important subject. Before *On the Bowery,* filmmakers had taken candid looks at depressing topics and had offered practical solutions, but few had devoted an entire film to a problem for which there are no easy remedies. Like Flaherty, Rogosin uses keen observation and deep compassion in telling the story from the inside. Also like Flaherty, he used his portable equipment to record the sights and sounds of a world that his audience knew mostly through stereotype.[28] Unlike Flaherty, however, he told a true story, not a fable.

On the Bowery surveys the world of the indolent men and women who live on New York's Bowery, a neighborhood of sleazy bars, flophouses, and Salvation Army Missions. Rogosin's central vision of this world is a cycle of despair. Men drink, fall down, are arrested and released; they drink again and are rehabilitated by evangelist missions; they drink again and fall down. There is a morning sequence in *On the Bowery* that is a nightmare vision straight from hell: men in every conceivable state of drunkenness and filth, lying in filthy gutters and doorways, shaking and shuddering as they awaken to face the new day. These men will do anything for a fellow alcoholic, but they will also do almost anything *to* him in order to get another drink. Ray, the main character, moving through an urban nightmare of isolation and loneliness, is both victor and victim. When he cannot sleep on the floor of a flophouse, he goes out in the night for a drink, is hustled by an alcoholic woman, and later is beaten and robbed. While Ray finds some hope in human companionship, the old men around him anticipate a darker fate. At the end of the film, Ray leaves the Bowery for some undisclosed destination, but we are told "He'll be back." If not Ray, his counterpart will enter this world of work for meager wages, trips to the pawnshop to get enough money to drink, and nights spent in bars and doorways. In another sequence, Rogosin's camera reveals a Bowery evangelist to be a hypocrite, and foreshadows the candor of later direct cinema portraits: Bob Dylan in Pennebaker's *Dont Look Back* (1966), Billy Graham in Richard Cawston's *I'm Going to Ask You to Get Up Out of Your Seat* (1966), and the salesmen in *Salesman* (1969) by Albert and David Maysles and Charlotte Zwerin.

New York was not the only city presented as an alienating environment; Los Angeles is the background for *The Savage Eye* (1959), a full-length film by Joseph Strick, Sidney Meyers, and Ben Maddow. Like *On the Bowery, The Savage Eye* suggests that the city is a terrifying, meaningless void, but it goes farther in depicting the overwhelming despair that finally drives the central character to attempt suicide. The film portrays Southern California as a place of sleazy bars, beauty and massage parlors, traffic jams, animal cemeteries, and faith healers. *The Savage Eye* depicts a city in which men and women are mired in their own depravity. Minor themes in the early European city symphony films, alienation and despair are now the filmmakers' dominant concerns. As Lewis Jacobs observes,

> *The Savage Eye* brought together all the isolated insights of city films made before and, in combining them with a deeper and more coherent social vision, became perhaps the best American example of a more profound kind of city film.[29]

With its images of postwar greed, spiritual emptiness, and brutality, *The Savage Eye* stands with many of its *film noir* counterparts as an authentic account of one individual's disillusionment and search for meaning in the postwar world. While the film does end with the protagonist's recovery, it nonetheless leaves behind a savage vision of a world without heroes or hope.

RANDOM OBSERVATIONS OF AMERICAN LIFE

In contrast to the alienation and *angst* of *On the Bowery* and *The Savage Eye*, other films provided delightful, random observations of American life. These include Valentine Sherry's *Coney Island* (1951) and Joseph Strick's *Muscle Beach* (1950), a lighthearted account of a stretch of the Venice Beach in Southern California where body builders work out for curious tourists and adoring fans alike. Although Strick was one of the codirectors of *The Savage Eye*, the sensuality and vanity of the bodybuilders are intended to be amusing in themselves, not symbols of some deeper, corrosive malaise in society. Bert Stern's *Jazz on a Summer's Day* (1959) not only documented the Newport Jazz Festival and the great vogue for jazz in the 1950s, but also anticipated films about rock music festivals made in the 1960s.

ETHNOGRAPHIC FILM RECORDS OF FOREIGN CULTURES

The anthropological or ethnographic film is one of the earliest types of the nonfiction film (see chapter 2), counting among its important early achievements Robert Flaherty's *Nanook of the North* (1922) and *Moana* (1926), Merian C. Cooper's and Ernest B. Schoedsack's *Grass*, Basil Wright's *Song of Ceylon* (1934), and Knud Rasmussen's *The Wedding of Palo* (*Palos brudefaerd*, 1934). Although the use of ethnographic film footage became common after the 1920s, particularly in the films that Gregory Bateson and Margaret Mead made in New Guinea, very few ethnographers actually completed films that could stand on their own as works of art until the period following World War II. At that point, serious ethnographic film making was influenced by the work of Jean Rouch, who was also a major influence on the development of cinéma vérité (see chapter 14). Rouch, along with Bateson, Mead, and Paul Fejos in the United States, and Gotthard Wolf in Germany, helped to make major advances in the production and critical reception of ethnographic films.[30]

The successful ethnographic film is measured by ethnographic, not cinematic standards. Flaherty said "First I was an explorer; then I was an artist": working as scientists, ethnographic filmmakers seek to compile empirical observation, not to create artistic form. They record raw data for analysis; relate specific observed behavior to cultural norms; strive for a holistic approach that seeks to observe and understand people and events in their social and cultural context; and they seek not to create a cinematic illusion of truth, but rather to recreate a physical and psychological verisimilitude. Ethnographic filmmaking attempts to be faithful to a cinematic realism in which space and time are preserved as closely as possible.[31]

Various attempts in the 1950s to make accurate films about other cultures included Lewis Jacobs's *Sponge Divers of Tarpon Springs* (1951) and Arnold Eagle's *Holy Week in Popayan* (1959); even Lionel Rogosin's *Come Back Africa* (1959) and Robert Flaherty's *Louisiana Story* (1948) have been classified as ethnographic films. A related mode of film, which satisfies a worldwide television audience insatiable for films about wildlife, includes the works of Jacques-Yves Cousteau (see chapter 12), Irwin Allen's *The Sea Around Us* (1952), based on the book by Rachel Carson, and the films produced by the Walt Disney Studios, including *The Living Desert, The African Lion,* and *White Wilderness* (all 1953), and *The Vanishing Prairie* (1954). Although the Disney films are beautifully photographed, they tend to anthropomorphize animal life, and charming as this may be to some, Disney's work cannot be ranked with the films of such scientists as Cousteau or the ethnographic filmmakers discussed here.

The most outstanding and influential ethnographic film of the decade was *The Hunters* (1958), a film by John Marshall and Robert Gardner about the Bushmen of the Kalahari desert. In the tradition of *Nanook of the North,* this film imposes a story upon factual footage and sometimes permits that story to take precedence over the truth. But it focuses on a whole people, not a single man and his family, and in its psychological understanding of the Bushmen, it goes beyond Flaherty's few rudimentary observations made about the psychology of the Inuit.

After *The Hunters,* Robert Gardner made *Dead Birds* (1963), which, although in the Flaherty tradition, was planned from the beginning, as Gardner says, to be "done by professionals trained and experienced in both film and anthropology."[32] The film's subject is the Dani people who live in the Central New Guinea Highlands. Like Flaherty, Gardner paid his subjects with objects that were useful and valuable—shells, salt, steel implements—and also like Flaherty, he had the advantage of working with a people who did not know what a camera was. Like Bateson and Mead, he made careful, thoughtful observations of people and events, and completed a film that is a remarkably thorough document of life among the Dani. *Dead Birds* was, according to Heider,

> a watershed for ethnographic film. . . . Before *Dead Birds,* there was a mere handful of films which could be called ethnography; in the decade since *Dead Birds,* literally dozens have been made. (34)

After *Dead Birds,* Gardner made *The Nuer* (1970) before completing his masterpiece, *Rivers of Sand* (see chapter 14).

FILMS ON ART

In the immediate postwar period, American nonfiction filmmakers made fewer films about art and artists than their European counterparts. During the 1960s, however, when art, artists, and the art market became the focus of cultural attention, and a significant number of American films on art and artists were produced (see chapter 14). The few films produced during the 1950s were generally conservative in their approach to a variety of artists.

After the war, the first important American film about an artist was Willard Van Dyke's *The Photographer* (1948), a record of a visit with Edward Weston, the pioneer American photographer who was also Van Dyke's mentor. The film is not only an excellent introduction to the art of photography, but is also one of the very first films from any country to regard photography seriously as an art form. Although *The Photographer* is notable for its intimate portrait of Weston, the commentary, written by Ben Maddow and Irving Jacoby, is banal and detracts from the beauty of Van Dyke's cinematography. Other films on art and artists included Erica Anderson's and Jerome Hill's *Grandma Moses* (1950); Weegee's (Arthur Felig's) *Weegee's New York* (1950); Irving Hartley's and Herbert Matter's *Alexander Calder: Sculptures and Constructions* (1948) and Herbert Matter's *Works of Calder* (1950); James Davis's *John Marin* (1951); Lewis Jacobs's *Mathew Brady: Photographer of an Era* (1953), Hans Namuth's and Paul Falkenberg's *Jackson Pollock* (1951).

Other films were concerned with artists from other countries and periods. These include James Johnson Sweeney's *Henry Moore* (1947), Peter Reithof's *Toulouse-Lautrec* (1951), and George Hoyningen-Heune's *God's Monkey: Hieronymus Bosch* (1955). Finally, there were several American films on diverse subjects: Jess Paley's *A New Way of Gravure* (1951), Sidney Peterson's *A Japanese House* (1955), and Charles and Ray Eames's *Textiles and Ornamental Arts of India* (1955).

FILM BIOGRAPHIES

This period marked the introduction of the nonfiction film biography, a genre that was to become extremely popular in the following years as part of the cult of personality. Such early films included Nancy Hamilton's *Helen Keller in Her Story* (1955); Richard Leacock's *Bernstein in Israel* (1956), about a tour by Leonard Bernstein and the New York Philharmonic Orchestra; Dave Butler's and Barnaby Conrad's *The Day Manolete Was Killed* (1957); and Jerome Hill's *Albert Schweitzer* (1956). Schweitzer was also the subject of Erica Anderson's *No Man is a Stranger,* (1958, with Dr. Nathan Kline) and *The Living Work of Albert Schweitzer* (1965).

DOCUMENTING WAR

War was an unpopular topic in the immediate postwar period. Although the Korean War lasted for three years, and inspired numerous narrative films, many of which were modelled after Hollywood's World War II films, there was virtually no official documentary film production about the Korean conflict.[33] As the cold war intensified, the American government preferred to produce USIA films about postwar foreign policy rather than films about the Korean conflict.[34] The American people, confused about foreign policy,[35] were less interested in learning about the Korean War—which was a police action, not a world war—than they were in pursuing prosperity at home. Those who wanted to keep abreast of the war could see the news on television.[36] Patriotic themes in general did retain their audience, and two nonfiction films about historic American battles won Academy Award Oscars as best documentaries: Dore Schary's *The Battle of Gettysburg* (1955), which made use of actual battle locations and voice-over narration, and Louis Clyde Stoumen's *The True Story of the Civil War* (1956), an outstanding compilation film that is very effective in its use of still photographs and other media.

PART FIVE

(1960–1985)

Continuing Traditions and New Directions

14

American Renaissance in the 1960s: The New Nonfiction Film

The decade of the 1960s encompassed a major social revolution, with many of its events exposing contradictions in an American society that had become complacent in the post–World War II period. Social historian Eric P. Goldman called the 1960s "the momentous decade," while novelist John Updike called it "a slum of a decade." On one hand, there was social progress and a quest for peace; on the other, there was social decay and outbreaks of violence at home and abroad. American society in the 1960s was strong enough to support a traditional culture and a counterculture, to be a secure postwar world and one whose values were under attack.[1] However, the strengths of the American democratic system could not prevent the serious domestic social conflicts that tore American society apart, and the decade represented a severe test of American values. As a result, American society, torn by turbulent extremes and currents of change, was transformed.

With the 1960s also came a new liberalism, a new economics, and a new idealism about social values. Soon after his eloquent 1961 inaugural address (" . . . ask not what your country can do for you; ask what you can do for your country"), President John F. Kennedy set out an ambitious domestic program, known as the New Frontier: tax reform; expanded federal aid to education, the space program, depressed areas, and medical care for the aged; and intensive attention to civil rights. With this spirit also evolved new concepts of government and new relationships among the Presidency, the establishment, the media, labor, minorities and ethnic groups. Nonetheless, the nation was divided by the assassinations of President Kennedy, Senator Robert F. Kennedy, Dr. Martin Luther King, Malcolm X, and Medgar Evers, and by social crises: black uprisings; campus protests and violence; a state of siege in many cities; worsening environmental conditions; widespread drug abuse; rising crime statistics; eroding confidence in national leadership; and the war in Vietnam.

The arts reflected this change and the spirit of liberation in American society. The spirited revival of cinema in the 1960s resulted partly from the rise of revolutionary politics throughout the western world and partly from the dominant youth culture that understood and embraced cinema as the most political of art forms. This generation understood, perhaps better than any before it, the language and affect of cinema. The spirit of the new waves that helped to fashion the European narrative film of the period also helped to shape the contours of a new nonfiction film.

During the 1960s, the nonfiction film was reborn. Not only were there an unprecedented number of films produced both for traditional distribution and television broadcasting, compared to previous decades, but the quality of these films also increased, as did the extent of their influence on audiences and later filmmakers. In addition, there was an increasing internationalization of the genre and a concurrent evolution of new cinematic languages. The American nonfiction film responded to the social dynamic of the decade, on the one hand, by reaffirming its traditions, and, on the other, by changing to meet the needs of society. The versatility of the nonfiction film provided a major key to its survival.

Among the reasons for the rebirth of the nonfiction film in the 1960s were the influences and achievements of the Anglo-American nonfiction film tradition in the post-World War II years; the beginnings of a stronger and more independent system of nonfiction film production and distribution; the potential of television as a medium for the exhibition of nonfiction film; experiments in the United States and abroad with cinematic forms seeking a free, direct expression of the realist impulse; the technological developments that produced lightweight, mobile equipment; the emergence of more women as producers, directors, and editors; and the development of the feature-length nonfiction film (ninety minutes or more). Although filmmakers continued to produce the traditional documentary film, it was in the development of cinéma vérité and direct cinema, experimental departures from these traditional roots, that the nonfiction film genre was revitalized. What, in the 1930s, John Grierson called "the documentary idea"—the use of film for reality-based didactic purposes—yielded in the 1960s to the idea of a new cinematic realism: the exploration and use of film for its own sake. This new approach evolved more from aesthetic than social, political, or moral concerns, an astonishing phenomenon considering the documentary film tradition and the social transformation that was shaping the decade.

CINÉMA VÉRITÉ AND DIRECT CINEMA

Cinéma vérité and direct cinema, which were cinematically, if not politically, radical, represented both a break with tradition and a unification of various American and European nonfiction film traditions.[2] Cinéma vérité appeared in France in the 1950s; direct cinema was developed in the United States in the early 1960s. They are two distinct genres, one building on the other, reaffirming two theoretical aspects of the nonfiction film: that the genre contained within itself limitless possibilities for cinematic expression and that all good nonfiction films take their shape from their subject matter.

Like most avant-garde movements, the achievement of this new cinematic language was to awaken filmmakers and audiences alike to a new way of revealing and recording life as it is. This realist impulse was born with the Lumières and developed by Flaherty and Vertov. But the most significant developments came after World War II—with Italian neorealism, British Free Cinema, and the postwar French cinema, the latter of which culminated in the New Wave; together, these constitute "the first efforts that were made to create a cinema that was not costly, that came closer to reality, and that was free from slavery to technique."[3]

After the war, the French cinema, unlike Italian neorealism or British Free Cinema, had neither leader nor manifesto, offering instead the continuation of independent film production, the fostering of apprenticeship opportunities for several of those directors who were to bring about the revolutionary New Wave in the late 1950s, and an intellectual and cultural climate that encouraged innovation. Among the important developments within postwar French film were a revival of the nonfiction film and the emergence of cinéma vérité.

Cinéma Vérité: Historical and Theoretical Origins

Cinéma vérité has its origins in Vertov. Its importance to the evolution of nonfiction cinematic technique was its experimentation with some traditional techniques: the interview (a device which was first used with Arthur Elton's and Edgar Anstey's *Housing Problems* in Great Britain in 1935); the biographical format (as old as Flaherty's *Nanook of the North*, 1922); the kaleidoscopic portrayal of city life (first attempted in Germany with Walther Ruttman's *Berlin: The Symphony of a Great City*, 1927, and developed further with Vertov's *The Man With the Movie Camera*, 1929); and the recording of ordinary people doing and saying ordinary things. Among the cinéma vérité pioneers in France and French-speaking Canada were Pierre Perrault, Chris Marker, Mario Ruspoli, Jacques Rozier, and Jean Rouch.[4]

Of these filmmakers, the best-known and perhaps most important is Jean Rouch.[5] The majority of his films, which he labels as "ethnographic fiction," represent a genre of their own. His *Chronicle of a Summer* (*Chronique d'un été*, 1961) had enormous influence upon the development of cinéma vérité.[6] A feature-length film that consists mainly of interviews with Parisians (who were asked " . . . are you happy?" and who answered with unpredictable and highly personal answers), *Chronicle of a Summer* was subtitled *"une experience de cinéma vérité,"* apparently in homage to Vertov.[7] With others who have experimented with the lightweight equipment and the direct approach, Rouch discovered the power of the camera to provoke people to behavior that was not typical of their everyday lives, and he saw in what he termed cinéma vérité[8] a means of liberating people from their limited selves.[9]

The appearance of cinéma vérité in the early 1960s showed that, once again in the history of cinema, technological developments preceded aesthetic impulses and strongly influenced the "look" of this new cinema. As Stephen Mamber has observed, cinéma vérité "indicates a position the filmmaker takes in regard to the world he films."[10] It was lightweight, portable equipment that made possible the achievement of that position, which is both physical and ontological.[11] Traditional Hollywood films had relied on the use of 35mm cameras and fine grain film stock, as well as the achievement of high studio production values.[12] But during World War II, the production of training, incentive, and combat films provided a new use for lightweight, compact, durable 16mm cameras with improved lenses and standardized, interchangeable parts. Unlike the Hollywood, "highly worked,"[13] image, these cameras generally produced a black-and-white image. Most important is that the camera was freed from the tripod; when the cameras were hand-held, the images, as a result, were sometimes shaky or blurred, but the audience perceived authenticity in these less-than-perfect cinematographic images. This widespread perception of footage shot by portable cameras as real and believable was only strengthened as television (also black-and-white at that time) emerged to accompany and then mostly to replace the other black-and-white media (newsreels and newspaper photographs) as this country's principal source of visual news reporting in the 1950s.

Advances in sound recording, also begun during World War II, were improved still further in the mid-1950s with the development of a magnetic tape recorder capable of synchronous sound and, around 1960, with the substitution in tape recorders of transistors for vacuum tubes. However, Monaco observes that "crystal synchronization provided the final necessary flexible link in this system, allowing cameraman and sound recordist to work independently, unhampered by the umbilical cord that used to unite recorder and camera" (50). Allen finds that "the difficulties in shooting synchronous sound on location stand out clearly in both neo-realist and traditional documentary films" (220). The use of transistors reduced the weight of the tape recorder from several hundred pounds to only twenty. The portable tape recorder offered the freedom to record actual synchronous sound; multitrack tape mixing equipment gave sound editors greater control over their material.

The "ideal" film thus became a possibility: it could be made anywhere, not just in the controlled studio environment; would require no more than available light, and thus avoid the theatrical look of much studio lighting; would have the option to record reality either in color or in "journalistic" black and white; and would record sound as it occurred in actuality, not as it was recreated in the studio.[14]

With its roots in *cinéma vérité*, direct cinema reflected two predominant, related influences—the desire for a new cinematic realism and the development of equipment necessary to achieving that desire. Direct cinema uses whatever cinematic properties are necessary to record reality and then to re-present it. Although different filmmakers take different approaches to creating direct cinema, the basic desire is the same: to capture a carefully selected aspect of reality as directly as possible, to record footage while events are happening rather than to create footage in the studio, to provide the viewer with the feeling of being there. To this end, direct cinema is unscripted and unrehearsed (although internal evidence in many films indicates some preparation). Direct cinema uses lightweight, portable equipment (with the camera mounted on the shoulder, rather than hand-held, as in *cinéma vérité*) in an informal attempt to break down the barriers between the filmmaker and the subject. The camera work is intimate, increasing the direct relationship between the filmmaker-subject-viewer; the sound recording is direct and synchronous, often clouded by pickup of extraneous noises that contribute to the sense of reality; and the editing tends to be continuous, rather than discontinuous, striving for a chronological, rather than dramatic, presentation of events. For the filmmaker, this practice involves a direct observation of reality; for the viewer, this results in a direct perception of reality.[15]

Direct cinema has often been mistakenly confused with other genres—candid eye, living cinema, concrete cinema; even more frequently, there has been an equation of its approaches and achievements with cinéma vérité. On the contrary, direct cinema is a distinct genre. The principal elements that distinguish it from other approaches to the nonfiction film are: (1) rejection of the nonfiction film tradition; (2) uncontrolled filming of real people in real situations; (3) rejection of traditional direction and script; (4) creation of a model of reality that includes many types of ambiguity; (5) spontaneous sense of the viewer's "being there"; (6) primacy of observation over narration; (7) use of lightweight, portable equipment; (8) live sound recording; (9) primacy of editing over long-take cinematography; (10) primacy of form over content.

Cinéma Vérité and Direct Cinema: A Comparison and Contrast

Direct cinema is not only different from cinéma vérité, but the term has replaced the more ambiguous cinéma vérité in designating the synchronous recording of image and sound. It is therefore essential to an understanding of direct cinema— what it is, what it is not—to understand how it is similar to, and just how much it differs from, cinéma vérité.

Cinéma vérité represents an application of nouvelle vague cinematographic practices to real events rather than staged ones. In a manner characteristic of French innovation in cinema, it added the conceptions of the camera as a catalyst, the filmmaker as an active participant behind and sometimes in front of the camera, the elimination of devices from fictional cinema, the shooting and recording of real events rather than staged ones, and a visual style that incorporated informality and spontaneity into its "look," including such unconventional "mistakes" as poor lighting and the optically violent movement of the camera, which was frequently hand-held. Overall, cinéma vérité brought about a redefinition of film aesthetics. In turn, this led to the development of a new self-reflexive cinema.[16]

The achievements of cinéma vérité created audience and critical reactions so diverse that the term cinéma vérité was applied to many innovative, experimental, or new developments in cinema after 1950 even if they had nothing in common with it. Moreover, it was applied pejoratively to many cinematic techniques, like direct cinema, whose fresh or startling qualities disturbed the status quo.

Both cinéma vérité and direct cinema are similar in that they are committed to reality; to the realistic observation of society, what James Monaco calls an "essentially ethnographic orientation" (51); to the advantages produced by the use of lightweight equipment; to a close relationship between shooting and editing; and to producing a cinema that simultaneously brought the filmmaker and the audience closer to the subject. At the heart of the relationship between cinéma vérité and direct cinema is the ancient question of the "truth" of a work of art, its fidelity to reality. But, as Peter Graham writes, the idea that either form achieves some absolute truth "is only a monumental red herring."[17] Both cinéma vérité and direct cinema are ways of seeing, of understanding, and of conveying the filmmaker's perception of the world. Each filmmaker defines the truth according to his or her own convictions, sensibility, and experiences, within a cultural context. In practical terms, more often than not the "truth" is what occurs to filmmakers during the moments of observing, shooting, and editing: not *the* truth, but a filmmaker's truth.[18]

Allied to the question of film truth is that of the filmmaker's approach, which Erik Barnouw defines as the difference between cinéma vérité and direct cinema:

> The direct cinema documentarist took his camera to a situation of tension and waited hopefully for a crisis; the Rouch version of *cinéma vérité* tried to precipitate one. The direct cinema artist aspired to invisibility; the Rouch *cinéma vérité* artist was often an avowed participant. The direct cinema artist played the role of uninvolved bystander; the *cinéma vérité* artist espoused that of provocateur.
>
> Direct cinema found its truth in events available to the camera. *Cinéma vérité* was committed to a paradox: that artificial circumstances could bring hidden truth to the surface.[19]

Both approaches raise such issues as the filmmaker's relationship to the material, the use of the camera, and the nature of the editing to be done. Cinéma vérité filmmakers are often participants in, and commentators on, the action they record; direct cinema filmmakers always avoid narration and rarely appear, either inadvertently or as *personae*, in their films. While editing is important to cinéma vérité, it may be the *most* important single element in direct cinema. In direct cinema, the film editor, more than the film editor of any other kind of cinema, produces a model of reality.

In direct cinema, the term "filmmaker" subsumes the functions denoted by the terms "director" and "cameraman" and "sound recorder" and "editor"; these are not obsolete functions, nor are they discrete functions in direct cinema, but rather singular operations incorporated by the more comprehensive term "filmmaker," and denoting what Richard Leacock calls the "integrated process" of this new style of filmmaking.[20] Inherent in this process, according to Bazin, is the filmmaker's awareness of, and obligation to preserve, a deeper psychological reality, as well as the audience's freedom to choose from a variety of interpretations of reality.[21] Central to direct cinema is the presentation of disparate material as if it were equivalent; the resultant ambiguity creates the illusion of reality itself. Direct cinema is a manifestation of cinematic time (more than space) in which memory and forgetting, objectivity and subjectivity, collide.

AMERICAN DIRECT CINEMA

The mutual impact of cinéma vérité and direct cinema redefined conventional realist theory and practice for many nonfiction filmmakers.[22] For a nonfiction filmmaker working in the 1960s, itself a decade shaped by chaos and liberation, direct cinema represented a change from tradition, an opportunity to confront directly the social forces of the time, and a challenge to bring closer together cinematic art and its relation to reality. In the United States, direct cinema at first appeared to have completely transformed the realist nonfiction film tradition with the freedom and clarity of its approach.

Major American Direct Cinema Filmmakers and Films

The development of American direct cinema in the 1960s was dominated by the distinct approaches of Robert Drew, Richard Leacock, D. A. Pennebaker, Albert and David Maysles, and Frederick Wiseman (the work of the Maysles brothers and Wiseman is discussed in chapter 15). Their belief in the spontaneous, uncontrolled cinematic recording of important events, issues, and personalities established an approach so strong that it dominated the further development of the form.[23] The pioneering work of all these filmmakers combined the unique properties of two mass communications media—journalism and the traditional documentary film— to develop a third: direct cinema.[24]

ROBERT DREW

Robert Drew, the father of American direct cinema, understood the limitations of the traditional documentary. Observing that the Griersonian documentary was little more than an illustrated lecture (Allen 223), Drew believed that he and others could find a way to make it less one-sided and more cognizant of reality. The means for this lay, not in the traditional nonfiction film, but in an adaptation of cinéma vérité for television.[25] In its earliest years, television was thought to be the appropriate environment for direct cinema development because the Federal Communications Commission had established the broadcasters' responsibility to address issues of general public interest through public affairs programming. (In fact, Drew later acknowledged his misjudgement in assuming that television would provide the regular airtime or programming environment necessary to establish the new form and to ensure the growth of audience understanding and acceptance.)[26]

Robert Drew Associates, the television production organization of Time, Inc., brought together such talented filmmakers as Richard Leacock, Gregory Shuker, Hope Ryden, James Lipscomb, Albert Maysles, and D. A. Pennebaker. ABC-TV, the network that provided the creative climate for Drew's initial experiments, differed from CBS-TV and NBC-TV in that it broadcast public affairs programming that was produced outside of its own news operations. Although ABC-TV had the lowest ratings and the least share of the viewing audience, it had a sponsor (the Bell & Howell Company) willing to support an incentive to try something different from traditional documentary film and ordinary television news programming. Drew's approach was characterized principally by its sync-sound location shooting of uncontrolled events and its reliance on images, rather than a narrator, to present the subject.

The resulting objectivity was important to the network and its sponsor in addressing the FCC's "Fairness Doctrine," in creating an impression of a disinterested network and a commercial company doing something valuable to raise the public consciousness, and in conforming to the prevailing political climate of consensus. Nevertheless, several factors discouraged the successful development of Drew's approach, including the lack of general audience interest in both public affairs and direct cinema, the ABC network's tendency to schedule public affairs programming where it would be seen by the least number of people, television's primary reliance on the "talking head," and the gradual absorption of many direct cinema methods into mainstream television news reporting.[27]

Robert Drew and his associates produced nineteen films on an astonishing choice and variety of subject matter. Before joining with ABC-TV, they made *Primary* (1960) and *On The Pole* (1960). For the ABC-TV "Close-Up!" series, they made four films: *Yanqui, No!* (1960), *X-Pilot* (1960), *The Children Were Watching* (1960), and *Adventures on The New Frontier* (1961). Their work also included two specials: *Kenya, Africa* (1961), for ABC-TV, and *On The Road To Button Bay* (1962), for CBS-TV. For the "Living Camera" series, they made *Eddie* (1961), *David* (1961), *Petey And Johnny* (1961), *Football* (also titled as *Mooney vs. Fowle*) (1961), *Blackie* (1962), *Susan Starr* (1962), *Nehru* (1962), *The Aga Khan* (1962), *Jane* (1962), *The Chair* (1962), and *Crisis: Behind A Presidential Commitment* (1962).

Of these films, the most influential are *Primary, Crisis: Behind a Presidential Commitment,* and *The Chair. Primary,* a film by Robert Drew, Terry Filgate, Richard Leacock, Albert Maysles, and D. A. Pennebaker, follows the Democratic Party campaign in the 1960 Wisconsin presidential primary through the eyes of the candidates, Hubert H. Humphrey and John F. Kennedy. The shoulder-mounted camera follows the two men closely, offering us an unprecedented view of the endless handshaking, speeches and street-corner electioneering that are the essence of American political campaigns. Within this intimate, behind-the-scenes look at the machinery of political campaigns, we see the usual spectacle, the predictable verbal abstraction, and the silly hullabaloo. But we also witness unpredictable and memorable moments: Humphrey directing a rehearsal of his own television program; Jacqueline Kennedy fidgeting while she recites a Polish sentence she has learned for a group of Polish supporters; Kennedy waiting in the night for the final results of his two-to-one victory over Humphrey.

Primary is a balanced, objective film report on politics; the filmmakers are there to record and to reveal, not to interpret. They let viewers judge for themselves, and attach no labels through editing that might have distorted the words or actions of either side. The sequences are well-balanced between the two sides; the narration is impartial, and there is little of it in comparison to the amount of direct sound recording. However, other "Living Camera" films had presented definite viewpoints on major issues of the time. *Yanqui, No!* (1960) followed the parallel rise of communism and anti-American feelings in Latin America; *The Children Were Watching* (1960) reported on the attempt in 1960 to integrate the public schools of New Orleans, and, for many television viewers, provided one of the first compassionate accounts of the ignorance and brutality of the white New Orleans community that surrounded this conflict; *Crisis: Behind A Presidential Commitment,* which was filmed partly from the offices of President Kennedy and Attorney General Robert Kennedy, and partly from the scene, was equally compassionate toward

Negro students as it followed the attempt by Governor George Wallace to defy court-ordered integration and bar them from the University of Alabama. *Crisis* raised serious questions that were later to become mainstays of direct cinema criticism: the validity and reliability of nonfiction footage shot in compliance with the participants; the possibility that the camera exploits personalities and issues; the ethics of the direct, unedited recording of conversations, particularly those involving issues of domestic security; and the ethics of imposing a dramatic structure (such as the paradigm of a "crisis") on nonfiction footage.

Of all of these films, *The Chair* has the most lasting value as an early demonstration of the antinomies inherent in the direct cinema style and the virtual impossibility of achieving objectivity about certain news events. Part crime reporting, part courtroom drama, part human interest story, *The Chair* is about what might have been the last few days and hours in the life of Paul Crump, a black man convicted of murder and sentenced to die in the Illinois electric chair. The film concentrates on the successful efforts of lawyers Louis Nizer and Donald Moore to convince the authorities that Crump has been rehabilitated during his years in prison and that his death sentence should be commuted to life imprisonment. While this tense film is structured, the drama is real.

The filmmakers—Leacock, Pennebaker, and Gregory Shuker—clearly favor the efforts of Nizer and Moore; since Moore was the principal lawyer, the film closely follows his activities. Nizer, a famous criminal lawyer, was retained at the last minute to add his prestige to the appeal. Moore is a remarkable presence on the screen, at times apparently aware of the camera with his theatrical gestures, and at other times oblivious to its presence, such as when he breaks down and cries after hearing that the Catholic archbishop of Chicago will issue a statement to aid his appeal; moments later, after composing himself, he adds spontaneously: "But I don't even believe in God!" But the partiality of the film does not stem from the filmmakers' own feelings; rather, it comes from the case itself. The prosecuting attorney, who does not seem to understand Paul Crump's position, bases his argument upon outdated and irrelevant legal and moral principles, making his points on incomplete evidence and calling unsupportive witnesses. When the parole board recommends and the Illinois Governor confirms the commutation, the filmmakers do not comment; they do not express regret or happiness that Paul Crump has been imprisoned for life, instead of being executed or released, for, again, the events speak for themselves. The film takes it stand on the matter of rehabilitation, not on the merits of the capital punishment argument.

The direct camera catches many fine moments in this tense struggle on Crump's behalf: the steel and concrete labyrinth of the Cook County Jail; his best friend, the warden, a tough, likable corrections official; an interview with his editor to put the final touches on a novel that will be published after his scheduled execution; his mother quietly listening to a discussion about whether her son should live or die; and a witness for the prosecution, making fine points about sin and contrition. All of these are dramatic touches, to be sure, but the difference between *The Chair* and a conventional television courtroom drama is that all of the events were true, and filmed directly as they were happening. The cinematography is unobtrusive and intimate, and the sound recording makes very effective use of telephone conversations, random comments, the sounds of bells and clanking steel doors, and the direct testimony in the hearing room.

Eventually, Leacock, Pennebaker, and others left Drew Associates to become independent filmmakers, rejecting the rigidity of the television format, the crisis structure that was not suitable for all subjects, and the manipulative editing used to secure this dramatic framework. Their disagreements suggested that if direct cinema were to develop further and realize its potential, it would not be the result of collaborative efforts for television, but rather would be an auteur's effort, carrying with it the stamp of an identifiable and controlling artistic intelligence.

RICHARD LEACOCK

Richard Leacock and D. A. Pennebaker worked with Drew Associates—most notably on *Primary, Eddie,* and *The Chair*—and have worked together as Leacock-Pennebaker on *Dont Look Back* (1966) and *Monterey Pop* (1968). Richard Leacock's early career in direct cinema included directing for the landmark television show "Omnibus" (e.g., *Toby and The Tall Corn,* 1954) and developing lightweight motion picture production equipment.[28] In this early part of his career, his most significant films were *Happy Mother's Day* and *A Stravinsky Portrait.*

Happy Mother's Day (1963), codirected by Joyce Chopra and Leacock (his first film after leaving Drew Associates), records the reaction of a small South Dakota town to the birth of quintuplets by Mrs. Fisher, a local woman. It is a masterpiece of objective observation and ironic narrative, confirming the codirectors' gift for balancing objectivity with intimacy. Because of this, it is never clear whether or not their implicit judgments are more important than their direct reportage. They are amused, as we are, at the human comedy in the townspeople's display of happiness, hypocrisy, commercial exploitation, and an attempt to maintain the family's privacy and dignity. Like the Maysles-Zwerin *Salesman* (1969), the film succeeds in not taking itself too seriously as it holds up a mirror to American society and values.

Leacock's camera focuses on many delightful details: the solemn discussion by the town's businessmen as they suggest ways to satisfy tourists and to protect the Fishers' privacy; the planning for a parade, commemorative souvenirs, and a testimonial luncheon; the refusal by the doctor who delivered the quints to join the parade. Perhaps the most remarkable, though, is the manner in which the Fisher family is almost completely ignored, how their "privacy and dignity" are discussed at the same time that city fathers are debating visiting hours, special facilities for viewing the quintuplets, and other impositions. Through all of this, Mrs. Fisher is both bewildered and calm, and her reaction seems somewhat like ours: she doesn't know whether to cry or to laugh. But it is society, not Mrs. Fisher, that is ridiculous, pretentious, and presumptuous. The Leacock-Chopra look at "Quint City" (the film was originally titled *Quint City, U.S.A.*) is direct, but not impartial; for instance, they do not let us know if any townspeople opposed the overblown hype that is being organized. Ultimately, the Leacock-Chopra viewpoint is best reflected in the sarcastic tone of the narrator, who, at the conclusion, after all this extraordinary activity, comments, "It was a typical day in Aberdeen, South Dakota." In fact, the true worth of *Happy Mother's Day* is not in the sarcasm of the narrator, the irony of the title, or the precision of the cinematography and sound recording, but, rather, in the mirror that it holds up to society.

Of Leacock's early films, the most revealing is *A Stravinsky Portrait* (1964), made in collaboration with Rolf Liebermann.[29] The challenge here was to make a film that would reveal both the man and his music, avoiding both the interview and the concert approaches. Leacock and Liebermann (the latter narrates and appears in the film) more than meet that challenge and provide the rare experience of watching a musical genius compose, discuss, and conduct his work. Leacock approaches Stravinsky with intelligence, understanding, and respect, and Stravinsky seems totally oblivious to the presence of the camera. We see the composer in intimate moments, at lunch and in discussions with his wife and friends. In one scene, Stravinsky and George Balanchine plan a ballet scenario for a Stravinsky score; they are drinking vodka, and Stravinsky urges, "Take some more, let's be drunk!" We hear him explain his work: "The creative process is the fun and pleasure of doing it." But it is the gentle, impelling enthusiasm of the great composer that makes this film; charming in explanation, delightful in humor, Stravinsky fills each sequence with his sparkling presence. *A Stravinsky Portrait* is a rare document, made possible by Stravinsky's candor and Leacock's unobtrusive observation, by a collaboration between two artists—one on either side of the filmmaking equipment.

Richard Leacock's later films include *Queen of Apollo* (1970), a unique glimpse of a New Orleans debutante at a Mardi Gras ball; *Light Coming Through: A Portrait of Maud Morgan* (1980), codirected with Nancy Raine, about the New York artist Maud Morgan; and *Community of Praise* (1982), codirected with Marisa Silver.

DONN ALAN PENNEBAKER

After leaving Drew Associates, Donn Alan Pennebaker's first work reflected his determination to make films that would reveal the "spiritual energy" of the people he chose as subjects.[30] His early films include *Opening in Moscow* (1959); *David* (1961); *Jane* (1962); *Lambert & Co.* (1964, a film by Pennebaker, Robert van Dyke, Nicholas Proferes, and Nina Schulman); *You're Nobody Until Somebody Loves You* (1964), an account of the wedding of the psychedelic guru Timothy Leary; *Dont Look Back* (1966); and *Monterey Pop* (1968). With the exception of *Opening in Moscow*, an account of the American exhibition there, *You're Nobody Until Somebody Loves You*, and *David*, which documents the efforts of a young jazz musician to free himself from drug addiction, these films provide an important chronicle of the performing arts in the 1960s.

With its grainy photography, poor lighting, and inadequate sound recording, *Dont Look Back* is closer in cinematic style to cinéma vérité than to direct cinema. Taking its title from a line in a Dylan song ("She's got everything she needs, she's an artist, she dont [sic] look back"), the film documents Dylan's 1965 tour of England. Bob Dylan is a charismatic performer, a vital element lacking in two of this film's more technically proficient predecessors, Pennebaker's *David* and *Jane*. It reveals him in candid interviews with newsmen and informal chats with teenagers, in concerts, in a room typing while Joan Baez sings. We see him arguing with hotel managers, dealing with his manager, and greeting a delightful lady Sheriff in an English town. However candid this portrait may be, it shows evidence of Dylan playing at being "Dylan," almost imitating a Dylan parodist. While this may invalidate what otherwise would have been a reliable portrait, the excitement of *Dont Look Back* results from the tension between Dylan, as he is, and Dylan, as he thinks the media and his fans want him to be. Putting words into his mouth, newsmen try to elicit answers that fit their preconceived notions of how a pop singer should behave. *Dont Look Back* is a touchstone for studying one of the enduring legends of 1960s pop culture.[31]

The first of the big rock festival films, Pennebaker's *Monterey Pop* (1968), is all the more enjoyable because it avoids the simple-mindedness of *Woodstock* and the obfuscation of *Gimme Shelter* (see chapter 15). The film preserves some memorable musical performances by The Who, Jimi Hendrix, Otis Redding, Ravi Shankar, Janis Joplin, The Mamas and the Papas, and Simon and Garfunkel. Beyond its value as social document and its excellent color photography and sound recording, *Monterey Pop* also reveals Pennebaker's admiration for music and musicians. While Pennebaker never achieves the cinematic intimacy with his subjects that, for example, Leacock does with Stravinsky, he is secure in his understanding and presentation of musicians. For his films to be successful, his belief in the "spiritual energy" of his subjects requires the equal interest of the audience.[32] Pennebaker makes an important contribution to the development of 1960s American nonfiction film with an intuitive approach to subject matter that is uniquely his.

Donn Pennebaker's later films reflect his continuing interest in the performing arts: *Original Cast Album: Company* (1971), *The Children's Theater of John Donahue* (1971), *Keep On Rockin'* (1972), *Ziggy Stardust and the Spiders From Mars* (1973), *Randy Newman Isn't Human* (1980), *Rockaby* (1982), a record of a Samuel Beckett play, and *Black Dance America* (1983). Another kind of theater is recorded in *Town Bloody Hall* (1971), a record of the famous Town Hall "Dialogue on Women's Liberation," featuring Germaine Greer, Diana Trilling, Norman Mailer, and others.

AMERICAN NONFICTION FILM OUTSIDE THE DIRECT CINEMA MOVEMENT

Although direct cinema was the most influential development in American nonfiction film of the 1960s, the independent nonfiction film, the mainstay of the American tradition, continued to flourish. It was a period of diverse and creative accomplishment in both traditional and nontraditional modes. Filmmakers were not only challenged by the central issues of the decade, but also by such professional issues as new technologies and expanding opportunities for longer nonfiction films and theatrical showings. Paramount among these challenges was the advent of commercial television.

The years between 1947 and 1951 marked a critical juncture in the history of mass communications: television began to replace the motion picture as the major communications force of the second half of the twentieth century. By 1949, the years of experimenting with the medium's technical potentialities had ended successfully, and regular television broadcasting (first local, then network broadcasting) had begun throughout the country. While television offered the public alternative popular entertainment at home, it seriously threatened the motion picture industry. Its appeal to the lowest common denominator of public taste resulted in a pattern of television programming that Newton Minow, Chairman of the Federal Communications Commission, referred to in 1961 as a "vast wasteland," a metaphor that sparked a widespread concern with the substance and quality of television programming.

Yet, ironically, television had a beneficial, even a profound effect on the nonfiction film.[33] It fostered the continuing development of the traditional nonfiction film, one advantage of which—in contrast to the flat, dull "look" of early television—was the relatively pure "look" of the cinematic form. Moreover, television itself not only offered the promise of improved technology (e.g., lightweight video cameras and videotape recording), but also brought the highest standards of reporting to such major news programs, "specials," and series as "See It Now," "CBS Reports," and "The Twentieth Century."[34] Television fostered the growth of the nonfiction film by providing the two supporting elements that had also aided the development of the early British documentary movement: sustained sponsorship and a creative atmosphere in which a dedicated group could pursue a common journalistic aim. Early television history in the 1960s was dominated by such major producers as Burton Benjamin, Robert Drew, and David Wolper, and by such narrators (and anchormen) as Edward R. Murrow, Walter Cronkite, Eric Sevareid, and Howard K. Smith. Later, public, or nonprofit, television became a major producer and exhibitor of the nonfiction film.[35] To these achievements, television added what no filmmaker, independent or working in a group, had ever enjoyed: the attraction of a new medium of mass communications and a vast audience that could enjoy it for virtually no cost beyond the initial investment in a television receiver.

In the following discussion of independent and television films by subject category, the emphasis is on those that, for their achievements, deserve continuing attention; films produced for television are designated by a bullet (•).

National Politics, Elections, and Leaders

John F. Kennedy, the man of the decade, was the subject of numerous films. These include *Primary* (see above), about the 1960 Kennedy-Humphrey primary race in Wisconsin; and Mel Stuart's *The Making of the President* (•1960), based on Theodore White's book, an account of the Kennedy-Nixon presidential election; and *Adventures On The New Frontier* (1961), a film by Richard Leacock, D. A. Pennebaker, Albert Maysles, and Kenneth Snelson about the President's first year.[36] Other films were about Kennedy's assassination: Mel Stuart's *Four Days in November* (1964), Bruce Hershenson's *John F. Kennedy: Years Of Lightning, Day Of Drums* (1966), made by the United States Information Agency,[37] which, considering the subject and the impact of the assassination, is a surprisingly bland biography; and Emile De Antonio's *Rush to Judgment* (1967), a study of the Warren Commission Report on the assassination (see chapter 15). Other films about politics include *Milhouse: A White Comedy* (1971)—De Antonio's scathing portrait of Richard M. Nixon, the man of the next decade—and *Campaign Manager* (1964; also titled *Republicans: The New Breed*), a film by Richard Leacock, Noel Parmentel, and Nick Proferes, about the man behind Barry Goldwater's 1964 presidential bid, and notable as one of the few American films that looks at conservative politics. Films about black leaders include Lebert Bethune's *Malcolm X: Struggle for Freedom* (1967), William Klein's *Eldridge Cleaver* (1970), and Marvin Worth's and Arnold Perl's *Malcolm X* (1972).

Justice and Civil Rights

The struggle to affirm civil rights for all Americans, especially blacks and other minorities, became one of the central social issues of the 1960s.[38] The civil rights movement, under the moral leadership of The Reverend Martin Luther King, Jr., and the political leadership of Presidents Kennedy and Lyndon B. Johnson, encouraged the passage of the Civil Rights Act of 1964, the most comprehensive civil rights legislation in United States history. King organized the 1963 March on Washington, which brought more than 200,000 to the nation's capital to witness King's "I Have a Dream" speech. Two outstanding films record this historic event: Haskell Wexler's *The Bus* (1964) and James Blue's *The March* (1964).

Films that help viewers to understand some of the background issues of the struggle to ensure civil rights for all citizens include Nicholas Webster's *Walk in My Shoes* (•1961), William C. Jersey's *Prisoner at Large* (•1962), Fred W. Friendly's *Storm Over the Supreme Court* (•1963), Arthur Barron's *My Childhood: Hubert Humphrey's South Dakota and James Baldwin's Harlem* (•1964), George Stoney's *The Run from Race* (1964), Harold Becker's *An Interview with Bruce Gordon* (1964), Richard Leacock's and David Lowe's *Ku Klux Klan—The Invisible Empire* (•1965), Adam Gifford's *Head Start in Mississippi* (1968), and William Greaves's and William Branch's *Still a Brother* (1969).

The battle for civil rights was fought not only in the nation's capitol, but also in dozens of regional conflicts. Many of these incidents, focussing on school integration, were violent. Films on regional incidents include Albert Wasserman's *Sit-In* (•1960), Stuart Schulberg's *The Angry Voices of Watts* (1966), Edward Pincus' and David Newman's *Black Natchez* (1967), *Cicero March* (1968) and *Chicago: The Seasons Change* (1969), both by the Film Group of Chicago, Perry Wolff's *The Battle of East St. Louis* (1970), and Peter Biskind's *On the Battlefield* (1972), a film about racial confrontation in Cairo, Illinois. The most memorable films were Charles Guggenheim's *Nine From Little Rock* (1963), a USIA film that won the 1964 Oscar as best documentary, and William C. Jersey's *A Time for Burning* (1966).

A Time for Burning, made for Lutheran Film Associates, involves us directly in the plight of L. William Youngdahl, a white Lutheran minister in Omaha who encourages his parishioners to open a dialogue with their black neighbors, and, for his efforts, is forced by them to resign. Race relations is the subject, but Youngdahl is the focus. Jersey took the direct cinema approach, reporting on black and white alike, recording and revealing their prejudice and anger, hope and fear. By his superb structuring and development of these themes, he has created a nonfiction film as remarkable for his mastery of the direct cinema technique as for his personal commitment to its subject. Not suprisingly, rejected (like its subject) by his community, Jersey's film was never shown by CBS.

Another battle in the civil rights struggle was fought on the nation's campuses, and recorded in three outstanding films: Arthur Barron's *The Berkeley Rebels* (1965), *Columbia Revolt* (1968), the Newsreel Group's inside view of the student occupation of Columbia University buildings, and Emile De Antonio's *Underground* (1976; see chapter 15).[39]

Youth

Perhaps the most colorful aspect of 1960s society was the youth movement, or so-called counterculture, which was evidenced by the peace movement, campus protests, rampant anti-intellectualism, experiments with drugs, eccentric clothes, and folk and rock music. It is surprising that filmmakers did not make more films about these activities. While aspects of the counterculture could be seen in certain films on rock music, no major nonfiction film made in the 1960s covered the subject as a whole. Films on youth centered on two areas: drugs and family life.

The use and abuse of drugs, previously associated with junkies and outcasts, first became associated in the 1960s with mental and spiritual enlightenment, but, then, spreading throughout society, became a scourge that killed drug apostles, rock star idols, hard-core users, and innocents alike. Films about drugs include Pennebaker's *David* (1961), *Marijuana* (1969), *The New Morality* (•1967), *The Addicted* (•1969), *Pull the House Down* (•1970), *The Trip Back* (1970), and Martha Coolidge's *David: Off and On* (1973), and *Drop-Out* (1963). Those about dropping-out include *From Runaway to Hippie* (1969), and Ed Pincus's and David Newman's *One Step Away* (1968).

The changing values of family life in this turbulent decade are the focus of such films as Arthur Barron's two-part study of attitudes of small-town teenagers toward parents, education, and family life: *Sixteen In Webster Groves* (•1966) and *Webster Groves Revisited* (•1967); Kent MacKenzie's studies of teenagers, *Teen-Age Revolution* (•1965) and *Saturday Morning* (•1971), and Craig Gilbert's *An American Family* (•1973). *An American Family*, a landmark in the development of direct cinema, raised many issues not only about family life—an American "institution" previously neglected by filmmakers—but also about the validity of the direct cinema approach.[40] The twelve one-hour segments of this controversial television series bring us remarkably close to the relationships, values, conflicts of the Loud family. Although there is some family harmony, the Louds are on the verge of a family breakup. Mr. and Mrs. Loud discuss divorce; Mrs. Loud mugs before the camera; Lance Loud, the older of five children, is alienated by this discord and by his homosexuality. Not until the Maysles' *Grey Gardens* (1975; see chapter 15) was direct cinema used so well to juxtapose the dynamic polarities of a family's relationships.[41] More traditional views of American youth and family life are found in two memorable films, distinguished by the light-handed humor of Richard Leacock: *On The Road To Button Bay* (1962), about the fiftieth anniversary of the Girl Scouts, and *A Happy Mother's Day* (1963; see above).

Poverty

The social legislation for a "Great Society," adopted in the administration of President Lyndon B. Johnson, included a nationwide "war on poverty." Although Johnson devoted considerable energy to establishing antipoverty programs in the nation's cities, these achievements were eclipsed by his escalation of the Vietnam War. However, the nation's efforts to combat poverty were documented in a group of nonfiction films, including two outstanding titles: Arthur Zegart's *The Battle of Newburgh* (•1962) and William C. Jersey's *Manhattan Battleground* (•1963). Other films include *War on Poverty* (1965), *Challenge of Urban Renewal* (1966), Martin Carr's and Peter Davis's *Hunger in America* (•1967), Jay McMullen's *The Tenement* (•1967), *Cities Have No Limits* (1968), *Incident in Roxbury* (1968), *Smalltown U.S.A.* (1968), *The View From City Hall* (1968), Morton Silverstein's *Banks and the Poor* (•1970), *The Besieged Majority* (1970), and *Appalachia: Rich Land, Poor People* (•1969)—a film by Fred Willis, Richard Pierce, and Adam Giffard.

Vietnam

During the 1960s and into the 1970s, the most serious and controversial social issue in the United States was the nation's undeclared war in Vietnam. While the principal years of U.S. involvement were 1961–73, the conflict itself began in 1954 and ended with the signing in 1973 of a peace treaty between the United States, North Vietnam, South Vietnam, and the provisional government of the National Liberation Front. Thoroughly covered by the media, the Vietnam War was dubbed the "living room war." However, unlike the World War II films, which were remarkable for their consistent support of the role of the United States and its allies, the nonfiction films (as well as television coverage) about Vietnam reflect divergent viewpoints and the polarization of American society into those who supported and those who opposed the war.[42]

Several films, all of which opposed the continuation or escalation of the conflict, presented and discussed issues in the war's background. These included Beryl Fox's *The Mills of the Gods* (1965), *Saigon* (1967), and *Last Reflection on a War* (1968); David Schoenbrun's *Faces of Imperialism* (•1967); Morley Safer's *Morley Safer's Vietnam* (•1967); David Loeb Weiss's *No Vietnamese Ever Called Me Nigger* (1968); the films of the Newsreel Groups;[43] Joris Ivens's *The Seventeenth Parallel* (*17e parallèle*, 1967) and *The People And Their Guns* (*Le peuple et ses fusils*, 1970); Michael Rubbo's *Sad Song of Yellow Skin* (1970); and the ambitious French-American production, *Far From Vietnam* (1967), codirected by Alain Resnais, Jean-Luc Godard, Joris Ivens, Agnes Varda, Claude Lelouch, Chris Marker, and William Klein. Yet, it took the courageous Emile de Antonio, with his *In The Year Of The Pig* (1969), to present a broad political, historical, and cultural analysis of the Vietnam conflict (see chapter 15).

The position of the United States government was expressed in several films, including John Ford's *Vietnam! Vietnam!* (1971), produced for the USIA. With its hard line against Communism, it resembled government propaganda of the 1950's; however, for all its patriotism, it reflected nothing of Ford's mastery of war propaganda in *The Battle of Midway*. The strongest statement of U.S. Vietnam policy was articulated in *Why Vietnam?* (1966), made by the Department of Defense. Its name and its purpose allude to Frank Capra's "Why We Fight" series (1943–45), but, aggressive and prowar as it is, it had as little in common with Capra's masterful achievement as the war in Vietnam had in common with World War II. Like the Capra films, it was produced to indoctrinate troops on their way to battle, to trace the historical background of the conflict, and to show actual combat footage interspersed with official comment (in this case, the remarks of President Lyndon B. Johnson). However, it is also a distorted, deceptive (one might even say desperate) attempt to justify the war's escalation to the millions of Americans, who nightly saw the actual effects of war on television. In fact, it convinced those who supported the war, and it outraged those who were against it.[44] However, the film's interpretation of the war ("We will not surrender and we will not retreat") had, according to Gallagher, "become embarrassing by the time of its release, and, after a few overseas showings in U.S. Information Agency libraries and cultural offices, it was withdrawn from circulation" (544). Several years later, Peter Davis's *The Selling Of The Pentagon* (1971) exposed the falseness of the government's justification of its escalation of the war.

The actual fighting in Vietnam was broadcast daily by American television networks, making combat films, which are slower to produce and release, far less necessary than they were in World War II. However, several combat films are worth notice, including Pierre Schoendorffer's *The Anderson Platoon* (1967), Peter Gessner's *Time of the Locust* (1967), and Eugene S. Jones' *A Face Of War* (1968). Jones's film, one of the best films made about Vietnam, takes a humanistic approach. Through a record of the daily experiences of American soldiers in the Seventh Marine Regiment, Jones makes a strong antiwar statement—the enemy is not the Viet Cong but war itself. Two films about North Vietnam gave Americans an insight into the people, the issues, and the society on the other side of the struggle: James Cameron's *Eyewitness North Vietnam* (1966) and Felix Greene's *Inside North Vietnam* (1967).

Another perspective about Vietnam was provided in films from other countries, most of which were not legally available for screening in the United States. From North Vietnam came *Nguyen Hun Tho Speaks to the American People* (*Chu tich Nguyen Hun Tho noi chuyen voi nhan dan my*, 1965); *The Way to the Front* (*Duong ra phia truoc*, 1969); and *Some Evidence* (*Vai toibac cua de quoc my*, 1969). From Cuba came Santiago Alvarez's *Hanoi, Tuesday the 13th* (*Hanoi, martes trece*, 1967), *Laos, The Forgotten War* (*La guerra olvidada*, 1967), *The 79 Springtimes of Ho Chi Minh* (*Las 79 primaveras de Ho Chi Minh*), 1969. From East Germany came Walter Heynowski's and Gerhard Scheumann's *Pilots in Pyjamas* (*Piloten in Pyjama*, 1967). In Japan, Junichi Ushiyama made *With a South Vietnamese Marine Battalion* (*Minami betonamu Kaiheidaitai Senki*, 1965). From Great Britain came

The Demonstration (1968) and *The Back-seat Generals* (1970). Other films came from Syria—Nabil Maleh's *Napalm* (1970); Poland—Andrzej Brzozowski's *Fire* (*Ogien,* 1969); and Australia—*Arts Vietnam* (1969).[45]

Finally, other films recorded war's aftermath. These include Michael Rubbo's *Sad Song of Yellow Skin* (1970) and Paul Ronder's *Part of the Family* (1971), which investigates three families who lost loved ones in the brutal struggles of the Vietnam War and in the domestic conflicts at Jackson State and Kent State Universities. Joseph Strick's *Interviews with My Lai Veterans* (1971) confirmed the My Lai atrocities and, together with *Woodstock,* won the Academy Award Oscar for the Best Documentary Films of 1970. No two films could better demonstrate the polarities of genocide and flower power that characterized the 1960s. Although it is comprised largely of World War II footage, Paul Brekke's *Outtakes: Paysage de Guerre* (1979) is a film whose images of bombing and its destruction bring to mind the atrocities of the My Lai massacre.

The best single film about Vietnam is Peter Davis's *Hearts and Minds* (1974). In contrast to the global, overwhelming, and frightening conflict of World War II, which mobilized the entire nation, the Vietnam War had been edited to fit the nightly news, and, in the perception of many Americans, was a war that seemed little, orderly, and comprehensible. During the 1960s, it was common to say that the Vietnam War was "fought on television." During World War II, Americans could easily discern allies from enemies; but during Vietnam, the political background was far more complex than a struggle of fascism against democracy. As the antiwar movement was strengthened by the disclosures of the Pentagon Papers and the My Lai massacre, it appeared that we, as well as the Viet Cong, were the enemy. That is, at least, what Peter Davis's *Hearts and Minds* would have us believe. Its compilation technique, influenced by Marcel Ophuls's *The Sorrow and the Pity* (1970), combines appalling combat footage, domestic scenes shot in the United States and Vietnam, and interviews with military leaders, civilian figures, fighting men, wounded soldiers, and grieved families. By juxtaposing the bad guys against the good guys, it forces the audience to take sides, to see the war as the result of America's history of racism and anticommunism, and, as such, as an immoral, illegal, and desperate abuse of this country's military power. Then as now, that conclusion seems inescapable. As an analysis of American culture, *Hearts and Minds* can be superficial in its analysis of the American and Vietnamese political, economic, and cultural backgrounds of the war. Like all propaganda films, it relies too heavily on manipulative editing. Perhaps, at the time, there was no other way to make this film, but the complexities of the war deserve a less biased treatment, as did its truths deserve a less manipulative one. Still, despite its coercive elements, it is an extraordinary achievement. No other film about Vietnam used so expansive a frame in its coverage, or was supported by such lavish Hollywood financing. A year after the war had ended, when the film was released, official Hollywood could afford to discover its conscience and to take sides. A major supporter of the military-industrial complex and one of the principal contributors to the culture that the film so strongly criticizes, Hollywood gave *Hearts and Minds* the 1974 Academy Award for Best Documentary Feature.

Hearts and Minds (Peter Davis, USA, 1974)

Unlike *Hearts and Minds,* which was necessarily limited in its coverage, *Vietnam: A Television History* (•1983), a twelve-part television series, is a masterpiece of exhaustive research and restrained reporting that is comprehensive and thorough in covering the complex, controversial history of the Vietnam War. Like *The Sorrow and the Pity,* its style is plain, but unlike that film, it does not seek to manipulate the audience. The series, which was underwritten and broadcast by public television, presents a range of viewpoints, including those of Americans, South Vietnamese, and North Vietnamese, as well as those of people in other countries. Moreover, its format allows for careful investigation of the major issues that characterized the war's background, development, and eventual termination.[46]

National Defense
While foreign affairs in the 1960s were overshadowed by the Vietnam War, other aspects of national security and defense served as the focus of several films, including Albert Wasserman's *The U–2 Affair* (•1960),[47] Donald B. Hyatt's *That War in Korea* (•1963), Len Giovannitti's *Cuba: Bay of Pigs* (•1964) and *Cuba: The Missile Crisis* (•1964), Peter Davis's *The Selling of the Pentagon* (•1971), and Paul Ronder's *Hiroshima-Nagasaki: August, 1945* (1970), about the U.S. atomic bombs dropped over Japan, and *Fable Safe* (1971), about the arms race.

Society
During the 1960s, nonfiction filmmakers studied many aspects of American society, including, as we have seen, the struggles for social justice and civil rights, the struggle in Vietnam, the youth revolution, and the war on poverty. They also investigated issues of health, industry and labor, and sports.

Outstanding films about health include Fred W. Friendly's *Business of Health:*

Medicine, Money, and Politics (•1961), which warned that the growing health "industry" was becoming detached from the best interests of people's health, and George Stoney's *A Cry for Help* (1962), which trained police how to cope with suicide. Stoney's later films include *How to Look at a City* (1964), *Vera and the Law: Toward a More Effective System of Justice* (1975), *Southern Voices: A Composer's Exploration With Doris Hays* (1984), *We Shall Overcome* (1988), and *You Are On Indian Land* (see below). Related films include William Weston's *The Miner's Lament* (•1963), about unsafe working conditions in the nation's mines, and Willard Van Dyke's and Wheaton Galentine's *Rice* (1964), which explains the vital role that rice plays in alleviating world hunger.

While the underside of American industry was explored in such films as Jay McMullen's *Biography of a Bookie Joint* (•1961), and Arthur Zegart's *The Business of Gambling* (•1963), more familiar aspects were studied in Morton Silverstein's *What Harvest for the Reaper?* (•1967),[48] a study of black migrant workers in the tradition of *Harvest of Shame* (see above); Jack Willis's *Hard Times in the Country* (1970), about the struggle of family farmers to survive in an economy dominated by chain food stores; and Arthur Barron's *Factory* (1969), a film about a factory worker, his family, and his friends.

For the first time, American nonfiction filmmakers made films about sports in the 1960s. These include James Lipscomb's *Football* (•1961); Bruce Brown's *Endless Summer* (1966), about surfing; Brown's *On Any Sunday* (1971), about motorcycling; and Robert Kaylor's *Derby* (1971), about roller skating. As a study of the football rivalry between two Miami high schools, Lipscomb's film successfully reflects the strengths of the "crisis" approach so closely associated with early direct cinema, and is a charming study of a classically American subject. William Klein's film about boxer Muhammad Ali, *Float Like a Butterfly, Sting Like a Bee* (1969), provides a good portrait of the boxer and an amusing view of the environment in which he worked. From Japan, Kon Ichikawa's exceptional *Tokyo Olympiad* (1964) reflects the influence of Leni Riefenstahl's masterpiece, *Olympia* (1938), and deserves comparison with it.

In a style reminiscent of Flaherty's *The Land,* as well as the work of Pare Lorentz and Willard Van Dyke, and with subject matter similar to Flaherty's *Louisiana Story,* Jules Victor Schwerin's *Indian Summer* (1960) concerns the plight of farmers who are being relocated so that their land can be flooded to build a new reservoir to supply water to cities. Although Schwerin is folksy and subtle in his treatment of a likable farmer, his theme is not clear. He seems to sympathize with the farmer, but also to indict progress; ultimately, this film lacks the bitterness of *The Land* and the charm of *Louisiana Story.*

Native Americans

The social awareness of the 1960s included a renewal of interest in the history and status of Native Americans.[49] In an impressive project that combined anthropology and nonfiction filmmaking, Sol Worth and Jon Adair taught a group of Navajo Indians the rudiments of filmmaking to enable them to make films depicting their culture and themselves through their own eyes. Working together, the Navajos made the following seven films: Johnny Nelson's *The Navajo Silversmith* (1966) and *The Shallow Well Project* (1966); Susie Benally's *A Navajo Weaver* (1966); Mrs. Benally's *Second Weaver* (1966); Mike Anderson's *Old Antelope Lake* (1966); Clah's *Intrepid Shadows*; and Maxine and Mary J. Tsosie's *The Spirit of the Navajos* (1966). As indicated by the titles, most of these films are straightforward accounts of agricultural and artistic activities. The most abstract of these films is Alfred Clah's *Intrepid Shadows* (1966), which strives to present visual images that convey Navajo spiritual truths. In a muddled style more reminiscent of the experimental than the nonfiction film, Clah conveys ideas about the concepts Navajos have of their gods, but its images are too subjective to evoke more than spiritual moods.

Foreign Subjects

During this period, a large number of American nonfiction films, both independent and television, reflected a new concern with a wide range of subjects about foreign countries. Films about Europe include Burton Benjamin's *Paris in the Twenties* (•1960), *Ireland: The Tear and the Smile* (•1961), Willard Van Dyke's *So That Men Are Free* (•1962), Reuven Frank's *The Tunnel* (•1962), Nicholas Webster's *Meet Comrade Student* (•1962), Helen Jean Rogers' *Britain: Ally on the Verge* (•1962), John Secondari's *The Vatican* (•1963), Arnold Eagle's *Easter Island* (1969), Abe Osheroff's *Dreams and Nightmares* (1974), Nicholas Broomfield's *Who Cares* (1971) and Broomfield's and Joan Churchill's *Tattooed Tears* (1978), and Susan Sontag's *Promised Lands* (1974). Outstanding among these is Robert M. Young's and Michael Roemer's *Cortile Cascino* (1961), an extraordinarily moving film about urban poverty in Italy that combines nonfiction and narrative techniques.

Films about Africa include Lionel Rogosin's *Come Back Africa* (1960), which exposed the atrocities of the South African policy of *apartheid* and deserves attention as a serious attempt to deal with a major issue of human rights. Also noteworthy are Richard Leacock's *Kenya, Africa* (•1961), which offered an uneven political analysis of an emerging African nation; Robert M. Young's *Angola: Journey to a War* (•1961); and Robert Gardner's *Rivers of Sand* (1974).

Rivers of Sand, a film about the Hamar people in Ethiopia, is, like Gardner's *Dead Birds* (1963), a model ethnographic film.[50] The focus of the film is the story of a woman's oppression and pain, told against a larger canvas of the tribe's life and activities. Gardner, like Flaherty, succeeds almost completely in avoiding criticism and judgement, especially when the film shows behavior that is repulsive to viewers from another culture. Even the gory, unfamiliar rituals of life and death are explained clearly and without passionate comment. However, there is a sense of foreboding throughout the film that, implicit as it is, reveals just how different the Hamar are from us. In technique, the film is outstanding in its intimate color cinematography, direct sound recording, and use of such optical devices as the freeze frame, zoom lens, and slow motion. Gardner's subsequent films include *Deep Hearts* (1981), *The Shepherds of Berneray* (with Allen Moore and Jack Shea, 1981), *Sons of Shiva* (with Akos Ostor, 1985), *Serpent Mother* (with Akos Ostor and Allen Moore, 1985), *Loving Krishna* (with Akos Ostor and Allen Moore, 1985), *Forest of Bliss* (1986), and *Ika Hands* (1988).

Rivers of Sand (Robert Gardner, USA, 1974)

Various aspects of life in Latin America were covered in *Yanqui, No!* (•1960), a film by Richard Leacock, D. A. Pennebaker, and Albert Maysles; James Blue's *The School at Rincon Santo* (1963); David Brinkley's *Report on Haiti* (•1963); and Saul Landau's and Haskell Wexler's *Brazil: A Report on Torture* (1971), a series of interviews with a few Brazilian revolutionaries and victims, from among the thousands of political prisoners who underwent torture at the hands of a totalitarian government. *Yanqui, No!*, made by Drew Associates for television, aroused awareness of strong anti-U.S. feelings in Latin America, warning that the entire region would fall through Communist revolutions unless the United States did something to show its concern. Although it tries to present a balanced view of this issue, *Yanqui, No!* is more important for providing an early view of Castro's Cuba than for its social analysis. In a more helpful way, Blue's *The School at Rincon Santo,* made for the USIA, actually showed how the Alliance for Progress made progress through the construction of a school in Colombia. Blue also made *The Olive Trees of Justice* (1962), about one family's involvement in the Algerian war, and *Letter from Colombia* (1964), about agricultural reform in Colombia.

While most 1960s nonfiction films about Asia were concerned in one way or another with the Vietnam War, others include Felix Greene's *China!* (1965), Willard Van Dyke's *Pop Buell, Hoosier Farmer* and *Taming the Mekong River* (•1965), and Tom Davenport's *T'ai Chi Chu'uan* (1968).

Portraits

Before the 1960s, nonfiction filmmakers tended to be more interested in world events than in the people who played a role in those events. This began to change as the decade of the 1960s gave birth to a new cult of personality in which rock stars replaced movie stars, and politicians were elected on the basis of their charisma rather than their ideas. This cult was fostered by television audiences, which seemed to have an insatiable appetite for biographies of successful and powerful people, both notorious and celebrated. The most prevalent film portraits are those of personalities from the arts and popular entertainment. Such profiles raise the issue of whether a personality accustomed to performing for the public can do anything but perform before the camera. Early efforts include *Susan Starr* (1962), an account by Hope Ryden and D. A. Pennebaker of a young pianist preparing for a competition; *Jane* (1962), an uneven film about the young Jane Fonda by Pennebaker, Leacock, Ryden, Shuker, and Abbot Mills; the Albert and David Maysles *Showman* (1962), a very amusing portrait of film producer Joseph E. Levine, and *Meet Marlon Brando* (1965); John Magnuson's *Lenny Bruce* (1967), which reveals little more than the comedian's self-indulgence; Leacock's *A Stravinsky Portrait* (1964); Pennebaker's *Dont Look Back* (1966); and Nelly Kaplan's *Abel Gance: Yesterday and Tomorrow* (1962), an outstanding film about one of cinema's greatest innovators. Other nonfiction film portraits about musicians include Bert Stern's *Jazz on a Summer's Day* (1960), Thomas Reichman's *Mingus* (1960), Arthur Barron's *Johnny Cash!* (1969), and Bernard Chevry's *Artur Rubinstein: The Love of Life* (1969). Films about entertainers include Ray Garner's *Will Rogers: A Self Portrait* and *Vincent Van Gogh: A Self Portrait* (•1961); and Eugene S. Jones's *The World of Bob Hope* (•1961); Jones also made *The World of Billy Graham* (1961) and *The World of Jacqueline Kennedy* (•1962); also of interest is Richard Cawston's film about Billy Graham, *I'm Going to Ask You to Get Up Out of Your Seat* (1966). Films about authors include Satyajit Ray's *Tagore* (1961), Robert Hughes's *Robert Frost: A Lover's Quarrel with the World* (1963), Kirk Browning's *The World of Carl Sandburg* (1966), and Harold Mantell's *I Am Pablo Neruda* (1967).

Some memorable titles about rock music, musicians, and festivals (beyond those listed dealing with personalities) include the Maysles brothers' *What's Happening! The Beatles In The U.S.A.* (1964), Pennebaker's *Monterey Pop* (1968) and *Keep On Rockin'* (1970); and Richard Heffron's *Fillmore* (1972), a film ostensibly about the closing of the Haight-Ashbury auditorium devoted to rock music, but which concentrates mostly on its founder, Bill Graham. The most significant and enduring of these are Michael Wadleigh's *Woodstock* (1970) and *Gimme Shelter* (1970; see Chapter 15).

Other films were about world figures of political and cultural importance.

Films about Adolf Hitler include Paul Rotha's *Life of Adolf Hitler* (1961), Erwin Leiser's *Mein Kampf,* Louis Clyde Stoumen's *The Black Fox* (1962), and Burton Benjamin's *The Plots Against Hitler* (•1963). Other film portraits about international figures include *Nehru* (1962) and *The Aga Khan* (•1962), films by Robert Drew Associates; Len Giovannitti's *The Death of Stalin* (•1963); Richard Kaplan's *The Eleanor Roosevelt Story* (1965); Erica Anderson's *The Living Work of Albert Schweitzer* (1965); and two films about Fidel Castro: *Fidel* (1970), by Saul Landau and Irving Saraf, and *Waiting for Fidel,* by Michael Rubbo (see below).

Miscellaneous film portraits included *X–Pilot* (•1960), a film by Terence Macartney-Filgate and Albert Maysles about the final test flight of the X–15 by pilot Scott Crossfield; Wade Bingham's *The Burma Surgeon Today* (•1961); George Freeland's *High Wire: The Great Wallendas* (•1964), about the family circus trapeze artists; *Portrait of Jason* (1967), Shirley Clarke's study of a black homosexual hustler; Frank Simon's *The Queen* (1968), about drag queens; Harry Booth's *A King's Story* (1967), the story of the Duke of Windsor; Richard Cawston's excellent *Royal Family* (1969), about Queen Elizabeth II; *Chiefs* (1969), by Richard Leacock and Noel Parmentel, a short, amusing film about a convention of police chiefs in Hawaii; Herbert Di Gioia's and David Hancock's *Chester Grimes* (1972), about a Vermonter who lives a traditional life; and two films about newspapers, Sam Rosenberg's *Vanishing Breed: Portrait of a Country Editor* (•1963), and Jerry Bruck's *I. F. Stone's Weekly* (1973), an impressive study of the independent Washington, D.C., newspaper publisher who was a mainstay in the anti-Vietnam movement.

Of the hundreds of American nonfiction films made during the 1960s, the scope of this study permits mention only of those that—by their choice of subject matter, or cinematic innovation, or influence (or, rarely, all three)—constitute the most significant corpus of achievement. Some films are difficult to classify. Three films about historical events call attention to the use of archival footage. Frédéric Rossif's *To Die in Madrid* (1964), through the dramatic use of narration and music, provides an eloquent insight into the Spanish Civil War. *Guns Of August* (1965), Nathan Kroll's adaptation of Barbara Tuchman's study of Europe just before World War I, is noteworthy for its judicious use of the relatively scarce footage from that period. Arthur Barron's *Birth And Death* (1969) juxtaposes the emotional experiences in the weeks before a child's birth and a man's death; in the process, it raises the familiar issue of the extent to which ordinary people are conscious of the camera. Other notable films on miscellaneous subjects include Donald B. Hyatt's *The Real West* (•1961); Burton Benjamin's *New York in the Twenties* (•1961); Guy Blanchard's *Shakespeare: Soul of an Age* (•1962); John G. Fuller's *Fire Rescue* (•1962); Ray Garner's *Greece: The Golden Age* (•1963); Ray Hubbard's *The Innocent Fair* (1963); Thomas Priestly's *Orient Express* (•1964); Jacques-Yves Cousteau's *World Without Sun* (1964); Paul Barnes's *Black Five* (1968), a beautifully photographed color film about a legendary British locomotive; and Nell Cox's *French Lunch* (1968).

CANADIAN FILM

In Canada, one of the largest and wealthiest countries in the world, native film production was overshadowed by the United States until 1939, the year that the National Film Board (NFB) was founded (see chapters 9 and 12). John Grierson, the NFB's first commissioner (1939–45), established a two-fold purpose: to encourage an indigenous filmmaking effort that would provide Canadian alternatives to the American films that dominated the Canadian market, and to interpret Canada (i.e., to provide Canadian propaganda) to Canadians and citizens of other countries during the Second World War (see chapter 12).[51] Throughout the world, the NFB is recognized not only as Grierson's most important achievement, but also as a world leader in the production and use of the nonfiction and animated film.

Grierson's Canadian achievements were impressive. Most important of all was his continued insistence that filmmakers focus on ordinary working people. He established a climate receptive to the production of nonfiction films, and a distribution network to stimulate the widespread sharing of such films across Canada. He recruited well-known filmmakers to work alongside inexperienced Canadians. Such filmmakers as Stuart Legg, Stanley Hawes, Raymond Spottiswode, and J. D. Stevens from England; Joris Ivens and John Fernhout from The Netherlands; and Irving Jacoby from the United States helped to train a new generation of Canadian filmmakers, including James Beveridge, Tom Daly, Sydney Newman, Gudrun Parker, Evelyn Cherry, Julian Roffman, and Norman McLaren. During the war, their achievements included Stuart Legg's *Churchill's Island* (1941), the first documentary to receive an Oscar; McLaren's outstanding animated films; and the "Canada Carries On" and "The World in Action" series. The end of war brought Canadian innovations in cinéma vérité (or *cinéma direct*, as Canadians often called it), as well as developments in Griersonian documentary films dealing with social issues and such series as "Faces of Canada" and "Candid Eye," and, during the 1960s, "Challenge for Change."[52] During the 1970s, the Canadian Broadcasting Corporation became active in nonfiction film production, and the French-Canadian separatist movement reaffirmed the use of nonfiction film for revolutionary political purposes and produced a small, but significant group of films.

Canadian Arts, Culture, and Personalities

Among the important Canadian films made during the 1960s and after include those about Canadian arts, culture, and personalities. Some of these were made in the style of the traditional documentary, others in the cinéma vérité style. Roger Blais's *Grierson* (1973) provides a thorough account of John Grierson's career, including his contributions to the postwar Canadian filmmaking effort. Through the testimony of Grierson's colleagues (including Joris Ivens, Sir Stephen Tallents, Irving Jacoby, Arthur Elton, Harry Watt, Edgar Anstey, Forsyth Hardy, Basil Wright, Ross McLean, Stuart Legg), we get a rich portrait of the man whom the narrator calls "a holy terror." *Grierson* is both critical and sympathetic, and it does not overlook such important issues as the allegations that ruined his Canadian and

American career in the postwar period (see chapter 8) and his increasing difficulties, in later life, in finding the appropriate place for his creative energies.

A variety of films attest to the rich, diverse accomplishment of Roman Kroitor and Wolf Koenig, whose previous nonfiction films about native Canadian subjects included *Paul Tomkowicz: Street Railway Switchman* (1954), *City of Gold* (1957) and *Glenn Gould: Off the Record* and *Glenn Gould: On the Record* (1959; noteworthy also is John McGreevy's *Glenn Gould's Toronto,* 1980). Kroitor's and Koenig's *Lonely Boy* (1961), a film about the creation of Canadian pop idol Paul Anka, takes its place with such similar cinéma vérité studies of pop artists as D. A. Pennebaker's *Dont Look Back* (1966) and the Maysles brothers' *What's Happening! The Beatles in the U.S.A.* (1964). Two films about Canadian painters include Gerald Budner's *The World of David Milne* (1963) and Gary Johnson's and Barry Gray's *Leonard Brooks* (1976). Donald Brittain's *Ladies and Gentlemen . . . Mr. Leonard Cohen* (1965) provides a portrait of the poet and singer, and Caroline Leaf's *Kate and Anna McGarrigle* (1981) is about the outstanding singers from Quebec. Other films about various aspects of Canadian culture include Terence Macartney-Filgate's *The Days Before Christmas* (1958), which used a cinéma vérité style to provide an account of frenetic holiday activities, and *The Back-Breaking Leaf* (1959), a lyrical, but serious film about the tobacco harvest in Ontario; Gilles Groulx's and Michel Brault's *The Snowshoers* (*Les Raquetteurs,* 1958), a charming account of the 1958 International Snowshoe Congress; Arthur Lipsett's *Very Nice, Very Nice* (1961), an abstract, cynical study of the contemporary scene; Donald Brittain's and John Kemeny's *Bethune* (*Bethune: héros de notre temps,* 1964), a portrait of the legendary Canadian doctor who served with the Loyalists during the Spanish Civil War (he is the subject of Herbert Kline's *Heart of Spain;* see chapter 7) and with the North Chinese Army during the Chinese-Japanese war; Don Owen's *High Steel* (1965), about the Mohawk Indians of Caughnawaga, near Montreal, who are famed for their fearless work in the dangerous business of erecting skyscrapers and bridges; Bernard Gosselin's *Jean Carignan, Violinist* (*Jean Carignan, violoneux,* 1975), a portrait of a fiddler who preserves the French Canadian musical heritage; and *Going the Distance* (1979), a film by Paul Cowan, Georges Dufaux, Reevan Dolgoy, Beverly Schaffer, and Tony Westman that presents a straightforward account of the 1978 Commonwealth Games.

Notable among these films is *Wrestling* (*La lutte,* 1961), by Michel Brault (*Les raquetteurs,* 1958), Claude Jutra, Marcel Carrière, and Claude Fournier. *Wrestling* juxtaposes coverage of ordinary working people who want to be wrestlers with coverage of a championship tag-team match. There is no evidence of fakery here— just horrid, dirty wrestling at its best. It has all the faults of early cinéma vérité, including poor camera coverage of the wrestling match, an ironic narration (featuring the typically folksy voice), and the absence of any conclusion. In a different style, Brault joined Pierre Perrault (*La regne du jour,* 1967; *Les voitures d'eau,* 1968; *Un pays sans bon sens,* 1970; and *L'Acadie, l'Acadie,* 1971) and Marcel Carrière to make *Moontrap* (*Pour la suite du monde,* 1964), the first in a trilogy of films on Ile aux Coudres, a small island in the St. Lawrence River. Similar in structure to *Farrebique* and in subject to *Man of Aran, Moontrap* encapsulates the yearly routine of the islanders, including their farming, faith, and respect for tradition. With tradition as the focus of the film, we see an extensive communal attempt to revive the trapping of white whales (or porpoises, as the natives call them). As the natives argue inconclusively about where the tradition derived, either from the native Indian inhabitants or the French emigrant settlers, they enthusiastically learn old skills, build an elaborate fence-like trap, and eventually capture one porpoise, which is sold to the New York Aquarium. In light of the islanders' spirituality and mysticism, the tremendous effort is fascinating. Sixteen years later, after he photographed *Moontrap*, Bernard Gosselin (*Jean Carignan, Violinist* [*Jean Carignan, violoneux*], 1975) returned to the region to make *The Skiff of Renald and Thomas* [*Le canot à Rénald et Thomas*], 1980), which, although workmanlike in its depiction of another revived custom—the building of beautiful skiffs—lacks the mystical aura of *Moontrap*.

Human Relationships

Shortly after the war, the NFB's "Mental Mechanisms" series established a reputation for the serious exploration of a range of psychological and emotional problems. Later, in the 1960s, the director Allan King continued to deal with many of these issues, but set himself apart from his Canadian and American colleagues by a film approach that stressed empathy with his subject matter rather than observation of it. King's films (especially *Warrendale* and *A Married Couple*) reflect his empathy with individual people and their relationships. His cinematic style is evident in his nearly twenty other films, most of them made for the Canadian Broadcasting Corporation, including *Skid Row* (1956), which appeared at the same time and covered the same subject as Rogosin's *On the Bowery*.

That Allan King's films elicit strong viewer response is perhaps best demonstrated by *Warrendale* (1966), his controversial investigation into the therapy of disturbed young people. Warrendale, a center in Toronto, used a new therapy called "holding" instead of drugs and other conventional techniques. Simply put, this approach encouraged children to be violent so that they could then be enveloped in the protective (and presumably therapeutic) arms of a staff member. The young people's reactions to this therapy were unpredictable, but the overall achievement seems to be a strengthening of trust and love. King's camera achieves an extraordinary intimacy in recording the therapists and the children, particularly their violent reactions and their responses to the holding therapy. However, the film is not about the treatment so much as it is a "personal, selective record" of the experience, in which King clearly communicates his involvement as the filmmaker; perhaps that is why the absence of information about the holding therapy raises as many questions about its validity and effectiveness as about the cinematic technique used to observe it. Equally controversial was King's *A Married Couple* (1969), an account of a marriage on the rocks, which deserves comparison with Craig Gilbert's *An American Family*.

Other noteworthy Canadian films about people include Dennis Miller's *Summerhill* (1966), about the English boarding school where every student is his or her own teacher; Donald Winkler's *The Scholar in Society: Northrop Frye in Conversa-*

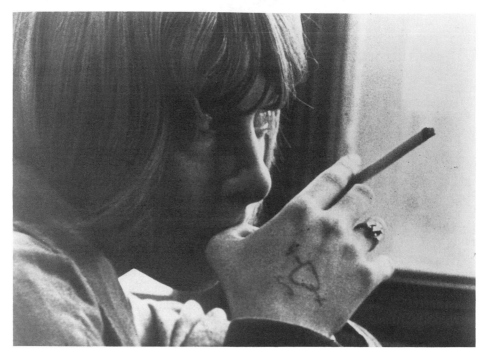

Warrendale (Alan King, Canada, 1966)

tion (1984); and Jan-Marie Martell's *Pretend You're Wearing a Barrel* (1978), about a woman's survival. Like *The Things I Cannot Change* and *Nell and Fred* (see below), Martell's film depicts Canadians who are tough and determined people in their quest for dignity.

Political Conscience

In the 1960s and 1970s, long after Grierson's departure from Canada, a new commitment among Canadian filmmakers affirmed one of his principal ideas: that art "is a weapon in our hands to see and to say what is right and good and beautiful, and hammer it out as the mold and pattern of men's actions."[53] While these new Canadian filmmakers were not members of a filmmaking group, in the usual sense of that word, they can be linked through their commitments to investigating social issues and to promoting social justice in Canada, the United States, and abroad. Some produced films for "Challenge for Change," an NFB program dedicated to the Griersonian tradition of social change, while others worked independently or for television networks. Noteworthy among them are Douglas Leiterman, Beryl Fox, and Michael Rubbo.

Leiterman's two best-known films are about American blacks: *One More River* (codirected by Beryl Fox, 1964) and *From Harlem to Sugar Hill* (1968). Leiterman, a Canadian, was perceived by many as an outsider in the United States, but he believed that his "very journalistic coverage plus a genuine compassion for the underprivileged"[54] would provide a useful perspective on the situation of blacks in the United States. The producers disagreed, and others believed that he distorted the issues he was trying to clarify. *One More River,* which was concerned with race relations in the American South, was produced by the International Television Federation (Intertel), a project of international cooperation in documentary production, and was shown on television in Canada, but not in the United States; *From Harlem to Sugar Hill,* which was concerned with the black middle class, was produced by CBS-TV, an American television network, but was also not shown in the United States.

Beryl Fox, who codirected *One More River* and directed *Summer in Mississippi* (1965), also about American race relations, has established a reputation as a prolific filmmaker committed to social change. In addition to films about women and American blacks, she has made three films on Vietnam: *The Mills of the Gods* (1965), *Saigon* (1967), and *Last Reflections on a War* (1968).[55] Michael Rubbo's films are *Sad Song of Yellow Skin,* about Southeast Asia (1970), *Wet Earth and Warm People* (1971), about Indonesia, and *Waiting for Fidel* (1974). *Waiting for Fidel* records the trip that Rubbo made to Cuba with Joseph Smallwood, the former Socialist premier of Newfoundland, and Geoff Stirling, a Canadian communications mogul. Rubbo believes that the Cuban Revolution is a success; Smallwood is as enthusiastic about Cuba's future as Stirling is pessimistic. Their intention was to interview Fidel Castro, who proves, as the title alludes, to be as elusive as Godot. As the group bides its time touring schools, housing projects,

Waiting for Fidel (Michael Rubbo, Canada, 1974)

hospitals, and even the beach of the Bay of Pigs, they argue about socialism and capitalism, all the time rehearsing their questions for Castro. While the film bristles with intelligent coverage, including a hilarious argument about the cinéma vérité method, it is overshadowed by the mood of anticipation, which, through the title's allusion, we know will be unfulfilled. Only Smallwood, dressed in a suit borrowed from the cameraman, has an unrecorded meeting with Castro at an official reception for the East German Premier. The film ends ironically, with official footage of Castro addressing a vast crowd, a conclusion that suggests that the Cuban Premier has time for almost everyone else but the filmmakers.

The "Challenge for Change" project, organized to inform Canadians about such social issues as poverty and family planning, produced some outstanding films, among them Tanya Ballantine's *The Things I Cannot Change* (1966; see below), Colin Low's *The Children of Fogo Island* (1967) and *The Winds of Fogo* (1969), Willie Dunn's *The Ballad of Crowfoot* (1968), Roger Hart's *A Memo from Fogo* (1972), George Stoney's *You Are on Indian Land* (1969; see below), and Richard Todd's *Nell and Fred* (1971). The astonishing characteristic of these films, produced with government funds, is that they present the subject's, not the government's point of view and are critical of government policies and practices. They serve effectively to call attention to the problems of the disregarded and disaffected, and, in so doing, to empower them in their struggle against bureaucracies. Ballantine's *The Things I Cannot Change,* an undirected observation of the life of a poverty-stricken family during a three-week period, is often clumsy in technique (for example, we hear the filmmaker prompting the family with questions), but its weaknesses are outweighed by its success in depicting the family's struggles to obtain official relief from their problems. While it is not difficult to get an audience's sympathy for people battling against the welfare system (cf. Frederick Wiseman's *Welfare*), this decent, stubborn couple are memorable for the love that keeps them and their nine children together and for their hope in the future. Stoney's *You Are on Indian Land* depicts the crisis that occurred when a group of Indians closed a bridge that traverses their Cornwall Island in the river between the United States and Canada. Narrated by an Indian participant, and made with the cooperation and assistance of members of the Akwasasne Indian Nation, we see Indian civil disobedience and the predictably routine response of the local police, and, finally, hear a long list of Indian grievances against the Canadian government's Department of Indian Affairs.[56] Todd's *Nell and Fred* records the plight of two old people, sharing a house, who weigh the advantages and disadvantages of moving to a new senior citizens home. After a tour of the facility, Nell decides to stay in her cozy house, but Fred moves into the modern complex, only to return shortly to Nell's comforting companionship. Technically, *Nell and Fred* has many of the faults of other cinéma vérité films—for example, we hear the filmmaker (who, incidentally, is Nell's grandson), asking and answering questions—but it is a touching tribute to Nell's and Fred's friendship, independence, and indomitable spirit.

15

Tradition and Change in the 1970s

The worldwide development of the nonfiction film in the 1970s was marked both by tradition and change. Few contemporary filmmakers were interested either in the identification of social abuses or in the cinematic experimentation that, a decade earlier, had created direct cinema. Thus, much of their output, mired in tradition, seemed bland. Nonetheless, there were several important historical developments. Among them were the emergence of a major new group of American and European film artists and a steady increase in the quantity and quality of American and European films on art.

NEW AMERICAN AND EUROPEAN MASTERS OF THE NONFICTION FILM

The nonfiction film of the 1970s produced several directors who are masters of the genre. This group includes Albert and David Maysles, Frederick Wiseman, and Emile De Antonio in the United States; Louis Malle in France; and Marcel Ophuls in Switzerland. While their films differ in subject, they are all technically superb and highly popular with the general public; several are epic in scope and length. Collectively, the work of these filmmakers marked a new direction in which the nonfiction film fulfilled its creative potential more fully than ever before.

Albert and David Maysles

Between 1959 and 1962, Albert Maysles worked as a cinematographer with Drew Associates on a number of films, but, in 1962, with his brother David, he formed an independent film production company.[1] Reflecting the influence of the Drew approach, their impressive body of work nevertheless has its own particular stamp. Stephen Mamber discussed the Drew influence on their early films:

Like the Drew films, the Maysles films consistently maintain a personality-oriented structure, and while not dependent upon the same sort of crisis conditions, they do have a sense of people trying to prove themselves (or, at least, to survive) in pressure situations. In Maysles films, however, the pressure never lets up. The contest never ends.[2]

Fascinated themselves by artists and the creative process, the Maysles perfected a direct cinema approach in which form and content are seamlessly joined. The Maysles brothers—Albert, the cameraman, linked to David, the sound recorder, by a symbiotic cable—are the eyes and ears of a highly sophisticated approach to direct cinema that (like the "nonfiction novel" of such writers as Truman Capote and Tom Wolfe) uses fictional techniques to shape the reporting of actual events. The Maysles were the first filmmakers to use the term *nonfiction* in describing their work, as well as calling it "direct cinema," rather than cinéma verité.[3]

Unlike Frederick Wiseman, for example, who edits his own films, the Maysles work closely with such gifted editors as Charlotte Zwerin, Ellen Hovde, Muffie Meyer, and Susan Froemke. This collaboration underscores the importance of editing to the development of the contemporary nonfiction film. (In fact, the art of the nonfiction film has always been, in large measure, the art of editing, as we have seen in the work of such influential editors as Sergei Eisenstein, Dziga Vertov, Leni Riefenstahl, Helen van Dongen, and William Hornbeck.) Since the Maysles brothers (as well as Wiseman) shoot without a formal script, following events as they occur, it is the editors, often working closely at the editing table with the filmmakers, who give the footage its structure and rhythm.[4] Although the Maysles acknowledge that the structure of their films is realized through editing, they differ from other great formalists—Eisenstein, in particular—in that the rhythm of the editing springs from the "spontaneous juxtapositions—in life itself."[5]

The Maysles films include numerous portraits of famous artists and personalities: *Showman* (1963), about movie mogul Joseph E. Levine; *What's Happening! The Beatles in the U.S.A.* (1964), a record of The Beatles' first trip to the United States; *Meet Marlon Brando* (1965); *With Love from Truman: A Visit With Truman Capote* (1966); *Mohammed and Larry* (1980), about Mohammed Ali and Larry Holmes preparing for the world heavyweight boxing championship; *Ozawa* (1985); and *Vladimir Horowitz: The Last Romantic* (1985). They have also made several films about the work of the conceptual artist Christo—*Christo's Valley Curtain* (1974), *Running Fence* (1978), *Islands* (1986)—as well as *The Burks of Georgia* (1976), a portrait of a family clan, and *Public Ed* (1985), a report on five different schools.

The most important and enduring Maysles films are *Salesman* (1969), *Gimme Shelter* (1970), *Christo's Valley Curtain* (1974), and *Grey Gardens* (1975), achievements that reveal the brothers' sensitivity to their subjects as well as their creation of the feeling of "being there."

Salesman, a film by Albert and David Maysles and Charlotte Zwerin, follows four representatives of the Mid-American Bible Company in their selling territories of Boston and Florida: Paul Brennan, known as "The Badger"; Charles McDevitt, "The Gipper"; James Baker, "The Rabbit"; and Raymond Martos, "The Bull."[6]

Salesman (Albert and David Maysles and Charlotte Zwerin, USA, 1969)

Paul Brennan is the focus of the film, not only because of his style, sales pitch, and introspection, but also because he is a natural actor, unaware of the camera, able to improvise, to reminisce, to laugh at adversity. Like his fictional counterparts, Willy Loman in Arthur Miller's *Death of a Salesman* and Harry Hickey in Eugene O'Neill's *The Iceman Cometh,* Paul represents more than just a salesman fallen on hard times.[7] He is caught in an existential dilemma, trapped between the meaning-lessness of his job and the dictates of his heart. He would be interesting if he were selling heavy machinery, shoes, or insurance; but he is selling the Bible, which is just another commodity to him. Carefully avoiding religious talk, he works up a sales pitch that is a combination of hard-sell phrases and a certain moral imperative that helps him to break down the resistance of customers. The larger themes about American society and its values that inform *Salesman* include the classic American conflict between material and spiritual values. Here, the Bible salesmen realize that their task is not so much to sell printed books, as it is to get customers to examine their faith. In that split second between faith and doubt (the books cost dearly), the sale is usually made.

However, *Salesman* is also about the lonely people who need an expensive Bible to confirm a faith engendered by a salesman's pitch; it is about the guilt they feel when they don't want the book or can't afford it. The film does not pretend to be deep social analysis; rather, its surface shimmers with unforgettable people, houses, and comments: the Irish mother and daughter in a Boston kitchen; the vice-president of the Bible publishing company, Melbourne I. Feltman, Ph.D., the "world's greatest salesman of the world's best seller"; the elderly widow whom Paul persuades into buying the book ("Well, I don't know how many years I have to read the Bible"); and the married couple straight out of a satire on American living customs—he in his undershirt, she with her hair in curlers, with a sound system playing a heavily orchestral version of The Beatles' "Yesterday." All of these moments, and many more, make *Salesman* a sociological document to be treasured.

Salesman bears the hallmark of direct cinema: control of the tension between film form and content. It is evident both in the film and in the filmmakers' comments that they cared for the subject and felt deeply about the film's implications.[8] It is Zwerin's editing that maintains the tension between the Maysles brothers' affection for Paul Brennan and their desire to remain objective in filming. The result is the intelligent, direct, and often witty handling of a sensitive subject, characterized by an understanding and respect for the line between fiction and fact.

Salesman is notable not only for its for its ability to sustain nonfiction reporting in a full-length film, but also for its superb cinematography and sound recording. Technically and conceptually, it is distinguished by its originality, intelligent handling of subject matter, and its fidelity to truth.

During the late 1960s and early 1970s, several successful nonfiction films documented folk and rock music: *Dont Look Back, Monterey Pop, Woodstock,* and *Gimme Shelter.* The latter two films—about rock festivals at Woodstock, New York, and Altamont, California—represent polarities, not only in the festivals themselves and their significance to the period's youth culture, but also in the ways in which the filmmakers made them. Michael Wadleigh's *Woodstock* (1970) is a lavish, lyrical tribute to the green, grassy splendors of a pastoral event claimed by its promoters to be a "state of mind." *Gimme Shelter* (1970), by the Maysles Brothers and Charlotte Zwerin, is a tight, jolting account of the violent rock concert held in 1969 in the dry hills of Northern California. *Woodstock* is a film about music, love, and fun; *Gimme Shelter* records music, hate, and horror. *Woodstock* features more than a dozen top performers and groups; *Gimme Shelter* features Mick Jagger and the Rolling Stones, and includes a brief appearance by Grace Slick and The Jefferson Starship. *Woodstock* marks the beginning of what many, despite the Vietnam War, believed was a period of youth, love, and peace—at least as it seemed to the performers and the mammoth audience; *Gimme Shelter* marks what appeared to be the abrupt end of that spirit, with the motorcycles of the Hell's Angels for a chorus and a murder for a climax.

Both films are dependent upon the immediacy of an historical event. *Woodstock* is a big, tightly controlled factual film—almost a newsreel of an historical event—as well as a documentary film that takes a lighthearted and positive view of the people and events it records. Wadleigh approached the festival as a reporter, not a commentator. The film is arranged in episodes that apparently followed the order of the performances, which are almost uniformly superb; although the sound is also excellent, the uneven quality of much of this footage is surprising.

Gimme Shelter (1970), a film about Mick Jagger and The Rolling Stones, is emblematic of the Maysles approach and of the critical debate it engenders. Like *Woodstock,* it is a social document of a rock music festival. Unlike *Woodstock,* however, it brings us close to violence at the tragic Altamont concert: a confrontation between some members of the Hell's Angels and the audience and the subsequent stabbing by a white of a black man; such behavior contradicts all that Woodstock symbolized. While the filmmakers seem genuinely to believe that they have made an objective film, *Gimme Shelter* raises serious questions about their fidelity to actuality. They set the Altamont incident in a larger context of the Stones' career, and intercut scenes of the Stones on and off the stage with scenes of Jagger and others watching the Altamont footage on an editing table. By creating distance from the event and playing down the violence, the Maysles reaffirm the film's broad coverage, but the detachment of the final result is unsatisfying precisely because it is so detached and thus overlooks the festival's significance as a major turning point of the decade. While the Maysles brothers achieved something less than their usual pure direct cinema of observation and juxtaposition, some audiences and critics wanted even more: a film that would analyze, cite causes, and place responsibility.[9] Direct cinema had reached a critical juncture: some viewers recognized it as art while they still seemed to yearn for the Griersonian interpretive viewpoint against which direct cinema developed.

Christo's Valley Curtain (1974)—a film by Albert and David Maysles and editor Ellen Giffard—is about Christo, the visionary artist who wraps buildings and monuments, hangs curtains or builds gates, and makes other aesthetic statements in actual environments. As such, Christo's work calls equal attention to the artist and his art.[10] We watch as Christo's idea takes shape in the studio and is then realized in the form of a colossal curtain hung in a Colorado valley named Rifle Gap. While the narrative is basically chronological—preparation, realization, aftermath—the editing employs two Maysles hallmarks: repetition and juxtaposition of three essential elements: the artist, the artwork, and the audience. Like other Maysles films, this is concerned with recording an event and with revealing the characters associated with it. We see Christo in his studio and in Colorado. The artwork is a curtain that is essentially enigmatic and transitory, that does not belong in a natural setting, that will obviously be gone soon, yet it is something that arouses strong reactions (pro and con) among its audience, which includes the artist, his wife, the construction workers, the casual onlookers at the site, and the film audience.

The film is about art, artists, and creativity. It challenges the notion that art is the province of the leisure classes by showing the artist and the construction crew working together with mutual respect and pleasure. Rigging the curtain is a formidable engineering feat, and one worker comments: "It's not the erection, it's the

Christo's Valley Curtain (Albert and David Maysles and Ellen Giffard, USA, 1974)

thought, it's a vision." The workers, who at first are "good old boys" nervously talking about their collaboration, actually become deeply involved in making the project succeed. When the curtain is finally hung, Christo proudly says: "It looks just like the drawing." The process of creation is seamless from conception to realization. Moreover, the film is about perception and, thus, about reality, how people perceive themselves in settings that are both familiar and unfamiliar. The curtain reflects the attitudes of the artist, the workers, the bystanders, and also the attitudes of the filmmakers. Their presence on screen not only reinforces the self-referential aspect of their style, but also their acknowledgement that they are but one part of the process. Inasmuch as the curtain reveals people, it, like the film that records it, is a mirror of reality.

Grey Gardens (by David and Albert Maysles, Ellen Hovde, Muffie Meyer, and Susan Froemke) is an complex film about an extraordinary relationship, one of the most profound, disturbing, and funny nonfiction films ever made. The relationship is between Edith Bouvier Beale and her daughter Edie, relatives of Jacqueline Bouvier Kennedy Onassis. Their relation to the famous Mrs. Onassis is only relevant in establishing a contrast between the glamorous social context in which these women were born and raised and the squalid circumstances in which they have

Grey Gardens (Albert and David Maysles, Ellen Hovde, Muffie Meyer, and Susan Froemke, USA, 1975) [left to right, Mrs. Edith Beale, David Maysles, Albert Maysles, Edie Beale]

now chosen to live together. In this exceptionally well-structured film, the Maysles brothers' overall premise is that the lives of these two women are too complex and contradictory to be reduced to standard categories or to a linear narrative. Their relationship goes beyond that of mother (Big Edie) and daughter (Little Edie).

The film's structure exemplifies one of the fundamental principles of direct cinema: when presenting unfamiliar subject matter, the filmmaker has a journalistic, as well as artistic, responsibility to try to be as objective as possible. Establishing the relationship of cinematic form to content becomes even more crucial when the artist is working with footage that documents a particular time, place, and situation. The film's appeal and strength derive not only from the Maysles' observation of these two women but also from the editing. Muffie Meyer, one of the film's editors, says that, in the evolution of the editing, there were times when Big Edie appeared much crueler and more dominating than she does in the film. Meyer and Ellen Hovde worked, through the editing, to achieve a certain balance between the two women.[11]

The structure of *Grey Gardens* is the process of accretion in which definite patterns emerge from a contrapuntal treatment of certain themes: older mother/ younger daughter, past/present, energy/lethargy, independence/dependence, freedom/confinement, love/hate, truth/lies, order/disorder, responsibility/irresponsibility. Little Edie says, "It's awfully hard to maintain the line between the past and the present," and the wistfulness in her voice sets a tone that is echoed in the film's structure. There is also visual and aural counterpoint and contradiction between the two women (e.g., static vs. dynamic energy), which achieves the "equality" for which the editors were striving: counterpoint between the past (in photographs, songs, stories, and other reminders, such as the dilapidated house set among well-kept mansions) and the cinematic present (what we see of the women today). About photographs (the past), Little Edie says: "You can't expose them to the light," yet now she is eager to be recorded by the camera.

An equal-sided triangle established between the two women and the cinematic process suggests that the camera (and microphone) is a character in the film. In fact, both Maysles appear in the film. The opening still shot of the brothers identifies them as Little Edie's "gentlemen callers"[12]; she asks "What do you want to do? Where do you want to go now?" The Beales talk with the Maysles, and, in one brilliant image that focuses characters and themes, we see Al, David (in a mirror), a lovely charcoal drawing of Big Edie on the wall, and Big Edie's voice on the soundtrack. The Maysles, like all the men in the Beales' lives, are important to the film as both protagonists and antagonists; the film's two key scenes of argument involve these various men.

The camera/microphone serves as a mute confidante. As Kenneth J. Robson has written, both Beales were and are performers; their lives are a series of rehearsals or cinematic "takes" for the full performance we never see.[13] This conversation exemplifies their involvement of the Maysles in their scenario:

> *Little Edie:* Darling David, where have you been all my life? Where have you been? All I needed was this man, David. David—I wish I'd had David and Al with me before this.
> *Big Edie:* You had your mother!
> *Little Edie:* Yeah.

At other times, Little Edie appeals her "case" to the camera. It seems as if she has been jailed at Grey Gardens, that the Maysles have given her the chance to send her story to the real world. Big Edie says: "You're wasting that thing [camera] on this [pointing to her daughter]. That's nuts!" And Little Edie responds: "You don't see me as I see myself, but you're very good with what you do see. . . . You see me as a woman. I see myself as a little girl." Through all of this, however, neither the camera nor the cameraman responds.

Ultimately, this unique relationship between the subjects and the creators of the film raises the issue of the Maysles brothers' point of view. In fact, there are various points of view in this precisely and formally structured film. The two women are almost always in each other's time and space, visually and aurally, on-screen and off-screen; perhaps most memorable is the sound of their voices. *Grey Gardens* never lets the viewer forget that these two women are inextricably linked, not just as mother/daughter, or as cohabitants, but also in the past/present, love/hate, dependency/independency pattern in which they have chosen to live. They are known as "big" and "little," and they call each other "woman" and "kid." It is this interplay (and the interplay between present reality and past history, mixed with memories) that gives the film its rich texture and complex structure. The Maysles brothers do not present the Beales as eccentrics or freaks, and they do not exploit them. The women, who are wealthy and have had all the advantages, are living their own way. The mother's strength is every bit as relevant as the daughter's dependence (and vice versa).

Grey Gardens exalts the Beales as two idiosyncratic people who have spent years alone and who have emerged basically sound. Big Edie is a woman of formidable strength, spiritual peace, and plain wisdom. For all her lack of talent, Little Edie is a woman of vitality and originality; she describes herself as "a staunch character, staunch woman." In one of the film's epiphanies, Little Edie asks assertively: "The hallmark of aristocracy is responsibility, is that it?" From a shot of her pensive face, the film cuts to a shot of Big Edie, who looks equally meditative. In *Grey Gardens,* the Beales, not the Maysles brothers, are the point of view.

Frederick Wiseman

Of the American masters of direct cinema, Frederick Wiseman is the only one not to have begun with Drew Associates. A practicing lawyer before he became a filmmaker, Wiseman worked alone in developing his own unique and enduring approach that gave to direct cinema what the "new journalism" gave to the print and broadcasting media.[14] He stretches the dimensions of reportage; maintains a strong narrative control over his material, without appearing in or narrating his films, either as a character or by accident; uses small, repeated experiences that represent the total experience; and shapes his films so unobtrusively as to conceal his hand completely. The basis of Wiseman's art of direct cinema is that it communicates its meaning not through a duplication of the real world, but through a selection that creates a model of it.[15]

A strong, inquiring intelligence—the hallmark of Wiseman's work—is generally implicit in his choice of subject, his shooting of sequences, and his editing. He does not, in his films, focus on one person, but rather concentrates on one institution, exploring its operations, concentrating on the workers, clients, their families, and others who are part of, or affected by, those operations. He defines an institution as "a series of activities that take place in a limited geographical area with a more or less consistent group of people being involved."[16]

Wiseman's approach to institutions is essentially metaphoric: limited, repeated experiences within the institution represent the total institution, and the institution represents elements in the larger society.[17] In his choice and handling of subjects, Wiseman reveals an intensity and concentration that set him apart from both tradition and his contemporaries. Like Grierson, Wiseman is fascinated by the internal operation of institutions, but in addition to showing *how* and *why* they work, he also provides us with enough material to determine for ourselves the quality of that operation. Wiseman uses much footage to establish an institution's environment and atmosphere. While this footage might at first appear gratuitous, it shows not only a fascination with architecture and design, but also with how a building's form often controls its functions (e.g., the labyrinth of the welfare system is embodied in the labyrinthine layout of the welfare agency's offices). Wiseman acknowledges the ambiguity of reality and refuses to trivialize complex structures with a simple cinematic treatment. He does not seem intent on indicting institutions, but rather on permitting them to reveal themselves. Thus, viewers have full opportunity to develop a wide range of interpretations; nothing stands between the viewer and the film.[18]

Wiseman's films include *The Titicut Follies* (1967), *High School* (1968), *Law and Order* (1969), *Hospital* (1970), *Basic Training* (1971), *Essene* (1972), *Juvenile Court* (1973), *Primate* (1974), *Welfare* (1975), *Meat* (1976), *Canal Zone* (1977), *Sinai Field Mission* (1978), *Manoeuvre* (1979), *Model* (1980), *The Store* (1983), *Racetrack* (1985), *Blind, Deaf, Adjustment and Work, Multi-Handicapped* (all 1986), *Missile* (1987), *Near Death*, and *Central Park* (both 1989). Of these twenty-three films, nineteen have been broadcast by the Public Broadcasting System in the United States and seen by millions of viewers (more people have seen his films than any other nonfiction films in history), and then distributed widely through Wiseman's production company; they have also been broadcast in many European countries. Wiseman's films have been screened in virtually every major film festival in the world, and have won countless awards.

The Titicut Follies, Wiseman's first and most controversial film, provides a view of the Bridgewater State Hospital for the criminally insane in Massachusetts.[19] While it echoes Peter Weiss's play *Marat/Sade* (1964), a fiction based on fact, the film is fact only. In setting out to expose injustice and inhumanity at Bridgewater, Wiseman reveals to us the ugly aspects of such institutions. *Titicut Follies* was

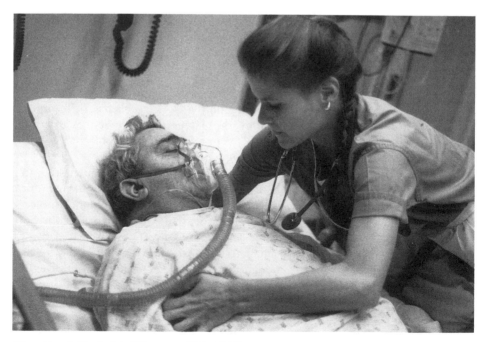

Near Death (Frederick Wiseman, USA, 1989)

perceived as so disturbingly candid by that state's citizens and by the media that it triggered considerable political controversy, a bitter legislative hearing, and a court censorship case that seems to have no end.[20] At issue is the propriety of the film's graphic footage of disturbing behavior (by inmates and guards alike) and its avoidance of narration and commentary.[21] Also at issue was the question of responsibility: the state's in permitting the foolish, degrading, and almost inhuman treatment of patients; Wiseman's in recording it. Undoubtedly, the discomfort felt by the lay audience must have been shared by the Massachusetts legislators and the institution's supervisors, for they charged Wiseman with violating the rights of patients and with breach of contract and banned showings of the film in Massachusetts.

Titicut Follies is a horrifying film about a modern-day Bedlam that many viewers might think had long been outlawed. Unlike Anatole Litvak's pioneering narrative film on this subject, *The Snake Pit* (1948), it does not need a dramatic structure to give intensity to the horrors; they were there, waiting to be filmed. *Titicut Follies* exposes more about us than it does about Bridgewater. It shows how supposedly rational and professional men demean and cheapen the quality of life; how they mistreat and humiliate the sick and incompetent; and how they betray the expectations of therapy and rehabilitation. The psychiatrists seem more interested in inmates' descriptions of sexual behavior than in ways in which they can help them, diagnose their problems, and prevent their unnecessary deaths (as they fail to do in one instance in this film). As seen through Wiseman's lens, the inmates are the victims of an inhumane institution that mocks and betrays its purpose.

Wiseman relies primarily on visual images and the words of his subjects to present the Bridgewater story; there is no narration or commentary to tell us what we are seeing or how we should feel. Indeed, in this, as in Wiseman's other films, the visual and auditory *are* the narration. However, *Titicut Follies*, like Allan King's *Warrendale*, combines material that may affect the audience's responses. Its sensational elements—naked inmates, a masturbating man, brutal treatment by guards, and unfeeling prison boards—may shock or even sicken some viewers. Wiseman reveals to us the ugly truth that institutions such as Bridgewater were built to hide. In his review of *Titicut Follies*, Arthur Knight asked, "But, inevitably, it must raise the ethical question: Where does the truth stop and common decency begin?"[22] If we had more films with the truth *and* common decency of *Titicut Follies*, he might not have had to ask such a question.

While *Titicut Follies* is Wiseman's most controversial film, it is also atypical; the others, less obviously polemic, conform to a more basic pattern in studying institutions that are more in the mainstream of American society. *High School* (1968) focuses on an institution that would at first appear to be at the opposite end of the social scale from Bridgewater State Hospital: Philadelphia's Northeast High School, an urban school with a functionally modern campus serving a predominantly middle-class, white student body. It seems to be a "model" school, and, to parents and administrators, it probably is; but to Wiseman, looking at it from the inside, it is a model of a very different reality. A common theme—and one apparent in other Wiseman films—links the film's many incidents: the rigid, mechanical, insulated nature of authority in a self-contained society.

Law and Order (1969), which focuses on the interactions of the Police Department and citizens of Kansas City, is concerned with American society's shift to the right, its emphasis on law and order at home, and its increasing armed aggression abroad.[23] However, like Wiseman's other 1960s films, *Law and Order* tries too hard to be objective, to balance scenes in presenting a multiple point of view; he succeeds neither in engaging our attention nor in providing a fresh perspective on a subject about which most people have definite opinions. With *Hospital* (1969), however, Wiseman reclaimed his approach and his audience.

Hospital provides an unpleasant picture of a massive social malady: inadequate health care for the urban poor. It is determined in its presentation, unflinching in its realism, and consistently intelligent in its viewpoint. Wiseman's position, like that of the medical and nursing staff, is detached and cool in its professional manner. (In fact, many of these workers do seem to be personally involved.) Whatever preconceptions his audiences may have about the quality of municipal health care service, Wiseman offers an uncontrived cinematic model of reality that balances breadth of coverage with depth. Equally important, we see the internal operations of this institution as well as its interdependence with other social service institutions, such as the police force and the welfare agency.[24] It might be argued that *Hospital* (1969) is not typical of Wiseman's best work, for it is not as critical as his other films. But his object seems to be incisive sociological analysis rather than direct criticism. A weak institution is its sharpest, most severe critic. The hospital is stronger than the high school, not perfect by any means, just more able to cope with its sizable and particular problems.

Basic Training (1971), which is about the training of military recruits, shares with Wiseman's *Essene* (1972) the distinction of presenting an institution that is relatively unfamiliar to the general viewer (*Essene* is about a monastery). During the early 1970s, when there were strong feelings for and against the war in Vietnam, and perhaps even now, the liberal viewer's first tendency might be to disregard the recruits as individuals and to associate them only with the nation's militarism. However, the film lets the viewer gently realize that they are the products of a dehumanizing process; the final destination of these men is Vietnam (as the final destination of the cattle is the slaughterhouse in Wiseman's *Meat*, 1976). Wiseman said that the film is about "killing," and that it presents a situation "even more depressing than I expected."[25] The process of socialization embodied by the military in *Basic Training* is symbolized by the educational institution in *High School*, the court system in *Juvenile Court* (1973), and the social service system in *Welfare* (1975); the military service in *Canal Zone* (1977), *Sinai Field Mission* (1979), and *Manoeuvre* (1980); fashion models in *Model* (1981);[26] and consumer buying habits in *The Store* (1983).

Wiseman's masterpiece, *Meat* (1976), is about the process by which cattle and sheep are raised, slaughtered, and prepared for market. *Meat* operates on several levels, exploring the relationship between process and product, and developing themes that are deeper and more provocative than any Wiseman had previously developed. Among these are the themes of life and death (the film opens with cattle pictured against the sky on the wide, open range and ends with a huge truck, also pictured against the sky, carrying meat to market), communication (very carefully edited sounds and voices of all kinds), self-determination (the cattle are led by the "Judas goat" to slaughter, while the men lose their identity through the labor union), and alienation (the cattle become chopped meat in a computerized plant, while the workers, listening to music through headphones in an atmosphere of deafening sounds, are separated by their work from any natural relationship with each other). These images of pens, traps, holding structures, and closing doors reinforce the interpretation that man's technology for processing animals entraps him as well. The company produces steaks and hamburgers, it also de-humanizes the men and women who prepare them.

This is the detailed, objective account of an efficient business as seen from the viewpoint of an outside observer. There is, of course, no narration, but the editing and people within the film "explain" various aspects of the process. The workers never comment on their work, but the session in which they discuss profit sharing reveals just how much they are dependent on, and are disregarded by, the company

Meat (Frederick Wiseman, USA, 1976)

for which they work hard. Wiseman's point of view is reflected in the structure, and, as in his other films, he develops the meaning through an accretion of images. The opening montage plunges us into the life of the institution, establishing environment and atmosphere. Although the film's structure is basically linear and chronological, the sequences build in a cumulative, not sequential, manner. Wiseman uses long, free scenes to preserve temporal and spatial reality, and to preserve the integrity of scenes in which institutional workers interact with customers. And, as in all of his films, direct sound recording is very important. Meat processing is hard, dirty work, and we are given sights and sounds, but not colors or smells (the film is in black and white). However, there is a paradox in Wiseman's approach, for while he is very close physically—through intimate camera work and sound recording—he is equally detached intellectually and emotionally. In *Meat,* content and cinematic form coalesce to a degree achieved only before in *Welfare*; *what* you see is *how* you see it.

Emile De Antonio

In the history of the American documentary film, Emile De Antonio is the unique master of a compilation genre that he created and can call his own. Although De Antonio's compilation films include the standard elements—interviews and archival footage—the result is anything but standard. Both subject and cinematic style are important. Like Marcel Ophuls, he made films that reflect his commitment to a cinema of truth and justice. His theme is always history; Pauline Kael wrote that the substance of his films was "the basic rottenness of America."[27] The hallmarks of his cinematic style are a rigorous critical intelligence, a Marxist point of view, and a refreshing iconoclasm about traditional nonfiction styles. Although De Antonio emerged as a filmmaker in the 1960s, he avoided the cinéma vérité approach:

> *Cinéma vérité* is first of all a lie, secondly a childish assumption about the nature of film. *Cinéma vérité* is a joke. Only people without feelings or convictions could even think of making *cinéma vérité*. I happen to have strong feelings and some dreams and my prejudice is under and in everything I do. (Quoted in Rosenthal 211)

De Antonio's films are always biased, continually challenging, and never dull. They were not "well-made," and their success and reputation are all the more astonishing when one considers that the period in which they were produced was one of great stylistic sophistication for the American nonfiction film.

De Antonio's films focus on many of the central events of the 1960s. They include *Point of Order* (1963); *Rush to Judgment* (1967), which raises many disturbing questions about the Warren Commission report on the assassination of President John F. Kennedy; *In the Year of the Pig* (1969); *America is Hard to See* (1970), about the failed 1968 candidacy of Senator Eugene McCarthy for the United States Presidency; *Milhouse: A White Comedy* (1972), a devastating satire on President Richard M. Nixon; *Painters Painting* (1972, see below); *Underground* (1976), featuring many of the key persons in the Weather Underground; and *In The*

King of Prussia (1983), a docudrama about the Plowshares Eight, a Catholic activist group, and the government's response to their antiwar activities.

Point of Order (1963), based on an idea of Daniel Talbot's, was compiled by De Antonio from the television coverage of the 1954 Senate Army–McCarthy hearings.[28] During the early 1950s, Senator Joseph McCarthy exploited the public's fear of Communism with a variety of tactics, using his role as Chairman of the U.S. Senate's permanent investigations subcommittee (Government Operations Committee) to bring national focus to his activities. In this endeavor, his ruthless and unprincipled tactics provoked widespread attack from the press and some of his Senate colleagues. In 1954, McCarthy accused Secretary of the Army Robert T. Stevens and his aides of attempting to conceal evidence of espionage among Army officers. The Army countered by accusing McCarthy, his chief counsel Roy Cohn, and a staff member of exercising improper pressure on the Army to gain preferential treatment for an Army private. After the stormy hearings, which were televised nationally, McCarthy and his aides were cleared of the Army's charges. Nonetheless, the Senate, acting on a motion of censure against him, voted to "condemn" Senator McCarthy for contempt of another Senate subcommittee and for insulting the Senate itself during the censure proceedings. While Senator McCarthy steadily lost his influence following this condemnation, his name gave birth to the term "McCarthyism," which denotes sensationalist tactics, including publicizing accusations of disloyalty or subversion with insufficient regard to evidence.

De Antonio organizes this complex historical subject through the use of interviews and compilation footage; there is no narrator. He begins *Point of Order* with a concise statement of the charges and countercharges, follows with a long sequence from a McCarthy speech on the "red menace," and throughout uses titles to keep us abreast of each stage of the hearings. To further set the issues in perspective, there is testimony from Army officials about McCarthy's and Cohn's conduct, as well as rebuttal from both of them. But the real conflict here is not between Secretary Stevens and Senator McCarthy, but rather between Robert Welch, counsel to the Army, and Roy Cohn, counsel to McCarthy. Their barbed interchanges are electric, the stuff of Hollywood courtroom drama. Long after the film has concluded, we remember Welch's harsh question to McCarthy: "Have you no sense of decency, sir? At long last, sir, no sense of decency?"

Through his editing, De Antonio attacks both McCarthy *and* the Army, and he has the final word. In the film's concluding sequence, as the hearing spectators walk out on McCarthy's ranting diatribe against Senator Symington, De Antonio leaves McCarthy to condemn himself. Scorned by his colleagues, with the television camera and hearing reporter as his only audience, McCarthy is a study in demagoguery. De Antonio does not show the actual conclusion of the hearings, which inform us that McCarthy was cleared of the charges against him, or refer to his subsequent condemnation by the Senate. Yet, he also makes the Army look less formidable than its array of generals would suggest. For those who lived through the era and for those who need an introduction to McCarthy, *Point of Order* provides a vivid portrait of what happens when power is fueled by paranoia.

In the Year of the Pig is the most original and provocative film yet to emerge about the origin and nature of the United States' involvement in the war in Vietnam. Like Peter Davis's *Hearts and Minds,* it is a biased, ambitious view of the war. Unlike Davis' film, which was made after the war, it was made during the war itself. And, unlike Davis's film (1974), it does not strive to balance arguments. De Antonio's purpose is to convince Americans that they do not understand the history of Vietnam, specifically the struggle of its people for independence, and that they therefore have no business fighting a war there. He dared to predict in 1969 that we would lose the war, and he was right. The film uses brilliant cinematic manipulation to let us see and hear for ourselves how the escalation of war represented the degradation of American values. What it lacks in serving the conventional responsibility of the nonfiction film, it gains in the sheer, cumulative forcefulness of its case against both the French and American involvement in Vietnam.

In both form and content, the film is a classic De Antonio statement: rough, provocative, and even outrageous. De Antonio's hero is Ho Chi Minh, and in a "wickedly manipulated" style (Rosenthal 205), he juxtaposes interviews, archival footage, and still photographs to portray the history of his leadership.[29] As the long struggle for Vietnamese independence is related, we hear French and American experts on Vietnamese culture and politics, as well as American politicians and government officers. All the major figures are here, although De Antonio sometimes neglects to identify them (a problem for younger viewers today). With its sharp juxtapositions of commentators—those supporting the war and those working to stop it—the film can be maddening, but beneath the cinematic trickery, there is the force of De Antonio's position.

In the end, *In the Year of the Pig* is concerned less with condemning our unthinking political and military leaders (whom, in contrast to the North Vietnamese, De Antonio does present as fools), than with presenting a tribute to the spirit of the North Vietnamese people. In the film's powerful ending over images of defeat and of dead and dying American soldiers, we hear the very ironic strains of "Glory, Glory, Hallelujah." No other American nonfiction film about war has ever taken such a radical stance. When we have been told "why we fight," we have been able to assume that we were on the side of victory, not defeat. Yet with history now underscoring the truth of De Antonio's prophecy for many Americans, other Vietnam films, such as John Ford's *Vietnam! Vietnam!* or the Defense Department's *Why Vietnam?,* seem like bland historical documents. Whatever its faults— and they are many, both scholarly and cinematic—there is no doubt that *In the Year of the Pig* is one of the most provocative and important nonfiction films ever made.

At first glance, De Antonio's *Painters Painting* would seem to be out of place in a corpus almost exclusively concerned with contemporary political issues. The film traces the evolution of modern painting from cubism through abstract expressionism and action field and color field painting, to pop art and op art; it features most of the most important artists in this evolution, talking about their different styles. There seem to have been at least several reasons why De Antonio made *Painters Painting.* First, he was understandably unhappy with other films on art:

I disliked the films on painting that I knew. They were either arty, narrated in a gush of reverence, as if painting were made by angelic orders, or filmed with violent, brainless zooms on Apollo's navel, a celebration of the camera over the god. They revealed nothing at all about how or why a painting was made. Dislike of other films is not a bad place for a film to begin.[30]

Second, he had known many artists for years, and was not only fascinated by, but intimately familiar with, how they think and work, and, more important, was able to photograph them in their studios, talking about their work. Third, he understood artistic freedom and wanted, in his own sprawling way, to provide a tribute to it. The iconoclasm of modern art is a natural subject for De Antonio. Modern painting is, after all, the history of reactions against representational art and classic aesthetic theories.

Painters Painting, which might more accurately have been titled "Painters and Critics Talking," is a typical De Antonio film in the provocative positions taken by some of the artists and critics who are featured and in its blunt compilation of footage of very uneven quality, most of it in color. De Antonio actually "signs" this canvas by appearing in the film, but his intellectual position on modern painting is not as clear as his conclusions on Senator McCarthy or Vietnam.[31] Perhaps one indication of De Antonio's position is in the film's conclusion, which not only repeats the remarks of Barnett Newman, with his emphasis on the "content" of modern painting, but also shows a 1960s crowd moving through an exhibition of modern paintings. The people look bewildered and uncomprehending, seemingly unmoved by either the form or the content of what they see. The art that has broken so completely with tradition seems not to be the art of the people. Yet, there is some poetic justice in this paradox, since this film (cinema is, after all, the art of the masses) provides an outstanding introduction to the subject.

Louis Malle

With the exception of *Phantom India* (1968), Louis Malle is not known as a director of nonfiction film. Although he worked with Jacques-Yves Cousteau on *The Silent World* (1956) and on other nonfiction films—*Vive le tour* (1966) and *Bons baisers de Bangkok* (1964)—Malle began his most significant work in the New Wave, and it is for feature narrative films that he is best known: *The Lovers* (*Les amants,* 1958), *Zazie* (*Zazie dans le métro,* 1960), *Murmur of the Heart* (*Le souffle au coeur,* 1970), *Lacombe, Lucien* (1975), and *Pretty Baby* (1978), among others. However, at the age of 39, in the mid-1960s, Malle decided to change his life. Abandoning his home and career, and seeking freedom from Western habits, he journeyed across the vast Indian subcontinent.

The result of this flight and quest was a nonfiction masterpiece: *Phantom India* (seven fifty-minute parts, 350 minutes total).[32] Made for television, the parts are titled "The Impossible Camera," "Things Seen in Madras," "The Indians and the Sacred," "Dream and Reality," "A Look at the Castes," "On the Fringes of Indian Society," and "Bombay—The Future India." While some Indians were offended at his political comments and leftist sympathies—the film was banned in

India but broadcast in Great Britain and the United States—*Phantom India* reflects considerable understanding and great affection for the country and its people. More important than its appreciation for India, however, is its exceptional insight into the process of perception as recorded by the camera.

Echoing Flaubert ("The novel is the mirror along the route"), Malle says "the camera is made a mirror along our route." And Malle's camera in this epic film takes many roles: recorder ("approaching reality at an angle"), weapon (perceived by some Indians as an evil eye), catalyst (which influences human behavior), voyeur ("who is the see-er and the seen?"), and intruder. Malle not only photographed this epic film, but also narrated it. Each film has a theme, but several consistent themes emerge: the coexistence of life and death in close and acceptable proximity; the inability of Western vocabulary to describe or explain Eastern civilization; the one and the many; colonialism and exploitation; India as a "Juggernaut with neither brakes nor steering"; and time (Malle says "I am a man of the West—a slave to time"). Approaching reality at an angle, Malle is aware of his role as an outsider, and thus expresses a humble awareness of the Westerner's identity ("plunderer," he calls himself).

Phantom India is both an extremely personal film and an extraordinarily beautiful film, providing an introduction to a country where the *Rig Veda* proclaims that "truth has a thousand names." As a Westerner, Malle says that he is able only to record shadows or spectres, what André Bazin called the "tracings of reality," and, thus, he creates a "phantom" India, one that exists for him by confirming his perceptions. Malle may not be able to "know" India, with its vast, pluralistic society, but he has created a brilliant record of his attempt to understand it. Indian reality contradicted his preconceptions and frustrated his conclusions, not only in contrast to the west, but also in its internal contradictions and complexities. For Malle, India embodied the multiple ambiguities that are reality.

He catches that reality with cinematic grace and intellectual insight. This is not only one of the greatest nonfiction films of all time, but also a fundamental text on cinematic perception and reality.

Marcel Ophuls

Unlike Louis Malle, Marcel Ophuls is known only for his epic nonfiction films.[33] Like Malle, he is concerned with perception and truth, but his focus is on the past, on historical events and people's perception of them. And like Malle, his work has been controversial for its attempt to find meaning in complexities and contradictions of those perceptions. His films include *Munich, or the Hundred-Year Peace* (1967), a study of the events leading up to World War II; *A Sense of Loss* (1972), about the "troubles" in Northern Ireland;[34] *A Memory of Justice* (1975), which examines Nazi war crimes, comparing them with what has happened since in other parts of the world, and *Hotel Terminus: The Life and Times of Klaus Barbie* (1988), another epic of crime and justice that opens the wounds of French collaboration with the Nazis in World War II. All of these films exhibit the qualities of psychological insight, careful observation of details, and ironic tension.

Ophuls's masterpiece, the epic compilation film on which his reputation is based, is *The Sorrow and the Pity* (*Le chagrin et la pitié,* 1970), an exhaustive inquiry into what happened during the Nazi wartime occupation of France.[35] The film, which is structured in two parts—"The Collapse" and "The Choice"—runs for four hours and twenty minutes, during which time Ophuls explores the idea that France was divided into those who joined the Resistance and those who supported the Vichy government's collaboration with the Nazis. It aroused opposition for its length, for its audacity at opening a controversial subject twenty-five years after the war, and for its point of view. When the film was released in 1971, in DeGaulle's France, it was refused screening on French television. Gaullists called it unpatriotic (and, indeed, DeGaulle is not glorified in the film). In 1972, it was released in French theatres, and, despite its length, was very successful with theatre and television audiences in the United States and Great Britain. Related nonfiction films are Claude Lanzmann's two-part *Shoah* (France, 1985), about the Nazi extermination centers; Victor Schonfeld's *Shattered Dreams: Picking Up the Pieces* (Great Britain, 1987), about forty troubled years of Israeli history; Josh Waletzky's *Image Before My Eyes* (1980); and Myriam Abramowicz' and Esther Hoffenberg's *As If It Were Yesterday* (1980).

For *The Sorrow and the Pity,* Ophuls invented a new compilation style.[36] Working from his own industrious research, Ophuls created this film on the editing table, moving between the past and the present, drawing heavily on wartime newsreels and other footage and juxtaposing this with provocative contemporary inter-

The Sorrow and the Pity [*Le chagrin et la pitié*] (Marcel Ophuls, France, Germany, Switzerland, 1970) [Helmuth Tausend, former Wehrmacht Captain stationed in Clermont-Ferrand]

views, to challenge the myth that all France supported the Resistance. On the soundtrack, Ophuls mixes narration with voices and voice-over translations. The conversational tone engages our interest and, to a certain extent, encourages our trust. Featured in the film are familiar names—Pierre Mendès-France, Georges Bidault, Anthony Eden, and Albert Speer; less familiar ones—René de Chambrun, the son-in-law of Pierre Laval, Premier of the Vichy government, and Christian de la Maziére, a Frenchman who was a member of the Nazi Waffen SS; and ordinary people from Clermont-Ferrand, an industrial city near Vichy, the headquarters of the government under Marshall Pétain. In this extraordinary range of people, we see and hear cowards and heroes; the guilty and innocent; those who were involved and those who were bystanders; participants, survivors, and their children. Some we believe; some we doubt; some we know are lying; others we cannot be so sure about. Some preconceptions about the French or the Germans are confirmed; others are challenged by new perceptions. While Ophuls's own point of view aligns him with the side of the resistance, he tries to be objective and leave final judgments to the viewer.

While Ophuls has created a cinema of political and moral commitment, using a rich texture and a heavily ironic tone, we must be careful in judging France on the basis of *The Sorrow and the Pity,* for, despite its length, a great deal of history is missing and a great many people are not interviewed. It is no criticism of Ophuls to acknowledge that the film distorts the truth through its process of selection. As Anthony Eden commented, people who did not live under the Nazi occupation should not judge the French too harshly.

Like such other complex nonfiction films as *Grey Gardens,* the interrelation of past and present and the multiplicity of viewpoints from which the situation is seen combine to form a complex work which, rather than telling the audience which attitude is the correct one, stresses how difficult any choice is within the inherent ambiguity of the situation that the film reveals. The film's title suggests the "pity and fear" that Aristotle says is the true result of all tragedy, and its internal dynamics reveal Ophuls's moral commitment that makes ambiguity impossible. Yet there are aspects of the film that resist any easy interpretation. Not only do the stories differ between the participating sides but the opinions within the same sides are shown to be, nearly always, at variance. The final sequence is particularly ambiguous. Here, Maurice Chevalier, the embodiment of French character, sings a lighthearted song typical of his nonchalance: "Let the whole world sigh or cry, I'll be up on a rainbow sweeping the clouds away." Does this song damn Chevalier and, through extension, the French, for avoiding reality? Or is it just another piece of wartime footage reminding us that history is a complex mosaic? Ophuls asks audiences to think for themselves about how others behaved, about how they might behave in the face of a great human challenge.

The Sorrow and the Pity is that rare film that asks audiences to sift through hours of information, to challenge their perceptions, to take moral positions, to reach conclusions. In doing this, Ophuls brought audiences worldwide to a new and positive conception of the power of the nonfiction film.

AMERICAN INDEPENDENT FILMMAKING

With the exception of the films made by Albert and David Maysles, Frederick Wiseman, and Emile De Antonio, American nonfiction filmmaking was less dynamic in the 1970s than it had been in the preceding decade when social and political fervor were high. In the 1968 campaign for the Presidency, Richard M. Nixon had appealed to a "middle America," a "silent majority" whose members, he believed, were dreaming of a return to a less turbulent world while continuing their present high incomes and enjoyment of material goods. Despite Watergate and Nixon's forced resignation, the will of that silent majority in the 1980s brought about the establishment of Ronald Reagan's new conservatism.

In this emerging conservative climate, many American nonfiction filmmakers were more inclined to observe society than to confront it. However, some of them made social documentaries that were committed to principles of social justice. These include the films of Peter Davis (*The Selling of the Pentagon*, 1971, and *Hearts and Minds*, 1974); Robert Machover and Norman Fruchter (*Troublemakers*, 1965); Mike Gray Associates (*The Murder of Fred Hampton*, 1971); Peter Biskind (*On the Battlefield*, 1972); Richard Cohen (*Hurry Tomorrow*, 1974); and Helen Whitney (*Youth Terror*, 1978). Several documentaries depicting social injustice reached a wider audience; these included Cinda Firestone's *Attica* (1973), about the September 1971 Attica Prison revolt in which forty-three men were killed; Barbara Kopple's *Harlan County, U.S.A.* (1976), and James Klein's and Julia Reichert's *Union Maids* (1976).

Kopple's *Harlan County, U.S.A.* expresses the simple, dignified, partisan voice of a community of Kentucky miners caught in a classic struggle with management. As such, it joins a distinguished group of films that also evoke the voice of the people, including Ivens's *The Spanish Earth*, Buñuel's *The Lost Ones*, Hurwitz's and Steiner's *Native Land*, and James Blue's *The Olive Trees of Justice*. While this partisan tone links Kopple's film to nonfiction film tradition, her use of human voices also provides a link with direct cinema, where language is an important element. The film's subtitles provide information and the music directs our reactions, but it is the direct cinematography and recording that bring us intimately close to the people talking about their plight.[37]

Reichert's and Klein's *Union Maids* is a compilation film interweaving archival footage with contemporary interviews to recount the role played by women in the American labor movement. Like Kopple, Reichert and Klein (who have made several important women's films) present labor history from the workers' viewpoint; management, police, and nonunion workers are ignored. Their interviews with three extraordinary women give the film a fresh approach to the struggle.[38]

The films of Danny Lyon have contributed to our understanding of the lives of Latino peoples in the Southwest, Mexico, and Central America. The people in his films are the victims of discrimination, poverty, and ignorance. Some live in communities with their families; others live on the fringes of society as fugitives, migrant workers, losers, and outcasts. Although women are present in these films, they are mostly about men's lives. Lyon's first film was *Soc. Sci. 127* (1969), about a

Texas tattooing parlor, but he is best known for a series of films about Chicano and Indian culture, including *Llanito* (1971), about the people of a Mexican town; *The Abandoned Children* (*Los niños abandonados*, 1974), a moving film about abandoned Colombian children; and *The Wetback* (*El mojado*, 1974), a short film about illegal Mexican migrant workers. Most impressive in this series are *Little Boy* (1977) and *The Other Side* (*El otro lado*, (1979).

Little Boy concerns the decline of Indian culture in the Southwest United States, a decline that resulted from the successive invasions of Spaniards and white men, including the arrival of the scientists who developed the atomic bomb in New Mexico. Lyon's focus is on a young man named Willie; the film's title refers to him as well as to the first atomic bomb, dropped on Hiroshima, which was named "Little Boy" (the second, dropped on Nagasaki, was named "Fat Man"). We see Willie as a little boy in black-and-white footage, and, in color footage, as a young man, just out of prison. He is a complex person, sometimes drunk and unappealing; at other times, engaging and touching in his hope for a new life. Lyon uses familiar characteristics of the straightforward direct cinema style, including frequent juxtapositions of people and symbols, as well as the less typical use of off-screen questions and comments to elicit on-screen responses from his subjects.

The Other Side—also in color, with some English subtitles, explanatory intertitles, and reenacted scenes—recounts the journey of a group of Mexicans who cross the border to pick oranges in Arizona. Like Lyon's other films, it is an extraordinarily straightforward account of the daily lives of people we know little about. Unlike the migrant workers in such films as Flaherty's *The Land,* whom we see in desperate straits because they are not working, these men go about their daily lives, picking fruit, cooking meals, washing clothes, and singing all the time. They appear to be relatively content, although they are fearful of being cheated by their employers and of being caught and deported by the U.S. immigration authorities. Lyon respects the dignity, hard work, companionship, and survival of these men, and he photographs them with sensitivity and affection.

Other notable nonfiction films of the period looked backward, focussing mostly on personal themes or recollections. These include Martin Scorcese's *ItalianAmerican* (1975), a film about his family; Abe Osheroff's *Dreams and Nightmares* (1975), an unusual account of the filmmaker's experiences in the Spanish Civil War; Jonas Mekas's *Reminiscences of a Journey to Lithuania* (1974); Manfred Kircheimer's *Stations of the Elevated* (1980), a tribute to New York's subway system that manages to make graffiti look beautiful; and David Loeb Weiss's *Farewell Etaoin Shrdlu* (1980), about the dramatic changes that occurred in the newspaper industry when production changed over from hot-type linotype to a cold-type computerized system. Other films focussed on contemporary issues, including Tom Davenport's *It Ain't City Music* (1973), about the oldest country music contest in the U.S.A.; Lucy Jarvis's *A Shooting Gallery Called America* (1975), which like *Murder in America* (1973), is about America's high rate of homicide; Mort Jordan's *Time and Dreams* (1976), a sensitive portrait of change in a black community in Alabama; Robert Fiore's and George Butler's *Pumping Iron* (1976) and Butler's *Pumping Iron II: The Women* (1985), both about bodybuilding; Nicholas Broomfield's and Joan Churchill's *Tattooed Tears* (1978), about a reform school; Nicholas Holmes' *We All Know Why We're Here* (1980), about inner city education; and Carol Mon Pere's and Sandra Nichols's *The Battle of Westlands* (1980), about land use in California's Central Valley.

The portrait film, a vital genre of the nonfiction film, proved to be successful at the box office as well. Among the more popular favorites were Howard Smith's and Sarah Kernochan's *Marjoe* (1972), a brilliant study of a teenage evangelist; Judy Collins' and Jill Godmilow's *Antonia: A Portrait of the Woman* (1974), a lovely account of a woman orchestra conductor;[39] and Barbet Schroeder's *General Idi Amin Dada* (1975), about the Ugandan dictator. Other portrait films include Yolande du Luart, *Angela Davis: Portrait of a Revolutionary* (1971); Charles D. Jones, *The Itinerary of Elie Wiesel* (1972); Lars Ullenstam and Tomas Dillen, *Harlem: Voices, Faces* (1973); Hal Walker, *Four Portraits in Black* (1974); Robert Snyder, *Anaïs Nin Observed* (1974); Howard Alk and Seaton Findlay, *Janis* (1974); Arnold Eagle, *The Pirogue Maker* (1975); Karen and David Crommie, *The Life and Death of Frida Kahlo* (1976); George Stoney's and James Brown's *The Shepherd of the Night Flock* (1980), about John Garcia Gensel, the pastor of New York's jazz community; Jack Shea's and Allen Moore's *The Shepherds of Berneray* (1981), a beautiful film (produced by Robert Gardner, who made *Dead Birds* and *Rivers of Sand*) about Scottish shepherds; Marc and Alan Levin's *Portrait of an American Zealot* (1982), a portrait of Ed McAleer, a leader of the Moral Majority movement; and Howard Brookner's *Burroughs* (1983), about writer William Burroughs.

BRITISH AND EUROPEAN INDEPENDENT FILMMAKING

After the creative development of the preceding two decades, the British nonfiction film of the 1970s became more traditional in approach. Through independent production, as well as public and private television, the British once again expressed their command of the possibilities of the genre.[40] Memorable films include Nicholas Broomfield's *Who Cares* (1971); Ben Lewsin's *Welcome to Britain* (1975), a blunt account of the discrimination faced by emigrants to Great Britain, especially blacks; Robert Vas's *Nine Days in '26* (1973) and *My Homeland* (1976), the first about the 1926 British general strike, the second about Hungary; *Ireland Behind the Wire* (1974), by the Berwick Street Collective, about the "troubles" in Northern Ireland; and Noël Burch's *Correction Please, or, How We Got Into Pictures* (1979), about the early evolution of cinema.

Joris Ivens remained a truly international filmmaker, working in the Netherlands, his native country, as well as in Italy, Cuba, and China. Between 1960 and 1980, he produced an astonishing group of films, including *Italy Is Not a Poor Country* (*L'Italia no e un paese povero*, 1960), an attempt to create better international relations for Italy; two films about Cuba—*Travel Permit* (*Carnet de Viaje*, 1961) and *Cuba, An Armed Nation* (*Cuba Pueblo Armado*, 1961); *The Sky and the Earth* (*Le Ciel, la Terre*, 1965) and *Meeting With President Ho Chi Minh* (1968), about Vietnam; *Rotterdam-Europort* (1966), film about the Dutch port city; *The*

People and Their Guns (*Le peuple et ses fusils,* 1970), a view of the war in the liberated zones of Laos; and films about China, including *Early Spring* and *600 Million People Are With You* (both 1958) and *How Yukong Moved the Mountains* (*Comment Yukong Deplaca les Montagnes,* 1973–75). *How Yukong Moved the Mountains* is a series of twelve films (lengths of 15 to 90 minutes) about everyday life in China; the comprehensiveness of Ivens' approach is seen in the titles: "The Drugstore," "The Oilfields," "The Generator Factory," "A Woman," "A Family," "The Fishing Village," "An Army Camp," "Impressions of a City (Shanghai)," "Professor Tchien," "The Football Incident: The High School," "In Rehearsal at the Peking Opera," "Behind the Scenes at the Peking Circus," and "Traditional Handicrafts." Ivens's longtime familiarity with Chinese leaders and his extraordinary rapport with the Chinese people make *How Yukong Moved the Mountains* a peerless record of a complex culture, comparable only to Louis Malle's *Phantom India.*

Other outstanding European films include the following: Jean-Louis Bertucelli, *Ramparts of Clay* (1969), and Christiane Gerhards and Malte Rauch, *Viva Portugal* (1976); Italy: Michelangelo Antonioni, *China* (1972); Ireland: *Ireland Behind the Wire* (1974); Germany: Werner Herzog, *La Soufrière* (1976); Yugoslavia: Aleksander Ford and Jerzy Bossak, *Fighting Poland* (*Polska Walczaca,* n.d.); Aleksander Ford and Jerzy Bossak, *Majdanek* (1944); Jerzy Bossak and Waclaw Kazimierczak, *Requiem for 500,000* (*Requiem de la 500,000,* 1963); Janusz Majewski, *Fleischer's Album* (*Album Fleischera,* 1962); Jerzy Ziarnik, *The Every-day Life of Gestapo Officer Schmidt* (*Powszedni dzien Gestapowca Schmidta,* 1963); Mica Milosevic, *Gymnastic Performance* (*Koncertogimnastiko,* 1962), *The Green Table* (*Za zelenim stolom,* 1965); and Vladimir Basara, *Hands and Threads* (*Ruke i niti,* 1964).

Within this rich diversity of European nonfiction film production, the most consistently rewarding films were made in Belgium. Frans Buyens's *Breendonk, Open Dialogue* (*Breendonk open dialoog,* 1971), is the first important Flemish documentary on the terrors of Nazism. Filmed at a concentration camp memorial, it records multiple conversations and discussions between two generations, survivors and students; reminiscent of Marcel Ophuls's *The Sorrow and the Pity,* it finds a lingering tendency among some Belgians to repress the truth of their memories. Another film about Nazism is Lydia Chagoll's *In the Name of the Fuhrer* (*In naam van de Führer,* 1977).

Later films concerned with domestic subjects include Edmond Bernhard's *Sunday* (*Dimanche,* 1961), which, like Henri Storck's early short films (1929–30), provides an impressionistic view of an idle Sunday: empty streets, closed windows, parks, the changing of the palace guard, anonymous faces in a stadium crowd, leisure activities. However, Bernhard's melancholy spirit is closer to that of the European "city symphonies" of the late 1920s than to Storck's playful sketches or to *Spare Time,* Humphrey Jennings's essay on leisure activities.

Beginning with *Borinage* (*Misère au Borinage,* 1933, codirected by Henri Storck and Joris Ivens) and *Houses of Misery* (*Les maisons de la misère,* 1937), Belgian filmmakers have pursued the potential of the social documentary film to address fundamental human issues. Paul Meyers showed continued concern for the

Borinage coal miners in *The Poor Flower has Already Flown Away* (*Déjà s'envole la fleur maigre*, 1960), as did Maurice De Wilde in *Mine Alarm* (*Mijnalarm*, 1966), and Frans Buyens in *Fight for Our Rights* (*Vechten voor onze rechten*, 1961), about major strikes that took place in the Winter of 1960; Buyens also made *East Germany* (*Deutschland, terminus ost*, 1964) and *Breedonk: Open Dialogue* (*Breendonk, open dialoog*, 1971). Ivo Berg's *Infernal Tempo* (*Tempo infernale*) (1969) recalls the pace of Chaplin's *Modern Times* in its depiction of work on an assembly linc in the automobile industry. In *The Love of Men* (*La passion des hommes*, n.d.), Jean Brismée celebrated the history and achievements of the Belgian Socialist Party, and in *Monsieur Plateau* (n.d.), he paid tribute to Joseph Plateau, whose Phenakistiscope, invented around 1832, was one of the most popular "persistence of vision" toys that preceded the invention of both photography and cinematography (see chapter 1). Jean Delire's *A Certain Belgium* (*Une certaine Belgique*, n.d.) provided a highly personal observation of the country, while Christian Mesnil was outright critical of the recent Belgian past in *The Royal Question* (*La question royale*, n.d.) and *From Zaïre to the Congo* (*Du Zaïre au Congo*, n.d.). Boris Lehman's *Magnum begynasium bruxellense* (1978) presents both a charming depiction of a threatened older quarter of Brussels and a denunciation of the urbanization of the Belgian capital.

Belgian television produced some excellent social documentaries, including Maurice De Wilde's two films concerned with Belgian wartime collaboration: *The New Order* (*De nieuwe orde*, 1980) and *The Collaboration* (*De kollaboratie*, 1981). Like Marcel Ophuls's *The Sorrow and the Pity*, they provide in unsurpassed information what they lack in cinematic distinction. De Wilde's *One Man's Meat is Another Man's Poison* (*De een zijn dood is de ander zijn brood*, 1973) concerns the Belgian arms industry. Other provocative work came from the Fugitive Group, including Robbe De Hert's and Guido Henderick's *The Death of a Sandwichman* (*De dood van een sandwichman*, 1971), about corruption in advertising and politics; De Hert's *Dockstrike* (*De dokstaking*, 1973), an agitfilm about the legitimate claims of striking workers and the bureaucracy of their unions; De Hert's and Chris Verbiest's *American Steak* (*Le filet americain*, 1978), a satirical view of contemporary Belgian politics; De Hert's *Eyewitness* (*Ooggetvige*, 1987), a portrait of Henri Storck; and Mark Schille's *Brussels* (1985).

AMERICAN AND EUROPEAN FILMS ON ART

The American and European film on art flourished during the 1960s and 1970s. These hundreds of films contributed not only to an audience's understanding of the subject, but also to the formal properties of the film on art.

American Films on Art

During the 1970s, the major American makers of films on art were Paul Falkenberg and Hans Namuth, Michael Blackwood, and Perry Miller Adato. Falkenberg and Namuth concentrated on modernist art; their films include *Louis Kahn: Architect* (n.d.), *Jackson Pollock* (1951);[41] *Dürer and the Renaissance* (1961), *Caravaggio and the Baroque* (1961), *Willem de Kooning: The Painter* (1966), *Joseph Albers: Homage to the Square* (1970), *Alfred Stieglitz: Photographer* (1981), *Alexander Calder: Calder's Universe* (1977).[42]

Michael Blackwood, whose films have been especially influential, concentrates on contemporary art. His work includes *Christo: Wrapped Coast* (1970), *Christo: Four Works in Progress* (1971), *Isamu Noguchi* (1971), *Larry Rivers* 1972), *Robert Motherwell* (1972), *American Art in the Sixties* (1973), *Philip Guston* (1973), *The New York School* (1973), *Claes Oldenburg* (1975), *Sam Francis* (1975), *Roy Lichtenstein* (1977), and *George Segal* (1979).

Perry Miller Adato specializes in biographical films, many of which have been about women artists. Her work includes *Gertrude Stein: When This You See, Remember Me* (1970), *Georgia O'Keefe* (1977), *Picasso: A Painter's Diary* (1980),[43] *Frankenthaler: Toward a New Climate* (1977), and *Mary Cassatt: Impressionist from Philadelphia* (1977).

Other American films about painters, sculptors, architects, and conceptual artists include Robert Gardner's *Mark Tobey: Artist* (1952) and *Mark Tobey Abroad* (1973), Wheaton Galentine's *The Corbit-Sharp House* (1965), Robert Snyder's *A Glimpse of De Kooning* (1961), Leo Hurwitz's *Journey Into a Painting* (1969), Robert Smithson's *Spiral Jetty* (1970), Michel Hugo's *Sort of a Commercial for an Icebag* (1971), about the work of Claes Oldenburg; Rudy Burckhardt's *Alex Katz: One Flight Up* (1971) and *Alex Katz Painting* (1979), Lana Yokel's *Andy Warhol* (1973), E. J. Vaughn's and John Schott's *America's Pop Collector: Robert C. Scull* (1974), Susan Fanshel's and Jill Godmilow's *Nevelson in Process* (1977), Francois de Menil's *North Star: Mark Di Suvero* (1977), Brian O'Doherty's *Hopper's Silence* (1981), and Courtney Sale's *In Search of Rothko* (1982).

Films on photographers include the following: David Myers's *Ansel Adams* (1958) and John Huszar's *Ansel Adams* (1981); Harold Becker's *Eugene Atget* (1963); Gordon Parks's *The Weapons of Gordon Parks* (1965); John Korty's *Imogen Cunningham* (1972); Thom Anderson's *Eadward Muybridge: Zoopraxographer* (1974); Edgar B. Howard's *Duane Michals* (1978) and Howard's and Seth Schneidman's *Harry Callahan: Eleanor and Barbara* (1983); Theodore R. Haimes's *Aaron Siskind* (1981); and Paul Falkenburg's and Hans Namuth's *Alfred Stieglitz: Photographer* (1981). Of these, the most impressive is Nina Rosenblum's *America and Lewis Hine* (1984).[44]

European Films on Art
Foreign films on art produced in this period include the following. From Great Britain: David Thompson's *The Pre-Raphaelite Revolt* (1967); Edward Bennett's *Hogarth* (1977); Michael Dibb's and John Berger's *Ways of Seeing* (four-part series, 1973); John Read's *Henry Moore at 80* (1978); Bryan Robertson's *Graham Sutherland* (1979); Pier Paolo Ruggerini's *Graham Sutherland* (1970); Ann Turner's *Point Counterpoint: The Life and Work of Georges Seurat* (1979); Gilbert and George's *The World of Gilbert and George* (1981); Ian Potts' *Return Journey* (1981); and Leslie Megahey's *Ingres: Slave of Fashion* (1985). From Norway: Peter Watkins's *Edvard Munch* (1976). From Italy: Giovanni Caradente's *Alberto*

Burri, The Artist in His Studio (*Alberto Burri, l'artiste dans son atelier*, 1960); and Marcello Grottesi's *Borromini* (1974). And from Switzerland: Pierre Koralnik's *Francis Bacon* (1964).

French films include Fabienne Tzanck's *Édouard Pignon, Ubac* (1960); Jean Lods's *Zadkine* (1960); Fabienne Tzanck's and Pierre Neurisse's *Zao Wou Ki* (1960); Jacques Brissot's *Objets animés, Arman* (1960); Carlos Vilardebo's *The Little Spoon* (*La petite cuillère*, 1960), *Mobiles* (*Les mobiles*, 1966), *Sandy's Colors* (*Les gouaches de Sandy*, 1973), *Une Statuette* (1970); Nelly Kaplan's *Gustave Moreau* (1961); Claude Fayard's *Man Ray Photograph* (*Man Ray Photographe*, 1961); Roger Kahane's *Jean Dubuffet* (1961); Michel Mitrani's *The Abstract Art in Question* (*L'art abstrait en question*, 1961), *Goya* (1962); Lauro Venturi's *Chagall* (1962), *Bonnard* (1965); Roger Leenhardt's *The Master of Montpellier* (*Le maître de Montpellier*, 1960), *The Man with the Pipe* (*L'homme à la pipe*, 1962), *Women and Flowers* (*Des femmes et des fleurs*, 1963), *Monsieur Ingres* (1967); Jacques Simonnet's and Guy Suzuki's *Gustave Singier, The Life and Work of Roger Bissiere, Jean le Moal* (all 1963); Jean Lhote's *The Origins of French Art* (*Les origines de l'art en France*, 1963); Edmond Levy's *The Life and Death of a Painter: Nicolas de Staël* (1963); Jean-Marie Drot's *Voyage to the Country of the Dead with Étienne Martin* (*Voyage au pays des demeures avec Étienne Martin*, 1962), *Giacometti* (1963), *Games of Chess with Marcel Duchamp* (*Jeux d'échec avec Marcel Duchamp*, 1964), *La bande à Man Ray* (1964); Michel Pamart's *Jean Le Gac and The Painter L.* (1983); Jean-Michel Meurice's *Jean-Paul Riopelle* (1963), *Dodeigne* (1963), *Françoise Sthaly* (1965), *Sonia and Robert Delaunay* (1967); Jacques Veinat's, Genevieve Bonnefoi's, and Claude Levet's *Henri Michaux or The Space Within* (*Henri Michaux ou l'espace du dedans*, 1964); Philippe Baraduc's *The Mad Fautrier* (*Fautrier l'enragé*, 1964); Roger Leenhardt's and Guy Bernard's *Corot* (1965); Jacques Baratier's *Le désordre à vingt ans* (1966); Jean Desvilles's *A Happy Week, or The Seven Elements* (*Une semaine de bonté ou les sept éléments*, 1966); Edgar Pillet's *Alberto Magnelli* (1968); André S. Labarthes's *Blue as an Orange* (*Bleue comme une orange*, 1968); Robert Hessens's *Multiples* (*Les multiples*, 1968), *Vasarely, le pré-cinétisme* (1970); Philippe Collin's *De Chirico* (1971); Clovis Prevost's *World Without God* (*Le monde sans Dieu*), *The Gods of the Night and of the Sun, Masters of the Unreal* (*Les maitres de l'irréal*, 1974); Catherine Binet's *Hans Bellmer* (1973); Jean-Louis Fournier's *Egon Schiele* (1977); Philippe Grandrieux's and Thierry Kuntzel's *Cubist Painting* (*La peinture cubiste*, 1981).

In Belgium, the major creators of films on art include Henri Storck, Jean Cleinge, Paul Haesaerts, and Luc de Heusch. Storck's films include *Felix Labisse, or the Happiness of Being Loved* (*Felix Labisse, ou le bonheur d'etre aimé*), 1962), *The Misfortunes of War* (*Les malheurs de la guerre*, 1962), *Paul Delvaux, or The Women Defended* (*Paul Delvaux, ou les femmes defendues*, 1970), and, with Patrick Conrad, *Permeke* (1985). Cleinge's films are *Ink* (*Encre*, 1964), *Van Eyck, Father of Flemish Painting* (*Van Eyck, père de la peinture flamande* (1972), and *Memling: Painter of Bruges* (1973). Haesaerts made *Cri et connaissance de l'expressionisme dans le monde à l'expressionisme en France* (1964), *La clef des chants surréalistes* (1966),

Ric Wouter's Joyous Folly (*La folle joie de Ric Wouters,* 1966), *Brueghel* (1969), and *Henri Evenepoel, Painter of Tenderness* (*Henri Evenepoel, peintre de la tendresse,* 1970). The films on art of Luc de Heusch are *Magritte, or the Object Lesson* (*Magritte, ou la leçon des choses,* 1960) and *Alechinsky d'après nature* (1971).

16 New Voices of the 1980s

The history of nonfiction film has been dominated by a relatively small number of masters, individual filmmakers whose unique cinematic vision and style were principal factors in shaping its development. But since the 1970s, this development has been shaped, not by a few masters, but by large number and wide variety of filmmakers. These new directors represent a wide spectrum of geographical, aesthetic, political, and sexual orientation, and their voices have diversified the committed viewpoints that have long been the hallmark of the social documentary. It is perhaps too soon to know which of them will take their places among the acknowledged masters, but many of these new filmmakers—with their insight into social problems, eagerness to share their experiences, and command of the cinematic medium—have already extended the potential and power of the nonfiction film. Notable among these new voices are the films of women, lesbians, and gay men, as well as those of artists in third world and non-western countries.

ISSUES SHAPING NONFICTION FILM IN THE 1980S

After its revitalization and international growth during the 1960s and 1970s, the nonfiction film continued to mature during the 1980s. In the two previous decades, its aesthetic growth had been sustained by several factors, including the influence of direct cinema on the prevailing theory of cinematic reality and the practice of recording it; the rise of the serious study of film history, theory, and production in colleges; the emergence of women and minorities into production; and the role of broadcast, cable, and satellite television in both production and exhibition. The ideological liberalism of the 1960s and 1970s was another explanation for the continued growth of the nonfiction film. J. Hoberman writes:

> The attraction to documentary—and particularly to social documentary—is, to
> some degree, a left-wing taste. The factors involved are an often puritanical antip-

athy to fantasy, a desire to educate (rather than "mystify") an audience, and a faith that the exposure of evil conditions will help ameliorate them.[1]

As this liberalism gave way to the conservatism of the 1980s, there was, despite the growth of the nonfiction film, some serious concern that its future was in jeopardy.[2] Direct cinema, for all of its impact, was not, in itself, sufficiently influential to offset the majority of mediocre films. In fact, direct cinema hindered the development of the social documentary, for its dispassionate objectivity meant that filmmakers did not take a stand. While the serious study of film in colleges had a promising start as a result of the curricular changes that students forced in the 1960s, this was soon stalled by the obstacles to securing the necessary academic approval and budget support for degree programs. More women and minorities made films about issues central to their lives, but few of them entered mainstream production. And while network and cable television provided an unprecedented showcase for nonfiction films, this outlet was not readily available to independent filmmakers, who had comparable problems in competing for the limited production funds made available by distributors, foundations, and government grants agencies. Another obstacle facing filmmakers, the young ones in particular, was the expense of motion picture production (which was eventually relieved in part by the use of video technology).

Out of these two decades of activity, marked by genuine achievements in the nonfiction film, there was some concern that the genre was moribund. Far from dying, the nonfiction film demonstrated again its capacity to revitalize itself. As Vincent Canby observed, the nonfiction film is "an eccentric hybrid,"[3] and filmmakers needed only the freedom to reassess and exercise the limitless possibilities of the genre. Thus it broke new ground and ensured its continued revitalization.

In the 1980s, the nonfiction film was shaped by other factors as well. The most important of these were the growth in the quantity and quality of nonfiction film production, the emergence of a new generation of filmmakers, the availability and influence of production in the video format, the emergence of new sources for financing and distribution, and the extraordinary popularity of the film on art, as well as such supportive factors as college-level study of film history, theory, criticism, and production; festivals devoted to nonfiction film (including the Anthropos Festival in Los Angeles, the world's largest showcase for nonfiction films); and more serious writing about nonfiction film.

Perhaps most notable among the forces shaping the contemporary nonfiction film has been the enormous growth in the quantity and quality of international nonfiction film production. In quantity, the total numbers are extraordinary; thousands of films are being produced each year. In quality, too, the production standards are outstanding. Moreover, many of these films have had commercial success. Good nonfiction films have always been popular with the general public, and there has been an increasing success of nonfiction films in the nation's commercial theatres. Full-length films, especially, such as *Harlan County, U.S.A., Shoah, The Atomic Cafe, The Times of Harvey Milk, Streetwise, The Thin Blue Line,* and *Roger and Me* have had unprecedented success. Reasons for this include

Harlan County, U.S.A. (Barbara Kopple, USA, 1976)

the excellent quality of the films, and the critical attention accorded them. On television, Frederick Wiseman's outstanding films continue to reach enormous audiences, as do many outstanding films on nature.

The new generation of nonfiction filmmakers includes women and members of minority groups, many of whom are not only familiar with film history, but also trained in filmmaking. Moreover, this new generation has been entrepreneurial in the pursuit of their goals, founding production and distribution collectives to bring their work to the attention of wider audiences. In addition, numerous commercial distributors have emerged to take advantage of the burgeoning audience and market for nonfiction film.

Major new filmmakers are producing nonfiction films in the United States, Great Britain, France, Belgium, and West Germany, as well as in the Soviet Union and Asia. Some of the new filmmakers to emerge in the United States in the last decade include Les Blank (*Burden of Dreams*, 1982, *J'ai été au bal*, 1989); Errol Morris (*Gates of Heaven*, 1978, and *The Thin Blue Line*, 1988); Kevin Rafferty, Jayne Loader, and Pierce Rafferty (*The Atomic Cafe*, 1982); Brent Owens (*The Bronx: A Cry for Help*, 1988); Renee Tajima and Christine Choy (*Who Killed Vincent Chin?*, 1988); Carol Mon Pere and Sandra Nichols (*The Battle of Westlands*, 1980); Jack Shea (*The Shepherds of Berneray*, 1981); Marc and Alan Levin (*Portrait of an American Zealot*, 1982); Nina Rosenblum (*America and Lewis Hine*, 1984, and *Through the Wire*, 1988); Philip Haas (*A Day on the Grand Canal with the Emperor of China*, 1988); John Cohen (*Sara and Maybelle*, 1981, *Musical Holdouts*,

1976, and *Mountain Music of Peru,* 1986); Jesus Salvador Trevino (*Yo soy Chicano,* 1972, and *Yo soy,* 1985); Henry Hampton, *Eyes on the Prize: America's Civil Rights Years, 1954–1965* and *Eyes on the Prize II: America at the Racial Crossroads, 1965–1985,* 1989); Diego Echeverria (*Los Sures,* 1983); Juan Christobal Cobo, Peter K. Hill, and Christopher C. Johnson (*Home,* 1986); Howard Brookner (*Burroughs,* 1983); Pedro Rivera and Susan Zeig (*Manjos a la Obra: The Story of Operation Bootstrap,* 1983); Claude Beller and Stefan Moore (*Presumed Innocent,* 1980); Michael Couturie (*Dear America: Letters Home From Vietnam,* 1987); Bruce Weber (*Broken Noses,* 1987, and *Chet,* 1989); William Greaves (*Booker T. Washington,* 1982, *From These Roots,* 1984); Geoffrey Dunn (*Miss . . . or Myth?,* 1986).

New filmmakers from other countries include Mary Pat Kelly (Ireland, *To Live for Ireland,* 1986); Anne Crilly (Ireland, *Mother Ireland,* 1988); Paul Hamann (Great Britain, *Execution: Fourteen Days in May,* 1988); Michael Apted (Great Britain, *28 Up,* 1985); Leslie Megahey (Great Britain, *David: The Passing Show,* 1985); Anthony Thomas (Great Britain, *The Death of a Princess,* 1980, and *Thy Kingdom Come, Thy Will Be Done,* 1988); Françoise Romand (France, *Call Me Madame,* 1988); Chantal Akerman (Belgium, *News From Home,* 1976, and *On Tour With Pina Bausch,* 1988); André Delvaux (Belgium, *To Woody Allen, From Europe With Love,* 1980); Stefan Decostere (Belgium, *The British Film Institute* [*Het Britse Filminstituut*], 1984); Jean-Claude Riga (Belgium, *Night Shift* [*Ronde de nuit*], 1984); Mara Pigeon (Belgium, *A Dry Season* [*Une saison seche*], 1984; Mark Schille, (Belgium, *Brussels,* 1985); Jan Neckers (Belgium, *As Big as a World Where Your Flag is Planted* [*Als een wereld zo groot, waar uw vlag staat gegplant*], 1986); Rob Rombout (Belgium, *Between Two Towers* [*Entre deux tours*], 1987); Werner Herzog (West Germany, *Last Words,* 1967; *Precautions Against Fanatics,* 1969; *Land of Silence and Darkness,* 1971; *The Great Ecstasy of the Sculptor Steiner,* 1975; *La Soufriere,* 1976; *How Much Wood Would a Woodchuck Chuck,* 1977; *God's Angry Man,* 1980; *Ballad of the Little Soldier,* 1984; *The Dark Glow of the Mountains,* 1984); Kazuo Haro (Japan, *The Emperor's Naked Army Marches On,* 1988); Hertz Frank (U.S.S.R., *Forbidden Zones,* 1975, and *Final Verdict,* 1988); Aleksandr Sokurov (U.S.S.R., *Evening Sacrifice,* 1988); Tatyana Chubokova (U.S.S.R., *Homecoming,* 1987); Nadezhda Khvorova (U.S.S.R., *Are You Going to the Ball?,* 1987); Vladimir Shevchenko (U.S.S.R., *Chernobyl: Chronicle of Difficult Weeks,* 1986).

The film on art continues to be extraordinarily popular, especially in France and the United States. Museums are experiencing a period of unprecedented growth and influence, and educational films on art extend their ability to reach large audiences. To this end, the Metropolitan Museum of Art in New York City and the J. Paul Getty Trust have established the Program of Art on Video and Film to foster the production of new films on art and the dissemination of information on existing films.

Other factors shaping the nonfiction film in the 1980s include an increase in the college-level study of film history, theory, criticism, and production; more festivals devoted to nonfiction film; and more serious writing about nonfiction film (theory in the academic journals, and criticism in both the academic journals and popular publications). Much of the new theory goes beyond the concerns of the founding fathers—Vertov, Grierson, Lorentz—and reflects the influences of structuralism, post-structuralism, and deconstruction in such concerns as modes of representation, ethics, narrativity, and readership and audience.[5] Equally important, and perhaps even more influential on the theory and criticism of nonfiction film, has been feminist film theory. And, finally, new books on nonfiction film and filmmakers have appeared, including histories of nonfiction film, anthologies of interviews and criticism, and specialized studies on Robert Flaherty, Dziga Vertov, John Grierson, Humphrey Jennings, Joris Ivens, Frederick Wiseman, direct cinema, feminist film, and Third World film.

LIBERATION FILMMAKING

The progressive atmosphere of the 1960s provided women, lesbians, and gay men with the social and political conditions necessary for presenting their view of themselves and the world to larger and more receptive audiences. To some participants, these efforts were seen as the direct outgrowth of the civil-rights, antiwar, and feminist movements of the earlier years of the decade. To many, especially gay and lesbian rights groups, these efforts were long overdue. At the same time, a great deal of the new film theory, including feminist theory, emerged in this ideological period; although most of it concerned narrative film, some theory was directed against the predominant realist modes in the nonfiction and documentary film as well as against what many perceived as a typically "male gaze."[6] Overall, the feminist film theorists emphasized, as Erens writes,

> the need for new forms, forms that would emphasize a feminist consciousness and ensure an alert, responsive audience. Their aim was not simply to replace the male voice with a female voice; they wanted to break down the traditional, passive way in which films are viewed.[7]

This dissatisfaction with prevailing modes was coupled with the practical need to use film for new purposes. Individual directors and filmmaking collectives in these liberation movements used film to raise consciousness and self-concept among themselves, to spread the word to people outside their movements, to record their activities and achievements, to help change power relations, and, perhaps most important, to serve as an alternative to the established media by presenting their own perspective on such issues as sexual identity, workplace equity, economic injustice, racism, abortion, educational opportunities, and role models. While the cinematic quality and sophistication of political analysis varies widely in these films, they have enriched the lives of their audiences and influenced the aesthetics and politics of the nonfiction film.[8]

Films by and about Women
Before the 1970s, "women's involvement in [American] documentary filmmaking was appallingly limited" (Erens 554). Since then, feminist nonfiction films have

depicted a broad and recognizable range of experiences in women's lives, a perspective that, in the beginning, was not only new, but also unique for most female audiences.[9] Julia Lesage writes that these films "speak to working women, encourage them in their public struggles, and broaden their horizons to make demands in other spheres as well."[10]

Among the first feminist films were those that presented the ordinary details of individual women's lives to primarily female audiences. These include Julia Reichert's and Jim Klein's *Growing Up Female: As Six Becomes One* (1969); Madeline Anderson's *I Am Somebody* (1970), *Being Me* (1975), and *Clementine Hunter, Artist* (1976); Kate Millett's *Three Lives*, 1971; Amalie Rothschild's *It Happens to Us* (1971), *Nana, Mom, and Me* (1974), and *Woo Who?, May Wilson* (1974); Liane Brandon's *Not So Young Now as Then* (1974); *The Woman's Film* (1971) by Louise Alaimo, Judy Smith, Ellen Sorin; Donna Deitch's *Woman to Woman* (1975); Deborah Schaffer's and Bonnie Friedman's *Chris and Bernie* (1974); Helena Solberg-Ladd's *The Emerging Woman* (1974), produced as part of the International Women's Film Project; Midge Mackenzie's *Women Talking* and *A Woman's Place* (both 1970); Herbert Risz's *Mukissi* (1974); and Diane Létourneau's *The Handmaidens of God* (*Les Servantes du Bon Dieu*, 1979).

Feminist films about women in history imply, as Patricia Erens writes, "that the women on the screen are representative of hundreds of others who lived these lives."[11] Thus, they not only reclaim for women their rightful place in history, but also bring that history alive for contemporary audiences. Prominent among such films are Harriet Hirshorn's and Lydia Pilcher's *Louder Than Our Words* (n.d.), a history of civil disobedience in the women's movement; Susan Clayton's and Jonathan Curling's *The Song of the Shirt* (1979), a unique and exciting film that combines nonfiction, fiction, and graphics footage to tell the story of 19th century sempstresses; Connie Field's *Rosie the Riveter* (1980); Barbara Kopple's *Harlan County, U.S.A.* (1976; see above); *The Wilmar 8* (1979); *With Babies and Banners* (1978); Julia Reichert's and Jim Klein's *Union Maids* (1976; see above); *Women of the Rhondda* (1973), a film about women involved in the 1926 general strike in a Welsh mining community, by Mary Capps, Mary Kelly, Margaret Dickinson, Esther Ronay, Brigid Segrave, and Humphrey Trevelyan; Elizabeth Barret's *Coalmining Women* (1982); Suzanne Bauman's and Rita Heller's *The Women of Summer: An Unknown Chapter of American Social History* (1985), about the Bryn Mawr Summer School for Women Workers that operated between 1921 and 1938; *Waiting Tables* (1985), by Linda Chapman, Pam LeBlanc, and Freddi Stevens Jacobi; and Vivian Kleiman's *Gold Rush Women* (1985). Other studies of about women in the workforce include *From Bedside to Bargaining Table* (•1984) by Tami Gold and Lyn Goldfarb; *Women of Steel* (•1984) by Mon Valley Media; *Trade Secrets: Blue Collar Women Speak Out* (1985) by Stephanie Antalocy; and *The Maids!* (•1988) by Sharon Conrad.

Film portraits that take pride in women's achievements include Yolande du Luart's *Angela Davis: Portrait of a Revolutionary* (1971), Perry Miller Adato's *Gertrude Stein: When This You See, Remember Me* (1971; see above for Adato's other films on women artists); Jill Godmilow's and Judy Collins's *Antonia: Portrait of the*

Woman (1973); Bonnie Friedman's and Deborah Shaffer's *Chris and Bernie* (1974); Mirra Bank's *Yudie* (1974); *Never Give Up: Imogen Cunningham* (1975) by Ann Hershey; Ellen Freyer's *Girls Sports: On the Right Track* (1976); *Elizabeth Swados: The Girl with the Incredible Feeling* (1977), by Linda Feferman; Nancy Porter's and Mickey Lemle's *A Woman's Place is in the House: A Portrait of Elaine Noble* (1977); Bonnie Friedman's *The Flashettes* (1977), about a girl's track team; *Love it Like a Fool* (1978), Susan Wengraf's film about Malvina Reynolds; Martha Sandlin's *Lady Named Baybie* (1979); Joanne Grant's *Fundi: The Story of Ella Baker* (1981); *Where Did You Get That Woman?* (1983) by Loretta Smith; Linda Post's and Eugene Roscow's *Doctora* (1983); *Miles to Go* (1983), a film by Deborah Boldt and Sarah Stein about women on a wilderness expedition; and Michelle Citron's *Parthenogenesis* (n.d.), an account of the filmmaker's sister learning the violin from a woman teacher. Films by differently abled women about differently abled women, an important part of women's film history, include *My Life Story* (•1988) by Barbara Jean Gregornik, and Sharon Conrad's *You Got Me Working Day and Night* (•1988).

Films by and about black women and other women of color include Madeline Anderson's *Clementine Hunter: Artist* (1976); Ayoka Chenzira's *Syvilla: They Dance to Her Drum* (1979); Carroll Blue's *Conversations With Roy DeCarava* (1984); and Barbara McCullough's *Horace Tapscott* (1984). Films by and about other minority women include Sylvia Morales's *Chicana* (1979); Lan Brooks Ritz's *Annie May: Brave-Hearted Woman* (1980); Allie Light's and Irving Saraf's *Mitsuye and Nellie* (1981); Ana Maria Garcia's *La operación* (1982); Loni Ding's *Nisei Soldier: Standard Bearer for the Exiled People* (1984); and *Mississippi Delta* (1984) by Christine Choy, Worth Long, and Allan Siegel.

Beyond these historical categories, there is a broad range of films covering a woman's life stages. Among the prominent films about motherhood include Lisa Joy Ross's *Homebirth* (•n.d.); Rachel Field's and Jackie Reiter's *Granny Midwives* (*Abuelitas de Ombligo,* •n.d.); Joyce Chopra's and Claudia Weill's *Joyce at 34* (1972);[12] Marjorie Keller's *Misconception* (n.d.); Geri Ashur's *Janie's Janie* (1971), which follows the self-realization of a white, single, working-class, welfare mother of five children; Peggy Stern's *Stephanie* (1986), about a young woman coping with adolescence; and Barbara Halpern Martineau's and Lorna Rasmussen's *Good Day Care: One out of Ten* (Canada, 1978). The most powerful of these films is Michelle Citron's *Daughter Rite* (1978), which explores relationships between mothers and daughters, and between sisters. Citron has made a rare and original contribution in combining various cinematic styles—traditional nonfiction forms, narrative fiction forms, and experimental film forms—in her examination of guilt, manipulation, trust, anger, competition, and love within the family. *Daughter Rite* is deservedly one of the most widely celebrated of all films by and about women.

Films about young women include Joel DeMott's and Jeff Kreines's *Seventeen* (n.d.), which, while not feminist analysis, is about teenage interracial dating; and *Streetwise* (n.d.), by Martin Bell, Cheryl McCall, and Mary Ellen Mark, which is about Seattle youngsters who panhandle, deal dope, pimp, and prostitute themselves. Other films on prostitution include *Ain't Nobody's Business* (1977), by

Sallary Barrett-Page and Ellen Grant, and *Hookers on Davie* (1984) by Holly Dale and Janis Cole. Films about menopause and old age, respectively, are Sabina Wynn's *Invisible Woman* (Australia, n.d.) and Barbara Halpern Martineau's *Tales of Tomorrow: Our Elders* (Canada, 1982). Women in the military are the subject of Nick Broomfield's and Joan Churchill's *Soldier Girls* (1981). Films about women in prison include Suzanne Jaspur's *Being a Prisoner* (n.d.); *Like a Rose* (1975) by Sally Barrett-Page and Ellen Grant of Tomato Productions; *We're Alive* (1971) by the California Institute for Women's Video and UCLA Women's Film Workshop; *Bail Fund Film* (1971) by a group of female NYU filmmaking students; and Janis Cole's and Holly Dale's *P4W: Prison for Women* (Canada, 1982), an intense study of five inmates of a Canadian prison. Much of the latter film's power comes from the women themselves, who speak about their lives, crimes, relationships inside and outside of prison, and, in two cases, the human warmth and love they found in prison that had evaded them on the outside. Even though the filmmakers make no judgments about these women, two impressions remain memorable: the extent to which the women measure themselves against society's established norms for female behavior and the lack of career training, which appears to be limited to preparing the prisoners to be hairdressers. *P4W: Prison for Women* provides an extraordinary and often heartbreaking glimpse into a women's world that few would otherwise ever see.

Some of the most important films about women have concerned healthcare issues. Prominent among these is *Self Health* (1974), by Catherine Allan, Judy Erola, Allie Light, and Joan Musante of the San Francisco Women's Collective, which defines women's sexuality on women's terms by showing women in a collective situation examining their bodies and sharing knowledge about them. This film sets a tone for many other films in this area: "We're learning from our bodies, teaching ourselves and each other how each of us is unique . . . and the same. . . . We see it as reclaiming lost territory that belonged to our doctors, our husbands, everyone but us" (quoted in Lesage 229). Other films include Susan Lambert's and Sarah Gibson's *Size 10* (n.d.); Kristin Porter's *Measure of Worth* (n.d.), about anorexia; Margaret Lazarus's *Taking Our Bodies Back* (n.d.); the Kartemquin Films *The Chicago Maternity Center Story* (n.d.); Denise Bostrom's and Jane Warrenbrand's *Healthcaring From Our End of the Speculum* (1977); and Frances Reid's and Elizabeth Stevens's *We All Have Our Reasons* (1981), about alcoholism.

Abortion, which continues to polarize the country, has been the subject of numerous films. Among the early films are Amalie Rothschild's *It Happens to Us* (1971); Bonnie Friedman's, Marilyn Mulford's, and Deborah Shaffer's *How About You?* (1974); Jerry Blumenthal's and Jennifer Rohrer's *The Chicago Maternity Center Story* (1976); and the London Women's Film Group, *Whose Choice?* (1976). Other films on abortion include Victoria Schultz's *Holy Terror* (1986), Gail Singer's *Abortion: Stories from North and South* (1984), and Thomas Goodwin's and Gerardine Wurzburg's *Personal Decisions* (1986). Films about rape include Martha Coolidge's *Not a Pretty Picture* (1974); JoAnn Elam's *Rape* (1976); Cambridge Documentary Films' *Rape Culture* (1978); and Meri Weingarten's *Waking Up to*

Rape (1985). Child molesting is the subject of Bobbie Birleffi's *Men Who Molest: Children Who Survive* (1984).

The role of women in the antiwar movement is the subject of *Dark Circle* (1982), about nuclear war, by Judy Irving, Chris Beaver, and Ruth Landy; *Carry Greenham Home* (n.d.) by Beeban Kidron and Amanda Richardson; and *Stronger Than Before* (n.d.), by the Boston Women's Collective. The Holocaust and women is the subject of Miriam Abramowicz's and Esther Hoffenberg's *As If It Were Yesterday* (Belgium, 1982), about Belgians who hid Jewish children from the Nazis; and Su Friedrich's *The Ties That Bind* (1984). Prominent among these Holocaust films is *Pink Triangles* (1982) by Cambridge Documentary Films.

Sexist attitudes are the subject of two films: Bonnie Sherr Klein's *Not a Love Story* (1981) and Lucy Winer's and Paula de Koenigsberg's *Rate It X* (1986). *Not a Love Story* relates the attempts of two women—filmmaker Bonnie Sherr Klein and stripper Linda Lee Tracy—to find out what pornography is, how it works, and how it affects relations between women and men. This journey explores the multi-billion-dollar industry of pornography—peep shows, strip joints, sex supermarkets, magazines—and interviews prominent feminists. Controversial as this film has been, its coverage of the degradation of, and violence against, women provides information vital to women's liberation. *Rate It X* presents a cross section of American men's views on women, sex, and sexuality, including Ugly George, the New York cable television personality who is a true sexist pig, a baker who creates cakes that resemble headless female torsos with large breasts, advertising executives, a group of aging American Legion members, and the head cartoonist for *Hustler* magazine, who justifies his appalling cartoons about child molesting with the comment that they make people "happy." Although the filmmakers present nothing new here—their examples all too familiar—their juxtapositions of these men's comments creates a strong feminist statement. Predictably, the men say their views are grounded in tradition, and they are pathetically unable to understand the sexist implications of their attitudes. While the filmmakers may seem to take a lighthearted approach—we see Lucy Winer's white-gloved hand holding the microphone as she interviews these men—they are neither distanced nor ambiguous in their conclusion: many aspects of American life should be rated "X" for their pornographic treatment of women.

Among the extraordinary array of films by and about women from European and Third World countries are Valeria Sarmiento's *A Man, When He is a Man* (Chile, 1982); Laleen Jayamanne's *A Song of Ceylon* (Sri Lanka, 1985); Laurette Deschamps's *No Longer Silent: Indian Women Struggle Against Injustice* (1986); Diane Kitchen's *Before We Knew Nothing* (1988); and Trinh T. Minh-ha's *Surname Viet Given Name Nam* (Vietnam, 1989).

In Canada, films by and about women have a history of strong support from the federal government. During John Grierson's tenure at the National Film Board, women were included at the highest levels of production.[13] Since 1974, Studio D, the National Film Board's women's unit, has provided a forum for women filmmakers in order to bring women's perspectives to the films it produces. An equally important activity has been the Federal Women's Film Program, which coordinates federal government departments and agencies to ensure the production and distribution of timely films that reflect women's perspectives on current issues affecting women and society.[14]

Outstanding Canadian films on women and women's issues include the following, listed by subject area. Women in history: *Great Grand Mothers: A History and Celebration of Prairie Women* (1976) by Anne Wheeler and Lorna Rasmussen; Janice Brown's *The Lady from Grey County* (1977), and Susan Trow's *Just a Lady* (1980). Marriage and family: Beverly Shaffer's *The Way It Is* (1982). Working mothers: " . . . *And They Lived Happily Ever After*" (1975) by Kathleen Shannon, Irene Angelico, and Anne Henderson; *The Spring and Fall of Nina Polanski* (1974) by Joan Hutton and Louis Roy; a series of films by Kathleen Shannon, including *Extensions of the Family, It's Not Enough, Like the Trees, Luckily I Need Little Sleep, Mothers are People, They Appreciate You More, Tiger on a Tight Leash, Would I Ever Like to Work* (all 1974), and *Our Dear Sisters* (1975). Women in the Workplace: Diane Beaudry's *Laila* (1980), Anne Henderson's *Attention: Women at Work!* (1983), Beverly Shaffer's *I Want to Be an Engineer* (1983), and Margaret Westcott's *Louise Drouin, Veterinarian* (1981). Women and the arts: Diane Beaudry's *Maud Lewis: A World Without Shadows* (1976), and Caroline Leaf's *Kate and Anna McGarrigle* (1981). Women and Politics: *Some American Feminists* (1977) by Luce Guilbeault, Nicole Brossard, and Margaret Wescott; *The Right Candidate for Rosedale* (1979) by Bonnie Sherr Klein and Anne Henderson; Terri Nash's *If You Love This Planet* (1982), winner of a 1983 Academy Award; and *Dream of a Free Country: A Message from Nicaraguan Women* (1983), which studies the heroic roles played by the women of Nicaragua in the people's revolution and their determined efforts to bring gender equality to their country. Older Women: Margaret Wescott's *Eve Lambart* (1978). Girls and Young Women: Barbara Greene's *Listen Listen Listen* (1976); Beverly Shaffer's *My Name Is Susan Yee* (1975); *I'll Find a Way* (1977, winner of an Academy Award), *Veronica* (1977), and *Julie O'Brien* (1981). Health and Sexuality: Gudrun Parker's *Your Move* (1973) and Diane Beaudry's *An Unremarkable Birth* (1978). Sexist Attitudes: Bonnie Sherr Klein's *Patricia's Moving Picture* (1978) and *Not a Love Story: A Film about Pornography* (1981; see above). Abortion: Paul Cowan's *Democracy on Trial: The Morgenthaler Affair* (1984). Sexual Abuse: Beverly Shaffer's *To A Safer Place* (1987). Finally, one of the NFB's most controversial films, Margaret Wescott's *Behind the Veil: Nuns* (1984).

Films by Lesbians and Gay Men

Among the earliest nonfiction films dealing with gay men were Shirley Clarke's *Portrait of Jason* (1967), about a black hustler, and Frank Simon's *The Queen* (1968), about a beauty contest among homosexual transvestites. While both were serious studies of people who had never before been the subject of nonfiction films, the real history of nonfiction gay and lesbian filmmaking began with those films that established the historical background and general issues in the struggle for gay and lesbian civil rights. These include Pat Rocco's *Mondo Rocco* (1970), a compilation of various liberation and oppression activities; John Shane's *Come Together* (1971) and *Britain 1971* (1971), about the Gay Liberation Front movement in London; Michael Rhodes's *A Position of Faith* (1974), an account of the events surrounding the eventually successful attempt of a gay man to be ordained as a minister in the United Church of Christ (cf. Ann Alter's *No Need to Repent: The Ballad of Reverend Jan Griesinger* [1989; see below]); *Rosa Winkel? Das ist doch schon lange vorbei . . . ,* by Peter Recht, Christiane Schmerl, and Detlev Stoffel, (West Germany, 1975), about the criminal prosecution of gays in West Germany; Lionel Soukaz's *Race d'ep!* (France, 1977), a record of major events in gay history; Jim Hubbard's *Stop the Movie Cruising!* (1979), a record of the protest against a film perceived to be homophobic; *Witches and Faggots—Dykes and Poofters* (1979) from the "One in Seven Collective" in Sydney, Australia; George Crile's controversial television study, *Gay Power, Gay Politics* (•1980); Gordon Keith's and Jack Lemmon's *Truxx* (1978) and *Enough is Enough* (1980), about police raids of gay bars and bathhouses in Toronto; *Before Stonewall: The Making of a Gay and Lesbian Community!* (1984) by Greta Schiller, John Scagliotti, and Robert Rosenberg; and Phil Zwickler's and Jane Lippman's *Rights and Reactions: Lesbian and Gay Rights on Trial* (1987). The best of these are *Silent Pioneers* (1984), by Lucy Winer, Harvey Marks, Paula de Koenigsberg, and Patricia G. Snyder, a timely, award-winning study of gay and lesbian elders, and Robert Epstein's *The Times of Harvey Milk* (1984), a portrait of the slain San Francisco homosexual rights leader that won an Academy Award for Best Documentary.

The process of "coming out"—acknowledging one's homosexuality to family and friends—is the subject of Vincent J. Sklena's *Out of the Closet* (1971); Arthur Bressan's *Coming Out* (1972); *Coming Out* (1973) by the Berkeley Lesbian Feminist Film Collective; and Bruce Glawson's *Michael, A Gay Son* (1980), a Canadian film about a young man coming out to his family. Outstanding among these films is *Word is Out* (1978), by the Mariposa Film Group, a gay collective, in which twenty-six gay men and women of diverse backgrounds discuss what it means to lead homosexual lives.

Homosexual lifestyles are the subject of Mervyn Nelson's *Some of My Best Friends Are* (1971); Kenneth Robinson's *Some of Your Best Friends* (1972); Barbara Hammer's *A Gay Day* (1973); Laird Sutton's *A Gay View/Male* (1975); the Document Associates's *Gay or Straight: Is There a Choice?, A Three Letter Word for Love,* and *Homosexuality and Lesbianism* (all 1976); Holly Dale's and Janis Cole's *Minimum Charge No Cover* (Canada, 1976), which shows the lives of prostitutes, homosexuals, transvestites, and transsexuals; Jesus Trevino's *Gay, Proud, and Sober* (1977); Dale Beldin's and Mark Krenzien's *Who Happen to be Gay* (1979); Armand Weston's *Radical Sex Styles* (n.d.); *Gay Voices, Gay Legends* (n.d.); and *On Being Gay: A Conversation with Brian McNaught* (n.d.).

Gay men's lifestyles are recorded in such films as Will Roberts' and Josh Hanig's *Men's Lives* (1975), Michael Chaite's and Len Grossman's *To Ourselves, Our Sons, Our Fathers: A Collection of Personal Statements by Men* (1978); and, from France, Luc Barnier's and Alain Lafargues's *Les oiseaux de nuit* (France, 1979). Foreign films on the subject include *Bögjävlar* (1977) from the Swedish Filmgruppen and Norbert Terry's *Homo-actualités* (1977), which features candid interviews with French gay writers and politicians.

Silent Pioneers (Lucy Winer, Harvey Marks, Paula de Koenigsberg, and Patricia
G. Snyder, USA, 1984) [left to right, Bruhs Mero and Gean Harwood]

Films about lesbian lifestyles include *The Continuous Woman* (1973), by the
Twin Cities Women's Film Collective, which includes five women, including one
lesbian, talking about women's issues; *Lesbians* (1975) by the Portland National
Organization of Women; Jan Oxenburg's *Home Movie* (1975), a self-portrait of the
filmmaker, compiled from old home movies and contemporary footage; Marie
Ashton's *Coming to Know* (1976), in which two young women talk about their
lesbian feelings; *The Woman in Your Life is You* (New Zealand, 1978); Anita
Clearfield's *Olivia Records: More than Music* (1977), which presents the lifestyle of
a lesbian feminist collective; Chi Yan Wong's *L'aspect rose de la chose* (France,
1980), a portrait of a gay and lesbian group in Grenoble, France; Susan Blaustein's
Susana (1979), a self-portrait of the filmmaker; *Just Because of Who We Are* (•1986)
by the Heramedia Collective; *Lesbian Tongues: Lesbians Talk about Life, Love, and
Sex* (•n.d.); and Pam Walton's *Out in Suburbia: The Stories of Eleven Lesbians*
(1988). Ann Alter's *No Need to Repent: The Ballad of Reverend Jan Griesinger* is an
excellent, straightforward account of the life of one of the few openly lesbian
Protestant ministers in the United States; it also shows how one group of feminists
are building a community of working and caring women. Films about lesbian
couples include Murray Markowitz's *August and July* (1973); Laird Sutton's *In
Winterlight* (1974); Elaine Jacobs' and Colleen Monahan's *Lavender* (1972); Greta
Schiller's and Thomas Seid's *Greta's Girls* (1978); and Kiki Zeldes's *Lifetime Commitment: A Portrait of Karen Thompson* (•1988). Other films about lesbians include

Constance Besson's *Holding* (1971), Ann Hershey's *We Are Ourselves* (1976), and Laird Sutton's *Gay Women Speak* (1979).

Lesbian and gay celebrities are the subject of several films. Ti-Grace Atkinson, Rita Mae Brown, and Kate Millett are profiled in the 1977 Canadian film, *Some American Feminists,* by Luce Guilbeault, Nicole Brossard, Margaret Wescott. Another Canadian film by Lydia Wazana and Kay Armitage presents the American journalist Jill Johnston: *Jill Johnston, October '75.* May Sarton, the author, is the subject of Marita Simpson's and Cathy Wheelock's film, *World of Light: A Portrait of May Sarton* (1980), and early women in the music business are the subjects of *International Sweet Hearts of Rhythm* (1986) and *Tiny and Ruby: Hell Divin' Women* (1988), both by Greta Schiller and Andrea Weiss. Films about gay artists include Tom Joslin's *Blackstar: Autobiography of a Close Friend* (1977); Philo Bregstein's *Whoever Says the Truth Shall Die* (1981), a study of the art, politics, and homosexuality of Italian film director Pier Paolo Pasolini; XXX's *Cadmus on Cadmus: Enfant Terrible at 80* (1986), Michelle Parkerson's *Storme: The Lady of the Jewel Box* (1987), about Storme DeLarverie, a star of America's first integrated female impersonation show; and the Italian television film, *The Rebels: Montgomery Clift* (•1985).

The struggle for homosexual civil rights has taken many forms, including local and national parades and demonstrations; many of these have been recorded on film, including Arthur J. Bressan, Jr.'s and David Pasko's *Gay U.S.A.* (1977), a record of the 1977 Gay Pride Marches around the country; Philip Quetschke's and Donald Smith's *March on Washington* (1979); Jim Hubbard's *March On!* (1979); Lionel Soukaz's *La marche gay* (France, 1980); Lucy Winer's *Greetings From Washington, D.C.* (1981); Phil Zwickler's and Jane Lippman's *Rights and Reactions: Lesbian and Gay Rights on Trial* (1987), a record of the 1986 New York City Council hearings on the gay and lesbian rights bill, which finally passed after sixteen years of debate; Joan E. Biren, *For Love and For Life: The 1987 March on Washington for Lesbian and Gay Rights* (•1988); *Never to be Forgotten* (•n.d.); *One Year After* (•n.d.); *Part of the USA: March on Washington* (•n.d.); and Barbara Hammer, *Sisters!* (1973), a record of the international women's day march.

The subject of gay and lesbian adoption and parenting provides the focus for *Sandy and Madeline's Family* (1973), by Sherrie Farrell, Peter Bruce, and John G. Hill, an account that also includes a child custody battle; *In the Best Interests of Children* (1977), a film about lesbian mothers and their children by Elizabeth Stevens, Cathy Zheutlin, Frances Reid; Liz Mersky's *Labor More Than Once* (1983); Christina Sinley's and Vicki Funari's *Alternative Conceptions* (1985); Debra Chasanoff's and Kim Klausner's *Choosing Children* (1985); Kevin White's *Not All Parents Are Straight* (1986); Linda J. Harness's *A Family to Me* (1986); Karen Sloe's *If She Grows Up Gay* (1986); and Aimée Sands' *We Are Family* (1987). Gay fathers are the subject of Richard James's and Jeffrey Lunger's *You Just Love Your Children* (1978).

Gay filmmakers have responded eloquently to the AIDS tragedy with such films as *The AIDS Epidemic, Till Death Do Us Part,* Wendy Dallas's and Marc

Huestis's *Chuck Solomon: Coming of Age* (1986), *Hero of My Own Life* (n.d.), Barbara Hammer's *Snow Job: The Media Mysteria of AIDS* (1986), Tina DiFeliciantonio's *Living With AIDS* (1987), Michael Aue's *I'm Still Alive* (1987), John Canalli's *Heroism: A Community Responds* (1987), *October 17, 1987: The Inaugural Display of the Names Quilt Project* (1988); Alain Klarer's *Bailey House: To Live As Long As You Can* (1988); Nick Sheehan's *AIDS: No Sad Songs* (1984); and David Thompson's *We Bring a Quilt* (n.d.); Robert Epstein's and Jeffrey Friedman's *Common Threads: Stories from the Quilt* (1989); Micki Dickoff's *Too Little, Too Late* (n.d.); and *Silence Equals Death* and *Positive* (1989), a collaboration between two filmmakers, Rosa von Praunheim from West Germany and Phil Zwickler from the United States.

NONFICTION FILM IN THIRD WORLD AND NON-WESTERN COUNTRIES

With the introduction of the Lumières' *cinématographe* in 1895, cinema became an international phenomenon. Within a year, films—simple nonfiction records of daily life—were being made and screened in Latin America, Asia, Africa, North America, and Europe. However, the first impulse in non-Western countries was not to capitalize on the mass-entertainment potential of this medium, but rather to use film to entertain colonial administrators and Western-educated native elites.[15] Throughout this period, filmmaking in "undeveloped" countries (which are largely unaffected by a capitalist economy) and "underdeveloped" countries (which are viewed as being at the bottom of the capitalist economic hierarchy) was dominated by foreign, and largely Western, distributors. And, since most films were shot by foreign filmmakers or recent immigrants from Europe, they "belong more to the history of how Europe and the United States have viewed the non-Western world than to an emerging expression of indigenous culture" (Armes 56).

In the period between 1895 and 1914, the beginning of World War I, the work of local pioneer filmmakers also began to make its appearance in non-Western countries. Armes writes that

> the national audience that non-Western film makers began to address with their films was almost invariably an underdeveloped one, which already accepted and enjoyed a Western consumer product and a Western conception of cinema as an undemanding form of mass entertainment—this is a situation that persists to the present day. (57)

Subsequently, the geographical and economic disruptions caused by the war created a climate more favorable to local film production in many countries, particularly in Asia, Africa, and Latin America. After this economic base had been established, local film production in third world countries was further strengthened by such diverse influences as the breakup of colonial empires, the development of national identity in emerging independent countries, the coming of sound, the development of a mass audience, and the emergence of individual directorial styles.

Third World cinema typically fuses social, political, and aesthetic concerns. In Third World countries, cinema is regarded as a compelling means of mass persuasion, cultural consolidation, and consciousness-raising. It tends to employ unusual production modes, independent of any existing studio system, and often "underground" or in collectives. And, in helping audiences to develop new ways of seeing and understanding their sociopolitical reality, it rejects prevailing cinematic aesthetics.[16] Italian neorealism was influential on the development of third world cinema because it used a limited mode of production to address the major social issues of postwar Italy. In emulation, certain governments, notably those of Cuba and India, sponsored filmmaking schools, controlled distribution, and forced the exhibition of nonfiction films.[17] The general tendency in third world countries was for filmmakers to use their cameras for similar purposes—to confront the reality of life around them and to use the power of cinema to awaken their people to a heightened awareness of this reality. In Latin America, especially, the new cinema was was known as a "militant" or "guerrilla" cinema.[18]

Since World War II, Third World cinema, in fulfilling its destiny, has been fostered by several factors: the growing international awareness of third world nations; state support for film schools and direct subsidies of production; revolution against colonialism and the emergence of more independent nations, especially in Latin America and Africa; widespread industrialization; and awareness of the role that film has played in these political, social, and economic developments. Inevitably, a large and lively body of aesthetic and political theory has emerged that is related to the special mission of Third World cinema. The writings of the Argentinian filmmakers Fernando Birri, Fernando Solanas, and Octavio Getino have been especially influential.

While there has been impressive quantity, quality, and stylistic diversity in the nonfiction filmmaking efforts in the developing countries with a market economy, significant obstacles—financial, practical, and ethical—have often impeded these achievements.[19] For example, funds for nonfiction filmmaking are often scarce in developing countries, thus outsiders rather than locals are apt to make the larger number of films. Furthermore, local audiences, still relatively unaccustomed to the cinematic art in general, tend to prefer native-made narrative films (which are often produced in the mode of Italian neorealist cinema) to nonfiction films about contemporary issues and problems. Moreover, the cinematic treatment of such issues and problems is often frustrated by government censorship. Indeed, filmmakers whose critical views do not please their governments have mysteriously disappeared or been jailed or exiled.

The history of the non-Western and Third World nonfiction film, yet to be written, must be presented outside the context of Western filmmaking. Such a study will need, first, to establish the complex political, social, artistic, and economic factors that shape non-western filmmaking; and, second, to emphasize, as Roy Armes has, "the role of Third World filmmakers in giving voice to peoples excluded from history and to ethnic minorities (or even majorities) normally denied expression. . . . ”[20] Within the scope of this study, it is possible to list only those films that have had a major influence on the overall development of third world cinema and that are available to Western audiences.

India

In postwar India, nonfiction filmmaking was a major means of expressing pride in Indian independence; in contrast to many underdeveloped countries, the nonfiction film was unusually prolific, chiefly because India's industrial base has been so much stronger.[21] Many young Indian filmmakers were trained in India by the German filmmaker Paul Zils (*Martila Dances of Malabar,* 1957), as well as in American film schools.[22] Although their early films focussed on Indian art and architecture, in recent years Indian nonfiction filmmakers have concentrated on more immediate socioeconomic issues, but government sponsorship and distribution, fraught with bureaucratic red tape, has hindered the further development of the independent Indian nonfiction film. Now, however, television, which has fostered nonfiction filmmaking in Europe and the United States, has begun to provide similar opportunities in India.

A major Indian nonfiction director is Vithalbhai K. Jhaveri, whose *Mahatma: Life of Gandhi, 1869–1948* (1968) is a five and one-half hour film that combines rare archival footage, still photographs, and drawings, as well as excellent Indian music; unfortunately, the poor archival recordings of Gandhi's voice weaken the film. Other important films include Fali Billimoria's *A Village in Travancore* (1957) and *The House that Ananda Built*—about a Bihari peasant family; S. Sukhdev's *An Indian Day* (1972), an impressionistic account of Indian life that was honored internationally; Mani Kaul's *Arrival* (1968)—an excellent, colorful study of life in Bombay, and *Mati Manas* (1985), about Indian potters; Saeed Mirza's *Slum Eviction* (1975); Kumar Shahani's *Fire in the Belly* (1975)—about drought and hunger; Shyam Benegal's *A Child of the Streets* (1967)—on vagrant and destitute children, *Nehru* (co-directed by Yuri Aldokhin, 1985), and *Satyajit Ray* (1985), a tribute to the great Indian filmmaker; Vinod Chopra's *Encounter with Faces;* and Ritwik Ghatak's *Where the Padma Flows* (1971).

East and Southeast Asia

In the Far East and Southeast Asia, as well as in Australia and the Pacific Islands, the nonfiction film developed more slowly than in India. From Japan came Nagisa Oshima's *Forgotten Imperial Army* (*Wasurerareta Kogun,* 1963), one of the few Japanese films to question the country's role in World War II; Noriaki Tsuchimoto's *Minimata* (1971); and S. Ogawa's *Peasants of the Second Fortress* (1971). From Vietnam came *On the Banks of the Ben-Hai River* (n.d.). In addition, there are many other films, mostly ethnographic or anthropological studies, that have been made about the peoples of various Far Eastern countries.

Latin America

The political turmoil and revolutionary climate in Latin America during the 1970s and 1980s provided, as it had in the Soviet Union in the 1920s (and perhaps in the

1990s), a fertile ground for the development of the nonfiction film. The result was that two of the most passionate political films ever made came out of Latin America: *The Battle of Chile* and *Hour of the Furnaces*. Patricio Guzman's *The Battle of Chile* (*La batalla de Chile*) is an account of the last year of democratic government in Chile before the 1973 military coup. Although Guzman's film is a masterpiece of political propaganda, *Hour of the Furnaces* (*La hora de los hornos,* Argentina, 1968), is the more important cinematically. This four-and-one-half hour film by Fernando Solanas and Octavio Getino vividly presents the Latin American struggle for freedom from neocolonialism and violence. As a compilation film of political liberation, it dynamically proclaims its message. Ideologically, it is a straightforward, Marxist account of history and contemporary culture that dramatically contrasts the leisurely life of the aristocracy with the grim reality of the people's everyday life. Cinematically, it is dynamic in its various styles, which include some sections made in a rapid, poster-like bluntness, some that use intertitles, motion picture footage, stills, narration, as well as ironic choral music, to denounce the imperialists from Great Britain and the United States (President Lyndon B. Johnson and the U.S. Alliance for Progress seem to be the arch enemies). *Hour of the Furnaces* is demanding on the viewer, for it is full of information, but the result is an unforgettable experience.

Other important Latin American films include the following, listed by country. Argentina: Raymundo Gleyzer's *It Happened in Hualfin* and *Mexico: The Frozen Revolution;* and Fernando Birri's *Throw Me a Dime* (*Tire-Die,* 1960), which clearly reflects the influence of Italian neorealism. Bolivia: Jorge Sanjinés's *The Courage of the People* (*El coraje del pueblo,* 1971) and *The Banners of the Dawn*

Hour of the Furnaces [*La hora de los hornos*] (Patricio Guzman, Argentina, 1968)

(*Las banderas del amanecer,* 1984). Colombia: Marta Rodriguez's and Jorge Silva's *The Brickmakers* (*Chircales,* 1968) and *Peasants* (*Campesinos,* 1976); G. Ignacio's *Los Gamines* (n.d.); Carlos Alvarez's *What is Democracy?* (*¿Qué es la democracia?,* 1971) and *The Sons of Underdevelopment* (*Los hijos del subdesarrollo,* 1975). El Salvador: the Cero a la Izquierda Film Collective's *Morazan* and *First Fruits* (*Los primos frutos,* both 1980); and Diego de la Texera's *El Salvador—The People Will Win* (*El Salvado—El pueblo vencéra,* 1980). Costa Rica: Ingo Niehaus's *Costa Rica, Banana Republic* (1976). Brazil: J. P. de Andrade's *Brasilia: City of Contradiction*; Leon Hirzsman's *Absolute Majority* (*Maioria absoluta,* 1964); and Arnaldo Jabor's *Public Opinion* (*Opiniao publica*). Cuba: Santiago Alvarez's *Now* (1965), *Hanoi: Tuesday, the 13th* (*Hanoi, martes trece,* 1967), *Always Until Victory* (*Hasta la victoria siempre,* 1967), *Laos: The Forgotten War* (*La guerra olvidada,* 1967), *The 79 Springs of Ho Chi Minh* (*Las 79 primaveras de Ho Chi Minh,* 1969), *The Tiger Leaps and Kills, But It Will Die . . . It Will Die* (*El tigre salto y mato, per morirá . . . morirá,* 1973); and O. Cortazer's *Por primera vez.* Mexico: Paul Leduc's *Reed: Insurgent Mexico* (*Reed: México insurgente,* 1973), *Ethnocide: Notes on Mesquital* (*Etnocido: notas sobre el mesquital,* 1976), and *Forbidden History of Pulgarito* (*Historias prohibitas del Pulgarito,* 1980). Uruguay: *Tupamaros* (1973), a film about the Uruguayan underground, directed by Swedish filmmaker Jan Lindquist.

The Middle East and Africa

There has been very litle nonfiction filmmaking of international importance in Iran, Turkey, or Egypt and the other Arab countries. However, three African films deserve mention: M. Traore's *Reous-takh* (Senegal, n.d.); Nana Mahomo's *Last Grave at Dimbaza* (South Africa, 1975); and *End of the Dialogue* (*Phela-ndaba* (South Africa, 1971)—an underground film about apartheid.

One Hundred Years of Nonfiction Film

In 1995, the nonfiction film will have ended its first century of development. This book has chronicled the stages and diversity of that development—actuality and factual films, documentary and propaganda films, cinéma vérité and direct cinema. The versatility and imaginative possibilities of the nonfiction film ensure that the genre will continue to stay alive and grow. While no two nonfiction filmmakers have ever agreed on a definition of the genre, most of them, would, in Vincent Canby's observation, "seem to share a compulsion to change things, to record history as it is happening or to call attention to some aspect of our lives that they believe deserves consideration."[1] That compulsion has ensured that the nonfiction film will thrive into the twenty-first century.

LEGACY OF THE 1980S

The 1980s brought a reaffirmation of the art and function of most genres of the Western nonfiction film: Griersonian social documentary, factual film, instructional film, direct cinema, journalistic reportage, even the personal film most closely associated with Flaherty. The social documentary, in particular, reclaimed its role as advocate—its Griersonian heritage—in shaping thought and discussion on the major issues of our time. Throughout the 1980s and into the 1990s, independent filmmakers around the world, in both industrialized and developing nations, continue to make serious statements about complex issues, to try to explain why social problems arise, and to offer suggestions for improvement.

The style of contemporary nonfiction films is as impressive as the content. Using state-of-the-art technology, artists are producing nonfiction films of the highest technical quality, creative statements that go far beyond what many audiences remember as the somber and fact-filled informational films of their classroom days. The hallmark of contemporary films is an intelligent questioning of things as they are, with little remaining of the illusory assumption, earlier fostered by cinéma vérité and direct cinema, that cinema can somehow see the truth more clearly than the naked human eye. The new documentary of the 1980s and 1990s respects the line between fiction and fact while it moves back and forth across it.

The evolving style of the nonfiction film has resulted in the gradual fading of the artificial distinctions that have traditionally separated fiction and nonfiction film. Filmmakers have consciously and deliberately defied the limitations of both genres, forcing them to overlap, to comment on each other, to coexist. This is not a movement toward the "semifictional documentary" or the "docudrama" (both of which are basically narrative genres based on real-life events), but rather (as the Maysles brothers did in *Grey Gardens*) the achievement, through editing, of a model that embodies the multiple ambiguities of reality. Influenced by direct cinema as well as by contemporary film theory, filmmakers today are concerned with reflexivity—with the film's ability to mirror itself as well as its world. According to Jay Ruby, the interest in reflexivity demonstrates "that films—all films, whether they are labeled fiction, documentary, or art—are created structured articulations of the filmmaker and not authentic truthful objective records."[2] As a result of this aspect of the complex, important, but often self-serving activity of contemporary film theory, both "film reality" and a viewer's perception of it are no longer taken for granted.

In order for this stylistic evolution to have occurred, theorists and critics have had to insist on an increased understanding of the limitations of the genre; audiences acquainted with film history and theory (especially students who have had some academic introduction to film) have had to be eager for cinematic experiences that transcended those limitations; and filmmakers have had to create a substantial body of work that embodies new ways of seeing and *re*-presenting reality. The continuing result of this hypothetical synergy between theorists, audiences, and filmmakers has been the further creative development of the nonfiction film—the evolution of a highly personal film distinguished by individual perception and expression. These films, like individual essays, are rich in style; they do not break rules: their creators either never learned the rules or deliberately chose to work outside potentially limiting circumstances (such as those, for example, that guided the British documentary film movement of the 1930s or the direct cinema movement of the 1960s). Today, nonfiction films explore not only facts, but also the way the camera (as well as the other elements of the cinematic process) records and interprets those facts to create its own reality. Sometimes, the nonfiction film of the 1980s shows an inevitable self-consciousness (in the sense that these films are self-reflexive); at other times, we are enabled to discover for ourselves that the boundaries between nonfiction and narrative film are arbitrary rather than fixed.

In the 1980s, the enormous growth in the quantity and quality of the international nonfiction film was influenced by the following circumstances that were external to the filmmakers' perception of their art, but extremely important to the production and distribution of their work and the reputation of the genre itself.

DEVELOPING TECHNOLOGIES

New technologies, especially video production, have now made nonfiction film production available to many persons who had not previously been able to make films; in that sense, this technology empowered a new generation of filmmakers with a diversity of voices. This lightweight equipment has effected a revolution comparable to that brought about by the filmmaking equipment developed in the early days of direct cinema and cinéma vérité.

FINANCING AND DISTRIBUTION

Nonfiction filmmakers have been further encouraged in their work by new sources of financing and distribution. Government agencies, such as the National Endowments for the Arts and the Humanities, as well as private foundations, have regularly made grants to filmmakers. Theatres such as New York's Film Forum and Public Theatre regularly feature nonfiction films, individually and in series or retrospective screenings. The public television stations are no longer alone in producing and exhibiting nonfiction film on television; they have been joined by other major producers and exhibitors, especially Home Box Office, the Discovery Channel, Arts & Entertainment, Showtime, and other cable channels that have devoted a significant portion of their budgets to the production of original nonfiction film. It goes without saying that there is significant audience interest in such programming, particularly among families, who also rent and buy nonfiction videocassettes at local stores. The most popular of these television programs are in the areas of science and technology, nature, history, human adventure, and world culture, with nature and world culture accounting for more than half of such programming.

Unfortunately, the dominant role of television in the production and distribution of nonfiction film has its drawbacks. However varied and successful its programming, television is seldom bold in its selection of subject matter and is particularly reluctant to underwrite committed films on social issues. As producer Arthur Barron writes, "To my knowledge, network television has never presented a film on the FBI, or the military-industrial complex, or on Congressional ethics, or on any number of other sacred cows."[3] Barron also observes that objective reportage remains the standard mode of nonfiction programming on television, with most programs made for the traditional purposes of informing and instructing the audience. While Barron acknowledges the advantages of this Griersonian influence, he laments the resultant lack of any substantial evidence of Flaherty's influence. In fact, as a public medium, television has generally valued journalistic objectivity above personal accounts or films of human revelation. Moreover, according to Barron, television producers prefer fact to feeling because they are reluctant to depict emotion, anger, and tenderness. There is, to be sure, more variety in the programming on public and cable television than on commercial television; but, overall, nonfiction programming on television is largely determined by commercial, rather than aesthetic, considerations.

FILM THEORY AND CRITICISM

Finally, the nonfiction film of the 1980s has been shaped by a growing awareness that it is a genre worthy of critical analysis. Recent years have seen an increase in the number of college-level courses and programs devoted to film history, theory, criticism, and production; more festivals devoted to nonfiction film; and more serious writing about nonfiction film (theory in the academic journals, and criticism in both the academic journals and popular publications). Much of the new theory goes beyond the concerns of the founding fathers—Vertov, Grierson, and Rotha—and reflects the influences of structuralism, post-structuralism, and deconstruction in such concerns as modes of representation, ethics, narrativity, and readership and audience.[4] Equally important, and perhaps even more influential on the theory and criticism of nonfiction film, has been feminist film theory. And, finally, many new books on nonfiction film and filmmakers have appeared, including histories of nonfiction film, anthologies of interviews and criticism, and specialized studies on such masters as Robert Flaherty, Dziga Vertov, John Grierson, Humphrey Jennings, Joris Ivens, Frederick Wiseman, as well as on such subjects as the British documentary film movement, the American leftist film, compilation film, newsreel, television documentary, direct cinema, feminist film, and third world film.

Almost one hundred years ago, Auguste and Louis Lumière established the nonfiction cinema believing that audiences would be interested in seeing films about each other, films that documented and illuminated their lives. From its beginnings in Paris, the nonfiction film was soon embraced in virtually every country of the world. In its subsequent history, it has played many roles and served many functions—factual film, documentary film, propaganda film, and direct cinema—and it has variously educated, enlightened, inspired, and sometimes outraged its audiences. Yet, in all of this diverse development, its primary functions have remained simple and steadfast: to record and interpret. In his foreword to the first edition of this book, Richard Dyer MacCann wrote that the mission of the nonfiction filmmaker "is to make complexity understood, to show that complex issues come from conflicting human needs and desires" (xiv). Its subject is human life, interpreted creatively. Thus, the nonfiction film is not a literal record of some event, a straightforward piece of argument, a twisted piece of propaganda, or an invented story. Rather, nonfiction film, like all film art, is a creative art; the nonfiction film, in John Grierson's term, is a "creative treatment of actuality."

Like most film efforts, the nonfiction film is the product of the collaborative efforts of many people. While some of the best nonfiction work has been done in groups, such as the British Documentary Movement, the genre cannot be easily identified with a place or time, as the narrative film can be identified with Hollywood or Pinewood or Cinecitta. To make nonfiction films, talented artists have worked together to produce something that integrates their individual visions of life and of truth. In this effort, the most distinguishing factor is a director with a strong, inquiring intelligence, one dedicated to a rational, critical, yet passionate examination of issues, events, and lives.

The nonfiction film can be informative, persuasive, useful, or all of these; but its true value lies in its insight into the human condition and its vision for improving it. As MacCann writes, the nonfiction film became "an ideal instrument for democratic communication, because it is so often concerned with measuring and valuing a present way of life by what it ought to be" (xiii). At the same time realistic and idealistic, the nonfiction film presents a paradox, a paradox that is resolved by its human focus. It is rooted in actuality and *re*-presents that reality, yet it is infused with a liberal idealism about life and an authentic sense of caring for the human condition. With these complementary purposes, the nonfiction film remains one of the most compelling and beneficial of cinematic forms.

Notes

PREFACE

1. This paraphrases slightly what my colleague and friend, the late Gerald Mast, wrote in the foreword to his *Film/Cinema/Movie: A Theory of Experience* (New York: Harper & Row, 1977).

1. REALITY PERCEIVED AND RECORDED

1. Charles Simond [Adolphe van Cleemputte, *pseud.*], *La Vie Parisienne au XIXè Siècle: Tome III, 1870–1900* (Paris: Librairie Plon, 1901).

2. Quoted in Jay Leyda, *Kino: A History of the Russian and Soviet Film*, 3rd ed. (Princeton: Princeton University Press, 1983), 407–08. The nature of Gorky's overall remarks indicates that he did not appreciate the importance of the new invention and found its presentation in a music hall to encourage vice, but his thoughts on its future are prophetic.

3. Dai Vaughan, "Let there be Lumière," *Sight and Sound* 50.2 (Spring 1981): 127.

4. "Monet, Lumière, and Cinematic Time," *Journal of Aesthetics and Art Criticism* 36.4 (Summer 1978): 441–47.

5. Robert Rosenblum and H. W. Janson, *19th-Century Art* (New York: Abrams, 1984), 254. The railroad was also a familiar subject in the works of such nineteenth-century photographers as Alexander Gardner, Andrew Russell, and James Mudd, as well as in early nonfiction films (see chap. 2).

6. Among the most popular early Edison films were those of celebrated railway trains of the day: see Raymond Fielding, *The American Newsreel: 1911–1967* (Norman: University of Oklahoma Press, 1972), 25.

7. *Cinema and Technology: Image, Sound, Colour* (Bloomington: Indiana University Press, 1985), 50.

8. Charles Dupêchez, *Histoire de l'Opéra de Paris: Un Siècle au Palais Garnier 1875–1980* (Paris: Librairie Académique Perrin, 1984).

9. Florian Bruyas, *Histoire de l'Opérette en France 1855–1965* (Lyons: Emmanuel Vitte, 1974).

10. The idea of the photograph as a memory of the past has been set forth by various writers, including Susan Sontag, *On Photography* (New York: Farrar, 1977); John Berger, "Ways of Remembering," *Camerawork* 10 (July 1978); and Roland Barthes, *Camera Lucida: Reflections on Photography* (New York: Hill, 1981). See also Neale's discussion, chap. 1.

11. See Neale, 7–9; and Gerald Mast, *Film/Cinema/Movie: A Theory of Experience* (New York: Harper, 1977), esp. chaps. 1–3.

12. Persistence of vision is an optical illusion, based on the delay between what the eye perceives and the brain interprets, that makes motion pictures possible. In recent years, the traditional explanation of this phenomenon has been challenged; for a concise discussion, see Neale, 29–31. See also Joseph Anderson and Barbara Fisher, "The Myth of Persistence of Vision," *Journal of the University Film Association* 30.4 (Fall 1978): 3–8; see also the special double issue of *Journal of the University Film Association* on "Cinevideo and Psychology" 32.1–2 (Winter and Spring 1980).

13. In *A Short History of the Movies*, Gerald Mast writes:

In Jean-Luc Godard's *Les Carabiniers*—Godard packs his films with historical tidbits—a farm boy watches his first movie, which is also a train arriving at a
station, using the same camera angle as the Lumières'. The boy shrieks and ducks,
just as the first movie audiences did in the café theatre. (21)

14. See C. W. Ceram's illustrated account of the "prehistory" of cinema: *Archaeology of
the Cinema* (London: Thames and Hudson, 1965), 9–73; and Georges Sadoul, *Histoire
générale du cinéma*, 6 vols. (Paris: Denoël, 1948–75), esp. vol. 1.

15. Other devices included Dubosq's Bioscope or Stéréofantascope, Anshutz's
Tachyscope, Reynaud's Praxinoscope, DuMont's Omniscope, Sellers's Kinematoscope,
Beal's Choreutoscope, and Cook and Bonnelli's Photobioscope; see Neale, 31–32.

16. Neale, 23–24.

17. Mast, 4th ed., 11.

18. Zola quoted in Susan Sontag, *On Photography* (New York: Farrar, 1977), 87.

19. "Photography/Cinematography," *Before Hollywood* (New York: American Federation of Arts, 1986), 74–75.

20. See Peter Galassi, *Before Photography: Painting and the Invention of Photography*
(New York: Museum of Modern Art, 1981), 12.

21. Among other achievements, he also originated the use of the words "positive" and
"negative" to describe the two principal stages in the production of a photographic image.

22. *The History of Photography*, rev. ed. (New York: Museum of Modern Art, 1982),
91. See also John Szarkowski, *Photography Until Now* (New York: Museum of Modern Art,
1989).

23. The role of technology in the development of American still photography is documented in Reese V. Jenkins, *Images and Enterprise* (Baltimore: Johns Hopkins Press, 1975).

24. See Barnouw, 4, for Georges Demeny's special application of Marey's technology of
series photography to teach lipreading to the deaf.

25. For an account of Muybridge's life and experiments, see Robert Bartlett Haas,
Muybridge: Man in Motion (Berkeley: University of California Press, 1976), esp. pp. 45–49
and 109–16; see also K. MacDonnell, *Eadweard Muybridge: The Man Who Invented the
Moving Picture* (Boston: Little, Brown, 1972) and A. V. Mozley et al., *Eadweard Muybridge:
The Stanford Years, 1872–1882* (Stanford: Stanford University Art Department, 1972).

26. *Documentary: A History of the Non-Fiction Film* (New York: Oxford University
Press, 1974), 3.

27. The American realist painter Thomas Eakins was also experimenting with series
photography; according to Newhall (121), Eakins, with Muybridge's assistance, devised a
camera similar to Marey's.

28. See A. R. Fulton, "The Machine." *The American Film Industry*, ed. Tino Balio.
(Madison: University of Wisconsin Press, 1976), 19–32. See also *A Technological History of
Motion Pictures and Television*, ed. Raymond Fielding (Berkeley: University of California
Press, 1967). According to David A. Cook, *A History of Narrative Film* (New York: Norton,
1981), "technological innovation necessarily precedes the aesthetic" (5) in the development
of the narrative cinema.

29. *Film Before Griffith*, ed. John L. Fell (Berkeley: University of California Press, 1983),
9. Acknowledging that the Skladanowsky brothers preceded the Lumière brothers by one
month by projecting motion pictures in Berlin, George C. Pratt, agreeing with Georges
Sadoul, nonetheless concludes that "in terms of repercussion, Lumière [sic] stands unchal-
lenged"; see "Firsting the Firsts," *"Image" on the Art and Evolution of the Film*, ed. Marshall
Deutelbaum (New York: Dover, 1979), 20.

30. See Gordon Hendricks, *The Edison Motion Picture Myth* (Berkeley: University of
California Press, 1961); *Thomas Eakins: His Photographic Works* (Philadelphia: Pennsylvania
Academy of the Fine Arts, 1969); W. K. L. Dickson and Antonia Dickson, *History of the
Kinetograph, Kinetoscope, and Kinetophotograph* (New York: Albert Bunn, 1895; reprinted,

New York: Arno Press, 1970). A brief account of Dickson's role in this development can be found in Cook, 5–7.

31. See Gordon Hendricks, "The History of the Kinetoscope," *The American Film Industry*, ed. Tino Balio (Madison: University of Wisconsin Press, 1976), 33–45.

32. Fritz Novotny, *Painting and Sculpture in Europe, 1780 to 1880* (Baltimore: Penguin, 1960), 1.

33. "Monet, Lumière, and Cinematic Time," *Journal of Aesthetics and Art Criticism* 36.4 (Summer 1978): 441–47.

34. Robert Rosenblum and H. W. Janson, *19th-Century Art* (New York: Abrams, 1984), 219.

35. In the United States, the brutality of the Civil War was recorded in photographs by Mathew Brady and his associates, Alexander Gardner, Timothy H. O'Sullivan, and George N. Barnard.

36. Gorky quoted in Leyda, *Kino: A History of the Russian and Soviet Film*, 3rd ed. (Princeton: Princeton University Press, 1983), 407.

37. Mimesis: *The Representation of Reality in Western Literature* (New York: Anchor, 1957), 489.

2. THE FIRST FILMS

1. *The American Newsreel: 1911–1967* (Norman: University of Oklahoma Press, 1972), 4. I am indebted to Fielding's excellent study for most of the information and titles in this section.

2. Fielding, 11. The distinguished point here is which audience was the first to *pay* for the privilege of seeing motion pictures. While the Lumières were the *first* to project films on March 22, 1895, it was not until December 28, 1895, that they showed them to a *paying* audience.

3. For a study of the first American audiences, see Garth Jowett, "The First Motion Picture Audiences," *Film Before Griffith*, ed. John L. Fell (Berkeley: University of California Press, 1983), 196–206.

4. See Francis Doublier, "Reminiscences of an Early Motion Picture Operator," *"Image" on the Art and Evolution of the Film*, ed. Marshall Deutelbaum (New York: Dover, 1979), 23.

5. Fielding comments that Edison copyrighted more than 250 news-film titles between 1896 and 1900 but that neither Biograph nor Vitagraph appears to have copyrighted a single film during that same period: "Whether this omission should be taken as a reflection of their contempt for the primitive copyright protection which they frequently and successfully defied, a disregard for the value of their own product, or simply a lack of fear of infringement is not clear" (27–28).

6. See Fielding, 9–16.

7. André Bazin says that "the cinema owes virtually nothing to the scientific spirit," in "The Myth of Total Cinema," *What Is Cinema?* (Berkeley: University of California Press, 1967), 17.

8. As Jean-Luc Godard joked in *La Chinoise*, the Lumière films now appear more fantastic than Méliès's "documentaries."

9. "French Cinema: Origins," *Cinema: A Critical Dictionary*, ed. Richard Roud, vol. 1 (New York: Viking, 1980), 394.

10. "Introduction," *Rediscovering French Film*, ed. Mary Lea Bandy (New York: Museum of Modern Art, 1983), 17.

11. "The Lumière Organization and 'Documentary Realism,'" *Film Before Griffith*, ed. John L. Fell (Berkeley: University of California Press, 1983), 159.

12. There was also a younger brother, Edouard.

13. Barnouw, 7.

14. Georges Sadoul, "Louis Lumière: The Last Interview," *Rediscovering French Film*, ed. Mary Lea Bandy (New York: Museum of Modern Art, 1983), 39. There is still very little scholarship in English on the Lumières' work. See Sadoul, *Louis Lumière* (Paris: Seghers, 1964) and Jacques Deslandes's *Histoire Comparée Du Cinéma*, 5 vols. (Tournai, Belg.: Casterman, 1966).

15. "Louis Lumière: The Last Interview," 40.

16. For a reminder of the variable speed by which silent films were projected, see Kevin Brownlow, "Silent Film: What Was the Right Speed?" *Sight and Sound* 49.3 (Summer 1980): 164–67.

17. This was not a paying audience.

18. Barnouw, 9.

19. "The Course of Realism," *Grierson on Documentary*, ed. Forsyth Hardy (London: Faber, 1966), 199; see also Michael J. Arlen, "The Air: on the Trail of a 'Fine Careless Rapture,'" *The New Yorker* (10 Mar. 1980): 73–79.

20. Dai Vaughan, "Let There Be Lumière," *Sight and Sound* 50.2 (Spring 1981): 126.

21. Marshall Deutelbaum, "Structural Patterning in the Lumière Films," *Wide Angle* 3.1 (1979): 30–31. See the entire article for an excellent close analysis of many of the films.

22. For an analysis of this film, see Dai Vaughan, "Let There Be Lumière," *Sight and Sound* 50.2 (Spring 1981): 126–27.

23. Raymond Fielding's translation of the title of this film suggests that the workers are leaving for lunch; see *The American Newsreel: 1911–1967* (Norman: University of Oklahoma Press, 1972), 4.

24. Lumière himself explains the length: "These films were all 17 meters long and it took about a minute to show them. This length of 17 meters may seem odd, but it was merely governed by the capacity of the spool-boxes holding the negative film when the pictures were taken." See "Louis Lumière: The Last Interview," 41. Barnouw writes that "at the turn of the century a one-reel film was one to two minutes long; five years later it was five to ten minutes long" (21).

25. Allen says (148) that the Lumières opened in May 1896 at Keith's Union Square Theatre; the prefatory titles of early Lumière films circulated by the Museum of Modern Art say that the Eden Musée was another theatre showing them; in *Tours de Manivelle* (Paris: Editions Bernard Grasset, 1933), Félix Mesguich says that he made the first presentation on 18 June at Koster and Bial's.

26. Reprinted in Jay Leyda, *Kino: A History of the Russian and Soviet Film*, 3rd ed. (Princeton: Princeton University Press, 1983), 407.

27. See Barnouw, 11–30; see Leyda, *Kino*, 405–06, for a list of the first nonfiction films made in Russia by Lumière, Pathé, and Alexander Drankov.

28. For the reproduction of a program of Lumière films shown to Queen Victoria, see Ceram, *Archaeology of the Cinema*, fig. 228.

29. Barnouw, 13.

30. Alan Williams also suggests that the subjects of the films were influenced by the tradition of French still photography, of which the elder Lumière was a master, and proposes categorizing them into three large groups: "(1) work and related activities (*Tearing Down a Wall*, but also *Watering the Gardener* and even in a sense *Feeding the Baby*); (2) ritual/ceremony (the countless military or governmental displays, but also *The Sack Race* and other 'happy worker' films, as well as the early film of debarking congress members); and (3) travel, most frequently with emphasis on physical transport (*Gondola Party, Arrival of a Train,* etc.) There would be other shorter lived (for the Lumières) groupings, such as 'family portraits,' perhaps a subcategory of ceremonials" (155).

31. Neil Harris, "A Subversive Form," *Before Hollywood* (New York: American Federation of Arts, 1986), 46.

32. "Vitascope/Cinematographe: Initial Patterns of American Film Industrial Practice," *Film Before Griffith*, ed. John Fell (Berkeley: University of California Press, 1983), 144. I am

indebted to Allen's excellent essay for this and other information on the Lumières' world-wide success, particularly in the United States.

33. "Louis Lumière: The Last Interview," 40.

34. Francis Doublier, "Reminiscences of an Early Motion-Picture Operator," *"Image" on the Art and Evolution of the Film*, ed. Marshall Deutelbaum (New York: Dover Publications, 1979), 23.

35. Gordon Hendricks, "The Kinetoscope: Fall Motion Picture Production," *Film Before Griffith*, ed. John L. Fell (Berkeley: University of California Press, 1983), 13–21.

36. For accounts of early film production and exhibition in Canada, Hungary, and Australia, respectively, see Peter Morris, "Images of Canada"; István Nemeskurty, "In the Beginning, 1896–1911"; and Eric Reade, "Australian Silent Films, 1904–1907: The Features Begin." These accounts are in *Film Before Griffith*, ed. John L. Fell (Berkeley: University of California Press, 1983); this valuable anthology contains other essays on early film.

37. Kevin Brownlow, *The Parade's Gone By* (Berkeley: University of California Press, 1968), 2.

38. Williams, 157–58.

39. Barnouw, 19.

40. Barnouw, 19–21. See also Jay Leyda, *Dianying/Electric Shadows: An Account of Films and the Film Audience in China* (Cambridge: MIT Press, 1972). The Lumière brothers may also have foreseen the larger factors that contributed to the general decline of the nonfiction film in the years before World War I.

41. Barnouw, 19.

42. Barnouw, 25.

43. *The History of the British Film, 1906–1914* (London: British Film Institute and British Film Academy, 1948), 147; see Low, chap. 4, for a discussion of the prewar British factual film.

44. See *Before Hollywood*, 89–136, for details on these films.

45. Raymond Fielding, "Hale's Tours: Ultrarealism in the Pre-1910 Motion Picture," *Film Before Griffith*, ed. John L. Fell (Berkeley: University of California Press, 1983), 118–19.

46. Fielding, 122.

47. Fielding, 123.

48. For an important study of film exhibition and audiences in Manhattan in the first decade of the twentieth century, see Robert C. Allen, "Motion Picture Exhibition in Manhattan, 1906–1912: Beyond the Nickelodeon," *Film Before Griffith*, ed. John L. Fell (Berkeley: University of California Press, 1983), 162–75. For an insight into film exhibition and American audiences outside of major cities, see Edward Lowry, "Edwin J. Hadley: Traveling Film Exhibitor," *Film Before Griffith*, ed. John L. Fell (Berkeley: University of California Press, 1983), 131–43.

49. See Robert C. Allen, "Motion Picture Exhibition in Manhattan, 1906–1912: Beyond the Nickelodeon," 162–75; and Garth S. Jowett, "The First Film Audiences," 196–206, *Film Before Griffith*, ed. John L. Fell (Berkeley: University of California Press, 1983).

50. See Barnouw, 25–26.

51. See Fielding, *The American Newsreel: 1911–1967*, 31.

52. "The American Vitagraph, 1897–1901: Survival and Success in a Competitive Industry," *Film Before Griffith*, ed. John L. Fell (Berkeley: University of California Press, 1983), 32.

53. Strebel, "Primitive Propaganda," 47.

54. Barnouw, 24.

55. Smith, quoted in Fielding, 31–32; see also 32n.

56. Strebel, "Primitive Propaganda," 45.

57. See his diary, *Biograph in Battle* (1901).

58. Albert E. Smith and J. Stuart Blackton, who made *Tearing Down the Spanish Flag*, one of the first war films, provide a fine account of how they recreated the Battle of

Santiago Bay in their New York studio for *Fighting with Our Boys in Cuba*; see Fielding, 32–33.

59. Strebel, "Primitive Propaganda," 45. For a dissenting opinion, see the remarks of Arthur Krows quoted in Fielding, 33.

60. Elizabeth Grottle Strebel, "Primitive Propaganda: The Boer War Films," *Sight and Sound* 46.1 (Winter 1976–77): 45; and "Imperialist Iconography of Anglo-Boer War Film Footage," *Film Before Griffith*, ed. John Fell (Berkeley: University of California Press, 1983), 264–71.

61. See Fielding, 110–15.

62. Kevin Brownlow, *The War, The West, and the Wilderness* (New York: Knopf, 1979), 4–5.

63. See Leyda, 92–93; and Fielding, 125–26.

64. *The War, The West, and The Wilderness*, 4.

65. Titles and information in this section were compiled from various sources, including Isenberg; Brownlow; Craig W. Campbell, *Reel America and World War I* (Jefferson, N.C.: McFarland, 1985), esp. pp. 224–39; Jack Spears, "World War I on the Screen," *Films in Review* (May 1966): 274–92 and (June–July 1966): 347–65; Rachel Low, *The History of the British Film: 1914–1918* (London: British Film Institute and British Film Academy, 1948); and *The National Film Archive Catalogue, Part I, Silent News Films 1895–1933* and *The National Film Archive Catalogue, Part II, Silent Non-Fiction Films 1895–1934* (London: British Film Institute, 1965).

66. See Fielding, 121, for a description of this innovative camera.

67. "World War I on the Screen," *Films in Review* (May 1966), 292; this article is continued in *Films in Review* (June–July 1966), 347–65.

68. Much of the information here on propaganda derives from M. L. Sanders and Philip M. Taylor, *British Propaganda During the First World War, 1914–18* (London: Macmillan, 1982).

69. *The War, The West, and The Wilderness*, 47.

70. Although Low lists *Munitions Makers*, it is not listed in *The National Film Archive Catalogue, Part II, Silent Non-Fiction Films 1895–1934* (London, 1960), which instead provides a notation of an untitled film, "Women's Munitions Work" (1917), produced by the Ministry of Munitions. Likewise, Low lists *The Destruction of a Zeppelin*, which *The National Film Archive Catalogue, Part I, Silent News Films 1895–1933* (London, 1965) does not list, but instead lists two films entitled *Zeppelin Destroyed*, both produced by Topical Budget; one was dated 4 Sept. 1916, the other 26 Mar. 1917.

71. Brownlow points out that *The Battle of the Somme* (1916) deeply shocked British audiences, who still had little conception of modern warfare, but that Americans were not so moved by it; see *The War, The West, and The Wilderness*, 52.

72. See Low, *The History of the British Film, 1914–1918*, 155ff, for a discussion of many of these films.

73. The following material is based on Rachel Low, *The History of the British Film, 1914–1918* (London: Allen and Unwin, 1950), pp. 148ff. Low frequently omits dates.

74. Although Low lists *The Ribemont Gas School, With the South African Forces*, and *Woolwich Arsenal*, they are not listed in *The National Film Archive Catalogue, I*, which lists films that seem similar: an untitled film listed as "Gas Attack Exercises" (produced by Pathé, c. 1916); *With Botha in South Africa: Bridge Building by South African Engineers* (produced by Gaumont, 31 May 1915); and *The One-Man Strike: 12,000 Woolwich Arsenal Employees Cease Work* (produced by Pathé, 3 July 1914) and *8,000 Men on Strike at Woolwich Arsenal: Scenes in Beresford Square* (produced by Topical Budget, 6 July 1914).

75. Again, there are discrepancies between the listings in Low and in *The National Film Archive Catalogue, I*. Low lists *Palestine, With the Australians in Palestine, The British Occupation of Gaza, The Advance in Palestine, 23rd–27th September 1918, With the Forces on the Palestine Front, The Occupation of Es Salt on May 16th, 1917, With the Forces in Mesopotamia*, and *The New Crusaders. The National Film Archive Catalogue* lists only one

film about Palestine in World War I: *Freed from Turkish Bondage: Mosque and Picturesque Scenes in Palestine Now Occupied by the British* (prod. by Topical Budget, 8 Apr. 1918). There are no relevant films listed for the date of 16 May 1917.

76. *The National Film Archive Catalogue, I* does not list *The King Visits His Armies in the Great Advance* or *The King's Visit to the Fleet*, but there is a film titled *Official Film: Recording Historic Incidents in His Majesty's Visit to His Grand Fleet* (no producer, listed 23 July 1918). Similarly, *The Royal Visit to the Battlefields of France* is not listed, but there is a film titled *His Majesty at the Front: King George Has Gone to France to Visit the "Contemptible Little Army"* (produced by Pathé, c. 1–5 Dec. 1914).

77. *Our Naval Air Power, The Way of a Ship on the Sea*, and *The Empire's Shield* are not listed in *The National Film Archive Catalogue, I*. However, *The Way of a Ship on the Sea* may be Low's title for similar untitled footage (c. 1918) held by the Archive.

78. Ludendorff quoted in *The War, The West, and The Wilderness*, 85.

79. Isenberg, 71ff; see also Richard Dyer MacCann, *The People's Films: A Political History of U.S. Government Motion Pictures* (New York: Hastings, 1973), 120–23; James R. Mock and Cedric Larson, *Words That Won the War: The Story of the Committee on Public Information, 1917–1919* (Princeton: Princeton University Press, 1939); George Creel, *How We Advertised America* (New York: Harper, 1920) and *Complete Report of the Chairman of the Committee on Public Information, 1917–1919* (Washington: Government Printing Office, 1920); and Larry Wayne Ward, "The Motion Picture Goes to War: A Political History of the U.S. Government's Film Effort in the World War, 1914–1918," diss. University of Iowa, 1981.

80. Fielding, 122.

81. Michael T. Isenberg, *War On Film: The American Cinema and World War I, 1914–1941* (London: Associated University Presses, 1981), 5.

82. *The War, The West, and The Wilderness*, 112–13.

83. *The War, The West, and The Wilderness*, 112.

84. See Barnouw, 114–15.

85. *The War, The West, and The Wilderness*, 131.

86. Isenberg, 73, reports this film as lost, but Brownlow, 570, lists it in the National Archives, Washington, D.C.; see also Campbell, 237.

87. Campbell, 238, lists this title as *If Your Soldier's Hit*.

88. Films about World War I that were released after the war include *The Price of Peace* (1919) and *Hiding in Holland* (1919), a film that makes fun of the Dutch Crown Prince on holiday.

89. Isenberg, 89.

90. Barnouw (29–30) says that by this time the basic roles of the nonfiction filmmaker had been established as promoter, reporter, propagandist, genre painter, travel lecturer, ethnographer, popular educator, and war reporter.

3. EXPLORATION, ROMANTICISM, AND THE WESTERN AVANT-GARDE

1. *Documentary Film* (New York: Hastings House, 1968), 79.

2. For further information on Holmes, see Genoa Caldwell, ed., *The Man Who Photographed the World: Burton Holmes, 1886–1938* (New York: Abrams, 1977); and Brownlow, 418–20.

3. Karl Baedeker was the publisher of a very reliable and popular series of guidebooks. Brownlow (xv–xvi) observes that it was not a filmmaker, but a former president of the United States, Theodore Roosevelt, who had the greatest impact on the development of the factual film and on the creation of a market for it.

4. Brownlow, 405–06. For information on the Kearton films, see *The Theodore Roose-*

velt Association Film Collection (Washington, D.C.: Library of Congress, 1986), 6–7, 126–28, 137, 152.

5. For further information on many of these early factual filmmakers, see Brownlow, chap. 3.

6. Barnouw, 410.

7. Brownlow (403) also mentions *Wild Heart of Africa*, the presumably lost record of the Walker-Arbuthnot expedition.

8. See George Pratt, "Osa and Martin Johnson: World Travellers in Africa," *Image* 22.2 (June 1979): 21–30.

9. See Brownlow, 425–33.

10. See Brownlow, 243.

11. Brownlow, 223.

12. See *Native Americans on Film and Video*, ed. Elizabeth Weatherford (New York: Museum of the American Indian, 1981).

13. See Brownlow, 338. Teri McLuhan's *The Shadow Catcher* (1974) is a film about Curtis.

14. Brownlow (406n and 337) cites two films on similar subjects that predated Flaherty's first film: William V. Mong's *The Way of an Eskimo* (1911) and John E. Maple's *Before the White Man Came* (1920).

15. See Richard Barsam, *The Vision of Robert Flaherty: The Artist as Myth and Filmmaker* (Bloomington: Indiana University Press, 1988).

16. During the filming, Flaherty was very much concerned with the safety of his cast, for his reenactment of the shark hunt placed great responsibility on his shoulders. See Pat Mullen, *Man of Aran* (Cambridge: MIT Press, 1970), 99–118. Another treatment of a similar narrative problem can be found in Luchino Visconti's film *La Terra Trema* (1948).

17. Grierson observes that there were both positive and negative attributes to this neo-Rousseauism (*Grierson on Documentary* 148).

18. Flaherty, *My Eskimo Friends*, 126; see also Rotha, ed. Ruby, 32ff.

19. Edmund Carpenter, *Eskimo* (Toronto: Toronto University Press, 1959).

20. For an account of Flaherty's work with the cast and shooting the storm sequence, see Frances Flaherty, "How *Man of Aran* Came into Being," *Film News*, 13.3 (1953): 4–6. See also Mullen, 188–99.

21. In *Robert Flaherty: A Guide to References and Resources* (Boston: Hall, 1978), William T. Murphy writes:

> The Flahertys had seen two persons tattooed previously. Although tattooing was officially discouraged, others have said that the practice was widespread. The Flaherty's believed it was one of those aspects of Samoan culture that was going to disappear, and so they would capture it on film. (15)

22. Flaherty assembled the footage in *Nanook* with the assistance of Charles Gelb, a technician otherwise inexperienced with film editing.

23. Brownlow, 482. See Calder-Marshall, 108–09, for the source of some of the confusion over Flaherty's use of panchromatic stock, which is repeated in my first edition of *Nonfiction Film: A Critical History*, 136, as well as in Murphy, 13–14 and in Rotha, *Robert J. Flaherty: A Biography*, ed. Ruby, 62ff.

24. See Calder-Marshall, 157–63; see also Hugh Gray, "Father of the American Documentary," 204–05.

25. Stephen Mamber suggests that Flaherty influenced the development of direct cinema; see his *Cinema Verite in America: Studies in Uncontrolled Documentary* (Cambridge: MIT Press, 1974), 9–14.

26. See Richard Barsam, "American Direct Cinema: The *Re*-presentation of Reality." *Persistence of Vision* 3–4 (Summer 1986), 131–56.

27. See Brownlow, 515–40.

28. See Brownlow, 515–29; and Merian C. Cooper, *Grass* (New York: Putnam's).

29. A new version of *Chang*, with a score by Bruce Gaston, was released in 1990.

30. *Alexander Dovzhenko: The Poet as Filmmaker, Selected Writings*, ed. and trans. by Marco Carynnyk (Cambridge: MIT Press, 1973), xxxviii.

31. Jay Leyda, *Kino: A History of the Russian and Soviet Film* (Princeton: Princeton University Press, 1983), 275.

32. Arthur Knight, "A Short History of Art Films," *Films on Art*, ed. William McK. Chapman (New York: American Federation of Arts, 1952), 8.

33. Alexander Hammid was formerly known as Alexander Hackenschmied.

34. Annette Michelson says that *Moscow* "seems to have influenced" both Ruttmann's film and Vertov's *The Man with the Movie Camera*; see *Kino-Eye: The Writings of Dziga Vertov*, ed. Annette Michelson (Berkeley: University of California Press, 1984), xxiv.

35. William Alexander says that the film was released as *New York the Magnificent* at the theater owner's insistence; see *Film on the Left: American Documentary Film from 1931 to 1942* (Princeton: Princeton University Press, 1981), 69; see also Scott Hammen, "Sheeler and Strand's *Manhatta*: A Neglected Masterpiece," *Afterimage* 6.6 (Jan. 1979): 6–7.

36. See Edgardo Cozarinsky, "Foreign Filmmakers in France," *Rediscovering French Film*, ed. Mary Lea Bandy (New York: Museum of Modern Art, 1983), 136–40. For further information on Cavalcanti, see Rodriguez Monegal, "Alberto Cavalcanti: His Career," *Nonfiction Film Theory and Criticism*, ed. Richard Barsam (New York: Dutton, 1976), 239–49; Claude Beylie, et al., "Alberto Cavalcanti," *Ecran* 30 (Nov. 1974): 49–59; and Wolfgang Klaue, *Alberto Cavalcanti* (Berlin: Staatlichen Filmarchiv der DDR, 1962).

37. "Style and Medium in the Motion Pictures," *Film Theory and Criticism*, ed. Gerald Mast and Marshall Cohen, 2nd ed. (New York: Oxford University Press, 1979), 246.

38. Vertov called it "absurd" to compare Ruttmann's *Berlin: Symphony of a Great City* with his *The Man with the Movie Camera*, since he believed Ruttmann's film to be conventional, not avant-garde; his disagreement notwithstanding, the film student will see in Ruttmann's work a genuine cinematic innovativeness and many similarities between the two films; see Vlada Petric, *Constructivism in Film: "The Man with the Movie Camera," A Cinematic Analysis* (Cambridge: Cambridge University Press, 1987), 79.

39. Mayer's name, synonymous with the German style of kammerspiel (literally, "intimate theatre" or "instinct" film) that superseded German expressionism, wrote some of the great films of the German silent period, including Robert Wiene's *The Cabinet of Dr. Caligari* and F. W. Murnau's *The Last Laugh*. Freund was responsible for the cinematography of many distinguished films of the German silent period, including Murnau's *The Last Man* (1924), Lang's *Metropolis* (1926), and E. A. Dupont's *Variety* (1925); his Hollywood films include Murnau's *Sunrise* (1927), Rouben Mamoulian's *Dr. Jekyll and Mr. Hyde* (1932), Tod Browning's *Dracula* (1931), and George Cukor's *Camille* (1935).

40. According to David Cook, he "edited the film to parallel the rhythms of a score by the German Marxist composer Edmund Meisel, whose stirring revolutionary music for Eisenstein's *Potemkin* helped to get that film banned in Germany" (131). The film may originally have been shown with sound accompaniment. See J. Kolaja and A. W. Foster, "Berlin: The Symphony of a Great City as a Theme of Visual Rhythm," *Journal of Aesthetics and Art Criticism* 23.3 (Spring 1965): 353–58.

41. See Barnouw, 80–81.

42. Barnouw (111) says that Ruttmann was reported to have died while making a film during World War II.

4. THE BEGINNINGS OF THE DOCUMENTARY FILM

1. See Jay Leyda, *Kino: A History of The Russian and Soviet Film*, 3rd ed. (Princeton: Princeton University Press, 1983). See also Michael J. Stoil, *Balkan Cinema: Evolution after*

the Revolution (Ann Arbor, MI: UMI Research Press, 1979) and *Cinema in Revolution: The Heroic Era of the Soviet Film*, ed. Luda and Jean Schnitzer and Marcel Martin (New York: Da Capo, 1973).

2. "Dziga Vertov: An Introduction," *Film Comment* 8.1 (Spring 1972): 38.

3. Sergei Eisenstein, *Film Essays and a Lecture*, ed. Jay Leyda (New York: Praeger, 1970), 25.

4. For a comparison of Vertov to Flaherty, see Seth Feldman, *Dziga Vertov: A Guide to References and Resources* (Boston: Hall, 1979), 32–33.

5. See Vlada Petric, *Constructivism in Film: "The Man With the Movie Camera," A Cinematic Analysis* (Cambridge: Cambridge University Press, 1987), viii. I am indebted to this superb study for much of my understanding of Vertov's life and work.

6. See Feldman, 9 and 38.

7. Grierson on Documentary, 128; see also 126–29.

8. *Documentary Film*, 90.

9. *Documentary: A History of the Non-Fiction Film*, 51–66.

10. *Theory of Film: The Redemption of Physical Reality* (New York: Oxford, 1960), 65.

11. "Introduction," *Kino-Eye: The Writings of Dziga Vertov*, ed. and with an introduction by Annette Michelson (Berkeley: University of California Press, 1984), xix.

12. For an account of Vertov's influence, see Petric, viii.

13. Boris Kaufman was an acclaimed cinematographer, who shot *A propos de Nice* (1929), *Taris* (1931), *Zéro de conduite* (1933), and *L'Atalante* (1933) for Jean Vigo before emigrating for the United States, where he worked with various American directors, including Elia Kazan and Sidney Lumet. Mikhail Kaufman, who began as Vertov's cinematographer, later produced documentaries in both the Soviet Union and the United States. He was born in Bialystok, which belonged to the Russian empire until 1918, and which now is part of Poland. As a youth, he studied piano, violin, and literature, reading widely in the works of American and British authors. In 1915, the Kaufman family moved from Bialystok to Moscow, where young Denis not only continued his studies of music but also began to write verse and science fiction. In 1916–17, in St. Petersburg (Petrograd), Vertov studied medicine and psychology at the Psychoneurological Institute, with a special interest in human visual and aural perception.

14. *Dziga* is a Ukrainian word meaning "spinning top" or "restless, fidgety, bustling person;" Vertov is derived from a Russian word meaning "to turn, spin, rotate, or fidget." Vlada Petric says that the closest English translation would be "Spinning Top That is Turning" (222). The pseudonym suggests Denis Kaufman's energetic personality, the whirring and turning of motion picture technology, the concern of Futurism and Constructivism with such technology, and the filmmaker's profession, the tireless activity of which is so adroitly portrayed in Vertov's masterpiece, *The Man With the Movie Camera* (1928).

15. See Seth Feldman, "Cinema Weekly and Cinema Truth: Dziga Vertov and the Leninist Proportion." *Sight and Sound* 43.1 (Winter 1973–74): 34–38.

16. See John Bolt, "Alexander Rodchenko as Photographer," *The Avant-Garde in Russia 1910–1930*, ed. Stephanie Barron and Maurice Tuchman (Los Angeles: Los Angeles County Museum of Art, 1980), 55; and Camilla Gray, *The Russian Experiment in Art: 1863–1922* (New York: Abrams, 1962), 271.

17. See Petric, 1–69, for an analysis of Vertov's relation to constructivism and the other avant-garde movements of his time.

18. See the Vertov filmography in *Kino-Eye: The Writings of Dziga Vertov*, ed. Annette Michelson, trans. Kevin O'Brien (Berkeley: University of California Press, 1984), 330–34.

19. Eisenstein's first film experience was with the *kinoks*; see Petric, 48–49.

20. "We: Variant of a Manifesto," *Kino-Eye: The Writings of Dziga Vertov*, 7.

21. The texts of many of these theoretical writings can be found in *Kino-Eye: The Writings of Dziga Vertov*.

22. For Mikhail Kaufman's recollections of working with Dziga Vertov and others, see "An Interview with Mikhail Kaufman." *October* 11 (Winter 1979): 54–76.

23. "Dziga Vertov as Theorist," *Cinema Journal* 1 (Fall 1978): 41–42.

24. For a provocative reassessment of Vertov's significance, see Jeremy Murray-Brown, "False Cinema: Vertov and Early Soviet Film," *The New Criterion* 8.3 (Nov. 1989): 21–33.

25. All but eight of these issues appeared under the *Kinopravda* title; for the titles of the others, see *Kino-Eye: The Writings of Dziga Vertov*, 331–32.

26. An early study of the film is Annette Michelson, "The Man with the Movie Camera: From Magician to Epistemologist," *Artforum* 7 (Mar. 1972), 60–72. For a close analysis of the opening shots, see Alan Williams, "The Camera-Eye and the Film: Notes on Vertov's 'Formalism.'" *Wide Angle* 3.3 (1980): 12–17. For frame enlargements from the film, see Petric, *Constructivism in Film*, 249–318.

27. "Dziga Vertov," *Cinema: A Critical Dictionary*, ed. Richard Roud (New York: Viking, 1980), vol. 2, 1024.

28. For differing views of its structure, see Petric, 72ff.; Bertrand Sauzier, "An Interpretation of *The Man With the Movie Camera*," *Studies in Visual Communication* 11.4 (Fall 1985): 34–53; and Seth Feldman, *Dziga Vertov: A Guide to References and Resources*, 98–110.

29. Annette Michelson writes: "The film was made, as Vertov expressly tells us, for the workers and peasants of the Soviet Union; the unavailability in both East and West informs us that its author indeed has no place in the picture; it is an index of the strangeness of his text" (xxii).

30. See Lucy Fischer, "Enthusiasm: From Kino-Eye to Radio-Eye" and "Restoring *Enthusiasm*: Excerpts from an Interview with Peter Kubelka," *Film Quarterly* 31.2 (Winter 1977–78): 25–34+.

31. See Petric, 48–60, for a summary of the controversy.

32. Jay Leyda, *Films Beget Films: A Study of the Compilation Film* (New York: Hill, 1971), 13. Paul Rotha seems to have coined the term "compilation film" in *Documentary Film*, and, as Leyda points it (9–10), it is an awkward term.

33. See Leyda, 15–16.

34. See Vlada Petric, "Esther Shub: Cinema is My Life," *Quarterly Review of Film Studies* 3.4 (Fall 1978): 429–56. This article includes the script for Shub's unrealized project, "Women" (1933–34), designed, according to Petric, "to show women in the historical context and through their sociopsychological evolution from 1914 to the early 1930's" (444).

35. For a discussion of *Old and New*, see Vance Kepley, Jr. "The Evolution of Eisenstein's Old and New," *Cinema Journal* 14.1 (1974): 34–50.

36. See Petric, 430, for a list of her books and other films.

37. This type of montage was criticized as achieving just the opposite; see Petric, 442–43.

38. See Elizabeth Sussex, *The Rise and Fall of British Documentary: The Story of the Film Movement Founded by John Grierson* (Berkeley: University of California Press, 1975); Jack C. Ellis, *John Grierson: A Guide to References and Resources* (Boston: Hall, 1986); Paul Swann, *The British Documentary Film Movement, 1926–1946*, diss. University of Leeds, 1979; Ian Aitken, *Film and Reform: John Grierson and the Documentary Film Movement* (London: Routledge, 1990).

39. See Forsyth Hardy, *John Grierson: A Documentary Biography* (London: Faber and Faber, 1979).

40. Anstey quoted in Sussex, 96.

41. For a discussion of Lippmann's influence, see Gary Evans, *John Grierson and the National Film Board: The Politics of Wartime Propaganda, 1939–1945* (Toronto: University of Toronto Press, 1984), 35–36.

42. See Evans, 38–40.

43. Storck quoted in G. Roy Levin, *Documentary Explorations* (New York: Doubleday, 1971), 156.

44. John Grierson, "E.M.B. Film Unit," *Cinema Quarterly* 1:4 (Summer 1933), 203.

45. Swann, 29.

46. "The EMB Film Unit," *Cinema Quarterly* 1 (1933): 203.

47. For a provocative analysis of Grierson's choice of the word documentary, see Dennis Giles, "The Name Documentary: A Preface to Genre Study," *Film Reader* 3 (1978): 18–22.

48. Stephen Tallents, *The Projection of England* (London: Faber, 1932), 31; see also Tallents, "The Documentary Film," *Journal of the Royal Society of Arts* (20 Dec. 1946): 68–85.

49. *Don't Look at the Camera* (New York: St. Martin's, 1974), 41.

50. Grierson and Basil Wright also edited *Conquest* (1930), a film compiled from footage from American westerns. See Jay Leyda, *Films Beget Films* (New York, 1964), 20–21.

51. Swann, 49–50. See also *The Factual Film: An Arts Enquiry Report* (London: Oxford University Press, 1947), 46; and Elizabeth Sussex, *The Rise and Fall of British Documentary: The Story of the Film Movement Founded by John Grierson* (Berkeley: University of California Press, 1975), 5.

52. Rachel Low, *The History of the British Film, 1918–1929* (London: British Film Institute and British Film Academy, 1971), 296.

53. Two autobiographies by filmmakers who were closely associated with it from the beginning provide personal views of the British documentary film movement: Harry Watt, *Don't Look at the Camera* (New York: St. Martin's Press, 1974); Basil Wright, *The Long View* (New York: Knopf, 1974).

54. The success of *Lumber* (1931), which was compiled from Canadian footage and made for theatrical distribution, encouraged Grierson's plans for producing more films for theaters, an interest that was to remain with him for years.

55. Margaret Dickinson and Sarah Street, *Cinema and State: The Film Industry and the British Government, 1927–84* (London: British Film Institute, 1985), 28.

56. Swann, 72–76, discusses the opposition of the film industry.

57. Swann, 69, says that Tallents "made it a condition of his new appointment to the Public Relations Department of the Post Office that the film unit should be taken over intact by the Post Office."

5. THE BRITISH DOCUMENTARY MOVEMENT

1. " 'Britain's Outstanding Contribution to the Film': The Documentary-Realist Tradition." *All Our Yesterdays: 90 Years of British Cinema*, ed. Charles Barr (London: British Film Institute, 1986), 72–97.

2. For a study of the filmmaking efforts outside the Grierson movement, see Bert Hogenkamp, *Film and the Left in Britain, 1929–39* (London: Lawrence & Wishart, 1986); includes filmography.

3. For commentary on the influence of Marxism on Grierson, particularly the Italian Marxist Antonio Gramsci, see Gary Evans, *John Grierson and the National Film Board: The Politics of Wartime Propaganda, 1939–1945* (Toronto: University of Toronto Press, 1984), 5ff.

4. Two essays address the autonomy, independence, and overall context in which the movement evolved; see Claire Johnston, " 'Independence' and the Thirties" and Annette Kuhn, "British Documentaries in the 1930s and 'Independence': Recontextualising a Film Movement," *British Cinema: Traditions of Independence*, ed. Don Macpherson and Paul Willmen (London: British Film Institute: 1980), 9–23, 24–33. This anthology reprints many relevant essays and reviews from the period. See also Sylvia Harvey, "The 'Other Cinema' in Britain: Unfinished Business in Oppositional and Independent Film, 1929–1984," *All Our Yesterdays: 90 Years of British Cinema*, ed. Charles Barr (London: British Film Institute, 1986), 225–51.

5. Paul Swann, in *The British Documentary Film Movement, 1926–1946* (25–27), attempts to discredit the idea, image, and cohesiveness of the movement. While I do not find

this aspect of Swann's argument to be convincing, he is persuasive in suggesting that Grierson's image might have been overdrawn by his followers. Nonetheless, Swann's study is valuable for its analysis of the political and organizational context in which the British documentary film movement developed.

6. See Swann, chap. 3, for an explanation of the organization and financing of film production at the GPO.

7. Stuart Legg made *Introducing the Dial* (1935), a film on the same subject, for the GPO.

8. See Richard Barsam, *The Vision of Robert Flaherty: The Artist as Myth and Filmmaker* (Bloomington: Indiana University Press, 1988), esp. chap. 4.

9. Rotha, *Documentary Diary: An Informal History of the British Documentary Film, 1928–1939* (New York: Hill, 1973), 50; Sussex, *The Rise and Fall of British Documentary: The Story of the Film Movement Founded by John Grierson* (Berkeley: University of California Press, 1975), 23–43.

10. *The War, the West, and the Wilderness* (New York: Knopf, 1978), 471.

11. *Industrial Britain* was released in 1933 with a package of five other E.M.B. films, all of which were widely shown; the other titles were *The Country Comes to Town, O'er Hill and Dale, Upstream, The Shadow on the Mountain,* and *King Log.*

12. For background on the making of this film, see Cecile Starr, "Basil Wright and *Song of Ceylon:* An Interview," *Filmmakers Newsletter* 9.1 (Nov. 1975): 17–21. For Wright's definition of documentary, see Sari Thomas, "Basil Wright on Art, Anthropology, and the Documentary," *Quarterly Review of Film Studies* 4.4 (Fall 1979): 465–81.

13. For a structural and Jungian analysis of the film's meaning, see Don Frederickson, "Jung/Sign/Symbol/Film (part 2)." *Quarterly Review of Film Studies* 5.4 (Fall 1980): 459–79.

14. In *Don't Look at the Camera,* Harry Watt describes the filming of *Night Mail* (79–97), insisting that he "directed every foot of the picture" (91) and was shocked by the main credit, "Produced by Basil Wright and Harry Watt" (96). In *The Long View,* Basil Wright does not refer to this. See Sussex, 65–78, for a discussion of the making of the film.

15. In existing prints, the final word of this narration seems to be "forgot," but W. H. Auden (in a letter to me, 17 Mar. 1972) says that "forgotten" is correct. For the full text, see W. H. Auden, *Plays* (Princeton: Princeton University Press, 1988).

16. Swann (119) claims that the GPO's need for self-advertisement caused it to exaggerate estimates of audience size at nontheatrical showings.

17. See Sussex, 82–83, for a statement of their purposes.

18. See Richard Barsam, "John Grierson: His Significance Today," *Image, Reality, Spectator: Essays on Documentary Film and Television,* ed. Willem De Greef and Willem Hesling (Leuven, Belg.: Acco, 1989), 8–16.

19. Grierson quoted in Jack Ellis, *John Grierson: A Guide to References and Resources* (Boston: G. K. Hall, 1986), 22.

20. *John Grierson and the National Film Board: The Politics of Wartime Propaganda, 1939–1945* (Toronto: University of Toronto Press, 1984), 47.

21. Grierson quoted in Ellis, 23.

22. Ellis, 23.

23. In *Don't Look at the Camera,* Watt spells it as Blewett; see also his comments in Sussex, 85–87, on the making of the film.

24. See "The Movement Divides," Sussex, 79–111.

25. Alan Lovell and Jim Hillier, *Studies in Documentary* (London: Secker and Warburg, 1972), 35; for a reassessment of the documentary-realist tradition, see Andrew Higson, " 'Britain's Outstanding Contribution to the Film': The Documentary-Realist Tradition."

26. "Alberto Cavalcanti: His Advice to Young Producers of Documentary," *Film Quarterly* 9 (Summer 1955): 354–55.

27. For an account of Cavalcanti's career, see Emir Rodriques Monegal, "Alberto

Cavalcanti: His Career," *Nonfiction Film Theory and Criticism*, ed. Richard M. Barsam (New York: Dutton, 1976), 239–49.

28. Films on air travel, sponsored by Imperial Airways, include *Air Outpost, The Future is in the Air*, and *Watch and Ward in the Air* (1937); and *African Skyways, Wings Over Empire* (1939), and *Sydney Eastbound* (1939).

29. See Swann, chap. 5, for a discussion of this.

30. For a favorable reassessment of Rotha's position, see Eva Orbanz, *Journey to a Legend and Back: The British Realistic Film* (Berlin: Volker Spiess, 1977).

31. See Swann, 180–84, for a discussion of this.

32. In a totally different area of creativity and expression, Len Lye made films that fuse brilliant graphics, bold colors, and inventive music and sounds to create whimsical but informative "posters" that are as fresh today as they were when they were made. Among the first to use color in nonfiction film, Lye's films include *Colour Box* (1935), *Rainbow Dance* (1936), *Trade Tattoo* (1937), *Musical Poster #1* (1939), *Swinging the Lambeth Walk* (1940), sometimes confused with C. A. Ridley's *Germany Calling*, 1941, an ironic compilation film that juxtaposed visuals of Nazi soldiers marching to the tune of "Swinging the Lambeth Walk."

33. See Swann, chap. 6.

34. Other Travel Association films include *So This is London, So This is Lancashire, St. James Park*, and *London on Parade*.

35. For several of my conclusions here, I am indebted to Basil Wright, *The Long View*, 109–13. Films from this period that I have not seen include *On the Way to Work, Kensal House, Cover to Cover, Rooftops of London, Heart of an Empire, The Key to Scotland* (1936); *New Architecture at the London Zoo, Here is the Land, Statue Parade, Job in a Million, Scratch Meal* (1937); *Duchy of Cornwall, The Tocher, London Wakes Up, Ile d'Orléans, Book Bargain, Mony a Pickle, Five Faces* (1938); *The Face of Scotland, Health for the Nation, Advance Democracy, Speed the Plough, British Made, Men in Danger, London on Parade, Wealth of a Nation, The Children's Story, Roads Across Britain, Do it Now* (1939); and *Big Money* (n.d.).

36. See Robert Colls and Philip Dodd, "Representing the Nation: British Documentary Film, 1930–45," *Screen* 26.1 (Jan.–Feb. 1985): 21–33.

37. See John Grierson, "Production Unit Planned: Mass Media to be Used for Peace," *UNESCO Courier* Feb. 1948: 3.

6. EUROPEAN AND ASIAN NONFICTION FILM: 1930–1939

1. *Documentary Film*, 268.

2. Arthur Knight, "A Short History of Art Films," *Films on Art*, ed. William McK. Chapman (New York: American Federation of Arts, 1952), 8.

3. Rodin is also the subject of Rene Lucot's *Rodin* (1942).

4. Knight, 11. After World War II, this film was held by the United States as enemy property, and various filmmakers—including Robert Flaherty, John Grierson, Helen Van Dongen, and others—were asked to reedit it, primarily to shorten it and improve the sound-track. While they all refused to edit another artist's work, Flaherty agreed to the use of his name as producer in the United States release of the film as *The Titan* in 1950. In 1951, Flaherty entered into a similar agreement with the film *St. Matthew Passion*, which was released with this credit: "Robert Flaherty Presents." Flaherty made no artistic contribution to either film.

5. See Joris Ivens, *The Camera and I* (New York: International Publishers, 1969) and Rosalind Delmar, *Joris Ivens: 50 Years of Film-making* (London: British Film Institute, 1979); Deborah Shaffer, "Fifty Years of Political Filmmaking: an Interview with Joris Ivens," *Ciné-*

aste 14.1 (1985): 12–16+; and Jerry Kuehl, "Arts and Entertainment—A Little Closer: The Films of Joris Ivens," *New Statesman* 98 (Nov. 2, 1979), 688 89.

6. For a critical filmography, see Delmar, pp. 8–72.

7. Pare Lorentz's unfinished *Ecce Homo!* (1939–40) contains what he called an "industrial symphony" sequence.

8. See Ivens, 81–93. For a discussion of Ivens's use of real events and staged sequences in *Misère au Borinage*, see Bert Hogenkamp, "Joris Ivens and the Problems of the Documentary Film," trans. M. Cleaver, *Framework* 11 (Autumn 1979): 22–25.

9. cf. Vertov's *Enthusiasm: Symphony of the Don Basin* (*Entuziasm: simphoniia Donbassa*, 1931).

10. See Ivens, 95, for his discussion of the film's editing.

11. Ferno was born Fernhout.

12. The editor was Henri Storck.

13. These qualities also distinguish *And So They Live* (1940), a film Ferno made in the United States.

14. For much of this historical background, I am indebted to Geert Van Wonterghem for his counsel and for translating sections of *Beeld & Realiteit: International Festival van de Documentaire Film en Televisie*, ed. Pascal Lefèvre and Geert Van Wonterghem (Leuven, Belg.: Catholic University of Leuven; Brussels, Hoger Institute of St. Lukas High School, 1987).

15. Important films about the Belgian Congo include Ernest Genval's *Le Congo Qui s'Eveille* (*The Congo Awakens*, 1925); Charles Dekeukeleire's *Terres Brulées* (*Burned Earth*, 1934); and Armand Denis's *Magie Africaine* (*African Magic*, 1938).

16. Until the liberation of the Flemish people after World War II, most films by Belgian filmmakers were produced in French.

17. André Bazin, "*Los Olvidados*," *The World of Luis Buñuel: Essays in Criticism*, ed. Joan Mellen (New York: Oxford University Press, 1978), 199; see also E. Rubinstein, "Visit to a Familiar Planet: Buñuel Among the Hurdanos," *Cinema Journal* 22.4 (Summer 1983): 3–17.

18. The official party name is the National Socialist German Workers Party (NSDAP); for an account of the history and organization of Nazi cinema, see David Welch, *Propaganda and the German Cinema 1933–1945* (New York: Oxford University Press, 1987), esp. chap. 1.

19. See David Stewart Hull, *Film in the Third Reich: A Study of the German Cinema, 1933–1945* (Berkeley: University of California Press, 1969), esp. 10–41.

20. Welch (236) says that Goebbels made a desperate attempt to radicalize the German cinema in 1944, but that the lack of information makes it difficult to assess the impact of this move.

21. *The Politics of Propaganda: The Office of War Information 1942–1945* (New Haven: Yale University Press, 1978), 19.

22. See Jacques Ellul, *Propaganda: The Formation of Men's Attitudes*, trans. Konrad Kellen and Jean Lerner (New York: Vintage, 1973).

23. See Welch, chap. 2.

24. Other studies of Nazi films include Siegfried Kracauer, *From Caligari to Hitler* (Princeton: Princeton University Press, 1947), esp. pp. 275–307; Kracauer, *The Conquest of Europe on the Screen: The Nazi Newsreel, 1939–1940* (Washington, D.C.: Library of Congress, 1943); David Stewart Hull, *Film in the Third Reich: Art and Propaganda in Nazi Germany* (New York: Simon, 1973); Roger Manvell and Heinrich Fraenkel, *The German Cinema* (New York: Praeger, 1971); and Erwin Leiser, *Nazi Cinema* (New York: Macmillan, 1975). Erwin Leiser's *Germany, Awake!* (1968) explains Nazi propaganda film tactics through a compilation of excerpts from narrative feature films.

25. For a list of election films, see William G. Chrystal, "National Party Election Films, 1927–1938," *Cinema Journal* 15.1 (Fall 1975): 29–47; for a list of propaganda and counter-

propaganda films, see *Propaganda und Gegenpropaganda im Film, 1933–1945* (Vienna: Österreichisches Filmmuseum, 1972).

26. Another film with the same title, Erwin Leiser's *Deutschland, erwache!* (*Wake Up, Germany!*, 1968) is a compilation film of sequences from Nazi feature films; see also Leiser's *Nazi Cinema* (New York: Macmillan, 1974).

27. In Britain, W. H. Auden, Stephen Spender, and C. Day Lewis wrote poems of praise to electrical pylons, machines, and railroads, and *Night Mail*, for which Auden wrote the narrative, idealizes the postal train (see chap. 5).

28. For an account of Zielke's background and work on *Olympia*, see Cooper C. Graham, *Leni Riefenstahl and "Olympia"* (Metuchen: Scarecrow, 1986), 41–45.

29. See Welch, 201–03, for an analysis of a typical *Deutsche Wochenschau* release.

30. "*Germany Awake*: Propaganda in Nazi Cinema," *Sightlines* 14.1–2 (Fall–Winter 1980): 12. See my *Filmguide to "Triumph of the Will"* (Bloomington: Indiana University Press, 1975); see also Steve Neale, "*Triumph of the Will*: Notes on Documentary and Spectacle," *Screen* 20.1 (Spring 1979): 63–86; Jill Caldwell, "*Triumph of the Will* and *Listen to Britain*: Propaganda—Militant/Non-militant," *Film Library Quarterly* 9.1 (Sept. 1976): 52–3.

31. When he saw the film, General Werner von Blomberg, Commander in Chief of the Army, complained to Hitler that Riefenstahl had neglected the importance of the German Army; to satisfy von Blomberg, she was asked to make *Tag der Freiheit—Unsere Wehrmacht* (*Day of Freedom—Our Armed Forces*, 1935), a beautifully photographed and edited film (no doubt produced from *Triumph* outtakes) that lacks any of the thematic or psychological interest of its famous predecessor.

32. See David B. Hinton, "*Triumph of the Will*: Document or Artifice," *Cinema Journal* 15.1 (Fall 1975): 48–57.

33. See my "Filmguide to *Triumph of the Will*"; the most recent controversy over Riefenstahl began with Susan Sontag's "Fascinating Fascism," *New York Review of Books* 6 Feb. 1975, which provoked a series of responses in that publication (esp. 20 Mar. 1975 and 18 Sept. 1975) and elsewhere, including Andrew Sarris, "Notes on the Fascination of Fascism," *The Village Voice* 30 Jan. 1978): 1+.

34. Carlos Fuentes, "The Discreet Charm of Luis Buñuel," *New York Times Magazine* 11 Mar. 1973: 87. When Willard Van Dyke was Director of the Museum of Modern Art Film Department, he told me that he withdrew the abridged version from circulation because he did not believe that any artist should edit another's work, no matter how eminent the person doing the editing or what the reason. The abridged version of the film, customarily attributed to Buñuel, is again available from the circulating film collection of the Museum, but its *Circulating Film Catalog* (1984) says "speculation that Luis Buñuel worked on the editing while employed at the Museum in the early forties has never been confirmed" (119).

35. See Cooper C. Graham, *Leni Riefenstahl and "Olympia"* (Metuchen: Scarecrow, 1986). Graham discusses the film's propaganda throughout the book, esp. chaps. 1 and 6. See also Hans Barkhausen, "Footnote to the History of Riefenstahl's *Olympia*," *Film Quarterly* 28.1 (Fall 1974): 8–12; Marcus Phillips, "Riefenstahl's 'Harrassment'," *Film Quarterly* 29.3 (Spring 1976): 62.

36. Riefenstahl published two books of outstanding photographs on the Nuba tribes of the Sudan: *The Last of the Nuba* (New York: Harper and Row, 1973) and *People of Kau* (New York: Harper and Row, 1976).

37. Cooper lists 45 cinematographers, 5 of whom were principal; Willy Zielke photographed the prologue.

38. Cooper (chap. 5) provides an extensive coverage of the history of the film after release.

39. *The Japanese Film: Art and Industry*, expanded ed. (Princeton: Princeton University Press, 1982), 146. See also *Japan in Film*, ed. Peter Grilli (New York: Japan Society, 1984);

and *Asian-American Media Reference Guide*, ed. Bernice Chu (New York: Asian CineVision, 1986).

40. See Erik Barnouw and S. Krishnaswamy, *Indian Film*, 2nd ed. (New York: Oxford University Press, 1980).

41. See Barnouw and Krishnaswamy, 123–24, for a list of these films.

42. Jay Leyda, *Dianying/Electric Shadows: An Account of Films and the Film Audience in China* (Cambridge: MIT Press, 1972), 1–14; see also the list of important Chinese films made by Chinese and foreign groups from 1897 to 1966, 392–414; unfortunately, Leyda concentrates almost exclusively on fiction films.

7. AMERICAN NONFICTION FILM: 1930–1939

1. Arthur Knight, "A Short History of Art Films," *Films on Art*, ed. William McK. Chapman (New York: American Federation of Arts, 1952), 9.

2. See Barsam, *The Faithful Vision: Robert Flaherty as Myth and Filmmaker* (Bloomington: Indiana University Press, 1988), 58–71.

3. By contrast, Georges Rouquier's *Farrebique* (1946), a film influenced by Flaherty, presents actuality without a staged conflict and structures the cinematic time to reflect the natural cycles of change throughout one year.

4. Robert Flaherty, "Filming Real People," *The Documentary Tradition: From Nanook to Woodstock*, ed. Lewis Jacobs, 2nd ed. (New York: Norton, 1979), 99. John Taylor was second cameraman; see interview with Taylor in Sussex, 28.

5. Joris Ivens, *The Camera and I* (New York: International Publishers, 1969), 138.

6. The group included John Dos Passos, Lillian Hellman, Ernest Hemingway, Archibald MacLeish, Clifford Odets, Dorothy Parker, and Herman Shumlin; see Alexander, 149–58; see also "Joris Ivens Interviewed by Gordon Hitchens," *Film Culture*: 53.55 (Spring 1972): 190–228.

7. "Men Cannot Act in Front of the Camera in the Presence of Death': Joris Ivens' *The Spanish Earth*," *Cinéaste* 12.2 (1982): 31.

8. See Ivens, 103–38, for a discussion of the shooting and Hemingway's active role in it.

9. Ernest Hemingway, *The Spanish Earth* (Cleveland: Savage, 1938), 19.

10. See Ivens, 130–38, for a summary of the critical response.

11. For Lorentz's views of Ivens's films, see Pare Lorentz, *Lorentz on Film* (New York: Hopkinson, 1975), 164–65, 190–91.

12. *Film on the Left: American Documentary Film From 1931 to 1942* (Princeton: Princeton University Press, 1981), 283.

13. Richard Dyer MacCann, *The People's Films* (103), suggests that the American quality of the film may also be due to the script which "the usually scriptless Lorentz asked Edwin Locke to help Ivens prepare. . . . "

14. For differing views on Ivens's accomplishments, see Cynthia Grenier, "Joris Ivens: Social Realist and Lyric Poet," *Sight and Sound* 27.4 (Spring 1958): 204–07; and R. Stebbins and J. Leyda, "Joris Ivens: Artist in Documentary," *Magazine of Art* 31 (July 1938): 392–99ff.

15. See Ivens, "Notes on Hollywood," *New Theatre and Film 1934 to 1937*, ed. Herbert Kline (New York: Harcourt, 1985), 294–99.

16. Early attempts in the 1930s to attack social problems in America through film include Seymour Stern's *Imperial Valley* (1931) and *Taxi, Sheriff*, and *City of Contrasts*. For a cursory analysis of the style of three filmmakers—Louis de Rochement, Pare Lorentz, and Leo Hurwitz—see Peter Rollins, "Ideology and Film Rhetoric: Three Documentaries of the New Deal Era," *Journal of Popular Film* 5.2 (1976): 126–45; for a list of them by category, see Tom Brandon, "Survival List: Films of the Great Depression: The Early Thirties," *Film Library Quarterly* 12.2-3 (1979): 33–40. An interesting anthology of essays and articles from

a left-wing arts magazine of the era is *New Theatre and Film 1934 to 1937*, ed. Herbert Kline (New York: Harcourt, 1985).

17. Russell D. Campbell, *Cinema Strikes Back: Radical Filmmaking in the United States, 1930-42* (Ann Arbor: UMI Press, 1982), 29; see also filmography, 313-19.

18. See William Alexander, *Film on the Left*; Roy Rosenzweig, "Working Class Struggles in the Great Depression: The Film Record," *Film Library Quarterly* 13.1 (1980): 5-14; Leo Seltzer, "Documenting the Depression of the 1930s," *Film Library Quarterly* 13.1 (1980): 15-21 and "The Film and Photo League," *Ovo Magazine* 10.40-41 (1981): 14-59; Steve Hutkins, "Unemployed Worker with a Camera: Leo Seltzer and the Film and Photo League," *Center Quarterly* 9.2 (Winter 1987-88): 8-11; and Victoria Wegg-Prosser, "The Archive of the Film and Photo League." *Sight and Sound* 46.4 (Autumn 1977): 245-47; and Anne Tucker, "The Photo League," *Ovo Magazine* 10.40-41 (1981), 3-9.

19. Others League members included Jack Auringer, Joseph Hudyma, John Shard, C. O. Nelson, Norman Warren, Kita Kamura, and Alfredo Valenti. See Fred Sweet, Eugene Rosow, Allan Francovich, "Pioneers: An Interview with Tom Brandon." *Film Quarterly* 26.5 (or 27.1) (1973): 12-24.

20. Nykino links New York with the Russian word for camera. See Joel Zuker, *Ralph Steiner: Filmmaker and Still Photographer* (New York: Arno, 1978).

21. See Evelyn Geller, "Paul Strand as a Documentary Filmmaker," *Film Library Quarterly* 6.2 (Spring 1973): 28-30.

22. See Alexander, 67-81.

23. This film was also known as *Air City*.

24. Independent of Frontier Films, Kline also directed two films that depict the human experience in the face of the impending world war: *Crisis* (1938), a record of the struggle of the Czech people for freedom from Nazi terrorism, and *Lights Out in Europe* (1940).

25. See Alexander, 207-42, for a discussion of this film.

26. "*Native Land*." *Film Quarterly* 26.5 (or 27.1) (Fall 1973): 61.

27. See Paul Strand, "Realism: A Personal View," *Sight and Sound* 19 (Jan. 1950): 23-26.

28. "*Native Land*: Praised then Forgotten." *Velvet Light Trap* 14 (Winter 1975): 15-16; see also John Hess and Michael Klein, "*Native Land* Reconsidered." *Jump Cut* 10-11 (Summer 1976): 63; Michael and Jill Klein, "*Native Land*: An Interview with Leo Hurwitz." *Cinéaste* 6.3 (1974): 2-7; and Joseph Goodwin, "Some Personal Notes on *Native Land*," *Take One* 4.2 (Nov.-Dec. 1972): 11-12.

29. It was to have been followed by another film, fifteen years later, showing the results of educational reform that was being introduced by the Alfred Sloan Foundation, its sponsor, but this second film was never made.

30. For the best assessment of Lorentz's career, see Richard Dyer MacCann, *The People's Films: A Political History of U.S. Government Motion Pictures* (New York: Hastings, 1973), esp. chap. 4, as well as his earlier work, "Documentary Film and Democratic Government: An Administrative History from Pare Lorentz to John Huston," diss. Harvard University, 1951. See also Robert L. Snyder, *Pare Lorentz and the Documentary Film* (Norman: Oklahoma University Press, 1968), a study that is heavily indebted to MacCann's original research.

31. For a study of various forms of American documentary expression during the 1930s, excluding documentary film, see William Stott, *Documentary Expression and Thirties America* (New York: Oxford University Press, 1973).

32. There are some obvious visual influences from *The Plow That Broke the Plains* on John Ford's screen version of *The Grapes of Wrath* (1940); and *Plow* can be effectively studied in contrast to King Vidor's *Our Daily Bread* (1934).

33. For a study guide to the film, see *The Plow That Broke the Plains* (Washington, D.C.: U.S. Film Service, 1938).

34. Today's conservationists do not support the kind of conservation exemplified by

the Tennessee Valley Authority projects and advocated by *The River*: flooding of vast valleys to create dams and cheap hydroelectric power.

35. Pare Lorentz, *The River* (New York: Stackpole, 1938), n. pag.

36. See Willard Van Dyke, "Letters from *The River*," *Film Comment*, 3.2 (Spring 1965): 38–60.

37. James Joyce said that the narration was "the most beautiful prose I have heard in ten years"; quoted in William L. White, "Pare Lorentz," *Scribner's* (Jan. 1939): 10; Carl Sandburg commented, "it is among the greatest psalms of America's greatest river" (quoted in Snyder 184).

38. For a different conclusion on Lorentz's films, see Andrew Bergman, *We're in the Money: Depression America and Its Films* (New York: New York University Press, 1971), 165–66.

39. Alexander, 256n. For Lorentz's scathing comment on some of these nonfiction filmmaking groups, see MacCann, *The People's Films*, 57.

40. For the background behind establishment of the USFS, see MacCann, *The People's Films*, chap. 5, and Snyder, 79–95.

41. For a discussion of the implications of government propaganda in a democratic society, with specific reference to the Congressional debate on the USFS, see MacCann, *The People's Films*, esp. 104–17.

42. While it was not particularly influential on succeeding filmmakers, it was well-received by both the medical and the lay communities; see MacCann, 96–99, and Snyder, 63–78.

43. See Snyder, 63–78, For Lorentz's instructions to Gruenberg.

44. After *The Fight for Life*, Lorentz entered the U.S. Air Force and made almost three hundred training films; after the war, he formed his own independent consulting and producing company, but never equalled his early achievements.

45. See Richard Barsam, *The Vision of Robert Flaherty: The Artist as Myth and Filmmaker* (Indiana University Press, 1988), esp. chap. 7.

46. John Huston is quoted in Calder-Marshall, *The Innocent Eye: The Life of Robert J. Flaherty* (New York: Harcourt, 1963), 196, as saying that this moment was worth all of John Ford's *The Grapes of Wrath*.

47. See Penelope Houston, "Interview with Flaherty," *Sight and Sound* (Jan. 1950): 16.

48. See Mike Weaver, *Robert Flaherty's "The Land"* (Exeter, Eng.: American Arts Documentation Centre, University of Exeter, 1979), 21.

49. See William T. Murphy, *Robert Flaherty: A Guide to References and Resources* (Boston: Hall, 1978), 35–36, for an account of the conflict surrounding the film's release.

50. See Raymond Fielding, *The American Newsreel, 1911–1967* (Norman: University of Oklahoma Press, 1972), 205–19.

51. See Raymond Fielding, *The March of Time: 1935–1951* (New York: Oxford, 1978) and *The American Newsreel: 1911–1967* (Norman: University of Oklahoma Press, 1972); A. William Bluem, *Documentary in American Television* (New York: Hastings, 1965); Robert T. Elson, *Time, Inc., The Intimate History of a Publishing Enterprise, 1923–1941* (New York: Atheneum, 1968); Robert T. Elson, "Time Marches on the Screen," *Nonfiction Film Theory and Criticism*, ed. Richard M. Barsam, (New York: Dutton, 1976), 95–114; Thomas W. Bohn and Lawrence W. Lichty, "*The March of Time*: News as Drama," *Journal of Popular Film* 2.4 (1973): 373–87; Bruce Cook, "Whatever Happened to Westbrook Van Voorhis," *American Film* 2 (Mar. 1977): 25–29; and Stephen E. Bowles, "And Time Marched On: The Creation of the *March of Time*," *Journal of the University Film Association* 29.1 (Winter 1977): 7–13.

52. See Robert L. Carringer, *The Making of CITIZEN KANE* (Berkeley: University of California Press, 1965), 18.

53. See Richard M. Barsam, " 'This is America': Documentaries for Theaters, 1942–1951," *Nonfiction Film Theory and Criticism*, ed. Richard M. Barsam (New York: Dutton: 1976), 115–35.

54. See Harrison Engle, "Thirty Years of Social Inquiry: An Interview with Willard Van Dyke," *Film Comment* 3.2 (Spring 1965): 24–37. See also Amalie Rothschild's film, *Conversations With Willard Van Dyke* (1977).

55. Van Dyke, "Letters from *The River*."

56. He photographed the opening sequences of an early version of *Native Land* discarded in favor of the extant film; see Van Dyke, "Letters from *The River*."

57. See Willard Van Dyke, "The Interpretive Camera in Documentary Film," *Hollywood Quarterly* 1.4 (July 1946): 405–09.

58. Richard Dyer MacCann writes that Pare Lorentz "made an important contribution in the form of a script outline." See "The City," *The International Dictionary of Films and Filmmakers*, vol. 1 (Chicago: St. James Press, 1984), 97.

59. For a critical catalog of the hundreds of films shown at the fair, see Richard Griffith, *Films of the World's Fair: 1939* (New York: American Film Center, 1940); see also Alexander, 255–56.

8. BRITISH FILMS FOR WORLD WAR II

1. See J. McDonald, "Film and War Propaganda," *Pubic Opinion Quarterly* (4 Sept. 1940), 519–22, and (5 Mar. 1940), 127–9.

2. Richard Griffith comments:

> His statement was open to two quite different interpretations: either he implied that motion pictures can be a powerful weapon as an opinion-building, attitude-directing, and emotion-stimulating medium; or he was speaking purely as a militaryman and had already foreseen that motion pictures were capable, in quite another manner and on a more technical level, of providing a new guide and a new arm to any High Command foresighted enough to utilise them. (Rotha, *Documentary Film*, 345)

3. During World War II, in the United States alone, the budget for nonfiction film production and distribution exceeded $50,000,000 a year, with similar amounts spent by other allies. See Richard Griffith, "The Use of Films by the U.S. Armed Services," in Paul Rotha, *Documentary Film*, 345. For a record of British production, see *The Factual Film* (London: Oxford, 1947).

4. My conservative estimate is that, in the United States and Great Britain alone, 1,200 to 1,500 films were produced during the war. However, once most of these films fulfilled their primary purpose in teaching or providing information, they had little subsequent value, except to historians, yet there is still a lamentable lack of accurate information on the scope of war film production. See Mayfield S. Bray and William T. Murphy, *Audiovisual Records in the National Archives of the United States Relating to World War II* (Washington: National Archives and Records Service, 1974).

5. See Sussex, "War and the Peak of Achievement," 112–60; see also chaps. 6–7 in Margaret Dickinson and Sarah Street, *Cinema and State: The Film Industry and the British Government, 1927–1984* (London: British Film Institute, 1985).

6. *Documentary Diary: An Informal History of the British Documentary Film, 1928–1939* (New York: Hill, 1973), 285.

7. The goal of "projecting" Britain was at the heart of Sir Stephen Tallents's efforts to establish the Empire Marketing Board in 1926.

8. Joseph Ball and Kenneth Clark; see Dickinson and Street, 112–14.

9. The most prolific directors of these MOI films were familiar names: Donald Alexander, Edgar Anstey, Geoffrey Bell, Ralph Bond, Andrew Buchanan, John Eldridge, Mary Field, Gilbert Gunn, Pat Jackson, Humphrey Jennings, Ralph Keene, Len Lye, Kay Mander,

Paul Rotha, Frank Sainsbury, Donald Taylor, Grahame Tharp, Margaret Thomson, and Harry Watt.

10. Cavalcanti's loyalties were not at issue, and he continued to direct films during the war, including *Yellow Caesar* and *Young Veterans* (1940) and *Three Songs of Resistance* (1943). The reasons for Dalrymple's resignation are discussed below.

11. MOI eventually produced 480 nonfiction films and acquired another 94, for a total wartime production of 574 nonfiction films. The yearly MOI production was, as follows: 1940, 74 films; 1941, 86 films; 1942, 160 films; 1943, 160 films; 1944, unknown. Films of all lengths were produced for general theatrical and nontheatrical distribution, for instruction and training, for domestic and overseas distribution. See *Documentary News Letter* 2 (1944): 19.

12. According to Sussex (116), the earliest was probably an inconsequential film telling people about how to act in an air raid.

13. Without questioning Jennings's overall contribution to this film, Sussex (128) expresses doubts about these directorial credits. *Britain Can Take It* [sic] is the alternative title of a shorter version released for domestic distribution.

14. Commenting on the tendency toward "art" in many wartime propaganda films, Swann writes: "it seems likely that Jennings' complex and sensitive films did not have the impact upon wartime cinema audiences which they had upon critics and film students in later years" (269). However, Hodgkinson and Sheratsky write that "no one who was in Britain between 1939 and 1945 can look at Jennings' wartime films without an emotional throat-catch of recognition and memory" (46).

15. Out of date by the time it was finished, the film was never used in Great Britain. An abbreviated American release of the film was titled *Flying Elephants*, which I incorrectly referred to as *Floating Elephants* in the first edition of this book.

16. The standard works on Jennings are Anthony W. Hodgkinson and Rodney E. Sheratsky, *Humphrey Jennings: More Than a Maker of Films* (Hanover: University Press of New England, 1982); *Humphrey Jennings: Film-Maker, Painter, Poet*, ed. Mary-Lou Jennings (London: British Film Institute, 1982); Alan Lovell and Jim Hillier, *Studies in Documentary* (London: Secker and Warburg, 1972); Lindsay Anderson, "Only Connect: Some Aspects of the Work of Humphrey Jennings," *Nonfiction Film Theory and Criticism*, ed. Richard Barsam (New York: Dutton, 1976), 263–70; also in *Humphrey Jennings: Film-Maker, Painter, Poet*, 53–59. For a study of Jennings's collaboration with his editor, see Dai Vaughan, *Portrait of an Invisible Man: The Working Life of Stewart McAllister, Film Editor* (London: British Film Institute, 1983).

17. For enhancing my understanding of this film, I am indebted to Kenneth J. Robson's unpublished thesis, "Tying Knots in History: The Films of Humphrey Jennings" (1979).

18. For a dissenting view, see Robert Colls and Philip Dodd, "Representing the Nation: British Documentary Film, 1930–45," *Screen* 26.1 (Jan.–Feb. 1985): 21–33.

19. Dai Vaughan, himself an editor, has written an excellent account of McAllister's career, including a spirited defense of his collaboration with Jennings; see *Portrait of an Invisible Man: The Working Life of Stewart McAllister, Film Editor* (London: British Film Institute, 1983).

20. See Jill Caldwell, "*Triumph of the Will* and *Listen to Britain*: Propaganda—Militant/ Non-militant," *Film Library Quarterly* 9.1 (Sept. 1976): 52–53.

21. Like the farming films, most gardening films were concerned with specifics: *Sowing and Planting* (1941); *Storing Vegetables Outdoors, Storing Vegetables Indoors, Garden Friends And Foes, Ditching* (1942); *Winter Work in the Garden, Saving Your Own Seeds*, and *Vegetable Harvest* (1943).

22. Films intended to call attention to the relationship between food and nutrition include *Green Food for Health, Oatmeal Porridge, Potatoes*, and *Steaming* (1940); *Emergency Cooking Stove* and *Simple Soups* (1941); and *Oven Bottling* and *Eggs and Milk* (1943).

23. Several are about childbirth (*The Birth of a Baby*, 1940) and maintaining children's

health (*Defeat Diptheria*, 1941, *Your Children's Teeth, Your Children's Eyes, Your Children's Ears*, and *Your Children's Sleep*, 1944).

24. Related are several films on nursing: *Nurse!* (1940), *Hospital Nurse* (1941), and *Student Nurse* (1943).

25. *The Pilot is Safe* (1941) is a more positive film about the Channel Rescue Service.

26. As to other films in color and other feature-length films, many of Len Lye's films were made in color, including *Colour Box* (1935) and *Musical Poster #1* (1939); from 1934 through 1944, British films one hour or longer include *B.B.C.: Voice of Britain* (1935, 60 mins.), *Dawn of Iran* (1937, 60 mins.), *For Freedom* (1940, 80 mins.), *The Birth of a Baby* (1940, 65 mins.), *World in Flames* (1941, 70 mins.), *Coastal Command* (1942, 73 mins.), *Desert Victory* (1943, 62 mins.), *Close Quarters* (1943, 75 mins.), *Neuro-Psychiatry* (1943, 68 mins.). The documentary-related feature film was a by-product of the mainstream documentary development—which, as before, tended to produce films that were shorter than the standard feature length of sixty to ninety minutes. While these films were fictionally based, they provided another demonstration of the uses of the nonfiction film mode. Moreover, cinema history shows that the fiction and nonfiction film have not developed exclusively of one another. Flaherty found it desirable to enhance fact with fiction in *Nanook of the North* and *Louisiana Story* (1948), and while films such as Harry Watt's *The Saving of Bill Blewitt* (1936), Pare Lorentz's *The Fight for Life* (1940), and Joris Ivens's *Power and the Land* (1940), to name only the most familiar, are all essentially nonfiction films, they are enhanced by their fictional aspects. In each of these films, as in many others, the need to dramatize and humanize certain subjects is clear. The same is true of those war films that make battle more specific through their concentration on the activities of a specific individual or, more often, a specific and identifiable group; films such as the British *Squadron 992*, or the American *Fighting Lady*, helped to give personal focus to the broad war effort. In Britain, though, more than in the United States, the commercial film industry successfully adapted documentary and nonfiction techniques to a number of feature films that were directly concerned with the war effort. The resources of the feature studios were made available to support the work of the Crown Film Unit and the Ministry of Information, and feature film directors contributed to the development of the wartime documentary with their artistry and sense of dramatic realism. Representative of these films (which often featured popular star performers) are Carol Reed's *The Way Ahead* (1944), humorous and effective in its depiction of a cross section of men as they were before and after their induction into the armed services; Frank Launder's and Sidney Gilliat's *Millions Like Us* (1943), a cross-sectional incentive film stressing the need for the cooperation of all citizens, especially women, in the war effort; Anthony Asquith's *Freedom Radio* (1942); Charles Frend's *The Foreman Went to France* (1942); and Thorold Dickinson's *Next of Kin* (1942), which examines the subject of security. Moreover, *Western Approaches* is significant as the last film that Ian Dalrymple produced before he left the Crown Film Unit because he believed that its bureaucratic system hindered the production of serious nonfiction films (quoted in Sussex, 151).

27. As far as I can determine, none of these films was directed by a woman.

28. Thompson's films include *Storing Vegetables Indoors* and *Storing Vegetables Outdoors* (1942), *Making Grass Silage, Making Good Hay, Saving Your Own Seeds*, and *Clean Milk* (1943); Field's films include *Handicraft Happiness* and *Raw Materials* (1940), *Winged Messengers* (1941), and *Water* (1942).

29. Unfortunately, this is only a partial listing, a task that is made even more difficult by the frequent occurrence of the British custom to use initials rather than a person's first name, thus sacrificing identity for some kind of equality. There is a substantial need for research on the many roles that women played in the British documentary film movement.

30. Ruby Grierson also codirected *Today We Live* (1937) with Ralph Bond.

31. *Germany Calling* [*Lambeth Walk*] should not be confused with Len Lye's *Swinging the Lambeth Walk* (1940).

32. See Hodgkinson and Sheratsky, 72.

33. For veterans, *Tomorrow is Theirs* (1940) and *The Way Ahead* (1943) provided a

general view of the future, while two other films provided more specific information: *Two Good Fairies* (1943), about the Beveridge Plan for postwar services to veterans, and *Farm Worker* (1944), about the pros and cons of farming as a career for veterans.

34. Of course, such an ideal situation was not always possible, as Flaherty discovered in the United States with *The Land* (see chap. 7), and his later success with the unprecedented commercial sponsorship and financing of *Louisiana Story* was a luxury that few filmmakers ever experience (see chap. 9).

35. For much of the information in this section, I am indebted to Gary Evans's study, *John Grierson and the National Film Board: The Politics of Wartime Propaganda, 1939–1945* (Toronto: University of Toronto Press, 1984); see also *The National Film Board of Canada: The War Years,* ed. Peter Morris (Ottawa: Canadian Film Institute, 1965).

36. For information on film production, see *Presenting NFB of Canada* (Ottawa: National Film Board, 1949); for information on the political scandal that led to Grierson's downfall in Canada, see Evans, chap. 7.

37. See Evans, 296–300, for a list of all the titles in these two series.

38. The wartime production of "Canada Carries On" encompassed the period April 1940 through June 1945; the series continued production until 1958.

39. See Basil Wright, "Documentary: Flesh, Fowl, or . . . ?" *Sight and Sound* 19.1 (Mar. 1950): 43–48.

9. EUROPEAN AND ASIAN FILMS FOR WORLD WAR II

1. Most of the factual information in this section on German propaganda films is derived from David Welch, *Propaganda and the German Cinema 1933–1945* (New York: Oxford University Press, 1987) and from Siegfried Kracauer, *From Caligari to Hitler* (Princeton: Princeton University Press, 1947), esp. pp. 275–307. Kracauer's book incorporates the material in his earlier short study: *Propaganda and the Nazi War Film* (New York: Museum of Modern Art Film Library, 1942). See also David Stewart Hull, *Film in the Third Reich* (Berkeley: University of California Press, 1969); and *Hitler's Fall: The Newsreel Witness,* ed. K. R. M. Short and Stephan Dolezel (London: Routledge, 1988).

2. They capitalized on the fact that war correspondents were in danger and died in the pursuit of their material, an approach opposite to that shown, for example, in the British *Cameramen at War.*

3. For information on the showing of such films to Germans, see these articles by Robert Joseph in *Arts and Architecture*: "Films for Nazi Prisoners of War" (62 [May 1945]: 16), "Film Program for Germany" (62 [July 1945]: 16), and "Germans See Their Concentration Camps" (63 [Sept. 1946]: 14). See also Erwin Leiser, *Nazi Cinema* (New York: Macmillan, 1974).

4. An interesting contrast is *Warsaw Capital* (*La Capitale s'appelle Varsovie,* n.d.), a Polish production, that includes unedited actual footage of Hitler's destruction of Warsaw. For a catalogue of Polish films shown in France, see *Films Polonais: Catalogue de film diffusés en France* (Paris: Régie Gouvernementale du cinéma en Pologne à Paris, 1954).

5. Barnouw, 143–44, cites as "one of the most extraordinary newsreel issues" the film that presents Goebbels's 1943 "total war speech."

6. Both Welch (43) and Hull (206–07) show the sharp decline in the production of political film.

7. See two articles in *Wide Angle* 1.4 (1977): Peter B. High, "The War Cinema of Imperial Japan and its Aftermath," 19–21, and Tadao Sato, "War as a Spiritual Exercise: Japan's National Policy Films," 22–24. See also Donald Richie, " 'Mono No Aware,' " *Film: Book 2, Films of Peace and War,* ed. Robert Hughes, Stanley Brown, and Carlos Clarens (New York: Grove, 1962), 67–86.

8. Franz Nieuwenhof, "Japanese Film Propaganda in World War II: Indonesia and Australia," *Historical Journal of Film, Radio, and Television* 4.2 (Oct. 1984): 161–77. For an

account of Australian filmmaking during the war period, see Graham Shirley and Brian Adams, *Australian Cinema: The First Eighty Years* (New York: St. Martin's, 1985).

9. Much of the information in this section is based on Marcia Landy, *Fascism in Film: The Italian Commercial Cinema, 1931-1943* (Princeton: Princeton University Press, 1986); the focus of this book is on narrative film. See also James Hay, *Popular Film Culture in Fascist Italy: The Passing of the Rex* (Bloomington: Indiana University Press, 1987), Mira Liehm, *Passion and Defiance: Film in Italy from 1942 to the Present* (Berkeley: University of California Press, 1984), and Vernon Jarratt, *The Italian Cinema* (London: Falcon, 1951).

10. See Jarratt, 45, and Landy, 253.

11. For a discussion of how contemporary viewers interpret historical footage, see Gideon Bachman, "Auto-Portrait du fascisme," *Cinéma* 183 (Jan. 1974): 77–85.

12. Richard Griffith in Rotha, *Documentary Film*, 345.

13. For a list of many films, see *Filme Contra Faschismus* (Berlin: Staatliches Filmarchiv der Deutschen Demokratischen Republik, 1965).

14. This section is based on Leyda, *Kino*, chap. 17. For an account of how Hollywood changed its portrayal of Russia after the Nazi invasion, see Robert Fyne, "From Hollywood to Moscow," *Film/Literature Quarterly* 13.3 (1985): 194–99.

15. See Robert Joseph, "The War of Russian Films," *American Cinematographer* 25.2 (Feb. 1945): 48–9.

16. Jay Leyda, *Films Beget Films: A Study of the Compilation Film* (New York: Hill, 1964), 56.

17. The first was directed by Yulia Solntseva and Yakov Avdeyenko; the second by Dovzhenko and Solntseva. These are not to be confused with Dovzhenko's project titled *Ukraine in Flames*, about which he writes deeply; see *Alexander Dovzhenko: The Poet as Filmmaker*, ed. and trans. Marco Carynnyk (Cambridge: MIT Press, 1973).

18. *Liberated France* was greatly admired by Eisenstein; his remarks are quoted in Leyda, *Films Beget Films*, 70.

19. Leyda, *Kino* (388), provides a glimpse into what happened to documentary and nonfiction filmmaking in the Soviet Union immediately after the war.

20. For the material in this section, I have relied heavily on Jay Leyda, *Dianying/Electric Shadows: An Account of Films and the Film Audience in China* (Cambridge: MIT Press, 1972), esp. chaps. 4 and 5.

21. See Leyda's appendix 2 for his list of important Chinese films made between 1897 and 1966; there were comparatively few films of any kind made during the war years.

22. See Evelyn Ehrlich, *Cinema of Paradox: French Filmmaking Under the German Occupation* (New York: Columbia University Press, 1985), which focuses on narrative films; André Bazin, *French Cinema of the Occupation and Resistance* (New York: Ungar, 1981); Roger Régent, *Cinéma de France sous l'Occupation: De "La Fille du Puisatier" aux "Enfants du Paradis"* (Paris: Editions d'Aujourdhui, 1975) and Jacques Siclier, *La France de Pétain et Son Cinéma* (Paris: Veyrier, 1981); the first chapter of Siclier's book, in English translation, appears as "The Psychology of the Spectator, or the 'Cinema of Vichy' Did Not Exist" in *Rediscovering French Film*, ed. Mary Lea Bandy (New York: Museum of Modern Art, 1983), 141–46.

23. Siclier, ed. Bandy, 141. Régent says that 220 features were produced during the Occupation; Siclier says the number was 280.

24. For a listing of these films, see "Remarquable Développement du Cinéma Documentaire Français," *Le cinéma Français 1945* (Paris: Editions de la Cinématographie Francaise, 1945), 15, 42–47.

25. See Jean-Pierre Bertin-Maghit, "Propaganda sociologique dans le cinéma français du 1940 à 1944," *La Revue du Cinéma* 329 (June 1978): 71–84; includes many film titles.

26. Paul Leglise, *Histoire de la Politique du Cinéma Français*, vol. 2 of *Le Cinéma entre Deux Républiques (1940-1946)*, ed. Pierre L'Herminier (Paris: Film Éditions, 1977).

27. For personal memoirs of wartime theatre-going, see Siclier and François Truffaut's introduction to Bazin.

28. Before it, Christensen had made *Sixty Million Horsepower* (1944) and *Citizens of the Future* (1945)

29. See Jytte Jensen, *Carl Th. Dreyer* (New York: Museum of Modern Art, 1988).

30. For an account of films shown after the Liberation, see "Analyse de tous des films inédits de long métrage projetés á Paris de la Liberation au 15 Octobre 1945," *Le Cinéma Français 1945*, vol. 2 (Paris: Editions de la cinématographie Française, 1945).

31. John Weiss, "An Innocent Eye?: The Career and Documentary Vision of Georges Rouquier Up to 1945," *Cinema Journal* 20.2 (Spring 1981): 39–63.

10. AMERICAN FILMS FOR WORLD WAR II

1. *The Politics of Propaganda: The Office of War Information, 1942–1945* (New Haven: Yale University Press, 1978), 157.

2. Alex Greenberg and Marvin Wald, "Report to the Stockholders," *Hollywood Quarterly* 1.4 (July 1946): 410–15; see also *Movie Lot to Beachhead*, ed. by editors of *Look* (New York: Doubleday, 1945).

3. In 1942, the Office of War Information (OWI) became the official liaison between the film industry and government.

4. As discussed above (see chap. 2), filmmaking during wartime was not a new idea; according to Richard MacCann,

> all the major film activities of World War II were used in World War I: newsreel distribution, nontheatrical showings, features and shorts for commercial theaters, and films for overseas, accomplished through government advice, then government sponsorship, and, finally, government production. (123)

5. During World War II, civilian audiences contributed almost $37,000,000 for war relief activities, while the Hollywood studios contributed another $2,000,000; see *Movies at War*, published in 1945 by the War Activities Committee of the Motion Picture Industry, vol. 4, 44. Looking back in 1945, James Agee wrote that viewing war films imposes special burdens on the audience:

> For all that may be said of our seeing these terrible records of war, we have no business seeing this sort of experience except through our presence and participation. . . . If at an incurable distance from participation, hopelessly incapable of reactions adequate to the event, we watch men killing each other, we may be quite as profoundly degrading ourselves and, in the process, betraying and separating ourselves the farther from those we are trying to identify ourselves with; nonetheless we tell ourselves sincerely that we sit in comfort and watch carnage in order to nurture our patriotism, our conscience, our understanding, and our sympathies. (See "Seeing Terrible Records of War," *The Nation* 24 May 1945: 342.)

6. Elmer Holmes Davis, "Report to the President," ed. and with an introd. by Ronald T. Farrar, *Journalism Monographs* 7 (Aug. 1968): 5–86.

7. Since World War II, in the shadow of nuclear holocaust, the major conflicts in Korea, Vietnam, and the Middle East, as well as many smaller wars, have changed American attitudes about the need to fight. During the Vietnam War, especially, increasing numbers of Americans withdrew their support of the government's policy; and, as it plainly became a war of politicians and diplomats, not a war supported by the majority of the people, it became an underground war, as far as propaganda forces were concerned. The films made about and for the Korean and Vietnam wars were mainly official ones for military purposes

or for television (see chap. 14). The few sponsored films that were made to support or to oppose the course of the Vietnam war have little importance as film or propaganda. By then, television coverage had replaced the government propaganda films of the Second World War and became the chief means of providing information for the American public.

8. "Post-War American Documentaries," *Penguin Film Review* 8 (1949): 92.

9. For a history of the OWI, see Winkler, *The Politics of Propaganda*; see also Mac-Cann, 118–151.

10. Raymond Fielding, *The American Newsreel: 1911–1967* (Norman: University of Oklahoma Press, 1972), 289–95.

11. After the war, the network established by OWI greatly contributed to the establishment of 16mm film as a major educational medium (MacCann 147).

12. "The Documentary and Hollywood," *Nonfiction Film Theory and Criticism*, ed. Barsam, 164.

13. Although the United Nations was established immediately after World War II, the name United Nations was coined by President Franklin D. Roosevelt in 1941 to describe the countries fighting against the Axis. On June 12, 1944, President Roosevelt established the Fort Ontario Emergency Refugee Shelter in Oswego. See Sharon R. Lowenstein, *Token Refuge: The Story of the Jewish Refugee Shelter at Oswego, 1944–46* (Bloomington: Indiana University Press, 1986) and Ruth Gruber, *Haven: The Unknown Story of 1,000 World War II Refugees* (New York: Coward, 1983).

14. For information on films made for the Inter-American Affairs division, including Walt Disney's *The Grain that Built a Hemisphere*, see MacCann, 147–51.

15. William T. Murphy said: "The production of these films was, and still is, the most ambitious effort to teach modern history with motion pictures." See "The Method of *Why We Fight*," *Journal of Popular Film* 1.3 (Summer 1972): 185.

16. *The Name Above the Title* (New York: Macmillan, 1971), 336–37.

17. Jay Leyda says that the Soviets were impressed with Capra's large historical plan and with his efficient handling of the material; see *Films Beget Films: A Study of the Compilation Film* (New York: Hill, 1971), 65.

18. See Herb A. Lightman, "Shooting Production Under Fire," *American Cinematographer* 26.9 (Sept. 1945): 296–97; Jeanine Basinger, *The World War II Combat Films* (New York: Columbia University Press, 1986), 281–82.

19. *John Ford: The Man and His Films* (Berkeley: University of California Press, 1986), 202.

20. See MacCann, 131–32.

21. *An Open Book* (New York: Knopf, 1980), 102–04. See also "The Courage of The Men: An Interview with John Huston," *Film: Book 2, Films of Peace and War*, ed. Robert Hughes, Stanley Brown, and Carlos Clarens (New York: Grove, 1962), 22–35.

22. See MacCann, 168.

23. See Huston, chap. 9.

24. See Charles Affron, "Reading the Fiction of Nonfiction: William Wyler's *Memphis Belle*," *Quarterly Review of Film Studies* 7:1 (Winter 1982): 53–59.

25. For producer Louis de Rochemont's account of making this film, see Ezra Goodman, "Fact Films to the Front," *American Cinematographer* 25.2 (Feb. 1945): 46–47+.

26. This quotation, which appears in the closing credits, is missing from some prints.

27. See Huston, *An Open Book*, chap. 10. For the script, see John Huston, "*Let There Be Light*," *Film: Book 2, Films of Peace and War*, ed. Robert Hughes, Stanley Brown, and Carlos Clarens (New York: Grove, 1962), 205–33.

28. About its suppression by the War Department, James Agee wrote: "I don't know what is necessary to reverse this disgraceful decision, but if dynamite is required, then dynamite is indicated" (*Agee on Film* [Boston: Beacon, 1958], 200).

29. See Erik Barnouw, "*Hiroshima-Nagasaki*: The Case of the A-Bomb Footage," *New Challenges for Documentary*, ed. Alan Rosenthal (Berkeley: University of California Press, 1988), 581–91.

11. BRITISH NONFICTION FILM AFTER WORLD WAR II

1. Margaret Dickinson and Sarah Street, *Cinema and State: The Film Industry and the British Government, 1927-1984* (London: BFI, 1985), 150ff.

2. See Winifred Holmes, "What's Wrong with Documentary?" *Sight and Sound* 16.65 (Spring 1948): 44-45; and John Grierson, "Prospect for Documentary: What Is Wrong and Why," *Sight and Sound* 17.66 (Summer 1948): 55-59.

3. American examples include *The Spanish Earth* (1937), *Native Land* (1942), and *The Fight for Life* (1941).

4. See Higson, 88.

5. See also Pierre Koralnik, *Francis Bacon* (1964, Swiss) and David Sylvestor, *Francis Bacon: Fragmente Eines Portrats* (1968, Germany).

6. Lindsay Anderson, "Free Cinema" and "Only Connect: Some Aspects of the Work of Humphrey Jennings" in *Nonfiction Film Theory and Criticism*, ed. Barsam, 70-74, 263-70; Kenneth J. Robson, "Humphrey Jennings: The Legacy of Feeling," *Quarterly Review of Film Studies* 7.1 (Winter 1982): 37-52; and *Humphrey Jennings: Film-Maker, Painter, Poet*, ed. Mary-Lou Jennings (London: British Film Institute, 1982).

7. The first Free Cinema screening featured French films by Georges Franju, Francois Truffaut, and Claude Chabrol; the American Lionel Rogosin's *On The Bowery*; and the early work of Lindsay Anderson, Karel Reisz, Tony Richardson, Guy Brenton, Claude Goretta, Lorenzo Mazzetti, and Alain Tanner. See Gavin Lambert, "Free Cinema," *Sight and Sound* 25.4 (Spring 1956): 173-77.

8. From the first Free Cinema program, quoted in David Robinson, *The History of World Cinema* (New York: Stein, 1973), 291-92.

9. Peter Davis, "Lindsay Anderson Views His First Feature Film," *Chicago Daily News* 28 July 1963: 21.

10. Stephen Mamber does not acknowledge this link; another view of the changing British tradition is Jack C. Ellis, "Changing of the Guard: From the Grierson Documentary to Free Cinema," *Quarterly Review of Film Studies* 7.1 (Winter 1982): 23-35; the many printer's errors in the Ellis article are corrected in the subsequent issue.

11. "Angles of Approach," *Sequence* 2 (Winter 1947): 5.

12. Elizabeth Sussex, *Lindsay Anderson* (London: Studio, 1969), 12-14.

13. See John Hill, esp. chap. 6.

14. Lindsay Anderson, "Only Connect: Some Aspects of the Work of Humphrey Jennings," *Nonfiction Film Theory and Criticism*, ed. Barsam (New York: Dutton, 1976), 263-70.

15. Guy Brenton also directed *The Vision of William Blake* (1958).

16. John Hill (151-53) discusses the influence of its use of sound on *A Taste of Honey* and *Saturday Night and Sunday Morning*.

17. Sussex, 33.

12. EUROPEAN, ASIAN, AND CANADIAN NONFICTION FILM AFTER WORLD WAR II

1. Ted Perry, "The Road to Neo-Realism," *Film Comment*, 14.6 (Nov.-Dec. 1978): 7-13; Eric Rhode, "Why Neo-realism Failed," *Sight and Sound* 30.1 (Winter 1960-61): 26-32.

2. Penelope Houston, *The Contemporary Cinema* (Baltimore: Penguin, 1963), 33.

3. "Some Ideas on the Cinema," *Sight and Sound* 23.2 (Oct.-Dec. 1953): 64-70.

4. See Peter Brunette, *Roberto Rossellini* (New York: Oxford University Press, 1987). In 1963, Rossellini produced *Blood on the Balcony* (Italian title: *Benito Mussolini*), directed by Pasquale Prunas. With a very ironic narration, the film recounts the rise of the fascist movement in Italy.

5. Leprohon, Pierre. *The Italian Cinema*, trans. Roger Greaves and Oliver Stallybran (London: Secker, 1972), 99.

6. *Antonioni* (New York: Praeger, 1968), 33.

7. Vernon Jarratt, *The Italian Cinema* (London: Falcon, 1951), 89.

8. Jarratt, 89; see 91–93 for a discussion of some lesser-known, but distinctive, filmmakers.

9. Lionello Torossi's 1969 English version, with narration by Richard Basehart, is titled *Giotto and the Pre-Renaissance*.

10. I am indebted to Geert Van Wonterghem, who provided me with his own summaries as well as notes and translations from various Belgian sources, including Pascal Lefèvre and Geert van Wonterghem, eds., *Beeld & Realiteit: International Festival Van de Documentaire film en Televisie* (Leuven, Belg.: Catholic University of Leuven and St. Hoger Institute of St. Lukas High School, Brussels, 1987); F. Bolen, *Histoire Authentique, Anecdotique, Folklorique et Critique du Cinéma Belge Depuis Ses Plus Lointaines Origines* (Brussels: Memo & Codec, 1978); Jan-Pieter Everaerts, *Oog Voor Het Echte* (Brussels: Brtuitgave, 1987). It is noteworthy that most early films of Flemish directors such as Storck and Dekeukeleire were made in the French language. After the war, the Flemish people sought greater cultural identity and most of their films were made in the Flemish language.

11. Also of interest are the British film by David Sylvester, *Magritte: The False Mirror* (1970), and the French film by Adrien Maben, *Monsieur René Magritte* (1978).

12. See Claude Goretta, "Aspects of the French Documentary," *Sight and Sound* 26.3 (Winter 1956–57): 156–68.

13. For the script, see Jean Cayrol, "*Night and Fog,*" *Film: Book 2, Films of Peace and War*, ed. Robert Hughes, Stanley Brown, and Carlos Clarens (New York: Grove, 1962), 234–55.

14. The full script is reprinted in Robert Hughes, ed., *Film: Book 2, Films of Peace and War* (New York: Grove, 1962).

15. "Four French Documentaries," *The Documentary Tradition: From Nanook to Woodstock*, ed. Lewis Jacobs (New York: Hopkinson, 1971), 318.

16. In addition to their films on art, the French excelled in television series on art. "Pleasures of the Arts" ("Plaisirs des arts") included such films by Michel Mitrani, Jean-Luc Dejean and Jacques Floran as *Léger* (1959), *Pevsner* (1959), *César* (1959), and *Pleasures of the Arts: Braque, Man Ray, Brown, Bryen, Bissière, les frères Loeb* (Plaisirs des arts, 1959). "Studios in France" ("Ateliers en France") included films by Fabienne Tzanck and Pierre Neurisse: *Henri Michaux* (1958), *Zao Wou Ki* (1960), *Ubac* (1960), and *Édouard Pignon* (1960). "Black Room" ("Chambre Noire") included Claude Fayard's *Man Ray Photograph* (*Man Ray photographe*, 1961), and "Terre des arts" included Michel Mitrani's *The Abstract Art in Question* (*L'art abstrait en question*, 1961) and *Goya* (1962); Roger Kahane's *Jean Dubuffet* (1961), and Jean Lhote's *The Origins of French Art* (*Les origines de l'art en France*, 1963). "Art and Men" ("*L'art et les hommes*") included Jean-Marie Drot's *Voyage au pays des demeures avec Étienne Martin* (1962), *Giacometti: A Man Among the Others* (*Giacometti, un homme parmi les autres*, 1963), *La bande à Man Ray* (1964), *Games of Chess with Marcel Duchamp* (*Jeux d'échec avec Marcel Duchamp*, 1964). "French Painters Today" ("Peintres Français d'aujourdhui") included Jacques Simonnet's and Guy Suzuki's *The Life and Work of Robert Bissière* (*La vie et l'oeuvre de Roger Bissière*, 1963) and *Gustave Singier* (1963). "Living Art" ("L'art vivant") included Jean-Michel Meurice's *Jean-Paul Riopelle* (1963), *Dodeigne* (1963), *Françoise Sthaly* (1965), and *Sonia and Robert Delaunay* (1967). The series "Les métamorphoses du regard, André Malraux" included Clovis Prevost's *Masters of the Unreal* (*Les maitres de l'irréel*, 1974), *The Gods of the Night and the Sun* (*Les dieux de la nuit et du soleil*, 1974), and *World Without God* (*Le monde sans Dieu*, 1974).

17. See Leenhardt, "L'evolution du film d'art," *Gazette des Beaux Arts* 6.102 (Jul.–Aug. 1983): 42–46.

18. See Leyda, *Films Beget Films: A Study of the Compilation Film* (New York: Hill, 1971), esp. chap. 5.

19. Films about the Nuremberg trials include Roman Karmen's *Judgement of the Na-*

tions (Soviet Union, 1946), Pare Lorentz's *Nuremberg* (USA, 1948), and Marcel Ophuls's *A Memory of Justice* (1976).

20. Leyda, 178. Among the very few West German films worth mentioning in the fifteen years after the war were films on art, including Walter Leckebusch's *Albrecht Dürer* (1954) and *The Age of Rococo* (1958).

21. See Erwin Leiser, *Nazi Cinema* (New York: Macmillan, 1974).

22. Ivens's film is notable for music by Dmitri Shostakovich and lyrics by Bertolt Brecht, sung by Paul Robeson.

23. Leyda (90) believes that the "coolness" of Resnais' *Night and Fog* is more effective than the heat of Hurwitz's film.

24. Other films that celebrate modern Russian history are the Thorndikes' *The Russian Miracle* (*Das Russische Wunder*, East Germany, 1963) and Carlo Infascelli's *Cavalcade of a Half Century* (*Cavalcata di mezzo Secolo*, Italy, 1951).

25. See Catherine de la Roche, "Arne Sucksdorff's Adventure," *Sight and Sound* 23.2 (Oct.–Dec. 1953): 83–6; and Forsyth Hardy, "The Films of Arne Sucksdorff," *Sight and Sound* 17.66 (Summer 1948): 60–63+.

26. See Erik Barnouw and S. Krishnaswamy, *Indian Film*, 2nd ed. (New York; Oxford, 1980).

27. During this same period, Satyajit Ray, India's most acclaimed film director, was winning international acclaim with his "Apu trilogy" of narrative films: *The Song of the Road* (*Pather Panchali*, 1955), *The Unvanquished* (*Aparajito*, 1957), and *The World of Apu* (*Apur sansar*, 1958).

28. See Donald Richie, *Japanese Cinema* (New York: Anchor, 1971).

29. See Jay Leyda, *Dianying/Electric Shadows: An Account of Films and the Film Audience in China* (Cambridge: MIT Press, 1979). Because of the prevalence of narrative films in Chinese postwar cinema history, Leyda focusses on them rather than nonfiction films. This brief account is heavily dependent on Leyda's comprehensive work.

30. See David Bickley, "Joris Ivens Filming in China," *Filmmakers Newsletter* 10.4 (Feb. 1977): 22–26; Deborah Shaffer, "Fifty Years of Political Filmmaking: An Interview with Joris Ivens," *Cinéaste* 14.1 (1985): 12–16+; Jane Rayleigh, "Joris Ivens in China," *Sightlines* 12.1 (Fall 1978): 21–3; and Robert Sklar, "Joris Ivens: The China Close-Up," *American Film* (June 1978): 59–65.

31. *John Grierson and the National Film Board: The Politics of Wartime Propaganda, 1939-1945* (Toronto: University of Toronto Press, 1985), 269.

32. Barnouw (201) says that "it inspired two projects that became television classics: *The Real West* (1961) and *End of the Trail* (1965)."

33. In *Universe* (1960), Roman Kroitor and Colin Low use similar techniques, as well as animation, to explore the solar system.

13. AMERICAN NONFICTION FILM AFTER WORLD WAR II

1. By contrast, 58,151 are recorded as Vietnam War deaths. By breakdown, in Korea, 33,629 are recorded as battle deaths, with 20,617 as other deaths; in Vietnam, 47,356 are recorded as battle deaths, with 10,795 as other deaths.

2. See William Lafferty, "A Reappraisal of the Semi-Documentary in Hollywood, 1945-1948," *Velvet Light Trap* 20: 22–26.

3. *The People's Films*, 174.

4. Thomas M. Pryor, "Films in the 'Truth Campaign,'" *The Documentary Tradition*, ed. Lewis Jacobs, 292.

5. See John W. Henderson, *The United States Information Agency* (New York: Praeger, 1969), esp. pp. 33–61 and 302–07.

6. This consolidation included those of the State Department, Mutual Security Agency, Technical Cooperation Administration, and those in the occupied areas administered by the

Defense Department; however, it did not include the educational exchange program, which remained in the State Department. The government's Reorganization Plan No. 2 of 1977 merged the USIA and the State Department's Bureau of Educational and Cultural Affairs, and changed the USIA's name to USICA. In a 1982 action, the agency's functions remained intact, but its name reverted to USIA. Despite this streamlining, the overseas operation is still known as the United States Information Service (USIS), as it has since the time of the OWI.

7. *U.S. Information Agency Fact Sheet* (United States Information Agency, Washington, D.C., Oct. 1989). See also MacCann, chap. 8.

8. Seltzer's *Visit to India* and *Visit to Pakistan* (1962) were combined as one film, retitled, and released as one film. This was made possible by a U.S. Senate resolution, in which the House of Representatives did not concur. See Henderson, 238, and Robert E. Elder, *The Information Machine: The United States Information Agency and American Foreign Policy* (New York: Syracuse, 1968), 279. Seltzer made many films for the USIA, including *Progress Through Freedom* (1962), a record of President and Mrs. Kennedy's trip to Mexico.

9. *Documentary in American Television* (New York: Hastings House, 1965), 59. See also *American History/American Television: Interpreting the Video Past*, ed. John E. O'Connor (New York: Ungar, 1983).

10. "Television and the Future of Documentary," *Film Quarterly* 9 (Summer 1955): 366–73.

11. "The Documentary Heritage," *The Documentary Tradition*, ed. Lewis Jacobs, 301.

12. See Bluem, 278–96, for a list of important films produced for television before 1965.

13. For a complete discussion, see Barsam, *The Vision of Robert Flaherty: The Artist as Myth and Filmmaker* (Bloomington: Indiana University Press, 1988), esp. chap. 8.

14. In Rotha, ed. Ruby, Frances Flaherty is quoted: "Bob was insistent that no one should show any affection for the boy except himself. He wanted sole control over him, as he had done with Sabu and Mikeleen" (236).

15. Thomson was awarded the 1949 Pulitzer Prize for the music, the first time this prize had been given for a film score. For the film, the score was played by the Philadelphia Orchestra under the direction of Eugene Ormandy. Thomson was further pleased that the two suites that he extracted from the film score have been played more than any other of his orchestral works.

16. See Barsam, 111–12, for Flaherty's final, unrealized projects.

17. "The Turn Toward Conservatism," 277.

18. See Sheldon Renan, *An Introduction to the American Underground Film* (New York: Dutton, 1967).

19. See Leo Seltzer, "Document of a Documentary: "Fate of a Child," *Studies in Visual Communication* 8.3 (Summer 1982): 41–54.

20. *In the Street* incorporates much footage intended for, but not used in, *The Quiet One*.

21. Stoney's other early films include *The Valiant Heart* (1953) and *A Cry for Help* (1962).

22. An outstanding exception to this is John Ford's masterpiece *The Grapes of Wrath* (1940); both the film and the Steinbeck novel on which it was based were the subjects of considerable controversy for their depiction of big business, labor unrest, and Depression-era social upheaval.

23. While the film employed nonprofessional actors, the lead, a professional actress named Rosaura Revueltas, gives a moving performance; reportedly, she was deported as a result of having appeared in the film, the crew were attacked by vigilantes, and a conspiracy formed which delayed completion of the film for about six months; see William Murray, "Films," *Nation* 178 (10 April 1954): 314

24. See Loren Cocking, *Francis Thompson: Analysis of an American Film Maker*, unpublished M.A. Thesis, Ohio State University, 1969.

25. Hurwitz rereleased the film in 1964 with an update on the civil rights movement, including coverage of the 1963 March on Washington.

26. Warren Miller, "Progress in Documentary," in *The Documentary Tradition*, ed. Lewis Jacobs, 247.

27. Guggenheim's *Nine From Little Rock* (1963), a USIA film about school integration, won the 1964 Oscar as best documentary feature. Other films on this subject include Lee Bobker's *All the Way Home* (1958).

28. See Mark Sufrin, "Filming Skid Row," in *The Documentary Tradition*, ed. Jacobs, 307–15.

29. "The Turn Toward Conservatism," 279.

30. Rouch's early ethnographic films, made in Africa, include *Hippopotamus Hunt* (*Chasse à l'Hippopotame*, 1946), *Cliff Cemetery* (*Cimétière dans la Falaise*, 1951), *The Rain Makers* (*Les Hommes Qui Font la Pluie*, 1951), and *The Foolish Masters* (*Les Maîtres Fous*, 1953). Other important titles include Conrad Bentzen's *Mokil* (1950) and those by Bateson and Mead—*Trance and Dance in Bali* (1952) and *Childhood Rivalry in Bali and New Guinea* and *Karba's First Years* (1952).

31. See Karl G. Heider, *Ethnographic Film* (Austin: University of Texas Press), 5–15.

32. "A Chronicle of the Human Experience: *Dead Birds*," in *The Documentary Tradition: From Nanook to Woodstock*, ed. Lewis Jacobs, 430.

33. See Jeanine Basinger, *The World War II Combat Film: Anatomy of a Genre* (New York: Columbia University Press, 1986).

34. Basinger lists only one documentary about the Korean War: *Cassino to Korea* (1950), which attempted to draw parallels between the Italian campaign of World War II and the Korean.

35. See MacCann, 179–80.

36. Although *That War in Korea* (Project XX) was not released until 1963, it remains the most outstanding television film about the war; see Bluem, 163.

14. AMERICAN RENAISSANCE IN THE 1960S: THE NEW NONFICTION FILM

1. There was what Morris Dickstein calls the "blissed-out side: the fascination with the occult, the attraction to Eastern gurus and meditative practices, the short-lived Nirvanas that come by way of drugs, polymorphous sexuality, or quickie therapies"; see *Gates of Eden: American Culture in the Sixties* (New York: Basic, 1977), viii. See also Eric P. Goldman, *The Crucial Decade—And After: America, 1945–1960* (New York: Vintage, 1960); Godfrey Hodgson, *America in Our Time* (New York: Vintage, 1978); William O'Neill, *Coming Apart: An Informal History of American Film in the 1960s* (Chicago: Quadrangle, 1971); Leonard Quart and Albert Auster, *American Film and Society Since 1945* (New York: Macmillan, 1984); and David E. James, *Allegories of Cinema: American Film in the Sixties* (Princeton: Princeton University Press, 1989).

2. For a more complete discussion of the historical and theoretical origins of cinéma vérité and direct cinema, see my "American Direct Cinema: The *Re*-presentation of Reality," *Persistence of Vision* 3–4 (Summer 1986): 131–56.

3. Louis Marcorelles, *Living Cinema: New Directions in Contemporary Film-Making* (New York: Praeger, 1973), 38.

4. Pierre Perrault (*Pour la suite de monde*, 1963, *La regne du jour*, 1967, *Les voitures d'eau*, 1968, *Un pays sans bon sens*, 1970, and *L'Acadie, l'Acadie*, 1971); Chris Marker (*Sunday in Peking* [*Dimanche à Pékin*], 1955, *Letter from Siberia* [*Lettre de Sibérie*], 1957, *Cuba* Si!, 1961, and *The Lovely May* [*Le joli mai*, 1963]); Mario Ruspoli (*Les Hommes de la baleine*, 1956, *Les inconnus de la terre*, 1961, and *Regard sur la folie*, 1961); Jacques Rozier (*Adieu Philippine*, 1963); and Jean Rouch (*The Manic Priests* [*Les maîtres fous*], 1955, *I, a*

Black [*Moi, un noir*], 1958, *Chronicle of a Summer* [Chronique d'un été], 1961, *Funeral in Bongo: Old Anai, 1849–1971*, 1979, and *Punishment*, 1963).

5. There is also a connection between Rouch, Vertov, Flaherty, and the Italian neorealists, but Rouch's work cannot be easily classified with theirs. See Jean-Andre Fieschi, "Jean Rouch" in *Cinema: A Critical Dictionary*, ed. Richard Roud, vol. 2, 901–09; Bruce Berman, "Jean Rouch: A Founder of the Cinéma Vérité Style," *Film Library Quarterly* 11:4 (1978): 21–23; *Anthropology-Reality-Cinema: The Films of Jean Rouch*, ed. Mick Eaton (London: British Film Institute, 1979); James Blue, "The Films of Jean Rouch (Including interviews with Blue and Jacqueline Veuve)," *Film Comment* 4.2–3 (Fall–Winter 1967): 82–91; and Robert Edmonds, *About Documentary: Anthropology on Film, a Philosophy of People and Art* (Dayton: Pflaum, 1974).

6. The film was coproduced with Edgar Morin, and photographed by Michel Brault, who later participated in the development of *cinéma direct*, a Canadian form of cinéma vérité.

7. That is but one source of the problem concerning the placement of his work in the history of nonfiction film. Another source is Rouch's comment that in *Chronicle of a Summer* he attempted to combine Vertov's theory and Flaherty's method. See "Table Ronde: Festival de Tours en Collaboration avec l'U.N.E.S.C.O.," *Image et Son* 160 (March 1963): 6.

8. Georges Sadoul claims that his 1948 translation of Vertov's *kino-pravda* into *cinéma vérité* was the first use of the term (See "Dziga Vertov," *Artsept* 2 [April–June 1963]: 18). Louis Marcorelles (34–35) claims that the term was first used in France in 1961 to describe *Chronique d'un Eté*, a film by Jean Rouch and Edgar Morin; others, including Mario Ruspoli, are credited with coining the term.

9. Eric Rohmer and Louis Marcorelles, "Entretien avec Jean Rouch," *Cahiers du Cinéma* 24.144 (June 1963): 1–22.

10. *Cinéma Vérité in America: Studies in Uncontrolled Documentary* (Cambridge: MIT Press, 1974), 1.

11. See Ed Pincus, "One-Person Sync-Sound: A New Approach to *Cinéma Vérité*," *Filmmakers' Newsletter* 6.2 (Dec. 1972): 24–30; Edmund Bert Gerard, "The Truth About Cinéma Vérité," *American Cinematographer* 50 (May 1969): 474–75; Mike Waddell, "*Cinéma Vérité* and the Documentary Film," *American Cinematographer* 49.10 (Oct. 1968): 754+; Colin Young, "Three Views on *Cinéma Vérité*: Cinema of Common Sense," *Film Quarterly* 17.4 (Summer 1964): 26–29+.

12. Robert C. Allen and Douglas Gomery, *Film History: Theory and Practice* (New York: Knopf, 1985), 219. As Allen observed, general familiarity with these techniques "might well have helped audiences to accept similar qualities of *vérité* style twenty years later, as well as giving *vérité* films an air of authenticity Hollywood films could not share" (221). See also James Wong Howe, "The Documentary Technique and Hollywood," *American Cinematographer* (Jan. 1944): 10; and Philip Dunne, "The Documentary and Hollywood," in *Nonfiction Film Theory and Criticism*, ed. Barsam, 158–66. In its attempts to recoup the vast audience from television, Hollywood exploited the technological advantages that motion pictures had over television. While some of these developments, such as the various widescreen processes, were not integrated into the nonfiction film, some were, including the almost total conversion to the use of color film stock; see Charles Barr, "CinemaScope: Before and After," in *Film Theory and Criticism*, ed. Mast and Cohen, 140–68.

13. James Monaco, "American Documentary Since 1960," *Cinema: A Critical Dictionary*, ed. Richard Roud (New York: Viking, 1980), vol. 1, 50; see also Robert C. Allen, 220–23.

14. The early direct cinema pioneers preferred a lightweight, shoulder-mounted 16mm camera such as the Auricon, but also used the Arriflex or French Eclair-NPR, and employed a compact, lightweight sound recorder using 1/4″ tape (usually a Nagra, Nagra Neo-Pilot, or Stellavox). To maintain sync with the camera, they used several devices, including a tiny radio transmitter and a method developed by Drew and Leacock that relied on a Bulova Accutron electronic watch (Allen 222–23).

15. The preceding discussion identifies American direct cinema as a radical solution to the problem of cinematic reality, one which severs almost entirely the nonfiction film from its backgrounds. For the filmmaker, there were two key events in this development. First was the replacement of the issue of social responsibility by that of the freedom of the artist to create a world of film that proved to be radically different from the traditional nonfiction genre. Second was a clear distinction between the process and product of nonfiction film-making: the uncontrolled nature of the profilmic process (lack of planning of the event to be filmed) followed by the controlled direct cinema product. Direct cinema is a disguised self-revelation, in which the filmmaker (either visible or invisible in the film) both expresses and conceals himself. For a different definition and interpretation of direct cinema, see Jean-Louis Comolli, "Detour par de direct—Un corps en trop," *Realism and the Cinema*, ed. Christopher Williams (London: Routledge, 1980), 224–58.

16. See Gerald Mast, *Film/Cinema/Movie* (New York: Harper, 1977), 158; James Blue, "Thoughts on *Cinéma-Vérité* and a Discussion with the Maysles Brothers," *Film Comment* 2.4 (Fall 1965): 23; and Jay Ruby, "The Image Mirrored: Reflexivity and the Documentary Film," *Journal of the University Film Association* 29.2 (Fall 1977): 3–12. Two negative views, asserting a Hollywood position that the techniques of cinéma vérité divert the audience's attention from what the filmmaker is saying, are: Mike Waddell, "*Cinéma Vérité* and the Documentary Film," *American Cinematographer*, 49.10 (Oct. 1968): 754+; and Edmund Bert Gerard, "The Truth About Cinéma Vérité," *American Cinematographer* 50 (May 1969): 474–75.

17. "*Cinéma Vérité* in France," *Film Quarterly* 17.4 (Summer 1964): 36.

18. Evoking the "nitty-gritty," a phrase indigenous to the 1960s, Henry Breitrose concludes that direct cinema should neither assume that there is a universal or absolute truth about objects or events, nor that it could capture this real essence, the "nitty-gritty" of reality; see "On the Search for the Real Nitty-Gritty: Some Problems and Possibilities in *Cinéma Vérité*," *Film Quarterly* 17.4 (Summer 1964): 36–40.

19. *Documentary: A History of the Non-Fiction Film* (New York: Oxford, 1974), 254–55.

20. Ian A. Cameron and Mark Shivas, "Interviews," *Movie* 8 (Apr. 1963): 17.

21. The achievement of "total" cinema remains an impossibility, despite the efforts of those who have tried with technology to create what Bazin called "total cinema." What brings us close to it, however, is the direct cinema artist whose vision (both philosophical viewpoint and physical point of view) controls the *re*-presentation of reality on film. See Bazin, "The Myth of Total Cinema," *What Is Cinema?* (Berkeley: University of California Press, 1967), 17–22.

22. To illustrate the international cross-pollination among these film movements, Jean-Luc Godard worked with Leacock, Pennebaker, and other Americans, as well as with a group he called the Dziga Vertov Group; see Richard Roud, "Jean-Luc Godard," *Cinema: A Critical Dictionary*, ed. Richard Roud (New York: Viking, 1980), vol. 2, 436–46.

23. Three articles in *Film Quarterly* 17.4 (Summer 1964) provide a comprehensive debate on the virtues and faults of early direct cinema; see Henry Breitrose, "On the Search for the Real Nitty-Gritty: Problems and Possibilities in Cinéma Vérité," 36–40; Peter Graham, "Cinéma Vérité in France," 30–36; and Colin Young, "Three Views on Cinéma Vérité: Cinema of Common Sense," 26–29+. In "Cinéma Vérité," *Film Quarterly* 18.2 (Winter 1964): 62–63, James Lipscomb, a member of Drew Associates, responds in an attempt to answer accusations that some scenes in Drew films were faked, to set the record straight, and to emphasize the collaborative nature of the group's work.

24. See Stephen Mamber, *Cinema Verite in America: Studies in Uncontrolled Documentary*, 23–114; and Robert C. Allen and Douglas Gomery, *Film History: Theory and Practice* (New York: Knopf, 1985), 213–41.

25. See Bluem, esp. chaps. 5 and 6. Drew's style was described in a typical news release that manages, in the mode of the carnival barker, to invoke Dziga Vertov: "It's unscripted,

it's unrehearsed . . . for the first time the camera is a man. It sees, it hears, it moves like a man." (quoted in Bluem 194).

26. Richard Lacayo, "Why Are Documentaries So Dull?", *The New York Times* 20 Feb. 1983, sec. 2: 29. See also "Television's School of Storm and Stress," *Broadcasting* 60 (Mar. 1961): 83.

27. See Allen and Gomery, *Film History: Theory and Practice* (New York: Knopf, 1985), 224–37. The "fairness doctrine" admonished broadcasters to "afford reasonable opportunity for the discussion of conflicting views on issues of public importance."

28. Ernest Callenbach, in "Going Out to the Subject," *Film Quarterly* 14.3 (Spring 1961): 38–40, recognized that Leacock's ability to go out to the subject enabled him to get into it as well. James Blue, in "One Man's Truth," *Film Comment* 3.2 (Spring 1965): 15–23, conducts a lengthy interview with the filmmaker that covers the overall approach of his direct cinema style. Another interview is "Richard Leacock," in G. Roy Levin, *Documentary Explorations: 15 Interviews with Film-Makers* (New York: Doubleday, 1971), 195–221. For information on Leacock's technological innovations, see Del Hillgartner's two-part article "Super Serious-8: Leacock-MIT Super-8 System," *Filmmakers Newsletter* 6.12 (Oct. 1973): 53–56, and 7.1 (Nov. 1973): 51–55; Louis Marcorelles, "Leacock at M.I.T.," *Sight and Sound* 18.2 (Spring 1974): 104–07; and Ed Pincus, "One-Person Sync-Sound: A New Approach to Cinéma Vérité," *Filmmakers Newsletter* 6.2 (Dec. 1972): 24–30.

29. Another excellent film about Stravinsky is Tony Palmer's *Once at a Border: Aspects of Stravinsky* (Great Britain, 1981).

30. See "Donn Alan Pennebaker" in G. Roy Levin, 223–70.

31. Ed Pincus, "New Possibilities in Film and the University," *Quarterly Review of Film Studies* 2.2 (May 1977): 159–78, in a good analysis of the history of direct cinema and what it has to offer for film production at the university level, considers the film as the best example for showing the aspirations and limitations of early direct cinema. See also D. A. Pennebaker, *Dont Look Back* (New York: Ballantine, 1968).

32. For another view, see William F. Van Wert, "The 'Hamlet Complex' or Performance in the Personality-Profile Documentary," *Journal of Popular Film* 3.3 (1974): 257–63. In discussing *Dont Look Back* and *Gimme Shelter*, among others, Van Wert's main point is that "whenever a documentary is of the personality-profile variety, and whenever that performer being filmed is most aware of the camera filming him (live interview, live concert), we can be reasonably sure that we are witnessing a lie and not a reality, an artifice as opposed to the truth, a performance as opposed to a true personality."

33. In writing about this relationship between television and the status of the documentary film in the postwar period, A. William Bluem observed that "television has given the documentary film its greatest impetus; it has all but rescued an ailing patient *in extremis*" (7). Bluem further observed that there was something almost historically inevitable in this relationship between television and the "documentary idea" (as defined first by Grierson and subsequently refined by others): "television *is* mass communication, and in this lies its strength as a documentary instrument" (16). For an account of the relationship between the documentary film tradition and early television, see Vance Kepley, "The Origins of NBC's 'Project XX' in Compilation Documentaries," *Journalism Quarterly* 61.1 (Spring 1984): 20–21. See also Paul Rotha, "Television and the Future of Documentary," *Film Quarterly* 9 (Summer 1955): 366–73; and Burton Benjamin, "The Documentary Heritage" in *Nonfiction Film Theory and Criticism*, ed. Barsam, 203–08.

34. Bluem (278–96) offers a list of significant early television documentaries. See also Richard C. Bartone, "A History and An Analysis of *The Twentieth Century* (1957–1966) Compilation Series," diss. New York University, 1985; and Jay Leyda, *Films Beget Films: A Study of the Compilation Film* (New York: Hill, 1971), 147–150.

35. For a later and more pessimistic view of the future for independently produced television documentaries, see Patricia R. Zimmerman, "Public Television, Independent Documentary Producer and Public Policy," *Journal of the University Film and Video Association* 34.3 (Summer 1982): 9–23.

36. A different view of Kennedy is seen in *Kennedy in His True Colours* (1962), made in the People's Republic of China; see Jay Leyda, *Films Beget Films: A Study of the Compilation Film* (New York: Hill, 1970), 118.

37. Because this film was released in the United States, it is listed here; however, this release was an exception to USIA policy, which stipulated that the agency's films were to be made only for release outside of the United States.

38. See William J. Sloan, "The Documentary Film and the Negro" in *The Documentary Tradition: From "Nanook" to "Woodstock,"* ed. Lewis Jacobs (rev. ed. 425–29).

39. See interview with Arthur Barron in Alan Rosenthal, *The New Documentary in Action: A Casebook in Film Making* (Berkeley: University of California Press, 1971), 131–48.

40. Craig Gilbert, "Reflections on *An American Family*, I" and "Reflections on *An American Family*, II," *New Challenges for Documentary*, ed. Rosenthal, 191–209, 288–307.

41. See Eric Krueger. "*An American Family*: An American Film." *Film Comment* (Nov. 1973): 16–19.

42. See Erik Barnouw, 268–83; Philip Knightley, *The First Casualty* (New York: Harcourt, 1975); and Michael Herr, *Dispatches* (New York: Knopf, 1977).

43. Bill Nichols, "Newsreel, 1967–1972: Film and Revolution," 135–53, and Dan Georgakas, *"Finally Got the News"* in *"Show Us Life": Toward a History of the Committed Documentary*, ed. Thomas Waugh (Metuchen: The Scarecrow Press, 1984), 154–67; see also Michael Renov, "The Imaging of Analysis: Newsreel's Re-Search For a Radical Film Practice," *Wide Angle*.

44. Erik Barnouw comments that "revelations later published in *The Pentagon Papers* showed the film to be even more deceptive than it had previously appeared to be" (272).

45. See Barnouw, 274–9.

46. *Vietnam: Anthology and Guide to A Television History*, ed. Steven Cohen (New York: Knopf, 1983); see also Lawrence W. Lichty, " 'Vietnam: A Television History': Media Research and Some Comments," *New Challenges for Documentary*, ed. Rosenthal, 495–505.

47. For an interview with Wasserman, see Alan Rosenthal, *The Documentary Conscience: A Casebook in Film Making* (Berkeley: University of California Press, 1980), 91–101.

48. For an interview with Silverstein, see Alan Rosenthal, *The Documentary Conscience: A Casebook in Film Making* (Berkeley: University of California Press, 1980), 102–112.

49. See *Native Americans on Film and Video*, ed. Elizabeth Weatherford (New York: Museum of the American Indian, 1981).

50. See Robert Gardner, "Chronicles of the Human Experience: *Dead Birds*," *Nonfiction Film Theory and Criticism*, ed. Barsam (New York: Dutton, 1976), 342–48, and Karl G. Heider, *The Dani of West Irian: An Ethnographic Companion to the Film "Dead Birds"*. (Andover, Mass.: Andover Modular Publications, 1972).

51. See Sally Bochner, "National Film Board of Canada: Four Decades of Documentaries and Animation," *Circulating Film Library Catalog* (New York: Museum of Modern Art, 1984), 231–38, and C. Rodney James, *Films As a National Art: NFB of Canada and the Film Board Idea* (New York: Arno Press, 1977).

52. Noteworthy also was an earlier effort, the multipart "Canada at War" (1940) series, directed by Stanley Clish, Peter Jones, and Donald Brittain.

53. "Art and Action," quoted in James, *Film as a National Art*, 81–82.

54. Interview with Douglas Leiterman in Alan Rosenthal, *The Documentary Conscience: A Casebook in Film Making* (Berkeley: University of California Press, 1980), 182.

55. See interview with Beryl Fox in Rosenthal, *The Documentary Conscience*, 227–31.

56. According to Rosenthal, *The Documentary Conscience*, another Canadian film, Dan Drasin's *Sunday*, "shows some of the same police officers from *Indian Land* trying to quell a folk music demonstration" (347).

15. TRADITION AND CHANGE IN THE 1970S

1. These include *Primary, On the Pole, Yanqui, No!, X-Pilot, Adventures on The New*

Frontier, Kenya, Africa, and *Eddie*. David Maysles is said to have worked as a reporter on *Adventures on The New Frontier* and on other Drew Associates films (see *Salesman* [New York, Signet, 1969], 125) although this contribution is not acknowledged in Mamber's more definitive filmography. David Maysles died in January, 1987.

2. *Cinema Verite in America: Studies in Uncontrolled Documentary* (Cambridge: MIT Press, 1974), 141.

3. See Hamid Naficy, " 'Truthful Witness': An Interview with Albert Maysles," *Quarterly Review of Film Studies* 6.2 (Spring 1981): 155–79; Calvin Pryluck, "Seeking to Take the Longest Journey: A Conversation with Albert Maysles," *Journal of the University Film Association* 28.2 (Spring 1976): 9–16; Bob Sitton, "An Interview with Albert and David Maysles," *Film Library Quarterly* 2.3 (Summer 1969): 13–18; James Blue, "Thoughts on Cinéma Vérité and a Discussion with the Maysles Brothers," *Film Comment* 2 (Fall 1964): 22–30; and Maxine Haleff, "The Maysles Brothers and 'Direct Cinema'," *Film Comment* 2.2 (Spring 1964): 19–23.

4. See interview with Charlotte Zwerin in *The New Documentary in Action: A Casebook in Film Making*, ed. Alan Rosenthal (Berkeley: University of California Press, 1971), 86–91, and with Ellen Hovde in *The Documentary Conscience: A Casebook in Film Making*, ed. Alan Rosenthal (Berkeley: University of California Press, 1980), 372–87.

5. See Robert Phillip Kolker, "Circumstantial Evidence: An Interview with Albert and David Maysles," *Sight and Sound* 40.4 (Autumn 1971): 183–86; Albert and David Maysles, "Direct Cinema," *Public Relations Journal* 38.9 (Sept. 1982): 31–33, "Financing the Independent Non-Fiction Film," *Millimeter* 6.6 (June 1978): 74–75, and "Maysles Brothers," *Film Culture* 42 (Fall 1966): 114–15; Charles Reynolds, "Focus on Al Maysles," *Popular Photography* (May 1964): 128–31; and "Albert and David Maysles" in G. Roy Levin, *Documentary Explorations: 15 Interviews with Film-Makers* (New York: Doubleday, 1971), 270–93.

6. See *Salesman* (New York: Signet, 1969); this publication contains the transcript, production notes, and an introduction by Harold Clurman.

7. A Canadian film with a similar subject is David Hoffman's *King, Murray* (1969).

8. See, for example, the interview with Albert Maysles in *The New Documentary in Action: A Casebook in Film Making*, ed. Rosenthal (Berkeley: University of California Press, 1971), 76–85.

9. See Albert and David Maysles, "*Gimme Shelter*: Production Notes," *Filmmakers Newsletter* 5.2 (Dec. 1971): 29–31; Paul Schrader, "Cinema Reviews: *Gimme Shelter*," *Cinema* 7.1 (Fall 1971): 52–54; Joel Haycock, "*Gimme Shelter*," *Film Quarterly* 24.4 (Summer 1971): 56–60; David Pirie, "*Gimme Shelter*," *Sight and Sound* 40.4 (Aug. 1971): 226–7; and David Sadkin, "*Gimme Shelter*: A Corkscrew or a Cathedral?", *Filmmakers' Newsletter* 5.2 (Dec. 1971): 20–27.

10. See Nancy Scott, "The Christo Films: *Christo's Valley Curtain* and *Running Fence*," *Quarterly Review of Film Studies* 7.1 (Winter 1982): 61–68.

11. See the interview with Ellen Hovde in *The Documentary Conscience: A Casebook in Film Making* (Berkeley: University of California Press, 1980), 372–87.

12. A reference which recalls the mother's expectations for her daughter in Tennessee Williams's *The Glass Menagerie*.

13. See Kenneth J. Robson, "The Crystal Formation: Narrative Structure in *Grey Gardens*," *Cinema Journal* 22.2 (Winter 1983), 42–53.

14. See Thomas W. Benson and Carolyn Anderson, *Reality Fictions: The Films of Frederick Wiseman* (Carbondale: Southern Illinois University Press, 1989); Liz Ellsworth, *Frederick Wiseman: A Guide to References and Resources* (Boston: Hall, 1979); Beatrice Berg, "I Was Fed Up With Hollywood Fantasies," *The New York Times* 1 Feb. 1970: 25–26. For an anthology of articles, see Thomas R. Atkins, *Frederick Wiseman* (New York: Monarch, 1976). See also David Denby, "The Real Thing," *New York Review of Books*, 37:17 (November 8, 1990): 24–28.

15. Wiseman has defined this approach several times; see interviews in G. Roy Levin, *Documentary Explorations*, 316–17, and in Alan Rosenthal, *The New Documentary in Ac-*

tion, 66–75; see also John Graham, " 'There Are No Simple Solutions': Frederick Wiseman on Viewing Film," *The Film Journal* (Spring 1971): 44–47 (also in Atkins); and Don Armstrong, "Wiseman's *Model* and the Documentary Project: Toward a Radical Film Practice," *Film Quarterly* 37.2 (Winter 1983–84): 2–10.

16. Rosenthal, *The New Documentary in Action*, 69. See Edgar Z. Friedenberg, "Ship of Fools: The Films of Frederick Wiseman," *The New York Review of Books* 17.6 (Oct. 1971): 19–22; Tim Curry, "Frederick Wiseman: Sociological Filmmaker?", *Contemporary Sociology* 14.1 (Jan. 1985): 35–39; Patrick Sullivan, " 'What's All the Cryin' About?': The Films of Frederick Wiseman," *Massachussetts Review* 13.3 (Summer 1972): 452–68.

17. It has become commonplace in some critical circles to debate the significance of this concern with institutions, specifically whether it implies his dislike or distrust of them. For example, in the first edition of this book, I wrote that "Wiseman clearly dislikes institutions, especially big, bureaucratic ones, but he does not pretend to suggest alternatives" (271). After having seen another ten years of his astonishingly consistent films, I would not only substitute *studies* for *clearly dislikes*, but also emphasize, more than before, the meticulousness with which his camera studies his subject and with which he edits the footage. However, both Pauline Kael and Michael J. Arlen admire Wiseman as a social reformer. Kael wrote: "What he's doing is so simple and so basic that it's like a rediscovery of what we know, or should know. . . . Wiseman extends our understanding of our common life." See "The Current Cinema," *The New Yorker* 18 Oct. 1969: 199–204. Similarly, Arlen wrote:

> For, despite Wiseman's by no means insincere self-explications of his interest in 'American institutions,' what he has been doing all along is to dare to show us ourselves without masks—to let the camera strip us bare, so that the camera may build us anew; in short, he has been working with the *kino* eye. (See "The Air: Fred Wiseman's 'Kino Pravda'," *The New Yorker* 21 Apr. 1980: 101.)

18. Arlen finds evidence of "some of the same obdurate, against-the-grain, though ultimately passionate, quality in Wiseman's films that may be found in the work of the pioneer Soviet realist Dziga Vertov" (96).

19. The film's title derives from a public benefit put on by the mental hospital's inmates and guards; they call it "Titicut Follies" (Titicut is the Indian name for the Bridgewater area) and scenes from this sad "entertainment" open and close the film.

20. See Carolyn Anderson and Thomas W. Benson, *Documentary Dilemmas: Frederick Wiseman's "Titicut Follies"* (Carbondale: Southern Illinois University Press, 1989); Carolyn Anderson, "The Conundrum of Competing Rights in *Titicut Follies*," *University Film Association Journal* 33.1 (1981): 15–22. See also Elliot Richardson's letter and Wiseman's response, "Letters: Focusing again on *Titicut*," *Civil Liberties Review* 1.3 (Summer 1974): 148–51.

21. Wiseman said that he provided "as complex a statement of the reality of the situation as possible" and that it is a "very polemical film," in Alan Sutherland, "Wiseman on Polemic," *Sight and Sound* 47.2 (1978): 82. See also Robert Coles, "Documentary: Stripped Bare at the Follies," *The New Republic* Jan. 1968: 18+; and Ronald Kessler's response, "Correspondence," *The New Republic* Feb. 1968: 35–6.

22. "Cinéma Vérité and Film Truth," *Saturday Review* 9 Sept. 1967: 44.

23. See Frederick Wiseman, "Reminiscences of a Filmmaker: Frederick Wiseman on *Law and Order*," *Police Chief* 36.9. (Sept. 1969): 32–35.

24. The film prefigures *Welfare* (1975), in which the welfare worker, Miss Hightower, actually appears to confirm the incompetence that we only hear about here.

25. Wiseman quoted in O'Connor, " 'The Film is About Killing'," *The New York Times* 3 Oct. 1971: 17.

26. See Dan Armstrong, "Wiseman's *Model* and the Documentary Project: Toward a

Radical Film Practice," *New Challenges for Documentary*, ed. Alan Rosenthal (Berkeley: University of California Press, 1988), 180–90.

27. Kael quoted in Rosenthal, *The Documentary Conscience*, 216; see also Gary Crowdus and Dan Georgakas, "History is the Theme of All My Films: An Interview with Emile de Antonio," *New Challenges for Documentary*, ed Alan Rosenthal (Berkeley: University of California Press, 1988), 165–79.

28. See Alan Rosenthal, *The Documentary Conscience: A Casebook in Film Making* (Berkeley: University of California Press, 1980), 205–26; see also Daniel Talbot, "Historic Hearings: From TV to Screen," *The Documentary Tradition: From "Nanook" to "Woodstock,"* 2nd ed., ed. Lewis Jacobs (New York: Norton, 1979), 392–94.

29. Helen Levitt (*The Quiet One*) was one of his two editors.

30. Emile de Antonio, "Flashback: My Brush with Painting," *American Film* 9.5 (Mar. 1984): 8+. The quote is on p. 10.

31. Even though modern art is the art of freedom, it is also the art of ideas, the subject of Tom Wolfe's caustic study, *The Painted Word* (1975).

32. See Todd Gitlin, "Phantom India," *New Challenges for Documentary*, ed Rosenthal, 536–41.

33. Ophuls made two narrative films, *Peau de banane* (1963) and *Feu à volonté* (1964), and a contribution to the multinational *Love at Twenty* (*L'Amour à vingt ans*, 1962).

34. Another film about Irish history is Robert Kee's *Ireland: A Television History*; see John Pym, "Ireland—Two Nations," *New Challenges for Documentary*, ed. Rosenthal, 480–87.

35. Another film on France and its people since World War I is collectively titled *French People, If You Only Knew* (*Français, si vous saviez*, 1973), codirected by Jacques Brissot and Luc Favory. Its three parts are *Passing By the Lorraine* (*En passant par la Lorraine*), *General, Here We Are* (*General, nous voila*), and *I Understood You* (*Je vous ai compris*). It was produced by André Harris and Alain De Sédouy, the executive producers of *The Sorrow and the Pity*.

36. See *The Sorrow and the Pity: A Film by Marcel Ophuls*, introd. by Stanley Hoffmann (New York: Outerbridge, 1972); see also André Bazin, *French Cinema of the Occupation and Resistance: The Birth of a Critical Esthetic*, introd. by François Truffaut (New York: Ungar, 1975), and James Roy MacBean, "*The Sorrow and the Pity*," *New Challenges for Documentary*, ed. Rosenthal, 471–79.

37. See Rosenthal, *The Documentary Conscience: A Casebook in Film Making*, 303–16; Gary Crowdus, "*Harlan County, U.S.A.*," *The Documentary Tradition*, ed. Lewis Jacobs (New York: Norton, 1979), 563–68.

38. See Rosenthal, *The Documentary Conscience*, 317–29.

39. See interview with Jill Godmilow in Alan Rosenthal, *The Documentary Conscience: A Casebook in Film Making* (Berkeley: University of California Press, 1980), 359–71.

40. See Richard Dyer MacCann, "Alternative Television: The British Model," *The American Scholar* 43.4 (Autumn 1974): 65–66.

41. See also Barbara Rose, *Lee Krasner: The Long View* (1978).

42. Among the many other films on Calder are Hans Richter, *Alexander Calder: From the Circus to the Moon* (1963), Herbert Matter, *Works of Calder* (1950), Carlos Vilardebo, *Calder's Circus* (1961, France), D. G. Hannaford, *The Calder Man* (1967, Great Britain).

43. See also Sir Roland Penrose, *Picasso The Sculptor* (1968, Great Britain).

44. See *Films and Video on Photography*, comp. by Nadine Covert et al. (New York: Program for Art on Film, Metropolitan Museum/J. Paul Getty Trust, 1990).

16. NEW VOICES OF THE 1980S

1. "Ain't Nothing Like the Real Thing," *American Film* 8.4 (Jan.–Feb. 1983): 59. Erik Barnouw put it differently, saying that the independent nonfiction film "is the very essence

of participatory democracy." Barnouw quoted in John J. O'Connor, "Is the Documentary Making a Comeback?," *The New York Times* 26 June 1988, sec. 2: 27.

2. See Alan Rosenthal, *New Challenges for Documentary* (Berkeley: University of California Press, 1988), 1–7; this anthology contains a selection of articles on many new trends and developments in nonfiction film.

3. "Documentaries: Limitless Eyes, Recording Civilization," *The New York Times* 3 Nov. 1985, sec. C: 20.

4. "Toward New Goals in Documentary," *The Documentary Tradition: From "Nanook" to "Woodstock,"* ed. Lewis Jacobs, 494.

5. See Dennis Giles, "The Name *Documentary*: A Preface to Genre Study," *Film Reader* 3 (1978): 18–22; Michael Renov, "Re-thinking Documentary: Toward a Taxonomy of Mediation," *Wide Angle* 8.3–4 (1986): 71–77; Bill Nichols, "The Voice of Documentary," *New Challenges for Documentary*, ed. Rosenthal, 48–63; Richard M. Blumenberg, "Documentary Films and the Problem of 'Truth'," *Journal of the University Film Association* 29.1 (Fall 1977): 19–22; and William Guynn, *A Cinema of Nonfiction* (Rutherford, NJ: Fairleigh Dickinson University Press, 1990).

6. See, for example, Eileen McGarry, "Documentary, Realism and Women's Cinema," *Women and Film* 2.7 (Summer 1975): 50–59.

7. Patricia Erens, "Women's Documentary Filmmaking: The Personal is Political," *New Challenges for Documentary*, ed. Alan Rosenthal (Berkeley: University of California Press, 1988), 561; this is a groundbreaking article in a field that deserves considerable further study; see also Erens, "Women's Documentaries as Social History," *Film Library Quarterly* 14.1–2 (1981), 4–9.

8. A key issue in the history of films by women, lesbians, and gays was the need to establish special distribution companies. Although a market existed, many companies would not distribute these films. Many of these filmmakers distribute their own films; others are distributed through the following organizations: Iris Films and Videos (Berkeley, California); New Day Films, Women Make Movies and Cinema Femina (New York City); and Women's Film Coop (Massachusetts). Because of the informality of some of these distribution arrangements, and the absence of catalogs and scholarly publications, it has not always been possible in this discussion to provide release dates or accurate information on format (film or video). Finally, because of these factors, the emphasis here is on American films.

9. Providing a historical perspective, E. Ann Kaplan writes:

> The first independent films by women situated themselves essentially in the realist tradition as it came immediately through the 1960s British free cinema movement and the work of the National Film Board of Canada, in conjunction with influences from the French New Wave. These movements in turn looked back to documentary efforts spurred by the First and Second World Wars. . . . But particularly important for women's documentaries was the work of the American Newsreel Collective, started in 1962 and largely inspired by Norm Fruchter on his return from working in England at the British Film Institute. (See *Women and Film: Both Sides of the Camera* [New York: Methuen, 1983], 126.)

Women filmmakers cited in other sections of this book include Perry Miller Adato, Erica Anderson, Cinda Firestone, Beryl Fox, Helen Grayson, Nelly Kaplan, Helen Levitt, Janice Loeb, Margaret Mead, Leni Riefenstahl, Esther Shub, Helen van Dongen, Nicole Vedrès, and Helen Whitney. Other feminist filmmakers, including Yvonne Rainer, Agnes Varda, and Chantal Ackerman, created films that bridge the fiction and nonfiction genres and defy easy categorization.

10. "Feminist Documentary: Aesthetics and Politics," *"Show Us Life": Toward a History and Aesthetics of the Committed Documentary*, ed. Thomas Waugh (Metuchen: Scarecrow, 1984), 245. See also Annette Kuhn, *Women's Pictures: Feminism and Cinema*

(London: Routledge, 1982), esp. 147–55; E. Ann Kaplan, *Women and Film: Both Sides of the Camera* (New York: Methuen, 1983), esp. 125–41; B. Ruby Rich, "Anti-Porn: Soft Issue, Hard World," *Films for Women*, ed. Charlotte Brunsdon (London: BFI, 1986), 31–43; Ruth McCormick, *Women's Liberation Cinema* in *The Documentary Tradition: From "Nanook" to "Woodstock,"* ed. Lewis Jacobs, 2nd ed. (New York: Norton, 1971), 523–35.

11. "Women's Documentaries as Social History," *Film Library Quarterly* 14.1–2 (1981): 4–9; see also Barbara Halpern Martineu, "Talking About Our Lives and Experiences: Some Thoughts about Feminism, Documentary, and 'Talking Heads'," *"Show Us Life": Toward a History and Aesthetics of the Committed Documentary*, ed. Thomas Waugh (Metuchen: Scarecrow, 1984), 252–73.

12. Weill also made *Girlfriends* (1977) and *The Other Half of the Sky* (with Shirley MacLaine, 1974).

13. For example, there were two women executive producers (Evelyn Cherry and Gudrun Parker), as well as women cinematographers and technicians. A letter to me from Gudrun Parker (18 April 1990) refutes the remark attributed to Grierson in the article by Chris Sherbarth cited below. Sherbarth writes:

> John Grierson, the Film Board's charismatic founder is sometimes praised for opening up a half dozen directing/producing jobs to women during the Second World War. The other side of the story, however, is that Grierson is on record asserting that film production was an area "where they [women] had ideas above the station to which it had pleased God to call them." (9)

Parker writes: "This quote is ludicrous. I worked for Grierson and if he did say this (which I doubt), it was most certainly ironically!!"

14. Chris Sherbarth, "Why Not D? An Historical Look at the NFB's Woman's Studio," *Cinema Canada* (March 1987): 9–13; see also *Beyond the Image: A Guide to Films about Women and Change*, 2nd. ed. (Montreal: National Film Board of Canada, 1984).

15. Roy Armes, *Third World Film Making and the West* (Berkeley: University of California Press, 1987), 55; see also *Questions of Third Cinema*, ed. Jim Pines and Paul Willemen (London: BFI Publishing, 1989).

16. See David A. Cook, *A History of Narrative Film* (New York: Norton, 1981), 599–600.

17. See *Indian Cinema: 1980–1985*, ed. Rani Burra (New Delhi: The Directorate of Film Festivals, 1985).

18. For example, it was called *cine liberación* in Cuba, *cinema nôvo* in Brazil, *cinema djidid* (new cinema) in Algeria, and *cinema motefävet* (New Iranian Cinema) in Iran.

19. See Helen W. Cyr, *A Filmography of the Third World, 1976–1983* (Metuchen: Scarecrow, 1985); Carl J. Mora, *Mexican Cinema: Reflections of a Society, 1896–1988*, rev. ed. (Berkeley: University of California Press, 1989); *Cinema and Social Change in Latin America: Conversations with Filmmakers*, ed. Julianne Burton (Austin: University of Texas Press, 1986); Michael Chanan, *The Cuban Image: Cinema and Cultural Politics in Cuba* (London: BFI Publishing, 1985); *World Cinema Since 1945*, ed. William Luhr (New York: Ungar, 1987); *The Political Companion to Film*, ed. Gary Crowdus (New York: Pantheon, 1987); Randal Johnson, *Cinema Novo X 5* (Austin: University of Texas Press, 1984); *Brazilian Cinema*, ed. Randal Johnson and Robert Stam (East Brunswick, N.J.: Associated Universities Press, 1982); Dennis West, *Curriculum Guide to Contemporary Brazilian Cinema* (Albuquerque: Latin American Institute, University of New Mexico, 1985); *Argentine Cinema*, ed. Tim Barnard (Toronto: Nightwood, 1986).

20. Armes, 311.

21. In 1948, the Indian government established the Films Division to produce films for public information, education, and motivation. By 1980, their annual output of 120 documentaries and 52 newsreels was seen each week in the country's 10,500 theatres. See B. D.

Garga, "The Long and Short of It," *Film India: The New Generation, 1960–1980*, ed. Uma da Cunha (New Delhi: The Directorate of Film Festivals, 1981), 35–40.

22. Among these filmmakers were Arun Chowdhary, *The Jain Temples*; Santi Chowdhury, *The Inner Eye, Amrita Shergil*; Clement Baptista, *Kailash at Ellora*; Jean Bhownagary, *Radha and Krishna*; Mohan Wadhwani, *Khajuraho*; P. Dasgupta, *Konarak*; Satyajit Ray, *Rabindranath Tagore* (1961); Girish Karnad, *Bendre* (1972), about D. R. Bendre, one of the greatest Indian poets of this century; and M. S. Sathyu, *Ghalib* (1969), about the 18th century poet.

AFTERWORD: ONE HUNDRED YEARS OF NONFICTION FILM

1. "Documentaries: Limitless Eyes, Recording Civilization," *The New York Times* 3 Nov. 1985, sec. C: 19.

2. "The Image Mirrored: Reflexivity and the Documentary Film." *Journal of the University Film Association* 29.1 (Fall 1977): 10.

3. "Toward New Goals in Documentary," *The Documentary Tradition: From "Nanook" to "Woodstock,"* ed. Lewis Jacobs, 494.

4. See Dennis Giles, "The Name *Documentary*: A Preface to Genre Study," *Film Reader* 3 (1978): 18–22; Michael Renov, "Re-thinking Documentary: Toward a Taxonomy of Mediation," *Wide Angle* 8.3–4 (1986): 71–77; Bill Nichols, "The Voice of Documentary," *New Challenges for Documentary*, ed. Rosenthal, 48–63; Richard M. Blumenberg, "Documentary Films and the Problem of 'Truth'," *Journal of the University Film Association* 29.1 (Fall 1977): 19–22; Carl Plantinga, "Defining Documentary: Fiction, Non-Fiction, and Projected Worlds," *Persistence of Vision* 5 (Spring 1987): 44–54; and William Guynn, *A Cinema of Nonfiction* (Rutherford, N.J.: Fairleigh Dickinson University Press, 1990).

Works Cited

Affron, Charles. "Reading the Fiction of Nonfiction: William Wyler's *Memphis Belle*." *Quarterly Review of Film Studies* 7.1 (1982): 53–59.

Agee, James. *Agee on Film*. Boston: Beacon, 1958.

———. "Seeing Terrible Records of War." *The Nation* 24 May 1945: 342.

Aitken, Ian. *Film and Reform: John Grierson and the Documentary Film Movement*. London: Routledge, 1990.

Alexander, William. *Film on the Left: American Documentary Film from 1931 to 1942*. Princeton: Princeton University Press, 1981.

Allen, Robert C. "Motion Picture Exhibition in Manhattan, 1906–1912: Beyond the Nickelodeon." *Film Before Griffith*. Ed. John L. Fell. Berkeley: University of California Press, 1983. 162–75.

———. "Vitascope/Cinématographe: Initial Patterns of American Film Industrial Practice." *Film Before Griffith*. Ed. John L. Fell. Berkeley: University of California Press, 1983. 144–52.

Allen, Robert C., and Douglas Gomery. *Film History: Theory and Practice*. New York: Knopf, 1985.

"Analyse de Tous Des Films Inédits de Long Métrage Projetés A Paris de la Liberation Au 15 Octobre 1945." *Le Cinéma Français 1945*. Vol. 2. Paris: Editions de la Cinématographie Française, 1945.

Anderson, Carolyn. "The Conundrum of Competing Rights in *Titicut Follies*." *University Film Association Journal* 33.1 (1981): 15–22.

Anderson, Carolyn, and Thomas W. Benson. *Documentary Dilemmas: Frederick Wiseman's "Titicut Follies."* Carbondale: Southern Illinois University Press, 1989.

Anderson, Joseph, and Barbara Fisher. "The Myth of Persistence of Vision." *Journal of the University Film Association* 30.4 (Fall 1978): 3–8.

Anderson, Joseph L., and Donald Richie. *The Japanese Film: Art and Industry*. Princeton: Princeton University Press, 1982.

Anderson, Lindsay. "Angles of Approach." *Sequence* 2 (Winter 1947): 5–8.

———. "Only Connect: Some Aspects of the Work of Humphrey Jennings." *Nonfiction Film Theory and Criticism*. Ed. Richard Meran Barsam. New York: Dutton, 1976. 263–70.

Archaeology on Film. Ed. Peter S. Allen and Carole Lazio. Boston: Archaeological Institute of America, 1983.

Arlen, Michael J. "The Air: Fred Wiseman's 'Kino Pravda.' " *The New Yorker* 21 Apr. 1980: 91–101.

———. "The Air: On the Trail of a 'fine careless rapture.' " *The New Yorker* 10 Mar. 1980: 73–79.

Armes, Roy. *Third World Film Making and the West*. Berkeley: University of California Press, 1987.

Armstrong, Dan. "Wiseman's *Model* and the Documentary Project: Toward a Radical Film Practice." *New Challenges for Documentary*. Ed. Alan Rosenthal. Berkeley: University of California Press, 1988. 180–90.

Atkins, Thomas R. *Frederick Wiseman*. New York: Monarch, 1976.

Atwell, Lee. "*Word is Out*" and "*Gay U.S.A.*" *New Challenges for Documentary*. Ed. Alan Rosenthal. Berkeley: University of California Press, 1988. 571–80.

Auden, W. H. *Plays*. Princeton: Princeton University Press, 1988.

Auerbach, Erich. *Mimesis: The Representation of Reality in Western Literature.* New York: Anchor, 1957.

Bachman, Gideon. "Auto-Portrait Du Fascisme." *Cinéma* 183 (1974): 77–85.

Barkhausen, Hans. "Footnote to the History of Riefenstahl's *Olympia.*" *Film Quarterly* 28.1 (1974): 8–12.

Barnouw, Erik. *Documentary: A History of the Non-fiction Film.* New York: Oxford University Press, 1974.

———. *"Hiroshima-Nagasaki": The Case of the A-Bomb Footage. New Challenges for Documentary.* Ed. Alan Rosenthal. Berkeley: University of California Press, 1988. 581–91.

Barnouw, Erik, and S. Krishnaswamy. *Indian Film.* 2nd ed. New York: Oxford University Press, 1980.

Barr, Charles. "CinemaScope: Before and After." *Film Theory and Criticism.* Ed. Gerald Mast and Marshall Cohen. 2nd ed. New York: Oxford University Press, 1979. 140–68.

Barron, Arthur. "Toward New Goals in Documentary." *The Documentary Tradition: From "Nanook" to "Woodstock."* Ed. Lewis Jacobs. 2nd ed. New York: Norton, 1979. 494–99.

Barsam, Richard M. "American Direct Cinema: The *Re*-presentation of Reality." *Persistence of Vision* 3–4 (Summer 1986): 131–56.

———. *Filmguide to "Triumph Of The Will".* Bloomington: Indiana University Press, 1975.

———. "John Grierson: His Significance Today." *Image, Reality, Spectator: Essays on Documentary Film and Television.* Ed. Willem De Greef and Willem Hesling. Leuven, Belgium: Acco, 1989. 8–16.

———. *Nonfiction Film: A Critical History.* New York: Dutton, 1973.

———, ed. *Nonfiction Film Theory and Criticism.* New York: Dutton, 1975.

———. " 'This Is America': Documentaries for Theaters, 1942–1951." *Nonfiction Film Theory and Criticism.* Ed. Richard M. Barsam. New York: Dutton, 1976. 115–35.

———. *The Vision of Robert Flaherty: The Artist as Myth and Filmmaker.* Bloomington: Indiana University Press, 1988.

Barthes, Roland. *Camera Lucida: Reflections on Photography.* New York: Hill, 1981.

Bartone, Richard C. "A History and an Analysis of *The Twentieth Century* (1957–1966) Compilation Series." Diss. New York University, 1985.

Basinger, Jeanine. *The World War II Combat Film.* New York: Columbia University Press, 1986.

Bazin, André. *French Cinema of the Occupation and Resistance: The Birth of a Critical Esthetic.* Introd. by François Truffaut. New York: Ungar, 1975.

———. "The Myth of Total Cinema." *What is Cinema?* Berkeley: University of California Press, 1967. 17–22.

———. "*Los Olvidados.*" *The World of Luis Buñuel.* Ed. Joan Mellen. New York: Oxford University Press, 1978.

———. *What is Cinema?* Berkeley: University of California Press, 1967.

Benjamin, Burton. "The Documentary Heritage." *Nonfiction Film Theory and Criticism.* Ed. Richard Meran Barsam. New York: Dutton, 1976. 203–08.

Benson, Thomas W., and Carolyn Anderson. *Reality Fictions: The Films of Frederick Wiseman.* Carbondale: Southern Illinois University Press, 1989.

Berg, Beatrice. "I Was Fed up with Hollywood Fantasies." *The New York Times* 1 Feb. 1970: 25–26.

Berger, John. "Ways of Remembering." *Camerawork* 10 (1978).

Bergman, Andrew. *We're in the Money: Depression America and Its Films.* New York: New York University Press, 1971.

Bergman, Bruce. "Jean Rouch: A Founder of the Cinéma Vérité Style." *Film Library Quarterly* 11.4 (1978): 21–23.

Bertin-Maghit, Jean-Pierre. "Propagande Sociologique dans le Cinéma Français du 1940 à 1944." *La Revue Du Cinéma* 329 (1978): 71–84.

Bessy, Maurice, and Lo Duca. *Louis Lumière*. Paris: Éditions Prisma, 1948.

Beylie, Claude, et al. "Alberto Cavalcanti." *Ecran* 30 (1974): 49–59.

Beyond the Image: A Guide to Films about Women and Change. Montreal: National Film Board of Canada, 1984.

Bickley, David. "Joris Ivens Filming in China." *Filmmakers Newsletter* 10.4 (1977): 22–26.

Blue, James. "The Films of Jean Rouch (Including Interviews with Blue and Jacqueline Veuve)." *Film Comment* 4.2–3 (1967): 82–91.

———. "One Man's Truth: Interview with Richard Leacock." *Film Comment* 3.2 (1965): 15–23.

———. "Thoughts on Cinéma Vérité and a Discussion with the Maysles Brothers." *Film Comment* 2.4 (Fall 1964): 22–30.

Bluem, A. William. *Documentary in American Television: Form, Function, Method*. New York: Hastings, 1965.

Blumenberg, Richard M. "Documentary Films and the Problem of 'Truth'" *Journal of the University Film Association* 29.1 (1977): 19–22.

Bochner, Sally. "National Film Board of Canada: Four Decades of Documentaries and Animation." *Circulating Film Library Catalog*. New York: Museum of Modern Art, 1984. 231–38.

Bohn, Thomas W., and Lawrence W. Lichty. "*The March of Time*: News as Drama." *Journal of Popular Film* 2.4 (1973): 373–87.

Bolen, F. *Histoire Authentique, Anecdotique, Folklorique et Critique du Cinéma Belge Depuis Ses Plus Lointaines Origines*. Brussels: Memo & Codec, 1978.

Bolt, John. "Alexander Rodchenko as Photographer." *The Avant-garde in Russia 1910–1930*. Ed. Stephanie and Maurice Tuchman Barron. Los Angeles: Los Angeles County Museum of Art, 1980.

Bordwell, David. "Dziga Vertov: An Introduction." *Film Comment* 8.1 (1972): 38–45.

Bowles, Stephen E. "And Time Marched On: The Creation of *The March of Time*." *Journal of the University Film Association* 29.1 (1977): 7–13.

Brandon, Tom. "Survival List: Films of the Great Depression: The Early Thirties." *Film Quarterly* 12.2–3 (1979): 33–40.

Breitrose, Henry. "On the Search for the Real Nitty-Gritty: Some Problems and Possibilities of Cinéma Vérité." *Film Quarterly* 17.4 (1964): 36–40.

Brownlow, Kevin. *The Parade's Gone By*. Berkeley: University of California Press, 1968.

———. "Silent Film: What Was the Right Speed?" *Sight and Sound* 49.3 (1980): 164–67.

———. *The War, the West, and the Wilderness*. New York: Knopf, 1979.

Brunette, Peter. *Roberto Rossellini*. New York: Oxford University Press, 1987.

Burch, Noel. "Four French Documentaries." *The Documentary Tradition: From "Nanook" to "Woodstock."* Ed. Lewis Jacobs. New York: Hopkinson, 1971. 318–26.

Burra, Rani, ed. *Looking Back: 1896–1960*. New Delhi: The Directorate of Film Festivals, 1981.

———, ed. *Indian Cinema: 1980–1985*. New Delhi: The Directorate of Film Festivals, 1985.

Burton, Julianne, ed. *Cinema and Social Change in Latin America: Conversations with Filmmakers*. Austin: University of Texas Press, 1986.

Calder-Marshall, Arthur. *The Innocent Eye: The Life of Robert J. Flaherty*. New York: Harcourt, 1963.

Caldwell, Genoa, ed. *The Man Who Photographed the World: Burton Holmes, 1886–1938*. New York: Abrams, 1977.

Caldwell, Jill. "*Triumph of The Will* and *Listen To Britain*: Propaganda—Militant/Nonmilitant." *Film Library Quarterly* 9.1 (1976): 52–53.

Callenbach, Ernest. "Going Out to the Subject." *Film Quarterly* 14.3 (1961): 38–40.

———. "*Native Land*." *Film Quarterly* 26.5 (1973): 61.

Cameron, Ian A., and Mark Shivas. "Interviews: Richard Leacock, Albert and David Maysles, William Klein, Jean Rouch, Jacques Rozier." *Movie* 8 (1963): 17–24.

Campbell, Craig W. *Reel America and World War I.* Jefferson, NC: McFarland, 1985.

Campbell, Russell D. "Radical Cinema in the United States, 1930–42: The Work of the Film and Photo League, Nykino and Frontier Films." Diss. Northwestern University, 1978.

Canby, Vincent. "Documentaries: Limitless Eyes, Recording Civilization." *The New York Times* 3 Nov. 1985, sec. C: 19–20.

Capra, Frank. *The Name Above the Title.* New York: Macmillan, 1971.

Carpenter, Edmund. *Eskimo.* Toronto: Toronto University Press, 1959.

Carringer, Robert L. *The Making of "Citizen Kane."* Berkeley: University of California Press, 1965.

Carynnyk, Marco, ed. and trans. *Alexander Dovzhenko: The Poet as Filmmaker, Selected Writings.* Cambridge: MIT Press, 1973.

Cavalcanti, Alberto. "Alberto Cavalcanti: His Advice to Young Producers of Documentary." *Film Quarterly* 9 (1955): 354–55.

Cayrol, Jean. "Night and Fog." *Film: Book 2, Films of Peace and War.* Ed. Robert Hughes, Stanley Brown, and Carlos Clarens. New York: Grove, 1962. 234–55.

Ceram, C. W. *Archaeology of the Cinema.* London: Thames and Hudson, 1965.

Chanan, Michael. *The Cuban Image: Cinema and Cultural Politics in Cuba.* London: BFI Publishing, 1985.

Chrystal, William G. "National Party Election Films, 1927–1938." *Cinema Journal* 15.1 (1975): 29–47.

Chu, Bernice, ed. *Asian-American Media Reference Guide.* New York: Asian CineVision, 1986.

Circulating Film Library Catalog: The Museum of Modern Art. New York: The Museum of Modern Art, 1984.

Cocking, Loren. "Francis Thompson: Analysis of an American Film Maker." Master's thes. Ohio State University, 1969.

Cohen, Steven, ed. *Vietnam: Anthology and Guide to a Television History.* New York: Knopf, 1983.

Coles, Robert. "Documentary: Stripped Bare at the Follies." *The New Republic* Jan. 1968: 18+.

Colls, Robert, and Philip Dodd. "Representing the Nation: British Documentary Film, 1930–45." *Screen* 26.1 (1985): 21–33.

Comolli, Jean-Louis. "Detour par de Direct: Un Corps en Trop." *Realism and the Cinema.* Ed. Christopher Williams. London: Routledge, 1980. 224–58.

Cook, Bruce. "Whatever Happened to Westbrook Van Voorhis." *American Film* Mar. 1977: 25–29.

Cook, David A. *A History of the Narrative Film.* New York: Norton, 1981.

Cooper, Meriam C. *Grass.* New York: Putnam's, 1925.

"The Courage of The Men: An Interview with John Huston." *Film: Book 2, Films of Peace and War.* Ed. Robert Hughes, Stanley Brown, and Carlos Clarens. New York: Grove, 1962. 22–35.

Cozarinsky, Edgardo. "Foreign Filmmakers in France." *Rediscovering French Film.* Ed. Mary Lea Bandy. New York: Museum of Modern Art, 1983. 136–40.

Craft Films: An Index of International Films on Crafts. Ed. Kay Salz. New York: Neal-Schuman, 1979.

Creel, George. *Complete Report of the Chairman of the Committee on Public Information, 1917–1919.* Washington: Government Printing Office, 1920.

———. *How We Advertised America.* New York: Harper, 1920.

Crowdus, Gary. "Harlan County, USA." *The Documentary Tradition: From "Nanook" to "Woodstock."* Ed. Lewis Jacobs. 2nd ed. New York: Norton, 1979. 563–68.

Cunha, Uma Da. *Film India: The New Generation, 1960–1980.* The Directorate of Film Festivals, 1981.

Curry, Tim. "Frederick Wiseman: Sociological Filmmaker?" *Contemporary Sociology* 14.1 (1985): 35–39.

Cry, Helen W. *A Filmography of the Third World, 1976–1983.* Metuchen, NJ: Scarecrow, 1985.

Davis, Elmer Homes. "Report to the President." Ed. Ronald T. Farrar. *Journalism Monographs* 7 (Aug. 1968): 5–86.

Davis, Peter. "Lindsay Anderson Views His First Feature Film." *Chicago Daily News* 28 July 1963: 21.

De Antonio, Emile. "Flashback: My Brush with Painting." *American Film* 9.5 (1984): 8.

Delmar, Rosalind. *Joris Ivens: 50 Years of Film-Making.* London: British Film Institute, 1979.

Denby, David. "The Real Thing." *New York Review of Books* 37:17 (November 8, 1990): 24–28.

Deslandes, Jacques. *Histoire Comparée Du Cinéma.* 5 vols. Tournai, Belg.: Casterman, 1966.

Deutelbaum, Marshall. "Structural Patterning in the Lumière Films." *Wide Angle* 3.1 (1979): 30–31.

Dickinson, Margaret, and Sarah Street. *Cinema and State: The Film Industry and the British Government, 1927–1984.* London: British Film Institute, 1985.

Dickson, W. K. L. *Biograph in Battle: Its Story in the South African War.* London: Fisher Unwin, 1901.

Dickson, W. K. L., and Antonia Dickson. *History of the Kinetograph, Kinetoscope, and Kinetophotograph.* New York: Albert Bunn, 1895. New York: Arno Press, 1970.

Dickstein, Morris. *Gates of Eden: American Culture in the Sixties.* New York: Basic, 1977.

Doublier, Francis. "Reminiscences of an Early Motion Picture Operator." *"Image" on the Art and Evolution of the Film.* Ed. Marshall Deutelbaum. New York: Dover, 1979. 23.

Dunne, Philip. "The Documentary and Hollywood." *Nonfiction Film Theory and Criticism.* Ed. Richard Meran Barsam. New York: Dutton, 1976. 158–66.

Eaton, Mick, ed. *Anthropology-Reality-Cinema: The Films of Jean Rouch.* London: British Film Institute, 1979.

Editors of *Look,* eds. *Movie Lot to Beachhead.* New York: Doubleday, 1945.

Edmonds, Robert. *About Documentary: Anthropology on Film, a Philosophy of People and Art.* Dayton: Pflaum, 1974.

Ehrlich, Evelyn. *Cinema of Paradox: French Filmmaking Under the German Occupation.* New York: Columbia University Press, 1985.

Eisenstein, Sergei. *Film Essays and a Lecture.* Ed. Jay Leyda. New York: Praeger, 1970.

Elder, Robert E. *The Information Machine: The United States Information Agency and American Foreign Policy.* New York: Syracuse, 1968.

Ellis, Jack C. "Changing of the Guard: From the Grierson Documentary to Free Cinema." *Quarterly Review of Film Studies* 7.1 (1982): 23–35.

_____. *John Grierson: A Guide to References and Resources.* Boston: Hall, 1986.

Ellsworth, Liz. *Frederick Wiseman: A Guide to References and Resources.* Boston: Hall, 1979.

Ellul, Jacques. *Propaganda: The Formation of Men's Attitudes.* Trans. Konrad and Jean Lerner Kellen. New York: Vintage, 1973.

Elson, Robert T. *Time, Inc., the Intimate Story of a Publishing Enterprise, 1923–1941.* New York: Atheneum, 1968.

_____. "Time Marches on the Screen." *Nonfiction Film Theory and Criticism.* Ed. Richard Meran Barsam. New York: Dutton, 1976. 95–114.

Engle, Harrison, "Thirty Years of Social Inquiry: An Interview with Willard Van Dyke." *Film Comment* 3.2 (1965): 24–37.

Erens, Patricia. "Women's Documentary Filmmaking: The Personal is Political." *New*

Challenges for Documentary. Ed. Alan Rosenthal. Berkeley: University of California Press, 1988. 554–65.

————. "Women's Documentaries as Social History." *Film Library Quarterly* 14.1–2 (1981): 4–9.

Evans, Gary. *John Grierson and the National Film Board: The Politics of Wartime Propaganda, 1939–1945.* Toronto: University of Toronto Press, 1984.

Everaerts, Jan-Pieter. *Oog Voor Het Echte: Het Turbulente Verhaal van de Blaamse Film-, Televisie-en Video Documentaire.* Brussels: Brtuitgave, 1987.

Everson, William K. "*Germany Awake:* Propaganda in Nazi Cinema." *Sightlines* 14.1-2 (1980): 12.

The Factual Film: An Arts Enquiry Report. London: Oxford University Press, 1947.

Feldman, Seth. "Cinema Weekly and Cinema Truth: Dziga Vertov and the Leninist Proportion." *Sight and Sound* 43.1 (Winter 1973–74): 34–48.

————. *Dziga Vertov: A Guide to References and Resources.* Boston: Hall, 1979.

Fell, John L., ed. *Film Before Griffith.* Berkeley: University of California Press, 1983.

Fielding, Raymond. *The American Newsreel: 1911–1967.* Norman: University of Oklahoma Press, 1972.

————. "Hale's Tours: Ultrarealism in the Pre-1910 Motion Picture." *Film Before Griffith.* Ed. John L. Fell. Berkeley: University of California Press, 1983. 116–30.

————. *The March of Time: 1935–1951.* New York : Oxford, 1978.

————, ed. *A Technological History of Motion Pictures and Television.* Berkeley: University of California Press, 1967.

Fieschi, Jean-André. "Dziga Vertov." *Cinema: A Critical Dictionary.* Ed. Richard Roud. Vol. 2. New York: Viking, 1980. 1022–26.

————. "Jean Rouch." *Cinema: A Critical Dictionary.* Ed. Richard Roud. Vol. 2. New York: Viking, 1980. 901–09.

Filme Contra Faschismus. Berlin: Staatliches Filmarchiv der Deutschen Demokratischen Republik, 1965.

Films Polonais: Catalogue de Film Diffusés en France. Paris: Régie Gouvernementale du Cinéma en Pologne à Paris, 1954.

Fischer, Lucy. "*Enthusiasm:* From Kino-Eye to Radio-Eye." *Film Quarterly* 31.2 (Winter 1977–78): 25–34.

————. "Restoring *Enthusiasm:* Excerpts from an Interview with Peter Kubelka." *Film Quarterly* 31.2 (Winter 1977–78): 35–36.

Flaherty, Robert. "Filming Real People." *The Documentary Tradition: From "Nanook" to "Woodstock."* Ed. Lewis Jacobs. 2nd ed. New York: Norton, 1979. 97–99.

————. *My Eskimo Friends.* Garden City: Doubleday, 1924.

Frederickson, Don. "Jung/Sign/Symbol/Film (part 2)." *Quarterly Review of Film Studies* 5.4 (1980): 459–79.

Friedenberg, Edgar Z. "Ship of Fools: The Films of Frederick Wiseman." *The New York Review of Books* 17.6 (1971): 19–22.

Fuentes, Carlos. "The Discreet Charm of Luis Buñuel." *The New York Times Magazine* 11 Mar. 1973: 87.

Fulton, A. R. "The Machine." *The American Film Industry.* Ed. Tino Balio. Madison: University of Wisconsin Press, 1976. 19–32.

Fyne, Robert. "From Hollywood to Moscow." *Film/Literature Quarterly* 13.3 (1985): 194–99.

Galassi, Peter. *Before Photography: Painting and the Invention of Photography.* New York: Museum of Modern Art, 1981.

Gallagher, Tag. *John Ford: The Man and His Films.* Berkeley: University of California Press, 1986.

Gardner, Robert. "A Chronicle of the Human Experience: *Dead Birds.*" *The Documentary Tradition: From "Nanook" to "Woodstock."* Ed. Lewis Jacobs. 2nd ed. New York: Norton, 1979. 430–36.

Garga, B. D. "The Long and Short of It." *Film India: The New Generation, 1960–1980*. Ed. Uma Da Cunha. New Delhi: The Directorate of Film Festivals, 1981.

Gartenberg, Jon, et al., eds. *The Film Catalog: A List of Holdings in The Museum of Modern Art*. Boston: Hall, 1985.

Geller, Evelyn. "Paul Strand as a Documentary Filmmaker." *Film Library Quarterly* 6.2 (1973): 28–30.

Georgakas, Dan. "*Finally Got the News*." "*Show Us Life*": *Toward a History of the Committed Documentary*. Ed. Thomas Waugh. Metuchen: The Scarecrow Press, 1984. 154–67.

Gerard, Edmund Bert. "The Truth About Cinéma Vérité." *American Cinematographer* 50 (1969): 474–75.

Gilbert, Craig. "Reflections on *An American Family*, I." *New Challenges for Documentary*. Ed. Alan Rosenthal. Berkeley: University of California Press, 1988. 191–209.

_____ . "Reflections on *An American Family*, II." *New Challenges for Documentary*. Ed. Alan Rosenthal. Berkeley: University of California Press, 1988. 288–307.

Giles, Dennis. "The Name *Documentary*: A Preface to Genre Study." *Film Reader* 3 (1978): 18–22.

Gitlin, Todd. "*Phantom India*." *New Challenges for Documentary*. Ed. Alan Rosenthal. Berkeley: University of California Press, 1988. 536–41.

Goldman, Eric P. *The Crucial Decade—And After: America, 1945–1960*. New York: Vintage, 1960.

Goodman, Ezra. "Fact Films to the Front." *American Cinematographer* 25.2 (1945): 46–47.

Goodwin, Joseph. "Some Personal Notes on *Native Land*." *Take One* 4.2 (1972): 11–12.

Goretta, Claude. "Aspects of the French Documentary." *Sight and Sound* 26.3 (Winter 1956–57): 156–58.

Graham, Cooper C. *Leni Riefenstahl and "Olympia"*. Metuchen, NJ: Scarecrow, 1986.

Graham, John. " 'There Are No Simple Solutions': Frederick Wiseman on Viewing Film." *The Film Journal* (Spring 1971): 44–47.

Graham, Peter. "Cinéma Vérité in France." *Film Quarterly* 17.4 (1964): 30–36.

Gray, Camilla. *The Russian Experiment in Art: 1863–1922*. New York: Abrams, 1962.

Gray, Hugh. "Father of the American Documentary." *The American Cinema*. Ed. Donald E. Staples. Washington, D.C.: U.S. Information Agency, 1973.

Greenberg, Alex, and Marvin Wald. "Report to the Stockholders." *Hollywood Quarterly* 1.4 (1946): 410–15.

Grenier, Cynthia. "Joris Ivens: Social Realist and Lyric Poet." *Sight and Sound* 27.4 (1958): 204–07.

Grierson, John. "The Course of Realism." *Grierson on Documentary*. Ed. Forsyth Hardy. London: Faber, 1966. 199–211.

_____ . "E.M.B. Film Unit." *Cinema Quarterly* 1.4 (1933): 203–08.

_____ . "Production Unit Planned: Mass Media to Be Used for Peace." *UNESCO Courier* Feb. 1948: 3.

_____ . "Prospect for Documentary: What Is Wrong and Why." *Sight and Sound* 17.66 (1948): 55–59.

_____ . "Robert Flaherty." Flaherty File, Film Study Center, Museum of Modern Art, New York. [United States]: n.p., n.d. N. pag.

Griffith, Richard. *Films of the World's Fair: 1939*. New York: American Film Center, 1940.

_____ . "Post-war American Documentaries." *Penguin Film Review* 8 (1949): 92–102.

Grilli, Peter, ed. *Japan in Film*. New York: Japan Society, 1984.

Guibbert, Pierre. *Les Premiers Ans du Cinéma Français*. Paris: Institut Jean Vigo, 1985.

Guynn, William. *A Cinema of Nonfiction*. Rutherford, NJ: Fairleigh Dickenson University Press, 1990.

Haleff, Maxine. "The Maysles Brothers and 'Direct Cinema.' " *Film Comment* 2.2 (1964): 19–23.

Hardy, Forsyth. "The Films of Arne Sucksdorff," *Sight and Sound* 17.66 (Summer 1948): 60–63.

————. *John Grierson: A Documentary Biography.* London: Faber and Faber, 1979.

Harris, Neil. "A Subversive Form." *Before Hollywood: Turn-of-the-Century Film from American Archives.* Jay Leyda and Charles Musser, Guest Curators. New York: American Federation of Arts, 1986. 45–49.

Harvey, Sylvia. "The 'Other Cinema' in Britain: Unfinished Business in Oppositional and Independent Film, 1929–1984." *All Our Yesterdays: 90 Years of British Cinema.* Ed. Charles Barr. London: British Film Institute, 1986. 225–51.

Hass, Robert Bartlett. *Muybridge: Man in Motion.* Berkeley: University of California Press, 1976.

Hay, James. *Popular Film Culture in Fascist Italy: The Passing of the Rex.* Bloomington: Indiana University Press, 1987.

Heider, Karl G. *The Dani of West Irian: An Ethnographic Companion to the Film "Dead Birds".* Andover, MA: Andover Modular Publications, 1972.

————. *Ethnographic Film.* Austin: University of Texas Press, 1976.

Hemingway, Ernest. *The Spanish Earth.* Cleveland: Savage, 1938.

Henderson, John W. *The United States Information Agency.* New York: Praeger, 1969.

Hendricks, Gordon. *The Edison Motion Picture Myth.* Berkeley: University of California Press, 1961.

————. "The History of the Kinetoscope." *The American Film Industry.* Ed. Tino Balio. Madison: University of Wisconsin Press, 1976. 33–45.

————. "The Kinetoscope: Fall Motion Picture Production." *Film Before Griffith.* Ed. John L. Fell. Berkeley: University of California Press, 1983. 13–21.

Herr, Michael. *Dispatches.* New York: Knopf, 1977.

Hess, John, and Michael Klein. "*Native Land* Reconsidered." *Jump Cut* 10–11 (1976): 63.

High, Peter B. "The War Cinema of Imperial Japan and Its Aftermath." *Wide Angle* 1.4 (1977): 19–21.

Higson, Andrew. " 'Britain's Outstanding Contribution to the Film': The Documentary-Realist Tradition." *All Our Yesterdays: 90 Years of British Cinema.* Ed. Charles Barr. London: British Film Institute, 1986. 72–97.

Hill, John. *Sex, Class and Realism: British Cinema 1956–1963.* London: British Film Institute, 1986.

Hillgartner, Del. "Super Serious-8: Leacock–MIT Super-8 System." *Filmmakers Newsletter* 6.12 (1973): 53–56.

————. "Super Serious-8: Leacock–MIT Super-8 System (part 2)." *Filmmakers Newsletter* 7.1 (1973): 51–55.

Hinton, David B. "*Triumph Of The Will:* Document or Artifice." *Cinema Journal* 15.1 (1975): 48–57.

Hitchens, Gordon. "Joris Ivens Interviewed by Gordon Hitchens." *Film Culture* 53.55 (1972): 190–228.

Hoberman, J. "Ain't Nothing Like the Real Thing." *American Film* 8.4 (1983): 59.

Hodgkinson, Anthony W., and Rodney E. Sheratsky. *Humphrey Jennings: More Than a Maker of Films.* Hanover, NH: University Press of New England, 1982.

Hodgson, Godfrey. *America in Our Time.* New York: Vintage, 1978.

Hogenkamp, Bert. "Joris Ivens and the Problems of the Documentary Film." Trans. M. Cleaver. *Framework* 11 (Autumn 1979): 22–25.

Holmes, Winifred. "What's Wrong with Documentary?" *Sight and Sound* 16.65 (1948): 44–45.

Houston, Penelope. *The Contemporary Cinema.* Baltimore: Penguin, 1963.

————. "Interview with Flaherty." *Sight and Sound* Jan. 1950: 16.

Howe, James Wong. "The Documentary Technique and Hollywood." *American Cinematographer* Jan. 1944: 10.

Hughes, Robert, Stanley Brown, and Carlos Clarens, eds. *Film: Book 2, Films of Peace and War*. New York: Grove, 1962.

Hull, David Stewart. *Film in the Third Reich: Art and Propaganda in Nazi Germany*. New York: Simon, 1973.

_____ . *Film in the Third Reich: A Study of the German Cinema*. Berkeley: University of California Press, 1969.

Huston, John. *An Open Book*. New York: Knopf, 1980.

_____ . "*Let There Be Light*." *Film: Book 2, Films of Peace and War*. Ed. Robert Hughes, Stanley Brown, and Carlos Clarens. New York: Grove, 1962. 205–33.

Isenberg, Michael T. *War on Film: The American Cinema and World War I, 1914–1941*. London: Associated University Presses, 1981.

Ivens, Joris. *The Camera and I*. New York: International Publishers, 1969.

_____ . "Notes on Hollywood." *New Theatre and Film 1934 to 1937*. Ed. Herbert Kline. New York: Harcourt, 1985. 294–99.

Jacobs, Lewis. "The Turn Toward Conservatism." *The Documentary Tradition: From "Nanook" to "Woodstock."* Ed. Lewis Jacobs. 2nd ed. New York: Norton, 276–82.

James, David E. *Allegories of Cinema: American Film in the Sixties*. Princeton: Princeton University Press, 1989.

James, Rodney. *Film as National Art: NFB of Canada and the Film Board Idea*. New York: Arno, 1977.

Jarratt, Vernon. *The Italian Cinema*. London: Falcon, 1951.

Jenkins, Reese V. *Images and Enterprise*. Baltimore: Johns Hopkins, 1975.

Jennings, Mary-Lou. *Humphrey Jennings: Film-maker, Painter, Poet*. London: British Film Institute, 1982.

Jensen, Jytte. *Carl Th. Dreyer*. New York: Museum of Modern Art, 1988.

Johnson, Randal. *Cinema Novo X 5*. Austin: University of Texas Press, 1984.

Johnson, Randal, and Robert Stam. *Brazilian Cinema*. East Brunswick, NJ: Associated Universities Press, 1982.

Johnston, Claire. " 'Independence' and the Thirties." *British Cinema: Traditions of Independence*. Ed. Don Macpherson and Paul Willmen. London: British Film Institute, 1980. 9–23.

Jones, D. B. "The Canadian Film Board Unit B." *New Challenges for Documentary*. Ed. Alan Rosenthal. Berkeley: University of California Press, 1988. 133–47.

Joseph, Robert. "Film Program for Germany." *Arts and Architecture* 62 (1945): 16.

_____ . "Films for Nazi Prisoners of War." *Arts and Architecture* 62 (1945): 16.

_____ . "Germans See Their Concentration Camps." *Arts and Architecture* 62 (1946): 14.

_____ . "The War of Russian Films." *American Cinematographer* 25.2 (1945): 48–49.

Jowett, Garth S. "The First Film Audiences." *Film Before Griffith*. Ed. John L. Fell. Berkeley: University of California Press, 1983. 196–206.

Kael, Pauline. "The Current Cinema." *The New Yorker* 45.35 (1969): 199–204.

Kaplan, E. Ann. *Women and Film: Both Sides of the Camera*. New York: Methuen, 1983.

Kaufman, Mikhail. "An Interview with Mikhail Kaufman." *October* 11 (1979): 54–76.

Kepley, Vance, Jr. "The Evolution of Eisenstein's *Old and New*." *Cinema Journal* 14.1 (1974): 34–50.

_____ . "The Origins of NBC's 'Project XX' in Compilation Documentaries." *Journalism Quarterly* 61.1 (1984): 20–21.

Kessler, Ronald. "Correspondence." *The New Republic* Feb. 1968: 35–36.

Klaue, Wolfgang. *Alberto Cavalcanti*. Berlin: Staatlichen Filmarchiv der DDR, 1962.

Klein, Michael. "*Native Land*: Praised Then Forgotten." *Velvet Light Trap* 14 (1975): 15–16.

Klein, Michael, and Jill Klein. "*Native Land:* An Interview with Leo Hurwitz." *Cinéaste* 6.3 (1974): 2–7.

Kline, Herbert, ed. *New Theatre and Film 1934 to 1937: An Anthology.* New York: Harcourt, 1985.

Knight, Arthur. "Cinéma Vérité and Film Truth." *Saturday Review* 9 Sept. 1967: 44.

———. "A Short History of Art Films." *Films on Art.* Ed. William McK. Chapman. New York: American Federation of Arts, 1952.

Knightley, Phillip. *The First Casualty.* New York: Harcourt, 1975.

Kolaja, J., and A. W. Foster. "*Berlin: The Symphony Of A Great City* as a Theme of Visual Rhythm." *Journal of Aesthetics and Art Criticism* 23.3 (1965): 353–58.

Kolker, Robert Phillip. "Circumstantial Evidence: An Interview with Albert and David Maysles." *Sight and Sound* 40.4 (1971): 183–86.

Kracauer, Siegfried. *The Conquest of Europe on the Screen: The Nazi Newsreel, 1939–1940.* Washington: Library of Congress, 1943.

———. *From Caligari to Hitler.* Princeton: Princeton University Press, 1947.

———. *Theory of Film: The Redemption of Physical Reality.* New York: Oxford University Press, 1960.

Krueger, Eric. "An American Family: An American Film." *Film Comment* Nov. 1973: 16–19.

Kuehl, Jerry. "Arts and Entertainment—a Little Closer: The Films of Joris Ivens." *New Statesman* 98 (1978): 688–89.

Kuhn, Annette. "British Documentaries in the 1930s and 'Independence': Recontextualising a Film Movement." *British Cinema: Traditions of Independence.* Ed. Don Macpherson and Paul Willmen. London: British Film Institute, 1980. 24–33.

———. *Women's Pictures: Feminism and Cinema.* London: Routledge, 1982.

Lacayo, Richard, "Why Are Documentaries So Dull?" *The New York Times* 20 Feb. 1983, sec. 2: 29.

Lafferty, William. "A Reappraisal of the Semi-Documentary in Hollywood, 1945–1948." *The Velvet Light Trap* 20: 22–26.

Lambert, Gavin. "Free Cinema." *Sight and Sound* 25.4 (1956): 173–77.

Landy, Marcia. *Fascism in Film: The Italian Commercial Cinema, 1931–1943.* Princeton: Princeton University Press, 1986.

Langlois, Henri. "French Cinema: Origins." *Cinema: A Critical Dictionary.* Ed. Richard Roud. Vol. 1. New York: Viking, 1980. 394–401.

Langman, Larry, and Edgar Borg. *Encyclopedia of American War Films.* New York: Garland, 1989.

Leenhardt, Roger. "L'evolution Du Film D'art." *Gazette Des Beaux Arts* 6.102 (1983): 42–46.

Lefèvre, Pascal, and Geert van Wonterghem, eds. *Beeld & Realiteit: International Festival Van de Documentaire Film en Televisie.* Leuven, Belg.: Catholic University of Leuven and St. Hoger Institute of St. Lukas High School, Brussels, 1987.

Leglise, Paul. "Histoire de la Politique Du Cinéma Français." *Le Cinéma Entre Deux Républiques (1940–1946).* Ed. Pierre L'Herminier. Paris: Film Éditions, 1977.

Leiser, Erwin. *Nazi Cinema.* New York: Macmillan, 1975.

Leprohon, Pierre. *The Italian Cinema.* Trans. Roger Greave and Oliver Stallybran. London: Secker, 1972.

Lesage, Julia. "Feminist Documentary: Aesthetics and Politics." *"Show Us Life": Toward a History and Aesthetics of the Committed Documentary.* Ed. Thomas Waugh. Metuchen, NJ: Scarecrow, 1984. 223–51.

"Letters: Focusing Again on *Titicut.*" *Civil Liberties Review* 1.3 (1974): 148–51.

Lévi-Strauss, Claude. *Tristes Tropiques.* Trans. John Russell. New York: Criterion, 1961.

Levin, G. Roy. *Documentary Explorations: 15 Interviews with Film-makers.* New York: Doubleday, 1971.

Leyda, Jay. *Dianying/Electric Shadows: An Account of Films and the Film Audience in China*. Cambridge: MIT Press, 1972.

———. *Films Beget Films: A Study of the Compilation Film*. New York: Hill, 1971.

———. *Kino: A History of the Russian and Soviet Film*. 3rd ed. Princeton: Princeton University Press, 1983.

Lichty, Lawrence W. " 'Vietnam: A Television History': Media Research and Some Comments." *New Challenges for Documentary*. Ed. Alan Rosenthal. Berkeley: University of California Press, 1988. 495–505.

Liehm, Mira. *Passion and Defiance: Film in Italy from 1942 to the Present*. Berkeley: University of California Press, 1984.

Lightman, Herb A. "Shooting Production Under Fire." *American Cinematographer* 26.9 (1945): 296–97.

Lipscomb, James. "Cinéma Vérité." *Film Quarterly* 18.2 (1964): 62–63.

Lorentz, Pare. *Lorentz on Film: Movies 1927 to 1941*, New York: Hopkinson, 1975.

———. *The River*. New York: Stackpole, 1938.

Lovell, Alan, and Jim Hillier. *Studies in Documentary*. London: Secker, 1972.

Low, Rachel. *The History of the British Film, 1906–1914*. London: British Film Institute and British Film Academy, 1948.

———. *The History of the British Film 1914–1918*. London: British Film Institute and British Film Academy, 1948.

———. *The History of the British Film, 1918–1929*. London: British Film Institute and British Film Academy, 1971.

———. *National Film Archive Catalog. Part I, Silent News Films 1895–1933. Part II, Silent Non-fiction Films 1895–1934*. London: British Film Institute, 1965.

Lowenstein, Sharon R. *Token Refuge: The Story of the Jewish Refugee Shelter at Oswego, 1944–46*. Bloomington: Indiana University Press, 1986.

Lowry, Edward. "Edwin J. Hadley: Traveling Film Exhibitor." *Film Before Griffith*. Ed. John L. Fell. Berkeley: University of California Press, 1983. 131–43.

Luhr, William, ed. *World Cinema Since 1945*. New York: Ungar, 1987.

MacBean, James Roy. "*The Sorrow and the Pity*: France and Her Political Myths." *New Challenges for Documentary*. Ed. Alan Rosenthal. Berkeley: University of California Press, 1988. 471–79.

MacCann, Richard Dyer. "Alternative Television: The British Model," *The American Scholar* 43.4 (Autumn 1974): 65–66.

———. "The City." *The International Dictionary of Films and Filmmakers*. Vol. 1 Chicago: St. James Press, 1984. 97.

———. "Documentary Film and Democratic Government: An Administrative History from Pare Lorentz to John Huston." Diss. Harvard University, 1951.

———. *The First Film Makers*. Metuchen, NJ: Scarecrow, 1989.

———. *Nonfiction Film: A Critical History*. Fwd. by Richard Meran Barsam. New York: Dutton, 1973. xiii–xv.

———. *The People's Films: A Political History of U.S. Government Motion Pictures*. New York: Hastings, 1973.

MacDonnell, K. *Eadweard Muybridge: The Man Who Invented the Moving Picture*. Boston: Little, 1972.

McCormick, Ruth. "Women's Liberation Cinema." *The Documentary Tradition: From "Nanook" to "Woodstock."* Ed. Lewis Jacobs. 2nd. ed. New York: Norton, 1979. 523–35.

McGarry, Eileen. "Documentary, Realism and Women's Cinema." *Women's Film* 2.7 (1975): 50–59.

Mamber, Stephen. *Cinema Verite in America: Studies in Uncontrolled Documentary*. Cambridge: MIT Press, 1974.

Manvell, Roger, and Heinrich Fraenkel. *The German Cinema*. New York: Praeger, 1971.

Marcorelles, Louis. "Leacock at M.I.T." *Sight and Sound* 18.2 (1974): 104–07.

———. *Living Cinema: New Directions in Contemporary Film-Making.* New York: Praeger, 1973.

Martineau, Barbara Halpern. "Talking About Our Lives and Experiences: Some Thoughts About Feminism, Documentary, and 'Talking Heads' " *"Show Us Life": Toward a History and Aesthetics of the Committed Documentary.* Ed. Thomas Waugh. Metuchen, NJ: Scarecrow, 1984. 252–73.

Mast, Gerald. *Film/Cinema/Movie: A Theory of Experience.* New York: Harper, 1977.

———. *A Short History of the Movies.* 4th ed. New York: Macmillan, 1986.

Maysles, Albert, and David Maysles. "Direct Cinema." *Public Relations Journal* 38.9 (1982): 31–33.

———. "Financing the Independent Non-fiction Film." *Millimeter* 6.6 (1978): 74–75.

———. "*Gimme Shelter*: Production Notes." *Filmmakers Newsletter* 5.2 (1971): 29–31.

———. "Maysles Brothers." *Film Culture* 42 (1966): 114–15.

Michelson, Annette. "*The Man With The Movie Camera*: From Magician to Epistemologist." *Artforum* 7 (1972): 60–72.

———, ed. *Kino-Eye: The Writings of Dziga Vertov.* Trans. Kevin O'Brien. Berkeley: University of California Press, 1984.

Miller, Warren. "Progress in Documentary." *The Documentary Tradition: From "Nanook" to "Woodstock".* Ed. Lewis Jacobs. 2nd ed. New York: Norton, 1979. 247–50.

Mock, James R., and Cedric Larson. *Words That Won the War: The Story of the Committee on Public Information, 1917–1919.* Princeton: Princeton University Press, 1939.

Monaco, James. "American Documentary Since 1960." *Cinema: A Critical Dictionary.* Ed. Richard Roud. Vol. 1. New York: Viking, 1980. 50–56.

Monegal, Rodriguez. "Alberto Cavalcanti: His Career." *Nonfiction Film Theory and Criticism.* Ed. Richard Meran Barsam. New York: Dutton, 1976. 239–49.

Mora, Carl J. *Mexican Cinema: Reflections of a Society, 1896–1988.* Rev. ed. Berkeley: University of California Press, 1989.

Morris, Peter. "Images of Canada." *Film Before Griffith.* Ed. John L. Fell. Berkeley: University of California Press, 1983. 67–74.

———. *The National Film Board of Canada: The War Years.* Ottawa: Canadian Film Institute, 1965.

Movies at War. Washington: War Activities Committee of the Motion Picture Industry, 1945.

Mozley, A. V., et al. *Eadweard Muybridge: The Stanford Years, 1872–1882.* Stanford: Stanford University Art Department, 1972.

Mullen, Pat. *Man of Aran.* Cambridge: MIT Press, 1970.

Murphy, William T. "The Method of *Why We Fight.*" *Journal of Popular Film* 1.3 (1972): 185.

———. *Robert Flaherty: A Guide to References and Resources.* Boston: Hall, 1978.

Murray, Williams. "Films." *Nation* 178 (1954): 314.

Murray-Brown, Jeremy. "False Cinema: Vertov and Early Soviet Film." *The New Criterion* 8:3 (Nov. 1989): 21–33.

Musser, Charles. "The American Vitagraph, 1897–1901: Survival and Success in a Competitive Industry." *Film Before Griffith.* Ed. John L. Fell. Berkeley: University of California Press, 1983. 22–66.

Naficy, Hamid. " 'Truthful Witness': An Interview with Albert Maysles." *Quarterly Review of Film Studies* 6.2 (1981): 155–79.

Native Americans on Film and Video. Ed. Elizabeth Weatherford. New York: Museum of the American Indian, 1981.

Neale, Steve. "*Triumph Of The Will*: Notes on Documentary and Spectacle." *Screen* 20.1 (1979): 63–86.

———. *Cinema and Technology: Image, Sound, Colour.* Bloomington: Indiana University Press, 1985.

Nemeskürty, István. "In the Beginning: 1896–1911." *Film Before Griffith.* Ed. John L. Fell. Berkeley: University of California Press, 1983. 75–80.

Newhall, Beaumont. *The History of Photography.* Rev. ed. New York: Museum of Modern Art, 1982.

Nichols, Bill. *Ideology and the Image: Social Representation in the Cinema and Other Media.* Bloomington: Indiana University Press, 1981.

———. "Newsreel, 1967–1972: Film and Revolution." *"Show Us Life": Toward a History of the Committed Documentary.* Ed. Thomas Waugh. Metuchen: The Scarecrow Press, 1984. 135–53.

———. "The Voice of Documentary." *New Challenges for Documentary.* Ed. Alan Rosenthal. Berkeley: University of California Press, 1988. 48–63.

Nieuwenhof, Franz. "Japanese Film Propaganda in World War II: Indonesia and Australia." *Historical Journal of Film, Radio, and Television* 4.2 (1984): 161–77.

Novotny, Fritz. *Painting and Sculpture in Europe: 1780 to 1880.* Baltimore: Penguin, 1960.

O'Connor, John E., ed. *American History/American Television: Interpreting the Video Past.* New York: Ungar, 1983.

O'Connor, John J. " 'The Film is About Killing'." *The New York Times* 3 Oct. 1971: 17.

———. "Is the Documentary Making a Comeback?," *The New York Times* 26 June 1988, sec. 2: 17.

O'Neill, William L. *Coming Apart: An Informal History of America in the 1960s.* Chicago: Quadrangle, 1971.

Orbanz, Eva. *Journey to a Legend and Back: The British Realistic Film.* Berlin: Volker Spiess, 1977.

Panofsky, Erwin. "Style and Medium in the Motion Pictures." *Film Theory and Criticism.* Ed. Gerald Mast and Marshall Cohen. 2nd ed. New York: Oxford University Press, 1979. 243–63.

Pennebaker, Donn Alan. *Dont Look Back.* New York: Ballantine, 1968.

Perry, Ted. "The Road to Neo-realism." *Film Comment* 14.6 (1978): 7–13.

Petric, Vlada. *Constructivism in Film: "The Man With The Movie Camera," A Cinematic Analysis.* Cambridge: Cambridge University Press, 1987.

———. "Dziga Vertov as Theorist." *Cinema Journal* 1 (Fall 1978): 29–44.

———. "Esther Shub: Cinema is My Life." *Quarterly Review of Film Studies* 3.4 (1978): 429–56.

Phillips, Marcus. "Riefenstahl's 'Harrassment.' " *Film Quarterly* 29.3 (1976): 62.

Pincus, Ed. "New Possibilities in Film and the University." *Quarterly Review of Film Studies* 2.2 (1977): 159–78.

———. "One Person Sync-sound: A New Approach to Cinéma Vérité." *Filmmakers Newsletter* 6.2 (1972): 24–30.

Pines, Jim, and Paul Willemen, eds. *Questions of Third Cinema.* London: BFI Publishing, 1989.

Plantinga, Carl. "Defining Documentary: Fiction, Non-Fiction, and Projected Worlds," *Persistence of Vision* 5 (Spring 1987): 44–54.

"The Plow That Broke The Plains". Washington: U.S. Film Service, 1938.

Pratt, George. "Osa and Martin Johnson: World Travellers in Africa." *Image* 22.2 (1979): 21–30.

Pratt, George C. "Firsting the Firsts." *"Image" on the Art and Evolution of the Film.* Ed. Marshall Deutelbaum. New York: Dover, 1979.

Presenting NFB of Canada. Ottawa: National Film Board, 1949.

Propaganda und Gegenpropaganda Im Film, 1933–1945. Vienna: Österreichisches Filmmuseum, 1972.

Pryluck, Calvin. "Seeking to Take the Longest Journey: A Conversation with Albert Maysles." *Journal of the University Film Association* 28.2 (1976): 9–16.

Pryor, Thomas M. "Films in the 'Truth Campaign.'" *The Documentary Tradition: From "Nanook" to "Woodstock"*. Ed. Lewis Jacobs. 2nd ed. New York: Norton, 1979. 292–95.

Pym, John. "Ireland—Two Nations." *New Challenges for Documentary*. Ed. Alan Rosenthal. Berkeley: University of California Press, 1988. 480–87.

Quart, Leonard and Albert Auster. *American Film and Society Since 1945*. New York: Macmillan, 1984.

Rawlence, Christopher. *The Missing Reel: The Untold Story of the Lost Inventor of Moving Pictures*. London: Collins, 1990.

Rayleigh, Jane. "Joris Ivens in China." *Sightlines* 12.1 (1978): 21–23.

Reade, Eric. "Australian Silent Films, 1904–1907: The Features Begin." *Film Before Griffith*. Ed. John L. Fell. Berkeley: University of California Press, 1983. 81–91.

Régent, Roger. *Cinéma de France Sous L'Occupation: De "La Fille Du Puisatier" Aux "Enfants Du Paradis"*. Paris: Editions D'Aujourdhui, 1975.

"Remarquable Développement Du Cinéma Documentaire Français." *Le Cinéma Française, 1945*. Paris: Editions de la Cinématographie Française, 1945. 15+.

Renan, Sheldon. *An Introduction to the American Underground Film*. New York: Dutton, 1967.

Renov, Michael. "The Imaging of Analysis: Newsreel's Re-Search For a Radical Film Practice." *Wide Angle* 6.3 (1984): 76–82.

———. "Re-thinking Documentary: Toward a Taxonomy of Mediation." *Wide Angle* 8.3–4 (1986): 71–77.

Reynolds, Charles. "Focus on Al Maysles." *Popular Photography* (May 1964): 128–31.

Rhode, Eric. "Why Neo-Realism Failed." *Sight and Sound* 30.1 (Winter 1960–61): 26–32.

Rich, Ruby. "Anti-Porn: Soft Issue, Hard World." *Films for Women*. Ed. Charlotte Brunsdon. London: British Film Institute, 1986. 31–43.

Richie, Donald. *Japanese Cinema*. New York: Anchor, 1971.

———. "'Mono No Aware.'" *Film: Book 2, Films of Peace and War*. Ed. Robert Hughes, Stanley Brown, and Carlos Clarens. New York: Grove, 1962. 67–86.

Riefenstahl, Leni. *The Last of the Nuba*. New York: Harper, 1973.

———. *People of Kau*. New York: Harper, 1976.

Rittaud-Hutinet, Jacques. *Le Cinéma des Origines*. Paris: Champ Vallon, 1985.

Robinson, David. *The History of World Cinema*. New York: Stein, 1973.

Robson, Kenneth J. "The Crystal Formation: Narrative Structure in *Grey Gardens*." *Cinema Journal* 22.2 (1983): 42–53.

———. "Humphrey Jennings: The Legacy of Feeling." *Quarterly Review of Film Studies* 7.1 (1982): 37–52.

———. "Tying Knots in History: The Films of Humphrey Jennings." Master's thes. The College of Staten Island/CUNY, 1979.

Roche, Catherine de la. "Arne Sucksdorff's Adventure." *Sight and Sound* 23.2 (Oct.–Dec. 1953): 83–86.

Rohmer, Eric, and Louis Marcorelles. "Entretien avec Jean Rouch." *Cahiers Du Cinéma* 24.144 (1963): 1–22.

Rollins, Peter. "Ideology and Film Rhetoric: Three Documentaries of the New Deal Era." *Journal of Popular Film* 5.2 (1976): 126–45.

Rosen, Miriam. "Louis Lumière." *World Film Directors*. Ed. John Wakeman. Vol. 1. New York: Wilson, 1987. 700–10.

Rosenblum, Robert, and H. W. Janson. *19th-Century Art*. New York: Abrams, 1984.

Rosenthal, Alan. *The Documentary Conscience: A Casebook in Film Making*. Berkeley: University of California Press, 1980.

———. ed. *New Challenges for Documentary*. Berkeley: University of California Press, 1988.

———. *The New Documentary in Action: A Casebook in Film Making*. Berkeley: University of California Press, 1971. 66–75.

Rosenzweig, Roy. "Working Class Struggles in the Great Depression: The Film Record." *Film Library Quarterly* 13.1 (1980): 5–14.

Rotha, Paul. *Documentary Diary: An Informal History of the British Documentary Film, 1928–1939*. New York: Hill, 1973.

———. *Documentary Film*. New York: Hastings, 1968.

———. *Robert J. Flaherty: A Biography*. Ed. Jay Ruby. Philadelphia: University of Pennsylvania Press, 1983.

———. "Television and the Future of Documentary." *Film Quarterly* 9 (1955): 366–73.

Rouch, Jean. "Table Ronde: Festival de Tours en Collaboration avec L'U.N.E.S.C.O." *Image et Son* 160 (1963): 6.

Roud, Richard. "Introduction." *Rediscovering French Film*. Ed. Mary Lea Bandy. New York: Museum of Modern Art, 1983. 13–36.

———. "Jean-Luc Godard." *Cinema: A Critical Dictionary, I*. Ed. Richard Roud. Vol. 1. New York: Viking, 1980. 436–46.

Rubinstein, E. "Visit to a Familiar Planet: Buñuel Among the Hurdanos." *Cinema Journal* 22.4 (1983): 3–17.

Ruby, Jay. "The Image Mirrored: Reflexivity and the Documentary Film." *Journal of the University Film Association* 29.4 (1977): 3–12.

Sadoul, Georges. "Dziga Vertov." *Artsept* 2 (Apr.–June 1963): 18.

———. Histoire générale du cinéma. 6 vols. Paris: Denoël. 1948–75.

———. "Louis Lumière: The Last Interview." *Rediscovering French Film*. Ed. Mary Lea Bandy. New York: Museum of Modern Art, 1983. 39–41.

———. *Louis Lumière*. Paris: Seghers, 1964.

"*Salesman*." Introd. by Harold Clurman. Notes by Howard Junker. New York: Signet, 1969.

Sanders, M. L., and Philip M. Taylor. *British Propaganda During the First World War, 1914–1918*. London: Macmillan, 1982.

Sarris, Andrew. "Notes on the Fascination of Fascism." *The Village Voice* 30 Jan. 1978: 1+.

Sato, Tadao. "War as a Spiritual Exercise: Japan's National Policy Films." *Wide Angle* 1.4 (1977): 22–24.

Sauzier, Bertrand. "An Interpretation of *The Man With The Movie Camera*." *Studies in Visual Communication* 11.4 (1985): 34–53.

Schnitzer, Luda, Jean Martin, and Marcel Martin, eds. *Cinema in Revolution: The Heroic Era of the Soviet Film*. New York: Da Capo, 1973.

Schrader, Paul. "Cinema Reviews: *Gimme Shelter*." *Cinema* 7.1 (1971): 52–54.

Scott, Nancy. "The Christo Films: *Christo's Valley Curtain* and *Running Fence*." *Quarterly Review of Film Studies* 7.1 (1982): 61–68.

Seltzer, Leo. "Documenting the Depression of the 1930s." *Film Library Quarterly* 13.1 (1980): 15–21.

———. "Document of a Documentary: *Fate Of A Child*." *Studies in Visual Communication* 8.3 (1982): 41–54.

Shaffer, Deborah. "Fifty Years of Political Filmmaking: An Interview with Joris Ivens." *Cinéaste* 14.1 (1985): 12–16+.

Sherbarth, Chris. "Why Not D? An Historical Look at the NFB's Woman's Studio." *Cinema Canada* (Mar. 1987): 9–13.

Shirley, Graham, and Brian Adams. *Australian Cinema: The First Eighty Years*. New York: St. Martin's, 1985.

Short, K. R. M., and Stephan Dolezel, eds. *Hitler's Fall: The Newsreel Witness*, London: Routledge, 1988.

Siclier, Jacques. *La France de Pétain et Son Cinéma*. Paris: Veyrier, 1981.

———. "The Psychology of the Spectator, or the 'Cinema of Vichy' Did not Exist."

Rediscovering French Film. Ed. Mary Lea Bandy. New York: Museum of Modern Art, 1983. 141–46.

Sitton, Bob. "An Interview with Albert and David Maysles." *Film Library Quarterly* 2.3 (1969): 13–18.

Sklar, Robert. "Joris Ivens: The China Close-up." *American Film* June 1978, 59–65.

Sloan, William J. "The Documentary Film and the Negro." *The Documentary Tradition: From "Nanook" to "Woodstock".* Ed. Lewis Jacobs. 2nd. ed. New York: Norton, 1979. 425–29.

Smith, Janet Adam. "Filming Everest." *Sight and Sound* 23.3 (Jan.–Mar. 1954): 138–40.

Snyder, Robert L. *Pare Lorentz and the Documentary Film.* Norman, OK: Oklahoma University Press, 1968.

Sontag, Susan. "Fascinating Fascism." *New York Review of Books* 6 Feb. 1975.

———. *On Photography.* New York: Farrar, 1977.

"The Sorrow And The Pity": A Film by Marcel Ophuls. Introd. by Stanley Hoffman. New York: Outerbridge, 1972.

Spears, Jack. "World War I on the Screen." *Films in Review* May 1966: 274–92; June–July 1966: 347–65.

Starr, Cecile. "Basil Wright and *Song Of Ceylon*: An Interview." *Filmmakers Newsletter* 9.1 (1975): 17–21.

Stebbins, Robert, and Jay Leyda. "Joris Ivens: Artist in Documentary." *Magazine of Art* 31 (1938): 392–99.

Stoil, Michael J. *Balkan Cinema: Evolution after the Revolution.* Ann Arbor, MI: UMI Research Press, 1979.

Stott, William. *Documentary Expression and Thirties America.* New York: Oxford University Press, 1973.

Strand, Paul. "Realism: A Personal View." *Sight and Sound* 19 (1950): 23–26.

Strebel, Elizabeth Grottle. "Imperialist Iconography of Anglo-Boer War Film Footage." *Film Before Griffith.* Ed. John L. Fell. Berkeley: University of California Press, 1983. 264–71.

———. "Primitive Propaganda: The Boer War Films." *Sight and Sound* 46.1 (1976–77): 45–47.

Sufrin, Mark. "Filming Skid Row." *The Documentary Tradition: From "Nanook" to "Woodstock".* Ed. Lewis Jacobs. 2nd ed. New York: Norton, 1979. 307–15.

Sullivan, Patrick. " 'What's All the Cryin' About?: The Films of Frederick Wiseman." *Massachusetts Review* 13.3 (1972): 452–68.

Sussex, Elizabeth. *Lindsay Anderson.* London: Studio, 1969.

———. *The Rise and Fall of British Documentary: The Story of the Film Movement Founded by John Grierson.* Berkeley: University of California Press, 1975.

Sutherland, Alan. "Wiseman on Polemic." *Sight and Sound* 47.2 (1978): 82.

Swann, Paul. "The British Documentary Film Movement, 1926–1946." Diss. University of Leeds, 1979.

Sweet, Fred, Eugene Rosow, and Allan Francovich, "Pioneers: An Interview with Tom Brandon." *Film Quarterly* 26.5 (1973): 12–24.

Szarkowski, John. *Photography Until Now* New York: Museum of Modern Art, 1989.

Talbot, Daniel. "Historic Hearings: From TV to Screen." *The Documentary Tradition: From "Nanook" to "Woodstock".* Ed. Lewis Jacobs. New York: Norton, 1979. 392–94.

Tallents, Stephen. *The Projection of England.* London: Faber, 1932.

———. "The Documentary Film," *Journal of the Royal Society of Arts* (20 Dec. 1946): 68–85.

"Television's School of Storm and Stress." *Broadcasting* 60 (1961): 83.

The Theodore Roosevelt Association Film Collection. Washington: Library of Congress, 1986.

Thomas, Sari. "Basil Wright on Art, Anthropology, and the Documentary." *Quarterly Review of Film Studies* 4.4 (1979): 465–81.

Thomas Eakins: His Photographic Works. Philadelphia: Pennsylvania Academy of the Fine Arts, 1969.

Trachtenberg, Alan. "Photography/Cinematography." *Before Hollywood: Turn-of-the-Century Film from American Archives*. Jay Leyda and Charles Musser, Guest Curators. New York: American Federation of Arts, 1985. 73–79.

U.S. Information Agency Fact Sheet. Washington: United States Information Agency, Oct. 1989.

Van Dyke, Willard. "The Interpretive Camera in Documentary Films." *Hollywood Quarterly* 1.4 (1946): 405–09.

———. "Letters from *The River*." *Film Comment* 3.2 (1965): 38–60.

Van Wert, William F. "The 'Hamlet Complex' or Performance in the Personality-Profile Documentary." *Journal of Popular Film* 3.3 (1974): 257–63.

Vaughan, Dai. "Let There Be Lumière." *Sight and Sound* 50.2 (1981): 126–27.

———. *Portrait of an Invisible Man: The Working Life of Stewart McAllister*. London: British Film Institute, 1983.

Waddell, Mike. "Cinéma Vérité and the Documentary Film." *American Cinematographer* 49.10 (1968): 754+.

Ward, Larry Wayne. "The Motion Picture Goes to War: A Political History of the U.S. Government's Film Effort in the World War, 1914–1918." Diss. University of Iowa, 1981.

Watt, Harry. *Don't Look at the Camera*. New York: St. Martin's, 1974.

Waugh, Thomas. " 'Men Cannot Act in Front of the Camera in the Presence of Death': Joris Ivens' *The Spanish Earth*." *Cinéaste* 12.2 (1982): 30–33.

———, ed. *"Show Us Life": Toward a History and Aesthetics of the Committed Documentary*. Metuchen, NJ: Scarecrow: 1984.

Weatherford, Elizabeth, ed. *Native Americans on Film and Video*. New York: Museum of the American Indian, 1981.

Weaver, Mike. *Robert Flaherty's "The Land"*. Exeter, Eng.: American Arts Documentation Centre, University of Exeter, 1979.

Wegg-Prosser, Victoria. "The Archive of the Film and Photo League." *Sight and Sound* 46.4 (1977): 245–47.

Weiss, John. "An Innocent Eye?: The Career and Documentary Vision of Georges Rouquier up to 1945." *Cinema Journal* 20.2 (1981): 39–63.

Welch, David. *Propaganda and the German Cinema 1933–1945*. New York: Oxford University Press, 1987.

West, Dennis. *Curriculum Guide to Contemporary Brazilian Cinema*. Albuquerque: University of New Mexico, 1985.

White, William L. "Pare Lorentz." *Scribner's* Jan. 1939: 10.

Williams, Alan. "The Camera-eye and the Film: Notes on Vertov's 'Formalism.' " *Wide Angle* 3.3 (1980): 12–17.

———. "The Lumière Organization and 'Documentary Realism' " *Film Before Griffith*. Ed. John L. Fell. Berkeley: University of California Press, 1983. 153–61.

Winkler, Allan M. *The Politics of Propaganda: The Office of War Information*. New Haven: Yale University Press, 1978.

Wiseman, Frederick. "Reminiscences of a Filmmaker: Frederick Wiseman on *Law And Order*." *Police Chief* 36.9 (1969): 32–35.

Wood, Robin. *Antonioni*. New York: Praeger, 1968.

Wright, Basil. "Documentary: Flesh, Fowl, or . . . ?" *Sight and Sound* 19.1 (1950): 43–48.

———. *The Long View*. New York: Knopf, 1974.

Young, Colin. "Three Views on Cinéma Vérité: Cinema of Common Sense." *Film Quarterly* 17.4 (1964): 26–29.

Zavattini, Cesare. "Some Ideas on the Cinema." *Sight and Sound* 23.2 (1953): 64–70.

Zimmerman, Patricia R. "Public Television, Independent Documentary Producer and Public Policy." *Journal of the University Film and Video Association* 34.3 (1982): 9–23.

Zuker, Joel. *Ralph Steiner: Filmmaker and Still Photographer*. New York: Arno, 1978.

Index of Film Titles

Included here are all films mentioned in the text and notes, each listed by its English title unless only the foreign one is available. Page numbers for illustrations are in italics.

Index of Names

*Included here are all nonfiction-film filmmakers,
filmmaking groups, and theorists mentioned in the text and notes,
as well as the names of quoted critics and other relevant persons and groups.
Page numbers for illustrations are in italics.*

Hardy, Forsyth, 323
Harlan, Veit, 201
Harness, Linda J., 369
Haro, Kazuo, 360
Harris, Neil, 30
Hart, Roger, 327
Hartley, Irving, 296
Harvey, Maurice, 103
Hathaway, Henry, 277
Haüssler, Johannes, 126
Hawes, Stanley, 323
Hearst, William Randolph, 31, 165
Heffron, Richard, 321
Heider, Karl G., 295
Heifitz, Josef, 210
Heisler, Stuart, 225
Heller, Rita, 362
Hellman, Lillian, 148, 397 n. 6
Hellwig, Joachim, 267
Hemingway, Ernest, 143, 397 n. 6
Henderick, Guido, 353
Henderson, Ann, 366
Henderson, John, 279
Henningsen, Poul, 122
Hepworth, C. M., 36
Heramedia Collective, 368
Herschel, Sir John, 7, 9
Hershenson, Bruce, 280, 311
Hershey, Ann, 363, 369
Herzog, Werner, 352, 360
Hessens, Robert, 262, 355
Heyerdahl, Thor, 264
Heynowski, Walter, 315
Higson, Andrew, 89
Hill, Jerome, 295, 296
Hill, John G., 369, 407 n. 16
Hill, Peter K., 360
Hippler, Fritz, 123, 174, 201, 202, 203, 204
Hirshorn, Harriet, 362
Hirzsman, Leon, 374
Hitchcock, Alfred, 277
Hitler, Adolf, 83, 108, 122, 124, 125, 129, 130–32, 201–04, 224, 228, 229, 259, 262, 267, 322
Hlvavaty, Kosta, 268
Hoberman, J., 357
Hodgkinson, Anthony W., 401 n. 14
Hodkinson, W. W., 40
Hoffenberg, Esther, 347, 365
Hollywood, 378
Holmes, Burton, 42, 135
Holmes, J. B., 97, 177, 188
Holmes, Nicholas, 351
Hornbeck, William, 330
Horner, William George, 7
Houseman, John, 222
Hovde, Ellen, 330, 334, 335
Howard, Edgar B., 354
Hoyningen-Heune, George, 296
Hoyt, Harry O., 45
Huang, Fu Ya, 272

Hubbard, Jim, 367, 369
Hubbard, Ray, 322
Huestis, Marc, 369
Hughes, Reginald, 247
Hughes, Robert, 321
Hugo, Michel, 354
Hugo, Victor, 6
Hulten, Pontus, 266
Hunter, Rosanne, 190
Hurley, Frank, 36
Hurwitz, Leo, 98, 146, 147, 148, 149, 151, 219, 268, 288, 292, 349, 354, 397 n. 16
Huston, John, 231–34, 236, 246, 277
Huszar, John, 354
Hutton, Joan, 366
Huxley, Julian, 109
Hyatt, Donald B., 281, 317, 322

Ibn al-Haytham (or Alhazen), 9
Ichikawa, Kon, 318
Ignacio, G., 374
Infascelli, Carlo, 257, 409 n. 24
Institut des Hautes Études Cinématographiques, 211
Instituto LUCE (L'Unione Cinematografica Educativa), 206
International Television Federation (Intertel), 327
Irving, Judy, 365
Isenberg, Michael T., 38, 40, 387 n. 86
Ivens, Joris, 59, 63–64, 68, 76, 79, 98, 100, 107, 112, 113, 115–118, 120, 122, 136, 137, 142–47, 148, 152, 159, 194, 224, 230, 267, 269, 272, 314, 323, 349, 351, 352, 361, 378, 402 n. 26, 409 n. 22
Iwasaki, Akira, 133

Jabor, Arnaldo, 374
Jackson, Pat, 182, 188, 189, 400 n. 9
Jackson, William Henry, 44
Jacobi, Freddi Stevens, 362
Jacobs, Elaine, 368
Jacobs, Lewis, 138, 285, 293, 295, 296
Jacoby, Irving, 223, 243, 278, 288, 296, 323
Jacquemain, André, 119
Jaenzon, Julius, 59
James, Richard, 369
Janssen, Pierre Jules César, 10
Jarratt, Keith, 257
Jarvis, Lucy, 350
Jaspur, Suzanne, 364
Jayamanne, Laleen, 365
Jeakins, A. E., 90
Jeapes Topical Films, 35, 36
Jennings, Humphrey, 98, 176, 179, 181, 182, 183, 184, 185, 186, 191, 194, 196, 243, 245, 249, 250, 251, 252, 253, 361, 378, 400 n. 9, 401 n. 14
Jersey, William C., 281, 312, 313, 314
Jhaveri, Vithalbhai K., 271, 372
Johnson, Christopher C., 360

RICHARD BARSAM is Provost of Pratt Institute in Brooklyn. His books include *The Vision of Robert Flaherty: The Artist as Myth and Filmmaker, Nonfiction Film Theory and Criticism, Filmguide to "Triumph of the Will"*, and *In the Dark: A Primer for the Movies*.